Handbook of Creativity

PERSPECTIVES ON INDIVIDUAL DIFFERENCES

CECIL R. REYNOLDS, *Texas A&M University, College Station*
ROBERT T. BROWN, *University of North Carolina, Wilmington*

Recent volumes in the series

THE CAUSES AND CURES OF CRIMINALITY
Hans J. Eysenck and Gisli H. Gudjonsson

HANDBOOK OF CREATIVITY
Edited by John A. Glover, Royce R. Ronning, and Cecil R. Reynolds

HANDBOOK OF MULTIVARIATE EXPERIMENTAL
PSYCHOLOGY
Second Edition
Edited by John R. Nesselroade and Raymond B. Cattell

HISTORICAL FOUNDATIONS OF EDUCATIONAL
PSYCHOLOGY
Edited by John A. Glover and Royce R. Ronning

THE INDIVIDUAL SUBJECT AND SCIENTIFIC PSYCHOLOGY
Edited by Jaan Valsiner

LEARNING STRATEGIES AND LEARNING STYLES
Edited by Ronald R. Schmeck

METHODOLOGICAL AND STATISTICAL ADVANCES IN THE
STUDY OF INDIVIDUAL DIFFERENCES
Edited by Cecil R. Reynolds and Victor L. Willson

THE NEUROPSYCHOLOGY OF INDIVIDUAL DIFFERENCES
A Developmental Perspective
Edited by Lawrence C. Hartlage and Cathy F. Telzrow

PERSONALITY DIMENSIONS AND AROUSAL
Edited by Jan Strelau and Hans J. Eysenck

THEORETICAL FOUNDATIONS OF BEHAVIOR THERAPY
Edited by Hans J. Eysenck and Irene Martin

A Continuation Order Plan is available for this series. A continuation order will bring
delivery of each new volume immediately upon publication. Volumes are billed only upon
actual shipment. For further information please contact the publisher.

Handbook of Creativity

Edited by

John A. Glover

Teachers College
Ball State University
Muncie, Indiana

Royce R. Ronning

University of Nebraska
Lincoln, Nebraska

and

Cecil R. Reynolds

Texas A&M University
College Station, Texas

Plenum Press • New York and London

ISBN 0-306-43160-2

© 1989 Plenum Press, New York
A Division of Plenum Publishing Corporation
233 Spring Street, New York, N.Y. 10013

Printed in the United States of America

This volume is dedicated to Dr. E. Paul Torrance

E. Paul and Pansy Torrance

Contributors

Bonnie B. Armbruster
Center for the Study of Reading
University of Illinois at Urbana-Champaign
Champaign, Illinois 61820

Patricia Bachelor
Department of Psychology
California State University at Long Beach
Long Beach, California 90840

Carolyn A. Ball
Department of Psychology
University of Missouri
Columbia, Missouri 65211

Michael Basseches
Massachusetts School of Professional
    Psychology, and
Clinical Developmental Institute
Belmont, Massachusetts 02178

Suzanne Benack
Department of Psychology
Union College
Schenectady, New York 12308

Bruce K. Britton
Department of Psychology
University of Georgia
Athens, Georgia 30602

Robert T. Brown
Department of Psychology
University of North Carolina at Wilmington
Wilmington, North Carolina 28403-3297

Roger Bruning
Department of Educational Psychology
University of Nebraska
Lincoln, Nebraska 68588-0641

Linda J. Carey
Center for the Study of Writing
Carnegie-Mellon University
Pittsburgh, Pennsylvania 15238

John Clement
Scientific Reasoning Research Institute
University of Massachusetts
Amherst, Massachusetts 01003

Carolyn A. Colvin
Department of Teacher Education
San Diego State University
San Diego, California 92182

E. Thomas Dowd
Department of Educational Psychology
Kent State University
Kent, Ohio 44242

Karen Fitzgerald
Department of Psychology
University of Missouri
Columbia, Missouri 65211

Linda Flower
Center for the Study of Writing
Carnegie-Mellon University
Pittsburgh, Pennsylvania 15238

John H. Flowers
Department of Psychology
University of Nebraska
Lincoln, Nebraska 68588

Calvin P. Garbin
Department of Psychology
University of Nebraska
Lincoln, Nebraska 68588

Shawn M. Glynn
Department of Educational Psychology
University of Georgia
Athens, Georgia 30602

Elizabeth M. Goetz
The Edna A. Hill Child Development Laboratory
    Preschools
Department of Human Development
University of Kansas
Lawrence, Kansas 66045

Patricia A. Haensly
Department of Educational Psychology
Texas A&M University
College Station, Texas 77843

John R. Hayes
Department of Psychology
Carnegie-Mellon University
Pittsburgh, Pennsylvania 15238

P. Paul Heppner
Department of Psychology
University of Missouri
Columbia, Missouri 65211

Dennis Hocevar
Department of Educational Psychology
University of Southern California
Los Angeles, California 90089-0031

Carolyn A. Jones
Department of Psychology
University of Missouri
Columbia, Missouri 65211

Leslie E. Lukin
Department of Educational Psychology
University of Nebraska
Lincoln, Nebraska 68588

Colin Martindale
Department of Psychology
University of Maine
Orono, Maine, 04469-0140

Linda F. Mattocks
Department of Educational Psychology
University of Georgia
Athens, Georgia 30602

Mary L. Means
Department of Psychology
Learning Research and Development Center
University of Pittsburgh
Pittsburgh, Pennsylvania 15260

William B. Michael
Department of Educational Psychology
University of Southern California
Los Angeles, California 90089

David Moshman
Department of Educational Psychology
University of Nebraska
Lincoln, Nebraska 68588

K. Denise Muth
Department of Elementary Education
University of Georgia
Athens, Georgia 30602

John A. O'Looney
Department of Language Education
University of Georgia
Athens, Georgia 30602

Robert Prentky
Research Department
The Massachusetts Treatment Center
Bridgewater, Massachusetts 02324; and
Department of Psychiatry
Boston University School of Medicine
Boston, Massachusetts 02118

Cecil R. Reynolds
Department of Educational Psychology
Texas A&M University
College Station, Texas 77843

Lyle F. Schoenfeldt
Department of Management
Texas A&M University
College Station, Texas 77843

Margaret Semrud-Clikeman
Department of Educational Psychology
University of Georgia
Athens, Georgia 30602

Barry S. Stein
Department of Educational Psychology
Tennessee Technological University
Cookeville, Tennessee 38505

Thomas Swan
Department of Psychology
Union College
Schenectady, New York 12308

P. E. Vernon
Late of the Department of Psychology
University of Calgary
Calgary, Alberta, Canada T3A 2E3

James F. Voss
Department of Psychology
Learning Research and Development Center
University of Pittsburgh
Pittsburgh, Pennsylvania 15260

Richard W. Woodman
Department of Management
Texas A&M University
College Station, Texas 77843

Claudia R. Wright
Department of Educational Psychology and
    Administration
California State University
Long Beach, California 90840

Preface

The motivation underlying our development of a "handbook" of creativity was different from what usually is described by editors of other such volumes. Our sense that a handbook was needed sprang not from a deluge of highly erudite studies calling out for organization, nor did it stem from a belief that the field had become so fully articulated that such a book was necessary to provide summation and reference. Instead, this handbook was conceptualized as an attempt to provide structure and organization for a field of study that, from our perspective, had come to be a large-scale example of a "degenerating" research program (see Brown, Chapter 1).

The handbook grew out of a series of discussions that spanned several years. At the heart of most of our interactions was a profound unhappiness with the state of research on creativity. Our consensus was that the number of "good" works published on creativity each year was small and growing smaller. Further, we could not point to a journal, text, or professional organization that was providing leadership for the field in shaping a scientifically sound framework for the development of research programs in creativity. At the same time, we were casting about for a means of honoring a dear friend, E. Paul Torrance. Our decision was that we might best be able to honor Paul and influence research on creativity by developing a handbook designed to challenge traditional perspectives while offering research agendas based on contemporary psychological views.

The contributors to our volume were selected with extreme care, because our intent was *not* to put together merely a collection of "name" individuals in creativity. Instead, we chose to solicit chapters from people of extraordinary ability who we believed could step beyond the context of the literature on creativity and address aspects of the field from the broader perspective of contemporary psychology. It is our contributors who must be credited for the positive features of this volume. In our judgment, our contributors wrote chapters of uncommon erudition, chapters, we believe, will "make a difference." The scholars represented in this volume made every effort asked of them and taught us a great deal about the meaning of scholarship. Any omissions or errors are our responsibility alone.

We had three major goals for this volume. First, we wanted to provide a critique of the level of development of research in creativity. Second, we wanted to articulate a series of research agendas that could lead to "progressive" rather than "degenerating" research programs. Third, we hoped to provide structure for the field either through intellectual leadership or, alternatively, by providing a target for researchers who wished to throw intellectual rocks at somebody. The first two goals are part and parcel of each chapter in this volume. The level of criticism ranges from questions about the utility of the concept itself (Brown) to the observation that there has been no research examining the role of perception in the creative process despite a great amount of talk about the issue (Flowers and Garbin, Chapter 8). The authors of each chapter also describe research agendas growing out of the contents of their chapters, agendas we believe could lead to fruitful, reinvigorated programs of research. Whether or not we have attained our third goal remains to be seen.

The handbook is organized into four parts. Part I, "The Nature of the Beast," consists of six chapters that examine basic issues related to the definition of creativity and how it is to be measured. Robert T. Brown begins with his chapter, "Creativity: What Are We to Measure?" which sets the tone for the volume as he analyzes the scientific utility of the global concept of creativity as well as the specific definitions of creativity that have appeared in the literature. The second chapter, prepared by Michael and Wright, is entitled "Psychometric Issues in the Assessment of Creativity," and follows directly from Brown's chapter but focuses entirely on issues often neglected in studies of creativity—the psychometrics involved in assessing the construct. In Chapter 3, "A Taxonomy and Critique of Measurements Used in the Study of Creativity," Hocevar and Bachelor build on the previous two chapters and provide an exhaustive analysis of currently available measures of creativity. Chapter 4, written by Woodman and Schoenfeldt, is entitled "Individual Differences in Creativity: An Interactionist Perspective." Their analysis of individual differences is followed by P. E. Vernon's chapter, "The Nature–Nurture Problem in Creativity." The final chapter in this part, "Creativity and Intelligence," was prepared by Haensly and Reynolds, who, in their chosen topic, return to the basic questions addressed in the first chapter concerning the nature of creativity.

Part II of the handbook, "Cognitive Models of Creativity," is devoted simply to that topic—the development and articulation of cognitively oriented models of creative thought. It opens with Hayes's chapter, "Cognitive Processes in Creativity." This general perspective then is followed by a focus on perception in the chapter written by Flowers and Garbin, "Creativity and Perception." Stein then emphasizes memorial processes in his chapter, "Memory and Creativity," and the focus shifts to how people think about their thinking in Armbruster's chapter, "Metacognition in Creativity." The last two chapters in this part of the book emphasize a developmental perspective. Moshman and Lukin examine the relationship between the development of reasoning and creative abilities in their chapter, "The Creative Construction of Rationality: A Paradox?" followed by Benack, Basseches, and Swan who discuss "Dialectical Thinking and Adult Creativity."

Part III of the volume is entitled "Personalogical Variables and Creativity." This section, featuring four different perspectives on creativity based on personality dimensions, opens with Martindale's chapter, "Personality, Situation, and Creativity," which provides a general perspective on personalogical approaches to creativity. Next, Dowd explores the construct of "self" and its relationship to creativity in "The Self and Creativity: Several Constructs in Search of a Theory." Prentky analyzes an extremely interesting topic in his chapter, "Creativity and Psychopathology: Gamboling at the Seat of Madness." Finally, Heppner, Fitzgerald, and Jones examine the role of creativity in therapeutic settings in "Examining Counselors' Creative Processes in Counseling."

The fourth part of the volume, "Applications," examines a broad array of issues involved in enhancing creative abilities. Three chapters emphasize the development of creativity in writing. Carey and Flower introduce the section with their chapter, "Foundations for Creativity in the Writing Process: Rhetorical Representations of Ill-Defined Problems," followed by one written by O'Looney, Glynn, Britton, and Mattocks, "Cognition and Writing: The Idea Generation Process." The last of the three chapters centered on writing takes a particularly effective applied approach as Colvin and Bruning examine "Creating the Conditions for Creativity in Reader Response to Literature."

Three chapters focus on science and social science. These chapters are organized by Clement's "Learning via Model Construction and Criticism: Protocol Evidence on Sources of Creativity in Science." A more applied approach can be seen in the chapter developed by Glynn, Britton, Semrud-Clikeman, and Muth, "Analogical Reasoning and Problem Solving in Science Textbooks." The last chapter in this sequence was developed by Voss and Means and is entitled "Toward a Model of Creativity Based upon Problem Solving in the Social Sciences."

The final two chapters in the volume are highly applied and emphasize the facilitation of creativity at different stages of life. Goetz's chapter, "The Teaching of Creativity to Preschool Children: The Behavior Analysis Approach," summarizes the last several years of her research program. The emphasis shifts to adults in Britton and Glynn's chapter, "Mental Management and Creativity: A Cognitive Model of Time Management for Intellectual Productivity."

A very large number of people were involved in putting this volume together—far too many for us to list in this brief space. Very grateful thanks, however, must be extended to some scholars who were particularly helpful. We thank Steve Benton and Barbara Plake for their erudite reviews. We thank Mike

Shaughnessy, former president of the National Association of Creative Adults and Children and editor of their journal, for frank discussions concerning the state of the field. John Zimmer, a man who needs no introduction, was his usual cogent and helpful self when asked to analyze difficult issues. We thank E. Paul Torrance, to whom this volume is dedicated, for his unflagging support and insistence on rigorous analyses of the area. Finally, we must thank Eliot Werner, our editor at Plenum, who encouraged the planning and development of the volume and was extremely helpful in shaping our thinking about the nature of this volume.

As is the case in any edited volume, the handbook did not turn out exactly as it was planned. Illnesses, family emergencies, job changes, and other circumstances sometimes defeat the best of plans. Consequently, chapters focusing on creativity in mathematics, creativity in music, and the development of cognitive skills in students were not included. Our greatest losses, though, were far larger and more deeply felt. Don MacKinnon, who was working on a chapter focused on the criterion problem, died last year. In addition, Philip E. Vernon died shortly after finishing his chapter for this volume. They will be sorely missed by their friends, family, and indeed all psychologists.

This volume does not represent a final effort. Hindsight shows us gaps and problems we should have foreseen but did not. In particular, we hope one day to be able to compile a more complete set of works focused on domain-specific creativity. We also hope to be able to examine the influence of journals and organizations on the quality of research in the area. In the meantime, we do very much hope that our readers find the chapters in this volume to be as interesting and exciting as we did.

JOHN A. GLOVER
ROYCE R. RONNING
CECIL R. REYNOLDS

Contents

PART I   THE NATURE OF THE BEAST

PART II   COGNITIVE MODELS OF CREATIVITY

PART III   PERSONALOGICAL VARIABLES AND CREATIVITY

PART IV   APPLICATIONS

Chapter 24   **Mental Management and Creativity: A Cognitive Model of Time Management**

for Intellectual Productivity 429

Bruce K. Britton and Shawn M. Glynn

PART I

The Nature of the Beast

This first part of the handbook attempts to define creativity, to examine issues related to its measurement, and to consider creativity in relation to other abilities. Of the six chapters comprising this part of the volume, Brown opens with an analysis of the concept of creativity and its value as a heuristic in psychology. Michael and Wright then examine psychometric issues involved in attempts to assess creativity. Their chapter is followed by Hocevar and Bachelor's critique of instruments designed to measure creativity. After this emphasis on measurement, the focus shifts next to Woodman and Schoenfeldt's analysis of individual differences in creativity, and then to Vernon, who considers the nature–nurture issue with regard to creativity. The first part closes with a return to questions centering on the nature of creativity in the chapter written by Haensly and Reynolds, as they seek to determine the relationship of creativity to intelligence.

CHAPTER 1

Creativity

WHAT ARE WE TO MEASURE?

Robert T. Brown

Creativity consists of at least four components: (1) the creative process, (2) the creative product, (3) the creative person, and (4) the creative situation (MacKinnon, 1970; Mooney, 1963). It has been studied from so many frequently incompatible theoretical perspectives, each with its own assumptions, methodologies, biases, and even meta-theoretical view, that coverage of all in a single chapter is not possible. This chapter concentrates on the divergent thinking approach to the study of the creative process—an approach that has the most explicitly developed theoretical base, underlies most creativity tests, and has generated the most empirical research. Along the way, information on some other components and theoretical approaches will be presented. Most other approaches are covered in detail in other chapters in this handbook, and general presentations of creativity theories are in Albert (1983), Bloomberg (1973), Busse and Mansfield (1980), and Vernon (1970).

A discussion of underlying processes does not exist in a vacuum; after all, one needs an observable guide to the unobservable. With creativity, unfortunately, even those guides are problematic, leaving questions about adequate anchor variables unresolved. For some people, performance on creativity

tests suffices, but focus is increasingly on actual creative performance. From the standpoint of empirical testing of a theoretical creativity construct, anchoring in performance is mandatory. This necessity, however, raises the issue of the criterion for creative performance, which is itself difficult and controversial. This chapter will discuss the issue as it pertains to creativity itself, but in an admittedly superficial way. Because some creativity theories are tied closely to particular creativity tests, criterion validity of the tests is important in evaluating these theories and will be considered in this chapter. That coverage will necessarily result in some overlap with other chapters in this handbook, particularly that of Hocevar and Bachelor.

What Is Creativity?

The question of what constitutes creativity needs to be addressed on two quite different levels: First, what individual and/or contextual factors or processes lead to a creative product? The answer to that psychological issue is the subject of much of this book. Fair warning: If you expect to find the answer in this chapter, skip it and try elsewhere. The best that you will get from me is a description and evaluation of some approaches to the question. That each approach has different answers with different

Robert T. Brown • Department of Psychology, University of North Carolina at Wilmington, Wilmington, NC 28403-3297.

implications for assessment and application reflects one of my own laws: When intelligent and informed people of good will disagree widely about something, chances are that nobody really knows what's going on.

Second, what is the status of creativity as a concept and what implications does that status have for theory development and evaluation? Most theorists explicitly or implicitly view creativity as both an intervening variable (MacCorquodale & Meehl, 1948; Turner, 1968), not directly observable but used to explain relations between stimuli and responses, and a trait, something that a person "possesses" and that varies among people. Since intervening variables are useful only under certain conditions and traits have certain general characteristics, we need to determine whether creativity meets the criteria of either.

Intervening Variables

In his classic analysis, Miller (1959) demonstrated that an intervening variable is efficient only if it mediates between multiple antecedents and outcomes. Although the cognitive revolution leaves us relatively free to pack constructs into the organism of interest, we should at some point pause to consider whether they serve an efficient explanatory purpose. Miller demonstrated that thirst was a useful intervening variable only when it could bridge at least three antecedent and three consequent variables. With fewer than three, the intervening variable used more connections than did simply directly linking antecedent and consequent variables. Given the many antecedent and outcome conditions to which intelligence can be related, its status is secure, however much we still argue over what the underlying construct actually is (e.g., Eysenck, 1979; Sternberg & Detterman, 1979, 1986). Does creativity mediate between sufficient antecedent and outcome variables to justify its status as an intervening variable? Evidence that we can vary different antecedents which may be presumed to affect a creative process, which, in turn, affects a variety of creative products, is not readily available.

An additional problem, to which I will return later, is multiple intervening variables that may affect a given outcome, leading to conceptual confusion. For example, informational content (factual knowledge the individual has acquired) and motivational-emotional factors (such as anxiety or achievement motivation) may facilitate or impair

performance on IQ tests (Zigler & Butterfield, 1968). As Zigler and Butterfield pointed out, interpreting changes in IQ as necessarily reflecting changes in intelligence is unwarranted. Indeed, they documented that increases in IQ consequent to nursery-school attendance reflected changes in variables other than intelligence.

In relation to creativity, as Wallach (1971, 1986) has detailed, researchers have often concluded that they have increased creativity itself on the basis of evidence that some manipulation increased performance on a creativity test. This would be true if creativity tests measured creativity and only creativity—a highly dubious contention as we shall see.

Traits

Traits, one type of intervening variable, are internal predispositions toward certain behaviors that are generally inferred through tests or attitude scales. Traits should be stable over some considerable period of time, show reliable individual differences, have some presumed or demonstrated genetic loadings, and predict particular behaviors in a variety of settings. Again, general intelligence, as measured by IQ tests, is a good example: It shows reliable individual differences, is fairly stable from age six years into adulthood, appears to have substantial genetic loading, and predicts overall school achievement fairly well and occupational level and income less well (Eysenck, 1979).

Whether creativity as measured by standard creativity tests actually meets the criteria of a trait appears doubtful. Individual differences are clear, but stability over time is not, and at least one study of genetic influences (Pezzullo, Thorsen, & Madaus, 1972) found no evidence for heritability of items from the Torrance Tests of Creative Thought. Of particular importance, people appear not to be more or less creative generally but more or less creative in relatively narrow areas. The creativity equivalent of Spearman's g, or general intellectual factor, appears to be the Holy Grail of creativity researchers.

Historical Antecedents

At least four approaches can be traced back to the early twentieth century, with creativity viewed as (a) an aspect of intelligence; (b) a largely unconscious process; (c) an aspect of problem solving; and (d) an associative process.

Creativity as an Aspect of Intelligence

In their 1896 paper on mental testing, Binet and Henri (as described in Freeman, 1924) proposed that 10 mental functions, including imagination, be measured by tests. Binet asked children to describe what they saw in an inkblot as a measure of imagination, but he and his colleagues could not develop a reliable scoring system and discarded the test. Binet and Simon's 1905 scale included three open-ended items that appeared to tap creativity—give rhyming words, complete sentences, and construct sentences containing three given words. Creativity researchers in the early twentieth century widely adopted such tests, which Guilford (1967) later used as measures of divergent thought. However, Binet dropped the items in later editions of his test, and the predictive success and interest in analysis of standard intelligence tests seem to have diverted attention from the potential value of open-ended tests.

Creativity as an Unconscious Process

In an often quoted passage, Poincaré (1913) recounted one of his discoveries:

> Just at this time I left Caen, where I was then living, to go on a geologic excursion under the auspices of the school of mines. The changes of travel made me forget my mathematical work. Having reached Coutances, we entered an omnibus to go some place or other. At the moment when I put my foot on the step the idea came to me, without anything in my former thoughts seeming to have paved the way for it, that the transformations I had used to define the Fuchsian functions were identical with those of non-Euclidean geometry. I did not verify the idea; I should not have had time, as, upon taking my seat in the omnibus, I went on with a conversation already commenced, but I felt a perfect certainty. On my return to Caen, for conscience' sake I verified the result at my leisure. (pp. 387–388)

Poincaré then proposed an influential theory on the generation of creative ideas: the "appearance of sudden illumination [is] a manifest sign of long, unconscious prior work" (p. 389). During a period of apparent rest, "great numbers of combination [of ideas are] blindly formed by the subliminal self" (p. 391). Most are useless and remain unconscious, but particularly "harmonious," "useful," and "beautiful" ones may break into consciousness. Poincaré further suggested that initial intense prior conscious work on the problem is necessary to "unhook" relevant ideas from fixed positions so that they are free to join during the unconscious process. Finally, the solution that has emerged from the unconscious is evaluated con-sciously. Thus, for Poincaré, conscious but unsuccessful effort to solve a problem sets in motion an unconscious process that leads to a random combination of ideas, one of which may emerge as an appropriate creative solution.

Creativity as an Element of Problem Solving

Several early problem-solving models have influenced both creativity theories and applied programs. As summarized in Table 1, each model views problem solving as a linear set of discrete steps. *Incubation* is the term used for unconscious generation of potential solutions. For Wallas (1926), incubation was more structured and guided than for Poincaré, and preparation, which included the individual's previous education, was a general orientation toward problem solving as well as the consideration of the problem at hand. A more recent investigation of scientific creativity (Busse & Mansfield, 1980; Mansfield & Busse, 1981) led to the conclusion that scientists go through a series of steps similar to those of Rossman (1931) and Wallas (1926): (1) selection of a problem, (2) extended effort to solve the problem, (3) setting constraints on a solution to the problem, (4) changing the constraints (transformation or restructuring), and (5) verification and elaboration.

Creativity as an Associative Process

Spearman (1931) claimed that the generation of novel ideas could be explained by three "neogenetic processes," those capable of generating new mental content: (1) the Principle of Experience—"A person tends to know his own sensations, feelings, and strivings" (p. 16); (2) the Principle of Relations—"When two or more items (percepts or ideas) are given, a person may perceive them to be in various ways related" (p. 18); and, most importantly, (3) the Principle of Correlates—"When any item and a relation to it are present to mind, then the mind can generate in itself another item so related" (p. 24). Spearman's basic model, shown in Figure 1, involves an active process in which associations with an initial idea can be freed from their relation to it and thus lead to something wholly new:

The final act in creativity must be assigned to the third neogenetic process; that of displacing a relation from the ideas which were its original fundaments to another idea, and thereby generating the further idea which is correlative to the past named, and which may be entirely novel. (p. 83)

Table 1. **Summaries of Problem-Solving Models**[a]

Rossman (1931) Invention	Wallas (1926) Creative production	Dewey (1910) Problem solving
1. Need or difficulty observed		1. A felt difficulty (problem found)
2. Analysis; problem defined	1. Preparation (problem stated; information obtained; attitude set toward appropriate solution)	2. Definition and location of difficulty (problem formulated)
3. Information surveyed; possible occurrence of incubation		
4. Many possible solutions formulated		3. Suggestion of possible solution(s)
5. Critical evaluation of solutions; sustained and ongoing incubation, particularly in complex problems	2. Incubation (unconscious generation of potential solutions)	4. Development of implications of solution(s) through reasoning
6. Formulation of new ideas, "inventions," and solutions	3. Illumination ("Eureka!" or "Aha!"—idea emerges from unconscious)	
7. Evaluation and refinement of most promising solution; acceptance of final solution	4. Verification (evaluation of solution)	5. Experimental corroboration of conjectural solution

[a]Based on and revised after Michael (1977).

These processes were conscious ones—Spearman suggested that preliminary work induced fatigue, which masked mental developments that were retained and appeared as if by a miracle (through some putative incubation process) when the fatigue had passed.

Although rarely cited, Spearman's Principle of Correlates is similar to several more recent concepts, including Guilford's (1967) transfer recall, Mednick's (1962) remote associations, Koestler's (1964) "bisociation of matrices," and Rothenberg's (1979) Janusian thinking, although Koestler returned the process to the unconscious.

A more recent antecedent to cognitive approaches to creativity should also be mentioned. As reported by Taylor and Ellison (1975), late in his career L. L. Thurstone and his colleagues began a study of creativity based on his factor-analytic model of intelligence and using open-ended tests. In one of these projects, Taylor (1947) isolated two factors, fluency of ideas and fluency of expressions, which appeared to be related to creativity and were reflected in subsequent work on divergent thought.

Creativity and Scientific Methodology

Although much of the discussion in this section is common knowledge, a brief review of some basic characteristics of scientific data and theory may be helpful as a referent against which to describe and evaluate positions on creativity. Because scientists and philosophers of science still argue over how science does or should work, what constitutes a "good" theory, and how data affect theory (e.g., Hacking, 1981; Harding, 1976; Lakatos & Musgrave, 1970), this presentation will be not only oversimplified but at odds with some positions.

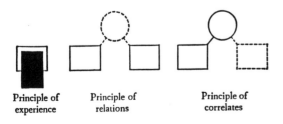

Principle of experience   Principle of relations   Principle of correlates

Figure 1. Spearman's three principles of creativity.

Theories, as explanations of observed phenomena, generally consist of a set of statements or models about processes that are themselves not directly observable. This set, the theory's "internal principles," is linked directly or indirectly to the observables by "bridge statements" (Hempel, 1966). Thus, "ideational fluency" may be seen as a bridge between particular observations and the concept of transfer recall in Guilford's theory of creativity. At a minimum, theories must meet two criteria: explanatory relevance and testability. A theory has explanatory relevance if it provides good grounds for believing that the phenomenon to be explained actually occurs (Hempel, 1966). The explanation, then, should relate directly to the explained.

A theory is testable if it makes clear and specific predictions about empirical phenomena, obviously about events unknown at the time. A dominant twentieth century view of an adequate theory has been Popperian falsificationism (e.g., Popper, 1935): For a theory to be scientific it must be falsifiable, and, in principle, a disconfirming crucial experiment should lead scientists to abandon the theory. A theory that does not make explicit predictions cannot be falsified and is not scientific. Thus, Popper's well-known pronouncement that Freudian theory was essentially pseudoscience was based on the apparent impossibility of falsifying it—any result could be accounted for. But most philosophers of science now agree that falsification of a theory does not lead to it being discarded. Confronting an anomalous result, scientists will either modify the theory or simply ignore the anomaly. Theories are discarded not on the basis of falsified predictions but in favor of a better theory (e.g., Conant, 1947; Lakatos, 1970).

Lakatos (1970, 1978) proposed an increasingly popular view of change in scientific theories that avoided problems associated with the falsificationism of Popper (1935) and the sociologically oriented scientific revolutions of Kuhn (1962). Lakatos dealt with broad "research programmes" that appear almost equivalent to Kuhnian paradigms. Although with creativity we are dealing with a narrower and lower-level set of concepts and research strategies, Lakatos's approach is still relevant, although he might object to its use. Lakatos contrasted "progressive research programmes" with "degenerating" ones and suggested that scientists tend to join the former and abandon the latter. The benchmark for differentiating between the two is that a progressive research program "leads to the discovery of hitherto unknown novel facts" whereas degenerating "theories are fabricated only in order to accommodate known ones" (Lakatos, 1978, p. 5). Beyond that,

the hallmark of empirical progress is not trivial verifications [;] "refutations" . . . are not the hallmark of empirical failure . . . since all programmes grow in a permanent ocean of anomalies. What really count are dramatic, unexpected, stunning predictions: a few of them are enough to tilt the balance; where theory lags behind the facts, we are dealing with miserable degenerating research programmes. (Lakatos, 1978, p. 6)

From this perspective, Freudian theory would be viewed as a degenerating program.

Other criteria for evaluating theories include power, the extent to which the theory accounts for what is known, and simplicity or parsimony, that other things being equal, the fewer explanatory statements used, the better. Criteria for selecting the simpler of two theories are not necessarily clear, however (Hempel, 1966).

Scientific data must also have certain characteristics (e.g., Hempel, 1966). First, by definition, they must be empirically verifiable and available for observation in principle by anyone. Thus, the frequent example: My dreams cannot be offered as data since they cannot be observed by anyone but me, whereas my dream *reports* are acceptable since anyone can read them. The distinction needs to be maintained; one should not slide from the report to the dream as data. Further, scientific data should be reliable; repeated observations should yield similar results. Statements about "who does what" and "who does what more than someone else" need to be based on appropriate samples and meet appropriate standards of probability. Bridge terms and all manipulatory and measurement terms should be operationally defined so that one can find one's way into the theory and back out. Problems arise if operational definitions for theoretical terms overlap in their observable referents. Without clear distinctions, an observation could reflect the operation of one of several theoretical constructs, leading to conceptual confusion.

Finally, to bridge the theoretical construct-empirical referent gap, operational definitions should be relevant to the phenomena of interest, not just the construct. If the operational referents of a construct refer only to that construct or its bridge statements and not to the phenomena to be explained by the construct, then the system may be internally cohesive but have no reality contact. The theory may then lack relevance.

Testing for Intelligence and Testing for Creativity

Comparing the development of intelligence tests with that of creativity tests may help to explain why the intelligence-testing movement, for all its flaws, has led to a better understanding of intelligence than the creativity-testing movement has of creativity.

As is well known, Francis Galton and James McKean Cattell both developed intelligence tests based on Galton's theory that individual differences in giftedness arose from differences in mental energy and psychophysical discriminability. While he was at Columbia University, Cattell in 1890 published in *Mind* a set of physical and psychophysical tests that was designed to determine stability of mental faculties over time, their interrelationships, and their variation across situations. The tests measured such qualities as strength of hand, visual and auditory acuity, pitch and weight discrimination, discrimination of two points on skin, free association to words, and memory. Note that the tests arose from a theory of intelligence, not from the goal of predicting intelligent behavior.

A classic study by Wissler (1901, as reported in Freeman, 1924) demonstrated the inadequacy of Cattell's tests and led to the abandonment of the "mental energy" theory of intelligence (but see Eysenck, 1979, for a contemporary resurrection). Wissler administered several tests to students and obtained information about their academic standing, both overall and in individual courses. Thus, he looked at both the internal consistency of the tests and their prediction of a presumed correlate of mental ability—college grades. Mental tests showed little intercorrelation ($r \approx .10-.20$), indicating that they were not tapping a common ability, and virtually no correlation with average class standing. But standing in a given class correlated ($r \approx .50-.60$) with standing in others, suggesting that a common factor, but one not tapped by the tests, underlay performance in different academic areas. In today's terms, Wissler's results demonstrated that Cattell's tests had neither construct nor criterion validity.

At about the same time, Binet and his co-workers were attempting to develop mental tests in Paris. Although Binet had a theory of intelligence and many of the tests were similar to those of Galton and Cattell, even his early work reflected a more practical approach. A list of proposed tests published in 1895 included memory of a short paragraph as well as immediate memory of numbers, mental images, attention, and comprehension. These tests tapped skills more directly related to what is commonly understood as intelligent behavior than did those of Galton and Cattell. Of particular interest, Binet compared performance of bright and dull children, attempting to develop tests that would differentiate between them. When asked in 1904 by the Minister of Public Instruction to develop tests to identify children who needed special instruction, Binet already had been trying to relate test performance to a criterion—school performance. With the development of intelligence tests that were standardized against a meaningful criterion, theories about intelligence, such as Spearman's two-factor theory, could be evaluated. Thus, Boring's (1923) classic statement, "intelligence is what intelligence tests test" had real meaning. The success of intelligence tests and research on intelligence rests, I suggest, on the initial establishment of *criterion* validity that enabled later theoretical constructs to be tied to observable behavior. Indeed, generally the most successful psychological tests may be those initially developed to meet a practical need and validated against a specific criterion.

Consider now the development of creativity tests. In his seminal American Psychological Association (APA) presidential address on creativity, which is detailed below, Guilford (1950) described several presumed components of creative thought and potential tests. He subsequently developed his theoretical multifactor structure of intellect and used specialized tests to identify the factors, particularly those associated with creative thinking. But the tests had not been validated against any external measure of creative productivity. In time, other researchers developed creativity tests according to their particular theoretical orientations, also without establishing criterion validity.

With little evidence that the creativity tests actually measured creative production in addition to some putative theoretical concept of creative thought, professionals began to use them for research and assessment. As indicated by Wallach (1986), the tests even became the evaluative criterion for programs to increase creativity. We should not be surprised that disillusionment began early (e.g., Hudson, 1966) and increased with the appearance of studies indicating that most tests were not internally consistent and that none reliably predicted actual creativity. The basic problem seems to be that creativity tests had only *apparent* construct validity and certainly not criterion validity—the same problem that doomed Galton and Cattell. Unfortunately, no Binet of creativity has appeared.

Problems with the Literature

Several problems in the research and theoretical literature contribute to the difficulty in elucidating the process(es) of creativity. Some disappear from notice as initial reports become summarized in secondary sources, but their effects may linger as contributions to the multiple inconsistencies in the area. Others seemingly are tolerated because of the nature of the process studied and typical methodologies used. Reasoning that would not be accepted in other areas abounds in the creativity literature; basic rules governing scientific data and theorizing are routinely ignored. Thus, some "findings" may be more apparent than real.

Use of Introspective and Retrospective Data

By their nature, self-reports and reports of events or people in the past are not open to empirical verification. Individuals tend to report what they think is relevant and can report only what they remember. Such data are open to alternative interpretations—rarely with any possibility of testing among them. This problem applies to virtually the entire psychoanalytic literature and is a major barrier to the psychoanalytic approach as a scientific one. (However, Ericsson and Simon, 1984, have provided evidence for the validity of their protocol analysis methods for studying concurrent and immediately retrospective self-reports.)

Other approaches suffer from the same limitation. One of the first books that expressly dealt with the process issue in creativity (Ghiselin, 1952) consists largely of autobiographical and biographical accounts of how various people came to create various things, frequently through some spontaneous or unconscious process. Although such reports may be valuable as sources for hypotheses for collection of future scientific data, we err in treating them as scientific data themselves, as somehow sufficient to justify postulating something like "incubation." The stories of Poincaré's sudden realization of the proof of Fuchsian equations, Kekule's daydream(?) of the benzene ring, and Coleridge's drug-induced dream of "Kubla Khan," however colorful and compelling, are simply stories whose literary merit outweighs their scientific value. The reporters, after all, were highly creative people, and that very

creativity affected their reports. See Weisberg (1986) for a critical discussion.

The one test (as far as I know) that purports to measure directly the creative process suffers from the same problem. Using the Creative Process Check List, Ghiselin, Rompel, and Taylor (1964) asked scientists to check words from two lists that applied to them before, during, and after they had grasped a new insight, solved a problem, or in some way brought "a new order into being within the field of [this] consciousness" (pp. 21–22). The word lists were adjectives describing "States of Attention" (focused, diffused, vague) and "States of Feeling" (tense, happy, uneasy). Selection of the words by Ghiselin *et al.* (1964) was based on assumptions about the effect of favorable or unfavorable states and feelings on creativity. The data clearly were introspective and, as the authors admitted, subjective. Further, the way in which replies would speak to the causal issue of process as opposed to correlates is unclear.

Use of Inappropriate Comparison Groups

Because high- and low-creative groups may differ on many dimensions other than those relevant to creativity, comparisons between them may not be clearly interpretable. Problems are compounded, when investigators' methods result in actual bias or confounding.

Consider a rarely mentioned confounding in MacKinnon's (1962, 1965) classic description of personality differences among more and less creative architects. His 40 highly creative architects came to the University of California at Berkeley in groups of 10, for a three-day interview and assessment; the two groups of less creative architects individually completed, in about six or seven hours at home, a selection of materials from the total battery. The extent to which differences in physical and social settings between the groups during assessment produced effects that were attributed to differences in creativity cannot be determined. One would expect, however, that the special attention would itself have significantly affected the creative architects' behavior.

Inferring Causality from Correlations

Virtually every undergraduate psychology major learns that correlational data rarely can be used to infer causality because of third-variable and directionality problems. Obviously one must do the best one can with data, but creativity research seems blithefully oblivious to these concerns. All too often, differences of some kind, say, in X, between "high-creative" and "low-creative" groups are inferred to cause differences in creativity with rarely a thought that they may result from differences in creativity. Next, someone develops a program to train X as a way to increase creativity! Further, if a test purportedly measures an underlying creativity trait, say, ideational fluency, then scores on that test are used as an index of that trait, regardless of the possible contribution of some other trait, say, obsessive-compulsiveness. This problem will be discussed in more detail later. Concerns about predictive validity are not reduced with reports that a particular test successfully predicted creative production when the creative production actually occurred some years *before* the tests were administered, as has been the case in several studies.

Inconsistent and Contradictory Findings

Intercorrelations among the same creativity tests and between those tests and measured intelligence vary widely from study to study, perplexing interactions are common, and failures to replicate are routine. Defenders of almost any position on any issue can find ample supporting citations. Those analyzing the creativity literature themselves need several personality characteristics commonly attributed to creative people—resistance to frustration and high tolerance for ambiguity and chaos, in particular.

Failure to Adhere to Principles of Statistical Inference

Research, even some classic studies, on correlates of high- and low-creative people commonly reflects many problems of statistical inference. Some errors which generally make Type I errors more likely include (a) failure to conduct overall analyses of variance before making multiple paired comparisons; (b) conversely, inference of a significant difference between two groups on the basis of an overall significant difference among many groups without making paired comparisons; (c) failure to cite any statistical analysis at all; and (d) failure to adjust alpha level when using multiple measures or correlations.

The last points warrant some amplification. Studies of creativity and creative individuals gener-

ally use multiple measures and/or intercorrelate many measures. In describing differences among his three groups of architects, MacKinnon (1962) only occasionally reported *any* statistical tests, leaving in doubt which differences actually were significant. Routinely, an alpha-level of .05 used with multiple tests or correlations is set, although the likelihood of chance effect being "significant" is increased as the number of tests increase. Two recent studies by well-respected researchers in standard journals of creativity and giftedness are examples of failure to adjust alpha levels. One used an alpha level of .05 in a correlation matrix of 78 correlations; the other used an alpha level of .10 to determine significance of analyses of variance of five measures of unreported degree of independence! One should not be surprised that studies using such procedures produce conflicting findings. See Mansfield and Busse (1981) for related criticisms.

Failure to Describe Methodology in Detail

Authors of studies comparing groups that supposedly differ in tested intelligence and/or creativity occasionally do not give actual test scores either of their groups or of the overall sample from which they were drawn. Further, they do not provide intercorrelations among their tests. Absence of such information prevents the reader from determining how different the groups really were.

Prevalence of Abstruse and Cryptic Writing

Perhaps because of the apparently almost "mystical" qualities of the process under consideration, otherwise sensible writers seem to lose their grip on linguistic reality when dealing with creativity. As Toscanini purportedly said of Bruno Walter, "He's an excellent conductor, but when he comes to a really beautiful piece of music, he melts." Fox (1963, pp. 123–124) suggested that failure to use critical faculties in the study of creativity "has resulted in a great deal of verbiage which would have been better left unprinted . . . the field has been inundated with a flood of words with little meaning." One's concern is hardly lessened when a well-known researcher explicitly introduces into his theory of creativity an unmeasurable and supernatural "cosmic" dimension which "may be regarded as the original creative life force, whose power and action manifest in all that is, the grand source of all creativity, products of which are but specific instances of it'' (Khatena, 1984, p. 57). Many authors could be brought up on charges of premeditated obfuscation.

Process and Product: The Criterion Issue

Recently, I asked the students at the beginning of one of my classes to draw the model of creative problem-solving that was presented by Albrecht (1980). The model is a fairly typical one: Divergent thought precedes convergent thought in a set of steps beginning with ''Problem Finding'' and ending with ''Evaluating Results.'' Usually conscientious, one of my students, Beth, obviously had not studied the model. However, after a short pause, she drew what appears here as Figure 2, certainly a most unexpected and novel response.

But does the novelty of the ''model'' qualify it as a creative product and by inference endow Beth with a degree of something called creative process? Ultimately, concepts of the creative process must be linked to creative products. After going so far as to say that ''there is no unique entity identifiable as the creative process'' (p. 134), Fox (1963) concluded that ''creativity has no meaning except in relation to the creative product'' (p. 140). As those who are familiar with the vagaries of criticism in the arts well know, identifying such products is difficult and controversial. The criterion issue is of such importance (e.g., Taylor & Holland, 1964) to an understanding of process that some coverage, however brief and inadequate, must be provided. Its complexity may be seen in the Criterion Committee Reports of the Utah Conferences on Creativity (e.g., Taylor & Barron, 1963).

In an influential conceptual paper relating criteria for creative products to characteristics of creators and the responses of others, Jackson and Messick (1967) gave novelty primacy:

No matter what other positive qualities it might possess, we generally insist as a first step that a product be novel before we are willing to call it creative. Indeed, the conjoining of novelty and creativeness is so deeply ingrained in our thinking that . . . novelty often comes to be used as the most common and, in some of our current paper-and-pencil tests of creativity, the only measure of a product's creativeness. (p. 4)

Beth's product meets that criterion—in hundreds of quizzes on the problem-solving model no one else has come close.

But Jackson and Messick stated, as have others

Figure 2. Beth's pop quiz ''problem-solving model.'' Figure is labeled ''Brooke Shields'' and is saying, ''Hi! I'm a problem-solving model! I have many problems to solve! Who to date? What to wear? How to handle my money and my mom? Whether to keep on being a virgin?'' Reprinted by permission of Elizabeth Riffe.

such as Fox (1963), that novelty alone is not enough: ''Somehow the mere oddities must be weeded out'' (p. 4). Appropriateness is a crucial conjoint criterion to unusualness. A product must fit the demands of the situation and needs of the creator, and with complex products, the individual parts must form a cohesive whole. Was Beth's product appropriate? Internally, it is certainly consistent, but it hardly meets the explicit demands of the situation. On the other hand, Beth knew both that a blank sheet of paper would have been worthless and that I rewarded last gasp efforts. So, to me, her drawing also met criteria of appropriateness; that decision is subjective, however, and others may have reacted quite differently. If appropriateness had been judged by the audience at the premier of Stravinsky's ''Le Sacre du printemps,'' after all, a second performance would never have taken place. Obviously, artists, scientists, and inventors may suffer neglect throughout their lives only to be "discovered" after they have died. Their products' novelty was apparent throughout—perhaps overwhelmingly so—but appropriateness was seen only in retrospect. The criterion of appropriateness, then, however appropriate, is easier to describe than to apply, particularly in the short term.

Jackson and Messick added two further criteria to determine the quality and level of creative products. "Transformation of constraint" involves combining elements in a way that breaks through tradition and leads to a new perspective or way of viewing reality. It occurs when a product is qualitatively different from its predecessors and may be inferred in part from the effect that the product has on the viewer. "Condensation" or "coalescence of meaning" is present in products which "do not divulge their total meaning on first viewing" (p. 10). Such products require repeated examination for complete understanding, allow for multiple interpretations, and may raise new questions while answering an old one. In Beth's "model," perhaps transformation is present but not condensation. My conclusion is that her product was indeed creative in the way that successful cartoons are (no small achievement), but that certainly nothing qualitatively new was apparent.

Jackson and Messick realized that criteria for creativity become more complex and ambiguous, going from novelty to condensation, and also that agreement on judgment of transformation and condensation would be more difficult. The fact that judges of creative products can agree, however, is seen in the work of those using consensual techniques. Although their methods differ, MacKinnon (1962), Getzels and Csikszentmihalyi (1976),

Amabile (e.g., 1983a,b), and Sternberg (1985) have all successfully used groups of judges to evaluate products in terms of creativity. What is of importance, however, is that such procedures generally involve experts using their own standards of creativity, thus avoiding the thorny issue of objectively defining specific criteria.

Realizing the importance of a unified view, Jackson and Messick (1967) considered the possible cognitive characteristics of creators, reactions on the part of viewers, and standards used in judgments, for each of their four criteria: "The creative person, his product, and the world's response to it combine to form the drama of human invention" (p. 18). A modification of their formulation is in Table 2. Jackson and Messick's description of their four criteria as being interrelated and of increasing complexity implies that products fall on a continuum from less to more creative and that people may have the characteristics in Table 2 to a lesser or greater extent. Creativity, then, would be distributed continuously like intelligence, as assumed also, for example, by Guilford (1950) and Amabile (1983a,b). But as others have noted, a continuous distribution of creativity is indeed an assumption.

An alternative proposal may be seen in Ghiselin (1963), who apparently subscribed to the Robert Benchley school of organization: "The world is divided into two groups of people, those who divide the world into two groups and those who do not." Ghiselin described creative products as being of two qualitatively different types: lower-level, secondary creativity simply extends some known concept into a new area of application, whereas higher-level, primary creativity "alters the universe of meaning itself" (p. 42) and dramatically changes the way in which we view reality. A requisite for

Table 2. Jackson and Messick's View of Relationships among Aspects of Creativity[a]

Property of creative products	Creative people		Others' responses to creative products	
	Cognitive style	Personal quality	Judgmental standard	Esthetic response
Unusualness (novelty)	Tolerance of incongruity and inconsistency	Original	Norms	Surprise
Appropriateness	Analytic and intuitive	Sensitive	Context	Satisfaction
Transformation	Openminded	Flexible	Constraints	Stimulation
Condensation	Reflective and spontaneous	Poetic	Summary power	Savoring

[a]Based on and revised after Jackson and Messick (1967).

primary creativity was true "production of insight" rather than "reproduction or copying of insight in any degree whatever" (p. 38). People who produce primary creativity are, then, qualitatively different from those who produce only secondary creativity. As Nicholls (1972) emphasized, studying "creativity" test results of normal people who will never produce anything actually creative may not help us understand the creative processes of those relatively few truly creative individuals. The issue of distribution of creativity has not been resolved. As his title suggested, Ghiselin's criteria were indeed "ultimate" and have not been translated into operational terms.

Giving quantum theory and the theory of relativity as examples of primary creativity, Ghiselin seems to have applied Kuhn's (1962) view of change in sciences to the entire creative process. As is well known, Kuhn proposed that science worked in two ways: "Normal" science involved the extension of a theory along the lines of its particular paradigm, whereas "revolutionary" science involved the overthrow of one paradigm and its replacement with a radically different one calling for a new view of the world. In the same volume as Ghiselin's chapter, Kuhn (1963) suggested that normal science actually involved considerable convergent thought whereas revolutionary science called for the flexibility and open-mindedness that characterize the divergent thinker. Whether more than coincidental similarity exists between their views is difficult to tell since neither referred to the other's chapter.

We will see in numerous sections in this chapter and in other chapters in this volume that the issues of what does and does not objectively qualify as creative and the way in which creativity is distributed have not been solved and remain as major problems for the field. As indicated above, the consensual approach provides an operational, but not conceptual, definition of the creative product. As my colleague Andy Jackson suggested to me, we are left with a version of the Potter Stewart approach to pornography ("I can't define pornography, but I know it when I see it.")—We cannot define a creative product, but we know it when we see it.

Guilford's Views on Creativity

Guilford's (1950) APA presidential address is generally viewed as the foundation of much contemporary research on creativity. As entire chapters in this volume are devoted to issues raised by Guilford, I will describe his address in some detail. Then I will present Guilford's well-known "structure of intellect", his concept of creativity as divergent thought, and his less well known problem-solving model of creativity.

General Characteristics of Guilford's (1950) Position

1. *Creativity is a set of traits.* Creativity is a "pattern of traits that are characteristic of creative persons" (p. 444). Until recently, the trait theory has dominated the study of creativity.

2. *Creativity should be stable.* By suggesting that creative potential might be discovered in childhood, Guilford indicated that underlying traits should show some long-term stability.

3. *Reliability of creativity tests will be low.* Considerable variations in actual creative productivity within people will lead to low reliability, which, although Guilford did not specifically say, presents considerable measurement problems.

4. *Completion tests are needed to measure creativity.* Tests of creativity should at least partly be open ended, allowing responders to generate their own answers instead of identifying a correct one.

5. *Creativity-test scores will show little correlation with intelligence-test scores.* Abilities tapped by standard intelligence tests are relatively unimportant for creative behavior and those underlying creativity are not tapped by intelligence tests. This presumed independence of creativity and intelligence anticipated the distinction between convergent and divergent thought in Guilford's structure of intellect and stimulated much research on creativity and creativity tests.

6. *Creative performance depends on more than creativity.* Motivational and temperamental traits determine whether an individual with creative abilities actually performs creative behavior.

7. *Creative abilities are continuously distributed.* "Whatever the nature of creative talent may be, those persons who are recognized as creative merely have more of what all of us have" (p. 446). We should therefore be able to study creativity in normal people.

Specific Creative Abilities

Guilford (1950) hypothesized that at least eight primary abilities underlay creativity. For most, he suggested some possible tests; one example will be given for each ability.

1. *Sensitivity to problems.* Creative people see problems where others do not, an ability possibly related to curiosity. *Test:* List things that are wrong with, or could be improved in, common household appliances.

2. *Fluency.* Those people who produce large numbers of ideas are more likely to have significant ideas. *Test:* State as many consequences as possible to a hypothetical situation, such as: "A new invention makes it unnecessary for people to eat" (p. 452).

3. *Novel ideas.* Creative people have unusual but appropriate ideas. *Test:* Note the frequency of remote verbal items (only those indirectly linked by mediators to the original item) in a word-association test.

4. *Flexibility.* Creative people should be able easily to change set. *Test:* Note the variety of types of answers to completion questions.

5 and 6. *Synthesizing and analyzing abilities.* "Creative thinking requires the organizing of ideas into larger, more inclusive patterns" (p. 453) and "symbolic structures must often be broken down before new ones can be built" (p. 453).

7. *Complexity.* Possibly related to synthesizing, complexity refers to the "numbers of interrelated ideas an individual can manipulate at once" (p. 453). (Guilford did not suggest tests for abilities 5–7.)

8. *Evaluation.* At some point, the value of new ideas must be determined. *Test:* Rank in order of excellence several correct solutions to a problem.

Guilford, then, saw creativity as a result of the action of several more-or-less independent traits. However, he and most others came to focus on fluency, flexibility, and to a lesser extent, novelty as the crucial aspects of creativity. Other factors, such as evaluation, were admittedly underplayed (Guilford, 1967). Given the general theoretical orientation of the period, we should not be surprised that Guilford ignored possibly important roles of situational factors. After all, traits were assumed to operate broadly across situations.

Of importance, Guilford (1950) explicitly stated that the first step in validating his tests should be factorial validity, a form of construct validity, de-

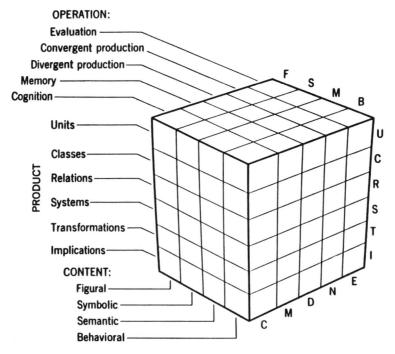

Figure 3. Guilford's "Structure of Intellect" model of intelligence. From *The Nature of Human Intelligence* by J. P. Guilford, 1967. New York: McGraw-Hill Book Co. Copyright 1967 by McGraw-Hill. Reprinted by permission.

termined by factor analysis of test answers. Only after identification of factors and development of appropriate tests would we be "justified in taking up the time of creative people with tests" (p. 453). Thus, criterion validity would follow construct validity—a position that had great impact on the way in which most researchers studied creativity thereafter.

The Three Faces of J. P. Guilford

Guilford's subsequent writings (e.g., 1967, 1977) suggest that he developed three psychological personalities. Although not as independent as Eve's, they make difficult a single description of his position on creativity. Brief profiles of these "faces" are: (a) "S. I." Guilford, psychometrician and factor analyst, who developed the *structure of intellect* (SI), which consisted of 120 virtually independent factors; (b) "D. T." Guil-

ford, who viewed *divergent thought* as a fairly general process underlying creative production; and (c) "P. S." Guilford, who developed a complex "structure of intellect *problem-solving* (SIPS)" model, which incorporated all five operations of the SI. "P. S." Guilford, less well known than either "S. I." and "D. T.", may well now be more in line with general trends in creativity research and theory. I shall describe each aspect of Guilford in some detail.

Structure of Intellect (SI). Guilford (1956, 1959, 1967) represented his tridimensional structure of intellect, which presented intelligence as much broader than would be assessed by standard intelligence tests, as the cube shown in Figure 3. Operations are the five ways in which humans can process four different kinds of informational contents that can lead to six different types of products (see Table 3 for brief descriptions). Guilford (1982)

Table 3. Brief Definitions of the Three Dimensions in Guilford's Structure of Intellect[a]

Operations	Contents	Products
Major intellectual processes; different ways in which humans deal with information	Types of information with which humans deal	Types of outcome of information processing
Cognition (C). Discovery or recognition of different forms of information; comprehension	Figural (F). Concrete visual, auditory, or other sensory forms	Units (U). Mutually exclusive items of information; "things"
Memory (M). Storage and potential availability of information in its original form	Symbolic (S). Denotative signs (letters, numbers, words, etc.) without consideration of meaning or form	Classes (C). Groupings of sets of items based on their common properties
Divergent production (D). Generation of variety and amount of information, based on given information; most involved in creative potential	Semantic (M). Meaning of words and occasionally pictures; important in verbal thinking and communication	Relations (R). Connections between items based on variables applying to them (e.g., relative size.)
Convergent production (N). Generation of conventionally accepted single best answer to a given problem	Behavioral (B). Nonverbals involved in human interactions, particularly concerning such things as moods, desires, and intentions	Systems (S). Organized, interrelating, or interacting groups of items or parts
Evaluation (E). Making judgments concerning extent to which a particular piece of information meets given criterion (adequacy, suitability, etc.)		Transformations (T). Various types of changes in existing information
		Implications (I). Extrapolations or elaborations of information in terms of, e.g., consequences or expectancies

[a]Based on and condensed from Michael (1977).

later split figural content into auditory and visual, resulting in five contents and 150 factors. Because auditory and visual appear not to have been well delineated, the earlier model is presented here. Guilford claimed that the 120 factors arising from this 5 × 6 × 4 matrix were essentially independent of one another; as opposed to Spearman, he proposed that intelligence had no even higher-level general factor. In successive reports, Guilford claimed to have located increasing numbers of SI factors, eventually over two-thirds of them. The degree to which he viewed the factors as actually independent is unclear, however, given his view on creative thought.

Divergent Production (DP) and Creative Thinking. "The greatest importance of divergent-production abilities is in connection with creative thinking, where many alternative ideas need to be brought to light with ease. Since creative thinking is an important aspect of problem solving, these abilities are also important in that connection" (Guilford, 1977, p. 108). Thus, the 24 DP factors arising from combinations of DP with various contents and products should be different elements of creativity. As shown in the examples in Table 4,

these factors include several types of fluency, originality, flexibility, and elaboration. Test of DP, then, should be useful as tests of creative productivity, although neither any one test nor any one overall creativity score is feasible as a predictor (Guilford, 1975). Guilford (1975) suggested, however, that higher-order factors related to divergent thought (DT) might emerge.

Structure of Intellect Problem-Solving (SIPS) Model. Guilford (e.g., 1967, 1977) presented a conceptual model for problem solving that incorporated the five operations and four contents of the SI. As can be seen in Figure 4, Guilford synthesized many of the steps in the earlier problem-solving models of Dewey (1910), Wallas (1926), and Rossman (1931), the feedback-based TOTE (test-operate-test-exit) model of Miller, Galanter, and Pribram (1960), and basic elements of SI into an information-processing model involving evaluation at each step. One of the relatively few summaries of SIPS is in Michael (1977), on whose detailed presentation much of this section is based. In the three inputs, "E" refers to information from the external environment and "S" to that from the internal environment or soma in terms of motivational, emo-

Table 4. Examples of Specific Divergent-Production Factors and Tests[a]

Factor	Label	Definition	Sample of tests
Semantic units	DMU	Appropriate meanings given to stimulus term (ideational fluency)	Consequences of a given event (What if people didn't need to sleep?); utility test (uses for a brick or a coat hanger)
Semantic relationships	DMR	Appropriate relationships given to stimulus term (associational fluency)	Synonyms and/or antonyms of given words
Symbolic units	DSU	Words of appropriate surface characteristic given to stimulus term (word fluency)	Words rhyming with a given word; words with given first and last letter
Semantic systems	DMS	Complex ideational systems given to stimulus term (expressional fluency).	Sentences of four words with first letter of each word specified
Semantic transformations	DMT	Unusual, remotely related, or clever responses to stimulus term (originality)	Rare associations to words; remote consequences of a given event
Semantic classes	DMC	Different classes of categories given to stimulus term (flexibility).	Different types of uses for a brick
Semantic implications	DMI	Going beyond information given in terms of e.g., detail or consequences (elaboration)	Steps specified to make a given plan work

[a]In all cases, (a) factors should be read "Divergent production of . . ." as in "Divergent production of semantic units"; (b) definitions are in terms of ability to produce indicated information; and (c) tests are scored in terms of number of specified responses given. Based on information in Guilford (1967, 1977).

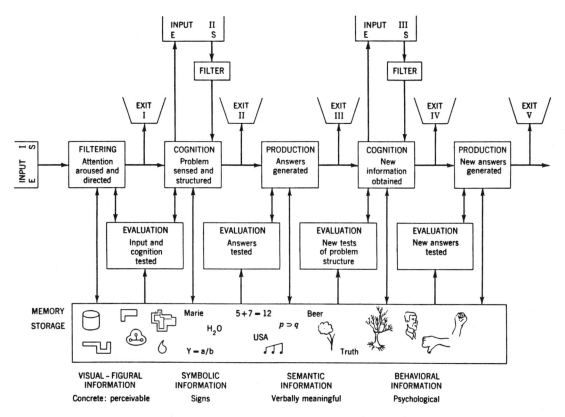

Figure 4. Guilford's "Structure of Intellect Problem-Solving (SIPS) Model." From *The Nature of Human Intelligence* by J. P. Guilford, 1967, New York: McGraw-Hill Book Co. Copyright 1967 by McGraw-Hill. Reprinted by permission.

tional, and temperamental tendencies. The latter influence the effort that will be expended in solving the problem. The array of the four contents displayed in memory is illustrative only; all types can be searched at each step, and new information can also be stored in memory during problem solving. The various exits indicate that the individual may decide the problem is trivial and not worth pursuing (Exit I) or give up at various later points. Also, if the problem is not solved after the second production stage, in which novel or creative solutions are suggested, the entire process can be repeated as in TOTE.

New solutions are generated through what Guilford called "transfer recall," in which information is retrieved

from a partial set of cues in the memory storage and the using of this information in a new context and in novel ways. This transformed use of retrieved information is effected largely by flexibly reclassifying, reinterpreting, or redefining well-organized

information within the memory storage in relation to the demands of a clearly defined problem. (Michael, 1977, p. 159)

An active search, then, can free information in memory from the context and cues with which it was remembered so that it can appear as a novel solution to a problem. New combinations of present and past information may presumably also be associated, allowing for truly novel ideas. Although not cited by Guilford, Spearman's (1931) principle of correlates appears highly similar to transfer recall. For Guilford (1967), transfer recall was an important feature of divergent production, but he also explicitly stated that SIPS does not distinguish between convergent and divergent production: "The production stages in the model actually represent both" (p. 316). Guilford appears to have designed SIPS to show how SI would function in real world problem-solving situations, but the collapse of convergent thought (CT) and DT into "production" seems to damage the presumed independence of those processes in SI and leads to conceptual confusion.

Evaluation of Guilford's Views on Creativity

An overall evaluation of Guilford's system is beyond the scope of this chapter; however, because of their implications for his views on creativity, some general criticisms must be presented. (For a more detailed evaluation, see Eysenck, 1979.) From the initial publication of *The Nature of Human Intelligence* (1967), reviewers have criticized Guilford's factor-analysis procedures. Of course, someone will criticize *anyone's* factor-analysis procedures, a situation that led Detterman (1979) to his

Law VIII. Never factor analyze anything. . . . First, it is impossible to conduct a factor analysis on data which are completely suitable. . . . Second, even if it were possible to extract factors correctly, determining an acceptable rotation has never been accomplished by anyone in the history of Western civilization. (p. 169, italics in original)

Guilford's approach is particularly troublesome. For one thing, he appears largely to have first constructed SI and then set about verifying it. Although some theoretical orientation is necessary for scientific data gathering, Guilford seems to have committed the error about which Sherlock Holmes warned Doctor Watson: ''It is a capital mistake to theorize before one has data. Insensibly, one begins to twist facts to suit theories, instead of theories to suit facts.'' As many (e.g., Carroll, 1968; Horn & Knapp, 1973; Humphreys, 1962) have commented, Guilford's Procrustean method of targeted rotations in factor analysis is so subjective as almost to guarantee identification of the desired structure.[1] Using targeted rotations, Horn and Knapp (1973) identified factors as accurately by determining targets randomly as by use of SI!

Additional problems further weaken the integrity of SI. Many of the tests had low reliability, such that failure of results of one test to correlate with those of others could reflect error variance (Eysenck, 1979), and many of the factors were identified using small numbers of tests on small numbers of subjects from restricted populations. A full si-

multaneous test of the independence of the 120 factors was never undertaken, a task which Eysenck (1979) estimated would have called for 192,000 test-taking hours from 2,400 subjects!

But more serious from the standpoint of the scientific status of Guilford's theory, the SI is essentially an encapsulated system, dealing with analysis of tests, but rarely the actual behavior they supposedly measure. A problem common to virtually all trait-test approaches to creativity is that the hypothetical creativity constructs were not clearly anchored to observable real-world creativity. As others (e.g., Eysenck, 1979; Wallach, 1986) have commented, creativity test results became identical with creative production itself. The issue became even more confused when educators or those in the private sector developed programs to increase creativity and then used performance on creativity tests as a criterion to evaluate performance, which as Wallach (1986) has documented, is common practice. The obvious difficulty, as indicated above, is that creativity tests have construct validity but not criterion validity. Paraphrasing Guthrie's criticism of Tolman: Guilford leaves the person poised in divergent thought.

Particularly troublesome for Guilford's view of DT as creativity, other than its theoretical confusion with CT in the SIPS, is disconfirmation of particular predictions about its distinctiveness. For example, according to SI, Divergent Production of Semantic Units (ideational fluency) should be essentially independent of Divergent Production of Semantic Transformations (originality). Hocevar (1979) administered three of Guilford's DT tests, which can be scored for both ideational fluency and originality (Alternate Uses, Plot Titles, and Consequences) to college students. The originality scores showed high internal consistency and significant convergent validity, as reflected in correlations between tests (that is, for example, originality on Alternate Uses correlated with that on Consequences). However, partialing out the effects of ideational fluency from the originality scores virtually eliminated both reliability and validity of originality, leading to serious questions about the actual construct validity of originality (Hocevar, 1979).

Results of analyses of the dimensionality of CT and DT are as troublesome. In an approach reminiscent of Wissler's study of Cattell's intelligence tests, Thorndike (e.g., 1963), Wallach and Kogan (1965), and Wallach (1970, 1971) suggested that Guilford's distinction between the dimensions of divergent and convergent thought should be de-

---

[1] ''Procrustes, in Greek legend, was a robber of Attica, who placed all who fell into his hands on an iron bed. If they were longer than the bed he cut off the redundant part, if shorter he stretched them till they fitted it; he was slain by Theseus'' (*Brewer's*, 1962, p. 731).

monstrable correlationally: DT tests should correlate more with each other than with standard tests of CT, such as IQ tests, which should also intercorrelate. In more concrete terms, creative behaviors should be coherent and should be distinguishable from other sets of behaviors (Thorndike, 1963). Thorndike found that six CT tests showed moderate intercorrelations; but DT tests showed no more consistency among themselves than they did with the CT tests. Other studies, reviewed in Wallach (1970), similarly indicate that Guilford's concept of DT is not empirically distinct from standard tests of CT.

The SI, then, was not a progressive research program that led to important confirmed predictions. Because of this, and the difficulty of distinguishing empirically among different factor analytic approaches, interest in SI in particular and factor-analytic models in general declined with the emergence of other approaches (e.g., Sternberg & Detterman, 1979, 1986). Unfortunately, the empirical limitations of Guilford's approach have not prevented some (e.g., Meeker, 1969) from urging its application to classroom, reflecting once again the tendency to go directly from theory to application, bypassing adequate empirical confirmation.

With all the criticisms, one may all too easily lose sight of Guilford's lasting contributions. Regardless of his quixotic tilt at the windmill of Spearman's ''g,'' Guilford nevertheless focused attention on aspects of cognitive processing other than traditional intelligence that underlie adaptive behavior. Delineating between divergent and convergent thought led to a reconsideration of processes involved in problem solving and the

development of a variety of applied programs for creative problem solving. His emphasis on the need for a theory of tasks (Sternberg, 1979) has had continuing influence. Finally, Guilford's conception of intelligence as multifaceted is reflected in contemporary theories as divergent themselves as those of Sternberg (1986) and Gardner (1983).

Other Divergent Thought Approaches: Creativity as an Associative Process

Many approaches to creativity, including Spearman's, are implicitly associationistic: A creative idea results from the novel combination of two or more ideas that have been freed from their normal correlates. Mednick (1962; Mednick & Mednick, 1964) offered an explicitly associationistic theory of creativity based on introspective accounts of creativity (e.g., Ghiselin, 1952). Suggesting that creative solutions could occur through serendipity, similarity, or, most importantly, mediation, Mednick (1962) defined the creative thinking process as

the forming of associative elements into new combinations which either meet specified requirements or are in some way useful. The more mutually remote the elements of the new combination, the more creative the process or solution. (p. 221)

For Mednick (1962), creativity was a function of people's ''associative hierarchy,'' which is the way in which they produce associations to words or problems. As can be seen in Figure 5, these hierarchies resemble generalization gradients of differ-

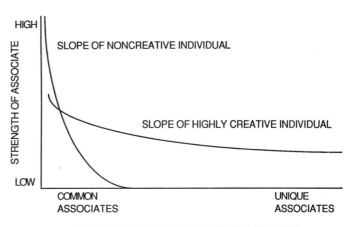

Figure 5. Mednick's concept of associative strength and gradients. Hypothetical gradients are shown for steep and shallow degrees of associative strength to a stimulus word. After Wallach and Kogan (1965).

ent degrees of steepness, with associations to word or problems ranging from common to unique. Individuals with relatively steep gradients tend to give common associations at high strength but few or no uncommon associations. In extreme, their responses may be rigid and stereotyped. Those with relatively flat gradients also initially give more common responses, but, as shown to the right in Figure 5, will then more likely make uncommon or unique associations—remote from the initial stimulus.

Mednick (1962) attempted to deal with a still serious problem concerning creative products: differentiating between the actually creative and the merely bizarre. As discussed earlier, open-ended tests involve no evaluation of appropriateness of solution. Mednick suggested that a product's actual creativeness depends on the number of requirements it meets and thus brought convergent thought back into a theory of creativity.

In order to measure ability to make remote associations and evaluate their appropriateness, Mednick (1962) developed the Remote Associates Test (RAT). The RAT consists of 30 sets of three more or less independent words sharing a common but remote association. The subject's task is to locate a particular experimenter-defined mediator that links the words. Thus, the three words "rat, blue, cottage" all share the mediating association "cheese," and "out, dog, cat" all share "house." Mednick (1962) reported some very promising reliability and validity data: (a) RAT scores generally correlated negatively with grades and not at all with measured intelligence; (b) high RAT scorers were more flexible, had more atypical views, and had interests similar to those of artists, psychologists, physicians, and authors; (c) RAT scores correlated positively with number of associations to a list of words and quantity and originality of anagram construction; and (d) RAT scores correlated with the originality score of the Institute of Personality Assessment and Research (IPAR) Questionnaire in MacKinnon's study of eminent architects.

However, more recent reviews of the RAT in Buros (1972, 1978) indicate that RAT scores correlate with standard intelligence test scores but only poorly, if at all, with actual creative productivity. Then, at least as measured by the RAT, the concept of associative hierarchies appears to be an intriguing but questionable basis for creative thought.

Wallach and Kogan (1965) adopted Mednick's basic theoretical view that creativity is an associative process but suggested that creative people's reports emphasized the importance of having a permissive or playful set. They defined the creative process as involving two elements: "first, the production of associative content that is abundant and that is unique; second, the presence in the associator of a playful, permissive task attitude" (p. 289). The divergent thought component largely focused on ideational fluency, and led to the construction of a battery of verbal and visual tests, many similar to those of Guilford. Each test had several items; one example of each will be given. The verbal tests asked for (a) instances ("Name all the round things you can think of"), (b) alternate uses ("Tell me all the different ways you could use a newspaper"), and (c) similarities ("Tell me all the ways in which a potato and a carrot are alike"). The visual tests were (a) abstract patterns (e.g., five small circles around a vertical straight line) and (b) straight or curved lines. In each case, subjects were to tell all the things the pattern or line made them think of. Of importance for Wallach and Kogan's theoretical views and the topic of much subsequent research and controversy (see Wallach, 1971, 1986, and Kogan, 1983, for summaries), the tasks were presented in a gamelike setting with no time limit. Each test was scored for both number and uniqueness of responses.

In a study of fifth graders, Wallach and Kogan's (1965) test battery proved to have two important characteristics: First, the 10 creativity scores intercorrelated strongly for both boys and girls, the average correlation being .41. Second, scores on their battery essentially were independent of a battery of 10 traditional measures of aptitude and achievement, the average correlation being only .09. Further, the aptitude and achievement scores also showed high intercorrelations, averaging .51. Thus, Wallach and Kogan's two test batteries appeared to tap two unitary and coherent but independent thought processes, one convergent, comparable to traditional concepts of intelligence and the other divergent, loading heavily on ideational fluency. Wallach and Kogan (1965) concluded that their fluency tests measured creativity, and compared on a variety of measures the four groups of children who scored high or low on the intelligence and/or creativity tests. The groups differed on cognitive, affective, and school behavior variables. Further, several interactions among the intelligence and creativity variables occurred. Although the results were not entirely consistent, the creativity test battery tapped a dimension that related in important ways to the children's behavior. For example, the high creativity–high intelligence children were said to "exercise within themselves both control and freedom," whereas the low creativity–high intelligence children were "'addicted' to school achievement" (p. 303).

Wallach (1970) considered his earlier research (Wallach & Kogan, 1965) and Mednick's (1962) work in relation to Maltzman's (1960) approach to training of creativity. He concluded that "what matters most is the generating of associates; once produced, the evaluation of their relevance and appropriate action in the light of this judgment seems to pose little difficulty" (pp. 1254–1255). He further suggested that the process actually underlying the generation of many associates was attention deployment. Creative individuals can attend to many aspects of a given stimulus and thus produce more and more varied associations.

A number of studies have confirmed that Wallach and Kogan's test battery shows internal consistency and relative independence from measures of intelligence (see Wallach, 1970, 1971, 1986 for reviews). However, several authors, including Wallach, have expressed concern about what construct DT tests actually tap, a topic dealt with in the next section.

Overall Evaluation of Creativity as Divergent Thought

Guilford's initial conception of a large number of more or less independent DT factors was supplanted primarily by a focus on ideational fluency as a general associative process, a sort of "g" factor, underlying virtually all types of creativity. This theoretical shift, in turn, led to the development of creativity tests that were narrower in focus than Guilford's battery, more unitary, and designed to be independent of traditional tests of intelligence. In spite of Kogan's (1983) suggestion that DT tests can be used to study divergent thought regardless of their criterion validity, the tests are so closely related to particular theoretical viewpoints that criterion and construct validity appear to be greatly interwoven. Evaluation of divergent thought as the major process underlying creativity then itself becomes intertwined with evaluation of DT tests as predictors of creativity productivity.

The problems become further complicated with consideration of the fact that, as others have suggested, hypothetical constructs other than divergent thought may affect performance on DT tests. Thus, scores on DT tests may or may not reflect DT. Since open-ended DT tests generally are scored in terms of number of associations, any process increasing productivity in general will increase scores on DT tests. Obviously, such a process may also increase actual creative productivity, which itself may result from the sheer amount of ideas generated (e.g., Campbell, 1960). But in this case, neither DT-test performance nor actual creativity would be due to DT but to some other process. Indeed, authors (see, Eysenck, 1979; Hocevar, 1980; Wallach, 1971, 1986) have nominated several possibilities: extroversion, obsessiveness, compliance with experimenter demands, suggestibility, overachievement, persistence, and, from my perspective, need for achievement or approval. Kogan (1983), summarizing evidence for the relative independence of quantity and quality of associations, concluded that most confounding factors would either affect quantity only or interfere with quality. However, several studies by Hocevar (e.g., 1979) indicate that ideational fluency, in terms of quantity, underlies originality scores. Hocevar used college students, and perhaps different processes operate at different ages, but, at present, differentiation between effects of DT itself and other factors on DT test performance appears difficult at best.

The crucial issue is whether DT tests actually predict creative production. As early as 1971, Wallach raised doubts about the extent to which tests of ideational fluency predict real-world creativity. With acute reasoning and after a close evaluation of the literature, he questioned the use of tests of ideational fluency which by name became "creativity tests," but did not have criterion validity, either to study the process of creativity or to evaluate programs designed to increase creativity. At the same time, Cattell (1971), a persistent critic of creativity tests, concluded that

the verdict that a test measures creativity is only a projection of the test constructor's personal view about what creativity is. Thus in the intellectual tests developed by Guilford's students and many others who have worked on creativity in this decade, creativity has finished up by being evaluated simply as oddity or bizarreness of response. . . . This indeed comes close to mistaking the shadow for the substance. (pp. 408–409)

Unfortunately, the issues regarding the importance of setting in which testing occurs (gamelike vs. testlike), relative value and independence of number and uniqueness of answers as criteria for creativity, and predictive validity of ideational fluency tests remain unresolved. Inconsistent and contradictory findings allow almost any conclusion (see Kogan, 1983, and Wallach, 1971, 1986, for some opposing views). Here again is the problem of a construct adrift and unanchored to meaningful criteria.

Even individual studies with apparently clear results present difficulties. Consider Wallach and Wing's (1969) study of "predictive" validity of intelligence and creativity tests. They mailed incoming freshman volunteers at Duke University four tasks from the Wallach and Kogan (1965) battery, asking them to give as many responses as possible, and also to list a variety of creative accomplishments in high school. Wallach and Wing scored the task results for number (ideational productivity) and uniqueness (ideational uniqueness) of associations, and used students' SAT scores to measure intelligence. They then classified students into the top and bottom third of scorers in terms of SAT, ideational productivity, and ideational uniqueness. Although the upper third of all three groups had higher high school grades than did the lower third, SAT scores predicted freshman grades at Duke better. Ideational productivity and uniqueness showed only slight and inconsistent relationship to grades. Of primary interest to the authors, students in the top third on both ideational measures generally reported having significantly more creative accomplishments in high school than did those in the lower third, whereas students of high and low intelligence reported essentially no significant differences in high school creativity. The commonly drawn conclusion that ideational fluency tests significantly predicted creative productivity is, however, problematic. Feldman (1970) noted several technical problems with statistical analyses, representativeness of their sample (V + Q SAT = 1264!), and overlapping representation of given students in their three measures. Beyond those issues is a serious logical flaw: The ideational fluency tests said to "predict" creative productivity were given *after* the creative productivity had occurred, producing a bit of a directionality problem. Actually, creative productivity predicted performance on tests of ideational fluency. In all fairness, one must note that Wallach later changed his views on the value of creativity tests.

In their review, Barron and Harrington (1981, p. 447) stated that even after 80 years, we do not have a satisfactory answer to "the vitally important question of whether divergent thinking tests measure abilities actually involved in creative think-

ing." Their conclusion that "some divergent thinking tests, administered under some conditions and scored by some sets of criteria, do measure abilities related to creative achievement and behavior in some domains" (p. 447) hardly inspires confidence in divergent thought as *the* important factor in creativity. Increasingly, the validity of DT tests is being questioned (e.g., Cronbach, 1984; Nicholls, 1972; Simonton, 1984). Amabile (1983a,b) opted for a consensual definition and Sternberg (1985) suggested that they "capture at best only the most trivial aspects of creativity" (p. 618).

Barron and Harrington's (1981) concern about the convergent-divergent thought distinction also is worth repeating:

> Divergent thinking in fact goes hand in glove with convergent thinking in every thought process that results in a new idea. The aha! comes when the process reaches a conclusion. But process is precisely what is invisible in the usual DT tests used in creativity research. A problem is set, and a written answer is obtained. What happens in between is anybody's guess, except the respondent's, who hasn't been asked. (p. 443)

Perhaps, but only with the great benefit of hindsight, we can see why the initial promise of divergent thought has not been fulfilled. Implicitly or explicitly, creativity theorists viewed divergent thought as a fairly general process that would account for a variety of creative activities. But several lines of research and theory (e.g., Albert, 1983; Amabile, 1983a,b; Feldman, 1986; Gardner, 1983; Hocevar, 1981; Wallach, 1986) are converging on the conclusion that talent and creativity are domain specific whether by dint of "natural" proclivity, extensive training, and/or education. As Barron and Harrington (1981) suggested, more domain-specific aspects of divergent thought may underlie creative productivity.

As a further problem, however, divergent thought and other approaches treat creativity as an intrapersonal trait. Although traits have explanatory value (e.g., Eysenck & Eysenck, 1985), since the pioneering work of Mischel (1968), psychologists have become increasingly aware of the importance of situational factors in determining behavior. The importance of such factors was seen by Getzels and Csikszentmihalyi (1976) in their study of artists, appears in Feldman's (1980, 1986) account of the importance of mentors in the development of prodigies, and is given prominence in Amabile's (e.g., 1983a,b) model and research program. The role of sheer chance (Austin, 1978; Campbell, 1960) also needs to be considered.

At the very least, as Wallach (1971, 1986) and others (e.g., Nicholls, 1972) have emphasized, the use of DT tests as a criterion for, or classifying measure of, creativity is unwarranted, although papers defending such use still appear (e.g., McCrae, 1987). As Nicholls (1972, p. 724) concluded, divergent thinking tests should not be called tests of creativity. Divergent thinking is of research interest, but not as "constrained by preconceptions about creativity."

Problem Finding as Creativity

Some writers in recent years have reemphasized the importance of *problem finding*, in addition to *problem solving*, as a crucial element of true creativity. Related to Guilford's (1950) notion of "sensitivity to problems" and the everyday meaning of curiosity, creative individuals' problem finding actively refers to their looking for discrepancies or something they do not understand. Darwin, according to Gruber (1981), demonstrated "purposefulness" in seeking out variability in species as well as ways to account for it. Feldman's (e.g., 1980, 1986) six prodigies initially were recognized when they showed great—and frequently persistent—interest in some particular area. My informal interviews with creative scientists consistently reveal an early preoccupation with some observation or reading that troubled them—something wanted further investigation. In some cases, that preoccupation became a long-term career interest.

Gestalt psychologists (e.g., Henle, 1962, 1974; Wertheimer, 1959) in particular have emphasized the importance of posing the correct question. Henle (1974) argued that the perception of "dynamic gaps" incites the creative process: "And yet posing the right question may be the most creative part of the whole process. As James Stephens once remarked, 'A well-packed question carries its answer on its back as a snail carries its shell' (1920, p. 68)" (p. 25). Henle described six conditions leading to the perception of gaps: (1) contradictions of all kinds; (2) unexpected similarities between one phenomenon and an apparently unrelated one; (3) strange, new phenomena; (4) in science, a hypothesis derived from theory; (5) again in science, difficulties with prevailing explanation, and of great importance; and (6) the presence of a "welcoming mind," actively looking for those gaps.

In a unique longitudinal study of prospective artists, Getzels and Csikszentmihalyi (1976, p. 79) conceptualized the creative process as problem solving consisting of "formulation of a problem, adoption of a method of solution, and the reaching of solutions." They differentiated between "presented problem situations" in which one can apply known answers to all three steps and "discovered problem situations" in which one must both identify the problem and develop new ways to solve it. In the latter situation, "the problem solver must become a problem finder" (p. 81). Although difficult to interpret at times because of its complexity and numerous correlated measures, the Getzels and Csikszentmihalyi study deserves detailed description.

Getzels and Csikszentmihalyi administered tests of intelligence, personality, and fluency to art students at the Art Institute of Chicago and obtained teacher ratings of the students' artistic potential. They then presented fine arts students with 27 objects (e.g., a small manikin, a bunch of grapes, a brass horn) and asked them each to select whatever ones they wished, arrange them into a composition, and then complete a drawing. The investigators recorded each student's behavior throughout the process, took several photographs, and interviewed each student after he or she completed the drawing.

Getzels and Csikszentmihalyi scored each student on problem finding at the formulation stage (which and how many objects the student handled and how thoroughly the student examined them), problem finding during problem solution stage (time each student took to develop the structure of the drawing, whether objects were rearranged or drawing paper was changed, and the extent to which the student transformed objects in drawing them), and overall concern for problem solving (based on the interview). These were combined into a total problem-finding score. Groups of judges (artists, art teachers, mathematics students, and business students) evaluated the drawings on overall aesthetic value, originality, and craftsmanship.

Of major interest, artist–critics' and art teachers' evaluations of the drawings correlated with students' problem-finding scores. Thus, problem finding had at least short-term criterion validity as one element of artistic creativity. Further, the behavioral protocols and interviews indicated that students with low problem-finding scores "saw" their drawing's final form much sooner than did those with high problem-finding scores. Getzels and Csikszentimihalyi (1976, p. 154) suggested that low scorers adopted a known solution whereas high scorers attempted to discover something new in the objects: ''In a sense, the one looks on the problem as familiar, the elements as new; the other looks on the elements as familiar, and the problem as new.'' It seems only a slight translation to suggest that the low scorers coalesced early on convergent problem solving whereas the high scorers maintained a divergent approach.

Also of interest is what did *not* correlate with success in school. Although instructors rated high achievers in art courses (B or above) higher on artistic potential than low achievers (C+ or below), the two groups showed essentially no differences on tests of fluency and flexibility (e.g., unusual uses test) or IQ. In fact, on the majority of tests, low achievers had *higher* fluency and flexibility scores.

Seven years after initial testing, Getzels and Csikszentmihalyi located as many former subjects as they could and rated the artistic success of each on the basis of judgments of a gallery director, an art critic, and the information gained in the follow-up itself. A number of family factors influenced success—successful artists were more likely to be first-born and come from wealthy families, for example. But neither fluency, intelligence, nor values tested the scores, and only one personality factor (low concern with social approval) correlated with success. Teachers' evaluations of artistic potential were slightly correlated with success, but academic grades were inversely related.

Of major interest, problem-finding total scores in the drawing exercise significantly predicted success as an artist seven years later ($r = .30$), demonstrating long-term predictive validity for the problem-finding concept. Getzels and Csikszentmihalyi (1976) pointed out that their findings may not apply to truly great artists, bringing up the criterion issue again. But their project not only reveals an important role of problem finding, but also represents a scientifically sound and potentially progressive, albeit complex and time-consuming, research program.

Unfortunately, their procedures do not allow for clear separation among a number of the components of creativity described in Guilford's (1950) original paper. One can infer, for example, that evaluation was an ongoing process among all the students during the drawing exercise, but that the more creative ones avoided premature closure. In any event, the processes underlying question asking appear to be important ones. At least one program designed to stimulate creativity in children emphasizes training in question asking (Landau, 1985), and Sternberg and Davidson (1986) have recently concluded that

gifted individuals have exceptional problem-finding ability.

Evaluation as a Creative Process

Although apparently not the subject of much research, evaluation of potential solutions may be an important aspect of creativity, as suggested by Mednick (1962). It certainly is an element of virtually all models of problem solving. My students' attempts at creative problem solving are often frustrated by their persistent failure to evaluate potential solutions. As a result, incorrect solutions are offered frequently—and confidently. For example, given the classic problem, ''How can you make four equilateral triangles out of six sticks of equal length?'' about half the students submit drawings of two sticks as diagonals inside a square made of the other four. When queried, the students indicate that they had not checked to see whether any of their triangles were equilateral or whether the two diagonals actually reached the corners. Their premature acceptance of an obvious but incorrect solution precluded further search that might have yielded a more creative and appropriate solution.

Evaluation in the form of ''selective retention'' is a crucial aspect of Campbell's (1960) theory of creativity, which will be discussed more fully in the next section. A variety of potential solutions is of little value if ''there is not the precise application of a selective criterion which weeds out the overwhelming bulk of inadequate trials'' (pp. 391–392). Campbell went on to suggest that solutions may be evaluated against a number of criteria, and that more creative thinkers may be able to keep track of and apply more criteria at one time.

Given the research devoted to other elements of creative problem-solving models, some might well be invested in evaluations of evaluation.

Should We Just Leave It All to Chance?

Most recent psychological accounts suggest that the creative process is an intrapersonal trait and is goal-directed. In the writings of philosophers and scientists, however, one finds considerable emphasis on internal and external chance factors. Campbell (1960) quoted a variety of mainly nineteenth-century views: ''With reference to originality . . . there is an active turn, a profuseness of energy, put forth in trials of all kinds on the chance of making lucky hits'' (Alexander Bain); ''le principe de l'invention est le hasard'' [the principle of discovery is chance] (Sourioux); the title of a major address by Ernst Mach, ''On the Part Played by Accident in Invention and Discovery''; and the excerpt from Poincaré cited earlier.

The impact of external chance happenings or encounters is obvious enough to serve as a ''What if . . .'' parlor game: ''What if Semmelweis's colleague had not contracted fatal puerperal-feverlike symptoms after being nicked by a student with an autopsy-dirtied knife?'' ''What if the young Charles Ives had not heard two bands simultaneously playing different tunes?'' ''What if Picasso had not seen African art?'' and ''What if Alexander Fleming didn't really like to play water polo?'' Austin (1978), a neurologist, has used a variety of case studies to document the role of external chance factors and to support his own basic position: ''We are all creative, but often only to the extent that we are lucky'' (p. xii). He described four types of ''good luck'' and personality traits required to capitalize on them: Chance I is simple ''blind'' luck resulting from an accident; nothing is attributable to the individual. Chance II (serendipity) results from general exploratory behavior and follows what Austin terms the Kettering Principle: Chance favors those in motion. Individuals high in general curiosity and persistence may have ''happy accidents.'' Chance III is attributed to sagacity and involves the Pasteur Principle: Chance favors the prepared mind. Individuals with great specialized knowledge and a particular sensitivity will be likely to form and see the value of certain new associations. Chance IV results from personalized action, what Austin terms, ''altamirage,'' or ''the quality of prompting good luck as a result of personally distinctive actions'' (p. 203), particularly those ''far removed from the area of the discovery'' (p. 78). It follows from the Disraeli Principle: Chance favors the individualized action. As an example of Chance IV, Austin suggests that Fleming might never have discovered penicillin if he had not liked to play water polo! The London hospital where Fleming chose to work had a swimming pool. As a result, it was damp and fostered bacterial cultures. Austin used other elements of Fleming's story to buttress his position that the greatest discoveries occur when all four aspects of chance operate.

From a scientific standpoint, Austin's account is of limited value since it offers only *post hoc* and anecdotal accounts of the role of chance. In fairness, Austin did not claim to offer a theory, but wanted to show the reality of research ''in all its haphazard, unpredictable complexity'' (p. xii).

In a fascinating if quirky paper, Campbell (1960) put the role of chance inside the individual. He proposed that the generation of multiple potential solutions to problems through ''thought trials'' was determined by chance:

Real gains in knowledge must have been the products of exploration going beyond the limits of foresight or prescience, and in this sense, blind. In the instances of such real gains, the successful explorations were in origin as blind as those which failed. (p. 381)

Campbell claimed that a ''blind-variation-and-selective-retention'' process was fundamental to all cases where induction leads to a creative advance in knowledge. The process is similar in its essentials to Darwinian evolution, in which mutations are not guided by any purposive or teleological force but natural selection preserves those which have advantageous effects. In considering individual examples of great creativity, Campbell says that our tendency to ''see marvelous achievements rooted in equally marvelous antecedents'' (p. 390) is no more than the ''fallacy of accident'' and ''*post hoc, ergo propter hoc.*'' Indeed, Campbell suggests that if a dozen equally brilliant people proposed guesses about something unknown and if one guess should be correct, it would inform us about the unknown but not about the ''greater genius'' of the correct guesser, who ''just happened to be where lightning struck'' (p. 390). No more than we impute ''foresight'' to a successful mutant allele should we ''expect marvelous consequents to have had equally marvelous antecedents'' (p. 390).

Individual differences in creativity will exist, according to Campbell, in terms of people's accuracy and details of representation of the world, which reduce to differences in information and intelligence; the number and variety of thought trials they can produce with a correct solution more likely by chance with greater frequency and variety; and differences in evaluative criteria, discussed above.

In a sense, blind-variation could be viewed as a form of divergent thought except that it is usually given a goal-directed quality explicitly absent from Campbell. Similarly, Newell, Shaw, and Simon's (1962) maze/model of creative problem solving explicitly includes heuristics for choosing subsets of all possible solutions to explore. Crovitz's (1970) relational algorithm could be described as an organized blind-variation. One might suggest that Campbell has failed to consider the importance of explicitly remote associations and differences in ability to make them. He seems to have difficulty in accounting both for the consistently creative person and for the highly productive but noncreative person, who should by chance alone have a hit once in a while. But if Campbell leaves too much to chance, he serves as a valuable reminder of the error of leaving too little to it.

Simonton (e.g., 1984) has most explicitly incorporated Campbell's (1960) basic concept that creative thought results from the combination of truly chance combination of ideas with retention only of the useful ones. He extends the model to actual creative productivity by emphasizing the importance of creators' leadership skills in determining whether or not their products have been actually accepted.

Indeed, in addition to stating that creators are leaders, Simonton (1984, p. 2) goes so far as to subsume creativity under leadership: ". . . creativity becomes a variety of leadership." Using a "historiometric" approach, Simonton (1984) has used archival data to generate a number of quantitative relationships, for example between creativity and age and birth order. Although Simonton's approach is itself novel and intriguing, he has not in detail clearly defined some important concepts including creativity and genius. Of course, as with all essentially psychohistorical approaches, relationships, no matter how quantified, are limited by the archival sources that are available and actually used. Such relationships are thus always open to alternative interpretations. But Simonton's (1984) emphasis on leadership is itself an important contribution to considerations of what underlies creative productivity.

Amabile's Componential/Social Psychological Approach

Given the general failure of divergent thinking and cognitive trait models to account for creative productivity, the role of other factors should be considered. Numerous authors (e.g., Barron, 1968; Barron & Harrington, 1981; Cattell, 1971; Mac-Kinnon, 1965, 1970; Nicholls, 1972; and Welsh, 1975, 1986) have suggested that personality and motivational factors underlie much of the individual differences among people in creativity. Cattell (1971) proposed that other than intelligence and specific talents, personality factors most determine

actual creative productivity. In addition to emphasizing diligence, a motivational characteristic, Welsh (1986) has amassed considerable support for the importance of two personality variables, which he calls *origence* and *intellectance*. Based on his review, Nicholls (1972) suggested that intrinsic, or task, motivation may be an important and overlooked factor. This chapter will conclude with a brief description of a recent interactive model of creativity that features intrinsic motivation as one of its main components.

Amabile (1983b, p. 358) argued that "creativity is best conceptualized not as a personality trait or a general ability but as a behavior resulting from particular constellations of personal characteristics, cognitive abilities, and social environments." As a working framework of the components involved in creative productivity, Amabile (1983a,b) proposed the model shown in Figure 6. Not only do the three major components interact, but each itself results from an interplay of several internal and external factors. The subprocesses traditionally viewed as being involved in the entire creative process appear in both the domain-relevant and creativity-relevant components.

Domain-relevant skills are the most basic; one cannot be truly creative unless one knows a great deal about a particular area, has the skills necessary to produce in that area, and has "talent," which Amabile also puts in quotation marks, for that particular area. Such skills comprise "the individual's complete set of response possibilities" (1983b, p. 363) from those involved in synthesis of the new response to those involved in evaluation, and include all knowledge about the domain, including facts, paradigms, esthetic criteria, and technical skills.

Creativity-relevant skills are those cognitive and personality characteristics that have traditionally been viewed as underlying generation of potentially creative responses. Briefly, cognitive style skills are: breaking perceptual set; breaking cognitive set, or trying new problem-solving strategies; keeping response options open, or delaying closure; suspending judgment; using "wide" categories; remembering large amounts of information accurately; and breaking out of performance scripts or algorithms. As indicated in Figure 6, also in this component are knowledge and use of heuristics, or sets of rules, for generating novel responses. Conducive workstyles include abilities to concentrate for long periods of time and to abandon fruitless strategies. Relevant personality characteristics are

1 DOMAIN-RELEVANT SKILLS	2 CREATIVITY-RELEVANT SKILLS	3 TASK MOTIVATION
INCLUDES: – KNOWLEDGE ABOUT THE DOMAIN – TECHNICAL SKILLS REQUIRED – SPECIAL DOMAIN-RELEVANT "TALENT" DEPENDS ON: – INNATE COGNITIVE ABILITIES – INNATE PERCEPTUAL AND MOTOR SKILLS – FORMAL AND INFORMAL EDUCATION	INCLUDES: – APPROPRIATE COGNITIVE STYLE – IMPLICIT OR EXPLICIT KNOWLEDGE OF HEURISTICS FOR GENERATING NOVEL IDEAS – CONDUCIVE WORK STYLE DEPENDS ON: – TRAINING – EXPERIENCE IN IDEA GENERATION – PERSONALITY CHARACTERISTICS	INCLUDES: – ATTITUDES TOWARD THE TASK – PERCEPTIONS OF OWN MOTIVATION FOR UNDERTAKING THE TASK DEPENDS ON: – INITIAL LEVEL OF INTRINSIC MOTIVATION TOWARD THE TASK – PRESENCE OR ABSENCE OF SALIENT EXTRINSIC CONSTRAINTS IN THE SOCIAL ENVIRONMENT – INDIVIDUAL ABILITY TO COGNITIVELY MINIMIZE EXTRINSIC CONSTRAINTS

Figure 6. Amabile's components of creativity (see text for explanation). From The social psychology of creativity: A componential conceptualization by T. M. Amabile, 1983, *Journal of Personality and Social Psychology, 45,* 357–376. Copyright 1983 by the American Psychological Association. Reprinted by permission of the author and the American Psychological Association.

those commonly reported as correlates of creative people, including self-discipline, ability to delay gratification, perseverance, and absence of conformity.

The final component, task motivation, is the focus of Amabile's own research. Her emphasis has been on the role of intrinsic motivation, that "generated by the individual's reaction to intrinsic properties of the task" (1983b, p. 364), and which involves engaging in an activity for its own sake. An individual's task motivation is specific to a particular task and has two basic elements: baseline attitude toward the task, determined by an appraisal of the degree to which the task matches the person's own interests, and perceptions of motivation for undertaking the task, largely determined by external social/environmental factors. In particular, Amabile is concerned about extrinsic factors that may control the person's performance, such as rewards. She has adopted the "overjustification principle" from attribution theories, which states basically that external constraints on an individual's involvement in a task are inversely related to intrinsic motivation. Thus, "extrinsic constraints will, by impairing intrinsic motivation, have detrimental effects on creative performance" (1983b, p. 365).

A possible schematic framework representing interactions among the components in actual creative production is shown in Figure 7. As with the components themselves, the framework synthesizes earlier approaches with Amabile's own focus. For example, as Amabile stated, Steps 1–5 at the top are clearly based on earlier models of problem solving. An individual's level of each component on a given task determines overall creativity on that task.

The framework deals with the entire creative process, from problem finding to evaluation, and involves feedback from Step 5. Briefly, problems are presented in Step 1, either from the individual's intrinsic interest or from someone else, but the individual will be more motivated to solve problems that arise intrinsically. Step 2 is preparatory to actual response generation and reactivates or acquires information relevant to the task. As Amabile suggests, Step 2 may involve a considerable investment of time if the individual has to acquire the information afresh. In Step 3, novel potential solutions are generated through use of both cognitive problem-solving pathways and potentially useful elements in the environment. Evaluation of potential solutions in Step 4 occurs through use of domain-relevant skills. Finally, a decision is made in Step 5 that determines whether or not the process can be terminated or must be rerun from Step 1. Feedback from success or failure may increase or decrease task motivation for future involvement with similar problems.

The framework is admittedly tentative and appears to have some shortcomings. Although feedback is explicitly involved, problem solving is presented as an essentially linear process in which failure or partial success leads to a return to Step 1. Given close evaluation of shortcomings of a potential solution, however, one might well return to Step 2 or even 3 rather than Step 1. The multiple feedback loops in Guilford's SIPS model may more accurately depict actual problem solving. Also, the

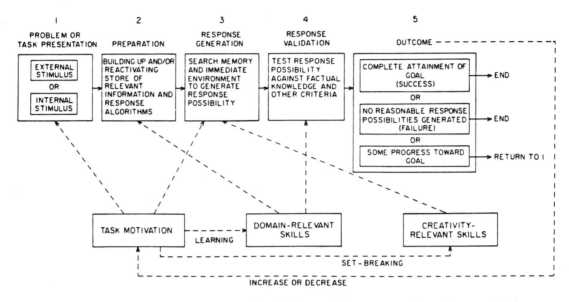

Figure 7. Amabile's componential framework of creativity. Solid arrows indicate sequence of steps in process; broken arrows indicate influences among factors. From The social psychology of creativity: A componential conceptualization by T. M. Amabile, 1983, *Journal of Personality and Social Psychology, 45,* 357–376. Copyright 1983 by the American Psychological Association. Reprinted by permission of the author and the American Psychological Association.

role of specific goals for the process is not clear. Without such goals, response validation is itself problematic. Further, each of the three components influences directly only one or two of the steps, whereas they might well affect virtually all. For example, task motivation stops directly guiding the process at Step 3, but as has been noted earlier in this chapter, problem solving frequently breaks down at the evaluation step, with a failure to compare a proposed solution with the requirements of the task. This failure would be particularly likely to occur on tasks induced through extrinsic motivation in which the individual has little interest.

Criticisms aside, however, Amabile has provided a model explicit and clear enough to be both rich in testable hypotheses, some of which are detailed in Amabile (1983a,b), and easily modified to account for new information. Her research has led to an impressive body of information on the role of situational factors in the production of creative solutions. She has adopted a functional approach to creativity, varying antecedent and consequent environmental factors and measuring their effect on creative productivity. Creativity of her subjects' products has been evaluated by a consensual technique, using groups of informed judges. A brief summary of some of her results, largely from Amabile (1983a), will show the power of the ap-

proach and indicate the importance of so-cial/contextual factors on creative productivity: (a) for both children and adults, external evaluation or expectation of evaluation lowers creative productivity on verbal and artistic tasks; (b) external rewards generally decrease creative productivity; (c) choice in whether or how to engage in a particular problem activity increases creativity; and (d) expressed interest in an activity is positively related to creative performance. These results support the intrinsic-motivation approach, although Amabile appears not to have dealt with the crucial issue of the origin of that intrinsic motivation. Of greater interest from the perspective of this chapter, Amabile has provided a novel answer to the question of what we should measure about creativity, focusing on observable and manipulable determinants of actual creative products rather than on underlying process. Her approach has led to a number of confirmed predictions and can synthesize a variety of previous research. As such, it represents a particularly progressive research program.

Conclusions

1. Much theorizing about creativity has not been clearly linked to observable antecedent and conse-

quent conditions. Constructs hang suspended in the ether, being tied to reality by neither adequate bridge statements nor clear and distinctive operational definitions. One cannot determine specifically how they relate to creative productivity or can lead to predictions. Such theories may be questioned on the basis of both relevance and testability.

2. Several theoretical approaches, including the psychoanalytic and factorial, may be described as degenerating and of questionable value. Interest in Guilford's structure of intellect among researchers, if not educators, has greatly diminished, reflecting an awareness of its limitations. The fact that some professionals continue to offer psychoanalytic explanations is itself a phenomenon worthy of study, perhaps in terms of dissonance reduction.

3. Clear operational discriminability needs to be established among concepts. As informational content, emotional, and motivational factors influence performance on intelligence tests, they also may influence performance on creativity tests, particularly fluency tests. Unfortunately, we cannot now easily determine whether fluency tests tap creativity or some other construct. One might suggest that, given the general stability of cognitive processes, if *short-term* programs increase creative productivity, the effect is probably on a motivational-emotional variable rather than on creativity itself.

4. The search for a "g" factor of creativity in terms of a divergent process is problematic; it does not seem to involve a progressive research program. Creativity appears much more domain-specific than intelligence and likely to consist of a number of processes. Although it may consist of essentially the same set of steps across domains, individuals highly creative in one area will not likely be in others. The ability to generate remote associations appears in so many accounts of creativity that its role should be pursued, but in domain-specific ways. The appearance of an occasional "Renaissance man" may reflect nothing more than chance combination of domain-specific factors.

5. Within domain, creativity is multifactor and consists of more than ability to generate associations. Guilford's (1950) original description of the entire creative process, from problem finding to evaluation, appears more accurately to reflect what leads to a creative product. As such, creativity may best be seen as an aspect of general problem solving (e.g., Newell *et al.*, 1962) in which all steps, and not just that involving production, are important.

6. Creativity research needs a more reliable and verifiable data base. Self-report data and retro-

spective case histories are generally unverifiable. Further, no control comparisons are possible in which the effect of presence or absence of given factors can be assessed. Generally accepted principles of statistical inference should be consistently followed.

7. All too often, authors have followed Detterman's (1979, p. 174) Law XXI. "Lacking reliability and or validity, theorize." The dictum, "Thou shalt not infer causality on the basis of correlations," is frequently ignored by theorists trying to explain creativity. As a result, much explanation falls into the logical trap of *post hoc, ergo propter hoc*.

8. The possibility that individual differences in creativity reflect differences in personality and motivation rather than cognitive variables needs to be reexamined in light of the current status of cognitive-trait approaches. The importance of such factors has, of course, been emphasized by numerous researchers.

9. In studying creativity, many psychologists appear to have committed the "fundamental attribution error" (e.g., Jones, 1979; Ross, 1977), underestimating the role of situational factors and overestimating the role of unique intrapersonal factors. The role of situational in addition to intrapersonal factors in influencing creative productivity needs to be considered more consistently in research. Both Stein (e.g., 1953) and Torrance (e.g., 1961, 1975) persuasively and persistently argued the importance of situational and cultural factors in determining actual creative productivity. Amabile's (1983a,b) experimental-social and Feldman's (1980, 1986) developmental-process approaches are but two examples that examine situational factors. Consideration of creativity as resulting from person-situational interactions brings the area more in accord with trends in psychology as a whole.

A general implication is that we should, however reluctantly, question the presumed existence of any such *thing* as creativity. I cannot improve on Claridge's observation (1987, p. 134) concerning another construct, except to substitute the word "creativity" for "arousal": "I have often felt that as an explanatory concept in psychology, 'creativity' has many of the qualities of a difficult but persuasive lover, whom reason tells one to abandon yet who continues to satisfy an inescapable need." Finally, as an indication of our current level of understanding, I offer in Figure 8 a "Confusional Model of Creativity."

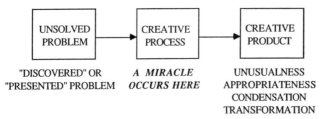

"DISCOVERED" OR   *A MIRACLE*   UNUSUALNESS   **Figure 8.** Brown's "Confusional Model of
"PRESENTED" PROBLEM   *OCCURS HERE*   APPROPRIATENESS   Creativity." As in Sidney Harris's classic cartoon,
                                              CONDENSATION   on which it is obviously based: "We need to be more
                                              TRANSFORMATION   specific in step 2."

ACKNOWLEDGMENTS. The author thanks William
B. Michael, Lee A. Jackson, Cecil R. Reynolds,
and especially John A. Glover for many useful discussions about creativity and suggestions for this
chapter and Martha Jo Clemmons and Lydia R.
Woodard for assistance in editing. He also thanks
George S. Welsh for conversations some years ago
that helped to focus attention on issues concerning
the study of creativity.

References

Albert, R. S. (Ed.). (1983). *Genius and eminence.* New York:
    Pergamon.
Albrecht, K. (1980). *Brain power.* Englewood Cliffs, NJ: Pren-
    tice-Hall.
Amabile, T. M. (1983a). *The social psychology of creativity.*
    New York: Springer-Verlag.
Amabile, T. M. (1983b). The social psychology of creativity: A
    componential conceptualization. *Journal of Personality and
    Social Psychology, 45,* 357–376.
Austin, J. H. (1978). *Chase, chance, and creativity.* New York:
    Columbia University Press.
Barron, F. (1968). *Creativity and personal freedom.* Princeton,
    NJ: Van Nostrand.
Barron, F., & Harrington, D. M. (1981). Creativity, intel-
    ligence, and personality. *Annual Review of Psychology, 32,*
    439–476.
Bloomberg, M. (Ed.). (1973). *Creativity: Theory and research.*
    New Haven, CT: College and University Press.
Boring, E. G. (1923). Intelligence as the tests test it. *New Re-
    public, 35,* 35–37.
Brewer's dictionary of phrase and fable. (1962). (6th ed.). Lon-
    don: Cassell.
Buros, O. K. (Ed.). (1972). *The seventh mental measurement
    yearbook.* Highland Park, NJ: Gryphon Press.
Buros, O. K. (Ed.). (1978). *The eighth mental measurement
    yearbook.* Highland Park, NJ: Gryphon Press.
Busse, T. V., & Mansfield, R. S. (1980). Theories of the cre-
    ative process: A review and a perspective. *Journal of Creative
    Behavior, 14,* 91–103, 132.
Campbell, D. T. (1960). Blind variation and selective retention
    in creative thought as in other knowledge processes.
    Psychological Review, 67, 380–400.
Carroll, J. B. (1968). [Review of *The nature of human intel-
    ligence* by J. P. Guilford]. *American Educational Research
    Journal, 73,* 105–112.

Cattell, R. B. (1971). *Abilities: Their structure, growth, and
    action.* Boston: Houghton Mifflin.
Claridge, G. (1987). Psychotism and arousal. In J. Strelau & H.
    J. Eysenck (Eds.), *Personality dimensions and arousal.* New
    York: Plenum Press.
Conant, J. B. (1947). *On understanding science.* New Haven,
    CT: Yale University Press.
Cronbach, L. J. (1984). *Essentials of psychological testing* (4th
    ed.). New York: Harper & Row.
Crovitz, H. F. (1970). *Galton's walk.* New York: Harper &
    Row.
Detterman, D. K. (1979). Detterman's laws of individual dif-
    ference research. In R. J. Sternberg & D. K. Detterman
    (Eds.), *Human intelligence* (pp. 165–175). Norwood, NJ:
    Ablex.
Dewey, J. (1910). *How we think.* Boston: D. C. Heath.
Ericsson, K. A., & Simon, H. A. (1984). *Protocol analysis.*
    Cambridge, MA: M.I.T. Press.
Eysenck, H. J. (1979). *The structure and measurement of intel-
    ligence.* Berlin: Springer-Verlag.
Eysenck, H. J., & Eysenck, M. W. (1985). *Personality and
    individual differences.* New York: Plenum Press.
Feldman, D. H. (1970). Faulty construct-ion. *Contemporary
    Psychology, 15,* 3–4.
Feldman, D. H. (1980). *Beyond universals in cognitive develop-
    ment.* Norwood, NJ: Ablex.
Feldman, D. H. (1986). *Nature's gambit.* New York: Basic
    Books.
Fox, H. H. (1963). A critique on creativity in science. In M. A.
    Coler (Ed.), *Essays on creativity in the sciences* (pp. 123–
    152). New York: New York University Press.
Freeman, F. N. (1924). *Mental tests.* New York: Houghton
    Mifflin.
Gardner, H. (1983). *Frames of mind.* New York: Basic Books.
Getzels, J. W., & Csikszentmihalyi, M. (1976). *The creative
    vision: A longitudinal study of problem solving in art.* New
    York: Wiley.
Ghiselin, B. (Ed.). (1952). *The creative process.* New York:
    Mentor.
Ghiselin, B. (1963). Ultimate criteria for two levels of creativity.
    In C. W. Taylor & F. Barron (Eds.), *Scientific creativity: Its
    recognition and development* (pp. 30–43). New York: Wiley.
Ghiselin, B., Rompel, R., & Taylor, C. W. (1964). A creative
    process check list: Its development and validation. In C. W.
    Taylor (Ed.), *Widening horizons in creativity* (pp. 19–33).
    New York: Wiley.
Gruber, H. E. (1981). *Darwin on man* (2nd ed.). Chicago: Uni-
    versity of Chicago Press.
Guilford, J. P. (1950). Creativity. *American Psychologist, 5,*
    444–454.

Guilford, J. P. (1956). The structure of the intellect. *Psychological Bulletin, 53,* 267–293.

Guilford, J. P. (1959). Three faces of intellect. *American Psychologist, 14,* 469–479.

Guilford, J. P. (1967). *The nature of human intelligence.* New York: McGraw-Hill.

Guilford, J. P. (1975).Creativity: A quarter century of progress. In I. A. Taylor & J. W. Getzels (Eds.), *Perspectives in creativity* (pp. 37–59). Chicago: Aldine.

Guilford, J. P. (1977). *Way beyond the IQ.* Buffalo, NY: Creative Education Foundation.

Guilford, J. P. (1982). Cognitive psychology's ambiguities: Some suggested remedies. *Psychological Bulletin, 89,* 48–59.

Hacking, I. (Ed.). (1981). *Scientific revolutions.* Oxford: Oxford University Press.

Harding, S. G. (Ed.). (1976). *Can theories be refuted?* Boston: Riedel.

Hempel, C. G. (1966). *Philosophy of natural science.* Englewood-Cliffs, NJ: Prentice-Hall.

Henle, M. (1962). The birth and death of ideas. In H. E. Gruber, G. Terrell, & M. Wertheimer (Eds.), *Contemporary approaches to creative thinking* (pp. 31–62). New York: Atherton.

Henle, M. (1974). The cognitive approach: The snail beneath the shell. In S. Rosner & L. E. Abt (Eds.), *Essays in creativity* (pp. 23–44). Croton-on-Hudson, NY: North River Press.

Hocevar, D. (1979). Ideational fluency as a confounding factor in the measurement of originality. *Journal of Educational Psychology, 71,* 191–196.

Hocevar, D. (1980). Intelligence, divergent thinking, and creativity. *Intelligence, 4,* 25–40.

Hocevar, D. (1981). Measurement of creativity: Review and critique. *Journal of Personality Assessment, 45,* 450–464.

Horn, J. L., & Knapp, J. R. (1973). On the subjective character of the empirical base of Guilford's structure of intellect model. *Psychological Bulletin, 80,* 33–43.

Hudson, L. (1966). *Contrary imaginations.* London: Methuen.

Humphreys, L. G. (1962). The organization of human abilities. *American Psychologist, 17,* 475–483.

Jackson, P. W., & Messick, S. (1967). The person, the product, and the response: Conceptual problems in the assessment of creativity. In J. Kagan (Ed.), *Creativity and learning* (pp. 1–19). Boston: Houghton Mifflin.

Jones, E. E. (1979). The rocky road from acts to dispositions. *American Psychologist, 34,* 107–117.

Khatena, J. (1984). *Imagery and creative imagination.* Buffalo, NY: Bearly Limited.

Koestler, A. (1964). *The act of creation.* New York: Macmillan.

Kogan, N. (1983). Stylistic variation in childhood and adolescence: Creativity, metaphor, and cognitive styles. In P. H. Mussen, J. H. Flavell, & E. M. Markman (Eds.), *Handbook of child psychology* (4th ed., Vol. 3, pp. 630–706). New York: Wiley.

Kuhn, T. S. (1962). *The structure of scientific revolutions.* Chicago: University of Chicago Press.

Kuhn, T. S. (1963). The essential tension: Tradition and innovation in scientific research. In C. W. Taylor & F. Barron (Eds.), *Scientific creativity: Its recognition and development* (pp. 341–354). New York: Wiley.

Lakatos, I. (1970). Falsification and the methodology of research programmes. In I. Lakatos & A. Musgrave (Eds.), *Criticism and the growth of knowledge* (pp. 8–101). Cambridge: Cambridge University Press.

Lakatos, I. (1978). *Philosophical papers. Vol I: The methodology of scientific research programmes* (J. Worrall & G. Currie, Eds.). Cambridge: Cambridge University Press.

Lakatos, I., & Musgrave, A. (Eds.). (1970). *Criticism and the growth of knowledge.* Cambridge: Cambridge University Press.

Landau, E. (1985). Creative questioning for the future. In J. Freeman (Ed.), *The psychology of gifted children* (pp. 379–392). New York: Wiley.

MacCorquodale, K., & Meehl, P. E. (1948). On a distinction between hypothetical constructs and intervening variables. *Psychological Review, 55,* 95–107.

MacKinnon, D. W. (1962). The personality correlates of creativity: A study of American architects. In S. Coopersmith (Ed.), *Personality research,* Vol. 2 of G. S. Nielsen (Ed.), *Proceedings of the XIV International Congress of Applied Psychology* (pp. 11–39). Copenhagen: Munksgaard.

MacKinnon, D. W. (1965). Personality and the realization of creative potential. *American Psychologist, 20,* 273–281.

MacKinnon, D. (1970). Creativity: A multi-faceted phenomenon. In J. D. Roslansky (Ed.), *Creativity: A discussion at the Nobel conference* (pp. 17–32). Amsterdam: North-Holland.

Maltzman, I. (1960). On the training of originality. *Psychological Review, 67,* 229–242.

Mansfield, R. J., & Busse, T. V. (1981). *The psychology of creativity and discovery.* Chicago: Nelson-Hall.

McCrae, R. R. (1987). Creativity, divergent thinking, and openness to experience. *Journal of Personality and Social Psychology, 52,* 1258–1265.

Mednick, S. A. (1962). The associative basis of the creative process. *Psychological Review, 69,* 220–232.

Mednick, S. A., & Mednick, M. T. (1964). An associative interpretation of the creative process. In C. W. Taylor (Ed.), *Widening horizons in creativity* (pp. 54–68). New York: Wiley.

Meeker, M. (1969). *The structure of intellect: Its interpretation and uses.* Columbus, OH: Merrill.

Michael, W. B. (1977). Cognitive and affective components of creativity in mathematics and the physical sciences. In J. C. Stanley, W. C. George, & C. H. Solano (Eds.), *The gifted and the creative: A fifty-year perspective.* Baltimore: Johns Hopkins University Press.

Miller, G. A., Galanter, E., & Pribram, K. H. (1960). *Plans and the structure of behavior.* New York: Holt.

Miller, N. E. (1959). Liberalization of basic S-R concepts: Extensions to conflict behavior, motivation and social learning. In S. Koch (Ed.), *Psychology: A study of a science* (Vol. 2, pp. 196–292). New York: McGraw-Hill.

Mischel, W. (1968). *Personality and assessment.* New York: Wiley.

Mooney, R. L. (1963). A conceptual model for integrating four approaches to the identification of creative talent. In C. W. Taylor & F. Barron (Eds.), *Scientific creativity: Its recognition and development* (pp. 331–340). New York: Wiley.

Newell, A., Shaw, J. C., & Simon, H. A. (1962). The processes of creative thinking. In H. E. Gruber, G. Terrell, & M. Wertheimer (Eds.), *Contemporary approaches to creative thinking* (pp. 63–119). New York: Atherton Press.

Nicholls, J. G. (1972). Creativity in the person who will never produce anything original and useful: The concept of creativity as a normally distributed trait. *American Psychologist, 27,* 717–727.

Pezzullo, T. R., Thorsen, E. E., & Madaus, G. F. (1972). The heritability of Jensen's level I and II and divergent thinking. *American Educational Research Journal, 9,* 539–546.

Popper, K. R. (1935, trans. 1959). *The logic of scientific discovery.* New York: Basic Books.

Poincaré, H. (1913). *The foundations of science.* Lancaster, PA: Science Press.

Ross, L. (1977). The intuitive psychologist and his shortcomings: Distortions in the attribution process. In L. Berkowitz (Ed.), *Advances in experimental social psychology* (Vol. 10, pp. 174–220). New York: Academic Press.

Rossman, J. (1931). *The psychology of the inventor: A study of the patentee.* Washington, DC: Inventors Publishing Co.

Rothenberg, A. (1979). The emerging goddess: The creative process in art, science, and other fields. Chicago: University of Chicago Press.

Simonton, D. K. (1984). *Genius, creativity, and leadership: Historiometric inquiries.* Cambridge, MA: Harvard University Press.

Spearman, C. (1931). *Creative mind.* New York: Appleton.

Stein, M. I. (1953). Creativity and culture. *Journal of Personality, 36,* 311–322.

Sternberg, R. J. (1979). Intelligence research at the interface between differential and cognitive psychology: Prospects and proposals. In R. J. Sternberg & D. K. Detterman (Eds.), *Human intelligence* (pp. 33–60). Norwood, NJ: Ablex.

Sternberg, R. J. (1985). Implicit theories of intelligence, creativity, and wisdom. *Journal of Personality and Social Psychology, 49,* 607–627.

Sternberg, R. J. (1986). A triarchic theory of intellectual giftedness. In R. J. Sternberg & J. E. Davidson (Eds.), *Conceptions of giftedness* (pp. 223–243). Cambridge: Cambridge University Press.

Sternberg, R. J., & Davidson, J. E. (1986). Cobnitive development in the gifted and talented. In F. D. Horowitz & M. O'Brien (Eds.), *The gifted and talented: Developmental perspectives* (pp. 37–74). Washington, DC: American Psychological Association.

Sternberg, R. J., & Detterman, D. K. (Eds.). (1979). *Human intelligence.* Norwood, NJ: Ablex.

Sternberg, R. J., & Detterman, D. K. (Eds.). (1986). *What is intelligence?* Norwood, NJ: Ablex.

Taylor, C. W. (1947). A factorial study of fluency in writing. *Psychometrika, 12,* 239–262.

Taylor, C. W., & Barron, F. (Eds.). (1963). *Scientific creativity: Its recognition and development.* New York: Wiley.

Taylor, C. W., & Ellison, R. L. (1975). Moving toward working models in creativity: Utah creativity experiences and insights.

In I. A. Taylor & J. W. Getzels (Eds.), *Perspectives in creativity* (pp. 191–223). Chicago: Aldine.

Taylor, C. W., & Holland, J. (1964). Predictors of creative performance. In C. W. Taylor (Ed.), *Creativity: Progress and potential* (pp. 15–48). New York: McGraw-Hill.

Thorndike, R. L. (1963). Some methodological issues in the study of creativity. In *Proceedings of the 1962 Invitational Conference on Testing Problems* (pp. 40–54). Princeton, NJ: Educational Testing Service.

Torrance, E. P. (1961). Factors affecting creative thinking in children: An interim research report. *Merrill-Palmer Quarterly of Behavior and Development, 7,* 171–180.

Torrance, E. P. (1975). Creativity research in education: Still alive. In I. A. Taylor & J. W. Getzels (Eds.), *Perspectives in creativity.* Chicago: Aldine.

Turner, M. B. (1968). *Psychology and the philosophy of science.* New York: Appleton-Century-Crofts.

Vernon, P. E. (Ed.). (1970). *Creativity.* Harmondsworth, Middlesex, England: Penguin Books.

Wallach, M. A. (1970). Creativity. In P. H. Mussen (Ed.), *Carmichael's manual of child psychology* (3rd ed., pp. 1211–1272). New York: Wiley.

Wallach, M. A. (1971). *The intelligence/creativity distinction.* New York: General Learning Press.

Wallach, M. A. (1986). Creativity testing and giftedness. In F. D. Horowitz & M. O'Brien (Eds.), *The gifted and talented: Developmental perspectives* (pp. 99–123). Washington, DC: American Psychological Association.

Wallach, M. A., & Kogan, N. (1965). *Modes of thinking in young children.* New York: Holt, Rinehart, & Winston.

Wallach, M. A., & Wing, C. W., Jr. (1969). *The talented student.* New York: Holt, Rinehart, & Winston.

Wallas, G. (1926). *The art of thought.* New York: Harcourt Brace.

Weisberg, R. W. (1986). *Creativity: Genius and other myths.* New York: W. H. Freeman.

Welsh, G. S. (1975). *Creativity and intelligence: A personality approach.* Chapel Hill, NC: Institute for Research in Social Science.

Welsh, G. S. (1986). Positive exceptionality: The academically gifted and the creative. In R. T. Brown & C. R. Reynolds (Eds.), *Psychological perspectives on childhood exceptionality: A handbook* (pp. 311–343). New York: Wiley.

Wertheimer, M. (1959). *Productive thinking* (enlarged ed.). New York: Harper & Row.

Zigler, E., & Butterfield, E. C. (1968). Motivational aspects of changes in IQ test performance of culturally deprived nursery group school children. *Child Development, 39,* 1–14.

CHAPTER 2

Psychometric Issues in the Assessment of Creativity

William B. Michael and Claudia R. Wright

Overview

In this first section, an overview of the remaining seven divisions of the chapter is presented. The second section affords a brief description of categories of instrumentation to provide the reader with a foundation within which the psychometric issues in the assessment of creativity can be viewed. In the third section, psychometric concerns pertaining to construct validity, content validity, and criterion-related validity are addressed. Subsequent to an abbreviated review of the meaning of reliability, concerns regarding optimal approaches to the estimation of reliability of creativity measures are considered in the fourth section. The impact upon reliability and validity of scoring procedures is examined in the fifth section with particular emphasis on the presence of fluency as a confounding factor in the interpretation of scores of measures of divergent thinking. The sixth section provides a survey of a number of the difficulties encountered in establishing normative data for the understanding of scores on measures of

creativity. A cursory exploration of a few selected issues in the administration of tests of creativity follows in the seventh section, and the eighth section contributes a concluding statement.

Alternative Methods for Measurement of Creativity

Considerable diversification exists in the types of measures used in the assessment of creativity. Although pencil-and-paper tests probably account for the majority of measures employed in research studies, other techniques are commonly used. In a comprehensive review and critique of currently available techniques for the measurement of creativity, Hocevar (1981) arrived at a taxonomy of 10 categories. He evaluated these alternative approaches to assessment of creativity in terms of reliability, discriminant validity, dimensionality, and convergent validity. These 10 categories included (a) tests of divergent thinking, (b) attitude and interest inventories, (c) personality inventories, (d) biographical inventories, (e) teacher nominations, (f) peer nominations, (g) supervisor ratings, (h) judgments of products, (i) eminence, and (j) self-reported creative activities and achievements. Hocevar concluded that an inventory of self-reported creative endeavors and achievements is the

William B. Michael • Department of Educational Psychology, University of Southern California, Los Angeles, CA 90089. **Claudia R. Wright** • Department of Educational Psychology and Administration, California State University, Long Beach, CA 90840.

33

most defensible approach for identifying creative individuals. In Chapter 3 of this volume, Hocevar and Bachelor have given a detailed critique of instruments designed to assess creativity.

Concerns Relating to Validity

Most psychometricians as well as theorists who have worked in the area of creativity probably would agree that validity of creativity assessment is the single most important consideration. As Wolf (1982) has so aptly pointed out, the validity of a test is anchored to three concerns: (a) what a test is supposed to be measuring, (b) what the score derived from the administration of a test means, and (c) how the score of an individual on a measure is related to other observable facts regarding that individual. Wolf has indicated that this third concern is the essence of the validation of the interpretation of a test score—a concern that in many instances could be as significant as, if not more important than, the validation of the test itself.

Within this broad context, three major types of validity—construct, content, and criterion-related—are examined, especially as they relate to the assessment of creative endeavor. These three types of validity are based on *Standards for Educational and Psychological Testing* prepared by the Committee to Develop Standards for Educational and Psychological Testing of the American Educational Research Association, the American Psychological Association, and the National Council on Measurement in Education which was published in 1985 by the American Psychological Association. Several general texts dealing with problems of psychological and educational measurement also have treated these three types of validity on the basis of content in an earlier edition entitled *Standards for Educational and Psychological Tests and Manuals* (American Psychological Association, 1974). A representative sampling of writings that present information about standards or criteria for validity would include contributions by Anastasi (1982), Campbell (1976), Crocker and Algina (1985), Cronbach (1971, 1980), Nunnally (1978), Thorndike (1982), and Wolf (1982). In the context of the assessment of creativity, validity issues have been treated by a number of writers (e.g., Golann, 1963; Guilford, 1971; Thorndike, 1963; Treffinger & Poggio, 1972; Treffinger, Renzulli, & Feldhusen, 1971).

Construct Validity

In this discussion, the topic of construct validity as a psychometric concern in the assessment of creativity is considered, followed by five major issues that are presented in subsequent sections: (1) construct validity is defined in general terms with reference to theoretical as well as statistical perspectives; special attention is given to definitions of creativity which emphasize several constructs, such as fluency, originality, flexibility, and elaboration; (2) a review is presented of the techniques of exploratory factor analysis and confirmatory factor analysis employed in the study of construct validity; (3) the application of multitrait–multimethod approaches to the problem of construct validity is considered in general, with specific attention given to its application to the domain of creativity; (4) the use of three other methodologies comprising experimental, longitudinal, and computerized imaging studies in the process of validating constructs of creativity is examined; and (5) some pertinent questions are posed central to inquiry about construct validity.

Definition and Rationale

Construct Validity Viewed from a Theoretical Orientation. Underlying the process of construct validation is the development of a conceptual linkage or network among selected variables identified within any given behavioral domain (such as locus of control, intelligence, or creativity) which when taken together form a composite or construct considered to hold promise as an indicator of the manifestation of the target behavior. It is assumed that the process of construct validation requires an inferential leap from observed patterns of response consistency (to which some meaning is attached) to a specific construct which purports to account for the observed consistency. As Messick (1975) pointed out, typically two major requirements, based on the pioneer work of Campbell and Fiske (1959), exist for establishing construct validity. The first requirement is *convergent* validation, the demonstration that a selected measure of a given behavior is related to other measures linked to the same construct as well as to other criterion-related variables which have a theory-based relationship to the construct. The second requirement involves *discriminant* validation which shows that the selected measure is not linked to other measures and variables which theoretically support distinctly different constructs. These requirements are also reflected in the technical standards related to construct validity listed in the previously cited *Standards for Educational and Psychological Testing* (American Psychological Association, 1985). Additional contributions concerned with the integration of evidence for construct validity may be found in the writings of Cronbach (1971, 1980), Cronbach and Meehl (1955), Fiske (1987), Tenopyr (1977), and Wolf (1982).

Construct Validity Viewed from a Psychometric Orientation. Statistical procedures central to psychometric methods often have been used to afford a relatively objective basis for arriving at the selection of measures to represent response consistencies that are conceptually linked to a construct. The statistical procedures most frequently employed to support the construct validation process include correlational and factor-analytic approaches, such as (a) the simple reporting of coefficients obtained between total scores or subscores of different measures selected on the basis of similarity in operational definitions and/or conceptualizations to indicate the strength of interrelationships among the measures; (b) multitrait–multimethod analyses for addressing convergent and discriminant validity concerns with particular attention applied to disentanglement of method and trait variance (Campbell & Fiske, 1959; Fiske, 1987); (c) exploratory factor analysis (Gorsuch, 1983; Nunnally, 1978); and (d) confirmatory factor analysis (Gorsuch, 1983; Jöreskog, 1969; Jöreskog & Sörbom, 1981), which can be subsumed under causal modeling (Bentler, 1980). Despite the usefulness of various psychometric procedures to facilitate evidence of the validity of a construct, it should be noted, as Cronbach (1971) has stated, that "one validates, not a test, but an interpretation of data arising from a specified procedure" (p. 447).

Defining Constructs Related to Creativity. If creativity is organized as a complex of interrelated constructs, the problem of construct validity must focus upon the operationalization of key theoretical constructs which are thought to underlie creative behaviors. Among the most commonly cited constructs are those originally proposed by Guilford in his structure-of-intellect (SOI) model. They include fluency, originality, flexibility, and elaboration in divergent thinking and transformations involving the application of convergent thinking to the arrival at unique solutions, often in an unfamiliar or for-

eign context (Guilford, 1963, 1967, 1968, 1970, 1971; Guilford & Hoepfner, 1971; Guilford & Tenopyr, 1968; Michael, 1977; Torrance, 1966).

The first four constructs rely heavily on conceptualizations associated with divergent thinking abilities. In the instance of fluency of verbal expression, the ability is conceptualized as the divergent production of semantic units, relations, and systems within the SOI model. It usually is operationalized in terms of the quantity of elements that can be generated. Originality (adaptative flexibility) has been defined in terms of measures indicating statistical infrequency, that is, those responses considered to be a rare occurrence either in comparison of a given response of a subject to all of his or her previous responses, or in comparison of that given response to all responses from different subjects (a within vs. a between comparison). The construct of flexibility generally applies to that of spontaneous flexibility in which a shift from one class of responses to another is involved as in the listing of alternative uses of an object, such as a shoe. In divergent thinking, elaboration may be measured in terms of the number of occupations that might be associated with a given symbol, such as a key. In contrast to these four constructs indicative of divergent production, the fifth construct involving the product of transformations arises frequently in the determination of a unique solution to a problem with many constraints as in mathematics or invention—a problem often involving a novel or ingenious use of a familiar object or process in a new or foreign context.

Treffinger *et al.* (1971) have emphasized that the measures of most common creativity constructs have been based on simple quantitative rather than qualitative dimensions. This quantitative emphasis may run the risk of leading the investigator to ignore in one hypothesized construct qualitative characteristics in behaviors that actually reflect other constructs in need of operational specification. Definition of these other constructs in the form of new measures would permit an initial determination of the place of the original construct within an ordered network of hypothesized and measurable constructs in an expanded domain of human behavior. Moreover, it should be emphasized that a simple numerical count of frequency of responses to reflect a construct of originality could overlook the occurrence of two or three highly significant responses on the part of one examinee that qualitatively would be worth a hundred fairly mundane responses of another examinee. Thus, the individual with the low quantitative score could be unfairly penalized in his manifestation of what would be judged truly original behavior.

Factor-Analytic Approaches

The use of factor-analytic approaches to construct validation often constitutes an attempt to explain the intercorrelations among test (item) variables in terms of a small number of psychologically meaningful dimensions. An attempt is made to interpret each dimension as an operational representation of a latent trait or construct in terms of shared or common process and content characteristics of these measures that serve to define or describe the dimension. An indication of the degree of relationship of a test or item variable to a dimension is often expressed as a coefficient of correlation, usually termed a factor loading or factor weight.

Frequently, hypotheses regarding the nature of cognitive abilities or affective characteristics are tested through use of factor-analytic techniques by choosing in advance three or four measures thought to represent a common construct. If in the resulting factor analysis the test or item variables hypothesized to represent the construct are loaded or weighted on a factor but are not correlated substantially with any other factor, evidence is viewed as being affirmative for that particular hypothesis. This form of evidence for the validity of a construct can occur in either exploratory or confirmatory factor analyses if adequate conceptualization has occurred and if corresponding care has been exercised in the selection of measures to portray the constructs hypothesized.

Exploratory Factor-Analytic Techniques.

Exploratory factor-analytic approaches provide not only a statistical method for tentative testing of initial hypotheses derived from a rather tentative theoretical conceptualization, but also a strategy for trying to effect some degree of parsimony in understanding a large complex of intercorrelated variables in a domain of inquiry about which the researcher has limited knowledge or insight. Generally, the overall goal in exploratory factor analysis is to identify factors that will explain the greatest amount of covariance among the variables. Depending upon the statistical technique employed, the first mathematically extracted factor typically accounts for most of the covariance in the data, with each subsequently extracted factor ac-

counting for smaller and smaller amounts of the variability left to be explained. As the initial factors generated in the mathematical procedure are usually difficult to interpret, a procedure known as the rotation of factor axes (the axes constituting mathematical representations of initially derived dimensions to describe the intercorrelations among the variables in a correlation matrix) takes place to improve the psychological meaningfulness and interpretability of the dimensions. As mentioned earlier, the variables loaded or weighted on the rotated factor axis are examined for common characteristics to provide a basis for definition or description of the factor as a psychological construct. Additional information regarding factor-analytic procedures may be found in standard texts, such as those by Gorsuch (1983) and Harman (1976).

Confirmatory Factor-Analytic Techniques.

Exploratory factor analysis traditionally has made use of arbitrary methods not only for estimating communalities (sum of common factor variance for each test or item variable), which are inserted in the diagonal of a correlation matrix prior to factor extraction, but also for rotating factor axes. The results frequently have led to a lack in uniformity and replicability of the dimensionality of a specified group of correlated variables. In contrast, confirmatory maximum likelihood factor analysis affords a comparatively objective approach of providing evidence to support or to disconfirm not only hypotheses obtained from exploratory factor analyses (especially in the instance of a new data base), but also conceptually based hypotheses derived from a researcher's theory. Specifically, the method of confirmatory maximum likelihood factor analysis, which has been made feasible in light of the availability of a set of computer programs in LISREL V (Jöreskog & Sörbom, 1981), furnishes a means through which the consistency of observed patterns of intercorrelations among measurable variables can be compared with the configuration of intercorrelations predicted from a group of hypothesized latent variables (constructs). These hypothesized variables that appear within a covariance structure (causal model) are related to one another in a manner harmonious with a researcher's theory. After the theoretical constructs, or latent variables, and their indicators (e.g., test measures) have been specified, the interrelationships among the various constructs can be indicated to constitute what is called a *structural model,* and the relationship of each construct to its measure (sometimes referred to as the *measurement model*) can be indicated.

Constituting the major components of a causal model, sets of regression, or structural, equations are formulated that express the relationship of measurement variables (dependent variables) to latent variables (independent variables). These equations designate the hypothesized effects associated with specific predictor variables upon one or several criterion variables. Understandably, a major statistical goal in the model becomes that of estimating its parameters as accurately as is feasible and of determining (generally, through employment of a chi-square test) how closely the proposed model fits the data acquired from the measured variables for the particular group of subjects studied. If the judgment is reached that the model does not afford an appropriate fit to the data, the investigator may reject it as a plausible representative of the hypothesized causal structure describing the measured variables. On the other hand, if application of significant tests does not result in the rejection of the model (the null hypothesis being tenable), then the model may be considered as providing a reasonable representation of the hypothesized (causal) structure. Ordinarily, in confirmatory maximum likelihood factor analysis, a given factor model is evaluated against numerous alternative factor models to provide a means of determining which model furnishes the most nearly adequate psychological interpretation of the data as well as the optimal degree of fit from a statistical viewpoint in reproducing the entries in a given correlation model (Khattab, Michael, & Hocevar, 1982).

Applications of Confirmatory Maximum Likelihood Factor Analysis to Guilford's SOI Model. The published works of Guilford and his associates (e.g., Guilford, 1967; Guilford & Hoepfner, 1971) have made use of various factor-analytic techniques that would be classified as exploratory. Many researchers (e.g., Harris & Harris, 1971; Horn & Knapp, 1973; 1974), however, have criticized Guilford's factor-analytic solutions as not providing strong evidence in support of the SOI model largely because objective criteria were not employed. In fact, Horn and Knapp declared that the Procrustean factor-analytic methods that Guilford had employed could afford almost as strong support for theories generated by random sampling procedures as for the SOI model itself.

To overcome some of these objections of subjectivity, reanalyses, using confirmatory maximum

likelihood factor analysis, were completed of correlational data involving several creativity measures from Guilford's Aptitudes Research Project, which for many years was centered at the University of Southern California (Khattab *et al.*, 1982; Khattab & Michael, 1986; Mace, Michael, & Hocevar, 1985). The resulting analyses yielded somewhat mixed results, partly as a function of which tests were incorporated within the correlation matrices. When a representative balance of ability measures intended to reflect the content, process, and product elements of hypothesized first-order and second-order SOI factors was included, reasonable support for hypothesized constructs of the SOI theory was forthcoming. Additional factor-analytic work with this comparatively new methodology needs to be carried out to substantiate the validity of the constructs in the SOI model that have been thought to reflect creative behaviors.

Concerns and Limitations in the Use of Factor-Analytic Approaches. Several conceptual and methodological concerns and limitations arise in the use of factor-analytic techniques in the study of a given psychological domain, such as creativity. Probably the one most important concern is that of having as sound and carefully conceptualized theoretical framework as is possible so that appropriate steps can be taken to design a study that will yield meaningful outcomes. Depending upon the stage of development of a given area of psychological inquiry, an integrated theoretical framework is necessary for the appropriate selection of variables to constitute the basis for operationalizing the hypotheses to be tested and to contribute to the design of the correlation matrix that subsequently will be analyzed. It is important that marker or anchor variables defining factors that already have been painstakingly established in the research of other investigators be included so that (a) well-established factors are not given new names or labels, (b) variance associated with previously defined dimensions is separated or removed from that associated with new constructs, and (c) an integration of new research findings can be made with those of previously conducted studies. In contrast to carefully planned analyses, the so-called shotgun approaches, in which variables are indiscriminately introduced within a correlation matrix without reflective considerations of their impact upon the solution, may well lead to psychologically meaningless or nonsensical results—a circumstance resembling the familiar expression in computer work of "garbage in—garbage out" (GIGO).

A number of psychometric and statistical concerns also arises in planning factor-analytic studies that hopefully will have the potential to yield definitive results. In the process of selecting variables, attention obviously needs to be given to constructing and/or selecting measures of as high reliability as possible so that significant amounts of systematic variance can be identified as being associated with newly isolated factor dimensions. Pilot studies may well be necessary to establish reasonably high reliabilities of the measures to be used and sufficient variance to permit the emergence of correlation coefficients that can be interpreted as reflecting genuine levels of association rather than inflated indices that have capitalized upon chance. In addition to the minimization of measurement error, sampling error also needs to be controlled by taking groups both representative of the population of interest and adequate in size so that the factor-analytic results do not reveal the capitalization upon random sampling error. Moreover, care should be exercised not to include too many variables for the number of subjects in the sample. Although investigators differ in the criteria that they employ, we have found that the ratio provided by the division of the total number of subjects in the sample by the total number of variables in the correlation matrix typically should be at least 15 to 20 if the measures are highly reliable (in excess of .80).

Several reservations need to be exercised in the interpretation of the outcomes of factor-analytic studies in terms of the particular features of methodology employed: (a) the number of factors extracted; (b) the type of estimate for the diagonal entries of the correlation matrix (unities, reliability coefficients, or communalities) depending upon the factor-analytic model selected; (c) the method of rotation to be employed—orthogonal or oblique (often a function of the theoretical position taken); (d) the selection of the particular statistical procedure for effecting either an orthogonal or oblique solution; (e) the choice of analyzing the intercorrelations of individual items or of composites of items (subtests) or of whole tests; (f) the setting of lower bounds in the magnitudes of factor loadings for meaningful interpretation to offset the impact of sampling and measurement error; (g) the optimal arrangement of the data presentation (as in trying to demonstrate the presence of a hierarchical solution in harmony with the hypothesized configuration of constructs within a particular theory); and (h) the

realization of numerous statistical assumptions, such as normality, linearity, homoscedasticity, and level of measurement (e.g., ordinal or interval). Variations in the extent or manner in which these several methodological features have been integrated into the factor-analytic approach can lead to rather different solutions that are open to conflicting interpretations. (For additional information pertinent to issues in factor analysis as a research technique, the reader is referred to Chapters 17 and 18 in Gorsuch, 1983.)

Multitrait–Multimethod Techniques

A useful procedure for operationally estimating construct validity between two or more traits or behavioral characteristics considered to be related to creativity is the multitrait–multimethod approach introduced by Campbell and Fiske (1959). This correlational technique provides for the simultaneous testing for convergent and discriminant validities of intercorrelated variables through the analysis of two or more theoretically related behaviors (traits) assessed by two or more methods of measurement. The basic idea of demonstrating convergent validity is that if two or more tests or measures, each employing different methods, provide relatively similar estimates of a target behavior, then one can have greater confidence in the strength of that inferred behavioral trait or characteristic and can maintain that evidence of convergent validity (that the multiple methods *converge* on a single behavioral characteristic) has been achieved. The concern of discriminant validity rests on the ability of the measures to discriminate among different behavioral traits. Thus, one can anticipate finding a relatively low degree of association between different behaviors measured by the same test.

To facilitate understanding of these principles, Figure 1, based upon fictitious data, is provided to illustrate the basic organization of the multitrait–multimethod matrix as it may apply to a construct-validity problem in the area of creativity. In this figure, the matrix is composed of the intercorrelations among three creativity traits (originality, flexibility, and fluency) which are measured by three different creativity tests (Guilford Test, Torrance Test, and Michael Test). To demonstrate construct validity from application of this methodology, at least two conditions must be addressed: (a) the first condition is a demonstration of convergent validity, meaning that a test should correlate highly with different tests which purport to measure the same

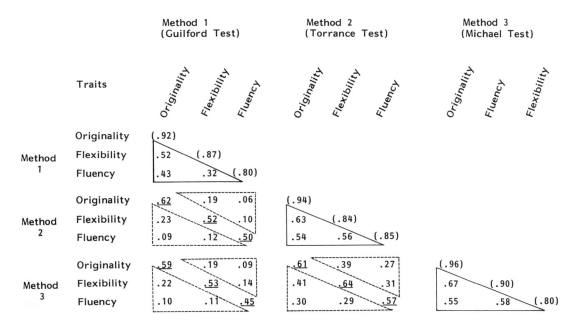

Figure 1. A demonstration of convergent validity. The main diagonal of values in parentheses comprises the estimates of reliability. The validity diagonal is represented by the underlined values. The heterotrait–monomethod comparisons are set off by the solid-line triangles and each of the heterotrait–heteromethod comparisons is provided in the broken-line triangles.

theoretical construct, and (b) the second involves a demonstration of discriminant validity—a condition in which a test is not statistically related to other measures from which it has been determined that the test should be conceptually and theoretically different. In the problem of demonstrating convergent validity, the entries in the validity diagonal represented by the underlined values in Figure 1 would be statistically significant and sufficiently large to justify a validity investigation. Additional support for convergent validity is found if higher correlations exist for the validity diagonal values than for those values associated with different traits measured by different measures (referred to as the heterotrait–heteromethod triangles which are shown as broken-lined triangles). Thus, in order to demonstrate convergent validity, the validity values for a given trait, such as originality (e.g., .62, .59, and .61) should be statistically significant, meaningful, and generally higher than the correlations obtained between originality and any other two traits (e.g., flexibility and fluency) measured by different methods.

According to Campbell and Fiske (1959), although convergent validation procedures emphasizing independence of methods provide key information for most validity problems, the demands

associated with establishing construct validity require additional analyses provided by discriminant validation techniques. Again, employing the multitrait–multimethod matrix, the first criterion for demonstrating discriminant validity which must be addressed requires that the correlations between similar traits measured by different methods (the convergent validities) exceed the correlations between different traits measured by different methods. (As noted previously, this comparison also supports the demonstration of convergent validity.) The second discriminant validity criterion considered is that the validity coefficients for each trait exceed the correlations between that trait and different traits measured by the same method. (This criterion is depicted by the heterotrait–monomethod values designated by the solid-line triangles in Figure 1.) If high intercorrelations are obtained across different traits (e.g., between originality and fluency) which are hypothesized to be conceptually and statistically unrelated employing the identical method or test, then a method effect is said to exist.

Marsh and Hocevar (1983) have summarized the major shortcomings of the multitrait–multimethod approach to include (a) the lack of objective criteria for defining satisfactory results; (b) the discrepancy between the conceptualization of the discriminant validity criteria with particular reference to the concept of trait covariation—the correlation between different traits that does not depend upon method; (c) the risk of realizing rather markedly an assessed method effect in one set of measures but not substantially in another set because of differential levels of correlation that arise as a function of systematic variation in the corresponding magnitude of reliabilities in one set or both sets of measures; and (d) the chance of obtaining inflated convergent validities also artificially increased by shared method variance among the traits. With reference to the second criticism (b), the existence of trait covariation for two of Campbell and Fiske's (1959) criteria can lead to conflicting interpretations. In one criterion, the occurrence of covariation is viewed as demonstrating a lack of discriminant validity, whereas the presence of covariation in the other criterion (a criterion for patterns of correlations) is interpreted as a demonstration of discriminant validity.

Use of Three Other Methodologies

Experimental Studies. Relatively few experimental investigations have been undertaken to demonstrate the validity of constructs associated with creativity. The basic methodology involves the comparison of an experimental group that has been exposed to an activity hypothesized to be associated with some aspect of creativity with a control group that has not been. A prediction would be made that the experimental group would perform at a higher level on a logically appropriate dependent variable, the standing on which would be anticipated to be elevated by participation in the planned intervention. One such investigation reported by Parnes (1964) indicated that students who had completed a creative problem-solving course performed at a higher average level on six out of eight creative ability measures than did those students who had not been exposed to the course.

Longitudinal Studies. In a number of biographical and longitudinal studies of creative or eminent mathematicians and scientists summarized by Michael (1977), personality characteristics, demographics, and home-related variables were identified. The primary goal of such longitudinal and archival investigations is not only to provide descriptions of salient characteristics of individuals classified as creative, but also to generate a pool of possible criterion variables from which to predict

creative behaviors. It is interesting to note in Michael's review of research studies that conclusions derived from intensive inquiry of life-history variables (Roe, 1951), based on in-depth interviews concerning the personal characteristics of creative individuals, were similar to those identified from use of standardized personality and ability measures chosen to reflect creativity (Guilford, 1963; MacKinnon, 1962, 1965).

Computerized Imaging of Cerebral Activity: Creativity Constructs and Physiological Correlates. Over the past decade, a revolution has taken place in the technological marketplace. Today, thanks to advances in medical technology which employ computerized imaging methods, such as computerized axial tomography (CAT)—sometimes referred to as the CAT-scan—procedures are available for the mapping of cerebral activity which provide opportunities for studying the generality or specificity of brain functions associated with human behavior. In a recent investigation on the relationship between neurological correlates and creative thought, Hudspith (1985) studied subjects who had been classified as either high-creative ($n = 10$) or low-creative ($n = 10$) based on their standing on three measures of creativity—the Remote Associates Test (RAT) (Mednick & Mednick, 1962, 1967) and two subtests from the Structure of Intellect Learning Abilities Test (SOILAT) (Meeker & Meeker, 1975), both of which were designed to reflect operations of divergent thinking applied to figural units and to semantic units. Each subject then received examinations of brainwave activity using the CAT apparatus during three experimental conditions—rest, word association, and spatial association. In each of the verbal and spatial conditions, "mental" manipulation, rather than a pencil-and-paper task, was required. For example, instructions for the word-association condition required the subject, with closed eyes, to listen to a pair of words and then to think of a word which has a common association with the pair. For the spatial condition, subjects were instructed to observe a three-dimensional model and then to imagine with their eyes closed the model folding open along a selected axis of the model.

Statistically significant outcomes were reported between the high-creative and low-creative groups in terms of mean and differential measures of electroencephalograph (EEG) recordings provided by the CAT output. In general, subjects classified as high-creative in relation to those identified as low-creative tended to produce lower occipital (visual cortex) amplitudes as well as a combination of lower occipital and higher prefrontal amplitudes in the three conditions of associational thinking investigated. This study, although preliminary in nature, points to the use of new methods for exploring creative activity and invites new hypotheses that will test neurological correlates of creativity constructs.

Some Pertinent Questions in Construct Validation

A central area of concern does exist in the accuracy of inferences regarding the manifestation of creative behavior in relation to the context in which it occurs. Addressing this important issue, Fiske (1988) has introduced the term *protocol,* which pertains to the conditions under which a study is conducted. His thoughtful paper has led to a number of questions that pertain to how method effects can contribute to construct invalidity. In the context of the study of creativity, the authors have taken the liberty of rephrasing and, in some instances, paraphrasing a number of his concerns in the form of the following sampling of questions (which is by no means exhaustive):

1. Is the creative behavior serendipitous—does it happen by chance?

2. Does the creative behavior occur under a structured situation during testing or does it manifest itself in an unstructured situation? Stated another way, does the creative behavior take place under specified demand characteristics that are determined in part by restricted materials or delimiting problem statements, or does the creative behavior arise in response to an open-ended question or situation?

3. Does the behavior occur following exposure to examples provided by models or in an apparently spontaneous manner from unidentifiable internal processes?

4. What is the minimum amount of information that can be given to a subject to evoke creative behavior?

5. Does the subject recognize his or her own product as creative?

6. How useful, if not essential, is the variable of time in formulating constructs about creative behaviors?

7. What are the relative merits of change scores over time or single scores at one point in time in the assessment of creative behaviors?

8. To what extent do measures rely on *a priori* judgments of what cognitive processes and abilities reflect creative behaviors?

These questions suggest a number of potential areas for research for clarifying the nature of creative behaviors and the context in which they occur. The reader is urged to study the paper by Fiske (1987) again and again for thoughtful stimulation and for its unlimited heuristic value.

Creativity versus Intelligence

The distinction between creativity and general intelligence has been a source of considerable controversy in the research literature (e.g., Dellas & Gaier, 1970; Getzels & Jackson, 1962; Golann, 1963; Guilford, 1967, 1968; Guilford & Hoepfner, 1971; Thorndike, 1963; Torrance, 1959). Although this concern about the distinction between creativity and general intelligence is primarily a conceptual one beyond the scope of this chapter, mention should be made of the fact that the realization of construct validity of the measures studied is essential to the demonstration of the relative independence or dependence of these two concepts. Clearly, the appropriate application of psychometric procedures and the fulfillment of the assumptions underlying them are necessary but not sufficient conditions for providing evidence regarding whether creativity constructs are independent of general intelligence or constitute a subset of abilities that can be subsumed under the rubric of general mental ability.

Closing Thoughts

The problems associated with establishing construct validity are pervasive regardless of the area of behavioral research. Special attention must be given, however, to the study of such behavioral domains as creativity because of the apparent complexity and potential interrelatedness of the constructs involved. Moreover, an improved understanding of what creativity is, on the assumption that it can be defined and understood, may lead to the design of teaching strategies and to the planning of educational environments so that maximal opportunities exist for creative behaviors to emerge in a technological and scientifically oriented society. Such a society will require the best creative talents that are available not only in the sciences, but also in the arts and humanities for the enrichment of the quality of life.

Content Validity

In the familiar context of achievement testing, content validity typically refers to the extent to which the behaviors associated with specific objectives of instruction or learning (both subject matter and process objectives) are representative samples of a relatively clearly defined broad domain or population of behaviors. Although an understanding of the construct or constructs underlying process objectives is essential to the realization of content validity of tasks involved in school learning, the importance of construct interpretation and hence of construct validity is probably relatively greater in the assessment of creative endeavor than it is in the evaluation of most cognitive tasks encountered in the classroom. Content validity would be relevant in the assessment of creativity primarily to the degree to which a teacher has devised an instructional unit specifically directed toward achieving certain instructional objectives reflecting original, unique, or flexible types of behaviors. Such instructional units, in the authors' experience, have been relatively rare at all levels of the educational process unless specifically funded as a special project, perhaps because they constitute a threat to the well-established status quo of student conformity or to the expectations of the instructor, who regards innovative activities as either a nuisance to a well-established routine or a challenge to his or her authority or status.

If a teacher is interested in bringing about the manifestation of creative behaviors, the steps that would be taken to realize content validity would parallel those associated with the evaluation of the nature and amounts of learning that have taken place in almost any instructional unit. Essentially, a two-dimensional grid is prepared in which topical or subject matter objectives are listed as headings in several adjacent columns (or rows) and the process objectives associated with various levels of thinking or cognitive activity are cited as headings along a series of adjacent rows (or columns). The intersection of a category from one dimension with that from a second dimension forms a cell for which one or more test items will be constructed to reflect the emphasis placed upon that particular content-process objective. For example, to find the cost to cover a kitchen floor with linoleum at a certain number of dollars per square yard would reflect in the grid the crossing of the topic of the determination of *areas of geometric figures* (subject-matter content) from the *use of an appropriate formula* along with the introduction of a cost coefficient in a

practical situation (process at the application level). This same methodology could be employed to develop items for a test of creative behavior in which several sets of items could represent different levels of complexity (a hierarchy) of a problem-solving process. Additional information concerning both the preparation of grids to portray instructional objectives and the common techniques for writing items to constitute the intended sampling emphasis within the grid can be found in standard textbooks in measurement and evaluation (Bloom, Hastings, & Madaus, 1971; Ebel, 1979; Gronlund, 1976; Mehrens & Lehmann, 1984; Sax, 1980; Thorndike & Hagen, 1977).

Criterion-Related Validity

Criterion-related validity of a test may be defined as the degree of accuracy with which the test is predictive of the behavior of an individual or group of individuals in a clearly defined situation typically amenable to measurement (customarily referred to as a criterion variable) (American Psychological Association, 1985; Thorndike & Hagen, 1977). For example, scores on a scholastic aptitude test often are employed to forecast standing on a criterion measure, such as grade-point average earned during the freshman year in college. Criterion-related validity is customarily differentiated into concurrent validity and predictive validity. In the instance of concurrent validity, the time lapse between the administration of the antecedent, or predictor, measure, such as a scholastic aptitude test, and the attainment of criterion data is minimal, if not virtually simultaneous. On the other hand, predictive validity implies the administration of a test to be used for selection, placement, or classification or for manifestation of a certain form of behavior (e.g., alcoholism, delinquency) often several weeks, months, or even years in advance of the collection of follow-up information that is intended to reflect the adequacy of performance or the adjustment of an individual as represented by his or her standing on one or more criterion measures.

Typically, the degree of criterion-related validity is indicated by a correlation coefficient that summarizes the amount of relationship between scores on a predictor variable with scores on the criterion measure. An alternative procedure that often precedes the calculation of the correlation coefficient is the preparation of a scatter diagram in which each dot or point represents the simultaneous standing of an individual on the predictor and criterion variables. Such a scatter diagram also can be cast into the form of an expectancy chart when the data have been grouped into intervals on each variable. In an expectancy chart, one can determine for those individuals falling within a given interval of scores on the predictor the probability of placing at or above the lower limit of any specified interval on the criterion measure. Both scatter diagrams and expectancy charts can provide the researcher with an indication of whether the trend of the data is linear or curvilinear and thus can afford evidence regarding the appropriateness of applying alternative statistical procedures for estimating the degree of relationship between the two variables and for making predictions of placement on one variable from knowledge of standing on the other.

Several limiting or modifying circumstances arise in conjunction with the meaningful interpretation of validity coefficients, particularly in the instance of creativity measures. Probably the most important concern in the realization of concurrent or predictive validity is that of identifying a truly satisfactory relevant criterion measure. In many instances, creative behaviors are likely to be multidimensional, complex, and difficult to define in operational terms. Almost inevitably, professional judgment based on rational considerations and extensive experience will be needed to determine the appropriateness of creative activities in an educational, working, or job-related situation. Decisions will need to be made concerning whether an observable product or an inferred process or a combination of these two components will be considered in the formation of criterion variables, because both product and process are inherent in the dimensionality of most creative acts.

A comprehensive understanding of alternative theoretical orientations regarding the nature of creativity will help the investigator to select those constructs that are psychologically meaningful and, at the same time, reasonably amenable to measurement. One approach to ascertaining the dimensionality of several criterion measures chosen to reflect creative behaviors would be that of the previously mentioned factor-analytic techniques that are used to identify the constructs of creativity. Specifically, criterion measures would be factor analyzed along with numerous psychological tests, the factorial composition of which has been reasonably well established. To forecast creative behaviors in a job-oriented situation, one would select those tests that duplicated the factors (empirical representations of constructs) identified in the criterion measures.

A second circumstance that can influence the interpretation of a validity coefficient, often adverse-

ly, would be the occurrence of criterion contamination in which the observer or evaluator of creative behaviors uses consciously or unconsciously information gained from previously administered tests as a basis of making a judgment of the adequacy of a subject's performance in one or more criterion measures (such as rating scales of creative behaviors). It cannot be sufficiently emphasized that any judgment regarding the amount and or quality of creativity represented by criterion measures must be made independently of any knowledge of standing on predictor variables.

A third area of concern, which is to be treated somewhat more extensively in the next section, is that of the degree of reliability of both the predictor and especially the criterion measure as a potentially attenuating element of the magnitude of any validity coefficient. In most circumstances, the reliability of the criterion measure is likely to be lower than that associated with the test. Essentially, if either the criterion variable or test variable is not stable or consistent within itself, it cannot be expected to be correlated highly or even moderately with any other measure. Painstaking care needs to be exercised in the construction of measures so that their reliability can be maximized through the selection and retention of the most discriminating items. Both seasoned professional judgment and empirical evidence derived from pilot studies involving extensive use of item analyses may be required to achieve an acceptably high level of reliability.

A fourth potentially limiting factor in the estimation of a correlation coefficient is that of restriction of range, a topic which Yamamoto (1965) considered at length. His paper was concerned with the influence of restriction of range as well as of lack of test reliability on the amount of correlation between measures of intelligence and creative thinking. As groups become more homogeneous and thus show limited variability in scores on either the predictor or criterion measure, the potential for realizing a high correlation coefficient is substantially reduced. As many investigations in the study of creativity are carried out in college or university settings in which the range of talent is quite restricted because of selective admissions policies, the obtained correlation coefficients will be considerably smaller than those found for members of a population without such restriction. Statistical corrections do exist for estimating what the correlation between two variables would have been had there been no restriction in range (Guilford & Fruchter, 1978; Gulliksen, 1950).

A fifth circumstance, which also is to be considered in the fifth section dealing with scoring, is that of cultural differences in groups that may be studied. Validity coefficients may fail to register statistical significance simply because either the predictor variable or the criterion task intended to emphasize creative activity may be so foreign to the subject that he or she fails to understand the requirements of either task relative to the expectations of significant others who may be from a quite different cultural background. In short, an insufficient knowledge base on the part of the examinee or subject or a paucity of shared values between the evaluator and the subject may exist. Moreover, what may be judged to be creative in one culture may not be judged as creative in another.

A sixth concern is a highly practical one of cost. In the judgment of management personnel either in a school or in a business or service organization, the enormous expense in research and development that may be required to devise appropriate predictor and criterion measures may not be warranted. The additional benefits in productivity associated with creativity (particularly in a routine or repetitive type of work situation) may not be viewed to be worth the time and cost in dollars necessary to develop predictors and to monitor the acquisition of criterion data supposedly indicative of creative behaviors.

It should be mentioned that relative to other measures of cognitive ability or even measures of affective characteristics, those of creativity have been used quite infrequently in the prediction of standing on a criterion variable. Cattell and Butcher (1968) have devoted a number of chapters to the prediction of achievement and creativity but have given relatively little emphasis to the prediction of creative behaviors from tests that in themselves were intended to be indicative of creative activities. What work they did in the choice of predictors was anchored toward personality variables rather than toward cognitive measures. The need for research to identify predictors for forecasting creative behaviors is a crucial one which may be expected to be quite difficult in view of the problems associated with defining operationally criterion measures indicative of relevant creative behaviors.

Concerns Relating to Reliability

As indicated earlier, reliability refers to the stability or consistency of scores on a given measure. In classical test theory, reliability is defined as the ratio of the variance of true scores (free of any error) to the total variance in obtained scores—a total which is the sum of the variance in true scores and that of the independent (uncorrelated) component of error scores. The standard deviation of the error scores is referred to as the standard error of measurement, which indicates the region within which approximately 68% of obtained scores for an individual would fall above or below his or her true score (a true score being the mean of an infinite number of obtained scores on a test form for an individual with practice and fatigue effects controlled). The higher the degree of reliability, the less the standard error of measurement (Guilford, 1954; Guilford & Fruchter, 1978; Nunnally, 1978; Thorndike & Hagen, 1977).

Three broad approaches exist for the estimation of test reliability: (a) the test–retest approach, which is the correlation between scores on the same form of a test administered at different points in time—a coefficient yielding an indication of stability of test scores, although practice effects and correlated errors may occur; (b) the equivalent or alternate (often called parallel) forms, the scores from each of which are correlated to yield an estimate of stability for different samplings of items—a procedure which controls in part for memory of items and correlated error; and (c) the internal-consistency approach, which is employed to estimate the reliability of a single test form administered once with the assumption being made that the items are relatively homogeneous in content and process characteristics—a method essentially revealing the ratio of the covariance of items to the total variance of the test. Coefficients of internal-consistency reliability are found in a number of ways, including use of the Kuder-Richardson formula 20 or 21 (Kuder & Richardson, 1937), Cronbach's (1951) alpha, the split-half technique in which scores on odd-numbered items are correlated with those on even-numbered items and then adjusted by the Spearman-Brown formula (Guilford & Fruchter, 1978) to afford an estimate of the reliability of the total test (twice as long as either half), and Hoyt's (1941) analysis of variance technique, especially useful in the determination of interrater reliability. Additional information regarding these approaches may be found in a number of texts, including those by Guilford and Fruchter (1978), Gulliksen (1950), Nunnally (1978), Thorndike (1982), and Thorndike and Hagen (1977).

In the estimation of reliability for tests of divergent thinking that tend to be open-ended and often complex, if not quite heterogeneous in the constructs that they represent, probably the most defensible procedure would be to use alternate forms. Many researchers who have only one form of a fluency measure frequently employ a test–retest approach—a procedure far more defensible than that of internal consistency. In addition to the possibility that the characteristics of item responses may be quite different (heterogeneous), the often speeded nature of measures of divergent thinking (especially fluency) is likely to lead to a spuriously high estimate if an internal-consistency approach is employed—a circumstance that is well known to investigators who have used tests of the perceptual speed factor. In such tests, there is a tendency for examinees to work at fairly constant rates over sets of items and to earn comparable scores on these sets because of the relatively low level of difficulty of most items.

In the instance of those tests of convergent thinking that often resemble fairly traditional multiple-choice measures in problem-solving tasks, the issues of estimating reliability are highly comparable to those found for most alternate choice examinations in which there is one correct answer. If the test portrays one construct or if each of the items in it is represented by a comparable factor structure (e.g., the presence of the same constructs to about the same degree from item to item), internal-consistency approaches may be quite appropriate.

For such other kinds of measures as a self-report inventories, which may have several subscales indicative of personality and interest traits, internal-consistency approaches to the estimation of reliability are commonly used. One needs to be alert to the possible presence of response sets, such as social desirability or acquiescence, that may lead to unwanted systematic variance that contributes to an inflated estimate of instrument reliability.

With respect to measures derived from observations of evaluators, as in the case of rating scales of creative behaviors or check lists for assessing creative merits of products as, for example, in the arts, internal-consistency approaches once again are commonly employed to estimate reliability—especially the analysis of variance technique initially suggested in generalized form by Hoyt (1941) and applied by Ebel (1951) specifically to ratings. In any type of evaluation involving observation, but especially in the instance of ratings, exaggerated estimates of reliability can occur because of the introduction of systemic variance attributable to response errors (sets), such as the halo effect, leniency, severity, or central tendency. One solution to such difficulties is to evaluate a series of behaviors in one category or the characteristics of one aspect of a product at a time across all individuals or specimens (in a manner analogous to scoring one essay question at a time across all examinees). It also is important that the observer or observers have received comparable amounts of training so that they are prepared to yield judgments based on equivalent levels of competency, although differences in values still can be expected to influence evaluations. It also has been found that the pooled judgments of several evaluators (typically three to five) will be considerably more reliable than those of one, with the estimates of reliability increasing very much in accordance with the well-known increments associated with the Spearman-Brown formula (Guilford, 1954; Guilford & Fruchter, 1978; Nunnally, 1978).

A host of miscellaneous factors may be cited that can influence the magnitudes of reliability coefficients. As in the instance of validity, a marked restriction in range of scores will be associated with attenuated estimates of reliability of either a criterion measure or its predictor. Likewise, if the level of difficulty of the vocabulary in the directions for taking a test or in the items to which subjects are responding is too great, reliability can readily approximate zero, as the scores may be indicative of chance responses. Unpredictable influences upon the size of reliability coefficients may occur if great differences exist in the motivational levels of individuals who are taking measures of creativity or who are being observed for creative acts in a school or occupational setting. The maturity of a subject, either in terms of chronological age or level of social awareness, also can lead to the realization of differential magnitudes of reliability estimates, not only as a result of the degree of attentiveness and/or commitment to the task at hand, but also as a function of the extent of cognitive development, especially in the instance of children or young adolescents. Substantial heterogeneity in the cultural backgrounds of members of a group can lead to the introduction of erratic and unpredictable amounts of error variance in creative ability test scores, self-report data, and observational judgments. Associated with this heterogeneity, differences in role expectations on the part of members of different cultural groups or of males and females within a given cultural group may contribute to unanticipated modality characteristics in distributions of scores and to differential patterns of response. The resulting scores need to be analyzed separately for each identifiable group rather than for a total sample. In other words, in the interpretation of test scores, attention should be directed to the existence of differential levels of reliability for subgroups that may be substantially different in cultural background, age, and previous opportunity for training.

The need for additional research in conjunction with reliability concerns in the assessment of creativity would not appear to be anchored to the development of new psychometric or statistical methodology, but to the improved application of existing procedures. Specifically, greater care should be exercised in the construction of measures and in the monitoring of their use—particularly in the instance of rating scales and related observational activities. A need continues to exist in any test-taking or observational situation to motivate both the subject and the observer (evaluator) to take seriously the task and to do one's best.

Concerns Relating to Scoring of Creativity Measures

General Considerations

In the assessment of creative endeavor, tests of divergent thinking are the ones most often used in educational settings and in educational and psychological research. As the responses are open-ended, considerable subjectivity often occurs in evaluating just how creative, original, or ingenious the answers posed to problem situations may be. In other circumstances, a judgment is formulated concerning how creative an observed product, as in visual art, or behavior in solving a complex social problem is thought to be. The scoring of responses is often differentiated along a continuum to reflect their being indicative of higher or lower levels of creativity.

One of the difficulties in formulating judgments on the part of two or more evaluators is that of obtaining a reasonable degree of agreement in the scoring procedure—a circumstance similar to that found in scoring essays in creative writing. In other words, judges or raters often have great difficulty in reaching a consensus regarding what is a truly creative or original response. Frequently, indices of interrater reliability, such as intraclass correlation coefficients, are employed to give some indication of the level of agreement.

Another method occasionally used to estimate the degree of manifested creativity is largely a normative one based on the statistical frequency of a response—the less frequent or more rare, the greater the amount of implied creativity. Once again, a judgment still must be made concerning whether an infrequent response is a bizarre or capricious one or one actually indicative of a creative thought. In a subsequent part of this section, consideration is given to an overriding concern in the scoring of tests of divergent thinking—namely, the confounding of ideational fluency with scores on each of several dimensions of creative endeavor.

In a few instances, objective tests of the multiple-choice or matching format are employed in which the examinee is required to select the most creative response cited in relation to an activity described in the stem of the item. As mentioned earlier, such tests may be particularly appropriate for problem-solving tasks in mathematics and the sciences for which only one solution or process involved in arriving at the desired answer can be judged as being both relevant and creative in terms of the collective wisdom of the test makers who constructed the key. As has been stated, the psychometric issues involving scoring such a test are basically analogous to those found for almost any multiple-choice examination in any academic discipline. As indicated previously, such tests are likely to reflect the product that has been named by Guilford (Guilford, 1967; Guilford & Hoepfner, 1971; Michael, 1977) as *transformations*, in which the examinee often has to find or devise a new use for a familiar object in a foreign context. Frequently, in higher mathematics, it is assumed that the solution of a difficult mathematics problem, in itself, requires a highly creative act to generate the unique solution—a form of thinking often termed as *convergent*.

Perhaps even more interesting than the unique solution is the process by which the examinee arrives at the answer. There may be many alternative approaches to reaching a unique solution with the element of creativity being on just how ingenious the process is in obtaining the answer. Once again, considerable subjective judgment may be required. Moreover, those individuals who have worked extensively in the psychology of creativity may be the least capable in making a judgment concerning just how ingenious a process employed in reaching the solution really is. Specialists in the field of creative endeavor frequently are called upon to render an evaluation in much the same way that distinguished scholars on editorial boards decide on the creative merits of manuscripts submitted for publication. Although checklists, outlines of desired solutions or processes for reaching them, rating scales, and other psychometric devices may facilitate the realization of improved degrees of objectivity, the overall process of scoring or judging is likely to remain a highly subjective one open to the idiosyncracies and preferences of the evaluator, who too often may not be too creative himself or herself.

In a not totally unrelated matter, creativity in the arts poses many unique problems of assessment. In the performing arts, such as acting, singing, conducting, and playing a musical instrument, the ongoing process, which may result in a final recorded product, is what needs to be evaluated. Fortunately, the use of videotapes with appropriate sound supplementation may provide a permanent record which numerous evaluators may judge on repeated occasions to arrive at some kind of consensus. Accompanying this approach might be rating scales on which observations can be recorded as well as comparative samples of parallel acts that can be employed as relevant standards (criterion measures). In any event, subjectivity in scoring will remain a central issue as will the degree of competence of the evaluators.

Perhaps somewhat easier to evaluate are final products, such as paintings or sculptured works, in which process is no longer the major consideration. In the instance of products, other products of more or less agreed upon creative merit can be used as standards against which to evaluate the newly completed works. In a supplementary fashion, rating scales can be employed along with critical reviews to arrive at some consensus. History has revealed only too often that what critics of one generation have judged as a mediocre work turns out in a later generation as a classic that may endure for centuries as an example of a truly creative contribution to world culture.

Fluency as a Confounding Factor

Fluency Scores as a Contaminating Influence

An area of concern in the scoring of divergent thinking tests has been the potential confounding of scores on tests of originality and flexibility with the factor of ideational fluency that may have inflated spuriously both reliability estimates and correlation coefficients indicative of convergent validity (Clark & Mirels, 1970; Hocevar, 1979). For example, in a review of 18 research studies in which 89 fluency/originality coefficients were cited, Hocevar (1979) noted an average coefficient of .69 with 82% of the coefficients exceeding .50. Moreover, he ob-

served that, in the nine studies in which it was feasible to apply the multitrait–multimethod standards proposed by Campbell and Fiske (1959), the criteria for discriminant validity could not be met. In addition, factor-analytic studies of intercorrelations of fluency and originality scores on two or more tests have yielded dimensions unique to each of the tests of originality rather than common factors of fluency and originality cutting across the originality measures (Kazelskis, 1972; Plass, Michael, & Michael, 1974; Yamamoto & Frengel, 1966).

In an attempt to address these difficulties, Hocevar (1979) found for a sample of 60 college students the intercorrelations of fluency and originality scores of three of Guilford's tests of divergent thinking—Alternate Uses (Christensen, Guilford, Merrifield, & Wilson, 1960), Plot Titles (Berger & Guilford, 1969), and Consequences (Christensen, Merrifield, & Guilford, 1958). It was hypothesized that when variance associated with fluency scores would be statistically controlled (partialed out of originality scores), the internal-consistency estimates of reliability would show marked decrements and also that the intercorrelations of originality scores (based on use of subjective judgment and on application of an objective criterion representing rarity or statistical infrequency of response) would drop substantially if not approximate zero. As considerable support was found for these two hypotheses with respect to either a subjective or an objective determination of scores, it was concluded that both the reliability and convergent validity of originality scores largely depend on individual differences in ideational fluency rather than on originality.

In a related investigation, Hocevar and Michael (1979) carried out two multitrait–multimethod studies to examine the effects of use of two scoring formulas on the discriminant validity of tests of divergent thinking. The first study involved 39 elementary school pupils in two fifth-grade classes whose teachers administered the Torrance Tests of Creative Thinking, Verbal Form A (Torrance, 1974). Scoring for fluency, flexibility, and originality made use of two procedures: (a) a *summing formula,* in which differential weights corresponding to responses of examinees were simply added according to criteria in the manual, and (b) *percentage scores,* requiring the flexibility and originality score for each item to be divided by the total number of responses (fluency score). The second study in which 60 college juniors and seniors participated employed the three tests of divergent thinking previously cited (Alternate Uses, Plot Titles, and Consequences), which were scored for fluency and originality. Use of the percentage score resulted in enhanced discriminant validity of subjectively determined originality scores, although application of an objective scoring procedure based on the statistical rarity was associated with alpha reliability coefficients approximating zero.

Fluency as a Possible Confounding Factor

The investigation by Clark and Mirels (1970) on fluency as a pervasive factor in the assessment of creativity also was concerned with the estimation of the extent to which fluency scores might account for the relatively low correlation sometimes reported between measures of creativity and those of general intelligence. Using 93 art school students ranging in age from 9 to 15 years, Clark and Mirels found the intercorrelations of five different scores intended to reflect creativity from a slightly modified version from Torrance's test concerned with figure completion (Thinking Creatively with Pictures) (Torrance, 1966) and scores on the Henmon-Nelson Tests of Mental Ability (Houghton Mifflin, 1931–1974). In addition to appearing in raw score form, the responses on the creativity measures were corrected or adjusted for fluency. Whereas the uncorrected creativity scores exhibited a mean intercorrelation of .45, the corrected ones displayed coefficients with a mean of .08. The correlational data failed to provide definitive information regarding the possible influence of fluency upon the correlation between scores on creativity measures and those on a test of general intelligence. For uncorrected creativity scores, the mean correlation with the intelligence measure was .09; for corrected scores, .13. It could well be that the figural nature of the material in the Torrance test simply portrayed constructs quite different from those found in a measure of general scholastic aptitude within which both semantic and symbolic content would be somewhat predominant. As Hocevar (1979) has pointed out, the tendency of several investigators to use a strategy to reveal that tests of creativity are highly intercorrelated and, at the same time, factorially distinguishable may be misleading because ideational fluency may be the component that contributes substantially to the high intercorrelations of creativity measures and to a factorial structure suggesting that these measures are distinct from intelligence tests.

Suggested Ways for Controlling for Fluency

To overcome mistaken conclusions regarding the effectiveness of training programs in creativity, in which the scores on measures (dependent variables) of originality and flexibility of those in experimental groups may have been inflated by ideational fluency in relation to those in control groups, and to minimize the occurrence of spuriously high correlation coefficients among creativity measures similarly confounded by ideational fluency, Hocevar (1979) has made a number of suggestions. In addition to the use of partial correlation techniques, one could score each response to a flexibility or an originality item and calculate an average for all responses rather than a total raw score. In mentioning Clark and Mirels' (1970) approach to scoring an equal number of responses for each examinee, Hocevar (1979) has indicated the possibility of requiring a given number of responses to every question. He illustrated this approach by suggesting that examinees be directed to cite the three most original or ingenious uses that they can think of for a specified object, such as a shoe. Fluency would be controlled in that each subject would present an equal number of responses. One difficulty with this approach, however, would be that the reliability of the measures could be quite low. Such a statement would also hold for the Clark and Mirels (1970) suggestion of scoring an equal number of responses. Both in this method and in the Hocevar suggestion (Hocevar, 1979), the more fluent respondent could be penalized by being denied the opportunity to give a comparatively large number of relevant responses indicative of originality or flexibility. To provide for a way of controlling for fluency without sacrificing originality or flexibility estimates, an alternative compromise approach may be useful. The respondent would be directed to generate as many possible uses for an object, such as a light bulb, and then be asked to choose a preselected number of the generated items (e.g., three) which the respondent considers to be the most ingenious.

Needed Research

The various suggested ways for controlling for fluency in conjunction with establishing the convergent and discriminant validity of creativity tests should be the subject of numerous empirical studies with a variety of individuals differing in test-taking experience, maturity level, and intelligence. Experimental studies incorporating as treatment variables differing instructions to examinees regarding how they should respond to a fluency test and alternative modes of scoring would be expected to provide some evidence that would afford a partial resolution of several of the concerns raised in the previous paragraphs.

Concerns Relating to the Use of Norms

The development of usable norms for the assessment of creativity constitutes a difficult task, as many individuals perceive creativity to be a process often resulting in a unique product with qualitative characteristics that may defy quantification. In the arts, in particular, a given work may be so original in its characteristics that there is no norm against which it can be immediately compared. At a philosophical level, perhaps the issue is one of the idiographic (individual) versus nomothetic (normative) characteristics of creativity—that is, the uniqueness or universality of creative acts or products. Certainly, when an artist is given a commission to create a new work—whether it be a symphony, a sculpture, or a painting—one cannot declare in advance what the product or the accompanying process will be. Reliance on evaluation of the merits of this work will depend upon the judgment of critics or peers in a similar area of endeavor. Even these individuals may find the product so foreign to their own background that they cannot make a meaningful evaluation, especially if this creative work foreshadows a new school of thought or the emergence of a new form of art (as in the introduction of modern electronic technology in the composition of music).

In the somewhat more common arena of school learning in which expectations are at least broadly defined for the use of educational or psychological tests specifically devised to give some indication of creativity as in measures of flexibility, fluency, or originality, it would appear reasonable to establish preliminary normative data. Care needs to be exercised in interpreting the performance of the student in relation to what would be anticipated for his or her age group. If in a given problem-solving task in science or mathematics, an 8-year-old child gives a response typical of an individual 12 to 14 years of age, it would appear that a judgment of precosity, if

not creativity, would be correct relative to that person's level of maturity. It would seem especially important to observe the process by which this child arrived at the answer, as this process may provide the evaluator with valuable information concerning whether an ingenious approach was employed in arriving at the solution or whether possibly the child had been given the answer by another or had been advised as to where to find the answer.

In the presentation of any set of norms, care must be taken to indicate clearly the population for which the norms are applicable according to age, cultural background, socioeconomic status, prior educational attainments, and existence of any special circumstances, such as the participation by the normative group in a gifted program or in a summer workshop directed toward the enhancement of creativity. Norms also should be provided for each subtest in a given battery of measures of creativity so that a profile of strengths and weaknesses in various components of creativity can be identified. One also needs to pay attention to scaling problems associated with ceiling and floor effects, as one or more measures may be either too easy or too difficult relative to the general maturity level or experiential level of the group being studied.

Research efforts may be directed toward the evaluation of alternative methods of presenting norms. In particular, attention could be given to how norms may be affected by the sequence in which particular tests within a battery are administered, by the level of comprehensiveness of instructions for test taking including practice exercises, by the shortening or lengthening of time limits especially for groups of culturally disadvantaged, and by the personality characteristics of those administering the tests.

Test Administration Issues

Issues in test administration are closely related to several of those cited in the previous section dealing with norms. If one is interested in a formal assessment of creativity so that comparative data can be realized, it is essential that a number of factors be reasonably well controlled: (a) the time allowed for the examinee to respond to questions or time allocated to observers to make their judgments; (b) the difficulty level of words and the mode of presentation of instructions, including comparable amounts of illustrative or practice material for all examinees (such as warm-up exercises); and (c) distracting influences, such as noise, inappropriate lighting, legibility of test format, and disturbing climatic factors (high humidity or extreme temperatures). Moreover, through pilot studies, a determination can be made of optimal time allocations and of the most effective sequence of administration of tests if more than one is being given.

In conjunction with the preceding section regarding norms, several suggestions were made for research that would be applicable to conditions of test administration. In particular, controlled research is needed to determine the effects of several of the factors cited in the first paragraph of this section. In addition, consideration should be given to identifying situations in which there is no time limit for a creative task to be completed, as in the instance of a mathematician or inventor who may be involved in the solution of a highly complex problem requiring considerable library research as well as time for reflection and meditation. In such situations, a few individuals may have what is sometimes referred to as a flash of brilliant insight that is difficult to explain other than its being essentially intuitive; others may reach the solution incrementally in a very systematic fashion that requires a great deal of trial and error and gradual elimination of alternative hypotheses or approaches associated with them.

Concluding Statement

It is apparent that many issues enter into the accurate assessment of creative behavior. As indicated earlier, the establishment of the validity of measures intended to reflect creativity is the most crucial concern—a concern that rests on a sound conceptualization of the constructs of interest and on the testing of hypotheses derived from a theory to which the constructs are central. It has been pointed out that sound principles of test construction that will yield highly reliable measures is also necessary if validity is to be achieved. The attainment of a high degree of validity and reliability will permit tests and scales intended to provide evidence of the manifestation of creativity to be useful in circumstances concerned with prediction, placement, diagnosis, prescription, and determination of competence levels in activities requiring creative behaviors.

In the presentation of any set of norms, care must be taken to indicate clearly the population for which the norms are applicable according to age, cultural background, socioeconomic status, prior educa-

tional attainments, and existence of any special circumstances, such as the participation by the normative group in a gifted program or in a summer workshop directed toward the enhancement of creativity. Norms also should be provided for each subtest in a given battery of measures of creativity so that a profile of strengths and weaknesses in various components of creativity can be identified. One also needs to pay attention to scaling problems associated with ceiling and floor effects, as one or more measures may be either too easy or too difficult relative to the general maturity level or experiential level of the group being studied.

Research efforts may be directed toward the evaluation of alternative methods of presenting norms. In particular, attention could be given to how norms may be affected by the sequence in which particular tests within a battery are administered, by the level of comprehensiveness of instructions for test taking including practice exercises, by the shortening or lengthening of time limits especially for groups of culturally disadvantaged, and by the personality characteristics of those administering the tests.

It is probably evident from the text that shortcomings in the application of psychometric procedures to the study of creativity have existed. It may well be that individuals who have contributed greatly to the conceptualization of creativity have lacked the requisite training in psychometrics and methodology to design well-controlled studies and to apply appropriate statistical procedures. The authors' impression is that the great surge of energy devoted by researchers to the study of creativity peaked in the mid-1960s. During the past 20 years, relatively few new ideas have been introduced. Perhaps this period from about 1965 to 1988 has been one of consolidation and reflection. What is very much needed at this time is a renewal of interest on the part of theoretically oriented psychologists who will combine their efforts with those of psychometricians, who are far better trained today than they were two decades ago, in formulating new conceptual frameworks and in applying sophisticated multivariate procedures to extract the maximum information concerning the tenability of multifold hypotheses that have been derived from conceptually evolving frameworks regarding creativity.

References

American Psychological Association. (1974). *Standards for educational and psychological tests and manuals.* Washington, DC: Author.

American Psychological Association. (1985). *Standards for educational and psychological testing*. Washington, DC: Author.

Anastasi, A. (1982). *Psychological testing* (5th ed.). New York: Macmillan.

Bentler, P. M. (1980). Multivariate analysis with latent variables: Causal modeling. *Annual Review of Psychology, 31*, 419–456.

Berger, R. M., & Guilford, J. P. (1969). *Plot titles*. Beverly Hills, CA: Sheridan Psychological Services.

Bloom, B. S., Hastings, J. T., & Madaus, G. F. (1971). *Handbook on formative and summative evaluation of student learning*. New York: McGraw-Hill.

Campbell, D. T., & Fiske, D. W. (1959). Convergent and discriminant validation by the multitrait-multimethod matrix. *Psychological Bulletin, 56*, 81–105.

Campbell, J. P. (1976). Psychometric theory. In M. D. Dunnette (Ed.), *Handbook of industrial and organizational psychology* (pp. 185–222). Chicago: Rand McNally.

Christensen, P. R., Merrifield, P. R., & Guilford, J. P. (1958). *Consequences*. Beverly Hills, CA: Sheridan Psychological Services.

Christensen, P. R., Guilford, J. P., Merrifield, P. R., & Wilson, R. C. (1960). *Alternative uses*. Beverly Hills, CA: Sheridan Psychological Services.

Cattell, R. B., & Butcher, H. T. (1968). *The prediction of achievement and creativity*. Indianapolis: Bobbs-Merrill.

Clark, P., & Mirels, H. (1970). Fluency as a pervasive element in the measurement of creativity. *Journal of Educational Measurement, 7*, 83–86.

Crocker, L., & Algina, J. (1985). *Introduction to classical and modern test theory*. New York: Holt, Rinehart & Winston.

Cronbach, L. J. (1951). Coefficient alpha and the internal structure of tests. *Psychometrika, 16*, 297–334.

Cronbach, L. J. (1971). Test validation. In R. L. Thorndike (Ed.), *Educational measurement* (2nd ed.) (pp. 443–507). Washington, DC: American Council on Education.

Cronbach, L. J. (1980). Validity on parole: How can we go straight? In W. B. Schrader (Ed.), *Measuring achievement: Progress over the decade* (pp. 99–108). San Francisco: Jossey-Bass.

Cronbach, L. J., & Meehl, P. E. (1955). Construct validity. *Psychological Bulletin, 52*, 281–302.

Dellas, M., & Gaier, E. L. (1970). Identification of creativity: The individual. *Psychological Bulletin, 73*, 55–73.

Ebel, R. L. (1951). Estimation of the reliability of ratings. *Psychometrika, 16*, 407–424.

Ebel, R. L. (1979). *Essentials of educational measurement* (3rd ed.). Englewood Cliffs, NJ: Prentice-Hall.

Fiske, D. W. (1987). Construct invalidity comes from method effects. *Educational and Psychological Measurement, 47*(2), 285–307.

Getzels, J. W., & Jackson, P. W. (1962). *Creativity and intelligence*. New York: Wiley.

Golann, S. E. (1963). Psychological study of creativity. *Psychological Bulletin, 60*, 548–565.

Gorsuch, R. L. (1983). *Factor analysis* (2nd ed.). Hillsdale, NJ: Erlbaum.

Gronlund, N. (1976). *Measurement and evaluation in teaching* (3rd ed.). New York: Macmillan.

Guilford, J. P. (1954). *Psychometric methods* (2nd ed.). New York: McGraw-Hill.

Guilford, J. P. (1963). Intellectual resources and their values as seen by scientists. In C. W. Taylor & F. Barron (Eds.), *Scientific creativity: Its recognition and development* (pp. 101–118). New York: Wiley.

Guilford, J. P. (1967). *The nature of human intelligence*. New York: McGraw-Hill.

Guilford, J. P. (1968). *Intelligence, creativity, and their educational implications*. San Diego, CA: Robert R. Knapp.

Guilford, J. P. (1970). Creativity: Retrospect and prospect. *Journal of Creative Behavior, 4*, 149–168.

Guilford, J. P. (1971). Some misconceptions regarding measurement of creative talents. *Journal of Creative Behavior, 5*, 77–87.

Guilford, J. P., & Fruchter, B. (1978). *Fundamental statistics in psychology and education* (6th ed.). New York: McGraw-Hill.

Guilford, J. P., & Hoepfner, R. (1971). *The analysis of intelligence*. New York: McGraw-Hill.

Guilford, J. P., & Tenopyr, M. L. (1968). Implications of the structure-of-intellect model for high school and college students. In W. B. Michael (Ed.), *Teaching for creative endeavor* (pp. 25–45). Bloomington, IN: Indiana University Press.

Gulliksen, H. (1950). *Theory of mental tests*. New York: Wiley.

Harman, H. H. (1976). *Modern factor analysis* (3rd ed.). Chicago: University of Chicago Press.

Harris, M. L., & Harris, C. W. (1971). A factor analytic interpretation strategy. *Educational and Psychological Measurement, 31*, 589–606.

Hocevar, D. (1979). Ideational fluency as a confounding factor in the measurement of originality. *Journal of Educational Psychology, 71*, 191–196.

Hocevar, D. (1981). Measurement of creativity: Review and critique. *Journal of Personality Assessment, 45*, 450–464.

Hocevar, D., & Michael, W. B. (1979). The effects of scoring formulas on the discriminant validity of tests of divergent thinking. *Educational and Psychological Measurement, 39*, 917–921.

Horn, J. L., & Knapp, J. R. (1973). On the subjective character of the empirical base of Guilford's structure-of-intellect model. *Psychological Bulletin, 80*, 33–43.

Horn, J. L., & Knapp, J. R. (1974). Thirty wrongs do not make a right: Reply to Guilford. *Psychological Bulletin, 81*, 502–504.

Houghton Mifflin. (1931–1974). *The Henmon-Nelson Tests of Mental Ability*. Boston: Author.

Hoyt, C. J. (1941). Test reliability estimated by analysis of variance. *Psychometrika, 6*, 153–160.

Hudspith, S. (1985). *The neurological correlates of creative thought: A comparison of the EEG activity of high and low creative subjects with an ergonomic presentation of the results for the lay person*. Unpublished doctoral dissertation, University of Southern California, Los Angeles.

Jöreskog, K. G. (1969). A general approach to confirmatory maximum likelihood factor analysis. *Psychometrika, 34*, 183–202.

Jöreskog, K. G., & Sörbom, D. (1981). *LISREL V: Analysis of linear structural relationships by method of maximum likelihood*. Chicago: National Educational Resources. (Distribution by International Educational Services.)

Kazelskis, R. (1972). The convergent, divergent, and factorial validity of the Torrance Figural Test of Creativity. *Southern Journal of Educational Research, 6*, 123–129.

Khattab, A-M., & Michael, W. B. (1986). The construct validity of higher order structure-of-intellect factors reflecting semantic and symbolic content abilities. *Educational and Psychological Measurement, 46*, 1029–1035.

Khattab, A-M., and Michael, W. B., & Hocevar, D. (1982). The construct validity of higher order structure-of-intellect abilities in a battery of tests emphasizing the product of transformations: A confirmatory maximum likelihood factor analysis. *Educational and Psychological Measurement, 42,* 1089–1105.

Kuder, G. F., & Richardson, M. W. (1937). The theory of the estimation of test reliability. *Psychometrika, 2,* 151–160.

Mace, D. E., Michael, W. B., & Hocevar, D. (1985). Validity of higher-order ability constructs in structure-of-intellect tests all involving semantic content and operations of cognition or evaluation: A confirmatory maximum likelihood factor analysis. *Educational and Psychological Measurement, 45,* 353–359.

MacKinnon, D. W. (1962). The nature and nurture of creative talent. *American Psychologist, 17,* 484–495.

MacKinnon, D. W. (1965). Personality and the realization of creative potential. *American Psychologist, 20,* 227–281.

Marsh, H. W., & Hocevar, D. (1983). Confirmatory factor analysis of multitrait-multimethod matrices. *Journal of Educational Measurement, 20,* 231–248.

Mednick, S. A., & Mednick, M. T. (1962). The associative basis of the creative process. *Psychological Review, 69,* 220–227.

Mednick, S. A., & Mednick, M. T. (1967). *The Remote Associates Test (RAT).* Boston: Houghton Mifflin.

Meeker, M., & Meeker, R. (1975). *Structure of Intellect Learning Abilities Test (SOILAT).* El Segundo, CA: SOI Institute.

Mehrens, W. A., & Lehmann, I. J. (1984). *Measurement and evaluation in education and psychology* (3rd ed.). New York: Holt, Rinehart & Winston.

Messick, S. (1975). The standard problem: Meaning and values in measurement and evaluation. *American Psychologist, 30,* 955–966.

Michael, W. B. (1977). Cognitive and affective components of creativity in mathematics and the physical sciences. In J. C. Stanley, W. C. George, & C. H. Solano (Eds.), *The gifted and the creative* (pp. 141–172). Baltimore: Johns Hopkins University Press.

Nunnally, J. C. (1978). *Psychometric theory* (2nd ed.). New York: McGraw-Hill.

Parnes, S. J. (1964). Research on developing creative behavior. In C. W. Taylor (Ed.), *Widening horizons in creativity* (pp. 145–169). New York: Wiley.

Plass, H., Michael, J. J., & Michael, W. B. (1974). The factorial validity of the Torrance Tests of Creative Thinking for a sample of 111 sixth-grade children. *Educational and Psychological Measurement, 34,* 413–414.

Roe, A. (1951). A psychological study of physical scientists. *Genetic Psychology Monographs, 43*(2), 121–235.

Sax, G. (1980). *Principles of educational and psychological measurement and evaluation* (2nd ed.). Belmont, CA: Wadsworth.

Tenopyr, M. L. (1977). Content-construct confusion. *Personnel Psychology, 30,* 47–54.

Thorndike, R. L. (1963). Some methodological issues in the study of creativity. In E. F. Gardner (Ed.), *Proceedings of the 1962 Invitational Conference on Testing Problems* (pp. 40–54). Princeton, NJ: Educational Testing Service.

Thorndike, R. L. (1982). *Applied psychometrics.* Boston: Houghton Mifflin.

Thorndike, R. L., & Hagen, E. P. (1977). *Measurement and evaluation in psychology and education* (4th ed.). New York: Wiley.

Torrance, E. P. (1959). Explorations in creative thinking in the early school years: VI. Highly intelligent and highly creative children in a laboratory school. *Research Mem.* BER-59-7. Minneapolis: Bureau of Educational Research, University of Minnesota.

Torrance, E. P. (1966). *Torrance Tests of Creative Thinking: Norms—technical manual.* Princeton, NJ: Personnel Press.

Torrance, E. P. (1974). *Torrance Tests of Creative Thinking: Norms—technical manual.* Lexington, MA: Ginn.

Treffinger, D. J., & Poggio, J. P. (1972). Needed research on the measurement of creativity. *Journal of Creative Behavior, 6,* 253–267.

Treffinger, D. J., Renzulli, J. S., & Feldhusen, J. F. (1971). Problems in the assessment of creative thinking. *Journal of Creative Behavior, 5,* 104–112.

Wolf, R. M. (1982). Validity of tests. In H. E. Mitzel, J. H. Best, & W. Rabinowitz (Eds.), *Encyclopedia of educational research* (5th ed., Vol. 4, pp. 1991–1998). New York: Macmillan.

Yamamoto, K. (1965). Effects of restriction of range and test unreliability on correlation between measures of intelligence and creative thinking. *British Journal of Educational Psychology, 35,* 300–305.

Yamamoto, K., & Frengel, B. (1966). An exploratory component analysis of the Minnesota Tests of Creative Thinking. *California Journal of Educational Research, 17,* 220–229.

CHAPTER 3

A Taxonomy and Critique of Measurements Used in the Study of Creativity

Dennis Hocevar and Patricia Bachelor

Creativity measurement itself has been a creative endeavor for both researchers and practitioners. When viewed as a group, the most salient characteristic of creativity measurements is their diversity. The initial purpose of this review is to integrate creativity measurements into a meaningful taxonomy and to illustrate the diversity of the available measurements by citing key examples of the many and varied ways in which creativity has been operationalized. It also is hoped that the numerous examples will give researchers a concise but thorough picture of the many options available when a measure of creativity is needed. The second goal of this review is to use the taxonomy as a framework for discussing the creativity construct in terms of several psychometric characteristics—namely, reliability, discriminant validity, and nomological validity. The third goal is to describe an analytic framework in which measurement issues can be better addressed.

In addition to the present review, readers interested in the measurement of creativity may want to refer to a number of previously published papers on the measurement of creativity and related issues (Crockenberg, 1972; Davis, 1971; Dellas & Gaier, 1970; Educational Testing Service, 1987; Kaltsounis, 1971, 1972; Mumford & Gustafson, 1988; Petrosko, 1978; Treffinger & Poggio, 1972; Treffinger, Renzulli, & Feldhusen, 1971; Tryk, 1968). In contrast to most previous reviews, the present review will cover a broad range of measurements rather than a more narrowly defined category of measurements (e.g., divergent thinking).

A Taxonomy of Creativity Measurements

In the following pages, we classify more than 100 examples of creativity measurement into eight categories: (1) tests of divergent thinking; (2) attitude and interest inventories; (3) personality inventories; (4) biographical inventories; (5) ratings by teachers, peers, and supervisors; (6) judgments of products; (7) eminence; and (8) self-reported creative activities and achievements. The categories

Dennis Hocevar • Department of Educational Psychology, University of Southern California, Los Angeles CA 90089-0031. Patricia Bachelor • Department of Psychology, California State University at Long Beach, Long Beach CA 90840.
Permission to reproduce sections of this article has been granted by the Society for Personality Assessment, Inc.

are meant to be descriptive and nonevaluative, and, in addition, they are not necessarily mutually exclusive.

Category 1: Tests of Divergent Thinking

Describing creativity in terms of divergent thinking is the most widely used approach to studying creativity. On the basis of Guilford's (1956) Structure-of-Intellect (SOI) model and over two decades of factor-analytic research, Guilford and his colleagues identified various intellectual abilities. Some of these abilities (e.g., fluency, flexibility, originality, redefinition, and elaboration) have been collectively labelled *divergent thinking*. A wide variety of tests have been developed by Guilford and his colleagues to measure divergent thinking, such as Alternate Uses (Christensen, Guilford, Merrifield, & Wilson, 1960), Plot Titles (Berger & Guilford, 1969) and Consequences (Christensen, Merrifield, & Guilford, 1958). Tests of divergent thinking are distinguished from traditional intelligence tests in that they require a multitude of responses rather than a single correct answer. For example, in the Alternate Uses test, subjects are asked to think of alternate uses for a variety of common objects (e.g., a shoe or a pencil). Similarly, in the Plot Titles test, subjects are asked to generate clever titles to two stories.

Guilford (1968) and others (most notably, Torrance, 1974; Wallach & Kogan, 1965; Wallach & Wing, 1969) have suggested that the more creative individual should possess the types of abilities measured by tests of divergent thinking, and the Guilford tradition has had considerable impact on the study of creativity. Two of the most widely used divergent-thinking test batteries, the Torrance Tests of Creative Thinking (Torrance, 1974) and the Wallach-Kogan creativity tests (Wallach & Kogan, 1965) may be seen as modifications and extensions of the Guilford tests. Also, an important adaptation of the Guilford tests at the elementary school level has been provided by Meeker and Meeker (1975), and this adaptation includes a divergent-thinking component (Thompson & Andersson, 1983).

Despite the considerable and valuable impact of divergent-thinking measures on the creativity literature, they have not gone without criticism, and a number of researchers have made suggestions as to how divergent-thinking tests might be revised to better suit both practitioners and researchers (Evans & Forbach, 1983; Fu, Kelso, & Moran, 1984; Harrington, 1975; Hattie, 1977, 1980; Hocevar,

1979a,b,c; Hocevar & Michael, 1979; Milgram, 1983; Milgram & Arad, 1981; Milgram & Milgram, 1976a,b; Milgram, Milgram, Rosenbloom, & Rabkin, 1978; Runco, 1986a,b; Seddon, 1983; Zarnegar, Hocevar, & Michael, 1988).

Category 2: Attitude and Interest Inventories

Some investigators have suggested that creativity can be identified in terms of interests and attitudes. This approach is based on the assumption that a creative person will express attitudes and interests favoring creative activities. For example, on the Group Inventory for Finding Interests (GIFFI) (Davis & Rimm, 1982; Rimm & Davis, 1976, 1980), subjects are asked to indicate their interest in a wide variety of activities like the following:

I have a good sense of humor.
I like to try new activities and projects.
I like to invent things.
I like to write stories.

Similarly, on the Holland and Baird (1968) Preconscious Activity Scale, individuals high on originality agree with items like the following:

I often daydream about unsolved problems.
I have to learn things in my own way rather than accepting ideas or relationships suggested in textbooks, etc.
If I had the necessary talent, I would enjoy being a sculptor.
I would like to be an inventor.

Finally, Khatena and Torrance (1976) have designed a personality inventory specifically for identifying creative adolescents. The Creative Perception Inventory has two subscales, ''Something about Myself,'' and ''What Kind of Person Are You?'' that are designed to identify the extent to which a respondent has interests, thought patterns, and personality characteristics that are thought to be creative. Items on the ''What Kind of Person are You?'' instrument call for the test-taker to select characteristics in a forced-choice format. For example, the creative person will describe him- or herself as curious rather than self-confident, a self-starter rather than obedient, intuitive rather than remembering well, and altruistic rather than courteous.

Other attitude and interest inventories useful in studying creativity are Basadur and Finkbeiner's (1985) measure of preference for ideation, the Creative Behavior Disposition Scale (Taylor & Fish, 1979), the Preference Inventory (Bull & Davis, 1982), the Childhood Attitude Inventory for Problem Solving (Covington, 1966), the Creative Attitude Survey (Schaefer & Bridges, 1970), the creative interests scale of the Guilford-Zimmerman Interest Inventory (Guilford & Zimmerman, 1963), the Opinion, Attitude, and Interest Survey (Fricke, 1965), the Allport-Vernon-Lindzey Study of Values (Heist, 1968), and a questionnaire developed by Holmes (1976).

Category 3: Personality Inventories

Some investigators have characterized creativity as a set of personality factors rather than cognitive traits. Consequently, several well-known personality inventories have been scaled to identify creativity. For example, in a number of studies, the Adjective Check List (Gough & Heilbrun, 1965) has been suggested as a potential measure of creativity (Domino, 1970; Gough, 1979; Lacey & Erickson, 1974; Smith & Schaefer, 1969; Welsh, 1977). The version that appears to have the most potential is Gough's (1979) Creative Personality Scale. Representative adjectives are: clever, individualistic, insightful, original, self-confident, and unconventional.

Additional personality inventories adapted to identify creativity are Heist and Yonge's (1968) Omnibus Personality Inventory (Heist, 1968), Gough's (1957) California Psychological Inventory (Helson, 1965), and Cattell and Eber's (1968) Sixteen Personality Factor Questionnaire (Cattell & Butcher, 1968).

Category 4: Biographical Inventories

The assumption that an individual's present behavior is determined by past experiences forms the basis for the use of biographical inventories in assessing creative talent. A number of studies indicate that "tailor-made" biographical inventories can predict creativity in an industrial setting (Buel, 1965; Buel, Albright, & Glennon, 1966; McDermid, 1965; Michael & Colson, 1979; Owens, Schumacher, & Clark, 1957). To illustrate, Michael and Colson (1979) developed a 100-item questionnaire by examining the research literature and identifying biographical correlates of creative endeavor. This questionnaire was then used to measure creative performance in a sample of electrical engineers in an industrial setting. Items generally

represent the occurrence of events rather than feelings and could be grouped into four categories: self-striving (e.g., displaying curiosity at an early age); parental striving (e.g., father holding a graduate degree); social participation and social acceptance (e.g., active participation in the YMCA); and independence training (e.g., setting one's own standards at an early age).

Two published biographical inventories are available: The Alpha Biographical Inventory by the Institute for Behavioral Research in Creativity (1968) and Schaefer's (1970) Biographical Inventory: Creativity. The Alpha Biographical Inventory is the result of an extensive research program carried out with National Aeronautics and Space Administration (NASA) scientists and engineers (Taylor & Ellison, 1964), and, consequently, it is limited to measuring creativity in the scientific areas. It consists of 300 items covering a wide variety of areas, such as hobbies, interests, childhood activities, self-ratings, and experiences, and it can be scored for both creativity and academic performance.

Schaefer's (1970) Biographical Inventory: Creativity is similar in nature but broader in applicability. One hundred and sixty-five questions are grouped into five sections: physical characteristics, family history, educational history, leisure-time activities, and a miscellaneous category. The inventory has several dimensions measuring different fields of creative endeavor. Boys are ranked on a math–science dimension and an art–writing dimension. Girls are ranked on a writing dimension and an art dimension. Several validation studies have been conducted using this instrument (Anastasi & Schaefer, 1969; Schaefer, 1969; Schaefer & Anastasi, 1968).

Category 5: Ratings by Teachers, Peers, and Supervisors

Category 5 is the least homogeneous of our eight categories in that researchers vary considerably in the criteria they use when asking for ratings of creativity. For this reason, this method of measuring creativity is more consistent methodologically than conceptually.

Teacher Nominations. A large portion of the research on creativity takes place in educational settings. Not surprisingly, teacher ratings are a commonly used criterion of creativity (e.g., Foster, 1971; Haddon & Lytton, 1971; Piers, Daniels, &

Quackenbush, 1960; Richards, Cline, & Needham, 1964).

Yamamoto's (1963) work is illustrative of the approach taken by several researchers. Yamamoto first established standards for teachers to use in their ratings. These standards involved identifying the most and least creative thinkers in the class. Creative thinking was defined as fluency (lots of ideas), flexibility (many different ideas), inventiveness (inventing and developing ideas), originality (unique ideas), and elaboration (detailed ideas).

Harrington, Block, and Block (1987) used a different approach to obtain teacher nominations. They compiled a list of personality traits that were cited in the research literature as characteristic of the creative personality. This list was then used as a 12-item checklist for teachers to use in making their judgments. Some illustrative items follow:

Tends to be proud of own accomplishments
Is resourceful in initiating activities
Has unusual thought processes
Is curious, exploring, eager for new experiences

Along the same lines, Renzulli, Hartman, and Callahan (1977) and Runco (1984) have developed rating scales for teachers which identify characteristics that theoretically relate to the creative personality.

Another common approach to teacher ratings is to have teachers give one or two global ratings. For example, in order to validate an inventory of creative interests, Rimm and Davis (1980) had teachers rate students on a 1- to 5-point scale, where 5 was defined as "highly creative, has many and original ideas related to art, music, class materials, or out-of-class interests (p. 38)" and 1 was defined as "very low creativity level, has rarely expressed any creative ideas in any verbal, musical or artistic form (p. 38)." At a secondary school level, Drevdahl (1956) asked faculty members in an arts and science department to rate their students on a 7-point scale of creativity. The raters were asked to make two judgments: one based on their own definition of creativity and one based on Drevdahl's definition. In an art school setting, Getzels and Csikszentmihalyi (1964) directed the art teachers to rate their students on a 4-point originality scale, where originality was defined as the "ability to originate ideas and to draw on personal resources in preparing assignments (p. 27)."

Teacher ratings have served as criteria in the validation of a number of creativity tests, such as Med-

nick and Mednick's (1967) Remote Associations Test (Karlins, Schuerhoff, & Kaplan, 1969; Mednick, 1963) and Schaefer's Biographical Inventory: Creativity (Schaefer, 1969; Schaefer & Anastasi, 1968) and Guilford and Torrance's tests of creative thinking (Houtz, Lewis, Shaning, & Denmark, 1983).

Peer Nominations. While recognizing some inherent limitations in using peer nominations as a criterion of creativity, Torrance (1974) has suggested that they may provide some useful data in the study of creativity. In order to eliminate the ambiguity in peer nominations, Torrance (1962) instructed young children to base their nominations on specific criteria, such as ideational fluency, unusual ideas, problem-solving ability, and inventiveness. Yamamoto (1964a,b), Foster (1971), and Reid, King, and Wickwire (1959) also have used peer nominations as a criterion of creativity and have developed questionnaires that include similar guidelines.

Surprisingly, peer ratings generally are used with children, although there are some exceptions. It is interesting to note that these exceptions stem from research in business and industrial settings. In working with research scientists, Taylor, Smith, and Ghiselin (1963) obtained creativity ratings, rankings, and nominations by peers in a research lab. Specher (1964) acquired peer descriptions on 12 characteristics taken to identify creative engineers. These characteristics included: skill in reporting results to others, persistence, liking for unusual and challenging problems, analytic thinking, ability to reach a decision on his own, fluency of ideas, working energetically, knowledge of the subject matter, friendly relations with co-workers, foresight, development of original approaches to problems, and development of valuable and worthwhile ideas. Finally, Keller and Holland (1978) asked employees from three applied research and development organizations to nominate from one to four co-workers who had contributed most to innovations in the organization. The number of innovations was used as an innovativeness index.

Supervisor Ratings. Particularly in industrial settings, supervisor ratings have proven to be a useful method of choosing creative employees (Keller & Holland, 1978; Meer & Stein, 1955; Taylor, 1958). Supervisors, like teachers, have the advantage of being familiar with the work of many individuals and of having the expertise to judge the work of these individuals.

Buel (1965) asked research supervisors in a large oil company to describe anonymously the most and the least creative researchers under their supervision. On the basis of their descriptions, Buel developed a list of creative behaviors which can be used as a descriptive checklist for helping supervisors identify creative research personnel. Taylor and his colleagues at the Institute of Personality Assessment and Research (IPAR) also employed supervisor ratings in their research with scientists in a government research lab (Taylor *et al.*, 1963). Immediate supervisors were asked to rate scientists on a number of traits including: productivity, drive, mathematical ability, integrity, desire for facts, independence, informative ability, flexibility, persistence, cooperation, and creation. Taylor also asked laboratory chiefs (higher level supervisors) to rate scientists with the aid of several checklists.

Category 6: Judgments of Products

It is self-evident that creative people should produce creative products. Understandably, identifying creative people in terms of one or more products is an approach that has encompassed virtually all areas of study and a varied sample of populations.

A little-known but ambitious example of this approach is a battery of tests developed by Foster (1971). Foster's assessment devices involve a broad range of activities typically associated with the secondary school. A brief description of these activities and their corresponding areas follow:

1. Sorting playing cards in sets of six that belong together (mathematics)
2. Creating mathematical equalities with a given set of numbers and symbols (mathematics)
3. Working in a physical education class with and without equipment (physical education)
4. Playing charades with several pieces of equipment, such as masks, hats, tools, etc. (drama)
5. Writing a story (literature)
6. Making a model out of one or several materials, such as buttons, feathers, wire, glue, corks, cloth, etc. (model-making)
7. Listening to music and painting a picture of what the music brings to mind (music)

Each of these products was then rated, using guidelines generally based on three criteria: fluency, flexibility, and originality.

More recently, Amabile's (1982) work is both important and illustrative of the creative product approach to measuring creativity. In the first of a series of eight studies, she provided 100 pieces of paper in multiple shapes, sizes, and colors to preadolescent girls and instructed them to make a collage that was ''silly.'' Designs then were evaluated by art teachers on a 5-point scale, ranging from very uncreative to very creative. In another study, Amabile extended her methods to literature by having her subjects write a cinquain, a 5-line stanza of unrhymed poetry. These poems were then evaluated using scales similar to the one described above by two groups of judges—advanced poetry students and published poets.

Numerous additional examples of research incorporating creative products are available in areas such as art (e.g., Brittain & Beittel, 1964; Bull & Davis, 1982; Csikszentmihalyi & Getzels, 1970; Jones, 1964; Sobel & Rothenberg, 1980), literature (Borgstadt & Glover, 1980; Davis & Rimm, 1982; Jones, 1964; Lynch & Kaufman, 1974; Malgady & Barcher, 1977, 1979; Rookey, 1974; Wallen & Stevenson, 1960), and science (Harmon, 1963; Pelz, 1963; Taylor *et al.*, 1963). In addition, products are sometimes defined less concretely as ideas (Graham, 1965; Ward & Cox, 1974).

The judges in product studies vary from experts to nonexperts, and the criteria vary from diverse definitions of creativity to social recognition (i.e., rewards or publication). Furthermore, subjective judgments usually are made on what products to choose and in what situation they will be obtained and, consequently, the products generally represent somewhat limited samples of behavior.

Category 7: Eminence

An impractical but valuable approach to the study of creativity is to study eminent people. Perhaps the most noteworthy research of this type is the work done at the IPAR (Barron, 1969; Hall & MacKinnon, 1969; Helson, 1971; Helson & Crutchfield, 1970; MacKinnon, 1962). The IPAR group initially asked a panel of professors of architecture to nominate the 40 most creative architects in the United States. On the basis of these nominations, 64 architects were asked to visit Berkeley for a weekend of intensive study at IPAR. Forty of these architects accepted. At IPAR, groups of creative writers and creative mathematicians also were selected by a similar process.

Another impressive programmatic analysis of eminence has been undertaken by Simonton (1976a,b,c, 1977a,b, 1979). By analyzing published historical and biographical records, Simonton has provided evidence on the effects of both individual (e.g., age) and social (e.g., political instability) variables on creative production in areas such as music, science, and others.

A number of older studies (e.g., Cattell, 1903; Cox, 1926; Ellis', 1904; cited in Gilcrist, 1972) attempted to identify persons of eminence through a variety of methods. Cox (1926) used Cattell's (1903) list of the 1,000 most eminent individuals in history. Cattell's criterion of eminence was the amount of space accorded to each individual in biographical dictionaries. Ellis (1904) based his definition of eminence on space devoted to individuals in the *Dictionary of National Biography,* a British anthology of eminent people. Cattell and Drevdahl (1955) selected eminent researchers, teachers, and administrators in the social sciences and physical sciences on the basis of committee selections and membership in a professional society. Roe (1951a) selected a group of physical scientists by asking a committee of scientists to rate a total of 69 men on a 3-point scale of excellence. Roe also chose a group of eminent biologists through a similar procedure (Roe, 1951b). In Ireland, Barron (1969) asked the staff of the Irish Management Institute, a 6,000-member management training group, to select individuals who were unquestionably leaders in Irish economic life.

The use of eminent people in the study of creativity raises the question of whether studying creativity in the highly gifted is tantamount to studying creativity in "normals." Although most researchers have treated creativity as a normally distributed trait, the argument that it is limited to a very small segment of the population is a worthwhile consideration.

Category 8: Self-Reported Creative Activities and Achievements

Perhaps the most easily defended way of identifying creative talent is in terms of self-reported creative activities and achievements. Although there is a problem in deciding which activities and achievements should be designated as creative, most of the lists that have been used in research have a reason-

able degree of face validity. Creative activities can take place in a number of fields recognized by society as important. In studying talent for the National Merit Scholarship Corporation, Holland and Nichols (1964) described lists of achievements and activities in science, art, literature, and music. The achievements described by Holland are rare, demand commitment, and generally are publicly recognized through prizes and publications. Some illustrative items are: placed first, second, or third in a regional or state science contest; exhibited or performed a work of art; had poems, stories, or articles published in a public newspaper; invented a patentable device; had minor roles or leads in plays produced by a college or university. Research incorporating this type of checklist has been published in a number of studies (Holland & Astin, 1962; Holland & Baird, 1968; Holland & Nichols, 1964; Holland & Richards, 1965; Richards, Holland, & Lutz, 1967a,b).

Another checklist of creative activities and accomplishments has been provided by Hocevar (1976; 1979d). Hocevar asked university students to name their three most creative accomplishments in each of six areas (art, mathematics and science, literature, music, performing arts, and a miscellaneous category). Another group of 50 college students then rated these activities and accomplishments on a scale ranging from most to least creative. These ratings were then used to create a 90-item inventory of creative activities and accomplishments that has six subscales: creativity in the fine arts, crafts, literature, music, performing arts, and math-science.

Other lists similar in content and emphasis to the Holland list have been developed by Runco (1986a), Torrance (1969), Skager, Schultz, and Klein (1965), and Wallach and Wing (1969). In general, the total creativity score is simply the number of activities checked. Although these lists have been used in educational and psychological research, there are no commercially available checklists.

Other Creativity Assessment Procedures

As stated earlier, these eight categories are meant to integrate some common techniques for assessing creative talent. Because of the varied nature of research on creativity, there are other measures of creativity that are tailor-made for specific situations that do not easily lend themselves to categorization.

A partial listing follows: Remote Associates Test (Mednick & Mednick, 1967); Starkweather Creativity Tests (Starkweather, 1971); Mosaic Construction Test (Hall, 1972); Barron-Welsh Art Scale (Barron & Welsh, 1952); Welsh Figure Preference Test (Welsh, 1959); Lundsteen Test of Creative Problem Solving (Rickborn & Lundsteen, 1968); Onomatopoeia and Images (Khatena, 1978); Pennsylvania Assessment of Creative Tendency (Rookey, 1971); Ingenuity Test (Flanagan, 1968); Sternberg's (1985) indices of people's implicit theories of creativity; the Rorschach VI. M scale (Frank, 1979); the problem-solving and creativity dimension of Marsh's (in press) Self-Description Questionnaire III, a series of cognitive measures developed by researchers at the Educational Testing Service (Frederiksen, Evans, & Ward, 1975); the measures of creativity fostering environments (Harrington *et al.,* 1987); Your Style of Learning and Thinking (Torrance, Reynolds, Riegel, & Ball, 1977; Reynolds, Kaltsounis, & Torrance, 1979); and the Lifetime Creativity Scales (Richards, Kinney, Benet, & Merzel, 1988).

In addition to the above, researchers also may want to examine measures of innovativeness, such as the Kirton Adaptation Inventory (Kirton, 1976), the Open Processing Scale (Leavitt & Walton, 1975); the Innovativeness Scale (Hurt, Joseph, & Cook, 1977) (see Goldsmith, 1986, for an analysis of these three scales). Finally, a number of intriguing measures of problem solving also could be useful to creativity researchers (see problems used by Milgram, 1983, and Houtz & Speedie, 1978, for examples).

The fact that the measures described in the previous two paragraphs do not fall neatly into any single category does not denigrate their potential usefulness. Indeed, as a group, they generally stem from sophisticated and highly original theories and offer much potential as new and interesting ways of further investigating creativity. In the next section, some general problems and criticisms of the eight major approaches to the measurement of creativity will be identified.

Discussion and Critique

Our discussion and critique of the measures used to assess creativity will focus on three commonly discussed psychometric qualities: reliability, discriminant validity, and nomological validity.

Reliability

Two forms of reliability, internal consistency and interjudge agreement, are particularly relevant to research on creativity , and each, therefore, will be discussed.

Internal Consistency. Internal consistency is important whenever a group of items on a test or questionnaire are summed to obtain a composite index. Such a practice is inherent to many of the previously described measurement approaches, namely, tests of divergent thinking, attitude and interest inventories, personality inventories, biographical inventories, and inventories of creative activities and achievements. Although a detailed analysis of the reported reliability coefficients in these studies is beyond the scope of this review, our subjective impression is that the internal consistency indices generally are satisfactory for research purposes in that most exceed .70. Internal consistency estimates are less relevant to supervisor ratings, teacher ratings, peer ratings, and product ratings because often only a single item (or product) is rated. Because of this practice, the extent to which these ratings would vary if another question had been asked or another product had been targeted has not been determined fully.

Interjudge Reliability. In comparison to internal consistency reliability, interjudge reliability is of more concern to creativity researchers. A number of the approaches identified earlier require people (i.e., experts, supervisors, peers, teachers) to make judgments about products, ideas, or other people. This technique presents a particular problem because the researcher must decide who the judges should be and what the judges should be looking for. To illustrate, when judgments of art products are made, there is some evidence that experts and nonexperts disagree (Golann, 1963; Knapp & Wulff, 1963). Skager *et al.* (1965) have identified at least three different points of view regarding art judgments. However, there also is evidence that expertise does not have a significant influence on ratings (Amabile, 1982).

Related to the problem of interjudge reliability is the problem of how the judges are asked to formulate their decisions. Not surprisingly, different researchers ask their judges to consider different criteria. The list of criteria is virtually unending, including fluency, originality and other cognitive characteristics, personality traits, self-expression, enthusiasm, productivity, and expertise. Some investigators use elaborate definitions of creativity; others use no definition at all. Some researchers train their judges; others believe that untrained judges should be employed. Furthermore, there is no guarantee that judges will understand and be guided by the sometimes complex definitions, and there is little research that shows the instructions even make a difference. To the contrary, when Drevdahl (1956) compared defined and undefined conditions with teacher nominations, no significant differences in the judgments of their most creative students were found. Similarly, Karlins *et al.* (1969) reported a correlation of .97 between defined and undefined ratings of creativity. Finally, to make matters even more complicated, with the exception of Amabile (1982), little is known about the extent to which extraneous factors (e.g., number of dimensions judged, number of products judged, and judges training) affect judgments of creativity.

Despite the concerns raised in the previous paragraph, a review of the numerous interjudge reliability indices, which were reported in studies that incorporate subjective judgments of people or products, finds that interjudge reliabilities usually exceed .70 and, consequently, are sufficient for research purposes. Practical constraints prevent our reviewing all these studies, but the interested reader is referred to Amabile's (1982) article, which represents the best work in the area of interjudge reliability. Nevertheless, there are still a number of unresolved issues, and a number of improvements in rating procedures have been proposed (Amabile, 1982; Korb & Frankiewicz, 1976; Malgady & Barcher, 1979; Richards *et al.*, 1988; Runco, 1984).

Discriminant Validity

A test of discriminant validity can be applied to the creativity literature in two ways. First, one may ask, ''Is the creativity construct different from other constructs?'' Second, ''Are the purported dimensions of creativity different from each other?'' Answers to each of these questions will be considered in the sections that follow.

Different from Other Constructs? Creativity is a scientific construct and thus it is reasonable to expect that it be different from other scientific constructs. In particular, because creativity is often subjectively assessed, one must hope that judges are able to distinguish creativity from other constructs, such as intelligence, achievement, and competence. Unfortunately, a review of some appropriate studies indicates otherwise. Holland (1959) had teachers, principals, and guidance counselors rate students on 12 traits, including originality. Originality correlated .72 with speaking skills and .84 with writing skills. The other nine correlations that involved originality ranged from .50 to .65. Wallen and Stevenson (1960) investigated creativity in fifth-grade writing and found that the teacher's judgments correlated .57 with IQ, .66 with school grades, and from .66 to .72 with three standardized achievement tests. In a study of research personnel, instructor ratings of creativeness correlated .68, .72, and .75 with grades, an officership rating, and a logical reasoning rating, respectively (Mullins, 1964). Finally, in a study involving faculty ratings of creativity in architecture, Karlins *et al.* (1969) found that ratings of creativity correlated from .79 to .95 with ratings of dependability, adaptiveness, need to know, independence, and productivity.

Regarding art judgments, the overall results are even more striking. Brittain and Beittel (1964) found that creativity scores determined by judgments on three art performances were correlated .89 with judged aesthetic quality. Csikszentmihalyi and Getzels (1970) found that originality ratings of a number of drawings correlated .76 with a rating of technical skill and .90 with a rating of overall aesthetic value. Similarly, in the Getzels and Csikszentmihalyi (1964) study, mean ratings on originality correlated with mean ratings on artistic potential .72 for males and .77 for females. Finally, Rossman and Gollob (1975) reported that among art students, peer ratings of creativity correlated .84 with peer ratings of intelligence. Likewise, faculty ratings of creativity correlated .59 with faculty ratings of intelligence.

Different Dimensions? Because judges have trouble discriminating creativity from other attributes, it follows that they will have even more trouble discriminating various dimensions of creativity. In the study cited earlier, Foster (1971) reported that the correlations between fluency, flexibility, and originality ratings were about .80 in physical education, painting, model-making, writing, and drama. Along the same lines, Yamamoto (1964b) found that when peer nominations were used to measure fluency, flexibility, and inventive level, their intercorrelations ranged from .62 to .82. Finally, Hocevar (1979a,b) and Hocevar and Michael (1979) conducted several studies collectively demonstrating that the dimensions of divergent thinking tests have questionable discriminant validity.

Additional Considerations. All the correlations reported in the previous two sections would be even higher if the data were free of measurement error (i.e., unreliability in the judgments). It is obvious that a considerable "halo" effect is present when creativity is based on subjective judgments. Judges seem only to be able to establish some overall opinion that influences all of their judgments. Because of this, they fail to discriminate creativity from other related constructs. The evidence indicates that asking judges to choose the most intelligent people or their favorite product is sometimes equivalent to obtaining judgments of creativity.

There are, of course, exceptions to the above findings. Rossman and Gollob (1975) demonstrated that subjects can make distinct judgments regarding creativity and intelligence. Harrington, Block, and Block (1983) found only moderate correlations in teacher ratings of creativity, general intelligence, and cooperativeness and, consequently, concluded that their creativity criterion possessed substantial discriminant validity. Sternberg (1985) presented evidence that individuals can discriminate creativity, intelligence, and wisdom. Amabile (1982) found that creativity could be distinguished from both aesthetic value and technical competence in judgments of art quality. Richards *et al.* (1988) presented procedures for discriminating creativity from intelligence and appreciation of creativity and for distinguishing vocational and avocational creativity. Finally, modifications in scoring techniques (Milgram, 1983; Milgram & Arad, 1981) and modifications in instructions (Runco, 1986b; Runco & Albert, 1985) seem to separate better the dimensions of divergent thinking.

These exceptions notwithstanding, researchers cannot assume that the creativity construct has discriminant validity, particularly when subjective judgments are involved. Empirical data as well as sophisticated statistical analysis are needed. The topic of statistical analysis is dealt with in a later section.

Nomological Validity

Nomological validity is achieved when variables relate to each other in a logical fashion.[1] Each of the previously defined approaches is a widely used and accepted technique for identifying creative talent. Because each method is purported to be measuring some aspect of creativity, it is reasonable to expect that the methods should yield scores that are correlated.

In a study of 166 scientists in a government laboratory, Taylor *et al.* (1963) collected scores on 52 criteria of creativity, including 11 supervisor ratings, six peer ratings, autobiographical information, and numerous product variables. Although scores based on the same method (e.g., the 11 supervisor ratings) tended to be highly related, scores obtained from different methods were not. For example, supervisor ratings had a low relationship to peer ratings, and self-rating scores were uncorrelated with the more objective autobiographical data. Furthermore, scores based on products, such as publications and reports, were not related to either supervisor or peer ratings. When factor analyzed, this array of criteria yielded a total of 14 relatively independent categories.

Davis and Belcher (1971) compared four methods of identifying creativity—two tests of divergent thinking, a biographical inventory, and a criterion composed of self-ratings on several creative activity questions. Except for the relationship of the biographical inventory and the criterion, the intercorrelations of these tests were low and generally nonsignificant for both males and females.

In their study of art students, Getzels and Csikszentmihalyi (1964) included 14 measures of creativity, including two teacher ratings, eight tests of divergent thinking, two personality inventories (Cattell's 16 Personality Factors and the Study of Values), grades, and IQ scores. The authors predicted some overlap among these criteria because they all have some claim as indices of creativity. Such was not the case. A factor analysis revealed only method factors rather than a general creativity factor. In another study of art students, Ellison

---

[1]We chose the term *nomological* rather than *construct* validity because construct validity is more all-encompassing; that is, construct validity usually subsumes all other types of validity. In addition, we chose not to use the term *convergent* validity because this type of validity is generally applied when one is studying different measures of a single construct. Our view is that the creativity instruments discussed herein measure a multitude of constructs.

(1973) found low and negative relationships between judged creativity on a pastel drawing, the Remote Associations Test, and the Barron-Welsh Art Scale. Along the same lines, Zimmer, Guip, and Hocevar (1988) provided data that point to a similar lack of nomological validity in that no significant relationship was found between creative attitudes and interests and a two-judge evaluation of art portfolios.

In the most ambitious analysis of the creative personality to date, Gough (1979) related seven different scales, all derived from the Adjective Check List, to criterion ratings of creativity in seven male samples and in five female samples. For six of the seven scales, only 17 of 72 validity coefficients were significant and only 1 of 72 exceeded .40. (Results were much more encouraging for the seventh scale, the Creative Personality Inventory, which had 10 of 12 validity coefficients significant at the .05 level.) Finally, the correlations of divergent thinking with other measures of creativity often indicate no relationship (Andrews, 1975; Barron, 1969; Beittel, 1964; Brittain & Beittel, 1964; Fitzgerald & Hattie, 1983; Getzels & Csikszentmihalyi, 1964; Goolsby & Helwig, 1975; Gough, 1976; Hadden & Lytton, 1971; Hocevar, 1980; Jordan, 1975; Karlins *et al.,* 1969; Kogan & Pankove, 1974; Popperova, 1972; Roweton, Farless, Donham, Wleklinski, & Spencer, 1975; Skager, Klein, & Schultz, 1967).

There are exceptions to the trends reported in the last several paragraphs. In particular, many studies report positive relationships among divergent thinking and various creativity criteria (Bartlett & Davis, 1974; Bennett, 1973; Cropley, 1972; Dewing, 1970; Halpin, Halpin, & Torrance, 1974; Harrington, Block, & Block, 1983; Haven, 1965; Hocevar, 1980; Jones, 1964; McCrae, 1987; Milgram & Milgram, 1976a; Rotter, Langland, & Berger, 1971; Runco, 1984, 1986a; Torrance, 1969; Wallach & Wing, 1969; Wallbrown & Huelsman, 1975; Zegas, 1976).

In addition to studies that involve divergent thinking, significant correlations between alternative approaches to measuring creativity have been reported in a variety of studies (e.g., Bull & Davis, 1982; Davis & Rimm, 1982; Keller & Holland, 1978; Michael & Colson, 1979; Rimm & Davis, 1980; Taylor & Fish, 1979; Taylor, Sutton, & Haworth, 1974). Nevertheless, it is important to recognize that in studies where significant positive correlations have been reported, the correlation is seldom higher than .30, suggesting that the two

alternative measures of creativity have less than 10% variance in common. When creativity is identified using multiple methods, individuals are ranked differently. High scorers on one method are not necessarily high scorers on another. This finding raises questions as to whether creativity should be viewed as a unitary disposition.

The inconsistent findings in relation to nomological validity have another important implication. Perhaps by using distinct techniques to assess creativity, researchers are actually studying different phenomena. If this is the case, conclusions must be limited to studies incorporating the same method, and theory integration in the area of creativity becomes even more difficult.

An explanation for the confusion is that many of the methods tagged with the creativity label really do not measure phenomena that society typically labels creative. In many cases, the methods are hypothesized correlates of real-life creative behavior. Guilford and the cognitive group have hypothesized that divergent thinking is somehow linked to creative behavior. The personality psychologists have hypothesized that some personality traits are linked to creative behavior. And others have hypothesized that attitudes and interests or past experiences are linked to creative behavior. Although there is some evidence to support the validity of these various hypotheses, the relationship of these measures to real-life creativity is not one-to-one. Therefore, caution should be taken in the uncritical use of correlates as criterion measures of creativity.

Conclusions

It is apparent that reliability, discriminant validity, and nomological validity cannot be taken for granted in creativity research. Even though findings are mixed, enough problems have been identified in the extant literature to point to a need for greater attention to measurement issues by those engaged in creativity research. It is noteworthy that throughout this review we have relied on assessing discriminant and nomological validity through the subjective interpretation of the size of correlations; that is, discriminant validity is indicated by low correlations and nomological validity is indicated by high correlations. There are problems with this approach. First, the correlations presented in most research reports are attenuated due to measurement error. Second, there is no agreed upon guideline for determining how low a correlation must be to demonstrate discriminant validity or how high a correlation must be to demonstrate nomological validity. Unfortunately, the literature itself necessitates this crude approach to discriminant and nomological validity. More sophisticated analytic approaches to discriminant validity have been available for many years (i.e., exploratory factor analysis; multitrait–multimethod [MTMM] analysis); however, these approaches largely have been unused by most researchers in the area of creativity. It is hoped that more modern structural modeling, such as Jöreskog and Sörbom's (1986) LISREL analytic paradigm and Bentler's (1985) EQS paradigm, will not be neglected similarly because these procedures offer much more precise and objective approaches to problems of discriminant and nomological validity. Such procedures are best used when at least two traits are measured by two different methods (i.e., the MTMM paradigm) (cf. Marsh & Hocevar, 1983, 1988). However, they also are applicable to the more common single-method studies in which the dimensionality of a test or questionnaire needs to be determined or to studies in which the discriminant validity of ratings on two or more traits needs to be evaluated (cf. Zarnegar et al., 1988). Finally, these procedures also would be applicable to the exploration of possible higher-order factor models (cf. Marsh & Hocevar, 1985) and to the analysis of factorial invariance (cf. Hocevar & El-Zahhar, 1984; Marsh & Hocevar, 1985).

Which approach to measuring creativity is best? Tests of ability, interests, and personality are appropriate when the researcher's goals are to explain something about creativity, but they are not acceptable as criteria of creativity. High scorers on these tests are not necessarily creative people. If a researcher is interested in the personality correlates of creativity or in the relationship of intelligence to creativity, or in evaluating educational programs designed to enhance creativity, why not go directly to the criteria that have face validity? This can best be accomplished through studying eminent individuals, evaluating creative products, or using an inventory of creative activities and accomplishments.

Because studies of eminent individuals are often impractical, assessing creativity through the analysis of creative products or through the administration of an inventory of creative activities and accomplishments are the best of the currently available assessment strategies. The kind of tasks analyzed by Amabile (1982) and Sobel and Rothen-berg (1980) (e.g., poems, collages, and sketches) and the kind of activities listed in the Holland and Nichols (1964) and Hocevar (1979d) inventories are recognized by society as being creative, and they are relatively rare. Most of the activities demand a high degree of commitment, and they are not something just anyone can master.

Although it can be argued that interest inventories, personality inventories, tests of divergent thinking, and other measures of creativity have predictive validity, past behavior is generally the best predictor of future behavior. The efficacy of this predictive strategy is evident in a number of areas (see Mischel, 1968, for a review). These findings appear to generalize to the area of creative behavior. MacKinnon (1968) reported that, in studies of creative persons in a variety of fields, earlier accomplishments were consistently predictive of later accomplishments.

The most compelling evidence for predicting future creative behavior with past creative behavior is found in two related studies (Holland & Nichols, 1964; Richards et al., 1967a). In a high-aptitude sample, Holland and Nichols predicted talented, nonacademic accomplishment in six areas: leadership, science, dramatic arts, literature, music, and art. Predictors included interests, goals, activities, self-conceptions, aptitudes, and personality traits. The results of this study indicated that past activities and achievements easily were the best predictors of creative achievement in college. The findings of this study have been replicated with a less select sample by Richards et al. (1967a).

In conclusion, our recommendation is that researchers interested in creativity focus on eminence, creative products, or an inventory of creative accomplishments and achievements. Three categories of creativity measurement—personality, interests, and divergent thinking—should not be accepted uncritically as criteria of creativity. Rather, they should be viewed as correlates of creativity that are possibly causally related but conceptually distinct from the creativity construct. Finally, the usefulness of ratings by others (teachers, peers, supervisors) and of autobiographical inventories as criteria of creativity is yet to be fully determined.

The possibility of using ratings by others deserves further consideration if the ratings focus on real-life creativity instead of its correlates and if satisfactory interjudge reliabilities, discriminant validities, and nomological validities can be obtained. Although much of the literature on ratings suggests that reliability and validity are problematic when people are asked to rate other people, there are isolated examples in which ratings have appeared to be promising. The work of Richards *et al.* (1988) on the Lifetime Creativity Scale is a case in point. They demonstrated that raters who independently evaluate the protocols of clinical interviewers could assess reliably lifetime vocational and avocational creativity in diverse samples of subjects, and that these assessments appeared to have content, discriminant, and construct validity.

Besides ratings by others, it is possible that autobiographical inventories offer some potential as measures of real-life criteria of creativity. This is because biographical inventories often include creative activities and accomplishments that are similar to the lists previously recommended. On the negative side, biographical inventories also often include life events that can only be classified as possible correlates of creativity. Suffice it to say that autobiographical inventories are diverse, and this diversity makes their usefulness as a criterion of creativity difficult to determine.

In marked contrast to our recommendation that real-life criteria of creativity be included in studies of creativity, prior studies often do not include such criteria. To illustrate, there are dozens of studies that relate correlates of creativity (e.g., divergent thinking) to other correlates (creative personality) or to other variables that represent distinct constructs (e.g., intelligence). Although these studies are valuable in that they help us understand the presumed correlates of creativity, they are limited in that they are one step away from actual real-life creativity.

Along the same lines, there are dozens of experimental studies that evaluate the effects of creativity-enhancing treatments without including a real-life criteria of creativity. Again, these studies are worthwhile in that it is of intrinsic interest to know whether the correlates of creativity (e.g., divergent thinking) are modifiable. Whether changes in these correlates can actually influence real-life creative behavior is another issue that can only be resolved when real-life criteria are included in the research design.

How can one best interpret the vast extant literature on creativity? A simple rule of thumb would be to focus on only those studies that include a measure of real-life creativity. Interestingly, this is the strategy generally employed by Mumford and Gustafson (1988) in their recent review of the creativity syndrome. In the main, their review focuses on studies in which eminence or real-life

creative production were outcomes. We agree with this approach.

Does the previous paragraph imply that studies that focus on divergent thinking or the creative personality can be discounted? The answer to this question is "clearly no" for two reasons. First, there is overwhelming evidence that divergent thinking and the creative personality are interesting constructs in their own right, and, consequently, deserve attention as distinct and important scientific constructs. Second, there is at least some evidence that these two constructs are potential causes of real-life creativity.

Agenda for Future Research on Measurement Issues

Rather than present a listing of "needed research," we will provide an expository example of an ideal hypothetical measurement study that is consistent with the conclusions just presented. Traditionally, measurement issues have been analyzed by computing reliability indices, inspecting attenuated correlations among measured variables, and possibly conducting an exploratory factor analysis. As discussed earlier in this review, this traditional approach fails to take advantage of modern developments in structural modeling. The intent of the following sections is to illustrate the use of structural modeling in a nontechnical manner and to expound on the advantages of this approach. When applied to measurement models, structural modeling is called *confirmatory factor analysis*. The statistical framework for confirmatory factor analysis presented herein is based mainly on the LISREL framework of Jöreskog and Sörbom (Jöreskog, 1969; Jöreskog & Sörbom, 1986).

Measurement research cannot be conducted without a concrete conceptual framework, and future research should reflect this fact. Thus, this illustration will follow one of many possible conceptual models. The hypothetical model is shown in Figure 1 (the parameter estimates should be ignored for the moment). In line with conventional practice (cf. Bentler, 1980), two types of variables are differentiated pictorially—measured or observed variables and nonmeasured or latent variables. The measured variables are shown in small squares and represent hypothetical responses to the following instruments:

VF1 = Wallach and Kogan's (1965) creativity battery (verbal fluency only)

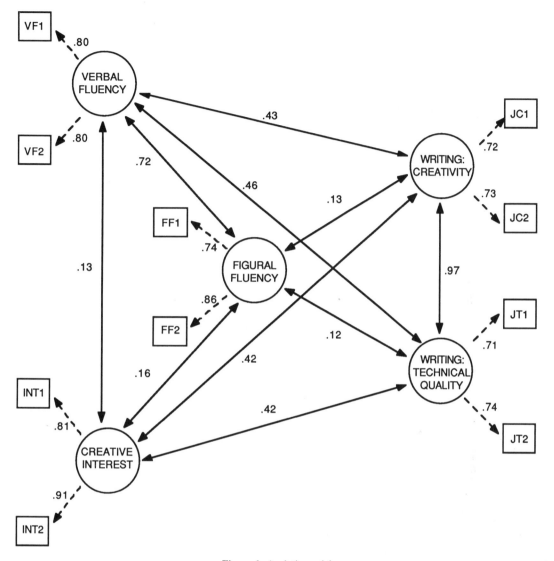

Figure 1. Analytic model.

VF2 = Torrance's (1974) Tests of Creative
Thinking (verbal fluency only)

FF1 = Wallach and Kogan's (1965) creativity battery (figural fluency only)

FF2 = Torrance's (1974) Tests of Creative
Thinking (figural fluency only)

INT1 = Group Inventory for Finding Interests
(Davis & Rimm, 1982; Rimm &
Davis, 1976, 1980) (odd items only)

INT2 = Group Inventory for Finding Interests
(Davis & Rimm, 1982; Rimm &
Davis, 1976, 1980) (even items only)

JC1 = Expert #1's judgments of the creativity of a short story written by each
subject

JC2 = Expert #2's judgments of the creativity of a short story written by each
subject

JT1 = Expert #1's judgments of the technical quality of a short story written
by each subject

JT2 = Expert #2's judgments of the technical quality of a short story written
by each subject

The latent variables are designated by circles. They represent five different hypothetical constructs: Verbal Fluency, Figural Fluency, Creative Interest, Writing: Creativity, and Writing: Technical Quality. In line with the discussion in the previous section, the conceptual model specifies that fluency and interest constructs are considered as distinct constructs.

One begins a confirmatory factor analysis by first deriving a correlation or covariance matrix among measured variables. A hypothetical correlation matrix is given in the Appendix. The next step is to determine which factor loadings will be estimated using theoretical considerations. Because both measured variables and latent factors are standardized, the factor loadings are correlations between measured variables and latent factors. The factor structure implied by Figure 1 is shown in Table 1. Two types of parameters are illustrated—factor loadings which were estimated and factor loadings which were set to zero. The general rule is that target factor loadings are estimated and nontarget factor loadings are set to zero; that is, measured variables are allowed only to load on the factors that they are hypothesized to measure. For example, the two verbal fluency measured variables, VF1 and VF2, are constrained to load on the Verbal Fluency factor. As illustrated in Table 1, 10 parameters were estimated in the factor-loading matrix, and 40 parameters were constrained to zero. In relation to Figure 1, factor loadings are represented by paths that go from hypothetical constructs (e.g., Verbal Fluency) to measured variables (e.g., VF1). These paths are shown as dotted lines.

In a confirmatory factor analysis, correlations between latent factors (10 parameters) can be estimated also. Correlations between latent factors are shown in Figure 1 as double-arrowed solid lines.

As will be clear from the discussion below, the interpretation of a confirmatory factor analysis is based on the factor loading and the factor intercorrelation parameter estimates previously mentioned. The mathematical objective of a confirmatory factor analysis is to find estimates of the parameters that yield a predicted correlation matrix that most closely fits the observed correlation matrix. Predicted correlations are determined by path multiplication.

The parameter estimates generated by the confirmatory factor analysis are shown in Figure 1. Single-arrowed dotted paths going from a hypothetical construct to a measured variable are factor loadings and they are correlations; double-arrowed paths going from one latent variable to another latent variable are between factor correlations. These correlations are corrected for measurement error (i.e., disattenuated) and, consequently, they are more useful than conventional attenuated correlations based on raw data.

The discussion and interpretation of our confirmatory factor-analytic results will focus on the three issues that formed the basis for our previous critique of creativity measurement; namely, reliability, discriminant validity, and nomological validity.

Reliability

In an earlier section, two types of reliability were identified as most relevant to the creativity researcher—internal consistency and interjudge.

Table 1. Factor-Loading Matrix

Measured variables	Latent variables (factors)				
	Verbal fluency	Figural fluency	Creative interest	Writing: creativity	Writing: technical quality
VF1	.80	0.0	0.0	0.0	0.0
VF2	.80	0.0	0.0	0.0	0.0
FF1	0.0	.74	0.0	0.0	0.0
FF2	0.0	.86	0.0	0.0	0.0
INT1	0.0	0.0	.81	0.0	0.0
INT2	0.0	0.0	.91	0.0	0.0
JC1	0.0	0.0	0.0	.72	0.0
JC2	0.0	0.0	0.0	.73	0.0
JT1	0.0	0.0	0.0	0.0	.71
JT2	0.0	0.0	0.0	0.0	.74

Internal Consistency. One approach to internal consistency is to correlate separate halves of a measure. The split-half technique is well known, and other techniques (e.g., coefficient alpha, Kuder-Richardson Formula 21) can be viewed as more refined methods of computing split-half reliabilities. In the present example, the split-half technique is illustrated for the Creative Interest construct. However, it also could have been applied to the Verbal Fluency and Figural Fluency constructs in a separate analysis or through a higher order factor analysis (cf. Marsh & Hocevar, 1988). In a confirmatory factor-analytic framework, a necessary but not sufficient condition for reliability is that the estimated correlations (i.e., factor loadings) between measured variables and their respective constructs be significant. For the first half of the Creative Interest measure (INT1), the factor loading is .81 and it is significant. (All the loadings in Figure 1 are significant, so the asterisks have been omitted from the diagram to simplify the figure.) The factor loading can be squared and subtracted from unity to yield an estimate of the percentage of error for any given measured variable. In this case, .81 squared is .66 and the error of measurement for INT1 is therefore .34 (i.e., $1 - .66$).

Because statistical significance can be obtained even when measurements are less than satisfactory, the degree of reliability also is important. With two measured variables, a sufficient reliability[2] is indicated when factor loadings exceed .70. The present example meets this rule of thumb for all ten factor loadings. A more precise indication of reliability is obtained by computing the reliability coefficient. The reliability coefficient is the percentage of "true" variation in a measurement, and it is given by the following formula:

$$\text{Reliability} = 1 - \frac{\text{Total error of measurement}}{\text{Total variance}}$$

where the total error of measurement is the sum of the errors across the measured variables, and the total factor variance is the observed variance of a factor composite that is created by adding the measured variables (in this case, the sum of the odd and even halves of the creative interests measure). To illustrate, the error for the first measured variable on the Creative Interest construct (INT1) is .34 (see above). By similar calculation, the error for INT2 is $1 - .91^2$ or .17. Thus, the sum of the errors is .51 (summing .34 and .17).

The total observed variance (S^2) is the sum of the variances of the observed variables ($1 + 1$ because we are analyzing a correlation matrix) plus two times their observed correlation ($2 \times .74$). In equation form: $S^2 = 1 + 1 + 2(.74) = 3.48$. Substituting into the formula given for reliability above, the reliability of the measurement of the Creative Interest factor is given as:

$$\text{Reliability} = 1 - \frac{\text{Total error of measurement}}{\text{Total variance}}$$
$$= \frac{.34 + .17}{3.48} = .85$$

A more strict test of internal consistency is the examination of the extent to which different measures (e.g., the Wallach-Kogan test and the Torrance test) of the same construct (e.g., Verbal Fluency) give consistent results. As shown in Figure 1, such a research question can easily be incorporated into a confirmatory factor analysis. To illustrate, both the Wallach and Kogan and the Torrance measures are constrained to load on Verbal Fluency latent variable. Both loadings are .80. These loadings easily exceed the .70 rule of thumb and the actual reliability coefficient, using the formula given above, is .78. These data point to the conclusion that both the Wallach-Kogan and the Torrance verbal fluency subtests are measuring the same construct in a satisfactory manner.

Interjudge Reliability. As previously discussed, subjective judgments of creativity are frequently employed by researchers. Such subjectivity requires that the extent to which independent judgments provide consistent results be assessed. In the present example, this assessment is accomplished by loading two independent judgments of creative writing (JC1 and JC2) on the same latent factor (Writing: Creativity). The procedure for computing and assessing interjudge reliability is identical to the internal consistency calculations discussed earlier, and the interjudge reliability for the Writing: Creativity indices (i.e., judgments) equals .69.

The reader may have realized that, up to this point, there is little that confirmatory factor analysis accomplishes that could not be accomplished with a

---

[2]The logic for the rule of thumb is as follows. If the loadings are equal to .70, the predicted correlation between measured variables is .49 (.70 × .70). Substituting .49 into the split-half formula, the reliability would be .66, which is usually regarded as sufficient or close to sufficient for research purposes. (The rule of thumb requires that one assumes that the predicted and observed correlations are roughly equivalent.)

more traditional approach to reliability (e.g., the split-half formula would yield almost identical results). This is correct, and the major advantages of confirmatory factor analysis fall into the areas of discriminant and nomological validity. However, it is important to point out that a confirmatory factor analysis requires that fundamental measurement issues be addressed. Also, in a confirmatory factor analysis, measurement findings automatically become integrated into the evaluation and interpretation of discriminant and nomological validity.

Discriminant Validity

In a previous discussion, two questions were identified as particularly relevant to the creativity literature. First, one may ask, "Are the dimensions of creativity different from each other?" Second, one may ask "Is creativity different from other constructs?" The following discussion will demonstrate how both questions can be examined in a confirmatory factor analysis.

Different Dimensions?   According to most authors, fluency has at least two dimensions: verbal and figural. Some authors have suggested that the dimensions of divergent thinking do not have discriminant validity when operationalized empirically. Others have disagreed, and it is likely that a consensus will occur only when the issue is examined in ways that are more precise than the subjective visual examination of attenuated correlations. Confirmatory factor analysis is tailor made for such an issue, because it provides a statistical test of whether or not two constructs differ.

To illustrate using the present example, the disattenuated correlation between Verbal Fluency and Figural Fluency is .72. Whether Verbal Fluency and Figural Fluency are actually different constructs can be determined by testing whether the disattenuated correlation (.72) is different from unity. This test is easily accomplished by testing whether the hypothesized model (Figure 1) better reproduces the observed correlation matrix than a model in which the Verbal/Figural correlation is set at unity. In this case, the original model does better reproduce the correlation matrix than the model in which the Verbal/Figural correlation equals unity. Thus, one would conclude that fluency has distinct Verbal and Figural dimensions.

Different Constructs?   A reasonable and frequent question in creativity research is the extent to which judges can discriminate creativity from other constructs. For example, in reference to Figure 1, can judges discriminate creativity in a short story from the technical quality of the short story? Inspection of attenuated correlations offers only an imprecise guess when answering questions about discriminant validity, but confirmatory factor analysis can answer such questions in a straightforward fashion. To illustrate, Figure 1 shows that the disattenuated correlation between Writing: Creativity and Writing: Technical Quality is .97. The sheer magnitude of this correlation clearly indicates that judges cannot discriminate creativity from technical quality. (An even more precise test could be accomplished in borderline cases by testing whether the correlation differs from unity.)

Although it might be tempting to argue that the above questions could be answered using more traditional correlational techniques, this is not the case. The inspection of uncorrected correlations is limited in that such correlations are attenuated because of measurement error and, consequently, can provide the illusion of discriminant validity. The present example is a case in point in that the attenuated correlations are only in the area of .50 (see the Appendix); yet there is clear evidence against discriminant validity in the confirmatory factor analysis. Simple correlational analyses are further limited in that discriminant validity requires the consideration of patterns of correlation rather than a single correlation. Such a process is unwieldy and difficult to interpret.

Traditional exploratory factor analysis has advantages over the visual inspection of attenuated correlations. Nevertheless, exploratory factor analysis is limited also in that the actual factors are determined using mathematical criteria rather than theory, and the correlations between factors are determined by arbitrary decisions that are set before the analysis, e.g., the type of rotation and the parameters (e.g., delta) that are set before the rotation.

Nomological Validity

Nomological validity is achieved if a construct correlates with other constructs in a logical fashion. For example, some logical relationships inherent in Figure 1 are:

1. Verbal Fluency should correlate with Writing: Creativity more highly than Figural Fluency because creative writing involves to a

greater extent the mental manipulation of ideas rather than figures.

2. Verbal Fluency should correlate more highly with Writing: Creativity than with Writing: Technical Quality because Verbal Fluency has been identified as integral to creative writing by numerous authors.

3. Creative Interest should correlate with Writing: Creativity; and this correlation should be greater than the correlation between Creative Interest and Writing: Technical Quality. By definition, this prediction is self-evident.

The disattenuated correlations in a confirmatory factor analysis can be used to check each of these hypotheses in a precise manner. To illustrate, Hypothesis 1 is supported because the correlation between Verbal Fluency and Writing: Creativity is .43, which is greater than the correlation between Figural Fluency and Writing: Creativity (.13). Hypothesis 2 is not supported because the correlation between Verbal Fluency and Writing: Creativity (.43) is slightly lower than the correlation between Verbal Fluency and Writing: Technical Quality (.46). Finally, Hypothesis 3 is partially supported. Creative Interest does correlate with Writing: Creativity (.42); however, this correlation is identical to the correlation between Creative Interest and Writing: Technical Quality. More precise tests for the difference between correlations in a confirmatory factor analysis are available (Jöreskog & Sörbom, 1986). Generally, in these tests, correlations are constrained to equality, and a statistical test is conducted to examine whether the fit of the constrained model shows a significant decrement.

Taken together, the results in reference to nomological validity are mixed and the reason for the mixed findings is clear: Judges fail to discriminate creativity in writing from the technical quality of writing.

Although it is possible to analyze nomological validity through visual inspection of attenuated correlation coefficients and with exploratory factor analysis, these approaches are less advantageous because low reliability can be mistaken for a lack of nomological validity. Further, nomological validity may necessitate the statistical comparison of correlations. Even though such tests can be accomplished using z transformations, it is more easily accomplished in a confirmatory factor analysis. Finally, though exploratory factor analysis can yield factor correlations that are disattenuated, exploratory factor analysis is limited in that factors are defined using atheoretical criteria, and correlations are estimated using arbitrary criteria for rotation.

Summary

Available creativity measures were classified into eight groups: tests of divergent thinking; attitude and interest inventories; personality inventories; biographical inventories; ratings by teachers, peers, and supervisors; judgments of products; eminence; and self-reported creative activities and accomplishments. These eight approaches to creativity measurement were collectively reviewed in terms of their reliability, discriminant validity, and nomological validity.

Both internal consistency reliabilities and interjudge reliabilities have been satisfactory for research purposes, although there remain many issues to be resolved in the analysis on interjudge agreement. A lack of discriminant validity continues to be a problem, both in terms of how creativity differs from other constructs and in terms of how the dimensions of creativity differ from each other. Much evidence points to a lack of nomological validity if one considers the eight categories of measurement as eight different ways of measuring some aspect of creativity; that is, measures that presumably relate to creativity frequently do not correlate with each other. The obvious conclusion is that different researchers are studying different phenomena by virtue of the measures that they select.

Researchers in the area of creativity have not taken advantage of modern developments in confirmatory factor analysis when assessing reliability, discriminant validity, and nomological validity. This chapter provides a concrete example of how confirmatory factor analysis might be applied to resolve measurement issues, and the advantages of the confirmatory factor analytic approach are discussed.

In reference to the issue of how creativity is best measured, peer nominations, supervisor ratings, and teacher nominations are often inadequate indicators of creativity due to the rater's inability to discriminate creativity from other traits. In addition, these methods do not guarantee that the raters will have the knowledge and intention to actually consider criteria that bear on real-life creativity in making their decisions. Divergent thinking, biographical characteristics, attitudes and interests, and personality characteristics are best described only as correlates of real-life creative behavior, and they should not be taken as direct measures of creativity. Research that has the most bearing on what society recognizes as actual creativity can best be accomplished by studying eminent women and men, analyzing creative products, and administering inventories of creative activities and accomplishments.

ACKNOWLEDGMENTS. The authors acknowledge the helpful comments of Susan Page Hocevar as contributing to this manuscript. This chapter is a revised and updated version of D. Hocevar (1981), Measurement of Creativity: Review and Critique. *Journal of Personality Assessment, 45,* pp. 450–64.

Appendix
Correlation Matrix: Hypothetical Data

	VF1	VF2	FF1	FF2	INT1	INT2	JC1	JC2	JT1
VF2	.64								
FF1	.45	.43							
FF2	.48	.49	.64						
INT1	.07	.06	.02	.04					
INT2	.12	.09	.13	.16	.74				
JC1	.25	.23	.11	.06	.27	.26			
JC2	.26	.27	.10	.07	.27	.28	.53		
JT1	.25	.29	.12	.10	.26	.29	.50	.51	
JT2	.28	.25	.09	.01	.28	.26	.53	.52	.53

Note: $N = 200$.

References

Amabile, T. M. (1982). Social psychology of creativity: A consensual assessment technique. *Journal of Personality and Social Psychology, 43,* 997–1013.

Anastasi, A., & Schaefer, C. E. (1969). Biographical correlates of artistic and literary creativity in adolescent girls. *Journal of Applied Psychology, 53,* 267–273.

Andrews, F. (1975). Social and psychological factors which influence the creative process. In I. A. Taylor & J. W. Getzels (Eds.), *Perspectives in creativity.* Chicago: Adline.

Barron, F. (1969). *Creative person and creative process.* New York: Holt, Rinehart & Winston.

Barron, F., & Welsh, G. (1952). Artistic perception as a factor in personality style: Its measurement by a figure preference test. *Journal of Psychology, 33,* 199–203.

Bartlett, M., & Davis, G. A. (1974). Do the Wallach and Kogan tests predict real creative behavior? *Perceptual and Motor Skills, 39,* 730.

Basadur, M., & Finkbeiner, C. T. (1985). Measuring preference for ideation in creative problem-solving training. *Journal of Applied Behavioral Science, 21,* 37–49.

Beittel, K. R. (1964). Creativity in the visual arts in higher education: Criteria, predictors, experimentation and their interactions. In C. W. Taylor (Ed.), *Widening horizons in creativity.* New York: Wiley.

Bentler, P. (1985). *Theory and implementation of EQS: A Structural equations program.* Los Angeles, CA: BMDP Statistical Software, Inc.

Bentler, P. M. (1980). Multivariate analysis with latent variables. In M. R. Rosenzweig & L. W. Porter (Eds.), *Annual review of psychology* (Vol. 31, pp. 419–56). Palo Alto, CA: Annual Reviews.

Bennet, S. N. (1973). Divergent thinking ability: A validation study. *British Journal of Educational Psychology, 43,* 1–7.

Berger, R. M., & Guilford, J. P. (1969). *Plot Titles.* Beverly Hills, CA: Sheridan Psychological Services.

Borgstadt, C., & Glover, J. A. (1980). Contrasting novel and repetitive stimuli in creativity training. *Psychological Reports, 46,* 652.

Brittain, W. L., & Beittel, K. R. (1964). A study of some tests of creativity in relationship to performances in the visual arts. In W. L. Brittain (Ed.), *Creativity and art education.* Washington, DC: National Art Education Association.

Buel, W. D. (1965). Biographical data and the identification of creative research personnel. *Journal of Applied Psychology, 49,* 318–321.

Buel, W. D., Albright, L. E., & Glennon, J. R. (1966). A note on the generality and cross-validity of personal history for identifying creative research scientists. *Journal of Applied Psychology, 50,* 217–219.

Bull, K. S., & Davis, G. A. (1982). Inventory for appraising adult creativity. *Contemporary Educational Psychology, 7,* 1–8.

Cattell, R., & Butcher, H. (1968). *The prediction of achievement and creativity.* Indianapolis: Bobbs-Merrill.

Cattell, R., & Drevdahl, J. (1955). A comparison of the personality profile (16 P.F.) of eminent researchers with that of eminent teachers and administrators and the general population. *British Journal of Educational Psychology, 46,* 248–261.

Cattell, R., & Eber, H. (1968). *Handbook for the Sixteen Personality Factor Questionnaire.* Champaign, IL: IPAT.

Christensen, P. R., Merrifield, P. R., & Guilford, J. P. (1958). *Consequences*. Beverly Hills, CA: Sheridan Psychological Services.

Christensen, P. R., Guilford, J. P., Merrifield, P. R., & Wilson, R. C. (1960). *Alternate Uses*. Beverly Hills, CA: Sheridan Psychological Services.

Covington, M. V. (1966). A childhood attitude inventory for problem solving. *Journal of Educational Measurement, 3*, 234.

Crockenberg, S. (1972). Creativity tests: Boom or boon-doggle? *Review of Educational Research, 42*, 27–45.

Cropley, A. J. (1972). A five-year longitudinal study of the validity of creativity tests. *Developmental Psychology, 6*, 119–124.

Csikszentmihalyi, M., & Getzels, J. W. (1970). Concern for discovery: An attitudinal component of creative production. *Journal of Personality, 38*, 91–105.

Davis, G. (1971). Instruments useful in studying creative behavior and creative talent. *Journal of Creative Behavior, 5*, 162–165.

Davis, G., & Belcher, T. L. (1971). How shall creativity be measured? Torrance tests, RAT, Alpha Biographical and IQ. *Journal of Creative Behavior, 5*, 153–161.

Davis, G., & Rimm, S. (1982). (GIFFI) I and II: Instruments for identifying creative potential in the junior and senior high school. *Journal of Creative Behavior, 16*, 50–57.

Dellas, M., & Gaier, E. L. (1970). Identification of creativity: The individual. *Psychological Bulletin, 73*, 55–73.

Dewing, K. (1970). The reliability and validity of selected tests of creative thinking in a sample of seventh-grade West Australian children. *British Journal of Educational Psychology, 40*, 35–42.

Domino, G. (1970). Identification of potentially creative persons from the Adjective Check List. *Journal of Consulting and Clinical Psychology, 35*, 48–51.

Drevdahl, J. E. (1956). Factors of importance for creativity. *Journal of Clinical Psychology, 12*, 21–26.

Educational Testing Service (1987). *Annotated bibliography of tests: Creativity and divergent thinking*. Princeton, NJ: Educational Testing Service.

Ellison, B. A. (1973). Creativity in black artists: A comparison of selected creativity measures using judged creativity as a criterion. *Journal of Non-White Concerns in Personnel and Guidance, 1*, 150–157.

Evans, R. G., & Forbach, G. B. (1983). Facilitation of performance on a divergent measure of creativity: A closer look at instructions to ''be creative.'' *Applied Psychological Measurement, 7*, 181–187.

Fitzgerald, D., & Hattie, J. A. (1983). An evaluation of the ''Your Style of Learning and Thinking'' inventory. *British Journal of Educational Psychology, 53*, 336–346.

Flanagan, J. C. (1968). Ingenuity Test. *Journal of Creative Behavior, 2*, 215–216.

Foster, J. (1971). *Creativity and the teacher*. London: Macmillan.

Frank, G. (1979). On the validity of hypotheses derived from the Rorschach: VI. M and the intrapsychic life of individuals. *Perceptual and Motor Skills, 48*, 1267–1277.

Frederiksen, N., Evans, F., & Ward, W. (1975). Development of provisional criteria for the study of scientific creativity. *Gifted Child Quarterly, 19*, 60–65.

Fricke, B. (1965). *Opinion, Attitude, and Interest Survey handbook: A guide to personality and interest measurement*. Ann Arbor, MI: OAIS Testing Program.

Fu, V. R., Kelso, G. B., & Moran, J. D., III (1984). The effects of stimulus dimension and mode of exploration on original thinking in preschool children. *Educational and Psychological Measurement, 44*, 431–440.

Getzels, J. W., & Csikszentmihalyi, M. (1964). *Creative thinking in art students: An exploratory study*. (Cooperative Research Project No. E-008). Office of Education, U.S. Department of Health, Education and Welfare, University of Chicago.

Gilchrist, M. (1972). *The psychology of creativity*. Melbourne, Australia: Melbourne University Press.

Golann, S. E. (1963). Psychological study of creativity. *Psychological Bulletin, 60*, 548–565.

Goldsmith, R. E. (1986). Convergent validity of four innovativeness scales. *Educational and Psychological Measurement, 46*, 81–87.

Goolsby, T., & Helwig, L. (1975). Concurrent validity of the Torrance Tests of Creative Thinking and the Welsh Figural Preference Test. *Educational and Psychological Measurement, 35*, 507–508.

Gough, H. (1957). *The California Psychological Inventory*. Palo Alto, CA: Consulting Psychologists Press.

Gough, H. (1976). Studying creativity by means of word association tests. *Journal of Applied Psychology, 61*, 348–353.

Gough, H. G. (1979). A creative personality scale for the Adjective Check List. *Journal of Personality and Social Psychology, 37*, 1398–1405.

Gough, H. G., & Heilbrun, A. B. (1965). *The Adjective Check List: Manual*. Palo Alto, CA: Consulting Psychologists Press.

Graham, W. R. (1965). Creative and constructive idea men and their participation in activities. *The Journal of General Psychology, 72*, 383–391.

Guilford, J. P. (1956). The structure of the intellect. *Psychological Bulletin, 53*, 267–293.

Guilford, J. P. (1968). *Intelligence, creativity, and their educational implications*. San Diego, CA: Robert R. Knapp.

Guilford, J. P., & Zimmerman, W. S. (1963). *Guilford-Zimmerman Interest Inventory*. Beverly Hills, CA: Sheridan Psychological Services.

Haddon, F. A., & Lytton, H. (1971). Primary education and divergent thinking abilities—four years on. *British Journal of Educational Psychology, 41*, 136–147.

Hall, W., & MacKinnon, D. (1969). Personality inventory correlates of creativity among architects. *Journal of Applied Psychology, 53*, 322–326.

Hall, W. B. (1972). A technique for assessing aesthetic predispositions: Mosaic Construction Tests. *Journal of Creative Behavior, 6*, 225–235.

Halpin, G., Halpin, G., & Torrance, E. P. (1974). Relationships between creative thinking abilities and a measure of the creative personality. *Educational and Psychological Measurement, 34*, 75–82.

Harmon, L. R. (1963). The development of a criterion of scientific competence. In C. W. Taylor & F. Barron (Eds.), *Scientific creativity: Its recognition and development*. New York: Wiley.

Harrington, D. M. (1975). Effects of explicit instructions to ''be creative'' on the psychological meaning of divergent thinking test scores. *Journal of Personality, 43*, 434–454.

Harrington, D. M., Block, J., & Block, J. H. (1983). Predicting creativity in preadolescence from divergent thinking in early childhood. *Journal of Personality and Social Psychology, 45*, 609–623.

Harrington, D. M., Block, J. H., & Block, J. (1987). Testing aspects of Carl Rogers's theory of creative environments: Child-rearing antecedents of creative potential in young adolescents. *Journal of Personality and Social Psychology, 52,* 851–856.

Hattie, J. A. (1977). Conditions for administering creativity tests. *Psychological Bulletin, 84,* 1249–1260.

Hattie, J. A. (1980). Should creativity tests be administered under testlike conditions? An empirical study of three alternative conditions. *Journal of Educational Psychology, 72,* 87–98.

Haven, G. A. (1965). Creative thought, productivity, and the self-concept. *Psychological Reports, 16,* 750–752.

Heist, P. (Ed.). (1968). *The creative college student: An unmet challenge.* San Francisco: Jossey-Bass.

Heist, P., & Yonge, G. (1968). *Manual for the Omnibus Personality Inventory—Form E.* New York: The Psychological Corporation.

Helson, R. (1965). Childhood interest clusters related to creativity in women. *Journal of Consulting Psychology, 29,* 352–361.

Helson, R. (1971). Women mathematicians and the creative personality. *Journal of Consulting and Clinical Psychology, 36,* 210–220.

Helson, R., & Crutchfield, R. S. (1970). Mathematicians: The creative researcher and the average PhD. *Journal of Consulting and Clinical Psychology, 34,* 250–257.

Hocevar, D. (1976). Dimensions of creativity. *Psychological Reports, 39,* 869–870.

Hocevar, D. (1979a). The unidimensional nature of creative thinking in fifth-grade children. *Child Study Journal, 9,* 273–277.

Hocevar, D. (1979b). Ideational fluency as a confounding factor in the measurement of originality. *Journal of Educational Psychology, 71,* 191–196.

Hocevar, D. (1979c). A comparison of statistical infrequency, subjective judgment, and random numbers as criteria in the measurement of originality. *Journal of Personality Assessment, 43,* 297–299.

Hocevar, D. (1979d). The development of the Creative Behavior Inventory. Los Angeles, CA: University of Southern California. (*ERIC* Documentation Reproduction Service No. ED 170 350).

Hocevar, D. (1980). Intelligence, divergent thinking and creativity. *Intelligence, 4,* 25–40.

Hocevar, D., & El-Zahhar, N. (1984). A paradigm for examining the psychometric characteristics of cross-cultural measurements. In H. M. van der Ploeg, R. Schwarzer, & C. D. Spielberger, *Advances in test anxiety research* (Vol. 4). New York: Erlbaum.

Hocevar, D., & Michael, W. B. (1979). The effects of scoring formulas on the discriminant validity of tests of divergent thinking. *Educational and Psychological Measurement, 39,* 917–921.

Holland, J. L. (1959). Some limitations of teacher ratings as predictors of creativity. *Journal of Educational Psychology, 50,* 219–223.

Holland, J. L., & Astin, A. W. (1962). The prediction of the academic, artistic, scientific, and social achievement of undergraduates of superior scholastic aptitude. *Journal of Educational Psychology, 53,* 132–143.

Holland, J. L., & Baird, L. L. (1968). The Preconscious Activity Scale: The development and validation of an originality measure. *Journal of Creative Behavior, 2,* 217–225.

Holland, J. L., & Nichols, R. (1964). Prediction of academic and extracurricular achievement in college. *Journal of Educational Psychology, 55,* 55–65.

Holland, J. L., & Richards, J. (1965). Academic and non-academic accomplishment: Correlated or uncorrelated? *Journal of Educational Psychology, 56,* 165–174.

Holmes, D. (1976). A questionnaire measure of the creative personality. *Journal of Creative Behavior, 10,* 183.

Houtz, J. C., & Speedie, S. M. (1978). Processes underlying divergent thinking and problem solving. *Journal of Educational Psychology, 70,* 848–854.

Houtz, J. C., Lewis, C. D., Shaning, D. J., & Denmark, R. J. (1983). Predictive validity of teacher ratings of creativity over two years. *Contemporary Educational Psychology, 8,* 168–173.

Hurt, H. T., Joseph, K., & Cook, C. D. (1977). Scales for the measurement of innovativeness. *Human Communication Research, 4,* 58–65.

Institute for Behavioral Research in Creativity (1968). *Alpha Biographical Inventory.* Greensboro, NC: Prediction Press.

Jones, C. A. (1964). Relationships between creative writing and creative drawing of sixth-grade children. In W. L. Brittain (Ed.), *Creativity and art education.* Washington, DC: National Art Education Association.

Jordan, L. A. (1975). Use of canonical analysis in Cropley's "A five-year longitudinal study of the validity of creativity tests." *Developmental Psychology, 5,* 117–126.

Jöreskog, K. (1969). A general approach to confirmatory factor analysis. *Psychometrika, 34,* 183–202.

Jöreskog, K., & Sörbom, D. (1986). *LISREL: Analysis of linear structural relations by the method of maximum likelihood.* Chicago: International Educational Resources.

Kaltsounis, B. (1971). Instruments useful in studying creative behavior and creative talent. *Journal of Creative Behavior, 6,* 268–274.

Kaltsounis, B. (1972). Additional instruments useful in studying creative behavior and creative talent. *Journal of Creative Behavior, 6,* 268–274.

Karlins, M., Schuerhoff, C., & Kaplan, M. (1969). Some factors related to architectural creativity in graduating architecture students. *Journal of General Psychology, 81,* 203–215.

Keller, R. T., & Holland, W. E. (1978). A cross-validation study of the Kirton Adaptation-Innovation inventory in three research and development organizations. *Applied Psychological Measurement, 2,* 563–570.

Khatena, J. (1978). Identification and stimulation of creative imagination imagery. *Journal of Creative Behavior, 12,* 30–38.

Khatena, J., & Torrance, E. P. (1976). *Manual for Khatena-Torrance Creative Perception Inventory.* Chicago: Stoelting.

Kirton, M. J. (1976). Adaptors and innovators: A description and measure. *Journal of Applied Psychology, 61,* 622–29.

Knapp, R. H., & Wulff, A. (1963). Preference for abstract and representational art. *Journal of Social Psychology, 60,* 255–262.

Kogan, N., & Pankove, E. (1974). Long-term predictive validity of divergent-thinking tests: Some negative evidence. *Journal of Educational Psychology, 66,* 802–810.

Korb, R., & Frankiewicz, R. (1976). Strategy for *a priori* selection of judges in a product-centered approach to assessment of creativity. *Perceptual and Motor Skills, 42,* 107–115.

Lacey, L., & Erickson, C. (1974). Psychology of scientist: XXXI. Discriminability of creativity scale for the Adjective Check List among scientists and engineers. *Psychological Reports, 34,* 755–758.

Leavitt, C., & Walton, J. R. (1975). Development of a scale for innovativeness. In M. J. Schlinger (Ed.), *Advances in consumer research* (Vol. 2). Ann Arbor, MI: Association for Consumer Research.

Lynch, M., & Kaufman, M. (1974). Creativeness: Its meaning and measurement. *Journal of Reading Behavior, 6*, 375–394.

MacKinnon, D. (1962). The nature and nurture of creative talent. *American Psychologist, 17*, 484–495.

MacKinnon, D. (1968). Selecting students with creative potential. In P. Heist (ed.), *The creative college student: An unmet challenge*. San Francisco: Jossey-Bass.

McCrae, R. R. (1987). Creativity, divergent thinking, and openness to experience. *Journal of Personality and Social Psychology, 52*, 1258–1265.

McDermid, C. D. (1965). Some correlates of creativity in engineering personnel. *Journal of Applied Psychology, 49*, 14–19.

Malgady, R. G., & Barcher, P. R. (1977). Psychological scaling of essay creativity: Effects of productivity and novelty. *Journal of Educational Psychology, 69*, 512–518.

Malgady, R. G., & Barcher, P. R. (1979). Some information-processing models of creative writing, *Journal of Educational Psychology, 71*, 717–725.

Marsh, H. (in press). *Self-Description Questionnaire (SDQ): III.* San Antonio, Texas: Psychological Corporation.

Marsh, H., & Hocevar, D. (1983). Confirmatory factor analysis of multitrait–multimethod matrices. *Journal of Educational Measurement, 20*, 231–248.

Marsh, H., & Hocevar, D. (1985). The application of confirmatory factor analysis to the study of self-concept: First and higher order factor structures and their invariance across age groups. *Psychological Bulletin, 97*, 562–582.

Marsh, H., & Hocevar, D. (1988). A new, more powerful method of multitrait–multimethod analysis. *Journal of Applied Psychology, 73*, 107–117.

Mednick, M. T. (1963). Research creativity in psychology graduate students. *Journal of Consulting Psychology, 27*, 265–266.

Mednick, S. A., & Mednick, M. T. (1967). *Examiner's manual: Remote Associates Test.* Boston: Houghton Mifflin.

Meeker, M., & Meeker, R. (1975). *SOI Learning Abilities test.* El Segundo, CA: SOI Institute.

Meer, B., & Stein, M. (1955). Measures of intelligence and creativity. *The Journal of Psychology, 39*, 117–126.

Michael, W. B., & Colson, K. R. (1979). The development and validation of a life experience inventory for the identification of creative electrical engineers. *Educational and Psychological Measurement, 39*, 463–470.

Milgram, R. M. (1983). Validation of ideational fluency measures of original thinking in children. *Journal of Educational Psychology, 75*, 619–624.

Milgram, R. M., & Arad, R. (1981). Ideational fluency as a predictor of original problem solving. *Journal of Educational Psychology, 73*, 568–572.

Milgram, R. M., & Milgram, N. A. (1976a). Creative thinking and creative performance in Israeli students. *Journal of Educational Psychology, 68*, 255–259.

Milgram, R. M., & Milgram, N. A. (1976b). Group versus individual administration in the measurement of creative thinking in gifted and nongifted children. *Child Development, 47*, 563–565.

Milgram, R. M., Milgram, N. A., Rosenbloom, G., & Rabkin, L. (1978). Quantity and quality of creative thinking in children and adolescents. *Child Development, 49*, 385–388.

Mischel, W. (1968). *Personality and assessment.* New York: Wiley.

Mullins, C. J. (1964). Current studies of the personnel research laboratory in creativity. In C. W. Taylor (Ed.), *Widening horizons in creativity.* New York: Wiley.

Mumford, M. D., & Gustafson, S. B. (1988). Creativity syndrome: Integration, application and innovation. *Psychological Bulletin, 103*, 27–43.

Owens, W. A., & Schumacher, C., & Clark, J. (1957). The measurement of creativity in machine design. *Journal of Applied Psychology, 41*, 297–302.

Pelz, D. C. (1963). Relationships between measures of scientific performance and other variables. In C. W. Taylor & F. Barron (Eds.), *Scientific creativity: Its recognition and development.* New York: Wiley.

Petrosko, J. (1978). Measuring creativity in elementary school: The current state of the art. *Journal of Creative Behavior, 12*, 109–119.

Piers, E. V., Daniels, J. M., & Quackenbush, J. F. (1960). The identification of creativity in adolescents. *Journal of Educational Psychology, 51*, 346–351.

Popperova, M. (1971, 1972). Some methodological problems relating to tests of creative thinking. [*Czskoslovenska Psychologie, 15*(4), 391–397.] *Psychological Abstracts, 49*, No. 5666.

Reid, J., King, F., & Wickwire, P. (1959). Cognitive and other personality characteristics of creative children. *Psychological Reports, 5*, 729–737.

Renzulli, J., Hartman, R., & Callahan, C. (1977). Scale for rating the behavioral characteristics of superior students. In W. Barbe & J. Renzulli (Eds.), *Psychology and education of the gifted* (2nd ed.). New York: Irvington.

Reynolds, C. R., Kaltsounis, B., & Torrance, E. P. (1979). A children's form of ''Your Style of Learning and Thinking'': Preliminary norms and technical data. *Gifted Child Quarterly, 23*, 757–767.

Richards, J. M., Cline, V. B., & Needham, W. E. (1964). Creativity tests and teacher and self judgments of originality. *Journal of Experimental Education, 32*, 281–285.

Richards, J. M., Holland, J. L., & Lutz, S. W. (1967a). Prediction of student accomplishment in college. *Journal of Educational Psychology, 58*, 343–355.

Richards, J. M., Holland, J. L., & Lutz, S. W. (1967b). Assessment of student accomplishment in college. *The Journal of College Student Personnel, 8*, 360–365.

Richards, R., Kinney, D. K., Benet, M., & Merzel, A. P. C. (1988). Assessment of everyday creativity: Characteristics of the lifetime creativity scales and validation with three large samples. *Journal of Personality and Social Psychology, 54*, 476–485.

Rickborn, I., & Lundsteen, S. (1968). The construction of and acquisition of reliability data for a test of qualitative levels in creative problem solving. *California Journal of Educational Research, 19*, 53–58.

Rimm, S., & Davis, G. (1976). GIFT: An instrument for the identification of creativity. *Journal of Creative Behavior, 10*, 178–182.

Rimm, S., & Davis, G. (1980). Five years of international research with GIFT: An instrument for the identification of creativity. *Journal of Creative Behavior, 14*, 35–46.

Roe, A. (1951a). A psychological study of physical scientists. *Genetic Psychological Monographs, 43*, 121–235.

Roe, A. (1951b). A psychological study of eminent biologists. *Psychological Monographs, 65* (No. 331).

Rookey, T. J. (1971). *The Pennsylvania assessment of creative tendency: Norms-technical manual*. Harrisburg: Pennsylvania Department of Education.

Rookey, T. J. (1974). Validation of a creativity test: The 100 students study. *Journal of Creative Behavior, 8*, 211–213.

Rossman, B. B., & Gollob, H. F. (1975). Comparison of social judgments of creativity and intelligence. *Journal of Personality and Social Psychology, 31*, 271–281.

Rotter, D. M., Langland, L., & Berger, D. (1971). The validity of tests of creative thinking in seven-year-old children. *Gifted Child Quarterly, 15*, 273–278.

Roweton, W. E., Farless, J. E., Donham, R., Wleklinski, D. J., & Spencer, H. L. (1975). Indices of classroom creativity. *Child Study Journal, 5*, 151–162.

Runco, M. A. (1984). Teachers' judgments of creativity and social validation of divergent thinking tests. *Perceptual and Motor Skills, 59*, 711–717.

Runco, M. A. (1986a). Divergent thinking and creative performance in gifted and nongifted children. *Educational and Psychological Measurement, 46*, 375–384.

Runco, M. A. (1986b). Maximal performance on divergent thinking tests by gifted, talented, and nongifted children. *Psychology in the Schools, 23*, 308–315.

Runco, M. A., & Albert, R. S. (1985). The reliability and validity of ideational originality in the divergent thinking of academically gifted and nongifted children. *Educational and Psychological Measurement, 45*, 483–501.

Schaefer, C. (1969). The prediction of creative achievement from a biographical inventory. *Educational and Psychological Measurement, 29*, 431–437.

Schaefer, C. (1970). *Manual for the Biographical Inventory Creativity (BIC)*. San Diego, CA: Educational and Industrial Testing Service.

Schaefer, C., & Anastasi, A. (1968). A biographical inventory for identifying creativity in adolescent boys. *Journal of Applied Psychology, 52*, 42–48.

Schaefer, C. E., & Bridges, C. I. (1970). Development of a creativity attitude survey for children. *Perceptual and Motor Skills, 31*, 861–862.

Seddon, G. M. (1983). The measurement and properties of divergent thinking ability as a single compound entity. *Journal of Educational Measurement, 20*, 393–402.

Simonton, D. K. (1976a). Biographical determinants of achieved eminence: A multivariate approach to the Cox data. *Journal of Personality and Social Psychology, 33*, 218–226.

Simonton, D. K. (1976b). The causal relation between war and scientific discovery: An exploratory cross-national analysis. *Journal of Cross-Cultural Psychology, 7*, 133–144.

Simonton, D. K. (1976c). Philosophical eminence, beliefs, and zeitgeist: An individual-generational analysis. *Journal of Personality and Social Psychology, 34*, 630–640.

Simonton, D. K. (1977a). Creative productivity, age and stress: A biographical time-series of 10 classical composers. *Journal of Personality and Social Psychology, 35*, 791–804.

Simonton, D. K. (1977b). Eminence, creativity and geographical marginality: A recursive structural equation model. *Journal of Personality and Social Psychology, 35*, 805–816.

Simonton, D. K. (1979). Multiple discovery and invention: Zeitgeist, genius, or chance? *Journal of Personality and Social Psychology, 37*, 1603–1616.

Skager, R. W., Schultz, C. B., & Klein, S. P. (1965). Quality and quantity of accomplishments as measures of creativity. *Journal of Educational Psychology, 56*, 31–39.

Skager, R. W., Klein, S. P., & Schultz, C. B. (1967). The

prediction of academic and artistic achievement at a school of design. *Journal of Educational Measurement, 4*, 105–117.

Smith, J., & Schaefer, C. (1969). Development of a creativity scale for the Adjective Check List. *Psychological Reports, 25*, 87–92.

Sobel, R. S., & Rothenberg, A. (1980). Artistic creation as stimulated by superimposed versus separated visual images. *Journal of Personality and Social Psychology, 39*, 953–961.

Specher, T. B. (1964). Creativity and individual differences in criteria. In C. W. Taylor (Ed.), *Widening horizons in creativity*. New York: Wiley.

Starkweather, E. K. (1971). Creativity research instruments designed for use with preschool children. *The Journal of Creative Behavior, 5*, 245–255.

Sternberg, R. J. (1985). Implicit theories of intelligence, creativity, and wisdom. *Journal of Personality and Social Psychology, 49*, 607–627.

Taylor, C. W. (1958). Some variables functioning in productivity and creativity. In C. W. Taylor (Ed.), *The second (1957) University of Utah research conference on the identification of creative scientific talent*. Salt Lake City: University of Utah Press.

Taylor, C. W., Smith, W. R., & Ghiselin, B. (1963). The creative and other contributions of one sample of research scientists. In C. W. Taylor & F. Barron (Eds.), *Scientific creativity: Its recognition and development*. New York: Wiley.

Taylor, I. A., & Fish, R. A. (1979). The Creative Behaviour Disposition scale: A Canadian validation. *Canadian Journal of Behavioral Science, 11*, 95–97.

Taylor, I. A., Sutton, D., & Haworth, S. (1974). The measurement of creative transactualization: A scale to measure behavioral dispositions to creativity. *Journal of Creative Behavior, 8*, 114–115.

Taylor, W., & Ellison, R. (1964). Predicting creative performances from multiple measures. In C. W. Taylor (Ed.), *Widening horizons in creativity*. New York: Wiley.

Thompson, B., & Andersson, B. V. (1983). Construct validity of the divergent production subtests from the Structure-of-Intellect Learning Abilities Test. *Educational and Psychological Measurement, 43*, 651–655.

Torrance, E. P. (1962). *Guiding creative talent*. Englewood Cliffs, NJ: Prentice-Hall.

Torrance, E. P. (1969). Prediction of adult creative achievement among high school seniors. *Gifted Child Quarterly, 13*, 223–229.

Torrance, E. P. (1974). *Torrance Tests of Creative Thinking: Norms-technical manual*. Princeton, NJ: Personnel Press/Ginn.

Torrance, E. P., Reynolds, C. R., Riegel, T., & Ball, O. E. (1977). "Your Style of Learning and Thinking" forms A and B: Preliminary norms, abbreviated technical notes, scoring keys, and selected references. *Gifted Child Quarterly, 21*, 563–573.

Treffinger, D. J., & Poggio, J. P. (1972). Needed research on the measurement of creativity. *Journal of Creative Behavior, 6*, 253–267.

Treffinger, D. J., Renzulli, J. S., & Feldhusen, J. F. (1971). Problems in the assessment of creative thinking. *Journal of Creative Behavior, 5*, 104–112.

Tryk, H. E. (1968). Assessment of creativity. In P. McReynolds (Ed.), *Advances in psychological assessment* (Vol. 1). Palo Alto, CA: Science and Behavior Books.

Wallach, M. A., & Kogan, N. (1965). *Modes of thinking in*

young children: A study of the creativity-intelligence distinction. New York: Holt, Rinehart & Winston.

Wallach, M. A., & Wing, C. (1969). *The talented student: A validation of the creativity-intelligence distinction.* New York: Holt, Rinehart & Winston.

Wallbrown, F. H., & Huelsman, C. B. (1975). The validity of the Wallach-Kogan creativity operations for inner-city children in two areas of visual art. *Journal of Personality, 43,* 109–126.

Wallen, N. E., & Stevenson, G. M. (1960). Stability and correlates of judged creativity in fifth grade writing. *Journal of Educational Psychology, 51,* 273–276.

Ward, W. C., & Cox, P. W. (1974). A field study of nonverbal creativity. *Journal of Personality, 42,* 202–209.

Welsh, G. (1959). *Preliminary manual for the Welsh Figure Preference Test.* Palo Alto, CA: Consulting Psychologists Press.

Welsh, G. S. (1977). Personality correlates of intelligence and creativity in gifted adolescents. In J. C. Stanley, W. C. George, & C. H. Solano (Eds.), *The gifted and the creative: A fifty-year perspective.* Baltimore, MD: Johns Hopkins University Press.

Yamamoto, K. (1963). Relationships between creative thinking abilities of teachers and achievement of pupils. *Journal of Experimental Education, 32,* 3–25.

Yamamoto, K. (1964a). Creativity and sociometric choice among adolescents. *Journal of Social Psychology, 64,* 249–261.

Yamamoto, K. (1964b). Evaluation of some creativity measures in a high school with peer nominations as criteria. *The Journal of Psychology, 58,* 285–293.

Zarnegar, Z., Hocevar, D., & Michael, W. (1988). Components of original thinking in gifted children. *Educational and Psychological Measurement, 48,* 5–16.

Zegas, J. (1976). A validation study of tests from the divergent production plane of the Guilford Structure-of-Intellect model. *Journal of Creative Behavior, 10,* 170–177.

Zimmer, J. W., Guip, D., & Hocevar, D. (April 1988). *Assessment of creativity—A longitudinal evaluation.* Paper presented at the annual meeting of the American Educational Research Association, New Orleans, Louisiana.

CHAPTER 4

Individual Differences in Creativity

AN INTERACTIONIST PERSPECTIVE

Richard W. Woodman and Lyle F. Schoenfeldt

Creativity seems to be one of those concepts understood by everyone in the world except behavioral scientists. Although some segments of the public might hypothesize other reasons for this state of affairs, we believe the reason for this seeming paradox is as simple as the difference between the terms *concept* and *construct*. As a concept used by laypersons, creativity carries meaning in everyday speech that, although somewhat imprecise, is nevertheless widely shared; any surplus meaning is relatively unimportant; and operationalization for measurement purposes is a nonissue. As a scientific construct, however, creativity is held to a higher (or, at least, different) standard, and the construct validity issues surrounding the term can be frustrating in the extreme for researchers interested in investigating the phenomena of creative behavior and creative persons.

How best to understand creativity? Many disciplines in the behavioral and social sciences have provided perspectives that may be, in some measure, useful. Several of these perspectives will be briefly reviewed here, pursuant to positing an interactionist model of creative behavior that attempts to combine elements of the personality, cognitive,

and social psychology perspectives on creativity. The proposed interactionist model provides a framework to explore in some detail a number of factors thought to be of importance in explaining individual differences in creative behavior. Finally, some conclusions and implications of our theoretical perspective will be presented.

Theoretical Explanations for Differences in Creative Behavior

The potential sources for individual differences in creativity are legion. Any categorization scheme is likely to be flawed; nevertheless, a potentially useful starting point is provided by an examination of creativity from the perspective of (a) personality differences, (b) cognitive style or ability differences, and (c) social psychology. Each of these perspectives on creative behavior will be examined in turn.

Personality

The study of personality characteristics associated with creative behavior has been a generally active area of research for some time, although such research has waxed and waned in popularity over the years (Helson & Mitchell, 1978). The research

Richard W. Woodman and Lyle F. Schoenfeldt • Department of Management, Texas A&M University, College Station, TX 77843.

and writing on personality factor–creative behavior relationships has tended to emerge in one of three ways: (a) attempts by personality theorists to explain creativity in terms of comprehensive theories of personality; (b) investigations regarding the personality and biographical characteristics of eminent creative individuals and/or creative activity in a variety of fields; and (c) more narrowly focused work that examines one or a few specific personality dimensions for possible relationships to creative behavior.

First, creativity as a construct has seemed to present a special challenge for personality theory, and many well-known personality theorists have made attempts to incorporate an explanation for creative behavior within their theoretical positions (Taylor, 1976; Woodman, 1981). The need for personality theory to explain creativity stems from its role as a general theory of behavior. As such, a personality theory that did not account for the creative act would seem incomplete, at least in the eyes of some critics. Of course, there is a great divergence across theories with regard to explanations of individual differences in creativity. This divergence can be traced, in part, to fundamental differences in perspective regarding the nature of human beings and their behavior that exist within various streams of psychological thought or research "traditions," that is, cognitive, humanistic, psychoanalytic, and behavioristic (Woodman, 1981).

A second major area of research within the personality framework has been the study of characteristics of creative persons. Good examples of investigations in this area are provided by the writings of Barron (1969), Helson (1971), MacKinnon (1970), Roe (1953), and Simonton (1977, 1986). These types of studies have attempted to catalogue personality correlates of creative productivity as well as biographical data that might be predictive of later creative behavior. Researchers have investigated similarities and differences in creativity across broad fields of endeavor, such as art, literature, music, and science. In addition, many researchers have focused on examining individual differences across more narrowly defined disciplines, such as architecture, physics, and mathematics (e.g., Weiss, 1981). In the most general sense, this research on creative persons and their creative products has delineated a set of "core characteristics" that are widely regarded as typifying the "creative personality." For example, after reviewing 15 years of research on personality characteristics of creative individuals, Barron and Harrington (1981) concluded:

> In general, a fairly stable set of core characteristics (e.g., high valuation of esthetic qualities in experience, broad interests, attraction to complexity, high energy, independence of judgement, autonomy, intuition, self-confidence, ability to resolve or accommodate apparently opposite or conflicting traits in one's self concept, and finally, a firm sense of self as "creative") continued to emerge as correlates of creative achievement and activity in many domains. (p. 453)

Despite such convergence in the research literature, the generalizability of any specific constellation of traits across fields of endeavor remains highly problematic.

Finally, a considerable body of literature has accumulated concerning specific personality dimensions related to creative behavior. Examples of heavily-researched traits which are thought to be important factors in creativity include locus of control (e.g., Bolen & Torrance, 1978), psychological femininity and masculinity (e.g., Barron & Harrington, 1981, p. 458), self-esteem or identity (e.g., Dellas, 1978), dogmatism (Faschingbauer, Moore, & Stone, 1978), and narcissism (Solomon, 1985) among many others. Trait-specific research has both benefited from and contributed to the research on creative persons discussed above, and, in addition, has close ties to the next major perspective to be discussed—explanations of creativity based on differences in cognitive styles or abilities.

Cognitive Style/Ability

Whether differences in creativity are best explained as a function of the personality or as a function of differences in cognitive styles, problem-solving approaches, or abilities continues to be debated (e.g., Eysenck, 1983). Without dismissing the importance of personality factors, a perusal of the literature suggests that much of the current research focus seems to have shifted to explorations of cognitive ability–creative behavior relationships. Cognitive factors thought to have important relationships to creativity include cognitive styles, such as field independence/dependence (e.g., Noppe & Gallagher, 1977; Spotts & Mackler, 1967), "creative" (e.g., "lateral," "reframing") thinking or problem-solving styles (Kershner & Ledger, 1985; Noppe, 1985), cognitive complexity (e.g., Quinn, 1980), divergent thinking or "production" (Guilford, 1967), ability to link remote "associations" among elements or ideas to achieve a creative solution (e.g., Mednick, 1962), ideational fluency (e.g., Basadur & Thompson, 1986; Carroll & Maxwell, 1979, pp. 615–616), and imagery and verbal fluency (e.g., Suler &

Aizziello, 1987). Many of these cognitive attributes or abilities are not sharply differentiated from each other, so additional work in modeling creative-thinking processes might be particularly instructive (e.g., Cagle, 1985). One of the better-known models in this regard is Guilford's (1967) "Structure-of-Intellect" (SOI) model. In Guilford's model, intelligence is defined as a collection of abilities or functions for processing information. Although many different mental functions relate to creativity, the operation of "divergent production" is seen as being particularly critical for creative behavior. This cognitive style or ability—perhaps identical to what other writers have called ideational fluency, adaptive flexibility, or the ability to generate logical alternatives—provides a good example of a cognitive ability–creative behavior relationship that is empirically well supported.

An extreme position is staked out by Eysenck (1983) who argues that creativity and originality are not aspects of operations of the mind, but instead are exclusively traits of personality and, as such, are essentially noncognitive. A more common position seems to be to treat both personality and cognitive factors as potentially important sources of individual differences in creativity (e.g., Arieti, 1976). Indeed, many examples of overlap between the personality and cognitive style perspectives on creativity can be found. For example, psychoanalytic theory places great emphasis on the critical role of "primary process thinking" in creative behavior. Suler (1980) describes this role as follows:

The creative act can be conceptualized as a special form of interaction between primary and secondary process thinking in which a novel idea or insight is generated by the loose, illogical, and highly subjective ideation of primary process and is then molded by secondary process into a context that is socially appropriate and meaningful to others. (p. 144)

This is essentially a cognitive explanation of creativity, although most explanations of creative behavior from the psychoanalytic tradition would fit most clearly within the personality framework.

In any event, the notion that creativity differences can be at least partially explained by some cognitive aspects seems reasonably well established. Researchers are in general agreement that some cognitive operations are more likely to lead to original ideas and to solutions to problems.

The Social Psychology of Creativity

In the overwhelming majority of psychological research on creativity, there has been a strong focus on the importance of internal determinants of creativity, but much less emphasis on external determinants; a concentration on creative persons, but generally little appreciation for "creative situations" or circumstances that might be conducive to creative behavior. In contrast, the social psychology of creativity seeks to understand and explain how particular social and environmental conditions might influence the creative behavior of individuals (Amabile, 1983b, p. 5).

Certainly, the important role of social interaction in creativity has long been recognized (cf., Hare, 1982). The groups in which an individual participates—from the earliest family experiences to later friendship and work groups—clearly have some impact on behavior, including creative behavior. A reasonable number of studies have investigated the effects of particular social and physical environments on creativity (e.g., Getzels & Jackson, 1961; Goyal, 1973; Klein, 1975; Torrance, 1965). Similarly, research on creativity and innovation in organizational settings has examined the effects of various contingencies in the organizational environment, including salient work group characteristics that might foster or inhibit creative behavior (Staw, 1984, pp. 655–657; Steiner, 1965; Woodman, 1983). Much of the biographical research (alluded to earlier) investigating the social and family backgrounds of creative persons has informed both the personality and the social psychological perspectives on creativity. Despite this body of work, the social psychology of creativity is probably theoretically less well developed than either the personality or cognitive style perspectives.

Possibly the most comprehensive social psychological explanations for creative behavior have been advanced by Amabile (1983ab). She has proposed, and investigated, a number of social and environmental influences on creative behavior, such as social facilitation, modeling, motivational orientation, evaluation expectations, effects of actual evaluations, use of rewards for creative behavior, task constraints, and opportunities for behavioral choices. A number of these social and environmental influences on creativity have been incorporated into the interactionist model of creative behavior presented next.

An Interactionist Model of Creative Behavior

Imagine a bird in a cage. This situation contains both the idea of "bird" and an easily definable current reality within which the bird finds itself. In this instance, the environmental press explains most, if not all, of the bird's behavior. Having accounted for 100% of the variance with the situation, is there anything left to say regarding the bird and its behavior? Indeed, there is; in fact, perhaps everything of importance remains to be explained. In other words, a careful description of the situation and the bird's responses to its environment do not begin to explain the behavior of all birds, all of the time. What other things might the bird do if the situation changed? Why might the bird do these things? For starters, we could imagine (armed as we are with other information) that the bird may well fly if the environmental constraint of "cage" is removed. Reasoning in this fashion helps to reveal some of the advantages found in an interactionist perspective on behavior. From an interactionist perspective, the behavior of an organism at any point in time is a complex interaction of the situation and something else—this something else is the nature of the organism itself. Both situation and organism and the interaction that unfolds over time must be explained to fully understand the organism-in-its-environment. Sometimes the contingencies of the current situation account for or can be said to explain the greater part of current behavior; sometimes the nature of the organism explains a great deal; sometimes both plus their reciprocal influences are necessary to even begin to understand what is going on. From an interactionist position, there is always something more to understanding behavior than just describing the observed behavior *per se*. This "something more" has to do with the essence of the organism and its behavioral potentiality.

Figure 1 posits an interactional model of creative behavior. The interactionist perspective has great promise for explaining human behavior in complex social settings, and interactional psychology provides a strong theoretical base from which to model complex behavioral phenomena (Schneider, 1983; Terborg, 1981). Figure 1 incorporates important elements of the personality, cognitive, and social psychology explanations of creativity.

Similar to a group of blind men describing an elephant, researchers from differing disciplines and theoretical perspectives seem to emphasize different aspects of Figure 1 in their attempts to explain creativity. For example, researchers and theorists who focus primarily on personality difference explanations of creativity might be said to emphasize most heavily the P-O-B linkages of Figure 1. Simi-

larly, cognitive explanations focus primarily on CS-O-B linkages. The social psychology perspective, which in many respects may be closest to the interactionist perspective (cf., Amabile, 1983a), nevertheless might be described as showing the most interest in explaining SI-O-B linkages, with somewhat lessened interest in CI-O-B or even A-SI-O-B and A-CI-O-B linkages. Going somewhat further, developmental psychologists, educational psychologists, and others interested in "gifted children" pay a great deal of attention to A-O-B, A-SI-O-B, and A-CI-O-B linkages, as does the previously discussed research that examines the social and family background of creative individuals. Much of the (limited) research on creativity and innovation in organizational settings could be described as being primarily concerned with the CI-O-B chain. Many "stage" models of the creative process seem to focus strongly on O-B-C-O linkages and on reciprocal influences and changes in this relationship over time. Finally, an operant-conditioning explanation of creative behavior (e.g., Skinner, 1974) might be conceptualized as emphasizing [A, CI, SI]-B-C linkages.

A true interactionist explanation of creative behavior contains all of these linkages as shown in Figure 1. Thus, a potential advantage of the interactionist model of creative behavior might be its ability to integrate these diverse perspectives, each of which perhaps captures variables of some explanatory power. Combining personality, cognitive, and social psychology explanations of individual differences in creative behavior could serve to improve our ability to understand creative persons, processes, and products. A number of the variables contained in Figure 1 will be examined more closely in the following section of this chapter.

Factors Underlying Individual Differences in Creativity

Creativity is not a single, unitary characteristic, but instead can be thought of as an imprecise category of behavior (Barron & Harrington, 1981). To quote Snow (1986), "Creativity is not a light bulb in the mind, as most cartoons depict it. It is an accomplishment born of intensive study, long reflection, persistence, and interest" (p. 1033). However defined, people differ in the extent to which they exhibit creativity (Nicholls, 1972). The major categories of variables delineated by the interactionist model shown in Figure 1—antecedent con-

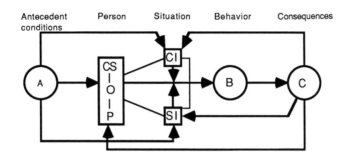

A = **Antecedent Conditions**   B = **Creative Behavior**   C = **Consequences**

Examples:
past reinforcement history;
early socialization;
biographical variables -- sex,
family position, birth order

O = **"Organism" (person)**

Gestalt of attitudes; values; intentions to behave; motivational orientations; and individual
differences.

CS = **Cognitive Style/Abilities**   P = **Personality Dimensions/Traits**

Examples: Examples:
Cognitive complexity   Locus of control
Divergent thinking   Dogmatism
Verbal/ideational fluency   Autonomy
Problem-Solving styles/approaches   Self-esteem
Perceptual openness   Narcissism
Field independence/dependence   Intuition

CI = **Contextual Influences**   SI = **Social Influences**

Examples: Examples:
Physical environment   Social facilitation
Culture   Evaluation expectations
Group/organization "climate"   Rewards/punishments
Task and time constraints   Role modeling

Figure 1. An interactionist model of creative behavior.

ditions, cognitive style/abilities, personality, contextual and social influences—provide a framework to examine some of the specific factors that account for or explain these differences in creative behavior or the capability to produce creative products.

Antecedent Conditions

Antecedent conditions refer to individual background characteristics that result in differences in creativity. The list of antecedent conditions that affect creativity is potentially lengthy, and includes such things as past reinforcement history (or learn-

ing), early socialization, and background characteristics.

Researchers have long been interested in the relationship between relatively immutable birth characteristics of individuals as explanatory factors in subsequent creativity. For example, the question of male versus female superiority in creative abilities has been of research interest for several decades. Studies show male superiority, female superiority, and no differences between the sexes, depending on age and the procedure for measuring creativity (Gupta, 1981). Both Gupta (1981) and Richardson (1986) found similar results among Indian and Jamaican adolescents, respectively. Sex differences were not found to be significant in the case of scores on verbal or nonverbal creativity. In the Indian study, Gupta (1981) observed that boys showed superiority on verbal fluency, verbal flexibility, and verbal transformations. Girls scored significantly higher on nonverbal dimensions, such as originality, complexity, and productive designing ability. The only difference between the Jamaican students was a significantly higher score for girls on the test of verbal fluency (Richardson, 1986). In a further study involving 110 Indian ninth-grade science students, Raina (1980) found no difference between the sexes on scores of fluency, flexibility, and originality from the Torrance Tests of Creative Thinking. Kershner and Ledger (1985) examined the effects of sex on creativity among average and gifted children and found that average and gifted girls scored significantly higher than boys on verbal and figural fluency.

It is possible that some of the sex–race differences on creativity tests requiring interpretation may be a function of examiner bias. Grim and Torrance (1977) assigned individuals trained at scoring and interpreting the Torrance Tests of Creative Thinking to one of four groups based on race (black/white) and sex (female/male) combinations. Each individual was given the same test record. To quote from Grim and Torrance:

Analysis of the free descriptive materials revealed biases favoring whites as more original, emotionally sensitive, intelligent, and quick. Boys were described more frequently than girls as being aware of the environment and socially skillful.

The data from the Ideal Child Checklist depicted blacks as more negative, less independent in judgment, less quiet, more talkative, more bored, more fearful, and less intuitive. Females were described as more timid and shy, less willing to take risks, less self-initiating, less preference for complex tasks, less truthful, more obedient and submissive, more willing to accept judgments of authorities, less self-confident, more neat and orderly, more visionary and idealistic, and less self-assertive. (p. 212)

All results were significant, and should inject a note of caution, at least with respect to results on tests of creativity subject to interpretation in the scoring.

Socioeconomic status has received attention as a variable associated with differences in creative expression. Several studies have reported that children from middle and lower socioeconomic levels have different strengths in creative expression (Deutsch, 1967; Gallager, 1975; Reissman, 1963; Torrance, 1974, 1977). In a study by Haley (1984), 47 black children from a private day care center (the advantaged) were compared to 42 black children attending a federally funded child development center located in a housing project for welfare families (the disadvantaged group) with respect to fluency and originality on verbal, kinetic, and integrative methods of expression. Results were consistent with previous studies in finding that lower socioeconomic status subjects were more kinetically creative whereas middle-class subjects excelled verbally. In addition, the disadvantaged generated a larger number of, but fewer original, solutions in studying creativity expressed through the integrative mode.

The relationship between handedness and creativity has received much attention (Katz, 1980; Peterson & Lansky, 1974), mainly as a result of the observation that many well-known creative geniuses have been left-handed. Recent examinations of the question of handedness as an explanatory construct in creativity (Hattie & Fitzgerald, 1983; Katz, 1980) have found little relationship. Hattie and Fitzgerald (1983) examined the relationship between handedness and some typical tests of creativity using a battery of tests administered to 103 eighteen-year-olds. Handedness was assessed using the Edinburgh Handedness Scale and, as a result, 29 of the subjects were classified as left-handed, 22 integrated or of mixed-handedness, and 52 right-handed. No differences were found with respect to creativity.

Another research approach in relating antecedent conditions to creativity has been biographical inquiry—historical information obtained on eminent creators. The original study was Galton's (1869) *Hereditary Genius* which became the prototype for the "historiometric" approach. Other studies include *The Early Mental Traits of Three Hundred Geniuses* by Cox (1926) which is a volume in Terman's monumental *Genetic Studies of Genius*. More recent works have included *Cradles of Eminence* (Goertzel & Goertzel, 1962), and *Three Hundred Eminent Personalities* (Goertzel, Goertzel, & Goertzel, 1978), the anthology *Genius and Eminence* (Albert, 1983), and *Genius, Creativity, and Leadership* (Simonton, 1984). In a 1986 study, Simonton subjected Goertzel's data to multivariate statistical analysis. The data included extensive measurements on over 50 biographical characteristics for 314 eminent individuals from over 40 countries. The individuals represented 20 distinct fields according to their chief contribution. The measurements included general demographic characteristics, family, education, and intellectual traits. The significance, in terms of antecedent conditions on eminence, included the following:

Nonfiction authors were more prone to come from urban centers, military figures from small towns; women were more likely to become nonfiction authors and performers, men to become athletes, politicians and artists (including composers and film makers); those from atheistic or agnostic backgrounds have the best chance of going into the military, nonfiction writing, science or revolution; authors of either fiction or nonfiction tend to come from unhappy home environments, while better home conditions produce scientists, religious leaders and philosophers, labor leaders, editors and publishers and reformers. . . . [L]arge families contain reformers and artists, small families poets and nonfiction authors; scientists, psychiatrists, politicians and reformers have the most formal education, while athletes, labor leaders, business persons, mystics or psychics, artists and performers the least; artists and composers are most likely to have had special schooling (e.g., in an art school or conservatory), business persons, explorers and editors or publishers to have gone to boarding school, while poets are the least likely to have had any kind of special school experiences. (pp. 17–18)

In terms of the interactionist model, antecedent conditions influence the cognitive and personality characteristics of the individual and, in addition, help define the situation existing for the individual at any given time. With this in mind, there can be little doubt that antecedent conditions provide some explanation of differences in creativity. Further, it is likely that different background characteristics relate to different types of creativity. On the other hand, it is not clear how much of the individual variation in creativity is accounted for by antecedent conditions. In all likelihood, much variation remains after background characteristics are taken into consideration.

Cognitive Factors

Most researchers regard cognitive factors as important in creativity. In addition to whatever else is involved, the development of creative products seems to have an intellective component. The important (and controversial) relationships between general intelligence and creativity clearly fit within the cognitive ability category. However, because intelligence–creativity relationships are the primary focus of another chapter in this volume, they will not be further explored here. Rather, we will examine several specific cognitive ability factors considered to be important in explaining differences in creative behavior.

Divergent Production. Much of the foundation for current thought with respect to the role of intellect in creativity comes from Guilford's (1967) research into the structure of intellect. Guilford's research on creative thinking has been based on factor

analysis. The Structure-of-Intellect (SOI) model organized factors that were developed from intellectual tests into a three-dimensional model involving content, operation, and product categories. The content categories refer to the organization of information used in the human cognitive process, and specifically include item types involving figural (subsequently termed visual), symbolic, semantic, and behavioral properties. (Later research added auditory as a fifth content category; see Guilford, 1975). The mental operations involved include evaluation, convergent production, divergent production, memory, and cognition. Finally, the products form an ascending scale: units, classes, relations, systems, transformations, and implications. A total of 120 SOI categories (factors) result by combining the four content categories with the five operations and six products.

Guilford's (1977, 1984) research is not the only taxonomy of cognitive abilities, and perhaps not even the approach most closely linked with the history of the factor analysis of abilities (Snow, 1986), but through the ability of divergent production, it is a research avenue associated with creativity. Thirty different divergent abilities have been distinguished as defined by the five content and six product categories. Each divergent ability is characterized by its unique combination of three features: its kind of operation, kind of content, and kind of product.

Further analysis by Guilford (1984) reported four second-order factors and a third-order factor. The four second-order factors follow along the lines of the contents, minus divergent-auditory dimensions. The six products (units, classes, relations, systems, transformations, and implications) form the divergent-visual dimensions. The same pattern is replicated for divergent-symbolic, divergent-semantic, and divergent-behavioral factors. Finally, a third-order ability of divergent thinking is derived. The essence of Guilford's work demonstrates that divergent production involves the cognitive processes of fluency, flexibility, originality, and elaboration. Taken together, these are the cognitive components of creative thinking.

In a subsequent publication, Guilford (1983) discussed the role of the transformation abilities in creativity. The 25 transformation abilities are formed by the combination of five operations (cognition, memory, divergent production, convergent production, and evaluation) and five contents (visual, auditory, symbolic, semantic, behavioral). One result of the research was a general cognitive style dimension, what Guilford (1980) called an intellectual executive function or disposition that prompts a person to employ a certain kind of intellectual ability to look for transformations.

Cognitive Style.   A converging line of research to cognitive aspects of problem solving is cognitive style. One of the most influential works on cognitive style has been that of Witkin, Dyk, Paterson, Goodenough, and Karp (1962). Following earlier work by Witkin, the group isolated two major approaches to a series of cognitive and perceptual tasks, field dependence and field independence. Individuals with high field independence have the ability to analyze the environment, breaking up the total field and attending to relevant features while withholding attention from the less salient aspects. Field-dependent individuals have difficulty separating more important from less important elements of a problem. Bloomberg (1967) was one of the early investigators to realize the relationship between field independence/dependence and creativity.

The work of Witkin and his colleagues stimulated many other investigations. Several studies related measures of cognitive style to those of various personality tests (Stuart, 1965; Wertheim & Mednick, 1958). Other investigators have examined the relationship between various cognitive styles and creativity (Del Gaudio, 1976; Dellas & Gaier, 1970; Quinn, 1980). Others, as exemplified by the work of French (1965), related measures of cognitive style to performance on other conceptual tasks. It was French who derived analogues to Witkin's field dependence and field independence in performance on cognitive tests. These dimensions were defined as a reasoned or systematic approach versus a less orderly scanning and visualizing.

In a further study, Noppe (1985) investigated the multivariate relationship between several measures of cognitive style and creativity. In addition to field dependence/independence, Noppe included measures of fixity-mobility, the degree of individual flexibility which permits cognitive functioning from both global as well as focused perspectives, and organismic interpretations or stagelike aspects of thought. Canonical analysis yielded a significant, positive correlation between the cognitive style variables and the measures of creativity. The relationship was such that it accounted for approximately 39% of the shared variance between the two sets of variables. The result was a clearer basis for a cognitive foundation of creative thought, especially with respect to stylistic variables.

The impact of the research on cognitive style was summarized by Shouksmith (1970):

It is often found that a particular individual adopts a certain strategy or group of strategies in his approach to a wide variety of problem situations. We use the term "cognitive style" to refer to this characteristic. Assessed over a wide range of situations, an individual's cognitive style is the amalgam of strategies that he typically adopts in his attempts to solve problems with which he is faced. . . . [C]ognitive style includes all those phenomena which have been variously referred to as "set," or "thinking mode," or the like. (p. 149)

The significance for creativity is the realization that the approach that is adopted to a task determines in part the level of success achieved in solving the problem. Thus, the score derived from an ability test may reflect a variety of factors, including elements of cognitive style. In this regard, creativity may be considered a form of problem solving (Guilford, 1964). Studies approaching creativity from this perspective have often suggested that creativity is a form of thinking, one for which stylistic considerations are important (Kendler & Kendler, 1962).

Other Cognitive Factors.   Other cognitive relationships are worthy of note. Firestien and Treffinger (1983) focused attention on another of the SOI operations, convergent production. Most research attention has been with respect to divergent production, the ability to generate imaginative ideas, but, as noted by Firestien and Treffinger (1983, p. 32), "without convergence, no action can take place, no decisions can be made." Firestien and Treffinger outline important benefits to be achieved through the ability to converge and a model for combining divergent and convergent talents to achieve an optimal group solution.

With respect to other taxonomies and resulting abilities that bear on creativity, Carroll (1985) reanalyzed previously collected data using modern methods. Three hierarchical levels resulted with general intelligence the sole dimension at the pinnacle. Seven second-order factors were specified, one of which, idea production, is most closely associated with creativity. The eight first-order factors that are part of idea production include (1) associative fluency, (2) fluency of expression, (3) figural fluency, (4) ideational fluency, (5) speech fluency, (6) word fluency, (7) practical ideational fluency, and (8) originality. Carroll's work does much to put the frequently cited structure of intellect in perspective as well as to bring to the fore other functions that may relate to individual differences in creativity.

Mathematical creativity of 476 ninth-grade Indian boys was studied by Tuli (1985). Each student was administered the Creative Ability in Mathematics Test, a subtest of the Differential Aptitudes Tests, and the Mathematics Attitude Scale. Examination scores on a standardized achievement test were the criterion. A significant relationship was found between mathematical creativity and achievement in mathematics. Creativity was not significantly related to attitude toward mathematics.

Summary. According to the interactionist model, cognitive style and ability are part and parcel of the individual, and thus help define and draw from the contextual and social influences. There can be little doubt that cognitive factors play a major role in the creative process, but just how this happens is not as clear as might be the case. In fact, a frequent argument is whether or not various cognitive factors are distinct from creativity (Jackson & Messick, 1965). For example, the work of Guilford, which regards creativity as a subset of the SOI, treats cognition as, in essence, embodying creativity, rendering the latter as superfluous.

A more enlightened approach would emphasize the process of cognitive functioning and would recognize that strategies or styles of thinking are important to the production of novel and useful problem solutions. A number of cognitive styles have been studied in relation to individual differences in creativity, and this appears to be a promising line of investigation, but further research is needed.

Personality Factors

As has been seen from the previous section, a reasonable conclusion from existing research would be that creativity is related to various cognitive activities and abilities. Another focus of the research has been with respect to the contribution of noncognitive factors (personality, interests, attitudes) toward individual differences in creativity.

In a recent review, Woodman (1981) concluded that "a theory of personality . . . which does not account for the creative act seems incomplete" (pp. 61–62). Woodman (1981) categorizes those theories that do attempt to explain creative behavior into one of three major streams: (a) psychoanalytic, (b) humanistic, and (c) behavioristic. Theorists writing

in the psychoanalytic tradition (e.g., Freud, Jung, Kubie) view creativity as stemming from the preconscious or the unconscious. Humanistic theories (e.g., Murray, Maslow, Rogers) typically relate creativity to the individual's quest for self-actualization. Behavioristic theories view creativity as novel or unusual behavior that is nevertheless learned, that is fundamentally no different than other behavior which can be explained in terms of stimulus-response or contingencies of reinforcement.

Several investigators have examined the relationship between locus of control (LOC) and creativity. Internal LOC individuals believe that rewards and reinforcements are primarily a result of their own actions. External LOC individuals believe that outcomes are largely governed by chance, luck, fate, or other systems over which they have no control. Yardley and Bolen (1980) explored the relationship of nonverbal creative abilities to LOC, sex, and race among 112 second-grade public school students in North Carolina. External females scored highest of all groups on fluency and flexibility, and were significantly higher than external males. The authors interpreted the results as suggesting that creative males were internal while creative females tended to be external in orientation. In another study, Aggarwal and Verma (1977) compared high-creative and low-creative high school students from India on LOC. High-creative students were significantly more internal than the low-creative students.

Kumar (1981) compared interest patterns of high- versus low-creative ninth-grade Indian students. It was found that patterns associated with literary, scientific, and fine arts interests characterized the high creatives. The low-creative students tended to be interested in household and outdoor activities. In a related study, Bachtold (1983) investigated whether university students differed in their potential for creativity according to their major field. It was found that art and economics students excelled on two measures of creativity (figural elaboration, verbal flexibility/originality). Social science students surpassed the other majors on verbal elaboration.

The interactionist model treats personality much as cognitive style and ability, as an essential component of the individual. Yet the measures of personality are less impressive in terms of both reliability and validity, hence the research evidence is less extensive than that for cognitive aspects of the individual. At the same time, biographical and experimental research studies have suggested that differences in creativity are a result of many factors and that among these qualities are patterns of personality traits.

Contextual and Social Influences

The contextual and social influences on creative behavior include such things as physical environment, culture, group or organizational climate, time/task constraints, expectations, rewards/punishments, and role models. Taken together, these are the elements of the environment and social setting in which the creative act takes place, and, as such, have the potential to contribute to or detract from individual differences in creativity.

Although the contextual and social factors have been implicit in much of the research, they have not been an explicit topic in a large number of studies. The previously cited research on biographical characteristics of eminent individuals is illustrative of one way knowledge about contextual and social factors can be developed. Yet, as Simonton (1986) noted, findings about eminent achievers raise the issue of how generalizations derived apply to others with much more modest accomplishments. We cannot automatically assume that the factors which differentiate a renowned individual also contribute to the creativity of those less acclaimed.

In a research report, Torrance (1961) outlined specific factors that affect creative thinking in children:

Of the factors in nature and society, . . . studies . . . thus far indicate that the following factors affect the development and/or expression of creative thinking:
1. Educational level
2. Differential treatment of boys and girls
3. Premature attempts to eliminate fantasy
4. Restrictions on manipulativeness and curiosity
5. Conditions resulting in fear and timidity, in both authority and peer relations
6. Misplaced emphasis on certain verbal skills, especially on mechanics
7. Overemphasis on prevention and on ''success''
8. Lack of resources for working out ideas
. . . [P]reliminary analyses indicate that the following experimentally manipulated variables affect significantly the production of ideas or functioning of the creative thinking abilities . . .
1. The composition of the group in which the thinking takes place (homogeneous or heterogeneous) . . .
2. Competition . . .
3. The teaching of principles for thinking up ideas . . .
4. The nature of the ''warm-up,'' instructions (quantity vs. quality), and practice (unevaluated vs. evaluated practice) . . .
5. Rewarding creative thinking (treating questions with re-

spect, treating imaginative ideas with respect, encouraging and evaluating self-initiated learning, etc.) . . .
6. Activities which help children to value their own ideas . . . . (pp. 171–172)

The research evidence presented by Torrance represents a major contribution to the understanding of social and contextual factors that influence individual differences in creativity. Actually, the factors outlined by Torrance are those that have the potential to foster creativity, that is, to give those individuals with the potential to be creative the chance to develop those skills. The maximization of opportunity increases individual differences in creativity as those with creative talents improve and those with more limited capabilities remain relatively unchanged.

In a major summary of the research literature on the social and environmental factors influencing creativity, Amabile (1983b) examined the topics of evaluation, rewards, modeling, and training. Among the conclusions from the review of research was the finding that the expectation of evaluation tends to undermine creativity. With respect to rewards, there is considerable research support for intrinsic motivation as facilitating creativity. An extrinsic reward tends to be detrimental to creative performance to the extent that it can lead others to view motivation as external. Conclusions with respect to social facilitation are more tentative. Results of group versus individual work are mixed. Exposure to models can improve performance, but only if the modeled behavior bears a high resemblance to the performance assessed. The Amabile (1983b) review provides a definitive summary of the literature on the social and environmental processes that contribute to individual differences in creativity.

In another study, Ekvall and Tangeberg-Andersson (1986) attempted to relate working climate to creativity in the field setting of a Swedish national daily newspaper. A total of 12 working-climate dimensions were measured (including challenge, support for ideas, richness in ideas, dynamism, and conflict) and were related to office creativity. The authors concluded that freedom and autonomy, combined with a largely democratic work organization, contributed to a creative climate not enjoyed elsewhere in the organization. To quote these authors:

The group shares certain basic values, although its members do not necessarily have the same political, social or other kinds of background. They approach the subjects discussed on the [woman's] page in the same sort of way (humanistic, holistic, and basically psychological), which makes it easy to discuss the factual content without wasting time and energy arguing about fundamental values, on convincing each other or testing one another's beliefs. Thus, the climate appars [*sic*] to be "soft" and conflict-free. (p. 222)

Norms that were reported include (a) everything is possible, nothing is fixed; (b) you create your own reality; (c) pursue your own ideas; and (d) question all rules. Findings from the research summary by Amabile (1983b) are related. Amabile (1983b) concluded that "work environments most conducive to the fulfillment of creative potential may include: a high level of worker responsibility for initiating new activities, a low level of interference from administrative superiors, and a high stability of employment" (p. 184). This summary is in agreement with the Swedish findings.

In summary, "research on creativity has led to a recognition of the fact that the kind of environment most likely to produce a well-adjusted person is not the same as the kind of environment most likely to produce a creative person" (Tyler, 1974, p. 114). This is to say, in terms of the interactionist model, antecedent conditions along with social and contextual influences can have an important impact on creativity. From the research evidence, it is clear that individual differences are a function of the extent to which the social and contextual factors nurture the creative process. Further, given the factors shown to be important, many children and adults do not operate in an environment that fosters creative achievements.

Summary and Conclusions: An Interactionist Approach to Individual Differences in Creativity

The topic of individual differences in creativity, or, for that matter, individual differences in any area of cognitive and noncognitive behavior, is inextricably bound to the issues of definition and assessment. Further, individual differences are a function of the criteria used to characterize creative behavior. In short, the base on which individual differences research is built can be no better than thinking and research on issues of definition, assessment, cognitive, and noncognitive models. With this in mind, it is the purpose of this section to review and pull together the evidence with respect to individual differences in creativity through ques-

tions of current knowledge, existing disparities, and needed knowledge.

What Do We Know?

Creativity can best be thought of in terms of accomplishments, "achievements that are original and make a meaningful contribution to culture" (Nicholls, 1972, p. 717). People differ in the extent to which they can be said to be creative, and these differences can be thought of as a function of the interactive influence of antecedent conditions, cognitive factors, personality, and surrounding contextual and social influences. The interactionist model presented in Figure 1 is an attempt to capture the gestalt of the relationships among these factors and creative behavior.

A plurality of research has focused on the role of cognitive factors as the source of differences among people with regard to creativity. Much of the research has concerned the role of divergent thinking and, more recently, convergent thinking.

There are ample examples of the unrelatedness between creativity and intelligence. Intellect is regarded as a threshold characteristic, a necessary but not sufficient condition for creativity. As a result, more recent research has concerned the role of cognitive strategies or styles of thinking as factors in explaining differences in creativity. Creative individuals tend to approach problems with greater amounts of intensity, reflection, and persistence than their colleagues of equal intelligence.

Concern for stylistic factors is, in effect, acknowledgment of the joint role of cognitive and personality (noncognitive) factors in creativity. There can be little doubt that noncognitive factors, such as intensity, persistence, and interest, play a role in creativity.

Finally, biographical studies have shown common antecedent conditions among creative individuals. At the same time, contextual and social factors can facilitate or retard creativity.

What Gaps Exist in Current Knowledge?

The major gaps are with respect to the operational definition of creativity along with the measurement of this concept. The vast majority of creativity research that now supports our understanding of individual differences in creativity is based on a small number of measurement instruments. Further, the construct validity of many of the instruments has not been adequately demonstrated.

The construct of divergent thinking and the closely related concepts of remote association and ideational fluency have dominated the measurement of creativity. To quote Nicholls (1972), "though there is some theoretical support for the notion that ideational productivity is important for creative achievement, the research evidence for the predictive validity of divergent thinking tests is far from impressive" (p. 719). Most research using one or more measures of ideational productivity assume that the resulting score or scores are synonymous with creativity, that is, no further confirmation is sought.

Another research gap has to do with the subjects used in many of the research studies. Most of those studied have been children or young adults, especially college-age students. Questions exist as to how the typical divergent thinking or novel uses scores taken as evidence of creativity among these groups translates into reshaping or extending achievement in a field, which would be closer to the definition of creativity among more mature individuals. The concentration of research on easily available individuals may have inhibited our understanding of individual differences in this important area.

How Will We Develop Needed Knowledge?

Clearly there is room for innovation with respect to research on individual differences in creativity. In addition, further work along traditional lines is needed.

Construct and empirical validation represent examples of research along accepted lines that would contribute to the understanding of individual differences in creativity. Empirical validation requires a criterion of creativity against which measures are validated. MacKinnon's (1964, 1965) research provides an example. Creative architects were compared to their less creative colleagues on a number of psychological dimensions. None of the dimensions were called creativity, as such, but instead were designed to provide a picture of how creative individuals differed from their normal colleagues.

Guilford's work on the structure of intellect, particularly the effort on relationships associated with the concepts of divergent and convergent thinking, is exemplary of construct validation. There are other examples of factor-analytic research's making contributions toward an understanding of creativity (Carroll, 1985). At the same time, other

techniques associated with construct validation have not been used in creativity research. For example, the multitrait–multimethod matrix developed by Campbell and Fiske (1959) has become a staple of construct-validation research, but has been seldom applied to research on creativity. The method requires the demonstration of convergent and discriminant validity. In other words, significant convergent agreement is required between measurements of the same construct using different methods. At the same time, a validity coefficient for a given variable must be greater than the correlation between the measurements of this variable and the measurements of all other variables with any other methods in order to demonstrate discriminant validity. Many of the measurement procedures used in creativity research, on which current knowledge is based, would not stand up to the requirements of the multitrait–multimethod matrix.

There are other more recent techniques of construct validation, such as meta-analysis, that may have applicability to creativity research. The point is that many of the techniques considered as basic to the establishment of construct validity of concepts have not been widely applied to the measurement of creativity.

In addition, an approach to explaining creative behavior, such as that illustrated by the interactionist model in Figure 1, could provide a useful heuristic or framework for programmatic research on creativity. In other words, perhaps what is needed at this point, in terms of theory development, is not yet another new "theory" of creativity but rather an integrative framework that would serve to combine diverse perspectives on creativity and thus build on current knowledge while, at the same time, suggesting promising avenues for future work. In short, we need a more complex system for integrating what we now know rather than a wholly new perspective on understanding differences in creative behavior. The interactionist perspective could possibly provide this more complex system.

Toward a Comprehensive View of Individual Differences in Creativity

Creativity is a valued trait in a democratic, free-enterprise society. Those with the talent for achievements that are original and make a meaningful contribution are rewarded and/or recognized for their accomplishments. Research efforts that are successful in guiding the selection and/or development of creative individuals will also have made a valued contribution. These are some of the reasons that make individual differences in creativity of general interest and concern.

The principle contribution of the present review is by way of the interactionist perspective adopted. Perhaps, understandably, researchers from different orientations have approached the problem from different perspectives. It would not be surprising that a cognitive psychologist would rely on principles of cognition as the basis of creativity, or that a social psychologist would postulate social facilitation as critical to creative accomplishments.

The interactionist model suggests that creativity is the complex product of a person's behavior in a given situation. The situation can be characterized in terms of the contextual and social influences that either facilitate or inhibit creative accomplishment. The person is influenced by various antecedent conditions, and brings to bear both cognitive abilities and noncognitive traits or predispositions.

Perhaps of greater importance, the model, in conjunction with the research evidence, leads to an understanding of the sources of individual differences in creativity. For example, research seems to suggest that cognitive factors are especially important. The specific abilities are those associated with divergent production or ideational fluency, along with convergent production. Creative accomplishment is more than cognitive ability; that more is personality and that ability area that bridges intellect and personality–cognitive style. Creative individuals seem to be more intense, more reflective, and more persistent. In short, they approach problems in a different manner from their less creative colleagues.

In sum, the interactionist model of creative behavior proposed here provides a comprehensive view of individual differences in creativity that incorporates important elements of the personality, cognitive, and social psychology explanations of creativity. Creative behavior is a complex person–situation interaction that is influenced by events of the past as well as salient aspects of the current situation. Within the person, both cognitive and noncognitive aspects of the mind are related to creative behavior. The interactionist perspective provides an integrating framework of sufficient complexity to incorporate diverse streams of research and to suggest exciting avenues for future programmatic research on creativity.

References

Aggarwal, Y. P., & Verma, L. K. (1977). Internal-external control of high creative and low creative high school students at different levels of socio-economic status. *The Journal of Creative Behavior, 11,* 150.

Albert, R. S. (Ed.). (1983). *Genius and eminence.* New York: Pergamon.

Amabile, T. M. (1983a). Social psychology of creativity: A componential conceptualization. *Journal of Personality and Social Psychology, 45,* 357–376.

Amabile, T. M. (1983b). *The social psychology of creativity.* New York: Springer-Verlag.

Arieti, S. (1976). *Creativity: The magic synthesis.* New York: Basic Books.

Bachtold, L. M. (1983). Differences in divergent thinking and temperamental traits among university students. *The Journal of Creative Behavior, 17,* 267.

Barron, F. (1969). *Creative person and creative process.* New York: Holt, Rinehart & Winston.

Barron, F., & Harrington, D. M. (1981). Creativity, intelligence, and personality. *Annual Review of Psychology, 32,* 439–476.

Basadur, M., & Thompson, R. (1986). Usefulness of the ideation principle of extended effort in real world professional and managerial creative problem solving. *Journal of Creative Behavior, 20,* 23–34.

Bloomberg, M. (1967). An inquiry into the relationship between field independence and creativity. *Journal of Psychology, 67,* 127–140.

Bolen, L. M., & Torrance, E. P. (1978). The influence on creative thinking of locus of control, cooperation, and sex. *Journal of Clinical Psychology, 34,* 903–907.

Cagle, M. (1985). A general abstract-concrete model of creative thinking. *Journal of Creative Behavior, 19,* 104–109.

Campbell, D. T., & Fiske, D. W. (1959). Convergent and discriminant validation by the multitrait-multimethod matrix. *Psychological Bulletin, 56,* 281–302.

Carroll, J. B. (1985, May). *Domains of cognitive ability.* Paper presented at the meeting of the American Association for the Advancement of Science, Los Angeles.

Carroll, J. B., & Maxwell, S. E. (1979). Individual differences in cognitive abilities. *Annual Review of Psychology, 30,* 603–640.

Cox, C. (1926). *The early mental traits of three hundred geniuses.* Stanford, CA: Stanford University Press.

Del Gaudio, A. C. (1976). Psychological differentiation and mobility as related to creativity. *Perceptual and Motor Skills, 43,* 831–841.

Dellas, M. (1978). Creative personality and identity. *Psychological Reports, 43,* 1103–1110.

Dellas, M., & Gaier, E. (1970). Identification of creativity: The individual. *Psychological Bulletin, 23,* 53–73.

Deutsch, M. (1967). *The disadvantaged child: Studies of the social environment and the learning process.* New York: Basic Books.

Ekvall, G., & Tangeberg-Andersson, Y. (1986). Working climate and creativity: A study of an innovative newspaper office. *The Journal of Creative Behavior, 20,* 215–225.

Eysenck, H. J. (1983). The roots of creativity: Cognitive ability or personality trait? *Roeper Review,* May, 10–12.

Faschingbauer, T. R., Moore, C. D., & Stone, A. (1978). Cognitive style, dogmatism, and creativity: Some implications regarding cognitive development. *Psychological Reports, 42,* 795–804.

Firestien, R. L., & Treffinger, D. J. (1983). Ownership and converging: Essential ingredients of creative problem solving. *The Journal of Creative Behavior, 17,* 32–38.

French, J. W. (1965). The relationship of problem-solving styles to the factor composition of tests. *Educational and Psychological Measurement, 25*, 9–28.

Gallager, J. J. (1975). *Teaching the gifted child.* Boston: Allyn & Bacon.

Galton, F. (1869). *Hereditary genius.* London: Macmillan.

Getzels, J. W., & Jackson, P. W. (1961). Family environment and cognitive style: A study of the sources of highly intelligent and of highly creative adolescents. *American Sociological Review, 26*, 351–359.

Goertzel, M. G., Goertzel, V., & Goertzel, T. G. (1978). *Three hundred eminent personalities.* San Francisco: Jossey-Bass.

Goertzel, V., & Goertzel, M. G. (1962). *Cradles of eminence.* Boston: Little, Brown.

Goyal, R. P. (1973). Creativity and school climate: An exploratory study. *Journal of Psychological Researches, 17*, 77–80.

Grim, C., & Torrance, E. P. (1977). Race and sex bias in interpreting creativity test results of children. *The Journal of Creative Behavior, 11*, 212.

Guilford, J. P. (1964). Creative thinking and problem solving. *Educational Digest, 29*, 29–31.

Guilford, J. P. (1967). *The nature of human intelligence.* New York: McGraw-Hill.

Guilford, J. P. (1975). Creativity: A quarter century of progress. In I. A. Taylor & J. W. Getzels (Eds.), *Perspectives in creativity.* Chicago: Aldine.

Guilford, J. P. (1977). *Way beyond the IQ: Guide to improving intelligence and creativity.* Buffalo, NY: Creative Education Foundation.

Guilford, J. P. (1980). Cognitive styles: What are they? *Educational and Psychological Measurement, 40*, 715–735.

Guilford, J. P. (1983). Transformation abilities or functions. *The Journal of Creative Behavior, 17*, 75–83.

Guilford, J. P. (1984). Varieties of divergent production. *The Journal of Creative Behavior, 18*, 1–10.

Gupta, A. K. (1981). Sex differences in creativity: Some fresh evidence. *The Journal of Creative Behavior, 15*, 269.

Haley, G. L. (1984). Creative response styles: The effects of socioeconomic status and problem-solving training. *The Journal of Creative Behavior, 18*, 25–40.

Hare, A. P. (1982). *Creativity in small groups.* Beverly Hills, CA: Sage.

Hattie, J., & Fitzgerald, D. (1983). Do left-handers tend to be more creative? *The Journal of Creative Behavior, 17*, 269.

Helson, R. (1971). Women mathematicians and the creative personality. *Journal of Consulting and Clinical Psychology, 36*, 210–220.

Helson, R., & Mitchell, V. (1978). Personality. *Annual Review of Psychology, 29*, 555–585.

Jackson, P. W., & Messick, S. (1965). The person, the product and the response: Conceptual problems in the assessment of creativity. *Journal of Personality, 33*, 309–329.

Katz, A. N. (1980). Do left-handers tend to be more creative? *The Journal of Creative Behavior, 14*, 271.

Kendler, H. H., & Kendler, T. S. (1962). Vertical and horizontal processes in problem solving. *Psychological Review, 69*, 1–16.

Kershner, J. R., & Ledger, G. (1985). Effect of sex, intelligence, and style of thinking on creativity: A comparison of gifted and average children. *Journal of Personality and Social Psychology, 48*, 1033–1040.

Klein, P. W. (1975). Effects of open vs. structured teacher-student interaction on creativity of children with different levels of anxiety. *Psychology in the Schools, 12*, 286–288.

Kumar, A. (1981). Interest patterns of high and low creatives. *The Journal of Creative Behavior, 15*, 270.

MacKinnon, D. W. (1964). The creativity of architects. In C. W. Taylor (Ed.), *Widening horizons in creativity.* New York: Wiley.

MacKinnon, D. W. (1965). Personality and the realization of creative potential. *American Psychologist, 20*, 273–281.

MacKinnon, D. W. (1970). The personality correlates of creativity: A study of American architects. In P. E. Vernon (Ed.), *Creativity.* Harmondsworth, Middlesex, England: Penguin Books.

Mednick, S. A. (1962). The associative basis of the creative process. *Psychological Review, 69*, 220–232.

Nicholls, J. G. (1972). Creativity in the person who will never produce anything new and useful: The concept of creativity as a normally distributed trait. *American Psychologist, 27*, 717–727.

Noppe, L. D. (1985). The relationship of formal thought and cognitive styles to creativity. *The Journal of Creative Behavior, 19*, 88–96.

Noppe, L. D., & Gallagher, J. M. (1977). A cognitive style approach to creative thought. *Journal of Personality Assessment, 41*, 85–90.

Peterson, J., & Lansky, L. (1974). Left-handedness among architects: Some facts and speculations. *Perceptual and Motor Skills, 38*, 545–550.

Quinn, E. (1980). Creativity and cognitive complexity. *Social Behavior and Personality, 8*, 213–215.

Raina, T. N. (1980). Sex differences in creativity in India: A second look. *The Journal of Creative Behavior, 14*, 218.

Reissman, F. (1963). *The culturally deprived child.* New York: Harper & Row.

Richardson, A. G. (1986). Sex differences in creativity among a sample of Jamaican adolescents. *The Journal of Creative Behavior, 20*, 147.

Roe, A. (1953). *The making of a scientist.* New York: Dodd, Mead.

Schneider, B. (1983). Interactional psychology and organizational behavior. *Research in Organizational Behavior, 5*, 1–31.

Shouksmith, G. (1970). *Intelligence, creativity and cognitive style.* New York: Wiley.

Simonton, D. K. (1977). Creative productivity, age, and stress: A biographical time-series analysis of 10 classical composers. *Journal of Personality and Social Psychology, 35*, 791–804.

Simonton, D. K. (1984). *Genius, creativity, and leadership.* Cambridge, MA: Harvard University Press.

Simonton, D. K. (1986). Biographical typicality, eminence and achievement styles. *The Journal of Creative Behavior, 20*, 14–22.

Skinner, B. F. (1974). *About behaviorism.* New York: Alfred Knopf.

Snow, R. E. (1986). Individual differences in the design of educational programs. *American Psychologist, 41*, 1029–1039.

Solomon, R. (1985). Creativity and normal narcissism. *Journal of Creative Behavior, 19*, 47–55.

Spotts, J. V., & Mackler, B. (1967). Relationships of field-dependent and field-independent cognitive styles to creative test performance. *Perceptual and Motor Skills, 24*, 239–268.

Staw, B. M. (1984). Organizational behavior. *Annual Review of Psychology, 35*, 627–666.

Steiner, G. A. (Ed.). (1965). *The creative organization.* Chicago: University of Chicago Press.

Stuart, I. R. (1965). Field dependency, authoritarianism and perception of the human figure. *Journal of Social Psychology, 66*, 209–214.

Suler, J. R. (1980). Primary process thinking and creativity. *Psychological Bulletin, 88,* 144–165.

Suler, J. R., & Aizziello, J. (1987). Imagery and verbal processes in creativity. *Journal of Creative Behavior, 21,* 1–6.

Taylor, I. A. (1976). Psychological sources of creativity. *Journal of Creative Behavior, 10,* 193–202, 218.

Terborg, J. R. (1981). Interactional psychology and research on human behavior in organizations. *Academy of Management Review, 6,* 569–576.

Torrance, E. P. (1961). Factors affecting creative thinking in children: An interim research report. *Merrill-Palmer Quarterly of Behavior and Development, 7,* 171–180.

Torrance, E. P. (1965). *Rewarding creative behavior: Experiments in classroom creativity.* Englewood Cliffs, NJ: Prentice-Hall.

Torrance, E. P. (1974). Differences are not deficits. *Teachers College Record, 75,* 472–487.

Torrance, E. P. (1977). *Discovery and nurturance of giftedness in the culturally different.* Reston, VA: The Council for Exceptional Children.

Tuli, M. R. (1985). Mathematical creativity: Its relationship to aptitude for achievement in and attitude towards mathematics among boys. *The Journal of Creative Behavior, 19,* 225–226.

Tyler, L. E. (1974). *Individual differences: Abilities and motivational directions.* New York: Appleton-Century-Crofts.

Weiss, D. S. (1981). A multigroup study of personality patterns in creativity. *Perceptual and Motor Skills, 52,* 735–746.

Wertheim, J., & Mednick, S. A. (1958). The achievement motive and field independence. *Journal of Consulting Psychology, 22,* 30–38.

Witkin, H. A., Dyk, R. B., Paterson, H. F., Goodenough, D. R., & Karp, S. A. (1962). *Psychological differentiation.* New York: Wiley.

Woodman, R. W. (1981). Creativity as a construct in personality theory. *The Journal of Creative Behavior, 15,* 43–66.

Woodman, R. W. (1983). A proposed process model of organizational innovation. *Southwest Division Academy of Management Proceedings,* 189–193.

Yardley, C. R., & Bolen, L. M. (1980). Relationship of locus of control to figural creativity in second-grade students. *The Journal of Creative Behavior, 14,* 276–277.

CHAPTER 5

The Nature–Nurture Problem in Creativity

P. E. Vernon

Very little discussion of the nature–nurture topic has appeared in the literature, mainly because of the complexities of the problem and the difficulties of collecting objective evidence. A useful attempt was made by Scheinfeld in his book, *Heredity in Humans* (1972), but this was a popular rather than a scientific treatment. A brief account by Zigler and Farber (1985) can also be recommended. In the absence of hard data from tests, sociological surveys, or controlled experiments, this chapter has to rely very largely on observational and interview studies, historical or biographic information, the opinions of critics or colleagues about creative individuals, and discussions of theories, all of which are liable to ambiguity and subjectivity.

The traditional view of creativity and genius ascribes these to creative abilities or traits within the individual; that is, they are a kind of gift that is inborn. But even the pioneer writers, such as Galton, Terman, Burt, and Cox, realized that genius is affected by environment and upbringing as well as the genes; also that such personality factors as persistence, drive, and commitment are at least as important as intellectual or cognitive abilities.

Genetic Theory

The common notion of hereditary or genetic versus environmental factors is much oversimplified. The genes do indeed provide for the transmission of hereditary qualities, but they do not *determine* an individual's height, or intelligence, or creativity. They are predispositions, whose effects develop differently in different environments; that is, they interact with environmental conditions or experiences and produce not a fixed effect but a certain "range of reaction." Nature and nurture are not opposed factors but are complementary to each other. Sometimes also the genes control or modify the environment, as when a highly intelligent child shapes his own environment by choosing books to read and other intellectual activities.

Nevertheless, it is possible to estimate quantitatively the relative strength of genetic and environmental differences in the growth of such qualities as intelligence; for example, by comparing the resemblance in intelligence quotients between various relatives (who share certain numbers of genes in common), or between foster children and their adopting parents. But, in practice, there are so many sources of error and unreliability in collecting and testing suitable groups of subjects that we still find wide disagreements between different writers in their estimates of genetic and other effects (e.g.,

P. E. Vernon • Late of the Department of Psychology, University of Calgary, Calgary, Alberta, Canada T3A 2E3.

Eysenck & Kamin, 1971). Doubtless the same lack of agreement will occur in attempting to estimate genetic variance in measures of creativity. The second half of this chapter surveys what evidence we have, and what answers it provides (see also Mistry & Rogoff, 1985).

Definitions

Let us first define the nature of creativity and other related variables, which might differ in their genetic-environmental components. Although numerous different definitions of creativity have been proposed (I. A. Taylor, 1959), there would be a considerable consensus on the following general statement. Creativity means a person's capacity to produce new or original ideas, insights, restructurings, inventions, or artistic objects, which are accepted by experts as being of scientific, aesthetic, social, or technological value. In addition to novelty as our major criterion, we must incorporate in our definition the acceptability or appropriateness of the creative product, even though this valuation may change with the passage of time.

Naturally we would expect differences between different types or areas of creativity. But the sciences—physical or biological, mathematical, psychological and social, and also engineering—do show a good deal in common. Likewise there are some resemblances, and also some differences between scientific and artistic creativity, as, for example, in literary, philosophical, musical, visual or decorative artistic, and sculptural creativity. Architecture seems to partake of both types (MacKinnon, 1962). Scientific creativity always involves some addition to our previous knowledge, either an improved theory or a new object or procedure, whereas artistic creation may give some new representation of life (e.g., a painting or poem) or feeling, but not usually a progression from previous representations. Another possible type of creativity might be termed social or spiritual (e.g., Mahatma Gandhi). But in my view, the performing arts (playing vs. composing music, acting, or dancing) do not merit the label creative, or only rather rarely, as, for example, Pavlova's dancing or Glenn Gould's highly interpretive piano music.

Gardner's recent book, *Frames of Mind* (1983), has attracted wide attention because it provides an alternative yet logical approach to the classification of creative abilities. He points out the present confusion between Galton's "eminence," Terman's "genius," general intelligence, and the factorists' *g*, or multiple-ability factors. He describes six domains of creativity, which he designates as "intelligences," namely, (1) verbal-linguistic, (2) musical, (3) logic-mathematical, (4) visual-spatial, (5) bodily-kinesthetic, and (6) social-personal. These domains are not causative entities, though they may involve some genetic differences. They were arrived at more from observational studies of child development and from real-life behavior, rather than from paper-and-pencil tests, such as the instruments that Thurstone, Guilford, and others have used. Each of these domains has a separate system of signals and, although relatively autonomous, they often work together in human problem solving and invention. Gardner provides considerable cross-cultural, neuropsychological, and other kinds of evidence to back his categorization.

There are several other terms that are linked to creativity and that are often used interchangeably; but it is better to distinguish them.

Talents are skills that differ in the different sciences and in the arts and that do appear typically in the performing arts. They almost certainly involve genetic components as well as learning and may occur, too, in idiots savant (e.g., in numerical or musical ability).

Genius is virtually identical with very high creative abilities, but one cannot specify *how* high. Because it also has other interpretations (e.g., a kind of inner spirit), it is better to avoid use of the term. Grinder (1985) gives a useful historical survey of conceptions of genius from Plato onward.

Prodigy refers to a child with skills or talents much superior to what is normal for his or her age. But the prodigy does not necessarily become a highly creative artist or scientist until he or she produces new work of accepted value; and this seldom occurs much before age 20. It has been said that all geniuses were prodigies (Agassi, 1985), but many exceptions come to mind (e.g., Darwin and Einstein).

Gifted applies to any child or adult of much above average ability; and most psychologists would agree that it is partly genetic in origin. It usually refers to those high in general intelligence or all-round ability. Thus, a child who is specially able in mathematics only would be talented rather than gifted.

Distribution of Creativity

Because some other qualifications are necessary, I would prefer to restrict the term *creative* to a very small proportion of scientists or artists whose productions are highly valued, say, the most eminent 2% or so of the total populations of Western or developed cultures. Although this conception is supported by Nicholls (1972), Mansfield and Busse (1981), and others, it runs counter to the popular views of Guilford, Torrance, and their followers, who believe that creative potential is present in all members of the population and that it can be treated as a normally distributed variable. For example, the householder who plans an attractive garden, or his wife who designs a new dress, would be continuous with, say, Leonardo da Vinci. These authors also provide tests which require simple tasks, such as Alternate Uses for a Brick or Torrance's Picture Completion, on which almost all children from kindergarten up can score something.

Now one would agree that there is some continuity between, say, a brilliant research chemist and his assistants who contribute more by teaching but who add a few novel ideas to his research. One cannot prove that the highly or genuinely creative scientist or artist differs qualitatively from those working at lower levels in the same fields (though this problem might be tackled by factor analysis). But the distribution of this productivity is nowhere near normal, and approaches more closely to the exponential or so-called J-curve. This distribution usually occurs when scores are affected by a large number of influences that interact with one another multiplicatively, and not additively. It applies, for example, to incomes, numbers of criminal acts, and populations of cities; and it explains why the top 5% or so of all scientists produce over 50% of the total publications in science. Price (1962) noted that such distributions must be S-shaped rather than J-shaped, because growth must slow down at some time, otherwise, for example, the total membership of the American Psychological Association would one day exceed the total American adult population.

These facts are important, because they imply that measures of creativity cannot be analyzed or treated statistically by conventional parametric techniques; and factor or principal component analysis would not be suitable for trying to analyze the chief underlying components of creativity variables. However, chi-squared or other non-parametric techniques could be used for comparing productivity indices with, say, socio-economic status (SES), age, or other relevant variables.

Sociology of Creativity

Most psychologists might be willing to give up the notion of creativity as a kind of ability or trait possessed by the artist or scientist (whether inherited or acquired) if they were better acquainted with the work of such sociologists as Merton (1968), Cole and Cole (1973), Brannigan (1981), Blackwell (1969), and Barber and Hirsch (1962). These authors stress the part played by the social climate or Zeitgeist in the production of creative ideas. Simonton (1977), among others, tabulated the productivity of large numbers of musical composers, philosophers, and writers in different countries and at different dates, and put forward hypotheses regarding the social conditions that might be expected to affect their work, for example, occurrence of wars, political stability, civil disturbances, or the existence of many other persons working in the same field of creativity. Each of these variables is carefully defined and measured by objective indices and then intercorrelated. Some of these hypotheses are confirmed by multiple correlations or path coefficients between the predictor variables and productivity. But often the correlations are too small to be significant (see also Narroll, Benjamin, Fohl, Fried, Hildreth, and Schaeffer, 1971).

Frequently, it has been noted in science that two or more authors report almost identical discoveries or theories at about the same date (e.g., Darwin and Wallace). Further, quite a large part in the appearance of a novel discovery is played by chance circumstances or observations (e.g., penicillin); though, at the same time, there must be sufficiently able scientists to recognize and work out the implications of the chance observation. F. C. Bartlett (1958) pointed out that the appearance of some new technique (e.g., the electron microscope) triggers off a whole series of new advances. Nowadays, also, advances in science are more likely to result from groups of scientists who are working together on some project rather than from the researches of individual geniuses; (this does not seem to occur in the arts).

It follows then that ascribing creative production to a creative mind is largely tautologous, because we have no evidence that a person is creative or not, other than by observing his or her productions and evaluating them (see also Agassi, 1985; Albert, 1975; Mistry & Rogoff, 1985). A topic that has been frequently discussed is that of the "unrecognized" or "potential" genius (see, e.g., Thomas Gray's "Elegy Written in a Country Church-Yard"). We would have to say that such a person is mythical, because he is not a genius until he has produced work of high creative quality. Thus, Gregor Mendel should not be so called until the value of his work was recognized long after his death. However, this is a tricky issue, for adolescents and young adults may produce work that strikes their teachers as promising, although they probably require greater maturity, knowledge, and skills before winning widespread recognition. Lenneberg (1980) described the difficulties young composers often face in getting their early works played or published. He suggested that this is exaggerated and that many innovative composers (e.g., Franz Schubert and Robert Schumann) were indeed recognized by their contemporaries, and their works were published quite soon after completion.

Finally, there are obvious cultural factors in creativity that are shown by the many differences in contents, styles, and skills, which characterize the artistic productions of different societies. These differences are more marked the more geographically remote one country is from another, but such cultural differences are much less common in the sciences. It is possible, however, that some of the artistic differences may have a genetic or racial basis. For example, it is quite likely that the North American Eskimo inherit certain genes for three-dimensional spatial ability, which help them to survive life in an Arctic environment and to produce their unique stone carvings.

Cognitive and Motivational Processes

Studies of creativity are often classified under three headings: the product, the process, and the personality. So far we have been mainly concerned with the first of these headings, and less attention will be given to the second, since it is covered in several other chapters. Also, there is little evidence to suggest that some creative processes are more likely to involve genetic factors than others.

The earliest cognitive analyses were those of von Helmholtz (1903), Poincaré (1924), Hadamard (1945), and Wallas (1926), who distinguished four main stages in creative activity. These stages were of limited value, as it was obvious that there was no rigid pattern of processing applicable to the arts as well as to the sciences. Naturally, also, there are variations between different creators and different products. The most interesting aspect of the stages is their recourse to unconscious mental processes, both in the incubation or cerebration stage and in the sudden flash of insight or inspiration. Ghiselin (1952) published a collection of descriptions by writers, musicians, and scientists of their own thoughts, methods, and feelings. More recent are Eiduson's (1962) and Rosner and Abt's (1970) books, with contributions from living scientists and other creative persons. Some of the authors recognize the importance of these subconscious processes, whereas others entirely reject them. Some point out that in any kind of thinking we retrieve large numbers of associations from long-term memory, which might be called preconscious. But they deny that the mind goes on working on an unsolved problem when they are engaged in other activities. This is the view favored in Perkins's (1981) detailed analysis of cognitive processes in creative thinking. He also allows that such thinking includes the appearance of sudden leaps to new conclusions, which are often accompanied by strong feelings of rightness or correctness.

In general, scientists rely less on inspirational flashes or sudden insights and claim that their creative discoveries depend far more on accumulating wide knowledge of the field, on elaboration and working out implications, and on evaluating new ideas. Artists are more likely to admit that their creative work is accompanied by strong emotions. Yet they, too, may make many drafts or modifications before they are satisfied. Compare, for example, Wolfgang Amadeus Mozart's rapid production of fully fledged compositions with Ludwig van Beethoven's painful striving. Richard Wagner was occupied with *The Ring* for 30 years; Edgar Allen Poe's "The Raven" was not completed until 20 years; and Charles Darwin's *The Origin of Species* took 23 years before publication.

Few psychologists or psychiatrists follow Freud's initial view of art as a sublimation of unconscious conflicts and sex drives. But many subsequent writers favor psychodynamic theories that involve Freud's primary process thinking as well as secondary process or rational thinking (e.g., Arieti, 1976; Biber, 1984; Kubie, 1958; Storr, 1972; Suler, 1980). This is interesting because primary and secondary process activities probably emanate from different areas or levels of the brain. Secondary process activity or conscious thinking would obviously depend to a much greater extent on learned skills.

Sternberg and Davidson (1985) gave a useful survey of theories of cognitive development among the highly talented and pointed out the weaknesses in (1) S-R theories, (2) Piagetian psychology, and (3) psychometric and factorial approaches. They had a preference for cognitive psychology, which studies the kinds and levels of information processing and aims to specify the main components in which highly able children or adults are much in advance of normal thinkers. For example, these individuals are characterized by the careful monitoring of their own thought processes and the correcting of their techniques when required. They not only have more knowledge but are better able to apply it. They have automatized many of their elementary skills, thus freeing their attention for focusing on novel tasks and seeing new concepts and relations. They also show exceptional drive and dedication in tackling new problems in their own field. Sternberg also concurred with Gardner (1983), Feldman (1982), and Gruber (1974) in believing that an individual case-study approach for tracing the methods of highly creative thinkers is more fruitful than trying to measure the main background factors or current abilities. Gruber's (1974) study of Charles Darwin's life and work is a good example.

A further survey by Rogers (1986) summarized 106 recent contributions to the characteristic problem-solving styles or strategies of highly gifted children, which include:

1. Preference for less structured or conventional materials
2. Taking responsibility for their own thinking (i.e., internal locus of control)
3. Independence of thought, as described by Witkin, rather than high verbal intelligence
4. Quick recognition of the nature of the problem, and the appropriate steps for solving it
5. Selecting relevant previous information and experience for application to the problem
6. Monitoring their thinking systematically
7. Exceptional insights in arriving at correct solutions

Although this work was not based on adult creative thinking, most of it probably could be so applied.

Doubtless there are great variations in the detailed processing for different areas (e.g., mathematical, biological, musical, literary); hence, we have not reached a stage of being able to specify an overall catalogue of creative operations. Some writers deny the existence of qualitative differences between creative processing and logical reasoning or problem solving in general (Campbell, 1960; Newell & Simon, 1972; Perkins, 1981; Rabinowitz & Glaser, 1985). Blackwell (1969) argued that there is no type of mental operation specific to creative work. Such work ranges all the way from the routine to the revolutionary. However, in my view, creative thinking and production should be differentiated. They involve a greater degree of free-flowing imagination and recourse to subconscious activities, such as incubation and inspiration. Although these activities appear more frequently with writers and musical and visual artists, they can be recognized in a good deal of scientific discovery. The roles of neurotic and affective processes are still obscure, but they, too, are evident among research scientists (Kubie, 1958). And, as pointed out in the introduction, creativity in the sciences and in the arts requires outstanding motivation and personality qualities besides cognitive skills.

The Relation of General Intelligence and Creativity

The analysis thus far suggests that creative production depends to some extent on general intellectual ability, and more so in scientists than in artists. But, insofar as it has been possible to measure both types of variables, we would expect the correlations to be moderate rather than high. Fortunately, there is a certain amount of hard evidence.

In their genetic studies of genius, Terman (1925) and Cox (1926) clearly believed that adult genius was directly connected to high intelligence in childhood. As is well known, they made estimates of the likely childhood (17-year) IQs of 300 eminent persons from history and found an overall average figure of about 135. But Cox provided good ground for regarding this as an underestimate, attributable to the paucity of information about many cases. She considered the correct figure to be nearer to 140–155. There were big variations, with some of her cases ranging up to 190 and a very few as low as 100. Some 16% of the cases were estimated as falling below an IQ of 120. When classified by type of achievement, philosophers were most able with mean IQs of 147. Writers (140) and scientists (135) were very high, artists were lower at 122, and soldiers were down to 115.

There are some more direct test results of living scientists. Gibson and Light (1967) gave the Wechsler Adult Intelligence Scale (WAIS) to 131 university scientists. Not many of these individuals, perhaps, were in the genius class, but they would all have made many creative contributions to research in their own areas. The mean IQ was 126.5. Chemists and mathematicians were highest at 130, agricultural scientists lower at 121.7. Notice, therefore, that quite a large proportion must have scored below 130. Little work has been done on more specialized talents or ability factors among those in different areas. Roe (1952), however, constructed and applied tests of verbal, spatial, and mathematical abilities to her groups of eminent scientists. Theoretical physicists were much higher than experimental ones in verbal ability, with biologists and social scientists intermediate. All physicists were high on spatial ability, biologists and anthropologists rather low. Biologists and psychologists were high on the mathematical test; (no mathematicians were tested).

Terman's (1925) major contributions were based on very high IQ children (135 upward), and he followed them through to adulthood. Although most of them achieved successful educational and occupational careers, very few showed such outstanding abilities as to merit the term *genius*. A large volume of subsequent psychometric studies has confirmed that the exceptionally creative tend to show high intelligence scores and vice versa; but there are many who are relatively high in one and lower on the other. MacKinnon (1962) and many other writers have subscribed to the "threshold hypothesis," namely, that there is a high correlation of intelligence with indices of creativity up to the average level. But when a certain threshold is reached, say, IQ 120, further gains in intelligence do not bring about much further rise in creative abilities. However, direct evidence for this hypothesis is often equivocal.

Despite continuing controversy regarding genetic factors in intelligence, it is widely agreed that the heritability variance is somewhere around .50. Insofar as there is a relation between creativity and general intelligence, this would suggest that creativity also has some genetic components; though there are obvious weaknesses and difficulties in such an argument.

Other Cognitive Indices of Creativity: Divergent Thinking

In MacKinnon's (1962) series of researches on eminent architects, writers, and other professional groups, the more creative individuals did not usually show better college grades than the less creative. Likewise, Hudson (1966) found that the Fellows of the Royal Society (who can be regarded as the most eminent living research scientists in Great Britain) had frequently obtained only mediocre BA or BS degrees at the university. This fact poses serious problems for the staff members of graduate programs, who try to select the most promising students for doctoral work. The shortage of good scientists in the Western world, the costs of training them, and the high drop-out rate in science and engineering courses are well known. Frequent use is made by academic selection committees of the Miller Analogies, the Terman Concept Mastery, or other difficult tests. But these instruments show quite low, if any, correlations with the quality of graduate theses. MacKinnon (1962) did obtain very high Concept Mastery scores in a sample of creative writers, though not among architects or scientists.

The most consistently predictive test in this area seems to be the Barron-Welsh Art Judgment test, which is based on preference for complex, asymmetrical designs over simpler, symmetrical patterns. Barron (1969) found considerable differences in mean scores between groups rated as high or low creative:

Artists	39
Highly creative architects	37
Research scientists	30½
Architects generally	26
Low-creative scientists	19
Normal college students	18

Welsh (1975) gave this test along with Concept Mastery to groups of able high school students and found interesting personality differences between high or low scorers on both measures. But these have not so far been related directly to creativity.

Guilford (1967), Torrance (1965), Wallach and Kogan (1965), and others have devised a large variety of tests of "divergent thinking," which contrast with the conventional "convergent" tests, and are claimed to measure original thinking. However, these tests are based on such trivial tasks as Alternate Uses, Similarities, and Verbal Fluency, which could not be expected to be of any relevance to real-life or high-level creativity (see the earlier section on "Distribution of Creativity"). In MacKinnon's study of architects, the divergent thinking tests clearly had no predictive value for creativity. Some more promising differences between children with high and low divergent scores have been reported by Getzels and Jackson (1962), Torrance (1965), and Wallach and Kogan (1965). But these studies have not been adequately replicated, and a more critical analysis of Wallach's results by Cronbach (1968) showed that they add very little to predictions based on ordinary general verbal intelligence measures. Hudson (1966) provided a brilliant discussion of why divergent thinking should not be confused with creativity (see also Vernon, Adamson, & Vernon, 1977). R. B. Cattell (1971) has made considerable use of ideational fluency tests from the 1930s on and now includes them as part of a general retrieval capacity, g_r, in his list of mental powers. But he has also found them to relate to his second-order personality factor, Exvia, which is not a characteristic of highly creative scientists.

However, several batteries of tests have been tried out on scientific researchers and other high-creative groups and have been found to yield multiple correlations of around .50 (Drevdahl, 1956; Shapiro, 1968; Vernon, 1972). Most of the tests were cognitive, that is, similar to divergent thinking, but usually at a more complex level. None has achieved wide usage, probably partly because of the time needed to give and score them, or because subjects' performance is too much affected by what they think the tests measure. Mednick and Mednick's (1967) Remote Associations Test is another example that has proved disappointing.

The most striking evidence that such tests may be of some value at adult level has been provided by Wallach and Wing (1969). They gave a divergent thinking battery to some 500 college freshmen, and inquired by questionnaire into their participation in creative extracurricular activities, such as writing, art, and scientific projects. Those who had participated substantially obtained higher divergent scores, though the degree of correlation was generally small. Bartlett and Davis (1974) confirmed this finding with correlations in the .30s, but Kogan and Pankove (1974) reported on the weak reliability of the creativity measures. It was noteworthy, in Wallach's study, that accomplishments in the performing arts (music and drama) were least well predicted.

Evidence for Genetic Factors in Creativity: Rarity of Genius

Six main types of evidence regarding the nature–nurture problem may be adduced. None of these is conclusive, but some are more favorable to genetic, others to environmental, determinants.

Many persons who are generally accepted as geniuses differ so remarkably from the norms as to seem inexplicable in terms of favorable environment. Clearly this applies to Mozart, who was not only performing music brilliantly by the age of 6 but was also composing. However, his most precocious compositions can hardly be said to have shown much originality until he reached about the age of 10. Now Mozart did grow up in a highly musical environment, indeed, under excessive pressure from his father, but his superiority was far greater than that found in other musicians who had equally stimulating environments. Regardless of all other kinds of evidence, Mozart by himself provides proof that genetic differences in creativity do exist.

Another compelling example is Leonardo da Vinci. Even though his artistic talents doubtless owed much to a favorable environment and good training, his almost equally outstanding scientific genius was almost wholly idiosyncratic, that is, self-initiated and self-developed. Madame Marie Curie and Sophie Germain (1776–1811) are very exceptional since so few women have specialized in physics or mathematics. The latter was almost wholly self-taught, and had no parental encouragement. An English girl, Ruth Lawrence, is currently attracting attention, because at age 13 she has surpassed all other mathematics students at Oxford University. She did receive, however, much help from her parents and schools. A considerable number of Stanley's (Stanley, Keating, & Fox, 1974) mathematical students (mostly males) were five years or more ahead of their age-peers, and some were graduated from college at age 13. Youthful prodigies appear to be much more rare in the literary and visual arts. However, Gardner's (1980) Nadia, an autistic girl who produced highly talented drawings at about age 5, was barely able to communicate orally with other children or adults. Thus, one might hesitate to ascribe her talent to some unusual genes, when she was so obviously psychotic and/or brain-damaged. Mention also should be made of idiots savant who show exceptional facility, particularly in mathematics or music. They could hardly be called creative, and their talent is often attributed to intensive practice and concentration in a very narrow field. But it seems reasonable to infer that they, too, must possess exceptional genes.

Neurological Factors

If particular types of creativity are associated with particular areas of the brain, this would provide strong evidence of genetic causation. We do know quite a lot about the language functions connected with Broca's and Wernicke's areas, though no evidence is known to me that exceptionally large growth in these areas is correlated with exceptionally high verbal abilities. Likewise vision is dependent on the occipital cortex and auditory sensitivity with the temporal lobe. Gardner's (1983) book does lay claims to cortical localization of his six areas of talent, though he also emphasizes the importance of upbringing and environment in the growth of such functions. We should further recognize that environmental stimulation can bring about neurological growth, that is, that the causation is not necessarily one way (Vernon, 1979). Most of the above evidence relates to sensation and perception and therefore may or may not have much application to creative thinking. However, Arieti (1976) discussed the role of different cortical areas in creativity, stressing the temporal, parietal, and prefrontal rather than the sensory areas.

Lateralization of function is, of course, an aspect of localization. Most of our knowledge of lateralization derives from brain-damaged persons who show very different symptoms according to whether the damage occurred to the left or right hemisphere. Also, many inferences have been made from the abilities or defects of commissurotomized patients. But impaired functioning observed when some cortical area is injured, or excised, does not necessarily mean that that area controls the same function in normal persons. Fortunately, there is other evidence from experiments with normals that left or right brain stimulation produces different effects, both in the visual and auditory fields. There are also differences in lateralization of visual and spatial functions between

males and females, which might presumably have something to do with sex differences in creativity (see below). Unfortunately, the importance of lateralization has been much exaggerated, and many writers believe that all verbal activities are left-brained, and all spatial and nonverbal activities right-brained. On the basis of quite inadequate evidence, it has been claimed that all creative activities are right-brained, so it is desirable for schools to try to train the right as well as the left (Gardner, 1978; Springer & Deutsch, 1981; Vernon, 1984). Ornstein's book, *The Psychology of Consciousness* (1977), has also had a considerable influence, though he is more concerned with the contrast between rational, logical, or Western-type thought, and intuitive, creative Eastern-type meditation. He claims that electroencephalograph (EEG) alpha waves and rapid eye movements in sleep are related to lateralization.

The grounds for crediting the right brain with such a wide range of functions, including creativity in general, are certainly weak; and it is much more probable that most, if not all, thinking and creative activities involve many parts and both sides of the brain. However, some relations to music and to drawing are fairly well established. Musical stimuli seem to be better recognized and recalled with the left ear (i.e., the right brain). But among trained musicians, the analytic perception of music as a series of relations between pitched tones is more a left-brain process. In visual art, Edwards (1979) has shown that drawing ability can be improved by reducing the influence of our verbal concepts of what objects, people, and trees look like. We all have stereotyped ideas of, for example, a chair, and we draw it, albeit inaccurately, to accord with these preconceptions. But if a chair is shown upside-down and we draw not the object but the spaces between the legs, seat, and back, our left brain is not interested in empty spaces, and the result is much more successful artistically. Conceivably, then, creative visual artists do have a different style of perceiving and reproducing visual stimuli than the average nontalented person.

Another reasonable hypothesis is that the right brain is mainly responsible for grasping the overall structure and contours of an object or scene to be drawn, while the left is more involved in recalling and delineating details. Further, a case might be made for the involvement of subcortical centers in the emotional aspects of creative thinking, though no direct evidence has been provided.

Chronological age is another physiological variable of some significance according to Lehman's (1953) finding that the peak of creative production in physicists tends to occur in the 20s or 30s, among biologists and social scientists more in the 40s, and much more spread out in writers and philosophers. His conclusions are strongly criticized by Dennis (1958). Highly original work occurs in most arts and sciences even up to 70 or later (e.g., Sophocles, Giusppe Verdi, Pablo Picasso, Goethe, Sigmund Freud, Bertrand Russell). Thus, although there may be some mental vigor or flexibility characteristic that tends to decline with age, we have not been able to specify it.

Consistency, or Predictability, from Early Childhood to Adulthood

On the analogy of human physical characteristics, such as height or red hair, which are known to be very largely genetically determined and are remarkably stable throughout most of the life period, one might expect mental characteristics, such as intelligence or creativity, to show considerable stability from early to later years, if they, too, depend on genetic factors. But there are many difficulties. Often the genes do not manifest their full effects until puberty. Certainly, measures of intelligence show big fluctuations from infancy until later childhood, though there are fairly high correlations between 12-year and early adult IQs, and even more consistency from then on until old age. Even physical attributes are to some extent modifiable by environmental conditions conducive to good or poor health; and mental attributes are likely to be much more liable. Hence, Gruber (1974) goes so far as to say that no link has been demonstrated between giftedness in childhood and creative genius in adulthood. Indeed, we can hardly expect high creativity to manifest itself much before age 20, because creative scientists and artists have to acquire a great deal of knowledge and skills to be creative with in the adolescent and early adult periods. Also, at least in the arts, it may be that the emotional maturity and drive necessary to creative production do not develop until late adolescence (with rare exceptions). Hence, although several investigations, such as Cox's (1926), Roe's (1952), and Eiduson's (1962), show most creative adults to have manifested considerable talents during childhood, there are probably many more equally talented who either fade out or achieve only quite

mediocre adult careers. On the whole, the most positive evidence is that collected by sociologists using Citation Indices, total numbers of publications, or other statistics on academic success, which show substantial correlations and reliability over 1 to 5 years or so. But, unfortunately, these do not seem to have been explored over longer periods.

Even if it did turn out that there is high consistency over, say, 30 years, it would be dubious to argue that stability in creative production is proof of genetic determination. It might be attributed, at least in part, to stability in environmental circumstances and stimulation. For example, persons brought up in continuously favorable artistic or scientific environments, with access to good universities and employment opportunities (say, as university teachers) might be more consistently creative than others reared under more unstable conditions.

Sex or Gender Differences

Considering the virtual unanimity of American social and differential psychologists on the cultural origins of differences between males and females in abilities, interests, attitudes, and personality, it may seem odd to cite sex differences in creativity as giving strong evidence of genetic factors. In secondary schools and colleges (in Western culture), far fewer girls than boys opt for science and mathematics courses (see Cole & Cole, 1971, 1973; Dresselhaus, 1984; Fox, Brody, & Tobin, 1980; Maccoby & Jacklin, 1974). Very few women obtain Ph.D.s in science. Cole quotes only 3% in the physical sciences in the 1970s; 8% in chemistry, 15% in biology, but 18% in sociology and 24% in psychology. He claims a considerable growth in their numbers during the 1970s, but it is difficult to disentangle this assertion when there are increasing numbers of women entering graduate work in all areas. Sometimes, too, the total number of female science students increases, but the number of males increases even more, so that the female proportion actually drops. The discrepancy is greatest in high-level employment, with extremely few women reaching full professorships in the natural sciences, though somewhat greater in the social sciences. The numbers of science publications by women also lag greatly behind those of men. Also women are more often employed as teachers than as research workers.

What is more surprising is that the numbers of highly creative women in most of the arts are about as low as in the sciences. This is true in music and the visual arts, including sculpture and architecture. However, there are many well-known female writers (though few poets). Probably there are more women than men in decorative and applied arts. The situation is very different, too, among performers. In music and drama, there is probably little difference in the totals of men and women, but in ballet dancing, women are clearly in the majority.

There can be no doubt that, in Western cultures, there are different pressures on boys or men and girls or women to engage in different kinds of interests, educational courses, and careers. From about the age of 1 year, boys are given different toys from girls, for example, bricks or cars as against dolls, cuddly animals, and books. Boys are encouraged to engage in physical activities and are expected to be more aggressive, girls are expected to be quieter, more conformist, and to express themselves more in verbal than in motor actions. The educational systems of Western society have accepted the same stereotyping, and often it is the influence of the teachers that deters girls from taking advanced mathematics and science courses and concentrating more in the arts, humanities, or domestic training. Girls themselves accept these differences, and a majority of them aspire to marriage or to a limited range of jobs, such as teachers, secretaries, hairdressers, or nurses, which they can readily abandon for marriage. But Fox *et al.* (1980) noted that the proportions of mathematically or scientifically inclined girls vary considerably from one high school to another, presumably because some schools have higher quality staff, or different traditions. Single-sex schools for girls tend to produce more scientists than mixed sex, because their students are less affected by fear of competition with boys. Most girls in ordinary mixed schools show some degree of "fear of success." That is, they prefer not to get higher marks or to appear to be better achievers than boys, because this makes them less attractive as potential marital partners.

There are, of course, large numbers of girls who reject these stereotypes and aim to become scientists or eventually to succeed in business careers. Some of them marry and bring up children as well. But these rebels against convention are a minority, and they may undergo considerable emotional stress as a result. Helson (1967) and Barron (1969) give good descriptions of the difficulties of women mathematicians in pursuing their careers.

Many writers, such as Cole (1979), have criticized the apparent discrimination against female scientific staff in universities. Their jobs are mostly lower grade, and their rate of promotion is below that of the male staff. They publish only about half as many books or articles, so that their Citation Indices tend to be low. They have more difficulty in getting research grants or other rewards. But Cole's analysis shows that, when their scientific qualifications are comparable to those of the male staff (e.g., whether they have Ph.D.s), their status and awards are much more similar. Although there is certainly discrimination generally, it is less marked in universities than is usually believed.

In their well-known book on sex differences, Maccoby and Jacklin (1974) showed how many of the widely accepted beliefs about the abilities and personalities of the sexes are traditional stereotypes that are not confirmed by controlled investigations; they also stressed the amount of overlapping when real differences do occur. Frequently, too, such differences as are found are rather specific to particular tests. For example, on many tests of verbal fluency and comprehension, females tend to score higher, but not on vocabulary or verbal information. They are usually lower, again, on Witkin-type tests of field independence, but not necessarily on all tests of spatial abilities. In both these areas, the differences could be explained as due to social expectations and stereotypes as by genetic factors. However, there are obvious biological differences in physical musculature and hormones that produce greater strength and suitability for fighting in males. Hence, it is highly probable that males are, by and large, more aggressive and dominant, females more submissive and concerned with child nurture and domestic activities. Such differences are by no means restricted to Western culture but, with few exceptions, apply throughout all human societies. Likewise they occur in many nonhuman mammalian species, where males do most of the hunting and fighting, and are less aggressive toward females than to males of their own species.

Thus, it is possible to make a case for certain biological sex differences, particularly those that are responsible for aggression, exploration, and initiative in males, and nurturance in females; and these traits might well underlie spatial, mechanical, and technological talents, even predisposing to scientific inclinations in males, and verbal and domestic inclinations in females. It is hardly possible to prove this, when social-environmental influences are so strong. But it is entirely implausible that human society should approve of females becoming highly talented performers of music, dance, and drama, and even allowing them to become creative writers, while, at the same time, disapproving of their becoming musical composers or painters. To me, this is the crux of the argument for attributing sex differences in creativity at least, in part, to genetic factors.

Family Resemblance

The statement that creativity or outstanding talent tends to "run" in families is frequently heard but is almost impossible to justify, because such resemblance between relatives can be attributed either to common genes, or to environmental influences, or to both, and we have no method to decide which. To my knowledge, no one has studied or compared the creativity of mono- and dizygotic twins or has used any other controlled techniques for providing more reliable evidence. However, many cases of identical twins who were reared apart, but who entered very similar occupational careers, have been reported.

According to Galton (1869), just half of his historically eminent persons had fathers or other close relations who were similarly gifted. Although this finding has not been replicated, Terman's (1925) gifted children came largely from upper-class families. But this fact was not universal. As many as 19% of Terman's group had unskilled or laboring-class parents, and many of the geniuses were of lower-class origins, neither the father nor mother showing any superior abilities (so far as their biographies indicated). For example, Immanuel Kant, Charles Dickens, Michael Faraday and John Bunyan all seem to have been raised in very poor circumstances, but the available data are often too patchy to allow quantitative measures of familial resemblance.

Many instances of resemblance among siblings could be cited, where two or more have shown outstanding creative talent: for example the Brontë sisters. Often siblings are eminent in different areas, for example, Aldous and Julian Huxley, one a writer, the other a biologist. Their grandfather, Thomas Huxley, was also an eminent scientist. In the area of music, Scheinfeld (1972) claimed that 70% of the children, both of whose parents are musical, are likely to be equally musical; with 1 musical parent, 60% of the children are the same, and when neither parent is musical, only 15% of the offspring are. This does not seem to have been confirmed.

Among the detailed pedigree tables that have been published, probably the most famous is that of the Bach family of musicians. From Veit Bach (died 1619) to Johann Christian Bach (died 1782), there is some information on 60 related males, spanning seven generations. Of these, 53 were well known as musicians, cantors, and/or organists, many of whom were eminent during their lifetimes. But it is noteworthy that only one of Johann Sebastian Bach's sons is still regarded as an important creative musician, namely, Carl Philipp Emanuel. A few others produced compositions that are still played, but none of these sons have lasting reputations comparable to their father's. Moreover, no other pedigree is anywhere near as striking, though several father–son resemblances are known, for example, Alessandro and Domenico Scarlatti. The pedigrees are even more rare in the other arts and in the sciences. Often one member of a pair is considered much more creative than the other, or they differ in their particular branch of science. For example, Robert Thorndike's area of specialization is largely different from that of his father, Edward. Surely, if there is a powerful genetic component in scientific research or other forms of creativity, one would expect it to last over several generations. Yet we must also remember that only half a parent's genes are passed on to his offspring, one quarter from the grandparent to the grandchild, and so on. Hence, even with a naive genetic theory, the underlying genes are rapidly diluted.

How far could parent–child resemblance be accounted for by environmental influence? In the home of a highly musical parent, one would expect the offspring to be exposed to a wide range of musical experience, from infancy through adolescence. This would be less true in the sciences, though an eminent physicist, for example, would very likely look out for any signs of scientific interests or skills in his children, even, say, in biology, and would usually give strong reinforcement by discussing and approving the child's activities, by providing scientific toys, books, and relevant TV documentaries. Moreover, many of the father's friends would also be scientists, who would give further encouragement. Yet, in other homes, it often occurs that adolescents rebel against parental pressures and set out to follow very different careers. Sometimes such offspring grow out of this stage and later revert to an occupation quite like the father's, but we have no convincing data for indicating how frequently these patterns of resemblance and difference occur, nor why.

Upbringing and Environment

Although our evidence for genetic determinants in creativity is rather weak, it should be possible to get better proof of the effects of home and school environment, and differences in upbringing. These factors appear to stimulate, or inhibit, creativity in general, or to affect certain types or aspects of creative production. Several investigations have been carried out using case studies, interviews, or biographical data obtained from highly creative scientists or artists. Other studies have used personality tests or biographical questionnaires, which have the advantages that they can be given to large groups and scored to yield quantitative measures. Besides Cox's (1926) work, Roe's (1952) surveys of several groups of scientists and Bloom and Sosniak's (1981) study of talent development are outstanding. Taylor and Ellison's (1964), Cattell and Butcher's (1968), and Chambers' (1964) investigations are characteristic of the second, more quantitative approach. MacKinnon's (1962), Barron's (1969), and Eiduson's (1962) studies combine both types of evidence. A useful overall survey of psychosocial development of highly gifted children is provided by Janos and Robinson (1985).

Although Cox drew attention to the importance of good home conditions and of the personality qualities of her geniuses, she also emphasized the great variations in upbringing and the wide personality differences. Roe likewise claimed that, in her groups of scientists, every personality was unique. Yet she arrived at a rather frequent basic pattern of childhood growth. A great many of her subjects showed a high degree of independence and solitariness; their relations with their parents were rather impersonal, though they were strongly encouraged in achievement and in intellectual interests. An unusual proportion of them were first born or only children, and many tended to show poor health, which reduced their contacts with other age-peers. Many, again, had been strongly influenced by another relative, adult friend, or an inspiring teacher. As adults they were rather detached and were much more strongly committed to their work than to social or sexual activities. Roe's study is exceptional in showing a very marked difference in the upbringing and personalities of 42 physicists and biologists on the one hand, and 22 social scientists on the other. The latter had had more stormy childhoods and conflicts with their parents, but were more gregarious as adults and more unstable emotionally; some 40% of them had been divorced as against 10% of the natural scientists.

Terman (1955) followed up all of his gifted children who had become scientists, contrasting them with those in business, law, or the humanities. The main difference, when first tested at about 11 years, was that the former already had considerable scientific interests and activities, and were lower in social participation than the nonscientists.

The work of MacKinnon (1962) and his colleagues tends to agree with and expand that of Roe. Creative architects and others usually show more radical, nonconformist attitudes, introverted and independent and often neurotic traits, though, as Barron (1969) argues, these are controlled by well-developed ego-strength. Taylor (1962) described a study of typical American male adults, as contrasted with creative individuals. They were generally conventional, extroverted, unimaginative, and concerned with home and sports rather than cultural or intellectual interests.

In the early 1960s, Taylor and Ellison (1964) realized that neither academic achievement, intelligence, nor other ability tests were of use in picking out industrial or research scientists, and tried instead to construct predictive biographical inventories. They included large numbers of items dealing with childhood and adolescent interests, favorable factors in home background, and current leisure activities. These inventories were given to adult scientists who had been rated high or low in creativity by their supervisors; and the best differentiating items were retained. When given to other rated groups, the scores correlated consistently at around .50 with the criterion. Several such inventories were prepared, but it appeared that items were somewhat unreliable over time; hence, an elaborate process of reconstruction and validation might be needed after a few years. Several other such instruments have been produced, for example, by Buel (1965) and by Schaefer and Anastasi (1968). Also Nichols and Holland (1963) found that similar questionnaires given to college freshmen yielded small but significant correlations with their self-rated accomplishments in scientific, musical, dramatic, and visual arts a year later. They further found predictive items in questionnaires given to parents, dealing with their own interests and social attitudes.

However, the above methods do not provide us with a kind of recipe for the "good" home, which produces creative adult offspring, nor a basis for differentiating those who are likely to be outstanding in any particular art or science. The questionnaires tend to support environmental explanations of creativity but not to prove them. Indeed, sometimes they contradict our expectations. Ammons and Ammons (1962) presented several case studies of eminent creatives (e.g., John Stuart Mill and Mozart) who as children were grossly over-pressured by their fathers. Apparently, the kind of conditions regarded by child psychologists as essential to mental health were entirely lacking. Some geniuses, also, seem to have been stimulated rather than impeded by opposition, for example, Galileo and Freud. However, the romantic notion that all great artists must have experienced suffering and conquered their stresses and hardships has no sound backing.

Bloom and Sosniak (1981) carried out a detailed inquiry into the development of outstanding talent among 25 men in each of 6 areas—2 scientific, 2 artistic, and 2 athletic. They emphasized the enormous amount of support and planning given by the homes from age 12, or even earlier. The boys commonly spent more time on practice and coaching in their talent areas than on ordinary schoolwork; and this training was more individualized and more intensive than they received at school. However, this applied more to the athletes and artists than to the scientists.

There is some evidence of a greater degree of authoritarianism than of permissiveness in the intellectual lives of future gifted scientists (Kennedy & Willcut, 1963). Parloff, Datta, Kleman, and Handlow (1968) gave a personality inventory to some 900 science talent scholars, who had produced creative scientific projects, and found that they scored highly on a personality factor designated as Disciplined Effectiveness. The subjects were not usually characterized by the nonconformist or rebellious traits found among MacKinnon's architects or among some of Roe's scientists. Hudson (1966) found English high school boys and college students, who were taking science, to be mainly convergent thinkers, whereas those taking literary courses were more often divergent thinkers. Storr (1972) suggested that many highly creative individuals can be classified under pathological headings, such as schizophrenic, manic depressive, or obsessional, but provided no empirical evidence.

Some of the earliest studies of environmental effects were James McKeen Cattell's (1906) demographic surveys of the backgrounds and careers of American scientists. He showed that the production of eminent scientists was greatest in those American states with good educational systems, many libraries and laboratories, and a high degree of tolerance and liberality toward scientific research. Knapp and Goodrich (1952) studied the types of colleges attended and the geographic areas which produced most scientists (see also Brannigan, 1981; and Coler, 1963). Clark (1957) surveyed the backgrounds and careers of American psychologists, and Moulin (1955) analyzed the countries of origin and other characteristics of Nobel prizewinners from 1901 to 1950. Other writers (e.g., Datta, 1967; Roe, 1952) found that religious background is influential, the greatest number of eminent scientists coming from Jewish or liberal Protestant homes, the fewest from fundamental Protestant or Catholic homes.

It has often been noted that "golden ages" occur in particular countries at particular periods, when a large number of creative individuals in one or more of the arts or in the sciences reach an outstanding level of creativity. Among the most notable were the dramatists, philosophers, and sculptors in classical Greece around 400–300 B.C., and the painters, architects, and writers of the fourteenth- and fifteenth-century Renaissance period in northern Italy. Certainly, such occurrences have environmental effects, though we have little or no knowledge as to why or how they occur.

Trainability

If the influence of genetic factors on the development of creativity is of minor or no importance, it should be possible to teach or train many aspects of creative thinking in much the same ways as educating to read and to do arithmetic. Currently, there is a strong trend in this direction. Many writers, such as Torrance (1965), de Bono (1970), and Parnes (1963), believe that, from the earliest school years, the curriculum should include extensive training in a variety of divergent thinking tasks, and that these should improve the all-around capacity to show imaginative, flexible thinking, leading up to creative problem solving. On the other hand, other psychologists, such as Mansfield, Busse, and Krepelka (1978), Cattell and Butcher (1968), and MacKinnon (1968), are highly critical of such an approach. They point out that the work of creative scientists and artists is totally unlike Osborn's brainstorming, de Bono's lateral thinking, or the numerous schemes and programs now being published for the enhancement of creative thinking. From the earliest days of educational psychology, the difficulties of bringing about transfer of training have been stressed. As G. M. Stratton (1922) put it: "what you do to the mind by means of education knows its place; it never spreads. You train what you train.'' In other words, coaching and practice may considerably improve ability in some particular activity, but they have limited or scarcely any transfer to other situations or tasks which might appear to be similar, or which have the same name.

Torrance (1972) published a survey of 142 follow-up studies of divergent thinking training and claimed that three-quarters of these gave positive evidence of improvement. But, in most of these cases, the criterion of creative thinking was much the same as the practice exercises, namely, scores on divergent thinking tasks. For example, scores on the Alternate Uses test may be affected by the training, but they cannot be taken to demonstrate generalization to real-life problem-solving or artistic productivity. Also few, if any, investigators appear to have carried out long-term follow-up studies, in which older students or adults, who have received so-called creativity training as children, were found to be superior as scientists or artists to those who received no such childhood training. Obviously, it would be very difficult to ensure that those without childhood experiences were equivalent to those with such experience in general intelligence, quality of schooling, and many other possible influences. Yet, until such evidence is forthcoming, we are not entitled to claim that creative ability is trainable.

Nevertheless, Stein's (1975) book, *Stimulating Creativity,* surveyed a number of relatively well-controlled experimental studies that make a better case for some positive short-term effects. Frederiksen (1984) demonstrated improvements in quite a range of complex problem-solving skills, which are more carefully defined and measured than creativity in general.

Rather more is known of the effects of organization of schools and the planning of suitable courses from such work as Stanley's and his colleagues on mathematically precocious adolescents (Stanley *et al.,* 1974; Daurio, 1979). Large numbers of mathematically gifted students were making very poor progress because of the slow pace at which school mathematics was taught, unless they happened to get help at home or obtained books for self-teaching. But when placed in special programs designed to let them progress at their own rates, they gained three or more years in grade standing and often obtained university degrees much earlier than usual. Unfortunately, there has been little attempt to follow them up several more years in order to see how many, as a result of this boost, have become research mathematicians or scientists. Although Stanley discovered far fewer mathematically gifted girls, he was able to pull many of them up much nearer the boys' standards by designing summer courses or other special classes.

Many books have doubtless been written on school or college teaching, which aim to show how to stimulate creative students and not merely implant conventional knowledge and skills. Brandwein's (1955) book, on the recruitment and teaching of promising science students at high school, may be an old one, but it brings together a wealth of data on stimulating interest in, and commitment to, science, the need for very high academic and intellectual standards among the students, the planning and individualization of courses, and the quality of the staff.

At the college level, Heist (1968) deplored the loss of potentially creative scientists because of their frustration with the rigidity and spoonfeeding of undergraduate science courses. Many requisite graduate courses can also be more stifling than stimulating; and similar criticisms apply to much course work in the fine arts. Chambers (1973) studied the characteristics of ineffective psychology and chemistry teachers by means of class observations and student ratings. ''Facilitating,'' as contrasted with ''inhibiting,'' teachers encourage class discussions and seldom read from notes. They are enthusiastically committed to their subjects and are readily available to students for consultations. Their courses are also intellectually demanding. Just as in home upbringing, permissive teaching can do more harm than good; and research students have to experience hard work, with frequent frustrations, in order to achieve the grounding necessary for creative research. At the same time, the more unconventional and rebellious students, who may be a nuisance to their instructors and supervisors, are likely to require more sympathetic handling and encouragement. But these problems are more matters of discussion and argument than of controlled research.

Summary and Conclusions

1. The difficulties of defining and measuring creativity are so great that no firm conclusions can be reached on the relative importance of genetic and environmental factors; the latter including sociological variables as well as individual differences in upbringing. Complex interactions occur among all these factors in the growth of creativity.

However, a considerable amount of psychological, sociological, biographical, neurological, and other types of evidence is available.

2. Creativity is taken to mean the production of novel ideas, theories, and objects, either in the sciences or in the arts, which are accepted by competent experts as original and valuable. Such productivity is quite rare and, though a matter of degree, tends to be concentrated among relatively small numbers of scientists and artists. Creative effort is not the same as an ability or trait that is presumed to underlie unconventional behaviors or to responses to ''divergent thinking'' tests, which do approximate to a normal distribution throughout the population.

3. In scientific discovery, the term *environment* includes not merely home, school, and cultural influences, but also the present state of knowledge and instrumentation, together with chance stimuli that suggest new ideas, favorable conditions of work, and cooperation or competition with other scientists. Thus, it should not be regarded as a kind of possession of the individual scientist, whether it be innate or acquired.

4. Descriptive and experimental approaches to the mental processes involved in scientific and artistic creativity are being fruitfully studied by cognitive psychologists and information theorists. But the degree to which creative thinking differs from other complex thinking is not yet decided. A great deal of observational and introspective evidence indicates the role of the subconscious processes in inspiration and in creativity, though—particularly in the sciences—rational processes of acquiring and analyzing knowledge and working out implications of new ideas tend to predominate.

5. Creative production correlates moderately with general intelligence. Scientists tend to show the highest IQs, but a great many exceptions occur. Thus, neither intelligence tests nor other cognitive tests, such as Terman's Concept Mastery or Guilford's divergent thinking, are valid predictors of future scientific or artistic creativity. This result should be expected in the light of the conclusions in numbers 1 to 3 above.

6. The strongest evidence for genetic factors is the appearance of persons of outstanding genius, both in the arts and the sciences, beyond what could reasonably be attributed to family upbringing and environment. There is also some evidence linking aspects of creativity with particular areas of the brain, though we cannot rule out the alternative theory that creative activity itself tends to stimulate brain growth. The popular view that creativity depends much more on the right than on the left side of the brain is too speculative to be acceptable. Likewise, changes in productivity with brain growth and later decay are of minor importance.

7. Giftedness observed during childhood and adolescence gives rather poor indications of creative productivity in adulthood. Although there is clearly some consistency and continuity in adults, fluctuations also occur that might be attributable more to changes in environmental circumstances or personality. Thus, this line of evidence neither confirms nor disproves genetic theories.

8. The numbers of creative women scientists and artists tend to be much lower than those for men. Most writers attribute this difference to sex-role stereotypes and differential pressures on the sexes that is exerted by parents, peers, schools, and society in general. However, there are obvious biological sex differences favoring more aggressive and dominant behavior in males and more compliant and nurturant behavior in females. These traits apply to most known human societies and to many mammalian species. Moreover, purely social causation could not readily explain the greater female achievement in particular areas, for example, in writing and in the decorative and the performing arts as against painting and musical composition.

9. Considerable resemblances are often observed between offspring, parents, sibs, and other relatives in creative production. But there are also frequent differences in achievement or in areas of specialization. Although genetic factors cannot be ruled out, such similarities are probably better explained by factors of upbringing and environment.

10. When highly creative scientists or artists are compared with less creative or normal individuals, a great many differences in personality, home background, and upbringing are found. Demographic differences are also associated with productivity. But because there is much overlapping, no particular personality or environmental factors differentiate in all cases. Thus, we cannot manipulate or control the development of creativity. Many outstanding creative individuals have succeeded despite apparently unfavorable home, school, or other conditions.

Differences between artists and scientists, or between those working in different areas, have also been observed, but again the results show many inconsistencies.

11. Several attempts to train or develop creative

talent by school activities and exercises are less effective than claimed. Specific skills can usually be trained by instruction and practice, but these seldom generalize or transfer to broader activities, such as creative production. No long-term follow-up studies can be quoted to show that such training produces more high-creative scientists or artists. However, progress is being made by cognitive psychologists in influencing the development of complex problem-solving skills. Better planning and organization of the curriculum in high schools and colleges have been shown to affect achievement (e.g., in mathematics). But so much depends on the motivation of the students and the quality of their teachers that it is difficult to specify general principles.

Future Developments

Readers of a chapter such as this might expect to be provided with a list of the most promising avenues for future research. But given the complexities of collecting any hard evidence, it is likely that every author would recommend a different list. We are still in the stage of carrying out fishing expeditions rather than recommending specific hypotheses and methods. However, two general considerations can be suggested. First, that the processes to be studied should be those that directly involve creative activities in one or more of the arts or sciences. There is no good reason for concentrating, as at present, on such simple tasks as those used in divergent thinking.

Second, the samples of subjects to be studied should be mainly adults of, say, 25 years or over, who can be assessed as genuine creatives (e.g., by their recent teachers). Adequate control samples who lack such creativity are also needed. As in Terman's follow-up of his gifted group, such creative individuals are likely to be interested in psychological investigations of their work and to cooperate in interviews or questionnaire surveys. There has been considerable progress in our knowledge of creativity over the past 30 years or so. Thus, given adequate funding, the prospects for further advances are favorable.

The major approach for experimentalists and theorists should be the extension of cognitive psychological studies, like those of Sternberg and of Frederiksen, which should cover genuine scientific research and discovery, or the actual production of musical, visual, or literary works.

The other line of recommended exploration is an extension of longitudinal studies similar to those of Roe and of MacKinnon. A large group of students identified as highly gifted at, say, 12 years might be followed through until they reached about 25 years, in order to find the home upbringing and school progress characteristics of those who end up as highly creative, and those who fade out and become mediocre adults. Fluctuations in interests and personality during adolescence would be particularly revealing. Less time-consuming studies might start with college freshman and attempt to analyze the college courses and avocations of those who, perhaps 6 years later, became really promising scientists or artists. Again, there seem to have been no follow-up studies of those designated as creative at age 25 to elicit the conditions under which they achieve further successes or declines over the next 10 or more years.

Quite short-term studies that would be of value could be based on work in progress. They should focus more on the motivational and emotional aspects of creativity than on the cognitive features. These studies, too, should cover several scientific and/or artistic areas.

Given a large enough sample of highly creative young adults (e.g., through public advertisements), it would be informative to study the backgrounds, present activities, and personalities of pairs of mono- and dizygotic twins, and a control group of siblings. The calculation of heritability indices would be of minor importance; but analyses of resemblances and differences by case-study methods could be quite fruitful.

References

Agassi, J. (1985). The myth of the young genius. *Interchange, 16,* 51–60.

Albert, R. S. (1975). Toward a behavioral definition of genius. *American Psychologist, 30,* 140–151.

Ammons, C. H., & Ammons, R. B. (1962). How to prevent genius: McCurdy revisited. *Proceedings of Montana Academy of Science, 21,* 145–152.

Arieti, S. (1976). *Creativity: The magic synthesis.* New York: Basic Books.

Barber, B., & Hirsch, W. (Eds.). (1962). *The sociology of science.* New York: Free Press.

Barron, F. (1969). *Creative person and creative process.* New York: Holt, Rinehart & Winston.

Bartlett, F. C. (1958). *Thinking: An experimental and social study.* London: Allen & Unwin.

Bartlett, M. M., & Davis, G. A. (1974). Do the Wallach and Kogan tests predict real creative behavior? *Perceptual and Motor Skills, 39,* 730.

Biber, B. (1984). *Early education and psychological development*. New Haven: Yale University Press.

Blackwell, R. J. (1969). *Discovery in the physical sciences*. Notre Dame: Notre Dame University Press.

Bloom, B. S., & Sosniak, L. A. (1981). Talent development vs. schooling. *Educational Leadership, 39*(2), 86–94.

Brandwein, P. F. (1955). *The gifted student as future scientist*. New York: Harcourt, Brace.

Brannigan, A. (1981). *The social basis of scientific discoveries*. New York: Cambridge University Press.

Buel, W. D. (1965). Biographical data and the identification of creative research personnel. *Journal of Applied Psychology, 49*, 318–321.

Campbell, D. T. (1960). Blind variation and student retention: Creative thought as in other knowledge processes. *Psychological Review, 67*, 380–400.

Cattell, J. McK. (1906). A statistical study of American men of science. III. The distribution of American men of science. *Science, 24*, 732–742.

Cattell, R. B. (1971). *Abilities: Their structure, growth and action*. Boston: Houghton Mifflin.

Cattell, R. B., & Butcher, H. J. (1968). *The prediction of achievement and creativity*. New York: Bobbs-Merrill.

Chambers, J. A. (1964). Relating personality and biographical factors to scientific creativity. *Psychological Monographs, 78*, No. 584.

Chambers, J. A. (1973). College teachers: Their effect on creativity of students. *Journal of Educational Psychology, 65*, 325–334.

Clark, K. E. (1957). *America's psychologists: A survey of a growing profession*. Washington, DC: American Psychological Association.

Cole, J. R. (1979). *Fair science: Women in the scientific community*. New York: Free Press.

Cole, J. R., & Cole, S. (1971). Measuring the quality of sociological research: Problems in the use of the Science Citation Index. *American Sociologist, 6*, 23–29.

Cole, J. R., & Cole, S. (1973). *Social stratification in science*. Chicago: University of Chicago Press.

Coler, M. A. (Ed.). (1963). *Essays on creativity in the sciences*. New York: Universities Press.

Cox, C. M. (1926). *The early mental traits of three hundred geniuses*. Stanford, CA: Stanford University Press.

Cronbach, L. J. (1968). Intelligence? Creativity? A parsimonious reinterpretation of the Wallach-Kogan data. *American Educational Research Journal, 5*, 491–511.

Datta, L. (1967). Family religious background and early scientific creativity. *American Sociological Review, 32*, 626–635.

Daurio, S. P. (1979). Educational enrichment versus acceleration: A review of the literature. In W. C. George, S. J. Cohn, & J. D. Stanley (Eds.), *Educating the gifted*. Baltimore: Johns Hopkins University Press.

De Bono, E. (1970). *Lateral thinking*. New York: Harper & Row.

Dennis, W. (1958). The age decrement in outstanding scientific contributions. *American Psychologist, 13*, 457–460.

Dresselhaus, M. S. (1984). A physicist's perspective on the complementary roles of the physical and behavioral sciences. *American Psychologist, 39*, 333–340.

Drevdahl, J. E. (1956). Factors of importance for creativity. *Journal of Clinical Psychology, 12*, 21–26.

Edwards, B. (1979). *Drawing on the right side brain*. Los Angeles: Tarcher.

Eiduson, B. T. (1962). *Scientists: Their psychological world*. New York: Basic Books.

Eysenck, H. J., & Kamin, L. (1981). *The intelligence controversy*. New York: Wiley.

Feldman, D. H. (Ed.). (1982). *Developmental approaches to giftedness and creativity*. San Francisco: Jossey-Bass.

Fox, L. H., Brody, L., & Tobin, D. (Eds.). (1980). *Women and the mathematical mystique*. Baltimore: Johns Hopkins University Press.

Frederiksen, N. (1984). Implications of cognitive theory for instruction in problem solving. *Review of Educational Research, 54*, 363–407.

Galton, F. (1869). *Hereditary genius*. London: Macmillan.

Gardner, H. (1978). What we know (and don't know) about the two halves of the brain. *Journal of Aesthetic Education, 12*, 113–119.

Gardner, H. (1980). *Artful scribbles: The significance of children's drawings*. New York: Basic Books.

Gardner, H. (1983). *Frames of mind: The theory of multiple intelligences*. New York: Basic Books.

Getzels, J. W., & Jackson, P. W. (1962). *Creativity and intelligence: Explorations with gifted children*. New York: Wiley.

Ghiselin, B. (1952). *The creative process: A symposium*. Berkeley: University of California Press.

Gibson, J., & Light, F. (1967). Intelligence among university students. *Nature, 213*, 441–442.

Grinder, R. E. (1985). The gifted in our midst: By their divine deeds, neuroses, and mental test scores we have known them. In F. D. Horowitz & M. O'Brien (Eds.), *The gifted and talented: Developmental perspectives*. Washington, DC: American Psychological Association.

Gruber, H. E. (1974). *Darwin on man: A psychological study of scientific creativity*. New York: Dutton.

Guilford, J. P. (1967). *The nature of human intelligence*. New York: McGraw-Hill.

Hadamard, J. (1945). *An essay on the psychology of invention in the mathematical field*. Princeton: Princeton University Press.

Heist, P. (Ed.). (1968). *The creative college student: An unmet challenge*. San Francisco: Jossey-Bass.

Helmholtz, H. von (1903). *Vortrage und Reden* (Fünfte Auflage). Braunschweig: F. Vierweg.

Helson, R. (1967). Sex differences in creative style. *Journal of Personality, 35*, 214–233.

Hudson, L. (1966). *Contrary imaginations*. London: Methuen.

Janos, P. M., & Robinson, N. M. (1985). Psychosocial development in intellectually gifted children. In F. D. Horowitz & M. O'Brien (Eds.), *The gifted and talented*. Washington, DC: American Psychological Association.

Kennedy, W., & Willcutt, H. (1963). Youth-parent relations of mathematically gifted adolescents. *Journal of Clinical Psychology, 19*, 400–402.

Knapp, R. H., & Goodrich. H. B. (1952). *Origin of American scientists*. Chicago: University of Chicago Press.

Kogan, N., & Pankove, E. (1974). Long-term predictive validity of divergent-thinking tests: Some negative evidence. *Journal of Educational Psychology, 66*, 802–810.

Kubie, L. S. (1958). *Neurotic distortion of the creative process*. New York: Noonday Press.

Lehman, H. C. (1953). *Age and achievement*. Princeton: Princeton University Press.

Lenneberg, H. (1980). The myth of the unappreciated (musical) genius. *Musical Quarterly, 66*, 219–231.

Maccoby, E. E., & Jacklin, C. N. (1974). *The psychology of sex differences*. Stanford, CA: Stanford University Press.

MacKinnon, D. W. (1962). The personality correlates of creativity: A study of American architects. *Proceedings of the*

XIV Congress of Applied Psychology (Vol. 2). Copenhagen: Munksgaard.

MacKinnon, D. W. (1968). Educating for creativity: A modern myth. In P. Heist (Ed.), *The creative college student*. San Francisco: Jossey-Bass.

Mansfield, R. S., & Busse, T. V. (1981). *The psychology of creativity and discovery: Scientists and their work*. Chicago: Nelson-Hall.

Mansfield, R. S., Busse, T. V., & Krepelka, E. J. (1978). The effectiveness of creativity training. *Review of Educational Research, 48,* 517–536.

Mednick, S. A., & Mednick, M. E. (1967). *Remote Associations Test*. Boston: Houghton Mifflin.

Merton, R. K. (1968). *Social theory and social structure*. New York: Free Press.

Mistry, J., & Rogoff, B. (1985). A cultural perspective on the development of talent. In F. D. Horowitz & M. O'Brien (Eds.), *The gifted and talented*. Washington, DC: American Psychological Association.

Moulin, L. (1955). The Nobel prizes for the sciences from 1901 to 1950. *British Journal of Sociology, 6,* 246–263.

Narroll, R., Benjamin, E. C., Fohl, F. K., Fried, M. J., Hildreth, R. E., & Schaeffer, J. M. (1971). Creativity: A cross-historical pilot survey. *Journal of Cross-Cultural Psychology, 2,* 181–188.

Newell, A., & Simon, H. A. (1972). *Human problem-solving*. Englewood Cliffs, NJ: Prentice-Hall.

Nicholls, J. G. (1972). Creativity in the person who will never produce anything original and useful: The concept of creativity as a normally distributed trait. *American Psychologist, 27,* 717–727.

Nichols, R. C., & Holland, J. L. (1963). Prediction of the first year college performance of high aptitude students. *Psychological Monographs, 77,* No. 570.

Ornstein, R. E. (1977). *The psychology of consciousness*. New York: Harcourt Brace Jovanovich.

Parloff, M. B., Datta, L., Kleman, M., & Handlow, J. H. (1968). Personality characteristics which differentiate creative male adolescents and adults. *Journal of Personality, 36,* 528–552.

Parnes, S. J. (1963). Education and creativity. *Teachers College Record, 64,* 331–339.

Perkins, D. N. (1981). *The mind's best work*. Cambridge: Harvard University Press.

Poincaré, H. (1924). *The foundations of science*. London: Science Press.

Price, D. J. (1962). The exponential curve of science. In B. Barber & W. Hirsch (Eds.), *The sociology of science*. New York: Free Press.

Rabinowitz, M., & Glaser, R. (1985). Cognitive structure and process in highly competent performance. In F. D. Horowitz & M. O'Brien (Eds.), *The gifted and talented*. Washington, DC: American Psychological Association.

Roe, A. (1952). *The making of a scientist*. New York: Dodd, Mead.

Rogers, K. B. (1986). Do the gifted think and learn differently? A review of recent research and its implications for instruction. *Journal for the Education of the Gifted, 10,* 17–39.

Rosner, S., & Abt, L. E. (Eds.). (1970). *The creative experience*. New York: Grossman.

Schaefer, C. A., & Anastasi, A. (1968). A biographical inventory for identifying creativity in adolescent boys. *Journal of Applied Psychology, 52,* 42–48.

Scheinfeld, A. (1972). *Heredity in humans*. Philadelphia: Lippincott.

Shapiro, R. J. (1968). The identification of creative research scientists. *Psychologica Africana, Monograph Supplements,* No. 4.

Simonton, D. K. (1977). Eminence, creativity, and geographical marginality: A recursive structural equation model. *Journal of Personality and Social Psychology, 35,* 805–816.

Springer, S. P., & Deutsch, D. (1981). *Left brain: Right brain*. San Francisco: Freeman.

Stanley, J. C., Keating, D. P., & Fox, L. H. (Eds.). (1974). *Mathematical talent: Discovery, description and development*. Baltimore: Johns Hopkins University Press.

Stein, M. I. (1974). *Stimulating creativity* (Vol. 1). New York: Academic Press.

Stein, M. I. (1975). *Stimulating creativity* (Vol. 2). New York: Academic Press.

Sternberg, R. J., & Davidson, J. E. (1985). Cognitive development in the gifted and talented. In F. D. Horowitz & M. O'Brien (Eds.), *The Gifted and Talented*. Washington, DC: American Psychological Association.

Storr, A. (1972). *The dynamics of creation*. London: Secker & Warburg.

Stratton, G. M. (1922). *Developing Mental Power*. New York: Houghton–Mifflin.

Suler, J. R. (1980). Primary process thinking and creativity. *Psychological Bulletin, 88,* 144–165.

Taylor, C. W. (1962). Who are the exceptionally creative? *Exceptional Children, 28,* 421–431.

Taylor, C. W., & Ellison, R. L. (1964). Predicting creative performance from multiple measures. In C. W. Taylor (Ed.), *Widening horizons in creativity*. New York: Wiley.

Taylor, I. A. (1959). The nature of the creative process. In P. Smith (Ed.), *Creativity: An examination of the creative process*. New York: Hastings House.

Terman, L. M. (1925). *Genetic studies of genius: Vol. 1. Mental and physical traits of a thousand gifted children*. Stanford, CA: Stanford University Press.

Terman, L. M. (1955). Are scientists different? *Scientific American, 192,* 25–35.

Torrance, E. P. (1965). *Rewarding creative behavior*. Englewood Cliffs, NJ: Prentice-Hall.

Torrance, E. P. (1972). Can we teach children to think creatively? *Journal of Creative Behavior, 6,* 114–143.

Vernon, P. E. (1972). The validity of divergent thinking tests. *Alberta Journal of Educational Research, 18,* 244–258.

Vernon, P. E. (1979). *Intelligence: Heredity and environment*. San Francisco: Freeman.

Vernon, P. E. (1984). Intelligence, cognitive styles, and brain lateralization. *International Journal of Psychology, 19,* 435–455.

Vernon, P. E., Adamson, G., & Vernon, D. F. (1977). *The psychology and education of gifted children*. London: Methuen.

Wallach, M. A., & Kogan, N. (1965). Modes of thinking in young children. New York: Holt, Rinehart & Winston.

Wallach, M. A., & Wing, C. W. (1969). *The talented student*. New York: Holt, Rinehart & Winston.

Wallas, G. (1926). *The art of thought*. London: Jonathan Cape.

Welsh, G. S. (1975). *Creativity and intelligence: A personality approach*. Chapel Hill, NC: Institute for Research in Social Science.

Zigler, E., & Farber, E. A. (1985). Commonalities between the intellectual extremes: Giftedness and mental retardation. In F. D. Horowitz & M. O'Brien (Eds.), *The Gifted and Talented*. Washington, DC: American Psychological Association.

CHAPTER 6

Creativity and Intelligence

Patricia A. Haensly and Cecil R. Reynolds

The Relationship between Creativity and Intelligence

Consideration of the relationship between creativity and intelligence during this past half-century has occupied the attention of psychologists with varied perspectives (e.g., Cattell, 1963a; Coler, 1963; Guilford, 1950, 1959, 1968, 1981; MacKinnon, 1962; Roe, 1951, 1963; Terman, 1954, 1955; Torrance, 1960, 1967). Scientists working in a variety of other disciplines from genetics to engineering (see Simonton, 1984, 1985; Taylor & Barron, 1963) also have been intrigued by the contribution of intelligence to creative discovery and invention. And philosophers from Aristotle and Plato to Immanuel Kant, Brand Blanshard, and Jacques Maritain (citing here only those of Western civilization) (Rothenberg & Hausman, 1976) have pondered the origin of creativity and its relationship to rational thought. Professionals and lay people alike are fascinated by the topic, and, even more so, by the consequences of applying creative effort and/or intelligent action, and by the implications for their nurturance and educability. This chapter will provide a brief overview of past perspectives regarding the nature and extent of a relationship between creativity and intelligence and will propose and

support a view of the two phenomena as integrated in optimal mental performance.

A frequently recurring theme in the consideration of the dual phenomena of creativity and intelligence has been that creativity is not independent of the general factor of intelligence (Yamamoto, 1965). Intelligence appears to be a necessary but not sufficient condition for creativity (Rossiman & Horn, 1971); that is, although intelligence appears to allow the development of creativity, it does not ensure that creative expression always will be forthcoming (Schubert, 1973). However, many, if not most, students of the phenomena hold the view that intelligent thinking must also include some degree of creative thinking. The most prevalent view, then, has been that creativity is a distinct category of mental functioning that has *limited overlap* with intelligence, both in the processes used and in the characteristics of individuals who exhibit them.

Because the terms *creativity* and *intelligence* carry strong valences in the images they convey, it is important that our examination not be hampered by conceptual biases stemming from images that may not be accurate. As deBono (1971) suggests, we must break "out of the old, self-perpetuating patterns [and generate] new ways of looking at things" (deBono, 1971, p. 11).

Transitions in Contemporary Perspective

The description of the relationship between creativity and intelligence has, throughout the his-

Patricia A. Haensly and Cecil R. Reynolds • Department of Educational Psychology, Texas A&M University, College Station, TX 77843.

111

tory of psychology, most often been approached from a position of defensiveness; that is, intelligence appears to be a "given," a characteristic organisms exhibit in varying degrees permitting them to adapt to their environment. Creativity, on the other hand, often is viewed as an appendage, an ancillary characteristic permitting humans to pursue roads not usually traveled. Creative endeavor has even been viewed as an alternate pathway itself, one not necessarily basic to survival or adaptation. Under these circumstances, creativity has been explained as something external to models of intelligence, something out of the realm of rational thought. We propose that such an approach has been incorrect and counterproductive in that it limits our understanding of how individuals function mentally. In fact, most of the research of the past 30 years or so on creativity has been inspired by the interests Torrance developed from his military work in survival training, in which creativity was seen as integral to survival.

Contemporary perspective or a "new think" (deBono, 1971) regarding the relationship has begun with consideration of the *process of development* of creative effort. However, in this development, the path by which an individual becomes creative cannot be described without first describing the nature of its context, that is, the environment or medium upon which the creative response acts (Csikszentmihalyi & Robinson, 1986). The nature of the response required to obtain the medium for its expression, or the experiences required to develop the skills necessary to express the creative responses, also must be described (e.g., Bloom, 1985; Feldman & Benjamin, 1986). Consider, for example, the elements of intelligence that had to be present for the mentally retarded artist Alonzo Clemons (a 26-year-old man reported to have the mental capacities of a 6-year-old) to become an accomplished sculptor (Harper, 1983). Once, when counselors at a state institution where Clemons grew up took away his modeling clay, Clemons sneaked onto the roof and scraped up tar with his fingernails from which he sculpted tiny black horses. Such a response required an analysis of what could be done with soft tar and the goal-oriented behavior to acquire it without being caught. Without "intelligence" within a very limiting context, could his creative expression have taken place?

Analyses from a neurological perspective also add insight to the relationship between intelligence and creativity. Gardner (1982), in describing the studies of the processes followed by "creative" artists and scientists conducted by himself and Howard Gruber, stated that such individuals focus their abilities in particularly adept ways. Gardner asserted that these individuals integrate the specialized activities of the left and right hemispheres of the brain in particularly effective ways (Gardner, 1982, pp. 352–353). In addition, Gardner and Gruber's findings verify Feldman and Benjamin's (1986) ideas regarding the effect of genetic, familial, motivational, and cultural factors in the outstanding contributions of the creative genius, and, more importantly, on their coincidence. The biographical observations suggested that only when these variables come together in an appropriate time and place does creative genius seem to occur.

The effect of these additional variables on creative productivity is seen in other biographical analyses as well. Simonton (1979) found that antecedents to creative production among Cox's 301 eminent geniuses included not only intelligence but also family background, role models, and formal education. Judging by the paucity of creative genius, the correct combination of these factors appears to be very difficult to assemble. Simonton even suggested that education at the graduate level may lessen one's chances of achieving eminence. Simonton described achieved eminence as, in part, a curvilinear or inverted U function of the amount of formal education a person has. Based on his data, he suggested that "excessive amounts [of intelligence] may inhibit creative development by enforcing an overcommitment to traditional perspectives" (Simonton, 1979, p. 81).

Even when intelligence is given primary focus, a similar view is perceived. Estes (1985), who described intelligence as adaptive behavior, stated that creativity or creative responses are often not adaptive for a particular setting or in a limited time frame. This may be seen, for example, in some academic settings, limited levels of scientific endeavor, traditional societal groups, in conventional business, and other such settings. Estes suggested that the more intelligent individuals are, the more likely they will block their creative output in order to produce an adaptive response to the particular setting. A problem exists in that, in the long run, this kind of blocking of creativity is likely to be maladaptive for the individual and for society.

The matter of choice in how and when an intelligent individual will allow his or her own creative expression may be seen in Krippner's systems approach to creativity (Krippner, 1983). Krippner suggested that different avenues for creative effort occur through expressed preferences for certain types of creative activity; that is, individuals exhibit preferences for the kinds of information they seek about their world, the mode through which they seek information, the way they process that information, and the way they make decisions regarding their processed information. Creative effort may arise in each of these preferences and will be exhibited accordingly. Thus, Krippner classified individuals who perceive information from their senses, who are practical and oriented to what is feasible now, as analytic scientists; he suggested that E. Paul Torrance is an example of this type and that one of Torrance's greatest creative contributions has been the set of principles by which the environment that would stimulate creativity in the learning process could be created. On the other hand, the individual who absorbs information through his or her imagination and reaches decisions based on values unique to that individual— the conceptual humanist—is exemplified in Rollo May who wrote *The Courage to Create* (1975). Intelligence, or adaptation to the perceived demands of one's environment, as well as preference for specific models of functioning may, in this way, elicit creative responses.

Although Jackson and Messick, as early as 1965 (Kagan, 1967), stated that efforts to distinguish empirically between the two phenomena lack significant *informative* power, contemporary efforts in this direction have continued. These efforts have focused on demonstrating, for example, that tests designed to elicit production of unusual responses bring into play distinctly different mental processes than tests designed to assess intelligence. In fact, the results of such efforts are somewhat arbitrary, since performance on the tests is, at best, a limited indicator of either phenomenon in practical situations (Sternberg & Wagner, 1986).

A Focus on Integration

Little attention has been given to the idea that creativity and intelligence may be viewed more informatively as two different facets of a singular function originating from mental ability. In such a view, each facet has a different type of endpoint and each manifests a different way of attending to information, retrieving and reorganizing it, and applying the resulting reorganization. Yet, together, both contribute to an integrated, fully adaptive response to a specific task or immediate environment. Al-though the difference between a dichotomous and the proposed unitary or integrated view may be subtle, the implications of the latter for application, nurturance, and educability are extensive.

To initiate this analysis of past thinking about the relationship between creativity and intelligence and to develop a foundation for the integrated view, some basic questions should be addressed. What specifically does creativity have to do with intelligence? Can an individual ever be creative without having intelligence? Can an individual demonstrate a high degree of intelligence that has no creativity associated with it? Creativity and intelligence—can they be isolated from each other in verbal context, or in any other context? Despite careful factor analysis, is it possible to verify that the clusters of traits that emerge are completely independent of each other? Would, for example, one cluster actually occur if other clusters had not preceded or accompanied its emergence?

More particularly, can creativity or intelligence be assessed as if one exists without the other? Is this any more possible than the culture-free assessment of intelligence? Indeed, have the psychometric instruments, so carefully designed to measure the degree to which individuals possess creativity or intelligence, been confounded by the presence of the other? This dilemma seems similar to that of verifying a wholly unique role for either heredity or the environment in human behavior. A resolution of this latter "problem" was proposed 30 years ago by Anastasi (1958), when she suggested that the intricate interweaving of the two components of heredity and environment had rendered the problem pointless, that the more vital consideration had become the determination of how each contributes to the final product, and what contexts would be most suitable for promoting maximal expression of each. Similarly, we might more profitably view mental functioning as a complex interweaving of intelligent and creative types of response, according to specific task demands and parameters, and dependent upon individual predilection or capacity for a particular response type.

Further, any consideration of mental functioning must include awareness of the effect of context. This environmental component, upon which genetically controlled ability may develop and act, not only permits the expression of ability, shapes and defines it, but also can limit it (Haensly, Reynolds, & Nash, 1986). Yet, as canalization theory (Fishbein, 1976) suggests, when adverse environments occur, the human's genetic plan tries to restore potential maximization. So too might mental ability, modified by context, attempt to manifest itself according to the individual's potential for different types of expression. The type and degree of response also may be shaped by the individual's *understanding* of task demands and his or her mental efficiency, which is defined by Sternberg (1984) as the internal world of the individual. Additional response shaping occurs through experiences that have developed or trained readiness for the task (the external world of the individual), and the receptiveness of the available audience (context), as described in Sternberg's componential theory of intelligence (Sternberg, 1984).

Attempting to isolate creativity from intelligence seems no more informative from an information-processing perspective of intelligence than from a developmental perspective, nor, for that matter, through analyzing the differential contributions of brain hemispheres and cortical specializations. When the individual confronts new information, is it perceived and encoded intelligently or creatively? Are the neurological patterns that arise intelligently planned and stored, or do they associate flexibly? And, depending upon the prior storage of patterns, do they organize predictably, or do they become established in novel arrangements? When retrieved from short- or long-term memory, what determines whether resulting information qualifies as an intelligent response or a creative response? Does this change when one considers the particular individual, or does it depend upon the aggregate of individuals who are privy to the response? Or, must it await the criterion of acceptance over time? How long must the novel or highly original response be available before others view it as an intelligent response to the task (Haensly & Roberts, 1983; Haensly *et al.*, 1986)?

Critical examinations of traditional views of intelligence and reconceptualizations of the processes involved (e.g., Case, 1978; Gardner, 1983; Pascuale-Leone, 1970; Piaget, 1972; Sternberg, 1985; Sternberg & Wagner, 1986) demand a reconsideration of the phenomenon of creativity as well. Unfortunately, there is no eluding the problem of terminology. To attempt to replace terms in current use will only decrease our ability to talk about mental functioning. We can, however, develop paradigms for description, explanation, and prediction inclusive of both creativity and intelligence. Such paradigms would demonstrate that optimal mental functioning occurs when there is appropriate alignment and balance between the various modes of

mental processing, according to the demands of the task addressed.

This chapter focuses on how and why creativity and intelligence should be viewed as a unitary phenomenon in which optimal mental functioning occurs in an integrated, complementary fashion. The remainder of the chapter will be devoted to (a) a brief examination of several early approaches to the assessment of creativity in order to describe the theoretical and empirical inclusion of intelligence in each, and (b) an examination of several approaches to assessment of intelligence in order to describe the theoretical and empirical inclusion of creativity in each. The intent in both of these examinations is to introduce and elaborate on the complementary nature of creativity and intelligence, rather than to review comprehensively all available theories. We then address a particular problem regarding the perceived relationship between creativity and intelligence that stems from the restricted range encountered in the assessment data of many studies. This is followed by a discussion of the synergistic effect between creativity and intelligence. The chapter concludes with a brief presentation of a perspective of mental processing that views intelligence as an intrinsic component of creative behavior in which creative expression is the ultimate extension of intelligence. It also notes some implications of the integrated viewpoint.

Intelligence as a Component in Theories and Assessment of Creativity

The Association Hierarchy

Among studies of creativity initiated with a focus on the creative process itself is that of Mednick (1962). Mednick defined creativity as "the forming of associative elements into new combinations which either meet specified requirements or are in some way useful" (p. 220). Based on this definition, Mednick established two immediate criteria for assessing creativeness: the degree of mutual remoteness of the elements of a new combination, and the combination's usefulness. For example, a propulsion device, chair, and parachute were once quite remotely associated elements, but their combination into an ejection seat has permitted individuals to safely depart precrash, in-flight vehicles. Mednick also postulated that the probability and speed of creative solutions would be affected by the condition of the organism. One of the most salient of those conditions is the repertoire of elements available to an individual. In other words, individuals who have larger repertoires resulting from quality of preparation and experience in a content area, experience in related content areas, or even in parallel systems will have a greater availability of elements. This state of the repertoire of available elements might well be equated with an individual's level of intelligence, if quantity of information and diversity of experiences with that information can be said to reflect intelligence. If this holds, then the more intelligent the individual, the higher the probability that a creative and useful association will arise quickly.

Other conditions that may affect the association of elements into new combinations include cognitive style, the way in which an individual originally organized the associative elements, and previous or current disposition to the problem at hand or to methods of approaching problems. Organization of information refers to encoding for efficient retrieval, which may include both visual and verbal representations. Again, the more intelligent an individual is, the more likely that the encoding will make available to the individual a wider and more complex hierarchy of associations in a variety of representations from which a creative solution could be selected.

Mednick's theory led to a simple assessment device, the Remote Associates Test (RAT), which was designed to elicit creative combinations and thus measure an individual's creative potential. Mednick focused on the semantic component of associations, and the RAT depends on a semantic mode of response. The contribution of intelligence to the establishment of a rich repertoire from which creative combinations can be generated can be seen clearly.

Guilford's Divergent Production Model

Guilford, too, approached the phenomenon of creativity from a process orientation, using the operations component of his *structure-of-the-intellect* (SOI) model to examine creativity (Guilford, 1968). The relevant operation from within his SOI model that is known as "divergent production" or "divergent thinking" (Guilford, 1959) frequently has been thought of as analogous to creativity. Yet Guilford asserted that "creativity and creative productivity extend well beyond the domain of intelligence" (Guilford, 1950, p. 445). He further suggested that having the requisite abilities does not

necessarily mean results of a creative nature will be produced; the latter would depend upon the presence of specific motivational and temperamental traits. Thus, Guilford addressed the genetic aspect in intellect (ability) and personality (temperament) yet did not exclude the contribution of environment (motivational factors) to the development of such traits.

Early in his studies of creative process, Guilford (1963) attempted to demonstrate how factors of intelligence fit into the operations used in creative thinking. He maintained that typical problem-solving models (e.g., Dewey, 1933) essentially describe the same phenomenon as typical creative production paradigms do (e.g., Wallas, 1926, 1945), with comparable, parallel steps or stages. Dewey's first stage of recognition of the problem was described by Guilford as the unique intellectual ability of sensitivity to problems. Further, he pointed out that Dewey's stage of solution-suggesting is comparable to Wallas's illumination or generation of ideas; the difference is that, in the latter case, the step occurs in a highly compressed timeframe, perhaps with unusual efficiency in mental processing. Guilford described the generation of ideas, whether in Wallas's illumination stage or in Dewey's solution-suggesting stage as retrieving information to be used in new forms or with new connections. This process invokes the phenomenon of transfer, which goes beyond just recalling associations to selectively reassociating pieces of information within the memory storage and with newly encountered problems.

In Guilford's description of intellectual operations, the degree of continuity in producing associations (in which speed might be an assumed characteristic) is termed *fluency* (see Guilford, 1968, p. 125). Fluency is applied to multiple types of content—figural, semantic, symbolic—and to the complexity of associations—units, relations, systems. Within Guilford's divergent production operation, generation of ideas may exhibit greater or lesser degrees of diversity in their basic categorization, which Guilford termed *flexibility*. Flexibility in idea production describes the ability to redefine problem parameters, a condition necessary for reducing functional fixedness, and, in so doing, providing a richer array of possibilities for problem solution. Thus, fluency and flexibility represent measures of the quantity and quality of divergent production taking place. It can be assumed that fluency depends, at least in part, on the quantity of ideas available in memory, and flexibility, on the variety of ideas. Both fluency and flexibility also depend not only upon the efficiency of the mental search but also on the manner of encoding—the variety of stimulus types (verbal, visual, tactile) and the organizational efficiency of the encoding (the categorization system).

Through incorporating the divergent production process as only one of the five basic operations in intellectual activity, Guilford's theory inextricably binds intelligence and creativity. Despite this theoretical amalgam, Guilford's search for correlational data to demonstrate a relationship between creativity and intelligence using traditional IQ tests resulted in data that do not necessarily support a direct relationship (Guilford, 1968). Using a battery of divergent production tests and a group intelligence test, the California Test of Mental Maturity (CTMM), Guilford and Hoepfner found that figural divergent production factors correlated lowest with CTMM IQ and with verbal comprehension. Second, they found that symbolic and semantic divergent production factors correlated higher with both of these latter criteria. For example, the mean of correlations between the figural divergent production tests and the verbal comprehension test was .10, and with the CTMM IQ, .22; the mean of correlations between the symbolic and semantic tests and verbal comprehension was .26 and .29, respectively, and with CTMM IQ, .40 and .37, respectively (Guilford, 1968, pp. 131–133). As Guilford pointed out, because the intelligence test reflects great complexity and thus has more sources of variance, using a limited *type* of divergent production test can greatly affect the resulting correlation. Further, Guilford stated that scatterplots developed from their data (see Guilford, 1968, pp. 132–134) vividly demonstrate that low-IQ individuals do not show high divergent production scores, whereas high-IQ individuals exhibit a wide range of divergent production scores. (This issue will be discussed further in the section ''Problems of Restricted Range in Studies of Creativity and Intelligence.'') From the theoretical foundations of Guilford's SOI model, it could be expected that the low-IQ individual (assessed on whatever intelligence measure) would lack the available quantity and quality of stored ideas to be either fluent or flexible. If efficiency of mental processing reflects intelligence, as previously assumed, retrieval of ideas and complex transference also would be lacking in low-IQ individuals. Likewise, it could be expected that, with increased intelligence, divergent production would access an increasingly wider

repertoire of ideas from which to retrieve, compare, combine, and transfer. In either case, in assessment, the more specific the divergent production test (i.e., semantic, figural, and symbolic content, and the units, relations, and systems products), the less likely will be a tight relationship with a broader based, general intelligence test.

It may be that theories generated to explain the creative and intelligence processes have not been matched with an appropriate system of verification, considering that reliance for verification has been on the interpretation of analyses from statistical procedures that confound rather than unravel the theories. Nevertheless, in Guilford's theory, intelligence appears not only to contribute to creative ability, but creativity is actually one form of the process of intelligence.

Torrance's Scientific View of Creative Process

''I defined creativity as the process of becoming sensitive to problems, deficiencies, gaps in knowledge, missing elements, disharmonies, and so on; identifying the difficult; searching for solutions, making guesses, or formulating hypotheses and possibly modifying them and retesting them; and finally communicating the results'' (Torrance, 1967, pp. 73–74). Thus, Guilford's (1963) elaboration of the unique intellectual ability of sensitivity to problems as Dewey's first stage of problem recognition has also become the cornerstone of Torrance's definition. In generating this definition for creativity, Torrance set the stage for an objective observation of an elusive process. It also provided a foundation from which to study the personal and environmental factors that facilitate or inhibit creative process. In reflecting on his definition, Torrance commented that some find it too loosely constrained, while others find it too narrowly oriented to scientific process to the exclusion of artistic endeavors. However, the definition was an attempt to find an area of focus in creativity that would be productive in helping scientists and lay people alike better understand the phenomenon.

Toward that end, Torrance's definition suggests, though does not specify, a relationship between creativity and intelligence. It fits closely Spearman's ideas (1930) about mental creativity as the power to transfer relations and generate new correlates and Newell, Shaw, and Simon's (1962) definition of creative problem solving. In each case, the focus is on process, that is, the use of particular mental abilities applied to some specific content in order to accomplish an end not previously in place.

Torrance's methods of assessment of creative potential, especially the figural and verbal forms of Torrance's Tests of Creative Thinking (1966), emphasized (as in Guilford's theory described earlier) the ability to generate many new ideas (fluency) that are unusual (originality) and represent a variety of categories (flexibility), as well as the ability to embellish the ideas (elaboration). This approach would seem to reflect Mednick's association hierarchy, and Guilford's divergent production strand of intelligence, more than a "sensitivity to problems and gaps in knowledge." However, Torrance's philosophical perspective suggests that ability represented in the listed behaviors will be applied with increasing frequency or transferred to any of the phases of problem solving. Torrance's approach to creativity and its implications for the transference of behaviors to multiple situations thus reflects an intrinsic inclusion of intelligence in creativity.

Creative Capacity, Constellation of Traits, and Their Application

The crux of the problem of defining creativity may lie in our seeming inability to separate the individual from the process, and the process from its application; that is, do we define creativity as the "things" one does, or as the ability to do them given the right conditions and circumstances, an ability that cannot be determined until the behavior is exhibited? Ausubel (1978), in fact, attributed confusion in our conceptualization of creativity to the failure to separate creativity as a trait (or cluster of traits) from the individual who possesses these traits to a singularly high degree. This may be compared to the difficulty in separating intelligence as a broad set of *characteristic behaviors* from the person who possesses these behaviors. But let us delay a discussion of this difficulty to address more immediately the process/application entanglement.

Ausubel (1978) maintained that semantic, if not theoretical, confusion results from a failure to distinguish "between creativity as a highly particularized and substantive capacity . . . a manifestation of talent in a particular field of endeavor [and] as a general constellation of supportive intellectual abilities, personality variables, and problem-solving traits" (p. 180). Ausubel's argument exemplifies the lack of separation of individual from process and process from application. He used

"manifestation of talent in a field of endeavor" to describe the process applied as well as the resulting product; "constellation of supportive intellectual abilities" describes the individual's internal "environment" from which the process emanated. In the former, we infer creativity based upon judgment of observed products (i.e., manifestation of talent). In the latter, supposedly, we must infer creativity based on observation of multiple behaviors (i.e., abilities, personality variables, problem-solving *traits*), across multiple situations. Thus, when Ausubel describes creativity as a "particularized substantive capacity" versus creative abilities that are "supportive intellectual-personality functions," we are faced with a recurrent dilemma of observability and measurement. How can capacity be separated from function, the capability to act from the act by which we may infer the capability? However, Ausubel suggested that a truly creative product only arises when the general constellation of supportive abilities is of such breadth and depth as to be manifested in a particularly rare and outstanding way. Is creativity's manifestation a question then of degree of breadth and depth of abilities to exhibit function (i.e., process)? Ausubel provided an answer to this (one already attributed to Anastasi & Schaefer, 1971, and to Eisner, 1965), when he said "Assessments of creative potentiality can only be based on expert judgments of actual work products, *suitably tempered by considerations of age and experience*" [italics added] (Ausubel, 1978, p. 181). We have thus returned to a focus on *application of the process* by which a judgment of the ability or capacity of the individual to deliver the process can be made. Apparently, not only must we return to process, but we must also consider the application of the process relative to what it might be, "tempered by . . . age and experience."

Ausubel (1978) saw confounding in yet another situation, resulting from discrepancies between cognitive trait data and assessment of ability data. He pointed out that cognitive traits associated with creativity (i.e., supportive of creativity) have been shown to correlate just as highly with intelligence as they do among each other, citing studies such as Anastasi and Schaefer (1971), Crockenberg (1972), and Getzels and Jackson (1962). Yet divergent thinking scores tend to correlate only moderately with measures of intelligence. The identified cognitive traits might then contribute but not be the sole support for creative expression, and/or they might contribute but not be sole support for intelligent behavior. Although Ausubel (1978) postulated that a minimal degree of intelligence is necessary for individual creative actualization, he balked at the idea that a relationship with creativity exists throughout the continuum of intelligence.

Using traits and personality variables to define and examine creativity has been a part of the approach of others as well. In their 1965 study, Wallach and Kogan identified a number of personality variables that appeared to characterize the individuals in their study (151 middle-class fifth graders) when they were grouped according to their intelligence and creativity. The continuum of intelligence in this sample represented a limited range and especially did not represent the lower end of the continuum. The type of characteristics derived included such things as high-creative–high-intelligent individuals exhibiting a minimal anxiety level, "as if they were bursting through the typical behavioral molds that the society has constructed" (Wallach & Kogan, 1972, p. 213). High-intelligent–low-creative individuals exhibited unwillingness to take chances, fear of errors, and reliance on conventional responses and were not disruptive but were aloof from peers. Both of these groups shared strong capacities for concentration on academic work and long attention span. Low-intelligent–high-creative individuals were least able to concentrate and maintain attention, were socially isolated, behaved disruptively, and possessed the lowest self-esteem. And finally, low-intelligent–low-creative individuals, who functioned better in the classroom than their highly creative counterparts in intelligence, showed the weakest aesthetic sensitivity. The personality traits associated with creativity thus appear to reflect a significant interaction with intelligence level, or at least with the way in which individuals of different intelligence levels are able to function.

More recently, Sternberg (1986) also addressed interactive effects on performance between the traits of creativity and those of intelligence. In his frequently described student typology, he specified that Student Alice does not have *synthetic* abilities and described Student Barbara as having been recommended as a tremendously creative woman with the ability to generate and follow through on creative ideas producing important research. Thus, we have a temporary definition for creativity, that is, synthetic ability, and a measure of it, that is, completed work based on new ideas or approaches. Elaborating his triarchic componential theory, Sternberg described the three basic processes of intelligent behavior—metaprocesses, performance,

and knowledge-acquisition processes. "Metaprocesses are used to plan, monitor, and evaluate one's problem solving . . . knowledge-acquisition processes are used to figure out how to solve the problems in the first place" (Sternberg, 1986, p. 145). Thus, if creativity is equated with qualitative problem solving, then both the metaprocesses and knowledge-acquisition processes represent creative behavior at some level of response. Sternberg suggested that conventional intelligence tests measure the metaprocesses directly (planning, monitoring, and evaluating one's strategies in solving posed problems) and knowledge-acquisition processes indirectly through measuring *past* effectiveness of acquisition of knowledge. It should be noted that there are inadequacies in the tests (the problems may not be as complex nor as practical as those faced in real life). Further, the tests cannot measure the effectiveness of the knowledge-acquisition processes of a child who has not had the opportunity to apply them in his or her environment on the type of material typical of intelligence tests. Synthetic abilities (as defined by Sternberg, 1986), then, are not assessed in conventional tests, and available creativity tests do not measure creativity at the level needed for significant intellectual contributions. However, Sternberg suggested that they probably do as good a job of predicting creativity in the artificial setting as intelligence tests do in the artificial setting of academia. We must therefore look for prediction of future creative behaviors to past manifestations of such behavior, that is, to products or observable accomplishments. With this conclusion, are we really making a leap in understanding or only digging a deeper hole?

A Synthesis: Intelligence as an Element of Creative Process

Varied views on the nature of creativity have been presented and the contribution to each of intelligence as a different *facet* of mental functioning, rather than a different phenomenon, has been discussed. Although a relationship between creativity and intelligence is evident, and commonalities apparent, differences in perspective hinder agreement on the relationship as one of "universal mutual origin," or even mutual purpose. For example, in Mednick's view, assessment involves creative responses that are essentially semantic in nature, an almost sure link with intelligence as we have known it. However, through focusing on the semantic component of associations and depending on the semantic mode of response, other forms of stored information that might be more typically associated with creative endeavor, such as the figural, images, or even kinesthetic patterns, may be ignored. From the standpoint of creative talent and development, another problem surfaces. The test ignores the individual's disposition to the specific problems, that is, his or her particular experiences with and interest in the problems presented for response. Individual differences in prior conditions available to the problem solver and familiarity or experience with the particular domain of terms included in the test also are not taken into account. Assessment depends on the individual's ability to generate uncommon associations based on a current store of knowledge and experience, even though this measure of fluency in divergent production may not be generalizable to situations in the individual's occupation or practical living conditions.

A statistical relationship, or lack of it, between *measures* of creativity and *measures* of intelligence, or between these measures and other characteristics of the individuals studied, frequently has been viewed as definitive evidence. Wallach and Kogan posed the thesis that such proof shows differences in cognitive capacity between creative individuals and intelligent individuals. The evidence takes a strange turn when the results focus on social and motivational differences (as discussed in the previous section) rather than on the actual cognitive processes, the social and motivational differences that have long been associated with failure to succeed in relation to peers. Capacity to perform might be inferred but the ability of these findings to distinguish a difference in capacity for creativity versus capacity for intelligence does not seem logically sound.

Comparisons also have been based on (a) the presence of specific, intact characteristics or clusters of traits and personality variables, used to infer capacity in individuals, (b) the expression of both creative and intelligent *process* by individuals, and (c) *products*, as in academic achievement, resulting from the application of the processes. Unfortunately, comparisons of intelligence with creativity often have been made that confound person, process, and product. For example, a process variable for creativity, such as divergent thinking, may be correlated with a product variable for intelligence, such as academic achievement. Several investigators (Getzels & Jackson, 1959, 1962; Torrance, 1960; Yamamoto, 1964a,b,c) have found correlations between Guilford-type and Torrance-type creativity tests with academic achievement, comparable to those found with intelligence test scores. However, Ausubel (1978, p. 184) asserted that it is "quite unlikely that creativity should be related to academic achievement, inasmuch as mastery of a given subject-matter discipline does *not* in any way presuppose conspicuous capacity for making original or creative contributions to that discipline." Additional confounding occurs when the expression of a specific process appears to be product-oriented yet lacks the essential integrity of a product; for example, assessment of creative potential based on the total number (fluency of responses) and uniqueness (originality of responses) of relevant associations (simulated product) in an *artificially defined* situation (Wallach & Kogan, 1965).

Contemporary theories of *intelligence* suggest similar problems of definition and measurement, as well as difficulties in extracting the process from its application or endproduct and the individual from the process. An even more informative parallel with these contemporary theories (already alluded to in the discussion of Mednick's association hierarchy) is the idea that context, age, and experience always must be taken into account when attempting to assess the presence of intelligence through application of the process; or when predicting the capacity of the individual to function in an intelligent way based on fragmented expressions of intelligence.

In fact, according to Sternberg and Davidson's theory of insight and problem solving (Sternberg & Davidson, 1983), or to deBono's theory of lateral thinking (deBono, 1971), creative problem solution entails selective combination of seemingly isolated pieces of information for creative associations, or seemingly illogical combinations, associations that, once examined, create breakthroughs in thinking about a problem. Further, these theories suggest that selective comparison of new problem situations to old bits of information or associations can become the extraordinary insights of creative problem solving. Whether Sternberg and Davidson considered these processes characteristic of creative behavior or of intelligent behavior is not clear, but, in either case, their studies indicated that a relationship between intelligence (assessed through group intelligence tests) and the various insight abilities is a positive one. Thus, the greater the intelligence, the greater the likelihood that individuals will employ spontaneously the selective comparison and combination (insights) necessary to solve insight problems.

There seems no doubt that intelligence is an element of the creative process. But is creativity as important an element of intelligence as it has been defined by various theoreticians? We continue with our examination of these phenomena, or the integrated phenomenon, as the case may be.

Creativity as a Component in Theories and Assessment of Intelligence

Intelligence as a hypothetical construct has been aptly described by Conger (1957) as a "scientific fiction" invented to help explain and predict behavior. Psychologists from Cattell to Wechsler to the present day have focused in various ways on three themes or components of this scientific fiction: capacity to act purposefully, that is, to learn or change one's behavior based on experiences; ability to think rationally and abstractly; and the ability to respond effectively to new situations in one's environment. Much earlier, however, Thorndike (1921) viewed this hypothetical construct in a more concrete way as facility in manipulating objects, in the use of symbols, and in interacting with other human beings. Remnants of these three themes may be found in each of the current views of intelligence. Through these themes the groundwork was laid for a translation of theoretical construct into observable and measurable behaviors. Notwithstanding this simplified thematic context and simplicity of measurement possibilities, four distinctly different theoretical approaches to understanding and measurement of intelligence have arisen (Maloney & Ward, 1976). Each places differential emphasis on the three possible themes and each has generated different methods for measurement. The four general approaches can be classified as learning, neurological-biological, psychometric, and developmental. We briefly describe, in turn, each general approach to intelligence, focusing on how the creative process is addressed in each. The purpose of this examination of a sample of available theories is to demonstrate that perspectives on intelligence typically have included creative process, whether or not it was labelled as such. (Some of these approaches, such as the developmental and psychometric, are addressed at length in other chapters of this handbook. They are included here in order to develop a point regarding the relationship of creativity with intelligence.)

Learning Theory

Classical learning theory focuses exclusively on process, and intelligence becomes "learning process functioning at its optimal level under appropriate situational conditions and satisfying some external value-type criteria not inherent in the behavior itself" (Maloney & Ward, 1976, p. 176). Learning theory claims to have the least use for individual characteristics, ignoring hereditary capacity in its consideration of what behaviors the individual emits and the circumstances under which those behaviors occur.

From this perspective, Thorndike (1926) focused on associations or connections as the "accumulation" of intelligence, in which greater intelligence occurs when a larger number of connections have been made. If creative production may be considered the result of accessing the more remote associations in one's mental storage (Mednick, 1962), then we can begin to see a tenuous notion of creativity and intelligence as having a common origin. One can further see the role a wide variety of prior learning experiences might play in establishing the vast and diverse hierarchy from which unique associations could be generated.

The influence of classical learning theory in the consideration of creativity may also be seen in the role of behavior modification in expanding originality in responses and creative production in problem solving. Studies by Brigham, Graubard, and Stans (1972), Goetz and Baer (1973), Glover and Gary (1976), Glover and Sautter (1977), Haensly (1979), Locurto (1974), Maltzman (1960), Nash (1975), Wallach and Kogan (1965), and others have focused on various ways to successfully modify stimuli for eliciting creative responses and increasing frequency of responses and their quality or originality.

Neurological-Biological Theory

The neurological-biological approach to intelligence seeks to understand behavior and the parameters that influence or determine behavior through looking for relationships within the underlying neurological system, its anatomy and physiology (Maloney & Ward, 1976). Attempts to verify earlier versions of this theory focused on trying to locate specific areas of the brain devoted to memory, reasoning, and judgment. In this approach, behavioral correlates of neuroanatomical and neurophysiological functioning are assessed.

Perhaps the most successful of these efforts was that of Broca who established the presence of a speech center in the posterior portion of the left frontal lobe of the brain. However, principles of mass action and equipotentiality formulated by Lashley (Maloney & Ward, 1976, p. 180), contradicted the efforts of those trying to localize specific functions in specific areas of the brain. This controversy continues to be addressed in research on hemispheric lateralization of the brain for abilities ranging from spatial to language expression and reading comprehension and from musical reception to mathematical abstraction (Gardner, 1983). This category of theory has been distinguished by Hebb's (1972) ideas on intelligence A and B and by Cattell's (1963b) theory of fluid and crystallized intelligence, referring, respectively, to innate biological capacity and to experience with the environment. The biological contribution in these latter theories refers to the intactness and efficiency of the nervous system.

Recent theories in this category have focused on the integrative functions within the brain and of the brain and nervous system, on the biochemical aspects within the brain and at the nerve endings, as well as on the measurable excitations of specific areas of the brain in response to specific types of tasks. Though perhaps difficult, it is not impossible to conceive of creativity and intelligence as differentiated either in chemical constituency or in area of cerebral localization.

A nebulous reference to creative production might be suggested for Hebb's intelligence A, with the assumption that biological capacity is related to problem-solving abilities, and for Cattell's fluid intelligence, with the assumption that untutored ability would represent the raw material of creative as well as intelligent responses. In this latter case, experiences with the environment could enhance creative responses only if the experiences did not overwhelmingly reinforce mundane responses.

Psychometric Theories

Psychometric theories view intelligence as a pattern of particularly adaptive abilities. Individuals differ in the specificity and extent of their abilities. With few exceptions these theories have arisen from data gathered on individual differences in abilities. Spearman's two-factor theory (1927), Thurstone's multiple-factor theory (1931), and hierarchical models with a general factor at the apex of the pyramid and specific factors breaking out from the general are models that depict a common origin for general mental functioning. These theories were devised to explain observed patterns of differences among individuals, particularly groups of individuals. They have been the product of two specific mathematical and statistical organizations of data, correlations, and their derivative procedure, factor analysis. Factor analysis by itself cannot provide answers about theoretical conceptions of intelligence. Interpretations must be developed for the observed relationships among specific abilities determined through correlations of performance on different types of tasks. These interpretations become quite critical as the statistical procedure becomes more detailed and complex in factor analysis. Frequently, several interpretations appear equally viable in explaining the data. Further, the origin of the data (i.e., the subject population from which the data are gathered) and its homogeneity or heterogeneity (sample selectivity) may greatly alter the results, as does the choice of variables for inclusion in the analysis.

Although two of the most frequently applied psychometric assessments of intelligence—the Binet and Wechsler scales—were constructed to sample a variety of intellectual abilities and are thus somewhat conceptually related to the multiple factor hypothesis (Maloney & Ward, 1976), their reliance on a single index would imply an assessment of the ''g'' or general factor. Nevertheless, the single quantitative index does not fit well with the factor approach, and the tests are a theoretically complex mix of such factors. Psychometric theory, which is basically qualitative in explanation (based on observed patterns of performance), does not seem to be represented well by these basically quantitative tests that result in an intelligence quotient. Current psychometric conceptualization continues to lean toward multiple factors, the number lying somewhere between the unacceptable extremes of too few (Spearman) and too cumbersome (Guilford). Interestingly enough, Gardner (1983), who professes extreme opposition to the psychometric ''IQ,'' has promoted a neurobiological theory that distinctly focuses on factors similar to those suggested by Thurstone.

Now, given these hedges, does creativity have a place in psychometric theories of intelligence? Since creativity and creative production are not exclusive to any content or domain and conceivably can encompass all manner of performance, it would seem inappropriate to assign it one specific ability slot in one of the factor theories. Vernon's model (1950) postulated two major group factors (verbal-numerical-educational and practical-mechanical-spatial-physical), one of which may be more function-oriented and the other content-oriented; creative production might find its niche in such a function-oriented factor. Within IQ tests themselves, little if any allowance has been made for divergent types of response; in fact, correctness in response is the mode. Yet the abilities assessed form the foundation from which creative endeavor must arise.

Although Guilford's theory falls into the psychometric category because it purported to measure individual differences in ability through performance, it is a reversal of typical approaches in that a *theory* of intelligence preceded the gathering of data for its verification. Most relevant to this discussion, it assigned creative function as one of the five types of mental operations, specifically, divergent thinking or divergent production (as described in a previous section of this chapter). This operation can take place with any of the four types of content, at any of the six increasingly complex levels of products. However, a problem arises in an exclusive assignment of creativity to the divergent production operation. Unless cognition is present, no content is available for memory. Unless memory is available, divergent production would be limited to responses in cases immediately at hand, and, without evaluation, divergent production cannot be usefully directed to form a creative contribution. Thus, we see that an intricate integration of operations must take place for divergent production to be realized as creativity. Such integration seems to reflect Sternberg's "synthetic ability" (Sternberg, 1986) —application of metaprocesses to knowledge-acquisition and performance processes. As in other assessments stemming from Guilford's theory, we must conclude that it is the *pattern* of integration that provides diversity among responses and among individuals. Even though various levels of the different types of operations might contribute to effective functioning, some minimal levels of each would be imperative. Creative genius would occur as each of the operations found its optimal balance for a particular content, operating on one of the six possible levels of products, in response to a particular environment with its specific demands, and criteria or qualifications.

Developmental Theory

Intelligence in the developmental perspective is conceptualized as action—dynamic, epigenetic, and ontogenetic—represented by mental organizational structures that change with maturation and experience. The third of the three all-purpose themes for the intelligence construct, the ability to respond effectively to new situations in one's environment, seems to dominate this perspective. Adaptation of the individual to the environment is the goal of intellectual activity, as it is the goal of all biological organisms.

Epistemological orientation, or emphasis on the genesis and growth of knowledge in the individual, is reflected in, for example, Piaget's concept of schema and his principles of assimilation, accommodation, and equilibration. Piaget emphasized that these internal organizational processes are available to all, and the focus is on universality rather than individuality. Intelligence is not only quantitatively different, at different ages, but also qualitatively different, and the age-related stages are sequential and hierarchical; that is, organizational processes or mental structures available to the individual are different at infancy than at adolescence. They are different in type of stimulus that activates response and different in type or mode of response generated, with each new stage interfacing with the structures or knowledge of the previous stage and, in this way, adding to the complexity of understanding.

Maloney and Ward (1976) suggested that these psychological structures have a neurological analogue. This possibility lends credence to Piaget's position that stage development is limited by neurological development; thus, maturation would exert an effect on capacity and performance. According to Piagetian perspective, individuals may differ in the rate at which they accomplish the conceptualization characteristic of a particular stage and, likewise, not all individuals will necessarily attain the highest stages. A critical element in the rate difference is the environment, with the individual dependent upon the appropriateness and richness of environmental experiences for optimization of knowledge growth and stage attainment. However, even with the richest environmental experiences, individuals would be limited in stage attainment by age-related neurological development. In practice, a few individuals with extraordinary mental capacity transcend these ordinary maturational limitations. Neo-Piagetian perspective (e.g., Case, 1978; Pasquale-Leone, 1970) proposed that some of such limitations have to do with the mental capacity available for processing increasing quantities of information. This perspective opens up the possibility that strategy awareness, training, or task simplification might permit responses not thought possible under strict Piagetian perspective.

From a developmental perspective, then, multiple creative possibilities exist in the schemata each individual constructs from his or her particularly unique interaction with the environment. Carrying this further, the concept of generative processing (Wittrock, 1974) proposes that, at any point in one's epistemological development, construction of knowledge is based on quantity and quality of one's prior, specifically individual experience. Therefore, no two individuals can have exactly the same construction and/or understanding of any concept, nor are they likely to have exactly the same view of events, persons, places, and things. Uniqueness becomes available to everyone. The quality of original ideas will greatly depend upon the appropriateness or "fit" with the understanding of others in the population. In turn, this may depend upon the extent to which an individual has developed related schemata, based on reliable experiences. The application of unique perspectives will depend upon the individual's problem-solving strategies (which will also evolve via the process described above) and on the opportunities for applying them—being in the opportune place at the opportune time.

The possibility of a contribution of creativity to intelligence from the developmental perspective becomes much more evident upon examination of Csikszentmihalyi and Robinson's (1986) elaboration of the time lines in development of talent. These authors superimposed Erikson's life-span transitions on Piaget's stages of cognitive development along with a time line for progression in a particular domain and in a particular field of endeavor. The latter two time lines may depend upon maturational factors, but even more importantly on the presence of appropriate training experiences at the most opportune intersects with cognitive and personality development. Further, the evolvement of an acknowledged creative contribution will depend upon its intersection with an appropriate and accepting audience at a time that will take maximum advantage of the individual's readiness and inclination to produce the creative contribution. Thus, outstanding creative contributions, generated to resolve problems, will occur when specific abilities have *coalesced* in a relevant *context,* and are emitted with sufficient quality, intensity, and duration (Haensly *et al.,* 1986).

A Synthesis: Integration of Creative Process with Intelligence

As stated earlier, the purpose of an examination of basic approaches to intelligence was to demonstrate that perspectives of intelligence do include or assume creative process as integral to intelligence, even when creative process is not so labeled.

In summary, classical learning theory appears not to distinguish between an intelligent and a creative response, viewing responses in general as observable and measurable behaviors, elicited and reinforced by attendant stimuli. On the other hand, neurological-biological theory may be seen as the most elusive of the four described approaches, yet the most promising for future investigation. Through microanalyses of physiological and anatomical correlates of behavior, the possibilities of differentiating the biochemical state in creative process from that in intelligent process, especially with relationship to antecedent conditions for the responses, is well within the realm of consideration. However, as of now, localization of response to specific content or domains of knowledge appears to have been the most productive application of this approach.

Despite bias regarding intelligence testing and its assumed exclusion of creative potential, psychometric theory provides an avenue for explaining the complementary nature of creativity and intelligence. However, it is developmental theory that appears most clearly suited to explanation of the mutual origin of creativity and intelligence in mental function, the interrelatedness of creative and intelligent responses within that function, and the reasonableness of universal goal-oriented adaptation. This adaptation is accomplished through appropriate application, timing, and intermingling of intelligent responses (planning, executing, and monitoring) and creative responses (extending beyond previously derived solutions to novel and useful ones).

Before proceeding to further elaboration of the

nature of an integrated relationship between creativity and intelligence as elements of a unitary phenomenon, we discuss a recurring barrier to such a view, a barrier resulting from interpretation of restricted-range studies.

Problems of Restricted Range in Studies of Creativity and Intelligence

Data accumulated from studies of the relationship between assessed creativity and intelligence have lent support to the idea that creativity *does* represent a function distinctly different from intelligence. In these studies, correlations between creativity and intelligence have often differed significantly between low or moderate levels of intelligence and high levels of intelligence. Some of these studies examined a restricted range of intellectual ability. Others focused on criteria of creativity that limited the options for creative response for particular subjects with specific backgrounds and thus may have wrongfully identified them as noncreative. Using a sample of relevant studies, problems arising from interpretation of this type of limited-range data are discussed in the following section. Interpretations of restricted-range data based on the idea of conceptual differences between creativity and intelligence will be described. The discussion will center, however, on alternative interpretations of statistical differences at low- and high-IQ levels.

Limited Range in Intellectual Ability

In a study designed to partially replicate with elementary, high school, and graduate school students the Getzels and Jackson 1958 study, Torrance (1962) found that a significant portion of students identified as most highly creative (upper 20%) on his battery of creative-thinking tasks (the Minnesota Tests of Creative Thinking) also were identified as most highly intelligent (upper 20%) on a variety of individual and group intelligence measures. Yet the overall correlations between creativity scores and intelligence were less than moderate, the highest, .32, in a sample where intelligence was assessed with the Otis Quick-Scoring Test of Intelligence. Among five samples of elementary school children, this overlapping highly creative-highly intelligent group comprised from 25% to 41% of the total sample; in a high school

sample of 272, 52% were among the top 20% in both creativity and intelligence as measured with the Lorge Thorndike Verbal Battery, a phenomenon Torrance attributed to the distribution of talent in this school or to the nature of the particular measure of intelligence used.

For comparison, however, the highly creative group (who did *not* rank in the upper 20% in intelligence) were contrasted on achievement measures with the highly intelligent group (who did *not* rank in the upper 20% on creative thinking). Using the Iowa Basic Skills Battery as criterion for achievement, the highly intelligent group consistently (but slightly) outscored the highly creative group, though the difference was not statistically significant in most samples. Torrance considered this evidence supportive of the Getzels and Jackson 1958 data and suggested that it also validated the Tests of Creative Thinking as measures of factors other than intelligence. He alluded to the possibility that the mental abilities sampled in measures of IQ may be more useful in certain kinds of achievement, whereas the creative-thinking abilities may be more useful in other kinds of achievement. Differences in the mean of intelligence between the highly creative and the highly intelligent group, a statistically significant difference in each sample, were further suggested as supporting a distinction between creative ability and intelligence. However, a difference in mean of intelligence between these two groups had to exist by virtue of the way in which the groups were comprised, with the most highly intelligent creatives eliminated from the comparison group just as the most highly creative intelligent individuals were eliminated from the intelligence comparison group. The results appear to support more appropriately the contention that a high degree of intelligence is more likely to be associated with a high degree of creativity, whereas at the same time, creative responses may be associated with intelligent responses at any level of either mode.

Using performance on the Remote Associates Test (RAT) (Mednick, 1962) as measure of creativity and the Scholastic Aptitude Tests of Verbal Ability (SAT-V), Mednick and Andrews (1967) found intelligence moderately related to creative ability in college populations, $r = .43$. Among 1,211 University of Michigan freshman, there was a slight tendency for the relationship to increase as the level of intelligence increased (from .09 to .19 over the six increments of SAT-V scores from minimal to maximal). Mednick and Andrews (1967) found no support for the suggestion that creativity and intelligence are more closely related at lower levels of intelligence, and that they are relatively independent processes among the brightest students. In this same data sample, the relationship between the SAT-Math scores and the RAT remained negligible across the same range, varying from .03 to .08, with an overall correlation of .20, as might be expected when using a verbal measure of creativity to correlate with an intelligence test focused on mathematics.

Guilford and Christensen (1973) used a divergent production (DP) battery of tests to demonstrate that a triangular scatter plot of the relationship between IQ and creative potential would be found more often than an elliptical scatter plot. These authors pointed out that the IQ as usually assessed probably represents most strongly semantic or verbal information. They hypothesized that, consequently, semantic divergent production tests would be more likely candidates for demonstrating the triangular type of relationship, with an elliptical relationship when visual-figural tests were used. As hypothesized, their data supported triangular scatter plots for semantic-DP tests and the more usual elliptical form for visual-figural DP tests. The data were obtained in a study of six groups of 40 to 95 children in each case, grades 4, 5, and 6, groups from which children with a Stanford-Binet IQ of 130 (California "gifted") or higher had been removed. The resulting triangular plots showed a continuous gradual shift in divergent production from low to high IQ with no breaks at any IQ level. Guilford and Christensen (1973) interpreted these findings to demonstrate that "the higher the IQ, the more likely we are to find at least some individuals with high creative potential" (p. 251). They further stated that their evidence does not support the threshold hypothesis regarding absence of relationship between IQ and creative potential above a critical IQ level, such as 120.

Guilford (1967) again emphasized the lack of correlation between creativity and intelligence at the upper end of the creativity range as he described the results of studies by Roe (1952), MacKinnon, Barron and associates (MacKinnon, 1960), and others. Scientists, writers, architects and mathematicians with an observable record of creative accomplishment do not appear to exhibit a verifiable statistical corelationship between creativity and intelligence—"the relation of creative potential and creative production to the traditional IQ has been found close to zero *where groups of superior IQ are*

concerned" [italics added] (Guilford, 1967, p. 9). However, when considering a wide range of IQ, for example, from 62 to 150, the relationship is substantial in the lower and middle area, but less strong at the upper end. Although Guilford suggested that IQ sets an upper limit on creative potential, other explanations should be considered. First, we may not have sophisticated or precise enough instruments to differentiate levels of creativity at its upper range. Second, limiting description to a linear model also may limit our understanding of the relationship. It may be that as the information base (intelligence) expands and an ever widening variety of possible responses becomes available, the type of intelligence tests and creativity tests must become more diversified as well. Guilford's emphasis on the importance of "transfer recall" (Guilford, 1967), or transformation in the understanding of insight within creative thinking, points to multidimensionality to explain the existing relationship. It very well may be necessary to use a three-dimensional model to demonstrate the corelationship of creativity with intelligence, especially to accommodate the upper end of the continuum.

Multiple Criteria for Assessing Creativity

Owens (1972) introduced a different type of concern into the creativity–intelligence question with regard to restricted range. In contrast to sampling only a portion of the *distribution of intelligence,* Owens referred to the limited range of *types of creative response* or application included in studies that focus on a specific field, such as psychology, architecture, mathematics. Thus, in Owens's study of research and development engineers, the type of creative response that may most frequently be expressed in relationship to the creativity criterion for engineers would be invention. Invention does not really represent the range of creative responses that might exist across other fields or occupations. As a matter of fact, in his study, Owens found that, in machine design, a specific, highly structured test with multiple definers for the product was a better predictor of creativity than a general ability test.

Whether the measures used to assess individual creativity actually possess criterion-related (construct) validity long has been a controversial issue and is addressed at length in another chapter of this volume. The following remarks specifically apply to the topic of restricted range. Dellas and Gaier (1970) addressed this issue citing MacKinnon's (1961) study of architects, in which the Guilford tests did not correlate highly with expert-peer judgment of the architects' creativity; Gough's (1961) data on the creativity of peer-rated research scientists exhibited low and even negligible correlations with the Guilford tests of Unusual Uses, Consequences, and Gestalt Transformations; Bittel's (1964) findings showed little relationship between measures of divergent thinking and performance in art; and Skager, Klein, and Schultz's (1967) study of artistic achievement at a school of design yielded inconsistent results. However, Barron (1963) found contradictory results using the Guilford tests with Air Force officers and Elliott (1964) with public relations personnel. As Dellas and Gaier (1970) pointed out, the criteria used for individual creativity nominations and judgments are a critical factor in whether or not the assessment measures can be expected to relate with the identifiers used in the practical applications of a particular field or occupation. The semantic nature of many of the divergent production tests may provide an optimal medium for the creativity of individuals who are engaged in advertising or public relations, but a much less appropriate medium for the expression of artistic, inventive, or discovery-based talent.

Della and Gaier's (1970) position goes beyond this suggestion of inappropriately constructed measures using an irrelevant medium. They emphasized that production of creative ideas simply may be, to use a medical metaphor, the "symptom" that exhibits when inherent potential meets with an appropriate intervening environment. The intervening environment, or intermediary factors, from which creativity symptoms might arise would be the mutually reinforcing clusters of personality characteristics (such as intuitiveness, unconventionality, openness to feelings, independence, empathic capability) and motivation variables (such as attraction to unconventional types of achievement, self-actualizing need, history of reinforcement for risk-taking endeavors). Reapplying the medical metaphor, the individual may experience pain and describe it, even suggesting its presumed source, but unless the diagnosing physician also views this pain as a recognizable symptom of condition X, the individual's pain remains a personal expression of an unrecognized condition. Although creative symptoms cannot evolve from a vacuum, but from an "effective use of intelligence" (Dellas & Gaier, 1970) that prepares the information and/or skills from which the creative response emanates, neither will they evolve without the fostering factors. Thus, some intelligent individuals go beyond to produce

creative responses while others with an equal capacity for intelligence *limit* their responses to the conventional and usual. What should be added to this fostering base is an environmental responsiveness to the particular direction of symptomatic behavior, without which the symptom cannot be recognized as creative even when the producer deems it is (Haensly & Roberts, 1983). Thus, according to Dellas and Gaier (1970), "the roots of creativity do not seem to lie in convergent or divergent thinking, but rather . . . in the personality and motivational aspects of character" (p. 68). Yet the organic entity that can produce the creative response remains the individual with at least a modicum of intelligence. Nevertheless, these authors stopped short of suggesting that either the personality characteristics or motivational factors are the determining factors for identifying who will or will not be creative.

In a retrospective view of creativity investigation, Taylor (1975) listed a number of definitions and criteria of creativity, including his own, which suggest the basic concept that new ideas are involved and that what is viewed as creative at one time and in one culture may not be so viewed at another time and culture. Wade (1968), who speculated on the role of environment in fostering the child's creativity, helps us focus on the possibility that variance in quantity and quality of creative responses may be a function of factors that permit the child to go beyond basic, intelligent responses. Factors, such as psychological safety and freedom, which provide a climate where external evaluation is not restrictive, may foster imagination, inventiveness, and fantasy. Although this type of environment should have little effect on development of the processes of efficient acquisition, effective storage, and successful retrieval of information needed for intelligent responses, it is likely to have a profound effect on the production of unusual combinations, innovative ideas, or highly elaborated "creative" responses. Wade's (1968) data on 105 tenth-grade students from upper-middle-class schools resulted in a correlation of .37 between creativity (using three Guilford tests of divergent thinking) and intelligence (using the Lorge-Thorndike Verbal test). As Wade pointed out, of greater importance is the finding that "in no case did any subject scoring within the *upper twenty percent on the creativity tests score below the mean on the verbal intelligence measure*" [italics added] (Wade, 1968, p. 99). The mean intelligence score for the total group was 111.5, but the mean for the highly creative subjects was 119. Additionally, the combination of intelligence and creativity was found to explain almost twice as much of the achievement variance (grade point average) as intelligence alone, a strong indication of "cognitive overlap" and the additivity of creativity in the intelligent response (Wade, 1968).

Even though MacKinnon (1962) supported the intelligence threshold concept and denied that his sample of architects represented a restricted range of intelligence, he admitted that this sample did *not* truly represent the entire range. MacKinnon's (1962) definition of creativeness included novelty, problem solving or accomplishment of a goal, and development of the response to its fullest. Additionally, his descriptors of the creative person included "a clear preference for the complex and asymmetrical" (MacKinnon, 1962, p. 488) and disposition "to admit complexity and even disorder into their perceptions without being made anxious by the resulting chaos . . . disordered multiplicity" (p. 489).

From an information-processing paradigm, this preference for complex stimuli can be seen as setting the stage for a wider scan of stored information and for holding open the possibilities of multiple associations between bits of information evolving in novel ways. Thus, Sternberg's selective combination and selective comparison that make up insight (Sternberg & Davidson, 1983) operate upon the richest of substrates—the more complex the set of perceptions made available, the greater the probability that a novel and appropriate response can be generated to accomplish a particular goal. The intensity and persistence with which this open-ended search and combination and selection of ideas proceed will affect the quantity and quality of creative responses. We can see then that the personality characteristics of openness, acceptance of ambiguity, and flexibility make possible special access to the same store of information available to a variety of intelligent individuals. The difference in response possibilities (conventional vs. creative) can occur because of differences in personality characteristics and in the motivational attitudes. MacKinnon's reservations about the relationship of creativity and intelligence could then be handled by viewing the process of derivation of creative responses from a specialized information-processing perspective. From such a perspective, the focus would be on insight as the creative variant of a basic sequence that exhibits intelligent encoding, manipulation, and retrieval of stored information.

It would seem that MacKinnon's ideas directly focused on the idea of a well-developed intelligence as the optimal medium from which creative response can arise, whether that creative response involves a skillful and sensitive use of an artistic medium to generate an original and worthy masterpiece or whether it involves discovering a unique solution for containing nuclear radiation. Restricted range and the resulting correlations, which have led to an assumption of a threshold of intelligence for the appearance of creativity and no relationship at higher levels of intelligence, may be more of a problem of accurate statistical description than of the functional relationship between creativity and intelligence.

Most of the studies to date that show either a threshold effect in the intelligence–creativity relationship, or that the two are independent at the "upper levels," have failed to control for regression effects on one of these variables or have fallen into the fallacy of conclusions that can result from the restriction of range phenomenon. It appears for now that intelligence and creativity are related across the full range of both variables, but the precise nature of the relationship remains unclear, largely for reasons described by Brown in Chapter 1 in this volume.

The Synergistic Effect between Creativity and Intelligence

"What is needed for the understanding of the relationship between creativity and intelligence is not only data at the correlational level, but conceptual reorganization as well" (Golann, 1963, p. 560).

Jackson and Messick (1967) pointed out that performance on tests does not provide the definitive foundation for that conceptual reorganization, even when the conventional tests for intelligence have appeared to require different abilities than tests designed to measure creative ability. They described the population, so to speak, of responses that might be considered to satisfy requirements for correctness in an intelligent response, and those that could be considered to satisfy requirements for "goodness," in a creative response. Although originality or unusualness of response might result from a request for uses of a tin can (e.g., compressing the tin can to use as convenient currency), the goodness of such a response results from the fact that compression for reuse has value for the conservation of resources. Thus, the concept of usefulness, appropriateness, or value, introduced by Mednick (1962), becomes superimposed as a requirement for creativeness, to be applied to that original response; the usefulness would not apparently have to be immediate, but useful in that the response leads to other responses of value. These populations of responses, the so-called intelligent and the so-called creative, become pools that have more or less of an overlap, as in a Venn diagram. The intelligent responses outside of the area of overlap lack the quality of goodness, are correct but mundane, suffice but do not move the solution forward to greater possibilities. The creative responses that lie outside of the overlap area are original and unusual, but, in so far as they lack justification, also lack ability to move the solution forward to possibilities of value. Yet a marvelously synergistic effect takes place when the two pools overlap. As described in Webster's dictionary (1980, p. 1174), synergism occurs as the result of "the cooperative action of discrete agencies such that the total effect is greater than the sum of the effects taken independently."

Jackson and Messick (1967) reflected that these overlapping criteria may apply in the aesthetic realm as well as in the realm of thinking and logic; for example, it can be assumed that there is a wide gap between the paint smattered canvas of the child and the abstract canvas of a Picasso, even though both have applied color to background in seemingly ill-structured representations or "spatial groupings." The child's painting, though it might be unusual, may lack the direction, substance, and correctness (sophistication?) of form present in the Picasso; the "goodness" criterion can then only be bestowed in comparison with the works of others with similar degrees of background and practice. Appropriateness of the response still may be questioned, and then only those individuals who have similar mental sets, or are in tune with the thinking of the artist, may be able to make that particular judgment—individuals with quite highly developed intelligence and/or creativity in such realms as engineering, medicine, or literature may fail to see meaning in Picasso's abstract shapes or to be moved to aesthetic appreciation of them. Yet those same individuals may see those "missing" qualities in an innovatively designed bridge span or in the symmetry of an anatomical arrangement. Returning from the aesthetic to the practical, we might see a similar need for judgment by an individual with comparable background, interests, and mindset to determine

whether an unusual idea for Arctic transportation also could be considered appropriate for inclusion in the overlap of pools between intelligent and creative.

"Correctness" and "goodness of fit" are complex criteria, and judgment of test performance is much more complicated than test constructors may have realized. In his model of intelligence, Guilford (1959) included a dimension of transformations, a particular dimension that allows for or considers leaps such as described above as an analyzable mode, different from the mode that addresses material and problems within their expected realm. Transformations, then, well may create new realms, realms that now can elicit their own expectations for response. Jackson and Messick (1967) discussed the personal impact of the products in each of these cases, describing their impact as surprise to the criterion of unusualness, satisfaction to appropriateness, and stimulation (of new ideas) to transformation.

Jackson and Messick (1967) added one further criterion to the intelligence/creativity collection that, perhaps in their judgment and in ours, is the most critical of all in considering these overlapping pools of responses characterized as having correctness and those having goodness. This fourth criterion of condensation refers to the bringing together of a set of ideas in such a simple way as to produce a sense of "why didn't I ever think of that before—it is so clearly fortuitous," yet of such complexity that different viewers will not only understand its simplicity in different ways, but also will be able to expand and generate entire new sets of understandings. Thus, Jackson and Messick (1967) described the recipient's response to the performance or product as one of pondering or "savoring."

This fourth criterion of condensation, as does that of transformation, requires judgment by individuals who have a sufficient foundation of information, have personally experienced transforming of ideas or understanding and appreciation of such transformations, and have the capacity to comprehend both the simplicity and complexity of the product, that is, of the response or performance. As Gowan has suggested, sometimes such individuals may not be available until a future time. In his words, he would donate copies of his books to libraries so that "when the future caught up with my thinking, it would be there" (Haensly & Roberts, 1983, p. 11). Actually, we may have few individuals who are prepared to make such judgments on the individual intelligence and/or creativity of many test performance responses. Such judgment presumes individuals do and will always exist who have equal or greater capacity than the test respondent.

Perhaps the most enlightening suggestion of Jackson and Messick's model (1967) is the idea that test performance or product formation is the element upon which assessment of intelligence and/or creativity must be applied, rather than upon the individual. This idea, however, is so obvious that critics must quickly respond "But of course, that was always the intention of intelligence tests, of creativity tests, to assess responses and thus categorize the individual as intelligent, as creative, or as both." Nevertheless, the entire body of research on the characteristics of creative individuals is predicated on the idea of defining clusters of traits that permit us to label an individual as intelligent or as creative. From this model, however, the personal characteristics, such as openmindedness, reflectiveness, spontaneity, playfulness, inconsistency, intuitiveness, sensitivity, and flexibility, can be seen to facilitate the *responses* that combine unusualness versus commonality with appropriateness versus lack of fit, transformation versus retaining a traditional or accepted form, and condensation versus ambiguous complexity or incorrect simplicity. These are the response characteristics that differentiate whether the response falls in the correctness pool, the unique idea pool, or the overlapping pool of ideas that transcend simple correctness and novelty.

Integration: A Model for Creativity and Intelligence

Wallach (1985) stated that "creativity may be best understood as what constitutes the work done at the cutting edge of a given field by those who have mastered it" (p. 117). Identification of such individuals remains a legitimate goal. In his Walter Bingham Lecture, MacKinnon (1962) referred to the loss to individuals and to society when individuals do not recognize their own possibilities for creative response and when environments fail to nourish or respond positively to creative expression.

In our examination of the relationship between creativity and intelligence, we have made an assumption that creativity is a phenomenon analyzable within a rational framework. In fact, we have avoided, for the most part, the humanistic and psychoanalytic perspectives of creativity which view it as the result of internal self-actualizing forces, or as a function of the subconscious shaped by elements of personality outside of the realm of individual control. We submit that, in so doing, we may be overlooking important qualities of creativity, ones that could contribute to its extraordinariness, uniqueness, and even mysteriousness.

Attempting to determine *how much* intelligence is associated with *how much* creativity would appear to be an exercise in small views of the universe of mental capability. Creativity and intelligence are an interrelated process and we propose that the intelligent response, at whatever level the individual is capable of, produces the ordinary, while the creative response lifts the ordinary into the realm of extraordinary. This interpretation may help us understand better Guilford's (1981) data, which indicated that a nonlinear relationship existed between verbal IQ and creativity test scores, with a higher correlation below 120 IQ and a lower one above 120 IQ. As Guilford emphasized in his earlier work (1968) on complex problem-solving tasks, each individual must produce his or her own strategy to capitalize on personal strengths and work around weaknesses. Individuals whose IQ exceeds 120 may be able to depend more often on convergent process to produce acceptable or correct responses to difficult and complex problems, whereas success for individuals whose IQ is below 120 may more directly depend upon the extent to which they can access divergent production. It would be of interest to repeat studies, such as Guilford's, using education as an independent variable, partialling intelligence from the relationship, and then repeating the work partialling education from the IQ–creativity relationship.

The annals of scientific invention, of musical and artistic accomplishment, of biological discovery, of mathematical logic or of governmental and political greatness are filled with descriptions of the creative process as it evolved in singularly extraordinary contributions. As deBono (1971) stated, some people have better developed capacities for generating new ideas than others. New ideas do not always come to those who have worked the hardest or learned the most about their domain. Yet some individuals go beyond deep thinking to bring into existence new ideas, new insights, and new breakthroughs at "the cutting edge" of their fields. These are the creative contributions. Not all of these creative acts are of the same importance or sophistication, nor are all recognized by a societal "medium" that is perhaps unreceptive to the particular creative application or insufficiently prepared to understand it. Yet each creative act may be the ultimate expression of intelligence, in which all of the cognition and comprehension that individuals have developed at that point in their time (age) and situation (context) with their degree of training (experience) have been brought to bear upon a particular idea or problem. We propose that creativity is not another "breed" of mental processing, but is the ultimate expression of that finely honed system of thinking we know of as intelligence.

References

Anastasi, A. (1958). Heredity, environment, and the question "How?" *Psychological Review, 65,* 197–208.

Anastasi, A., & Schaefer, C. E. (1971). Notes on the concepts of creativity and intelligence. *Journal of Creative Behavior, 5,* 113–116.

Ausubel, D. P. (1978). The nature and measurement of creativity. *Psychologia, 21,* 179–191.

Barron, F. (1963). *Creativity and psychological health: Origins of personality and creative freedom.* Princeton, NJ: Van Nostrand.

Bittel, K. R. (1964). Creativity in the visual arts in higher education. In C. W. Taylor (Ed.), *Widening horizons in creativity.* New York: Wiley.

Bloom, B. (1985). *Developing talent in young children.* New York: Ballantyne.

Brigham, T. A., Graubard, P. S., & Stans, A. (1972). Analysis of the effects of sequential reinforcement contingencies on aspects of composition. *Journal of Applied Behavior Analysis, 5,* 421–429.

Case, R. (1978). Piaget and beyond: Toward a developmentally based theory and technology of instruction. In R. Glaser (Ed.), *Advances in instructional psychology* (Vol. 1, pp. 167–228). Hillsdale, NJ: Erlbaum.

Cattell, R. B. (1963a). The personality and motivation of the researcher from measurements of contemporaries and from biography. In C. W. Taylor & F. Barron (Eds.), *Scientific creativity: Its recognition and development* (pp. 119–131). New York: Wiley.

Cattell, R. B. (1963b). Theory of fluid and crystallized intelligence: A critical experiment. *Journal of Educational Psychology, 54,* 1–22.

Coler, M. A. (1963). *Essays on creativity in the sciences.* New York: New York University Press.

Conger, J. J. (June, 1957). The meaning and measurement of intelligence. *Rocky Mountain Medical Journal, 54,* 10–12.

Crockenberg, S. B. (1972). Creativity tests: A boon or boondoggle for education? *Review of Educational Research, 42,* 27–45.

Csikszentmihalyi, M., & Robinson, R. E. (1986). Culture, time, and the development of talent. In R. J. Sternberg & J. E. Davidson (Eds.), *Conceptions of giftedness* (pp. 264–284). Cambridge, England: Cambridge University Press.

deBono, E. (1971). *New think.* New York: Avon Books.

Dellas, M., & Gaier, E. L. (1970). *Identification of creativity: The individual. Psychological Bulletin, 73* (1), 55–73.

Dewey, J. (1933). *How we think.* New York: Heath.

Eisner, E. W. (1965). Children's creativity in art: A study of types. *American Educational Research Journal, 2,* 125–136.

Elliott, J. M. (1964). Measuring creative abilities in public relations and in advertising work. In C. W. Taylor (Ed.), *Widening horizons in creativity.* New York: Wiley.

Estes, W. K. (1985). Learning, memory, and intelligence. In R. J. Sternberg (Ed.), *Handbook of human intelligence* (pp. 170–224). Cambridge, England: Cambridge University Press.

Feldman, D. H., with Benjamin, A. C. (1986). Giftedness as a developmentalist sees it. In R. J. Sternberg & J. E. Davidson (Eds.), *Conceptions of giftedness* (pp. 285–305). Cambridge, England: Cambridge University Press.

Fishbein, H. D. (1976). *Evolution, development, and children's learning.* Pacific Palisades, CA: Goodyear.

Gardner, H. (1982). *Art, mind, and brain. A cognitive approach to creativity.* New York: Basic Books.

Gardner, H. (1983). *Frames of mind.* New York: Basic Books.

Getzels, J. W., & Jackson, P. W. (1959). The highly intelligent and the highly creative adolescent: A summary of some research findings. In C. W. Taylor (Ed.), *The Third University of Utah Research Conference on the Identification of Creative Scientific Talent.* Salt Lake City: University of Utah Press.

Getzels, J. W., & Jackson, P. W. (1962). *Creativity and intelligence: Explorations with gifted students.* New York: Wiley.

Glover, J., & Gary, A. L. (1976). Procedures to increase some aspects of creativity. *Journal of Applied Behavior Analysis, 9,* 79–84.

Glover, J., & Sautter, F. (1977). Procedures for increasing four behaviorally defined components of creativity within formal written assignments among high school students. *School Applications of Learning Theory, 9,* 3–22.

Goetz, E. M., & Baer, D. M. (1973). Social control of form diversity and the emergence of new forms in children's block-building. *Journal of Applied Behavioral Analysis, 6,* 209–217.

Golann, S. E. (1963). Psychological study of creativity. *Psychological Bulletin, 60,* 560.

Gough, H. (1961). Techniques for identifying the creative research scientist. In D. W. MacKinnon (Ed.), *The creative person.* Berkeley: Institute of Personality Assessment and Research, University of California.

Guilford, J. P. (1950). Creativity. *American Psychologist, 5,* 444–454.

Guilford, J. P. (1959). Three faces of intellect. *American Psychologist, 14,* 469–479.

Guilford, J. P. (1963). *An informational theory of creative thinking.* Paper presented at the Convention of the Western Psychological Association, Santa Monica, CA. (Available in *USAF Instructors' Journal, 1,* 28–33.)

Guilford, J. P. (1967). Creativity: Yesterday, today, and tomorrow. *Journal of Creative Behavior, 1,* 3–14.

Guilford, J. P. (1968). *Intelligence, creativity and their educational implications.* San Diego, CA: Robert Knapp.

Guilford, J. P. (1981). Potentiality for creativity. In J. C. Gowan, J. Khatena, & E. P. Torance (Eds.), *Creativity: Its educational implications* (2nd ed., pp. 1–5). Dubuque, IA: Kendall/Hunt.

Guilford, J. P., & Christensen, P. R. (1973). The one-way relation between creative potential and IQ. *Journal of Creative Behavior, 7,* 247–252.

Haensly, P. A. (1979). *Behavior modification for problem solv-*

ing: Originality and creative production expanded. Unpublished manuscript. Texas A & M University, Gifted & Talented Institute, College Station, TX.

Haensly, P. A., & Roberts, N. M. (1983). The professional productive process and its implications for gifted studies. *Gifted Child Quarterly, 27,* 9–12.

Haensly, P. A., Reynolds, C. R., & Nash, W. R. (1986). Giftedness: coalescence, context, conflict, and commitment. In R. J. Sternberg & J. E. Davidson (Eds.), *Conceptions of giftedness* (pp. 128–148). Cambridge, England: Cambridge University Press.

Harper, T. (1983, October 4). Celebrated sculptor can't even read (Associated Press). Boulder, CO: *Bryan-College Station Eagle,* page 1C.

Hebb, D. O. (1972). *Textbook of psychology* (3rd ed.). Philadelphia: W. B. Saunders.

Jackson, P. W., & Messick, S. (1967). The person, the product, and the response: Conceptual problems in the assessment of creativity. In J. Kagan (Ed.), *Creativity and learning* (pp. 1–19). Boston: Houghton Mifflin.

Kagan, J. (Ed.). (1967). *Creativity and learning.* Boston: Houghton Mifflin.

Krippner, S. (1983). A systems approach to creativity based on Jungian typology. *Gifted Child Quarterly, 27,* 86–89.

Locurto, C. M. (1974). Verbal operant conditioning and self-reinforcement of originality. *Dissertation Abstracts International, 35,* 1945-B.

MacKinnon, D. W. (1960). The highly effective individual. *Teachers College Record, 61,* 367–378.

MacKinnon, D. W. (1961). Creativity in architects. In D. W. MacKinnon (Ed.), *The creative person.* Berkeley: Institute of Personality Assessment and Research, University of California.

MacKinnon, D. W. (1962). The nature and nurture of creative talent. *American Psychologist, 17,* 484–495.

Maloney, M. P., & Ward, M. P. (1976). *Psychological assessment: A conceptual approach.* New York: Oxford University Press.

Maltzman, I. (1960). On the training of originality. *Psychological Review, 67,* 229–242.

May, R. (1975). *The courage to create.* New York: Norton.

Mednick, S. A. (1962). The associative basis of the creative process. *Psychological Review, 69,* 220–227, 232.

Mednick, S. A., & Andrews, F. M. (1967). Creative thinking and level of intelligence. *Journal of Creative Behavior, 1,* 428–431.

Nash, W. R. (1975). The effects of warm-up activities on small group divergent problem solving with young children. *Journal of Psychology, 89,* 237–241.

Newell, A., Shaw, J. C., & Simon, H. A. (1962). The processes of creative thinking. In H. E. Gruber, G. Terrell, & M. Wertheimer (Eds.), *Contemporary approaches to creative thinking* (pp. 63–119). New York: Atherton Press.

Owens, W. A. (1972). Intellective, non-intellective, and environmental correlates of mechanical ingenuity. In C. Taylor (Ed.), *Climate for creativity* (pp. 253–268). New York: Pergamon Press.

Pascuale-Leone, J. (1970). A mathematical model for transition in Piaget's developmental stages. *Acta Psychologica, 32,* 301–345.

Piaget, J. (1972). Intellectual evolution from adolescence to adulthood. *Human Development, 15,* 1–12.

Roe, A. (1951). A psychological study of physical scientists. *Genetic Psychology Monographs, 43 (2),* 121–235.

Roe, A. (1952). *The making of a scientist.* New York: Dodd, Mead.

Roe, A. (1963). Psychological approaches to creativity in science. In M. A. Coler (Ed.), *Essays on creativity in the sciences* (pp. 153–182). New York: New York University Press.

Rossiman, T., & Horn, J. (1971). Cognitive, motivational and temperamental indicants of creativity and intelligence. *Journal of Educational Measurement, 9,* 265–286.

Rothenberg, A., & Hausman, C. R. (1976). *The creativity question.* Durham, NC: Duke University Press.

Schubert, A. (1973). Intelligence as necessary but not sufficient for creativity. *Journal of Genetic Psychology, 122,* 45–47.

Simonton, D. K. (1979). The eminent genius in history: The critical role of creative development. In J. C. Gowan, J. Khatena, & E. P. Torrance (Eds.), *Educating the ablest* (2nd ed., pp. 79–87). New York: F. E. Peacock.

Simonton, D. K. (1984). *Genius, creativity, and leadership: Historiometric inquiries.* Cambridge: Harvard University Press.

Simonton, D. K. (1985, December). Genius, creativity and leadership. *EEE Potentials,* pp. 31–32.

Skager, R. W., Klein, S. P., & Schultz, C. B. (1967). The prediction of academic and artistic achievement in a school of design. *Journal of Educational Measurement, 4,* 105–117.

Spearman, C. (1927). *The abilities of man: Their nature and measurement.* New York: Macmillan.

Spearman, C. (1930). *Creative mind.* London: Nisbet.

Sternberg, R. J. (1984). Toward a triarchic theory of human intelligence. *The Behavioral and Brain Sciences, 7,* 269–315.

Sternberg, R. J. (1985). *Beyond IQ: A triarchic theory of human intelligence.* Cambridge, England: Cambridge University Press.

Sternberg, R. J. (1986). Identifying the gifted through IQ: Why a little bit of knowledge is a dangerous thing. *Roeper Review, 8,* 143–147.

Sternberg, R. J., & Davidson, J. E. (1983). Insight in the gifted. *Educational Psychologist, 18,* 51–57.

Sternberg, R. J., & Wagner, R. K. (1986). *Practical intelligence: Nature and origins of competence in the everyday world.* Cambridge, England: Cambridge University Press.

Taylor, C. W., & Barron, F. (Eds.). (1963). *Scientific creativity: Its recognition and development.* New York: Wiley.

Taylor, I. (1975). A retrospective view of creativity investigation. In I. A. Taylor & J. W. Getzels (Eds.), *Perspectives in creativity* (pp. 1–36). Chicago: Aldine Publishing.

Terman, L. M. (1954). Scientists and nonscientists in a group of 800 gifted men. *Psychological Monographs: General and Applied, 68* (7, Whole No. 378).

Terman, L. M. (1955). Are scientists different? *Scientific American, 192(1),* 25–29.

Thorndike, E. L. (1921). Intelligence and its measurement. *Journal of Educational Psychology, 12,* 124–127.

Thorndike, E. L. (1926). *Measurement of intelligence.* New York: Teachers' College, Columbia University.

Thurstone, L. L. (1931). Multiple factor analysis. *Psychological Review, 38,* 406–427.

Torrance, E. P. (1960). Eight partial replications of the Getzels-Jackson study. *Research Memorandum BER-60-15.* Minneapolis: Bureau of Educational Research, University of Minnesota.

Torrance, E. P. (1962). *Guiding creative talent.* Englewood Cliffs, NJ: Prentice-Hall.

Torrance, E. P. (1966). *Torrance Tests of Creative Thinking: Norms-technical manual.* Princeton, NJ: Personnel Press.

Torrance, E. P. (1967). Scientific views of creativity and factors affecting its growth. In J. Kagan (Ed.), *Creativity and learning* (pp. 73–91). Boston: Houghton Mifflin.

Vernon, P. E. (1950). *The structure of human abilities.* London: Methuen.

Wade, S. (1968). Differences between intelligence and creativity: Some speculation on the role of environment. *Journal of Creative Behavior, 2,* 97–101.

Wallach, M. A. (1985). Creativity testing and giftedness. In F. D. Horowitz & M. O'Brien (Eds.), *The gifted and talented: Developmental perspectives* (pp. 99–124). Washington, DC: American Psychological Association.

Wallach, M. A., & Kogan, N. (1965). *Modes of thinking in young children.* New York: Holt, Rinehart & Winston.

Wallach, M. A., & Kogan, N. (1972). Creativity and intelligence in children. In A. Rothenberg & C. R. Hausman (Eds.), *The creativity question* (pp. 208–217). Durham, NC: Duke University Press.

Wallas, G. (1926, 1945). *The art of thought.* New York: Harcourt, Brace.

Webster's New Collegiate Dictionary (1980). Springfield, MA: G. & C. Merriam.

Wittrock, M. C. (1974). Learning as a generative process. *Educational Psychologist, 11,* 87–95.

Yamamoto, K. A. (1964a). Role of creative thinking and intelligence in high school achievement. *Psychological Reports, 14,* 783–789.

Yamamoto, K. A. (1964b). Threshold of intelligence in academic achievement of highly creative students. *Journal of Experimental Education, 32,* 401–405.

Yamamoto, K. A. (1964c). A further analysis of the role of creative thinking in high-school achievement. *Journal of Psychology, 58,* 277–283.

Yamamoto, K. A. (1965). Validation of tests of creative thinking: A review of some studies. *Exceptional Children, 31,* 281–290.

Cognitive Models of Creativity

Part II presents a collection of chapters in which the authors have developed models of creative thought based on contemporary cognitive psychology. Hayes begins with an overall perspective, "Cognitive Processes in Creativity." Flowers and Garbin then focus on the role of perceptual processes in their chapter, "Creativity and Perception." Next, Stein examines the role of memory in creative thought in "Memory and Creativity." Armbruster examines the potential roles in creativity of metacognition in her chapter on "Metacognition in Creativity." Moshman and Lukin take a cognitive-developmental perspective in their chapter, "The Creative Construction of Rationality: A Paradox?" This second part of the volume then closes with a look at the development of adult thought and creativity in the chapter by Benack, Basseches, and Swan, "Dialectical Thinking and Adult Creativity."

CHAPTER 7

Cognitive Processes in Creativity

John R. Hayes

"Creative" is a word with many uses. Sometimes it is used to describe the potential of persons to produce creative works whether or not they have produced any work as yet. Sometimes it is used to describe everyday behaviors as, for example, when a nursery school curriculum is said to encourage creative activities, such as drawing or storytelling. In this chapter, I will restrict the meaning of the term in two ways. First, I will be concerned solely with creative productivity, that is, with creativity expressed in the actual production of creative works and not with the unexpressed potential for producing such works. Second, I will be concerned only with creative acts at the highest level, that is, with the best and most valued works of artists, scientists, and scholars.

Society defines creative acts through a complex process of social judgment. It relies most heavily on the opinions of relevant experts in making such judgments—music critics, art historians, scholars, and scientists who are presumed to know the field. But even expert judgments are highly subjective and are frequently influenced by irrelevant factors. For example, judgments may be influenced by the experts' current focus of attention—Gregor Mendel had to wait decades before the appropriate experts recognized that his work was important—and by the reputation of the creator—it is difficult for an unknown writer to get a publisher's attention.

Despite the vagueries of such judgments, there appears to be a core of three evaluations that underlie the identification of a creative act: (1) The act must be seen as original or novel; (2) the act must be seen as valuable or interesting; and (3) the act must reflect well on the mind of the creator. All three of these criteria appear to be essential if an act is to be considered creative. No matter how well executed a work may be, it will not be considered creative unless it incorporates substantial new ideas not easily derived from earlier work. Thus, even the best copies of paintings are not judged creative, not, at least, if the source is known. And no matter how original an act is, it will not be considered creative unless it also is judged to be valuable. A composer may arrange notes in a novel and unexpected way, but the work will not be considered creative unless it also is judged to have musical value. Finally, an act will not be judged creative unless it reflects the intelligence of the person who is the creator. If a work is produced entirely accidentally, then it is not judged to be creative. This does not mean that chance cannot play a role in genuinely creative acts. Austin (1978) made an interesting distinction among four kinds of chance events. Chance I is just blind luck; it could happen to anyone and does not depend on any special ability of the person it happens to. In Chance II, luck depends on the person's curiosity or persistence in exploration. The fact that a curious person attends more, say, to the habits of beetles makes him or her more likely to discover something interesting about beetles than a person

John R. Hayes • Department of Psychology, Carnegie-Mellon University, Pittsburgh, PA 15238.

who regards beetles simply as something to be squashed. In Chance III, luck depends on the person's having extensive knowledge of the field that is not shared by most people. Thus, the discovery of radium by Pierre and Marie Curie depended on their recognizing that a certain mineral was more radioactive than it ought to be on the basis of the known elements it contained. Clearly, only a very knowledgeable person could make such a discovery. This is the sort of chance that Louis Pasteur was referring to when he said that "chance favors only the prepared mind." Finally, in Chance IV, luck depends on the person's particular and, perhaps, unique intellectual style or pattern of interests. Acts that involve chance events of the last three types do reflect credit on the mind of the actor and are thus potentially creative.

In the remainder of this chapter, I will discuss data that bear on two major questions: "What are the characteristics of creative people?" and "What cognitive processes are involved in creative acts?" Finally, I will present a theoretical framework to account for these data.

Characteristics of Creative People

Do Creative People Have High IQs? Yes and No

It is often assumed that creativity is closely related to IQ. Indeed, both Roe (1953), who did studies of eminent physicists, biologists, and social scientists, and MacKinnon (1968), who also studied distinguished research scientists, mathematicians, and architects, found that these creative individuals had IQs ranging from 120 to 177—well above the general average. However, these higher-than-average IQs cannot be taken as an explanation of the observed creativity and, indeed, may be unrelated to it.

Several studies have indicated that highly creative individuals in a particular field do not have IQs higher than the IQs of matched individuals in their field who are not judged to be creative. For example, Harmon (1963) rated 504 physical and biological scientists for research productivity and found no relation between creativity and either IQ or school grades. Bloom (1963) studied two sample groups of chemists and mathematicians. One sample consisted of individuals who were judged outstandingly productive by their colleagues. The other group consisted of scientists who were matched in age, education, and experience to the first sample, but who were not judged to be outstan-

dingly productive. Although the first group outpublished the second group at a rate of eight to one, there was no difference in IQ between them. In a similar study, MacKinnon (1968) compared scientists, mathematicians, and architects who had made distinguished contributions to their respective fields with a matched group who had not made distinguished contributions. There was no difference between the two groups in either IQ or in school grades.

How can it be that creative scientists and architects have higher than average IQs and yet IQ does not predict which one of two professionals will be the more creative? At least two alternative theories seem plausible. I will call the first alternative the "threshold theory." According to this theory, a person's IQ must be above some threshold value, say, 120, if that person is to be successful in creative activities. IQ differences above the threshold level, however, make no difference in creativity. The reason that there is no correlation between IQ and creativity among professionals is that schooling weeds out professionals with IQs that are less than 120.

I have proposed a second alternative theory which I call the "certification theory" (Hayes, 1978). According to the certification theory, there is no intrinsic relation between creativity and IQ. Being creatively productive, however, depends on attaining a position in which one can display creativity—such as a college professor, an industrial chemist, or an architect. Being considered for these positions typically requires a college or also a graduate degree. Because academic performance is correlated with IQ, it may be that one's opportunity to be creative depends on IQ simply because of the degree requirement. Thus, creative people may not need high IQs to be creative but they may need them to be certified to get jobs where they can put their creativity to work. This second alternative is worth considering, because, if it is correct, or even partly correct, our society inappropriately may be discouraging a large portion of the creative individuals in the population.

Other Cognitive and Personality Traits

A large number of studies have been conducted to identify the cognitive and personality traits that characterize creative people. Surprisingly, studies of cognitive traits generally have yielded disappointing results, with perhaps the most disappointing being the results on divergent thinking. Divergent thinking is widely believed to be an important part of the creative process (Guilford, 1967), and measures of divergent thinking constitute a major component in the most popular creativity tests (e.g., the Torrance Tests of Creative Thinking). However, Mansfield and Busse (1981) reviewed the studies of divergent thinking in scientific thought and concluded that essentially there is no evidence relating divergent thinking to creative performance in science. These same researchers also reviewed studies of 16 other cognitive tests and concluded that none "has consistently shown high correlations with measures of real-life creativity" (p. 50). Researchers have been more successful, however, in identifying personality traits in creative people. I will therefore review evidence concerning four traits that appear to differentiate more creative from less creative people: devotion to work, independence, drive for originality, and flexibility.

Devotion to Work. One of the most consistent observations about creative people is that they work very hard. Roe (1953) studied a group of top ranking physicists and biologists and described them in this fashion:

There is only one thing that seems to characterize the total group, and that is absorption in their work, over long years, and frequently to the exclusion of everything else. This was also true of the biologists. This one thing alone is probably not of itself sufficient to account for the success enjoyed by these men, but it appears to be a sine qua non. (p. 233–234)

Chambers (1964) and Ypma (1968) also reported that creative people work harder than others. Harris (1972) reported that University of California professors spend an average of 60 hours weekly on teaching and research. Herbert Simon, who received the 1978 Nobel Laureate in economics, spent about 100 hours per week for years doing the work for which he eventually won the Nobel Prize (personal communication, May 15, 1986).

Independence. Researchers consistently have found that creative people have a strong drive for independence of thought and action. In particular, they seem to want very strongly to make their own decisions about what they do. Chambers (1964) found that the creative scientist "is not the type of person who waits for someone else to tell him what to do, but rather thinks things through and then takes action on his own with little regard to convention or current 'fashion'" (p. 14). He also found that "when seeking a position, . . . the overwhelming choice for the creative scientists is the

opportunity to do really creative research and to choose problems of interest to them" (p. 6).

MacKinnon (1961) found that creative architects also strongly preferred independent thought and action rather than conformity. Ypma (1968) found that creative scientists were more likely than other scientists to say that they would like to have "a good deal of responsibility" in their jobs. Further, Ypma found that creative scientists were much more likely than others to answer yes to the question, "Did you ever build an apparatus or device of your own design on your own initiative and not as part of any required school assignment during your later school years?" (In this instance, "later school years" refers to high school and college.) This last result is interesting in the light of the success that the Westinghouse Science Talent Search has had in identifying outstandingly creative scientists. This talent search has selected 40 high school students each year since 1942 on the basis of self-initiated projects rather than written tests or grades. The projects are then evaluated for excellence by two scientists in the project's field. In the group of 1,520 students selected between 1942 and 1979, there are five Nobel prize winners, five winners of MacArthur Fellowships, and two winners of the Fields Medal in Mathematics. This remarkable performance suggests that the tendency to initiate independent action is, indeed, an important trait of the creative person and that it may be exhibited quite early in the person's career.

The Drive for Originality. Because creative acts are by definition original, it would not be surprising if creative people showed a special drive to be original. In fact, that is just what the research has shown. MacKinnon (1963) described the typical creative architect in his study as "satisfied only with solutions which are original and meet his own high standards of architectural excellence" (p. 276). Ypma (1968) found that when they are asked about their major motivations, the more creative scientists were likely to answer, "to come up with something new." Barron (1963) and Bergum (1975) have made similar observations.

Flexibility. Helson and Crutchfield (1970) administered the California Psychological Inventory to 105 mathematicians who had been rated for creativity by other mathematicians. The more creative mathematicians scored significantly higher on the flexibility scale than did the less creative mathematicians. In an extensive review of research on creativity in engineers, Rouse (1986) also found that flexibility was strongly correlated with creative performance. Creative engineers tended to mix algorithmic and associative thinking and to represent knowledge both visually and symbolically.

What Cognitive Processes Are Involved in Creative Acts?

In this section, I will present an analysis of creative acts in terms of familiar cognitive processes, that is, in terms of processes involved in everyday thought and action. Before doing so, though, I should note that there are (at least) two points of view which hold that such an analysis is impossible. The first of these is that creative acts are, in principle, unanalyzable and the second, that creative acts involve special processes not involved in other kinds of thought.

Are Creative Processes Unanalyzable?

Popper (1959) asserted quite forcefully that the process of scientific discovery is indeed unanalyzable. In his book, *The Logic of Scientific Discovery,* Popper claimed that

The initial stage, the act of conceiving or inventing a theory, seems to me neither to call for logical analysis nor to be susceptible of it. . . . My view of the matter, for what it is worth, is that there is no such thing as a logical method of having new ideas, or a logical reconstruction of this process. My view may be expressed by saying that every discovery contains "an irrational element," or "a creative intuition," in Bergson's sense. (pp. 31–32)

In their book, *Scientific Discovery: An Account of the Creative Processes,* Langley, Simon, Bradshaw, and Zytkow (1987) presented a position directly challenging Popper's view. These authors argued that it is indeed possible to account for scientific discovery in terms of well-specified heuristic procedures. In particular, they hold that discoveries are achieved when the scientist applies sensible heuristic procedures in drawing inferences from data. They argued quite convincingly for the adequacy of this view by incorporating such heuristics in computer programs and by showing that these programs can induce well-known scientific laws from data. For example, one program, BACON 1, incorporates the following search heuristics:

1. Look for variables (or combinations of variables) with constant value.

2. Look for linear relations among variables.
3. If two variables increase together, consider their ratio.
4. If one variable increases while another decreases, consider their product.

When provided with appropriate data, this program successfully induced Boyle's law, Kepler's third law, Galileo's law, and Ohm's law.

Lenat (1976) had demonstrated earlier that a well-specified set of heuristics, incorporated in his program AM (for Automated Mathematician), could make interesting discoveries in mathematics. For example, AM discovered de Morgan's laws, the unique factorization of numbers into primes, and Goldbach's conjecture.

Of course, these results do not mean that human creative processes can be accounted for entirely in terms of such search heuristics. If a person did make a discovery by applying search heuristics to data, it would still be interesting to ask what motivated the person to examine those data. However, the results do demonstrate the plausibility of accounting for an important part of the creative process through commonsense search heuristics.

Is There a Special Creative Process?

At present, the special process view appears to have achieved "straw man" status in the scientific literature on creativity and is much more frequently attacked than defended. Further, there are no live candidates for "special creative process" that have substantial empirical backing. Although we should not rule out the possibility that such special processes may be discovered someday, we should continue to exercise a healthy skepticism toward candidates proposed in the popular press (e.g., "lateral thinking" and "right-brain thinking"). Parsimony appears to be serving us well in this area.

The "Nothing-Special" Position

This position, due primarily to Simon and his coworkers (Newell, Shaw, & Simon, 1964; Simon, 1966), holds that creative acts are a variety of problem solving and involve only those processes that also are involved in everyday problem-solving activities. According to this view, creative acts are problem-solving acts of a special sort. First, they are problem-solving acts that meet criteria such as those above—that is, they are seen as novel and valuable and they reflect the cognitive abilities of the problem solver. Second, they typically involve ill-defined problems—that is, problems that cannot be solved unless the problem solver makes decisions or adds information of his or her own. Ill-defined problems occur frequently in practical settings. For example, in architectural practice, the client typically specifies a few of the properties of a building to be designed, but the architect must supply many more features before the design problem can be solved.

To describe creative activities as problem solving need not, but to many does, suggest that creation happens only when the creative person is in some sort of trouble. To an extent, this is true. Necessity *is* the mother of invention—at least, of *some* invention. But there are other sorts of situations that lead to creation. Creators are not always digging themselves out of trouble. In many cases, it is reasonable to think of them as taking advantage of opportunities, of recognizing the possibility of improving what is currently a satisfactory situation. Whether an individual is exploring an opportunity or resolving a difficulty, the important point is that he or she is setting goals and initiating activities to accomplish those goals.

Having reviewed these alternative points of view, I will now return to the analysis of creative acts in terms of familiar cognitive processes. I will discuss various cognitive processes for which there are either data or a plausible inference to suggest that they are especially important in creative acts.

Preparation

There is very wide agreement among researchers that preparation is one of the most important conditions of creativity (Mansfield & Busse, 1981; Wallas, 1926; Ypma, 1968). By preparation, we refer to the effort of the creative person, often carried out over long periods of time, to acquire knowledge and skills relevant to the creative act. Recently, I (Hayes, 1985) provided strong evidence that even the most talented composers and painters (e.g., Mozart and Van Gogh) required years of preparation before they began to produce the work for which they are famous. I surveyed all the composers mentioned in *The Lives of the Great Composers* (Schonberg, 1970) for whom there were sufficient biographical data to determine when they first became seriously interested in music (e.g., when they began piano lessons in earnest). Seventy-six composers were included in the study. Next, I identified the notable works of these composers and the dates on which they were composed. (For this study, I defined a notable work as one for which

at least five different recordings were currently available.) From these data, I calculated when in the composer's career, that is, how many years after the onset of serious interest, each work was composed. Out of more than 500 works, only three were composed before year 10 of the composers' careers, and these three works were composed in years 8 and 9. Averaged over the group, the pattern of career productivity involved an initial 10-year period of silence, a rapid increase in productivity from year 10 to year 25, a period of stable productivity from year 25 to about year 45, and then a period of gradual decline.

In the same paper, I reported a parallel study of 131 painters, using biographical data to determine when each artist became seriously involved in painting. I defined the notable works of these painters as those that were reproduced in any of 11 general histories of art. The pattern of career productivity for these painters was similar to that observed in the composers. There was an initial period of non-creativity lasting about six years. This was followed by a rapid increase in productivity over the next six years, then a period of stable productivity until about 35 years into their careers, and lastly a period of declining productivity.

Wishbow (1988) conducted a biographical study, similar to those just described, of 66 eminent poets. She defined a notable poem as one that was included in the *Norton Anthology of Poetry*. She found that none of her 66 poets wrote a notable poem earlier than five years into their careers, and 55 of the 66 poets produced none earlier than 10 years into their careers.

The early periods of inactivity observed in all three of these studies suggests that a long period of preparation is essential for creative productivity, even for the most talented of our composers, painters, and poets.

In conducting this research, both Wishbow and I encountered considerable skepticism expressed by experts in music, art, and literature that such investigations could produce any consistent result. Their skepticism was based on the following very reasonable argument:

1. These studies included individuals of very diverse aesthetic orientations (e.g., Richard Wagner and Erik Satie) who were attempting to do very different things.
2. These studies included individuals from four different centuries (the seventeenth through the twentieth) who produced their works in very different social contexts.

3. Therefore, there is no reason to expect that there would be consistency in the conditions favoring creative performance across such diverse times and groups.

There is nothing logically wrong with this argument. It might be that differences in social context and aesthetic goals would dominate all other conditions of creative productivity. As it turns out, they do not. Creators appear to require a long period of preparation despite differences in time and aesthetic objectives.

What is this period of preparation used for? Simon and Chase (1973) observed that chess players require about 10 years of preparations before they reach the level of grand master. They suggested that, during this time, the serious player learns a vast store of chess patterns through hundreds of hours devoted to study and play. They estimated that a player needs to know roughly 50,000 chess patterns in order to play at the grand-master level. One can easily imagine that composers, painters, and poets need a comparable period of time to acquire sufficient knowledge and skills to perform in their fields at world class levels.

Goal Setting

Goal setting often appears to be the most critical element in a creative act. According to Einstein and Infeld (1938),

Galileo formulated the problem of determining the velocity of light, but did not solve it. The formulation of a problem is often more essential than its solution, which may be merely a matter of mathematical or experimental skill. To raise new questions, new possibilities, to regard old problems from a new angle, requires creative imagination and marks real advance in science. (p. 92)

Pavlov's discovery of the conditioned reflex is another case in point. As part of a study of digestive processes, Pavlov was investigating the salivary reflex in dogs. Dogs salivate automatically when food is placed in their mouths. At first, the experiment went well but, after a while, the dogs began to salivate before the food was placed in their mouths. This development seriously complicated the study Pavlov was trying to carry out. However, rather than seeing it as an annoyance to be eliminated, he saw it as an interesting phenomenon to be investigated. Against the advice of his colleagues, Pavlov abandoned his original objective and set a new goal which led to his historic work on the conditioned reflex.

Janson (1983) claimed that Edouard Manet's painting, *Luncheon on the Grass,* was historically significant because it was "a visual manifesto" of a new set of goals—goals that emphasized the importance of visual effects on the canvas in contrast to social or literary "meanings" a painting might convey. He said, "here begins an attitude that was later summed up in the doctrine of Art for Art's Sake" (p. 607).

Of course, goal setting is not always difficult. There are many situations in which the goals are obvious even though the means for achieving them are not. Everyone knows that curing cancer and reducing auto accidents are valuable goals. What distinguishes the creative people in the examples described above is that they recognized an opportunity or a problem when other people did not. What might be responsible for differences in peoples' abilities to find problems or to recognize opportunities? Because we know very little about such processes, any account admittedly must be speculative. Here are some hypotheses.

1. Extensive knowledge of a field should give one increased ability to recognize both opportunities and problems by analogy to previous experience. For example, if a chess situation resembles one the player has been in before, it could signal an opportunity if the previous outcome was favorable, and a problem if it was not.

2. A unique pattern of knowledge outside of a field, which is acquired perhaps through hobbies or through switching professions, could provide a person with analogies that are not generally available to others in the field. Such analogies could suggest unsuspected possibilities or problems in the field. Consistent with this view, Gordon (1961) recommended that problem-solving teams in industry should include people from very diverse fields.

3. Strong evaluation skills may lead a person to recognize problems in a line of research that others fail to recognize and, as a result, to initiate new studies that others would not have thought of. Evaluation skills in the social sciences seem to depend heavily on the sorts of critical-thinking skills described in the rival hypotheses of Huck and Sandler (1979). Perhaps some aspects of creative performance could be improved through training in these skills.

These hypotheses could be viewed as examples of the operation of Austin's (1978) Chance III and Chance IV.

Representation

Because tasks that allow scope for creativity typically are ill defined, a person doing such a task is forced to make many choices in building a representation of the task. For example, an architect may be given the task of designing a shop together with specifications of the location, size, type of merchandise to be displayed, and clientele. To represent the design problem in sufficient detail so that it can be solved, the architect must make a great many decisions. For example, he may decide that the shop should have a certain kind of access, should be "transparent," and should have "levels" (see Hayes, 1978, pp. 206–210). Ill-defined problems offer a great deal of latitude in the way they can be represented or defined.

The way in which a person represents a task can have a critical impact on how hard the task is to do or even whether it can be done at all. Kotovsky, Hayes, and Simon (1985) showed that a problem represented in one way may be 16 times as hard to solve as the same problem represented in a different way. The 16-to-1 range almost certainly underestimates the full range over which changes in representation can change problem difficulty. Thus, choosing to represent a problem visually rather than verbally, or choosing to represent the problem by one metaphor rather than another, could make a sufficient difference in problem difficulty that one scholar may be able to solve the problem and another may not be able to. In some cases then, the creative person—the one who solved the problem when others could not—may be the person who chose the best representation of the problem.

Kotovsky, Hayes, and Simon (1985) compared different representations of the same problem. Even though the problem-solvers' representations of the problem were different in the sense that a problem element might be represented as a position in one case and as a size in another, the underlying problem was always the same. It is rare, though, for two people, acting independently, to define an ill-defined problem in the same way. If two architects were commissioned to design the same house, they would almost certainly interpret that commission in different ways, placing different emphases on the various design requirements. Each architect would define his or her own design task. It is tempting to speculate that creative people define "better" or "more interesting" tasks for themselves than do less creative people.

Although there are no studies comparing task definition in creative and noncreative people, there are some task-definition studies comparing experts and novices. These studies show that a very important part of the difference between experts and novices may lie in the way they define the task to be performed. Hayes, Flower, Schriver, Stratman, and Carey (1987) found that novice writers represented the task of revision as a sentence-level task; that is, they attended to each sentence separately, fixing the grammatical and lexical problems it contained, and concerned themselves rarely or not at all with global problems, such as transitions, coherence, and the effectiveness of the whole text. The experts, in contrast, were primarily concerned with global problems, although they fixed the local problems as well. The experts did a far better job of revision than did the novices, and it seems clear in this case that their better performance depended on their having defined a better task for themselves. One cannot really expect to do a good job of revision with a task definition that ignores a very important class of problems. Carey and Flower (Chapter 17 in this volume) provide an excellent discussion of how expert–novice differences in task definition influence expository writing.

Although these expert–novice studies cannot be taken as proof, they do make it seem plausible that creative people may differ from less creative people in some degree because they define better tasks for themselves.

Searching for Solutions

Many approaches to improving creative thinking, such as brainstorming (Osborn, 1948) and synetics (Gordon, 1961), focus on the fostering of divergent thinking, that is, on generating many alternative solutions to the same problem. These techniques appear to be useful for some kinds of group problem solving. However, as was noted above, divergent-thinking skills appear to be unrelated to the sort of creative productivity this chapter is concerned with.

It is interesting to contrast the emphasis in the creativity literature on the importance of generating many solution paths with the emphasis in the cognitive science literature (see Newell & Simon, 1972) on the importance of heuristic search, that is, with narrowing many solution paths down to a few. Perhaps high-level creative activities are more likely to demand heuristic searches than divergent thinking.

In an early, but still influential, discussion of creativity, Wallas (1926) claimed that incubation is one of the characteristic stages of the creative process. By incubation, he meant a stage in which the problem solver has stopped attending to the problem but during which progress, in any case, is being made toward the solution. Researchers have attempted to demonstrate the reality of this phenomenon experimentally. Typically, experimental and control subjects are given a complex problem to solve. The control subjects are allowed to work continuously on the problem until they solve it. The experimental subjects are interrupted in their solution efforts and are asked to attend to another task for a period of time before they are allowed to return to the problem and solve it. If the experimental subjects required less total time working on the problem to solve it than the control subjects, this would be taken as evidence of incubation. Although a number of early investigators failed to obtain positive results with this method, Cook (1934, 1937), and Ericksen (1942), more recent experimenters, have obtained positive results (Fulgosi & Guilford, 1968; Murray & Denny, 1969; Silviera, 1971).

The success of such experiments, however, cannot be taken as definite proof that incubation has occurred. As Ericsson and Simon (1984) pointed out, the problem is that it is very difficult to establish that the experimental subjects obeyed (or, indeed, could obey) instructions not to attend to the problem during the incubation period.

Even if incubation is real, it does not follow that it is characteristic of the creative process. In my reanalysis (Hayes, 1978) of the data on which Wallas based his conclusions (the testimony of creative individuals), I found many instances in which creative acts proceeded from beginning to end without any pause that would allow for incubation. Although Wallas's claims for incubation are interesting, it appears that there is little empirical evidence to support them.

Revision

In performing skilled activities, people often stop to evaluate what they have produced and to improve on any shortcomings they may find. This revision process appears to be especially important in creative activities because of the very high standards involved. Donald M. Murray, a Pulitzer prize-winning essayist, spoke eloquently about the importance of revision: "Rewriting is the difference between the dilettante and the artist, the amateur and the professional, the unpublished and the published." William Glass testified, "I work not by writing but rewriting." Dylan Thomas stated, "Almost any poem is fifty to a hundred revisions—and that's after it's well along." Archibald MacLeish

talked of "the endless discipline of writing and rewriting and rewriting" (Murray, 1978, p. 85).

Revision, of course, is not confined to writing. It happens in the development of scientific theory, in painting, and in musical composition. For example, in a letter, Tchaikovsky said,

Yesterday, when I wrote you about my method of composing, I did not enter sufficiently into that phase of the work which related to the working out of the sketch. This phase is of primary importance. What has been set down in a moment of ardour must now be critically examined, improved, extended, or condensed. (quoted in Vernon, 1970, p. 59)

If revision is an important part of creative activity, it is reasonable to expect that creative people may be better at revision than others. Although evidence on this issue is scant at best, the question is interesting enough to pursue. There are at least three possible factors which might make creative people superior revisors:

1. *Creative people may have higher standards for performance than others.* Although this is a very plausible assertion, its validity has been tested only in the area of standards for creativity. As was noted above, creative people aspire more than others to be creative. The impact this might have on performance is illustrated in a study carried out by Magone (personal communication). Magone collected think-aloud protocols of people who were taking a creativity test in which they were asked to complete a drawing in as many different ways as they could. She found that people who scored high on the test were much more likely than those who scored low to reject ideas as "trite" or "boring." Even though a creativity test probably does not predict real creativity, the study does illustrate the point that high standards for creativity can shape performance.

2. *Creative people may be more sensitive than others in perceiving that standards have not been met.* There are no studies comparing creative people with others in this skill. However, Hayes *et al.* (1987) have found that expert writers were far more sensitive detectors of text problems than novices.

3. *Experts may be more flexible than others in considering change.* Results of the personality surveys, which were cited above, suggest that creative people are, in fact, more flexible than others. Flexibility could increase a person's chances of performing creatively in a number of ways: A more flexible person might be more likely than others to drop everything to pursue a hot new lead as Pavlov did in the example presented earlier. A flexible per-

son might be more likely than others to sacrifice less important goals in order to accomplish more important ones. And, lastly, a more flexible person might be more likely than others to change problem representation if progress toward solution is unsatisfactory.

Summary

In this chapter, I explored two major questions. In answer to the question, "What are creative people like?" fairly good empirical evidence supports the following conclusions:

1. Creative people work very hard.
2. Creative people are more disposed to setting their own agenda and to taking independent action than are others.
3. Creative people strive for originality.
4. Creative people show more flexibility than others.
5. Creative people do not have higher IQs or get better school grades than others when we control for age and education. In fact, no cognitive abilities have been identified that reliably distinguish between creative and noncreative people.

The surprising thing about these findings is that all the variables that discriminate between creative and noncreative people are motivational. No cognitive abilities have been discovered that discriminate between these two groups.

In exploring the question, "What cognitive factors are involved in creative acts?" I have uncovered convincing evidence on two points:

1. Years of preparation are essential for creative productivity in many fields.
2. Goal setting is the critical element in many creative acts.

In addition, plausible arguments can be made for the importance of the following procedures in creative acts:

1. Choosing good problem representations
2. Defining good problems in ill-defined problem situations
3. Accurately evaluating the shortcomings of one's own work

4. Taking effective action to revise shortcomings

Clearly, both cognitive and motivational factors are involved in creative performance. However, the failure of cognitive ability measures, such as IQ, to predict creative performance leads me to propose that creative performance has its origin not in innate cognitive abilities but rather in the motivation of the creative person. Over a period of time, this motivation has cognitive consequences, such as the acquisition of large bodies of knowledge, that contribute in a critical way to creative performance; but the *origin* is in motivation, not cognition.

The creative person may be thought of as a vector special in strength and in direction. Motivation of great strength is necessary because creative people face daunting tasks. They must work for many years, perhaps for a decade or more, before they can begin to accomplish their creative goals. They may have to reject easily available rewards in order to pursue their fields. One of my students said, "I must like art a lot to be willing to go to school for four years in order to be out of work." Sometimes they may have to face active opposition as Pavlov did.

The direction of motivation is as critical as its strength. Success in many areas of life requires strong motivation and hard work. In many practical situations, the hard work must be directed to satisfying the demands of a boss, some set of standards, or the interests of the public. Creative people, however, are motivated to be in charge of their own actions, and, through those actions, to do something that has not been done before, perhaps has not even been thought of before.

The nature of their motivation may lead creative people to take different paths than others take. For example, creative people may choose fields, such as the arts or sciences, in which they believe they can exercise their interest in creative activities, rather than sales or medical practice, in which creative activities may not be appreciated.

Motivational differences can result in important differences in cognitive factors. If a person is willing to work longer and harder than others, he or she can acquire a larger body of information than others. In solving a problem, this extra information might be used directly to make an essential inference or might provide an analogy that would suggest a solution path. Willingness to work hard could also lead persons to define harder and better problems for themselves and in general to set higher standards for themselves. Higher standards could then lead them to be more critical of shortcomings in their own work.

The motivation to be independent would predispose persons to set their own goals and motivation to be creative would lead them to reject goals that were "trite" or "boring."

Finally, motivation to be flexible could make it easier to change direction completely when a new opportunity presents itself, to sacrifice minor objectives to accomplish major ones, and to change representations when progress is unsatisfactory. The primary thrust of the position I am presenting here is that differences in creativity have their origin in differences in motivation. These differences in motivation then cause cognition differences, and these motivational and cognitive differences account jointly for the observed differences between creative and noncreative individuals.

References

Austin, J. H. (1978). *Chase, chance, and creativity*. New York: Columbia University Press.

Barron, F. (1963). The disposition toward originality. In C. W. Taylor & F. Barron (Eds.), *Scientific creativity: Its recognition and development* (pp. 139–152) New York: Wiley.

Bergum, B. O. (1975). Self-perceptions of creativity among academic inventors and non-inventors. *Perceptual and Motor Skills, 40,* 78.

Bloom, B. S. (1963). Report on creativity research by the examiner's office at the University of Chicago. In C. W. Taylor & F. Barron (Eds.), *Scientific creativity: Its recognition and development* (pp. 251–264) New York: Wiley.

Chambers, J. A. (1964). Relating personality and biographical factors to scientific creativity. *Psychological Monographs, 78* (7, Whole No. 584).

Cook, T. W. (1934). Massed and distributed practice in puzzle solving. *Psychological Review, 41,* 330–335.

Cook, T. W. (1937). Distribution of practice and size of maze pattern. *British Journal of Psychology, 27,* 303–312.

Einstein, A., & Infeld, L. (1938). *The evolution of physics*. New York: Simon & Schuster.

Ericksen, S. C. (1942). Variability of attack in massed and spaced practice. *Journal of Experimental Psychology, 31,* 339–345.

Ericsson, K. A., & Simon, H. A. (1984). *Protocol analysis: Verbal reports as data*. Cambridge: MIT Press.

Fulgosi, A., & Guilford, J. P. (1968). Short-term incubation in divergent production. *American Journal of Psychology, 7,* 1016–1023.

Gordon, W. J. (1961). *Synectics*. New York: Harper & Row.

Guilford, J. P. (1967). *The nature of human intelligence*. New York: McGraw-Hill.

Harmon, L. R. (1963). The development of a criterion of scientific competence. In C. W. Taylor & F. Barron (Eds.), *Scientific creativity: Its recognition and development* (p. 44–52). New York: Wiley.

Harris, S. E. (1972). *A statistical portrait of higher education*. New York: McGraw-Hill.

Hayes, J. R. (1978). *Cognitive psychology: Thinking and creating*. Homewood, IL: Dorsey Press.

Hayes, J. R. (1985). Three problems in teaching problem solving skills. In S. Chipman, J. W. Segal, & R. Glaser (Eds.), *Thinking and learning skills* (Vol. 2, pp. 391–406). Hillsdale, New Jersey: Erlbaum.

Hayes, J. R., Flower, L. S., Schriver, K. A., Stratman, J., & Carey, L. (1987). In S. Rosenberg (Ed.), *Cognitive processes in revision*. Cambridge, England: Cambridge University Press.

Helson, R., & Crutchfield, R. S. (1970). Mathematicians: The creative researcher and the average Ph.D. *Journal of Consulting and Clinical Psychology, 34,* 250–257.

Huck, S. W., & Sandler, H. M. (1979). *Rival hypotheses: Alternate interpretations of data based conclusions*. New York: Harper & Row.

Janson, H. W. (1977). *History of Art*. (2nd ed.). Englewood Cliffs, N.J.: Prentice-Hall, and New York: Abrams.

Kotovsky, K., Hayes, J. R., & Simon, H. A. (1985). Why are some problems hard? Evidence from tower of Hanoi. *Cognitive Psychology, 17,* 248–294.

Langley, P., Simon, H. A., Bradshaw, G. L., & Zytkow, J. M. (1987). *Scientific Discovery*. Cambridge, Massachusetts: MIT Press.

Lenat, D. (1976, July). *AM: An artificial intelligence approach to discovery in mathematics as heuristic search, SAIL AIM-286*. Stanford CA: Stanford University, Artificial Intelligence Laboratory.

MacKinnon, D. W. (1961). Creativity in architects. In *The Creative Person*. Proceedings of a conference presented at the University of California Alumni Center, Lake Tahoe, Ca.

MacKinnon, D. W. (1963). Creativity and images of the self. In R. W. White (Ed.), *The study of Lives*. New York: Atherton Press.

MacKinnon, D. W. (1968). Selecting students with creative potential. In P. Heist (Ed.), *The creative college student: An unmet challenge* (pp. 101–118). San Francisco: Jossey-Bass.

Mansfield, R. S., & Busse, T. V. (1981). *The psychology of creativity and discovery*. Chicago: Nelson-Hall.

Murray, D. M. (1978). Internal revision: A process of discovery. In C. R. Cooper & L. Odell (Eds.), *Research on Composing: Points of Departure* (pp. 85–104). Urbana, IL: National Council of Teachers of English.

Murray, H. G., & Denny, J. P. (1969). Interaction of ability level and interpolated activity (opportunity for incubation) in human problem solving. *Psychological Reports, 24,* 271–276.

Newell, A., & Simon, H. A. (1972). *Human problem solving*. Englewood Cliffs, NJ: Prentice-Hall.

Newell, A., Shaw, J. C., & Simon, H. A. (1964). The process of creative thinking. In H. Gruber, G. Terrell, & M. Wertheimer (Eds.), *Contemporary approaches to creative thinking*. New York: Atherton Press.

Osborn, A. (1948). *Your creative power*. New York: Scribner.

Popper, K. R. (1959). *The logic of scientific discovery*. London: Hutchinson.

Roe, A. (1951). A psychological study of physical scientists. *Genetic Psychology Monographs, 43,* 121–235.

Roe, A. (1953). *The making of a scientist*. New York: Dodd Mead.

Rouse, W. B. (1986). A note on the nature of creativity in engineering: Implications for supporting system design. *Information Processing and Management, 22,* 279–285.

Schonberg, H. C. (1970). *The lives of the great composers*. New York: W. W. Norton.

Silviera, J. A. (1971). Incubation: The effects of interruption timing and length on problem solution and quality of problem processing (Doctoral dissertation, University of Oregon, 1972). *Dissertation Abstracts International, 32,* 5500B.

Simon, H. A. (1966). Scientific discovery and the psychology of problem solving. In R. G. Colodny (Ed.), *Mind and cosmos: Essays in contemporary science and philosophy* (Vol. III). Pittsburgh: University of Pittsburgh Press.

Simon, H. A., & Chase, W. (1973). Skill in chess. *American Scientist, 61,* 394–403.

Vernon, P. E. (1970). *Creativity*. Harmondsworth, England: Penguin Books.

Wallas, G. (1926). *The art of thought*. New York: Harcourt, Brace.

Wishbow, N. (1988). *Creativity in poets*. Unpublished doctoral dissertation, Carnegie-Mellon University, Pittsburgh, PA.

Ypma, E. G. (1968). Predictions of the industrial creativity of research scientists from biographical information (Doctoral dissertation, Purdue University, 1970). *Dissertation Abstracts International, 30,* 5731B–5732B.

CHAPTER 8

Creativity and Perception

John H. Flowers and Calvin P. Garbin

Informal thought about the nature of mental operations important to creative human behavior suggests that perceptual processes are of considerable importance. The ability to "see relationships among elements" is an attribution commonly made toward authors of major scientific discoveries or of noteworthy artistic achievements. For example, Shepard (1978, 1981) documented self-reports from several creative scientists and authors that strongly emphasize the role of visual imagery and the manipulation of visual codes in the creative process.

Given the anecdotal and self-report evidence for a relationship between creative behavior and aspects of perceptual processing, it initially may seem surprising that there is a notable *void* in either research or theoretical articles specifically focused on these issues. In preparing this chapter, for example, we noted that, during the last six volumes of the *Journal of Creative Behavior,* there was only one title that included the word *perception,* and that paper (Goodman & Marquart, 1978) was limited to a one-page abstract. In addition, we noted that among seven current textbooks in perception that presently reside on our bookshelves, *none* contain the term *creativity* in their indexes, nor is the term *creative ability* addressed at any point in the texts. Although references to the term *perception*

occasionally can be found in indexes of monographs specifically dealing with the topic of creativity, most of these references refer to research related to specific theories about individual differences in perceptual styles or processing modes, as opposed to broader contemporary issues of perceptual processing. Clearly, most researchers in the field of perception have not touched upon the topic of creativity, and relatively few researchers in creativity have chosen to integrate their work with perceptual issues.

Why Have Perceptual Psychologists Had Little to Say about Creativity?

One reason that may have inhibited psychologists who were studying aspects of perception from becoming involved in research on creativity is the fact that the term itself is not viewed as a scientifically "tight" concept of the variety preferred by relatively "operationalistic" behavioral scientists. As has been noted in earlier research (e.g., Stein, 1956; Taylor, 1960), as well as the contributors to this volume, providing an easily agreed upon operational definition of creativity that can be related to specific aspects of observable behavior or specific information-processing operations is problematic. Although there is general agreement among researchers in human thinking that a key component

John H. Flowers and Calvin P. Garbin • Department of Psychology, University of Nebraska, Lincoln, NE 68588.

of creativity is the process of generating novel mental representations, assessment of creativity by society is generally done on the basis of product; that is, does a particular solution, invention, discovery, or artistic contribution meet the joint criteria of novelty and worthwhileness? Obviously, a wide variety of mental operations and processes could contribute to the characteristics of a product that elicit those subjective evaluations.

The lack of existing literature explicitly relating issues in perception to the study of human creativity may also be attributable, in part, to fundamental differences in the "level of approach" among behavioral scientists who study fundamental characteristics of mental and behavioral processes common across individuals, as opposed to those having primary interest in differences among individuals. Both historically and at present, the majority of research efforts directed at understanding perceptual processes has been directed at theories, models, and descriptions of behavior that apply to perception in general, as opposed to individuals. The very term *creativity,* on the other hand, denotes an attribute that individuals presumably possess (or at least exhibit) in different amounts, hence, its study generally assumes an individual differences approach.

In our view, however, neither the fuzziness attributed to the definition of creativity nor its degree of association with ideographic rather than nomothetic approaches is as responsible for the lack of an existing body of literature relating creativity and perception as is the fact that perception traditionally has been studied as a process of *organizing* information within the nervous system, whereas studies of mental processes associated with creative behavior usually imply the *generation of novel representations* of information within the nervous system. At first inspection, these two classes of mental activity seem to have little to do with each other—or worse yet, they may even be viewed as incompatible operations.

Is Perceptual Organization Incompatible with Creative Thought?

Although individual theories of perception may differ substantially in their emphasis upon the importance of stimulus structure versus mental organizational processes (see, e.g., Hochberg, 1981, for a review), most theories approach perception as an information *reduction* process whereby noisy, variable, and impoverished patterns of environmental energy become resolved into stable and consistent internal representations optimal for human performance. Terms such as *perceptual organization* and *perceptual constancy* reflect emphasis on the information reduction processes. The latter term, in particular, emphasizes the role of perception in providing an individual with similar or identical mental representations of events that may have widely varying physical representations in the environment.

If a major function of "efficient" perceptual processing is to provide perceptual constancy, as well as to encourage different observers to obtain similar or identical representations from common environmental stimuli, then it does indeed seem that this organizational aspect of perception works against the generation of novel representations. One might therefore predict that some measures of perceptual performance that tap perceptual organizational processes would be negatively related to measures of creative ability. A potential consequence of such a relationship would be a positive association between perceptual *deficiencies* or handicaps and creative ability. Case study instances supportive of a relationship between perceptual handicaps and creative behavior can, in fact, be found in discussions of artistic and musical achievement. For instance, some of the innovative stylistic changes in Beethoven's later works are commonly attributed to the increasing severity of his hearing impairment.

However, there are many reasons to believe that some aspects of perceptual performance should be positively correlated with creative ability—or at least with the output of creative products. Many products of creative activity are not simple spontaneous generations, but result from effortful production, interspersed with the evaluation of feedback. Thus, handicapping the senses at a peripheral level (e.g., blindness or deafness) would certainly disrupt the ability to evaluate visual and auditory productions as they are being created. Despite what has been said about Beethoven's deafness, it seems absurd to predict that there would be a general negative relationship between basic measures of auditory sensitivity and frequency discrimination ability and creative output of music among composers, or a negative relationship between visual acuity measures and creative output of painters.

The Importance of Executively Controlled Processing

In our view, however, there are other aspects of perception for which performance measures ought to relate positively to creativity—in particular, processes under the conscious control of the perceiver. These include the ability to control various aspects of selective attention, to control figural organization when ambiguous sensory data are presented, to perform manipulations of internal visual and/or auditory representations of perceptual information, and the ability to equate perceptual experiences obtained from different sense modalities (cross-modal abilities). Although the earlier stages of perceptual processing leading to perceptual organization (e.g., sensory transduction, feature extraction, figural synthesis) typically are viewed as involuntary processes not under executive control, it is clear that perceptual organization and pattern recognition are influenced jointly by both involuntary or automatic and executively controlled processing.

At the level of perceptual organization, consider the examples of the Necker cube and of the reversible or ambiguous figures commonly found in most introductory psychology textbooks as well as in textbooks on perception (some examples are given in Figure 1). In each of these examples, there are contextual cues that cause a particular organization of the object to be perceived upon initial inspection. In most versions of these objects, observers have an ability to reverse the organization through voluntary changes in visual attention, although the time and effort required for such reversals, as well as which of the possible organizations is most likely to be initially seen, can be greatly influenced by modifying the contextual cues supporting either of the organizations. With some modifications, reversal becomes virtually impossible, and thus only one interpretation is obtained. Executively controlled processes can, within limits, significantly modify figural synthesis and organization, allowing a single physical stimulus to have multiple perceptual representations. Such processes may thus play a role in the generation of novel mental representations of information, which, in turn, could form the basis for creative products. Indeed, it is this kind of processing that appears to contribute to high-performance levels on tests, such as Guilford's (1967) divergent production test, that are specifically aimed at measuring individual differences related to creativity.

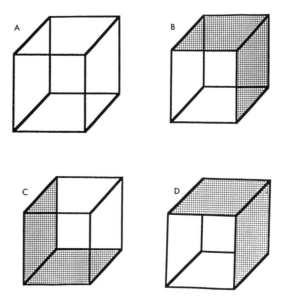

Figure 1. The Necker Cube—a familiar example of how controlled visual attention can change perceptual organization. In Example A, where the cube is essentially "transparent," two distinct organizations of depth can be obtained with moderate ease. In Example B, the shading and obscuring of the internal contours provide additional context making one organization dominant, although the second organization can still be obtained with effort. In Example C, shading of other parts of the figure makes the opposite depth organization dominant. In Example D, where the internal contours are totally removed, the alternative depth organization cannot be obtained at all (by typical subjects), even with considerable mental effort. Note also that, after viewing cube C, it is easier to view cube A (and even cube B) in the same organization as is dominant for cube C.

Thus, we see two distinct categories of perceptual processes for which individual variation among different observers might well relate to creativity. The first category contains the largely involuntary processes of perceptual organization. These are information-reducing processes that promote stability and organization of percepts, and thus normally tend to act against the formation of novel representations of information. The second category of perceptual processes, those under executive control of the observer, serve to modify and control the actions of the involuntary processes and also may serve to encourage the generation of novel representations of information. Extensive data exist on how each of these classes of processes affects performance as a function of stimulus and task parameters. Unfortunately, the data base on individual differences among either of these categories of processes is limited. Thus, it is difficult to relate directly specific empirical findings from existing perceptual studies to either the prediction of creative behavior in individuals or to modification of the environment to encourage creativity. We feel this indicates a need for additional basic research in individual differences *per se,* as well as research that directly relates these individual differences to creative ability.

A Configural Conception of Creativity

The particular topics (and perceptual tasks) that we will be discussing are selected largely because they focus on the joint role of involuntarily and executively controlled processes in perception. We are guided by a broad conception of creativity that assumes that there are essentially three factors that influence an individual's creative potential. One involves the relative ''looseness'' of involuntary organizational processes. An individual for whom the involuntary processes operate somewhat less deterministically (but perhaps less efficiently) is more likely to represent environmental data mentally (as well as data recalled from memory) in novel ways. The potential relationship between schizophrenia and creativity (Keefe & Magaro, 1980; Prentky, 1979) would seem to illustrate this factor.

The second factor involves the power of executively controlled processes, such as spatial selective attention, manipulation of mental images, and controlled cross-modal representation. Presumably, an individual having superior executive control of these processes is able to produce novel representations of information through effortful construction and modification of mental representations. This concept of ''creativity through controlled mental effort'' is very different from the concept of creativity attributable to ''loose organizational processes.'' For example, schizophrenics and individuals with schizotypic patterns of cognitive activity are notably weak on performance measures that presumably tap executively controlled mental processes.

The third factor, we feel, is of importance, particularly to creative thought that involves sudden insight, that involves processes not under executive control nor driven by sensory data, but that produces seemingly spontaneous mental representations, often involving visual imagery. Based largely upon self-reports of creative scientists and authors, Shepard (1978, 1981) attributed this aspect of creative activity to the same perceptual mechanisms that are normally coupled to the analysis of sensory input, and that are responsible for many aspects of perceptual organization. According to Shepard, these highly evolved and specialized perceptual mechanisms have the ability to operate upon data other than that obtained from normal sensory input, when decoupled from the sensory environment, as in such altered consciousness states as dreams. It is conceivable that the ability to use such spontaneously generated mental constructions in creative thought could be relatively independent of an individual's power of executively controlled mental operations, but *positively* correlated with the strength of perceptual organizational processes.

This three-factor view of creativity, directly based upon perceptual mechanisms, suggests therefore, a highly configural, nonlinear relationship between creative ability in the population and specific individual differences in mental processes. By looking—from an individual differences perspective—at various perceptual tasks that seem likely to tap differentially involuntary organizational processes and executively controlled processes, researchers may be in a better position to form a more detailed model relating specific representational and transformational processes to creative behavior. Additionally, such research might guide development of programs or products for the enhancement of creative ability.

Impairment of Sensory Processes

One of the most highly noticeable individual difference variables in perception is that of impairment of one or more of the primary senses—at least insofar as distinguishing normal individuals (including prosthetically correctable persons) from those who have apparent handicaps. Case study analyses of creative output from visually or auditorily handicapped individuals is a topic that deserves intensive study on its own; our limited mention of the topic here is merely to recognize that the broad categories of differences in perceptual and cognitive processes that characterize adaptation to severe defects in either hearing or vision obviously can affect the creative process, albeit in complex ways. It is a well-known principle of developmental psychobiology that prolonged deprivation of sensory experience, from birth or early in life, can result in permanent changes in neural structures that often prevent full recovery of function, even if the handicap is later repaired. Furthermore, neural structures may adapt functions qualitatively different from those assumed by corresponding structures in sensorily intact individuals. In human behavior, the consequences of sensory handicaps may affect aspects of memory and cognition that depend upon the use and manipulation of auditory or visual "codes," in addition to the ability to gain information from the environment. Recognition of this fact has led researchers and educators to develop specialized educational programs for hearing-impaired individuals that are specifically adapted to differences in modes of information processing among such individuals. In addition to producing performance differences *per se,* differences in memory codes, attention, and other control processes attributable to early sensory handicaps obviously have the potential for producing products that are novel when compared with norms of the general population of nonhandicapped individuals.

We see two major problems, however, in extrapolating general conclusions about creativity from the study of the perceptually handicapped. The first problem is the extreme degree of heterogeneity in types and degree of impairment among such individuals; not to mention potential differences in compensatory processes among individuals who share relatively similar physical impairments and developmental histories. The second problem is that the ease of retrieving examples of perceptually handicapped creative individuals from memory makes the topic ripe for attributions of correlations between the handicap and the creativity that may not be warranted (e.g., Kahneman & Tversky, 1973). One may be able to learn a great deal about the creative processes of a given handicapped individual through careful case study, protocol analyses, and other techniques, and such research potentially could be of tremendous value to the development of special therapeutic and educational approaches. As a simple individual difference variable to be applied for understanding the characteristics of creativity in the general population, the handicapped–nonhandicapped dichotomy does not, on the other hand, appear to be very useful.

Environmental Constraints on Sensory Input

It may be more useful to consider the effects, within unimpaired individuals, of different levels of sensory stimulation upon creative thought processes. In particular, the fact that common resources are used in executive control of mental representations and in the processing of corresponding forms of sensory data implies that perception within a particular modality may *interfere* with thought processes sharing a common form of representation. For instance, the generation and the manipulation of visual images are inhibited when a task requires processing visual input, and manipulations of linguistic representations may be inhibited by tasks requiring the processing of speech. The interference between perceptually generated and internally generated codes that share a common modality easily can be demonstrated by using a task developed by Brooks (1968). In this task, subjects are required to imagine a moving dot traveling around a mental image of a block drawn letter, such as a capital F (see Figure 2), and to respond orally yes or no based upon whether each corner constitutes an external angle (requiring a "right turn" on the part of the dot) or an internal angle (requiring a "left turn"). Time to complete the circuit with the oral response mode is generally much less than that required for the same task when subjects must check off Ys versus Ns in a visually presented answer sheet. However, when subjects are presented with a linguistic search task, requiring them to indicate whether successive words in memorized sentences are nouns versus other parts of speech, the visually guided check-response mode produces

Figure 2. An illustration of the sort of "imaginary stimuli" used by Brooks (1968) to study the effect of verbal or visually guided response processes on the ability to search visually coded information in active memory. Subjects were required to mentally construct an image of a letter, such as this capital F, and to indicate whether each corner passed by the imaginary asterisk consisted of an external or an internal angle. Subjects could perform better on this task if an oral yes-no response was used than if a visually guided manual response system was employed, indicating that manipulation of visual codes shares resources with visual perception.

considerably faster searches than does the oral yes-no mode. Modality specific interference between imagery and perceptual detection tasks also has been demonstrated by Segall and Fusella (1970), who asked subjects to construct mental images, such as the appearance of a tree (visual) or the ringing of a telephone (auditory), and showed selective deficits in the ability to detect weak auditory or visual signals.

Because documented self-reports of mental events associated with creative thought often include extensive use of mental imagery (Shepard, 1978, 1981), it seems plausible that creating an environment that minimizes potentially interfering sensory input might be useful in facilitating manipulations of mental image processing and, hence, contribute to creative thought. Additional research in how regulation of stimuli (visual and linguistic feedback from a display screen on a word processor) can affect the speed and quality of creative output is one area of applied perceptual research that has current value for product development. An increasing number of products are being released into the personal and professional software markets that are designed to aid the initial stages of manuscript planning and organization. These so-called idea processors are aimed specifically at the facilitation of creative output for a variety of applications (Kellogg, 1986). With the increasing use of small computers in a variety of settings, one might expect the developments of similar products to continue. One attribute of at least some of the existing hardware is that users are prevented from viewing previously entered text—a design feature that seems to assume that the availability of visual feedback, or at least the existence of printed text that stimulates the visual system of the user, is detrimental to performance.

As Kellogg (1986) pointed out, evaluative research on these products and on prototypes for future related software aids is woefully lacking. The same can be said for research that is not tied to a specific product but that provides general information about the production as a function of the presence of perceptual stimuli of, for example, text, figural design, and metaphorical or analogical relationships. Based upon the implications of such studies as those of Brooks (1968), it may be the case that the presence of auditory or visual stimuli, while an individual is attempting to "be creative," can have certain interfering stimulus-related costs for mental representation and transformation, and, hence, inhibit creative performance. The knowl-edge base that is generated from such a research effort might prove very useful in the development of both text-related products and picture-related software aids used in computer-assisted design. More generally, however, such knowledge might prove useful in the development of techniques for fostering increased output of creative activity in a much wider range of settings, through the teaching of specific strategies for minimizing perceptual interference with image-based mental operations and other forms of mental code transformations.

Altered and Transitional States—Decoupling Perceptual Mechanisms from Sensory Input

Our discussion above has concerned the overlap in resources between mechanisms normally tied to the involuntary processes of analyzing and organizing sensory stimulation and those of executively controlled construction and manipulation of visual and auditory images. A related issue concerns the potential role of the perceptual mechanisms normally driven by sensory input during unaltered states of observer consciousness, when those mechanisms are decoupled from sensory input. Dream states, and perhaps some drug-induced states, represent examples of such a decoupling. Shepard (1978, 1981) argued that transitions from such states represent a fertile ground for the development of creative ideas, because the perceptual mechanisms automatically linked to organizing the sensory world (which are normally transparent to our conscious experience) run "on their own," occasionally constructing novel and useful percepts and images from fragments of internal neural noise and loosely guided consultations with memory. According to Shepard (1981), contact with the linguistic system allows the abstract images and relationships to be translated into communicable form. Shepard clearly viewed the mechanisms of perceptual organization that involve spatial relationships in particular as a powerful source of general knowledge about relationships that can be analogically applied to invention and problem solving:

The creative productions of a brain presumably stem from whatever intuitive wisdom, whatever deep organizing principles have been built into that brain as a result of the immense evolutionary journey that has issued in the formation of that brain. If the arguments sketched out in this chapter have any merit, the most basic and powerful innate intuitions and principles underlying verbal and nonverbal thought, alike, may well be those governing the relations, projections, symmetries, and transformations of objects in space. (Shepard, 1981, p. 339)

Thus, Shepard described a very direct relationship between perceptual processes and creative thought, making the claim that (1) implicit knowledge of visual relationships among objects, and rules for transforming those relationships, may constitute the fundamental mental operations inherent in much of creative thought, and (2) that decoupling certain normally involuntary processes from their data source may allow those same mechanisms to operate as a primary generator of creative thought. It seems apparent from Shepard's descriptions of self-report data that this form of creative thought is not of the controlled variety (as discussed in the previous section) but is the product of involuntary mental operations that lead to spontaneous insight. Thus, the effects of decoupling of normal sensory input during alternative states of consciousness should be viewed as distinct from restricting sensory input in a normal-waking-state individual in order to prevent interference with controlled manipulation of perceptual codes.

In popular religious and scientific circles, vast amounts have been written about alternative states of consciousness that involve such decoupling of sensory input, although, in our view, it is sometimes difficult to determine into which of those circles a given piece of research/literature should be categorized. It is also apparent that, throughout much of the history of civilization, some human beings knowingly have exploited alternative states (including dreams) as a deliberate strategy for fostering creative behavior—not to mention the use of alternative consciousness states as a *causal* construct for particular creative acts. Like research relating either handicaps or psychopathology to creativity, selection biases and the availability heuristic can play havoc with attempting to relate existing literature on alternate states and creativity either to individual differences in creative potential or to research into conditions that foster creativity.

It may, however, be profitable to study the extent to which individual differences in dream recall might relate to instances of insightful creative thought, as well as to individual differences in attention and perceptual organization. Such data could provide for a better empirical grasp on the degree to which information processing in dream or

transitional states actually constitutes a major source of creative productions. Mental constructions occurring during an altered or transitional state can be useful only insofar as they are remembered, and insofar as they can be evaluated for application and worthwhileness. It may be that the degree to which decoupled automatic perceptual processes contribute to creative output has far more to do with facility in higher level cognitive processes, such as memory storage, retrieval, search, and comparison, than in individual differences in perceptual organization processes *per se*.

Consideration of the role of stimulus-decoupled perceptual organization processes as a fundamental source of creative thought, as Shepard proposed, leads to an interesting conjecture about the link between efficiency of perceptual organization and creativity—particularly with respect to how general cognitive defects, such as those associated with schizophrenia, might relate to creative thought. One common view of why individuals who possess some of the traits of schizophrenic thought might be viewed as creative is that deficiencies in the normal involuntary perceptual organization processes lead to an increased likelihood of an atypical representation of a perceptual event (see, e.g., Keefe & Magaro, 1980). In other words, it is the anomalous organization of sensory input, coupled with sufficiently good higher order processes to evaluate the potential worthwhileness of a mental construction (or, alternatively, the opportunity for a peer to notice the worthwhileness of a product even if the cognitively impaired individual cannot perform the evaluation), that lead to creative output. However, creativity that is attributable to looseness in perceptual organization in the presence of stimuli is very different from creativity that is attributable to perceptual organization processes decoupled from normal sensory inputs. An increased frequency of transitions from hypnopompic or hallucinatory states (as might be reasonably expected to occur in association with certain psychotic disorders), combined with *unimpaired* (or even superior) mechanisms of perceptual organization, thus represents a potential alternative route for contributing to creative thought by some individuals who possess dispositions toward cognitive disorders. Moreover, the relative weakness or looseness in organizational processes and the ability to exploit involuntary organizational processes decoupled from sensory input are suggested as *distinct* individual difference variables, both of which might relate to creativity in the general population.

Assessing Individual Variation in Perceptual Organization Ability

Our discussion thus far suggests that obtaining a better understanding of patterns of individual variation in perceptual organization tendencies might be highly useful in examining the role of perceptual organization processes in creative thought. Unfortunately, with the exception of various measures of embedded figures performance, Gestalt grouping processes and other related "automatic" processes of perceptual organization have not been subjected to systematic individual difference measurements. Performance measures on tasks, such as those involving embedded figures, often do not provide a convenient way of separating performance attributable to loose perceptual organization (failure to group), from performance attributable to strong, executively controlled focused attention (ability to break apart). It appears to us, however, that one should be able to separate the contributions of automatic organization and efficient focused attention, by selecting a combination of structurally similar tasks, including some in which perceptual organization is helpful to performance, and others for which perceptual organization is harmful.

As an example of such an approach, consider the example of the stimulus displays shown in Figure 3,

used by Pomerantz, Sager, and Stover (1977). The task required of the subject was to detect the "oddball" quadrant as rapidly as possible, and choice reaction time (RT) was the dependent variable. In Example A, the baseline task involves choosing the oddly oriented single parenthesis, located in this example in the upper left. This display requires a quite effortful scrutiny as the mean RT obtained by Pomerantz *et al.* was 2,400 msec. However, adding the four extra context elements in the display leads to a perceptual grouping phenomenon that makes the oddball element stand out, reducing the RT by nearly a second (for a group average obtained with college student subjects). Now, consider the display shown in Example B. Here, different context elements are added (rotated parentheses) for which the result of organizational processes produces objects perceptually less distinct than the single parentheses, resulting in an average increase in RT of 550 msec. Thus, in these examples, we have two highly similar tasks, one for which Gestalt organization helps, one for which it hurts.

Presumably, individuals with weak organizational processes would fail to gain as much benefit from the helpful context, in comparison with more typical subjects, while performing tasks such as that of Example A. On the other hand, such subjects also might be less susceptible to interference from context stimuli that disrupt performance of typical subjects. In contrast, subjects possessing nominal automatic grouping processes, but exceptionally powerful *executively controlled* focal attentional processes, might exhibit far less interference from the harmful context, while still maintaining benefits from the helpful context.

A related set of classification or sorting tasks that have the potential for separately assessing looseness of involuntary perceptual organization and the strength of voluntary visual attention is the one used by Pomerantz and Schwaitzberg (1975). In this experiment, there were three different basic sorting tasks required of a subject, and the stimulus response mappings for each of these is shown in Figure 4. In Condition A (the control condition), subjects sorted stimuli on the basis of orientation of the leftmost parenthesis; the orientation of the right parenthesis was held constant. In Condition B, which required subjects to divide attention and attempt to ignore the irrelevant rightmost parenthesis, the response assignment was determined by the left parenthesis, and the right parenthesis varied in a manner orthogonal to the left parenthesis. In this condition, classification times were considerably

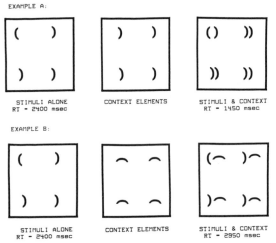

Figure 3. Examples of stimuli used in an "oddball quadrant" detection task employed by Pomerantz, Sager, and Stover (1977). In Example A, the addition of the context elements causes Gestalt grouping processes that make the unique quadrant more distinctive, whereas in Example B, the rotated context elements obscure the distinction (see text for details).

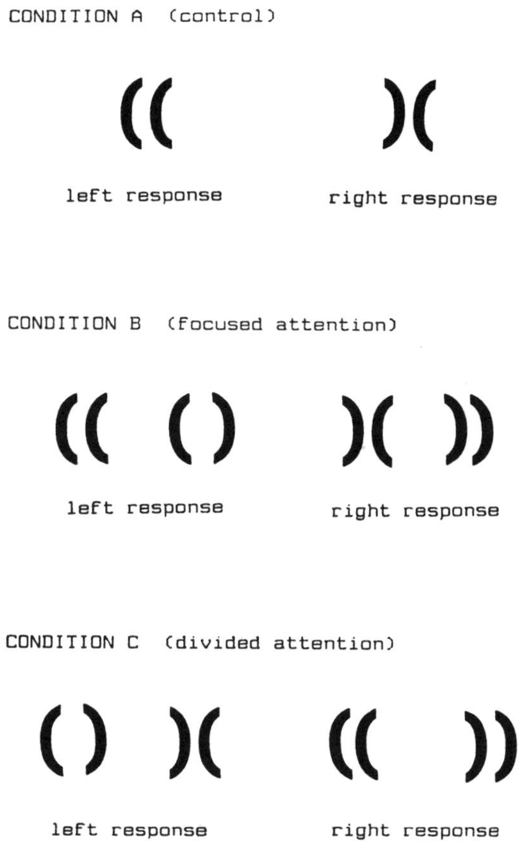

CONDITION A (control)

((   )(

left response   right response

CONDITION B (focused attention)

((()   )( ))

left response   right response

CONDITION C (divided attention)

())((( ))

left response   right response

Figure 4. Examples of stimuli used by Pomerantz and Schwaitzberg (1975) in a task illustrating how Gestalt grouping affects selective and divided attention in a visual classification task (see text for details).

slower than those of the control condition, provided the spatial separation between the parenthesis pairs was close. As the spatial separation between the elements was increased beyond a single typespace in other stimulus sequences, the interference from the irrelevant right parenthesis diminished.

Condition C required that subjects split the four possible pairings of parentheses into two groups, such that the response assignment was determined by the combination of both parentheses. Unlike either Condition A or Condition B, this task required an evaluation of *both* the leftmost and the rightmost parentheses. At close separations, such grouping seemed to occur involuntarily, as subjects reported perceiving the parenthesis pairs as single objects. In this case, classification times were actually shorter than for Condition B, because the objects assigned to each category appear to share common percep-

tual attributes (e.g., "the fat ones vs. the skinny ones"). However, at wider separations, in which involuntary grouping processes break down, subjects had to apply effortful *divided* attention processes, either to try to perceptually group the parenthesis pairs or to separately evaluate each parenthesis and apply a classification rule. A typical pattern of results for these three tasks is shown in Figure 5, in which sorting time is plotted as a function of separation of the parentheses. Again, these data are based upon the means of subjects' performances that were obtained by Pomerantz and Schwaitzberg (1975).

One might expect, however, that individual differences in the potency of involuntary organizational processes and individual differences in the executively controlled ability to break up perceptual configurations (as well as divide attention, in this case) would produce systematic differences in the functions from those shown in Figure 5. An appropriate application of psychometric scaling procedures to differences among such patterns, in addition to similar analyses of patterns in such tasks as the "oddball detection" examples in Figure 3, could lead to separate scales for strength of perceptual organization tendencies and power of voluntary selective attention.

To our knowledge, there is no existing research on patterns of individual differences in the costs and benefits of the configural effects that might be obtained by systematic administration of these or similar tasks to large numbers of individuals, in order to obtain an index of relative organizational power among different individuals that might be of use for determining its relationship to creative behavior. However, given that individual differences in more traditional measures of embedded figures tasks exist (even though the voluntary selective component has not been factored out), and given the recent evidence of the very unique and actually *superior* performance of schizophrenics (compared with normals) on tasks for which avoidance of grouping contributes to performance (Place & Gilmore, 1980; Wells & Leventhal, 1984), we believe that such individual differences exist, are potentially measurable, and probably do bear a relationship with other important cognitive attributes including creativity. Given that the presumed organizational looseness of schizophrenics is often related to creative thought in individuals who perhaps have a lesser degree of the deficiency (e.g., Keefe & Magaro, 1980), the data on the psychiatric populations are of considerable interest and are encourag-

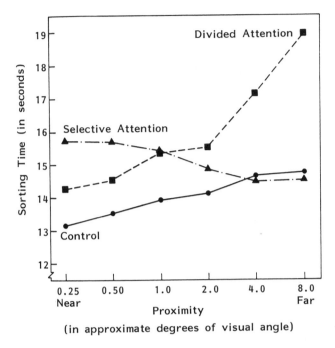

Figure 5. A graphical representation of results obtained by Pomerantz and Schwaitzberg (1975) for Tasks A, B, and C of Figure 4. Sorting times for decks of 32 cards displaying these stimuli are plotted as a function of the physical separation between the pairs of parentheses. Stimulus sets involving wide spatial separations between the two stimuli greatly slowed sorting in the divided attention task (Task C of Figure 4), while allowing subjects to avoid interference from perceptual grouping in Task B. Presumably the form of such functions might differ for subjects differing in the potency of their involuntary perceptual organization processes as well as the power of their controlled visual attention. Reprinted by permission of LEA Associates.

ing for clarifying the "creativity-madness" association that has been around for centuries.

Individual Variation in Intramodal Visual Code Transformation

In contrast to our lack of knowledge about individual variation in perceptual organizing ability, psychometric tests that directly tap the ability of individuals to compare transformed visual objects (e.g., rotated block drawings, folded and unfolded block figures) have been available for decades (e.g., see Guilford, 1967). Individual variation in abilities to perform such operations is clearly measurable, and it is apparent that performance on such psychometric tests correlates with performance of mental tasks or problems that appear to be mediated by use of visual analog codes.

One specific example is a study by Paivio (1978), who measured subjects' reaction times for deter-

mining which of two clock times (given as digital expressions) would produce the smallest angle between the hands of a standard analog clock. Paivio found that, in general, reaction time was a monotonic function of differences in the analog hand angles, providing strong evidence that the task was mediated by image comparison. In addition, however, subjects were divided into "high-imagery" and "low-imagery" groups, on the basis of a median split of performance on a composite of Guilford's Block Visualization Test, the Minnesota Paper Form Board, and the Thurstone Space Relations Test. High-imagery subjects produced RTs that averaged about 1 second faster at each level of angular difference than low-imagery subjects. In contrast, a similar split of the subject population on the basis of a verbal fluency measure (Paivio, 1971) produced no differences between groups. This study as well as numerous others (e.g., see Paivio, 1971, 1978 for a review) provide relatively convincing evidence that individual differences in ability to perform top-down manipulation and transformation of visuospatial codes can be predicted effectively with existing psychometric instruments.

Given the apparent importance of fluent visual coding in anecdotal reports of creative cognition, it seems intuitive that psychometric measures of such visual abilities should relate positively to measures of creative behavior, particularly for those individuals whose creative work is arrived at primarily through the effortful, voluntary route. One must keep in mind, however, that simple possession of a mental ability does not necessarily imply that ability will be used to produce novel and worthwhile products. Creative behavior requires an evaluative component for recognizing when a particular novel representation is of value. Given these considerations, and our configural view of the creative process, one should not expect extremely high linear correlations between measures of visual coding fluency and creative behavior *per se.*

One issue of importance in determining how specific information-processing characteristics relate to creativity is whether it is appropriate to view individual differences in performance of specific classes of perceptual tasks as measures of relatively narrowly defined information-processing abilities, or whether correlations among specific task performances suggest the existence of a general ability "factor." Guilford (1981, 1983) argued that processes, such as visual code manipulation and cross-modal transformations (which we will discuss presently), are all part of a general "transformational ability" that is a key component of creative thought. Indeed, one can make a rather strong psychometric argument for that position, as Guilford has done. On the other hand, perceptual psychologists who are aware that different neural structures may be involved in intramodal versus cross-modal transformations, and also that common neural structures may be involved in both voluntary and involuntary processing of visually coded information, are more likely to have interest in specific comparisons among tasks. One research question that bears upon the relationship between specific visual information-processing abilities and our configural model of creativity is whether fluency in controlled visual transformations might be related to the frequency of spontaneous insight in creative thought. We have thus far implied, as has Shepard (1978, 1981), that spontaneous novel constructions are basically the result of involuntary representational processes, decoupled from their normal sensory source of data. However, it must be noted that

most of the anecdotal reports of such spontaneous insight, summarized by Shepard and others, have come from individuals who were likely to score very high on measures of mental abilities *and* who were (or still are) known to have put in large amounts of controlled mental effort on problems related to their creative achievements. The *selection, refinement,* and *use* of images spontaneously generated during transitional or altered states likely may depend upon effortful executive processes, suggesting that spontaneous insight should not be viewed as a totally involuntary occurrence. Moreover, mental activity that substitutes for the sensory signals that normally drive mechanisms of perception, insofar as they are influenced by memory activities, may be highly structured by previous effortful mental code manipulations. In short, spontaneous insight may not be so spontaneous and is conceivably quite closely related to mental transformation abilities of both intramodal and intermodal varieties.

An Example of the Interplay of Involuntary and Executively Driven Creative Processes: Synesthesia and Cross-Modal Representations

Previously, we have posited that these two very different processes might produce similar creative products. In this section, we will look at two related processes, one perceptual (automatic) and one cognitively mediated (executively controlled), that do indeed seem to lead to similar and potentially creative representations of the environment.

Theorists and artists long have recognized the correspondences, interrelationships, and interdependencies of the senses as they are used to capture information about the world. Aristotle and other early thinkers posited various relationships of cross-modal process or product, and Bishop Berkeley added his notion of their ontogeny. More recently, Stevens (e.g., 1959), Gibson (1966), and Marks (e.g., 1978, 1982) have provided more refined theories and hypotheses about the nature, workings, and meanings of these correspondences. Particularly for Marks, the evidence of artistic awareness and of creative use of these correspondences adds weight to various laboratory studies that are in support of the theoretical ideas of cross-modal equivalences and sensory unity.

Most people are familiar with the use of onomatopoetic words, such as "hiss," "crack," and "woff," to convey the auditory characteristics of a sound as well as its semantic meaning. But the sounds of words also seem to convey other information. Kohler (1947) showed that most people matched the pseudowords "maluma" and "takete" with the rounder and the more angular of two line figures, respectively. As a demonstration, Marks (1978) replicated the finding using a production task in which two children were asked to draw the visual representations of these words. The drawing of takete was clearly the more angular for each person. As another example of how word sounds can supply nonauditory information, Sapir (1929) and later Newman (1933) asked subjects about the size of objects referred to by nonsense syllables and found the words containing the letter /a/ were judged to refer to larger objects than did those containing /i/. Finally, most people in our society are familiar with the relationships between colors and temperatures—red is "hot" whereas blue is "cool."

These types of correspondences are quite different from the wholly involuntary phenomena of true synesthesia, in which "a small minority of people experience a curious sensory blending, where stimulation of a single sense arouses a mélange of sensory images" (Marks, 1978, p. 83). In addition to truly synesthetic individuals, there are widespread reports of involuntary synesthesia produced by various consciousness-altering drugs, such as LSD and hashish.

As interesting and well-documented as true involuntary synesthesia is, it is not, in itself, a creative product, just as the novel representations of schizophrenic thought are not. Creative products require the additional processes of appropriate *selection* and *presentation* of those novel representations. Unlike the schizophrenics' art, which is often identified as creative after production, the synesthetics must choose whether or not to capture their mental representations and present their novel version of the world.

Furthermore, although loose perceptual organization is a *potential* source of novel representations for synesthetics (as for schizophrenics), documentation of creative products from *true* synesthetics is notably lacking. In part, the lack of documented examples simply may reflect the relative infrequency of true synesthetic individuals in the population, relative to schizotypic or schizophrenic individuals. But from each of these sources of anomalous per-

cepts, numerous products have arisen. According to Marks (1978), synesthesia has enjoyed two periods of extensive study, the first 40 years of the twentieth century, and an earlier period during the nineteenth century. It was during this earlier period, when synesthesia was of interest not only to scientists and physicians but also to musicians, that creative products were introduced that clearly sprang from the perceptual phenomena. Perhaps the best known of these were the multimodal concerts that mixed music with colored lights and occasionally with odor. Louis-Bertrand Castel built the first light organ in 1735. This organ and others like it produced a particular colored light along with each note as the keys were depressed. Numerous pieces were written for and performed with these instruments. Laser light shows are a more recent version of this same artistic use of the close relationship between color and tonality to produce desired affective responses.

Also, during the nineteenth century and later, there were numerous linguistic expressions of synesthesia-like experiences, or synesthetic metaphors. The following examples of such poetry are taken from Marks (1978): Charles Baudelaire's "Correspondences," "perfumes fresh as children's flesh, sweet as oboes, green as prairies," and Arthur Rimbaud's "Sonnet of the Vowels" "A black, E white, I red, U green, O blue." Examples of synesthetic metaphor in literature are (from Marks, 1982): "the sound of coming darkness" (Poe); "a soft yet glowing light, liked lulled music" (Shelley); and "music suddenly opened like a luminous book" (Conrad Aiken).

On interesting point concerning these uses of color–sound correspondence and poetic metaphor (which is an important difference between these productions and those of schizophrenics) is that none of these authors appear to have been truly synesthetic themselves (although one may conjecture about those authors who had a history of narcotic use, e.g., Poe). Yet they were able to produce creative results using these correspondences in ways so compelling that we not only understand and agree with their meanings, but often do not even immediately notice that there are "crossed" or "mixed" modality-specific adjectives and nuances. Marks provided experimental evidence that most persons have (or can develop) a strongly internalized correspondence of cross-modal relationship between certain visual and auditory characteristics (primarily brightness and loudness). Thus, we see that an automatic perceptual process—the capability and tendency toward cross-modal associations—is necessary for the appreciation of creative products generated by an executively controlled process.

In this discussion, we have tried to give an example of how knowledge of an infrequent, perceptual, and automatic phenomenon (synesthesia) can provide the impetus for the use of executively controlled processes to create artistic products. Finally, the appreciation of these creative products greatly depends upon the ability to "perceptually resonate" with those products, an ability that seems to be nearly universal and automatic.

Summary and Conclusions

We have argued that the generation of creative behavior can result from a combination of involuntary and executively controlled processes. These processes rely heavily on neural mechanisms and systems that have evolved primarily as *perceptual* systems. However, these systems, which embody highly sophisticated computational and inferential mechanisms, also serve to operate on mental codes actively retrieved from memory (e.g., conscious generation and modification of imagery). In addition, there is anecdotal evidence that these same mechanisms can be the source of spontaneously generated images or representations, when their normal driving source of sensory stimulation is decoupled, as in transitions from dreams or altered states. Such spontaneous generation, if appropriately selected and recognized as useful, perhaps can produce the sudden creative insights characterized by many self-reports from creative individuals.

According to our analysis, creativity thus can result from some combination of (1) novel percepts attributable to departures from the normal deterministic processes of perceptual organization, (2) effortful conscious mental activity involving manipulation and transformation of codes that generate novel representations, and (3) spontaneous generation of novel representations. Because the relative contributions of each of these to a specific creative achievement presumably varies markedly across both situations and individuals, the relationship between specific cognitive abilities or characteristics of processing and the likelihood of an individual's producing products judged to be creative is highly configural and thus difficult to measure. The configurality of factors is particularly

problematic in that individual differences in cognitive processing that affect these three "routes" to creative thought probably are not independent. For example, the looseness in perceptual organization that may characterize creative individuals with schizotypal thought patterns may well be negatively correlated with ability to make effortful mental transformations as well as the ability to recognize that a novel mental representation is worthwhile.

We do believe, however, that research efforts into individual differences in specific perceptual characteristics potentially can be useful in both increasing our understanding of their relationships to creative behavior, as well as for determining circumstances that might foster creative thought. As we have noted, research literature describing individual differences in perceptual organization tendencies is notably lacking. The study of individual differences in executively controlled transformations of mental representations has received considerably more research effort, due to a long existing presumption that such operations are closely related to measures of basic mental abilities. However, the "mental measurement" motivation for much of this research, has, in our view, directed researchers more toward the study of "common transformational ability factors" (e.g., Guilford, 1981, 1983) rather than toward the properties of specific types of mental code manipulations, such as synesthetic metaphor. Lastly, the literature on spontaneous generation of novel representations by perceptual mechanisms is, at present, highly speculative, and consists primarily of self-report anecdotes.

A Flow Diagram of the Creative Process and Its Implications

To summarize our view of how processes related to perception influence the creative process, we offer the flow diagram shown in Figure 6. In addition, Table 1 summarizes some of our conjectures about the relationships between various components of the flow diagram and some individual difference variables potentially measurable by existing or designable assessment instruments and surveys.

Essentially, Figure 6 is a visual summary of our previous discussions of a configural view of the creative process. It lists as *sources* of novel representations (1) atypical involuntary processes of perception, including both loose organizational processes and true synesthesia, (2) spontaneous (and

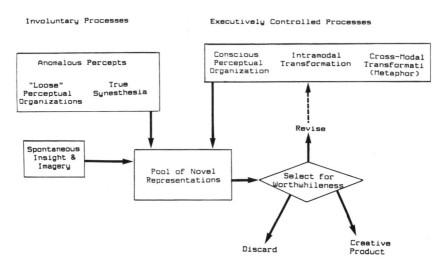

Figure 6. A schematic representation of our view of how involuntary and executively controlled perceptual processes contribute to creative thought (see text for details).

involuntary) generation of insight and imagery, (3) conscious perceptual organization, (4) conscious intermodal transformations of representations, and (5) conscious cross-modal transformations of representations. In addition, it includes the process of *selection* of novel representation and *feedback* to the executively controlled processes for purposes of refining the potential creative product.

In Table 1, we have chosen to relate the uses of each of the potential sources of novel representations discussed in this chapter together with an "efficiency" selection mechanism drawn from the following set of individual differences variables: (1) strength of perceptual organization, SPO; (2) imag-

ery ability, IM; (3) general measures of transformation ability, T; (4) schizotypal thought, ST; (5) drug usage, DU; (6) ability to report dreams, DR; and (6) amount of reported conscious effort expended on the problem for which a creative solution is found, EF. Note that these items constitute a nonexhaustive sample of *potentially* measurable individual differences variables. As we have mentioned previously, respected psychometric instruments exist that presumably tap some of these, whereas for others, instruments would need to be developed. Furthermore, measurement of some of the self-report variables (such as DR and EF) would most likely involve both validity and reliability problems

Table 1.   Hypothetical Associations between Modes of Generating and Selecting Creative Representations and Various Measures of Individual Differences[a]

Source	SPO	IM	T	ST	DU	DR	EF
Loose perceptual organization	−	−	−	+	+?	?	−?
Synesthesia	?	+?	?	−?	+	?	?
Spontaneous imagery	+?	+	+	−?	?	+	+
Conscious perceptual organization	+	+	+	−	−?	?	+
Intramodal transformation	+	+	+	−	−	?	+
Cross-modal transformation	?	+?	?	−	?	?	+?

[a]See text for a detailed explanation.

that we will not address here. Given those disclaimers, and with the additional disclaimer that nearly all the cell entries are based upon our own current personal speculations as opposed to existing data, we offer this table of hypotheses as a guide for potential future research. The cell entries themselves consist of + and − signs to indicate presumed positive and negative correlations, together with ? signs that specify either that no particular relationship is likely to exist, or, if there is one, we have no basis to speculate its directionality. Additionally, we have used the question mark as a modifier to indicate above average uncertainty about our speculations.

We should call attention to one pattern among these hypothetical intercorrelations that emphasizes our previous statements about the configural nature of creativity. That pattern is that individuals whose creativity stems largely from anomalous perceptual inputs (i.e., individuals with loose perceptual organization and perhaps a rare, creative, true synesthetic) are likely to be very different from creative individuals who rely more heavily upon executively controlled processes. Conceivably, this might bear upon differences in the *types* of creative products that are developed by individuals who rely predominantly upon anomalous percepts for novel representations, as opposed to those arising from some combination of executively controlled manipulations of representations and spontaneous imagery and/or insight. As a possible case in point, one often encounters examples of schizophrenic paintings and drawings, yet rarely does one encounter mention of schizophrenic poetry or sculpture.

As a final point, we do not wish to imply, by our apparent emphasis upon individual difference variables in this final section of this chapter, that research on conditions that affect the likelihood of creative behavior within a given individual is less important than research aimed at predicting patterns of creativity among individuals. Clearly, the two classes of research complement each other; by learning more about relationships between perception-related processes as varieties of creative behavior, we may discover strategies for optimizing creative production within individuals. Similarly, through applied research aimed at development of "thinking aids," "designing aids," and "writing aids," or through the evaluation of such products, we may discover additional relationships among perceptual and cognitive processes and the creative process.

References

Brooks, L. R. (1968). Spatial and verbal components of the act of recall. *Canadian Journal of Psychology, 22,* 349–368.

Gibson, J. (1966). *The senses considered as perceptual systems.* Boston: Houghton Mifflin.

Goodman, K. J., & Marquart, D. I. (1978). Creativity and perception: The neglected theory of Lowenfeld. *Journal of Creative Behavior, 12,* 279.

Guilford, J. P. (1967). *The nature of human intelligence.* New York: McGraw-Hill.

Guilford, J. P. (1981). Higher order structure of intellect abilities. *Multivariate Behavioral Research, 16,* 411–435.

Guilford, J. P. (1983). Transformation abilities or functions. *Journal of Creative Behavior, 17,* 75–83.

Hochberg, J. (1981). Levels of perceptual organization. In M. Kubovy & J. Pomerantz (Eds.), *Perceptual organization* (pp. 255–278). Hillsdale, NJ: Earlbaum.

Kahneman, D., & Tversky, A. (1973). On the psychology of prediction. *Psychological Review, 80,* 237–251.

Keefe, J. A., & Magaro, P. A. (1980). Creativity and schizophrenia: An equivalence of cognitive processing. *Journal of Abnormal Psychology, 89,* 390–398.

Kellogg, R. (1986). Designing ideal processors for document composition. *Behavior Research Methods, Instruments, and Computers, 18,* 118–128.

Kohler, W. (1947). *Gestalt psychology.* New York: Liveright.

Marks, L. (1978). *The unity of the senses.* New York: Academic Press.

Marks, L. (1982). Synesthetic perception and poetic metaphor. *Journal of Experimental Psychology: Human Perception and Performance, 8,* 15–23.

Newman, S. S. (1933). Further experiments in phonetic symbolism. *American Journal of Psychology, 45,* 53–75.

Paivio, A. (1971). *Imagery and verbal processes.* New York: Holt, Rinehart & Winston.

Paivio, A. (1978). Comparison of mental clocks. *Journal of Experimental Psychology: Human Perception and Performance, 4,* 61–71.

Place, E., & Gilmore, G. (1980). Perceptual organization in schizophrenia. *Journal of Abnormal Psychology, 89,* 409–418.

Pomerantz, J., & Schwaitzberg, S. (1975). Grouping by proximity: Selective attention measures. *Perception and Psychophysics, 18,* 355–361.

Pomerantz, J., Sager, L., & Stover, R. (1977). Perception of wholes and their component parts: Some configural superiority effects. *Journal of Experimental Psychology: Human Perception and Performance, 3,* 422–435.

Prentky, R. A. (1979). Creativity and psychopathology: A neurocognitive perspective. In B. Maher (Ed.), *Progress in experimental personality research* (Vol. 9, pp. 1–39). Academic Press.

Sapir, E. (1929). A study of phonetic symbolism. *Journal of Experimental Psychology, 12,* 225–239.

Segall, S. J., & Fusella, V. (1970). Influence of imaged pictures and sounds in detection of visual and auditory signals. *Journal of Experimental Psychology, 83,* 458–474.

Shepard, R. N. (1978). Externalization of mental images and the act of creating. In B. Randhawa & W. Coffman (Eds.), *Visual learning, thinking, and communication* (pp. 133–189). New York: Academic Press.

Shepard, R. N. (1981). Psychophysical complementarity. In M.

Kubovy & J. Pomerantz (Eds.), *Perceptual organization* (pp. 279–341). Hillsdale, NJ: Earlbaum.

Stein, M. I. (1956). A transactional approach to creativity. In D. W. Taylor (Ed.), *Research conference on the identification of creative talent*. Salt Lake City: University of Utah Press.

Stevens, S. (1959). Cross-modality validation of subjective scales for loudness, vibration and electric shock. *Journal of Experimental Psychology, 57*, 201–209.

Taylor, D. W. (1960). Thinking and creativity. *Annals of the New York Academy of Sciences, 91*, 108–127.

Wells, D., & Leventhal, D. (1984). Perceptual grouping in schizophrenia: Replication of Place & Gilmore. *Journal of Abnormal Psychology, 93*, 231–234.

CHAPTER 9

Memory and Creativity

Barry S. Stein

Although there are many ways to define creativity, creative behavior usually involves a product or response both novel and appropriate to the task at hand. Creative ideas and discoveries often provide new information and perspectives that were not apparent in the past. In contrast, the concept of memory is typically associated with ideas that are not novel or original. Indeed, the act of remembering is an attempt to recreate events and experiences that have occurred in the past. From this perspective, memory and creativity appear to involve very different kinds of activities.

From other points of view, the differences between memory and creativity may not be as distinct. For example, Bartlett (1932) noted that the way an event is remembered can change over successive recall tests. He found that information is sometimes deleted from the recollection of an event, and new information is sometimes added to the recollection of an event that was not present during the original experience. On the basis of these observations, Bartlett argued that remembering is not simply the reinstatement of previously experienced events but rather involves an imaginative reconstruction of the past.

The tendency for remembering to involve imaginative and interpretive processes is also consistent with other research. For example, what is remembered about an event can be affected by the kinds of

inferences people make during learning and by their expectations at the time of test (e.g., Johnson, Bransford, & Solomon, 1973; Loftus & Palmer, 1974; Pichert & Anderson, 1977). These findings suggest that some elements of creativity are involved in remembering.

Creative behavior can also involve elements of memory. For example, many creative works are based on the personal experiences of the artists and writers who produce them. The recollection of personal experiences necessarily involves aspects of memory. Creative behavior can also involve more abstract types of knowledge and skills. For example, a writer's linguistic skills or an artist's drawing skills reflect knowledge that is acquired through experience and represented in memory.

The preceding discussion suggests that although memory and creativity often involve different goals, they may frequently involve similar processes. In order to better understand the factors that influence creativity, it seems worthwhile to consider how previous experience affects creativity. This chapter explores both the positive and negative effects of memory on creativity and provides a conceptual framework for understanding the constraints that influence the creative transfer of knowledge. Consideration is also given to the types of experimental methods that can provide useful information about the creative transfer of knowledge. In addition, a heuristic framework is discussed that may facilitate the creative transfer of knowledge and provide ideas for further research.

Barry S. Stein • Department of Educational Psychology, Tennessee Technological University, Cookeville, TN 38505.

The Effects of Memory on Creativity

Negative Effects

The idea that previous experience can interfere with the development of creative solutions is supported by a variety of empirical studies. For example, Maier (1931) observed how remembering common properties of objects can adversely affect creative problem solving in the classic "two-cord" or "two-string" problem. In that study, people were asked to tie together two cords that were hanging from a ceiling. The cords were positioned far enough apart so that a person could not hold one cord while reaching the other. Although the participants in that study were given numerous hints to help them generate a particular solution, Maier found that many people failed to attach an available set of pliers to one of the cords to enable it to be swung like a pendulum (making it possible to reach one cord while holding onto the other cord). Maier's observations suggest that people fail to produce the creative pendulum solution because their previous experience with pliers as a gripping device prevents them from thinking of the pliers as a weight (see also Birch & Rabinowitz, 1951).

The term *functional fixedness* is often used to describe situations (like those that Maier observed) in which people tend to think about objects only with respect to their most characteristic function (e.g., Duncker, 1945). This tendency to think about objects in the way that they are most often used illustrates one way that our memory for past experiences can limit flexibility in thinking and can inhibit the production of creative solutions.

There are also other ways that memory can adversely affect creativity. For example, Perfetto, Bransford, and Franks (1983) found that previous experience with a problem can adversely affect the production of creative solutions. They presented people with problems such as this:

A man who lived in a small town in the U.S. married 20 different women of the same town. All are still living and he has never divorced one of them. Yet, he has broken no law. Can you explain?" (p. 25)

The participants in the experiment were given clues that could help them solve the problems prior to the presentation of the problems (e.g., "A minister marries several people each week"). Perfetto and his colleagues found that people were less likely to solve this problem correctly when given a hint to use the information presented earlier if they had attempted to solve the problem first without the hint. The negative effects of trying to solve the problem without the hint were found to be problem specific; that is, previous experience with a problem only affected subsequent performance on the same problem and not on other problems presented during the experiment.

The findings of Perfetto *et al.* (1983) suggest that memory for previous attempts to solve a problem can inhibit creative problem solving. Previous experience with a particular problem-solving strategy also may reduce the likelihood of using alternative and more effective problem-solving strategies (e.g., Luchins & Luchins, 1950). These findings demonstrate how memory for recent events or familiar concepts and strategies can interfere with creativity in problem solving.

Positive Effects

The preceding discussion illustrated some of the ways in which memory can inhibit creative problem solving; however, there are clearly many situations in which previous experience facilitates creativity. For instance, it is difficult to imagine any creative work in art or science that is not related in some way to an individual's previous experience. As Weisberg (1986) pointed out, many of the events and characters portrayed in creative works (e.g., *Crime and Punishment,* and *Tender Is the Night*) appear to be based on specific personal experiences of the artists. These observations suggest that remembering can be an important part of the creative process (cf. Campbell, 1960).

In other situations in which a particular experience is not the focus of creative behavior, the knowledge that is acquired through past experience is often useful in generating creative solutions (e.g., Amabile, 1983; Newell & Simon, 1972). For example, discovery of the double-helix structure for DNA by Watson and Crick required an understanding of biological concepts and X-ray diffraction techniques. Similarly, the skills that enable the artist to paint and the writer to write are also developed through previous experience. These observations suggest that the knowledge and skills that are acquired in a specific discipline provide the conceptual tools that are needed to develop creative solutions. Without that knowledge, our potential for creative works would be greatly diminished. As Amabile (1983) notes, "clearly, it is only possible to be creative in nuclear physics if one knows something (and probably a great deal) about nuclear physics'' (p. 70).

Contextual Constraints on Creative Transfer

One approach for explaining the differential effects of memory on creativity is to argue that certain kinds of knowledge are inherently more beneficial for creative problem solving than are other kinds of knowledge. For example, one might argue that remembering unusual facts or experiences (e.g., pliers can be used as a weight) will facilitate creative problem solving more than remembering familiar properties of objects (e.g., pliers can be used to grip things). It could also be argued that abstract knowledge and skills are more beneficial for creativity than is knowledge of concrete particulars. Indeed, there are a variety of dimensions that could be considered to explain the varying effects of memory on creativity (e.g., episodic vs. semantic knowledge; procedural knowledge vs. declarative knowledge).

Alternatively, one could argue that there are not inherent differences in the effects that different types of information have on creativity. Instead, the effects of any particular memory depend on the context in which it is remembered and how it is applied to the problem. For example, in Maier's two-cord problem, remembering that a set of pliers can be used as a gripping device would not help people generate the creative pendulum solution. However, in a different problem-solving context, remembering that same information could prove beneficial. For instance, in searching for some way to remove a hot pan from the oven, remembering that pliers can be used as a gripping device can lead to a creative solution (e.g., using a pliers as a pot holder). Within this alternative approach, the creative value of any information is only a function of the context in which it is remembered.

Consider another illustration of how the creative value of information can depend on the context in which information is remembered. For example, remembering that an igloo is a type of home that can be damaged by heat is not in itself a novel or creative thought. However, in the context of explaining the statement, ''The home was small because the sun came out,'' remembering that particular information about igloos can lead to a creative solution. What appears to influence the effect of any particular knowledge on creativity is not the unusual nature of the information remembered but

rather the appropriateness of that information for solving a particular problem.

An emphasis on the contextual determinants of creativity is consistent with other research that demonstrates the important role of contextual factors in learning phenomena (e.g., Bransford, 1979; Jenkins, 1974, 1979; Morris, Bransford, & Franks, 1977; Rosnow & Georgoudi, 1986; Stein, 1978). For instance, Jenkins (1979) noted that what is learned in any particular situation depends on the nature of the information presented, the activities performed by the learner, and the skills of the learner (see also Bransford, 1979). Jenkins also suggested that what is learned in any particular situation will affect the kinds of tasks that can be performed. For example, Stein (1978) and Morris *et al.* (1977) found that the effects of any particular learning experience depend on the nature of the test that is given to assess learning. Learning experiences that enhance performance on certain types of criterial tests do not facilitate performance on other types of criterial test (see also Roediger & Weldon, 1987).

From a contextualist's perspective, the creative transfer of knowledge is constrained by both the context in which information is to be used and the context in which information is learned. To understand the factors that affect creative problem solving, it is necessary to examine the relationship between different learning experiences and performance on creative problem-solving tasks.

Methods for Investigating Creative Transfer

One implication of the contextually sensitive nature of learning and transfer is that the contexts in which people are tested need to be carefully considered. As Jenkins (1979) notes, ''there is no assurance that our contrived and artificial situations will ever come to relate to anything that we care about in the real world'' (p. 443). From the standpoint of investigating creativity, there is no assurance that factors that affect performance on other types of tasks will also affect creative problem solving. Therefore, it is important to design experimental tasks that tap into the same processes that people use when solving problems creatively in natural settings.

There are several important features of creative problem-solving tasks. For instance, in these tasks, the individual must not only remember information but must also appropriately apply that information to a novel problem. Furthermore, creative problem-solving tasks usually do not include hints to use specific information to solve problems. In fact, determining what information is relevant for a problem and how to apply that knowledge is an integral part of creative problem solving.

In much of the research that investigates learning and memory, people are given implicit cues or instructions to use information presented earlier in the experiment at the time of test. For example, subjects are generally told at some point in the experiment that they are to recall the information presented to them earlier. In contrast, people seldom have such cues to select relevant experiences in creative problem-solving situations. Indeed, if a person has to be explicitly prompted to access and to apply information to a problem, then the resulting behavior is generally not considered creative. For example, if a person has to be explicitly prompted to use pliers to create a pendulum in Maier's two-cord problem, his or her solution would not be considered as creative as a solution that is produced without such prompting.

The preceding discussion suggests that ecologically relevant investigations of creative problem solving may involve different experimental procedures than are typically used in other studies of learning and memory. Specifically, it seems important to investigate factors that affect the spontaneous transfer of knowledge to novel problem-solving tasks. In spontaneous transfer experiments, people are not given hints to use specific information or experiences.

Investigations of Spontaneous Transfer

One method that has been used to investigate the spontaneous transfer of knowledge to problem-solving tasks is first to present information relevant to the solution of a problem and then, at some later point, to present the problem (e.g., Gick & Holyoak, 1980; Maier, 1931; Perfetto et al., 1983; Weisberg, DiCamillo, & Phillips, 1978). For example, Gick and Holyoak (1980) presented people with a descriptive passage during the initial phase of their experiment. This passage described a situation (a problem together with a solution) that was analogous to a problem presented later in the experiment. One of the passages presented early in the experiment involved a story about a general who was trying to capture a fortress. The general had a suffi-

cient force to overcome the fortress but could not bring his entire force as a unit to the fortress because the enemy had mined the roads, allowing only small groups to travel on the road without setting off the mines. The general's solution was to divide his troops into small units traveling on different roads that would eventually converge at the fortress.

In the second phase of the experiment, Gick and Holyoak (1980) presented people with an analogous problem to solve (Duncker's, 1945, "radiation problem"). In the radiation problem, people are asked to propose a procedure that could be used to destroy a malignant tumor using a special type of radiation. At a sufficient intensity level, the radiation will destroy the tumor. However, at an intensity level sufficient to destroy the tumor, the radiation will also destroy healthy tissue. At lower levels of intensity, the radiation will not destroy the tumor. Gick and Holyoak (1980) were particularly interested in whether people would transfer the solution proposed in the military problem to the radiation problem. For example, a solution suggested by the military situation is to have different beams of low-intensity radiation converge at the tumor and produce sufficient energy to destroy the tumor. Gick and Holyoak (1980) found that even when people memorized the military story beforehand, they did not frequently transfer the solution to the radiation problem unless they were given a hint to use the prior story to help them solve the problem.

The failure to find evidence of spontaneous transfer has been noted in other studies as well. For example, Maier (1931) found that people often failed to spontaneously transfer construction principles presented at the beginning of an experiment to a novel construction problem unless given specific directions to do so. Weisberg *et al.* (1978) also reported little spontaneous transfer of clues to a novel problem-solving task.

Other research by Perfetto *et al.* (1983) examined the frequency of spontaneous transfer in situations that involved a clear connection between the clues presented beforehand and a subsequent problem-solving task. For example, they presented people with problems, such as "Uriah Fuller, the famous Israeli superpsychic, can tell you the score of any baseball game before the game starts. What is his secret?" Prior to solving the problems, people were given a list of clues that included such statements as "Before it starts, the score of any game is 0 to 0." Perfetto *et al.* (1983) found that people did not transfer the clues to the problem-solving task unless they were specifically informed about the relevance of the information presented earlier in the experiment.

The findings discussed above suggest that the spontaneous transfer of information in memory to a novel problem-solving situation can be a difficult process. In fact, if these results are indicative of the frequency of spontaneous transfer in situations outside of the laboratory, one might expect very little creative transfer of knowledge.

Learning Activities That Facilitate Transfer

One reason people may have failed to spontaneously transfer information in the studies described above is that there was little perceived similarity between the original learning task and the subsequent problem-solving task. Indeed, other investigations of retention demonstrate that the accessibility of information in memory is influenced by the similarity between information encoded during acquisition and the information available at the time of test (e.g., Barclay, Bransford, Franks, Mc-Carrell, & Nitsch, 1974; Tulving & Thomson, 1973). The latter investigations suggest that the probability of transfer in problem-solving tasks should increase as the similarity between the learning and transfer tasks increases.

Although creative thinking implies an ability to bridge the gap between previous experience and new situations, it is not clear when and how creative people prepare for bridging that gap. There is abundant evidence to indicate that people spontaneously elaborate information that they are trying to understand and learn (e.g., Franks, Vye, Auble, Mezynski, Perfetto, Bransford, Stein, & Littlefield, 1982; Pichert & Anderson, 1977; Rohwer, 1980; Rumelhart & Ortony, 1977; Stein, Bransford, Franks, Owings, Vye, & McGraw, 1982). For example, Stein *et al.* (1982) found that successful learners tend to elaborate confusing relationships in ways that help them better to understand and remember those relationships. There is also evidence to indicate that the elaborations that people spontaneously generate during learning are influenced by their interests, goals, and expectations (e.g., Anderson, Reynolds, Schallert, & Goetz, 1977; Pichert & Anderson, 1977). The failure to find spontaneous transfer in certain laboratory experiments may result from people not having clear expectations about how information (problem clues) might be used. Without appropriate goals for comprehension and transfer, people may not perform appropriate elaboration activities that are needed for transfer.

In learning environments in which people have clear goals and expectations for using information, it is more likely that they will perform appropriate elaboration activities. For instance, creative problem solvers might think of potential applications for the information they are studying. These elaborations could increase the similarity between the information represented in memory and the information available in subsequent problem-solving tasks. The similarity in appearance between a new situation and a previously experienced event has been found to facilitate spontaneous remembering (e.g., Gentner & Landers, 1985; Ross, 1984). Indeed, many mnemonic strategies are based on the principle of elaborating new information with cues that are available in the retrieval environment (e.g., Bransford & Stein, 1984; Hayes, 1981). However, the creative transfer of memory to novel problems often requires more than just accessing a relevant concept in an appropriate context.

Creative transfer also depends on the appropriate application of concepts (Simon, 1980). For example, a student may remember an appropriate physics formula during problem solving but be unable to apply it to the problem situation. The successful transfer of information to novel situations depends on understanding the particular relevance of a concept or strategy (e.g., Brown, Bransford, Ferrara, & Campione, 1983). Elaborations that help people understand the relevance of concepts for solving specific problems may facilitate the spontaneous transfer of knowledge to similar problem situations.

An Investigation of Elaboration and Spontaneous Transfer

Stein, Way, Benningfield, and Hedgecough (1986) examined the effects that different types of elaborations have on the spontaneous transfer of information to novel problem-solving tasks. In this study, people were asked to provide plausible explanations for seemingly implausible events (e.g., "The home was small because the sun came out"). These problems were adapted from a set of difficult-to-comprehend sentences used by Auble, Franks, and Soraci (1979). Prior to the presentation of these riddles, the participants were presented with clues that could help them solve the problems (e.g., "igloo"). These clues were embedded in one of four different types of elaborative contexts.

The elaborative contexts used by Stein *et al.*

(1986) differed in terms of whether they used content words that were similar or dissimilar to those found in the problem statements (surface structure similarity). The elaborative contexts also differed in terms of whether they emphasized relevant or irrelevant properties of the key concepts that were needed to solve the problems (contextual relevance). For example, given a problem, such as "The home was small because the sun came out," a statement with a relevant context and dissimilar surface structure is "An igloo can be damaged by heat." This elaborative statement uses the key word *igloo* in a relationship that emphasizes the deleterious effects of heat on that type of structure. An example of a statement with a relevant context and a similar surface structure is "An igloo is a home that can be damaged by the sun." The latter statement emphasizes relevant properties of the key concept (igloo), and it includes two content words that are also found in the problem statement (e.g., home, sun). In contrast, consider a statement with an irrelevant context and dissimilar surface structure, such as "Some eskimos live in an igloo." The latter statement does not emphasize properties of an igloo relevant to the problem statement, nor does it include similar surface structure features.

Stein *et al.* (1986) found that elaborative statements that did not prompt people to consider relevant properties of the key concepts resulted in little or no spontaneous transfer. These findings are consistent with other research that has failed to demonstrate spontaneous transfer effects (e.g., Gick & Holyoak, 1980; Perfetto *et al.*, 1983; Weisberg *et al.*, 1978). Stein *et al.* (1986), however, also found that the elaborations that prompted people to consider relevant properties of the key concepts resulted in significant levels of spontaneous transfer particularly when the elaborative contexts and the problem statements had similar surface structures (Experiments 1 and 2). These findings demonstrate that the spontaneous transfer of information to novel problems can be facilitated by elaborative activities that are performed during learning.

Stein *et al.* (1986, Experiment 3) also examined the different effects that elaborations can have on accessing information and appropriately applying information to problem-solving tasks. For example, the similarity in surface structure between elaborations and problem statements primarily influenced the accessibility of clue information during problem solving (see also Gentner & Landers, 1985). In contrast, the contextual relevance of elaborations (i.e., the extent to which they emphasized

relevant properties of the key concepts) primarily influenced the appropriate application of the key concepts to the problems. The fact that little or no spontaneous transfer was found when the elaborations did not emphasize relevant properties of the key concepts (similar or dissimilar surface structures) suggests the relative importance of learning experiences that help people understand how to apply concepts to novel problems.

More recent investigations provide additional support for the idea that spontaneous transfer in problem-solving tasks is affected by the similarities between how information is elaborated during prior learning experiences and how the problem is encoded on the subsequent transfer task. For example, Holyoak and Koh (1987) found that similarities in surface structure and in the deeper relational properties of clues and problems affect spontaneous transfer. Other research by Adams, Kasserman, Yearwood, Perfetto, Bransford, and Franks (1988) and Lockhart, Lamon, and Gick (1988) indicates that spontaneous transfer can be enhanced when the clue information is presented in the same type of question–answer format that is found in subsequent problem-solving tasks.

Differences between Informed and Spontaneous Transfer

The findings discussed above seem particularly significant because many studies have been unable to find evidence of spontaneous transfer in novel problem-solving tasks. Investigating the factors that affect spontaneous transfer can also be difficult because laboratory testing environments often provide implicit cues about the relatedness of initial learning experiences and subsequent transfer tasks. For example, consider a study conducted by Gick and Holyoak (1983). They asked people to solve problems such as Duncker's (1945) "radiation problem" after receiving various types of learning experiences with analogous problems (that included solutions). An important feature of Gick and Holyoak's (1983) study is that it examined transfer in situations in which people were not informed about the relevance of the analogous stories for solving the radiation problem.

Gick and Holyoak (1983) found that transfer in the uninformed conditions was facilitated by certain types of learning experiences. For example, little spontaneous transfer was found when the participants in the study simply read the analogous stories prior to solving the radiation problem; however, considerably more spontaneous transfer was observed when people received two examples of analogous stories and accurately summarized the abstract relationship that was common to both stories prior to solving the radiation problem.

The findings reported by Gick and Holyoak (1983) appear to be relevant for understanding the constraints that affect the creative transfer of knowledge because people transferred the solution strategies that were described in the analogies without any hints. More recent research by Spencer and Weisberg (1986) suggests, however, that people may often implicitly assume that information presented earlier in an experiment is relevant to subsequent tasks because of the continuity of the experimental setting. Spencer and Weisberg (1986) used a procedure similar to that employed by Gick and Holyoak (1983) but that also included an experimental condition in which the acquisition and testing contexts were made to seem clearly unrelated (i.e., they used different experimenters and testing rooms). Although Spencer and Weisberg (1986) were able to replicate Gick and Holyoak's (1983) findings in situations that involved highly similar acquisition and testing contexts, they did not replicate Gick and Holyoak's results when the acquisition and testing contexts were made to seem unrelated.

The results of Spencer and Weisberg's (1986) study raise the question whether the learning experiences that Gick and Holyoak (1983) found to affect uninformed transfer in the laboratory will also affect spontaneous transfer in creative problem-solving situations outside of the laboratory. An important issue to consider from the standpoint of designing research to investigate the creative transfer of knowledge is whether the processes that underlie transfer in informed conditions are fundamentally different from the processes that underlie spontaneous transfer.

From one perspective, it could be argued that both informed and spontaneous transfer tasks provide information about constraints that affect the creative use of knowledge, as both tasks assess transfer to novel problems. Alternatively, one could argue that there are some important differences in how information may be accessed in informed and spontaneous transfer situations. For example, Stein et al. (1986, Experiment 3) found that problem-solving performance in informed transfer conditions was highly related to whether the problem clues were remembered on a free recall test given prior to the problem-solving task. In con-

trast, problem-solving performance in the spontaneous transfer conditions was unrelated to whether the relevant clues could be recalled prior to the problem-solving task.

The relationship Stein et al. (1986) observed between problem-solving performance and free recall in the informed transfer conditions may result from a particular strategy that people use in informed transfer tasks. For instance, consider that in most laboratory studies of transfer the relevant clues for solving problems are presented within the context of a relatively small set of irrelevant information. If people know that some of the information presented earlier may facilitate problem solving, they could serially recall each clue presented and evaluate its applicability to the problem. The effectiveness of this strategy would depend on knowing that the information presented earlier in the experiment was relevant to the problem-solving task and on being able to consciously recall that information during problem solving. In situations in which people use such a strategy, one would expect to find a strong relationship between free recall performance and problem-solving performance.

Although a problem-solving strategy based on free recall may be effective in certain laboratory situations, it is doubtful whether such a strategy would be useful in other natural problem-solving situations that require creativity. For instance, it would be difficult to apply a strategy based on serial recall to problem-solving tasks that involve a large set of potentially relevant experiences (i.e., the content of a semester course or a college education). In problem-solving situations in which there is a relatively large set of potentially relevant experiences to consider, it would be difficult, if not impossible, to recall each experience and then analyze how it might be appropriately applied to the problem. In fact, the benefits of being prompted to consider a set of previous experiences in any problem-solving situation may diminish as the number of potentially relevant experiences in that set increases.

Effects of Set Size and Similarity on Informed and Spontaneous Transfer

Stein and Hedgecough (submitted) conducted two experiments to examine differences in how knowledge is accessed in informed and in spontaneous transfer tasks. In the first experiment, the effect of acquisition set size was examined. It was hypothesized that increasing the amount of irrelevant information presented together with problem-solving clues would negatively affect informed transfer because it would make it more difficult to recall each relevant clue. In contrast, acquisition set size was not expected to affect spontaneous transfer, as the latter task does not involve explicit memory.

Experiment 1 employed a transfer task similar to that used by Stein *et al.* (1986, Experiment 1). Each of the 80 undergraduates who participated in the study read a list of statements that contained clues (e.g., "igloo") to help them solve problems presented later in the experiment (e.g., "The home was small because the sun came out. Can you explain?"). The clues were embedded in two types of elaborative statements that Stein *et al.* (1986) found to influence transfer. The statements either prompted people to consider properties of the key concept relevant to the problem (e.g., "An igloo can be damaged by heat") or prompted people to consider irrelevant properties of the key concept (e.g., "Some Eskimos live in an igloo"). The clue statements were presented in a list with either 10 or 40 unrelated filler statements during the first phase of the experiment. Before the transfer problems were presented, half of the participants in the study were given hints to consider the information presented earlier. In the spontaneous transfer conditions, the participants were led to believe that the two tasks were unrelated. All treatments were manipulated between subjects.

The mean percentage of problems solved correctly in each condition is presented in Table 1. There was significantly ($p < .05$) less transfer in the

Table 1. Mean Percentage of Problems Solved[a]

| Group | Clue statement | |
	Relevant contexts	Irrelevant contexts
Informed		
15 Items	68	36
45 Items	50	12
Uninformed		
15 Items	40	12
45 Items	32	8

[a]From *Differences between Spontaneous and Informed Transfer in Problem-Solving Tasks: The Effects of Set Size and Clue-Problem Similarity* (Experiment 1) by B.S. Stein and C.A. Hedgecough, submitted.

informed conditions with larger acquisition set sizes (31%) than in the informed conditions with smaller acquisition set sizes (52%). In contrast, acquisition set size did not significantly affect transfer in the uninformed conditions (20% vs. 26%).

The fact that informed transfer was negatively affected by larger acquisition sets is consistent with the notion that people may use a consciously directed recall strategy to access information in informed tasks. As acquisition set size increases, this recall-based strategy becomes less effective because it is more difficult to remember each episode. Spontaneous transfer, on the other hand, is not as strongly affected by acquisition set size. One explanation for the latter finding is that spontaneous transfer involves an implicit knowledge activation process that is not dependent on consciously directed recall. This implicit activation process is presumably dependent on the similarity between information encoded during problem solving and during previous experience (see also Holyoak & Koh, 1987).

To investigate potential differences in how similarity might affect informed and spontaneous transfer, Stein and Hedgecough (Experiment 2, submitted) varied the surface structure similarity of clues and problems. Note that in earlier research it was found that manipulating deeper relational similarities between clues and problems significantly influenced the ability to apply accessible clue information to the problems. By varying the surface structure similarity of clues and problems (e.g., the use of two or three identical content words in the clue and problem statements), Stein and Hedgecough hoped to clarify potential differences in the way similarity affects access to relevant knowledge in informed and spontaneous transfer tasks.

The procedure was similar to that of Experiment 1 except that only relevant clue contexts were used. As mentioned earlier, Experiment 2 varied the surface structure similarity of clue and problem statements by using two or three identical content words in the clue and problem statements. In addition, Experiment 2 assessed each participant's ability to recall the clues before the problem-solving task in order to assess the relationship between the ability to recall clue information and subsequent transfer.

The mean percentage of problems solved correctly in each condition is presented in Table 2. As in Experiment 1, larger acquisition sets yielded significantly less transfer in the informed conditions (51.4%) than smaller acquisition sets (65.3%). In contrast, there was little difference in the amount of

Table 2.   Mean Percentage of Problems Solved[a]

Group	Clue statement surface structure	
	Similar	Dissimilar
Informed		
15 Items	70.8	59.7
45 Items	62.5	40.3
Uninformed		
15 Items	44.5	19.5
45 Items	40.3	19.4

[a]From *Differences between Spontaneous and Informed Transfer in Problem-Solving Tasks: The Effects of Set Size and Clue-Problem Similarity* (Experiment 1) by B.S. Stein and C.A. Hedgecough, submitted.

spontaneous transfer found in conditions with large acquisition sets (29.9%) and small acquisition sets (32.0%). The results of Experiment 2 also reveal differences in how surface structure similarity affects problem solving in informed and in spontaneous transfer tasks. In the small acquisition set conditions, surface structure similarity did not significantly affect informed transfer, a finding that is consistent with the idea that access to relevant information in informed transfer tasks is accomplished through consciously directed recall. In contrast, surface structure similarity significantly affected spontaneous transfer in the small and the large acquisition set conditions. The latter findings suggest that the similarity between information encoding during problem solving and during previous experience is an important determinant of access in spontaneous transfer tasks.

Differences between informed and spontaneous transfer tasks were also found when the relationship between recall and subsequent problem solving was analyzed. For example, the probability of solving problems in the informed conditions was significantly greater if the relevant clue could be recalled ahead of time (84.8%) than if the clue could not be recalled (53.1%). In contrast, there was not a significant difference in the probability of solving problems in the spontaneous transfer conditions if the clue could be recalled ahead of time (37.7%), relative to when the clue could not be recalled ahead of time (34.9%). The latter findings are consistent with the idea that consciously directed remembering plays a more important role in informed transfer tasks than in spontaneous transfer tasks.

The findings discussed above indicate that there are important differences between how knowledge is accessed in informed laboratory tasks and spontaneous transfer tasks. The differences between informed and spontaneous transfer appear to be most dramatic when small acquisition sets are used in an experiment. These differences may become less significant, however, as increasing amounts of information are learned. For example, in the larger acquisition set conditions, Stein and Hedgecough found that surface structure similarity significantly affected performance in both the informed and uninformed transfer conditions. Furthermore, the difference in prolem-solving performance between the informed and uninformed conditions declined as acquisition set size increased. The latter results may reflect a change in the type of strategy used by people in the informed transfer conditions as acquisition set size increases. For instance, it may become increasingly difficult to use a strategy that is based on consciously directed remembering when there is a large number of potentially relevant experiences that must be considered during problem solving. In such cases, people may rely on more implicit knowledge activation processes that depend on the similarity between information encoded during problem solving and during previous experience.

Creating Opportunities for Transfer

The preceding discussion considered the types of experimental tasks that can be used to investigate the effects of different learning experiences on the creative transfer of knowledge. It was noted that learning experiences that help people understand how to apply concepts to novel problem-solving tasks can facilitate spontaneous transfer. In the research by Stein *et al.* (1986), the elaborations that facilitated spontaneous transfer to novel problem-solving tasks (e.g., ''An igloo can be damaged by heat'') were supplied by the experimenter. Stein and his colleagues argued that similar elaborations could also be generated by people when learning new information. For example, it is not difficult to imagine people who are learning about igloos asking themselves such questions as What would happen to igloos if the climate suddenly changed and it became warmer? The latter type of question might prompt one to consider the deleterious effects of heat on igloos. Experiences that lead people to explore the applications and limitations of concepts have often been considered valuable for promoting understanding (e.g., Bransford, Sherwood, & Sturdevant, 1986). The current discussion suggests that such experiences may also help facilitate the creative transfer of knowledge.

It is important to note that there are many different ways of elaborating new concepts. Furthermore, different problem-solving contexts may require very different types of elaborations to facilitate transfer. For instance, elaborations that focus learners on the sensitivity of igloos to heat may provide little transfer to problems that require knowledge about the shape of igloos or how to build them. In other words, the properties of a concept that are relevant in one context may be irrelevant in another context. In view of this, the benefits of any particular learning experience for creativity are contextually limited.

One obvious and yet important implication of arguments about the contextually sensitive nature of transfer is that learning strategies that improve performance on tests of retention may not facilitate the creative transfer of knowledge. For example, Stein *et al.* (1986) and Weisberg *et al.* (1978) found that memorizing the clues presented in a spontaneous transfer study had little effect on whether people spontaneously transferred the memorized information to a novel problem-solving task. Other research also demonstrates the limitations of learning strategies that are based on mnemonic techniques. For instance, Stein, Brock, Ballard, and Vye (1987) found that learning experiences involving visual images can sometimes lower performance on tasks that assess people's understanding of verbal relationships. These findings illustrate the potential shortcomings of learning strategies or learning environments that emphasize rote retention.

Learning Is Problem Solving

The contextually sensitive nature of learning and transfer suggests that it is important to select an appropriate learning strategy. Selecting an appropriate learning strategy, however, necessarily involves some understanding of how information will be used and the effects that different learning strategies can have on transfer. The importance of establishing goals and planning appropriate strategies during learning indicates that learning is, itself, a problem-solving process.

One approach that emphasizes the important role

that problem solving plays in learning is discussed by Bransford and Stein (1984). They describe five problem-solving activities that underlie effective learning. The acronym, IDEAL, is used to represent these activities. Within this approach, effective learning depends on *identifying* the existence of a learning problem and the contextually sensitive nature of transfer; *defining* the type of criterial task to be performed with the information; *exploring* appropriate learning strategies to accomplish these goals; *acting* on the selected strategies; and *looking back* at the effects of using these strategies to determine the effectiveness of the problem-solving approach.

Bransford and Stein's heuristic framework emphasizes the importance of defining one's learning goals before selecting an appropriate learning strategy. Indeed, different learning experiences are often needed to accomplish different learning goals. Note, for instance, that the learning experiences that would enable a person to build an igloo are certainly different from the learning experiences that would enable a person to solve a problem, such as the home was small because the sun came out. From the perspective of the current chapter, the actual process of defining one's learning objectives may be an important component of creative transfer. For example, defining the context for transfer may help people identify potential applications of the concepts being studied.

It is important to note that, in many laboratory studies of learning, people are not encouraged to define their own learning goals and to identify potential applications of the information presented. For instance, in many experiments, people are instructed to perform tasks (e.g., rating comprehensibility) that may prevent or discourage them from considering realistic learning goals. These laboratory investigations may inadvertently prevent people from engaging in the types of learning and problem-solving activities that foster creative transfer.

In order to better understand the constraints that affect the transfer or knowledge to novel problems, more attention needs to be given to the decisions that people make about learning strategies. It seems particularly important to examine differences in the way people approach learning problems and how these approaches to learning affect spontaneous transfer to novel problems. Investigations that address these issues may reveal important differences in the way creative and less creative individuals define their learning goals.

The Effects of Problem Definitions on Transfer

The preceding discussion considered how the creative transfer of knowledge may be influenced by the kinds of activities people perform during learning. The creative transfer of knowledge may also be affected by the activities people perform in the transfer task. For example, how people define and interpret a problem situation can affect what information is accessed during problem solving (e.g., Adams, 1979; Bransford & Stein, 1984).

To illustrate the effects problem definitions can have on the type of knowledge accessed in problem-solving situations, consider the experiences of a group working at Tennessee Technological University to develop new ways of protecting people from injury in automobiles. In the initial stages of problem solving, the group found that many of the concepts people were considering (e.g., safety nets, automatically activated harnesses, force fields) were derived from a particular way of defining the problem (e.g., how to restrain people during a crash). It was not until people considered alternative ways of defining the problem (e.g., how to make the interior of a car less likely to cause injury to an unrestrained person or how to help people avoid crashes) that other types of creative solutions were considered.

Adams (1979) also provided examples of how problem definitions can affect the type of solutions that are considered. In one example, he described the experiences of a group of engineers who were trying to design an improved method for mechanically picking tomatoes that would be less likely to damage the fruit. The engineers considered a variety of strategies for improving mechanical pickers, such as increasing the padding on the picking arms and reducing the speed of the picking arms. An alternative way of defining the problem facing the tomato pickers is How can they make the tomatoes less likely to be bruised while being picked mechanically? This alternative definition of the problem suggested other creative ideas for solving the problem, such as developing new strains of tomatoes that are less likely to be bruised.

Generating Alternative Definitions of Problems

The examples discussed above demonstrate how different definitions of a problem situation can fa- cilitate the creative use of knowledge. Given the effects that problem definitions can have on creativity, it seems important to examine factors that can influence the quality and diversity of problem definitions. For example, consider the research by Chi, Glaser, and Rees (1982) that examined differences between novice and expert problem solvers within the domain of physics. Chi *et al.* (1982) found that novices often have a limited ability to generate inferences and relations not explicitly stated in the problem because of their less developed knowledge base. In contrast, the more developed knowledge base of experts permits greater elaboration of the problem situation (see also de Groot, 1965; Newell & Simon, 1972). An expert's ability to elaborate new problems could allow them to bridge the gap between novel problems and previous experience by framing the problem in terms of concepts and relationships that correspond more closely to previous experience. Indeed, one might predict that an expert's ability to transfer knowledge to problems in that domain should be less affected by surface structure similarities than someone with less expertise in that domain. In fact, recent research on spontaneous transfer by Novick (1988) provides some support for the latter idea. Novick (1988) found that people with higher levels of expertise in a domain were less likely to be affected by surface structure similarities between new problems and previous experience than people with lower levels of expertise in the problem domain. In contrast, people with higher levels of expertise in the problem domain were influenced more by deeper relational similarities between the problems and previous experience than were people with lower levels of expertise in the problem domain. These findings suggest that the knowledge and skills acquired from past experience can provide the conceptual tools needed to define problems in ways that can improve transfer to novel situations.

Although the knowledge and skills an individual acquires in a content domain can affect how problems are defined and elaborated, there are also other variables that affect the quality and diversity of problem definitions. For instance, it was noted earlier that people may fail to consider alternative approaches to problem solving because of their familiarity with a particular approach. People may also fail to consider alternate approaches to problems because of implicit assumptions about how a problem should be defined (e.g., Adams, 1979; Bransford & Stein, 1984).

One way to achieve greater creativity in problem solving is to state explicitly the assumptions and definitions that are guiding one's thinking (Bransford & Stein, 1984; Polya, 1957). For instance, Bransford and Stein (1984) suggested that developing creative solutions to problems involves such activities as defining the problem in different ways and then evaluating the adequacy of those definitions by examining the appropriateness of the assumptions in each approach. It was noted earlier that creative problem solving often involves looking back at the assumptions that limit the types of solutions being considered (e.g., the only effective way to prevent automobile injuries is by restraining the occupants). By making problem definitions explicit and by evaluating the assumptions underlying those definitions, people can recognize the limitations of particular approaches and begin to explore other definitions of the problem that may lead to creative solutions (e.g., How to prevent accidents? How to reduce the velocity of automobiles immediately before a crash? How to position people so that they are less likely to suffer severe injuries in a crash?).

Implications for Future Research

The preceding discussion considered how various cognitive activities that are performed during the acquisition of new information and during attempts to solve problems can affect the creative transfer of knowledge. For example, it was noted that different definitions of a problem situation can influence the type of knowledge that is accessed during problem solving. However, further research is clearly needed to explore the relationship between problem definition activities and the creative transfer of knowledge. For instance, are creative abilities related to the way individuals approach and define problem situations (e.g., Getzels & Csikszentmihalyi, 1975)?

Further research is also needed to explore how people can be prompted to consider alternative ways of defining problems that might enhance the creative transfer of knowledge. For example, preliminary findings indicate creative transfer can be enhanced by prompting people to consider alternative definitions of problems during problem solving (Stein & Moore, unpublished manuscript). Additional research is needed to evaluate the effects of more general training in problem definition skills

on creative transfer. For instance, can training with heuristic frameworks like that proposed by Bransford and Stein (1984) facilitate creative transfer?

It was noted earlier that the types of cognitive activities that are performed during the acquisition of new information can also affect creative transfer. Indeed, learning experiences that optimize the transfer of information to certain tasks may not promote transfer to other tasks. The idea that there does not appear to be any single best learning strategy that can be used to optimize transfer to all problem situations is consistent with theoretical frameworks like that which was proposed by Jenkins (1979). One implication of contextualism is that we should stop searching for an optimal learning activity or strategy that will enhance transfer to all tasks. Instead, future research should attempt to identify the potential benefits of different learning activities and delineate the conditions under which such activities promote transfer. The latter approach promotes research exploring "spheres of influence" for particular learning activities/strategies rather than a search for the single "best" learning strategy.

An emphasis on the contextual nature of learning and transfer also illustrates the value of treating learning itself as a problem-solving experience. For instance, successful learners must define their learning goals and select an appropriate learning strategy that will optimize transfer to future problem-solving tasks. Further research is needed to explore differences in the way people define learning problems and modify their methods of study to accomplish different goals. For example, my colleagues and I are currently exploring differences in the way that successful and less successful students approach various learning problems. Our preliminary findings indicate that successful students tend to be better able to define learning problems and are more flexible in selecting strategies to accomplish different learning goals than less successful students. It is also important to study the types of learning activities that creative individuals use in natural learning contexts to optimize transfer. The latter type of research may help clarify whether creative individuals are more likely to identify or anticipate potential problem situations that new information may help them solve (e.g., Stein *et al.*, 1986).

Finally, an emphasis on the contextual nature of learning and transfer suggests that to understand creative transfer in natural environments, our investigations must incorporate testing contexts that reflect real-world problem-solving constraints. In most natural problem-solving tasks, the problem solver must spontaneously access and apply appropriate information to the problem; however, in many laboratory investigations, the participants are given direct or indirect hints to use specific clues to solve the problem. There appear to be some important differences between the constraints that govern the spontaneous transfer of knowledge to problem-solving tasks and the constraints that govern transfer in situations in which people are informed about the relevance of previously studied information. Specifically, transfer in informed problem-solving tasks may be directly affected by the ability to intentionally recall previously presented clue information. In contrast, the spontaneous transfer of previously learned information to problem-solving tasks does not appear to be related to factors that influence free recall performance (e.g., set size).

Conclusion

That previous experience can have both positive and negative effects on creativity is a consequence of the contextually sensitive nature of learning and transfer. Although creativity implies an ability to bridge the gap between previous experience and novel problems, it is not clear when or how creative people prepare for bridging that gap. This chapter considered how the activities people perform during learning and problem solving can affect the transfer of knowledge to novel problems. For example, it was noted that people may enhance the creative transfer of knowledge during learning by imagining appropriate applications of the information that is being studied. It was also noted that people's definitions of problem situations can restrict or enhance the creative application of knowledge. Clearly, additional research is needed to investigate these issues and to examine factors that affect transfer in natural problem-solving contexts.

ACKNOWLEDGMENTS. I thank Karla Brock and Ada Haynes for their helpful comments on an earlier version of this chapter.

References

Adams, J. L. (1979). *Conceptual blockbusting* (2nd ed.). New York: Norton.

Adams, L. T., Kasserman, J. E., Yearwood, A. A., Perfetto, G.

A., Bransford, J. D., & Franks, J. J. (1988). Memory access: The effects of fact-oriented versus problem-oriented acquisition. *Memory and Cognition, 16,* 167–175.

Amabile, T. M. (1983). *The social psychology of creativity.* New York: Springer-Verlag.

Anderson, R. C., Reynolds, R. E., Schallert, D. L., & Goetz, E. T. (1977). Frameworks for comprehending discourse. *American Educational Research Journal, 14,* 367–382.

Auble, P. M., Franks, J. J., & Soraci, S. A. (1979). Effort toward comprehension: Elaboration of "aha"? *Memory and Cognition, 7(6),* 426–434.

Barclay, J. R., Bransford, J. D., Franks, J. J., McCarrell, N. S., & Nitsch, K. E. (1974). Comprehension and semantic flexibility. *Journal of Verbal Learning and Verbal Behavior, 13,* 471–481.

Bartlett, F. C. (1932). *Remembering: A study in experimental and social psychology.* New York: Macmillan.

Birch, H. G., & Rabinowitz, H. S. (1951). The negative effect of previous experience on productive thinking. *Journal of Experimental Psychology, 41,* 121–125.

Bransford, J. D. (1979). *Human cognition: Learning, understanding, and remembering.* Belmont, CA: Wadsworth.

Bransford, J. D., & Stein, B. S. (1984). *The ideal problem solver: A guide for improving thinking, learning, and creativity.* New York: W. H. Freeman.

Bransford, J. D., Sherwood, R. D., & Sturdevant, T. (1986). Teaching thinking and problem solving. In J. B. Baron & R. J. Sternberg (Eds.), *Teaching thinking skills* (pp. 162–181). New York: W. H. Freeman.

Brown, A. L., Bransford, J. D., Ferrara, R. A., & Campione, J. C. (1983). Learning, remembering and understanding. In J. H. Flavell & E. M. Markman (Eds.), *Carmichael's manual of child psychology* (Vol. 1). New York: Wiley.

Campbell, D. (1960). Blind variation and selective retention in creative thought as in other knowledge processes. *Psychological Review, 67,* 380–400.

Chi, M. T. H., Glaser, R., & Rees, E. (1982). Expertise in problem solving. In R. J. Sternberg (Ed.), *Advances in the psychology of human intelligence* (pp. 7–76). Hillsdale, NJ: Erlbaum.

de Groot, A. D. (1965). *Thought and choice in chess.* The Hague: Mouton.

Duncker, K. (1945). On problem solving. *Psychological Monographs, 58,* 270.

Franks, J. J., Vye, N. J., Auble, P. M., Mezynski, K. J., Perfetto, G. A., Bransford, J. D., Stein, B. S., & Littlefield, J. (1982). Learning from explicit versus implicit texts, *Journal of Experimental Psychology: General, 111,* 414–422.

Gentner, D., & Landers, R. (1985, November). Analogical access: A good match is hard to find. Paper presented at the annual meeting of the Psychonomic Society, Boston, MA.

Getzels, J. W. & Csikszentmihalyi, M. (1975). From problem solving to problem finding. In I. A. Taylor & J. W. Getzels (Eds.), *Perspectives in creativity* (pp. 90–116). Chicago: Aldine.

Gick, M. L., & Holyoak, K. J. (1980). Analogical problem solving. *Cognitive Psychology, 12,* 306–355.

Gick, M. L., & Holyoak, K. J. (1983). Schema induction and analogical transfer. *Cognitive Psychology, 15,* 1–38.

Hayes, J. R. (1981). *The complete problem solver.* Philadelphia: Franklin Institute Press.

Holyoak, K. J., & Koh, K. (1987). Surface and structural similarity in analogical transfer. *Memory and Cognition, 15,* 332–340.

Jenkins, J. J. (1974). Remember that old theory of memory? Well, forget it! *American Psychologist, 29,* 785–795.

Jenkins, J. J. (1979). Four points to remember: A tetrahedral model of memory experiments. In L. S. Cermak & F. I. M. Craik (Eds.), *Levels of processing and human memory* (pp. 429–446). Hillsdale, NJ: Erlbaum.

Johnson, M. K., Bransford, J. D., & Solomon, S. (1973). Memory use for tacit implications of sentences. *Journal of Experimental Psychology, 98,* 203–205.

Lockhart, R. S., Lamon, M., & Gick, M. L. (1988). Conceptual transfer in simple insight problems. *Memory and Cognition, 16,* 36–44.

Loftus, G. R., & Palmer, J. C. (1974). Reconstruction of automobile destruction: An example of the interaction between language and memory. *Journal of Verbal Learning and Verbal Behavior, 13,* 585–589.

Luchins, A. S. & Luchins, E. H. (1950). New experimental attempts at preventing mechanization in problem solving. *Journal of General Psychology, 42,* 279–297.

Maier, N. R. F. (1931). Reasoning in humans. II. The solution of a problem and its appearance in consciousness. *Journal of Comparative Psychology, 12,* 181–194.

Morris, C. D., Bransford, J. D., & Franks, J. J. (1977). Levels of processing versus transfer appropriate processing. *Journal of Verbal Learning and Verbal Behavior, 16,* 519–533.

Newell, A., & Simon, H. (1972). *Human problem solving.* Englewood Cliffs, NJ: Prentice-Hall.

Novick, L. R. (1988). Analogical transfer, problem similarity, and expertise. *Journal of Experimental Psychology: Learning, Memory and Cognition, 14,* 510–520.

Perfetto, G. A., Bransford, J. D., & Franks, J. J. (1983). Constraints on access in a problem solving context. *Memory and Cognition, 11,* 24–31.

Pichert, J., & Anderson, R. C. (1977). Taking different perspectives on a story. *Journal of Educational Psychology, 69,* 309–315.

Polya, G. (1957). *How to solve it.* Garden City, NY: Doubleday Anchor.

Roediger, H. L., & Weldon, M. S. (1987). Reversing the picture superiority effect. In M. A. McDaniel & M. Pressley (Eds.), *Imagery and related mnemonic processes; theories, individual differences, and application* (pp. 151–176). New York: Springer-Verlag.

Rohwer, W. D., Jr. (1980). An elaborative conception of learner differences. In R. E. Snow, P. A. Frederico, & W. E. Montague (Eds.), *Aptitude, learning, and instruction* (pp. 23–46). Hillsdale, NJ: Erlbaum.

Rosnow, R. L., & Georgoudi, M. (1986). The spirit of contextualism. In R. L. Rosnow & M. Georgoudi (Eds.), *Contextualism and understanding in behavioral science* (pp. 3–24). New York: Praeger.

Ross, B. H. (1984). Remindings and their effects in learning a cognitive skill. *Cognitive Psychology, 16,* 371–416.

Rumelhart, D. E., & Ortony, A. (1977). The representation of knowledge in memory. In R. C. Anderson, R. J. Spiro, & W. E. Montague (Eds.), *Schooling and the acquisition of knowledge* (pp. 99–135). Hillsdale, NJ: Erlbaum.

Simon, H. A. (1980). Problem solving and education. In D. T. Tuma & F. Reif (Eds.), *Problem solving and education: Issues in teaching and research* (pp. 81–96). Hillsdale, New Jersey: Erlbaum.

Spencer, R. M., & Weisberg, R. W. (1986). Context-dependent effects on analogical transfer. *Memory and Cognition, 14,* 442–449.

Stein, B. S. (1978). Depth of processing reexamined: The effects of precision of encoding and test appropriateness. *Journal of Verbal Learning and Verbal Behavior, 17,* 165–174.

Stein, B. S., & Hedgecough, C. A. (submitted) Differences between spontaneous and informed transfer in problem-solving tasks: The effects of set size and clue-problem similarity.

Stein, B. S., & Moore, S. (1988). *The effects of problem definitions on transfer in problem-solving tasks.* Unpublished manuscript.

Stein, B. S., Bransford, J. D., Franks, J. J., Owings, R. A., Vye, N. J., & McGraw, W. (1982). Differences in the precision of self-generated elaborations. *Journal of Experimental Psychology: General, 111,* 399–405.

Stein, B. S., Way, K. R., Benningfield, S. E., & Hedgecough, C. A. (1986). Constraints on spontaneous transfer in problem solving tasks. *Memory and Cognition, 14,* 432–441.

Stein, B. S., Brock, K. F., Ballard, D. R., & Vye, N. J. (1987). Constraints on effective pictorial and verbal elaboration. *Memory and Cognition, 15*(4), 281–290.

Tulving, E., & Thomson, D. M. (1973). Encoding specificity and retrieval processes in episodic memory. *Psychological Review, 80,* 352–373.

Weisberg, R. W. (1986). *Creativity: Genius and other myths.* New York: W. H. Freeman.

Weisberg, R. W., DiCamillo, M., & Phillips, D. (1978). Transferring old associations to new situations: A nonautomatic process. *Journal of Verbal Learning and Verbal Behavior, 17,* 219–228.

CHAPTER 10

Metacognition in Creativity

Bonnie B. Armbruster

The process of creation is a cognitive process. Perceiving, learning, thinking, and remembering—this is the stuff of creativity. The creative process involves the acquisition of knowledge and skills, the transformation of knowledge into new forms, and the rendering of these forms into a shareable product. Each stage in the process entails cognition. It seems appropriate, therefore, to inquire about a cognitive model of creativity. In one way or another, the chapters in this part of the book all address this issue. The purpose of this chapter is to examine the creative process from the perspective of one particular aspect of cognition—metacognition.

What Is Metacognition?

Modern-day cognitive psychology recognizes the hierarchical nature of psychological processes that are involved in cognition. At the top of the hierarchy are the executive processes that oversee, regulate, and orchestrate the activities of cognition. These executive processes are known as *metacognition*. Metacognition includes both the *knowledge* and the *control* that individuals have over their own cognitive processes. Control, or self-regulation, includes setting goals and subgoals, planning the next

cognitive move, monitoring and evaluating the effectiveness of cognitive strategies, and revising cognitive strategies (Baker & Brown, 1984).

Metacognition is currently a hot topic in cognitive psychology. In the past 15 years, literally hundreds of studies have been conducted in the name of metacognition. This research has had a significant influence on the area of learning, particularly learning from reading. Early metacognitive research focused on how, when, and why students have difficulty studying and learning. The research generally indicated that metacognition is a late-developing skill, with younger and poorer readers displaying less effective metacognitive skills than older and better readers. Later research in metacognition has concentrated on intervention research that is designed to overcome metacomprehension problems. This research has demonstrated the value of including metacognitive training in three areas: (1) *skills*—training and practice in task-specific strategies; (2) *self-regulation*—instruction in the orchestration, overseeing, and monitoring of skills; and (3) *awareness*—information concerning a skill's evaluation, rationale, and usefulness (Baker & Brown, 1984). Adding these metacognitive components has contributed substantially to the success of cognitive skills training programs.

Given the impact of metacognition on theory and practice in the area of learning, it seems appropriate to inquire about the relevance of metacognition to the study of one of the most intriguing of cognitive processes—creative thinking. Specifically, what is

Bonnie B. Armbruster • Center for the Study of Reading, University of Illinois at Urbana-Champaign, Champaign, IL 61820.

creativity from the perspective of metacognition? What metacognitive processes might distinguish creative from less creative individuals? In attempting to answer these questions, I will use the framework of a four-part stage model of the creative process as proposed by Wallas (1970).

Wallas first proposed the model in his book, *The Art of Thought,* in 1926. Why use such an old model? First, the model seems at least implicit in what many other writers have written about the creative process. Second, the self-reports of creative individuals tend to corroborate the model. Third, I was unable to find a better model. Finally, the stage model provides a useful way to organize a discussion of the creative process. However, there is a danger in using Wallas's model, because it implies that the process of creativity is linear. Creativity is much more likely to be interactive and iterative, with much communication among stages. With that caveat in mind, I will now move to a discussion of the four stages of creativity as proposed by Wallas.

At least implicit in Wallas's writing is the idea that the creative process actually begins with a problem or a question. The creative act starts with "an eager search . . . a strong conscious desire for something—the solution of a problem or the construction of a work of art" (Sinnott, 1970, p. 112). The recognition of a "strong conscious desire for something" is the first instance of metacognition in the creative process. The individual is aware of a goal or purpose; this goal becomes the guiding force behind the rest of the creative endeavor.

Wallas, however, does not include the establishment and recognition of a goal or purpose as a specific stage in his model.

Stage 1: Preparation

The first of Wallas's stages of the creative process is "preparation," which includes "the whole process of intellectual education" (Wallas, 1970, p. 92). During this stage, individuals are laying the foundation for their later creative acts by acquiring the requisite knowledge and skills of their field. Creative individuals must work hard to acquire a particularly rich background of knowledge and experience (Ghiselin, 1952; Sinnott, 1970). As industrial designer George Nelson puts it, "people identified as creative people don't just walk around and have ideas. The ideas are a result of a considerable amount of delving into the problem" (Rosner & Abt, 1970, p. 256).

According to cognitive psychology, what is hap-pening during this learning phase? One popular cognitive theory is *schema* theory. In schema theory, information is thought to be stored in the mind in the form of abstract knowledge structures called *schemata.* Rumelhart and Norman (1978) suggested three different kinds of learning within schema theory: (1) *accretion,* or the encoding of new information in terms of existing schemata; (2) *tuning,* or the modification and refinement of a schema due to its use in different situations; and (3) *restructuring,* or the process of creating new schemata through *patterned generation* (patterning by analogy on existing schemata) or *schema induction* (inducing from experience).

All three types of learning are probably happening during the preparation stage of creativity. Yet the most important type of learning is undoubtedly the learning that takes place prior to or during restructuring, since restructuring seems to be what creativity is all about.

Spiro and his colleagues (Spiro, Vispoel, Schmitz, Samarapungavan, & Boerger, 1987) were apparently thinking of restructuring when they referred to the importance of a flexible knowledge representation. They speculated that one key factor affecting the ability to think independently, productively, and flexibly (i.e., to think creatively) is the *flexibility* with which relevant prior knowledge is initially represented in memory. A flexible knowledge representation is one in which fragments of knowledge are not represented in a rigid, prepackaged, compartmentalized schema but can be moved about and reassembled into new knowledge structures. A flexible knowledge representation increases the potential for the unique recombinations and reorderings of knowledge fragments that are the essence of creativity.

Spiro and Myers (1984) further suggested how individuals might attain a flexible representation of knowledge during the preparation stage: by encoding (representing in memory) a lot of information; by encoding the same information in many different ways; and by using different modes or styles of thought (e.g., verbal and visual-perceptual) in encoding information. In sum, the analysis of Spiro and his colleagues suggests that, in the preparation stage, creative individuals construct very rich, interconnected, flexible cognitive structures that are the raw materials for restructuring in the act of creation to follow.

Metacognition may function in two ways at the preparation stage. First, creative individuals may be especially attuned to the state of their cognitive representations of knowledge. In other words, they may know whether their knowledge is full, rich, and flexible enough to provide the potential for creative restructurings. Second, creative individuals may be particularly adept at controlling or regulating the encoding of a flexible representation of knowledge. For example, they may know and use some of the strategies Spiro and his colleagues mention as ways to ensure flexible knowledge.

Stage 2: Incubation

The second of Wallas's stages of the creative process is "incubation." During the incubation stage, or "gestatory period" (Cowley, 1963, p. 256), the problem is not consciously pursued; rather, incubation is characterized by the "free working of the unconscious or partially conscious processes of the mind" (Wallas, 1970, p. 95). Introspecting on his own creative process, George Nelson states that "you turn off your conscious mind with all its buzzing and scurrying, and just coast. Then the subconscious does the work" (Rosner & Abt, 1970, p. 257).

What is the "work" the mind is doing during the incubation stage? Some scholars of creativity recognize that mental work is somehow controlled by inherent organizational processes of the mind. For example, Sinnott (1970) wrote:

Here mental work is being done. Here, quite without conscious participation, choices are being made and ideas fitted together into patterns. . . . One must recognize the operation in the unconscious of such an organizing factor, for chance alone is not creative. Just as the organism pulls together random, formless stuff into the patterned system of structure and function in the body, so the unconscious mind seems to select and arrange and correlate these ideas and images into a pattern. (pp. 111–112)

Apparently, during the incubation stage the interconnected network of flexibly organized knowledge acquired during the preparation stage is being restructured into new schemata; that is, elements of the original representation are being recombined and reordered to create new mental structures. Of course, exactly how this process occurs is still unknown.

One noteworthy characteristic of creative individuals during the incubation stage appears to be a metacognitive skill—their "mastery or control" over the reworking of their flexible cognitive representations (Spiro *et al.*, 1987). Presumably, the individual shapes the restructurings ever closer to that which will fulfill the purpose or goal of the creative enterprise. Creative individuals may have a superior metacognitive ability to separate the wheat from the chaff; that is, to control efficiently and effectively the restructuring of their schemata.

Metacognition at the incubation stage of creativity, however, is quite unconscious. Indeed, conscious attempts to guide and control creativity too early in the process seem doomed to failure. Amy Lowell, for example, writing on the process of making poetry, stated that "no power will induce it if the subconscious is not ready" (Lowell, 1952, p. 112). And George Nelson claimed, "It is my experience anyway that unless you turn off the active conscious mind, [the] idea quite possibly won't arrive" (Rosner & Abt, 1970, p. 257).

Stage 3: Illumination

Wallas's third stage of creativity is called "illumination." Illumination is "the final 'flash' or 'click'" (Wallas, 1970, p. 96) that is the culmination of the incubation stage. Illumination is inspiration, revelation, insight; it is the "Eureka!" or "Aha!" experience. At illumination, what has previously been unconscious suddenly becomes fully conscious.

Many creative individuals have described illumination, yet they are clearly at a loss to explain how it happened. The new ideas "arise spontaneously in the mind, often seemingly out of nothing and at a time when a person may be thinking of something quite different" (Sinnott, 1970, p. 109). In the words of Tennessee Williams,

The process by which the idea for a play comes to me has always been something I really couldn't pinpoint. A play just seems to materialize; like an apparition, it gets clearer and clearer and clearer. (Plimpton, 1984, p. 84)

Isaac Bashevis Singer described illumination in this way:

Somehow it [a story] comes to you. It comes "out of the blue," as you say. . . . In some cases you have a feeling as if some little imp or devil is standing behind you and dictating to you. . . . How our subconscious works we never really know. No man can ever describe how an idea comes to him. (Rosner & Abt, 1970, p. 230)

Shrouded in mystery, illumination seems to be a metacognitive event. Interestingly, Wallas refers to illumination as a "click," which is the same term Anderson (1979) chose for the awareness of successful comprehension. Indeed, I think the clicks of comprehension and of creativity are similar phenomena. In both cases, the clicks involve the recognition of a coherent cognitive representation. In the case of comprehension, it is recognition of the successful interpretation of information; in the case of creativity, it is recognition of a mental representation that fulfills, or has the potential of fulfilling, the goal of the creative enterprise. Creative individuals may be particularly attuned to the click of illumination. They may have a superior metacognitive awareness of when an insight is a good one, worthy of pursuit.

The creative process *may* end at the illumination stage; some creations are fully formed at illumination. For example, Robert Frost reported that, one winter evening, as he stepped outside into the snow for a breath of air, the entire poem, "Stopping by Woods on a Snowy Evening," came into his head (Sinnott, 1970, p. 109). Similarly, Conrad Aiken reflected, "It seized me at lunch, the first section, and I had to leave the table to put it down. Then it finished itself. In a way I had little to do with it" (Plimpton, 1974, p. 36). The illumination of a fully formed work is not the usual case, however. Ghiselin (1952) stated that "spontaneous appearance of inventions very fully formed is not extremely rare, but it is by no means ordinary. Spontaneity is common, but what is given is usually far from complete" (p. 15).

Stage 4: Verification

In the typical case, then, the incomplete product of illumination is subjected to a fourth and final stage of the creative process, "verification." Verification involves "the work of verification, correction, or revision that ordinarily follows the more radical inventive activity and completes or refines its product" (Ghiselin, 1952, p. 28). Although illumination is a sudden, often joyful experience, verification is frequently sustained and painful.

One of the most demanding aspects of creative discipline is the revision process: artists and scientists clarify their condensed thoughts through the successive drafts (or revisions) of their work. . . . The process is like a dialogue between the artist and his or her product. (John-Steiner, 1985, p. 75)

Verification is a stage in which metacognition clearly plays a significant role. The "dialogue"

between artist (or scientist) and product that John-Steiner refers to probably entails two types of metacognition. The first type involves verifying or measuring the product against an *internal* standard—the original purpose of the creative enterprise and the mental image formed during illumination. The second type of metacognition involves verifying the product against an anticipated *external* standard—a would-be audience.

Rosenblatt (1986) referred to these two types of metacognition in the writing process when she mentioned two kinds of "authorial reading" (the reading by authors of their own writing during the verification stage). In the first "purpose-oriented" authorial reading, "the writer tries to satisfy, while refining, a personal conception" (p. 19). In the second kind of authorial reading, "the writer dissociates from the text and reads it with the eyes of potential readers" (p. 19).

Creative individuals mention both kinds of metacognition in the verification process. For example, author John Cheever seemed to be referring to metacognition regarding an internal standard when he commented, "It's a question, I guess, of trying to get it to correspond to a vision. There is a shape, a proportion, and one knows when something that happens is wrong" (Plimpton, 1981, p. 132). Author Gabriel García Marquez was clearly referring to metacognition regarding an external standard when he said,

In general, I think you usually do write for someone. When I'm writing I'm always aware that this friend is going to like this or that another friend is going to like that paragraph or chapter, always thinking of specific people. In the end all books are written for your friends. (Plimpton, 1984, p. 322)

The conscious metacognition of the verification stage is apparently a skill that can be refined and perfected over time. Creative individuals may be able to hone both their sensitivity to the internal and external standards and their ability to respond to these standards. As author Arthur Koestler put it, there is "a very curious built-in control which develops as the years go by, with your experience" (Rosner & Abt, 1970, p. 152).

In sum, creative individuals seem to be especially adept at the conscious metacognitive skills that are required during the verification stage. They may be unusually sensitive to both internal and external standards and particularly able to revise the creative product accordingly. Creative individuals may also be especially good at improving these abilities with experience and practice.

Concluding Remarks

The foregoing analysis suggests that metacognition plays a very important role in creativity. Indeed, metacognition is probably a significant component of each stage in the creative process. Therefore, it seems that future studies of creativity might benefit from a closer look at the role of metacognition in the creative process. Likewise, cognitive psychology might benefit from a closer look at the creative process as a fascinating and informative example of cognition and metacognition in action.

Personally, I would like to see research efforts in three areas. First, I would like to see studies on expert–novice differences in metacognition and creativity. What are the differences between an expert creator and a novice creator in their metacognitive abilities at each stage of the creative process? A related question is the development of metacognitive abilities with practice. For instance, it was suggested that the conscious metacognition of the verification stage develops over time and with experience. Is this true of metacognition at other stages? What is it that people are learning over time?

Second, I would like to see a line of research directed at the purported relationship between ''flexible'' knowledge and creativity. We need to research the speculations of Spiro and his colleagues that flexible knowledge is a prerequisite for schema restructuring and, hence, creativity. If this relationship is verified, we then need to know more about how flexible knowledge is and could be acquired.

A third potentially profitable research area is intervention studies that are designed to teach metacognitive skills in creativity. It seems likely that some of the principles of metacognitive skills instruction that are derived from intervention studies in learning could be fruitfully applied to creating. Indeed, this potential has already been demonstrated by Scardamalia and Bereiter in the area of writing. These researchers have completed a number of studies in which students receive instruction and help in various cognitive and metacognitive skills that are associated with writing; for example, planning a composition, making evaluative judgments about their writing, and diagnosing text problems (Scardamalia & Bereiter, 1983a,b, 1985). Similar research should be carried out in other areas of creative endeavor.

Doubtless there are many other useful lines of research in the area of metacognition and creativity. The possibilities are limited only by our creativity as researchers!

References

Anderson, T. H. (1979). Study skills and learning strategies. In H. F. O'Neil, Jr., & C. D. Spielberger (Eds.), *Cognitive and affective learning strategies* (pp. 77–78). New York: Academic Press.

Baker, L., & Brown, A. L. (1984). Metacognitive skills and reading. In P. D. Pearson (Ed.), *Handbook of reading research* (pp. 353–394). New York: Longman.

Cowley, M. (Ed.). (1963). *Writers at work: The Paris Review interviews* (Second Series). New York: Viking Press.

Ghiselin, B. (1952). Introduction. In B. Ghiselin (Ed.), *The creative process: A symposium* (pp. 11–31). New York: New American Library.

John-Steiner, V. (1985). *Notebooks of the mind: Explorations of thinking*. Albuquerque, NM: University of New Mexico Press.

Lowell, A. (1952). The process of making poetry. In B. Ghiselin (Ed.), *The creative process: A symposium* (pp. 109–112). New York: New American Library.

Plimpton, G. (Ed.). (1974). *Writers at work: The Paris Review interviews* (Fourth Series). New York: Viking Press.

Plimpton, G. (Ed.). (1981). *Writers at work: The Paris Review interviews* (Fifth Series). New York: Viking Press.

Plimpton, G. (Ed.). (1984). *Writers at work: The Paris Review interviews* (Sixth Series). New York: Viking Press.

Rosenblatt, L. M. (1986). *Writing and reading: The transactional theory*. Paper presented at the Reading/Writing Conference, University of Illinois at Champaign-Urbana, Illinois, October 19–21.

Rosner, S., & Abt, L. E. (Eds.). (1970). *The creative experience*. New York: Grossman Publishers.

Rumelhart, D. E., & Norman, D. A. (1978). Accretion, tuning, and restructuring: Three modes of learning. In J. W. Cotton & R. L. Klatzky (Eds.), *Semantic factors in cognition*. Hillsdale, NJ: Erlbaum.

Scardamalia, M., & Bereiter, C. (1983a). Child as co-investigator: Helping children gain insight into their own mental processes. In S. Paris, G. Olson, & H. Stevenson (Eds.), *Learning and motivation in the classroom* (pp. 61–82). Hillsdale, NJ: Erlbaum.

Scardamalia, M., & Bereiter, C. (1983b). The development of evaluative, diagnostic, and remedial capabilities in children's composing. In M. Martlew (Ed.), *The psychology of written language: A developmental approach* (pp. 67–95). London, England: Wiley.

Scardamalia, M., & Bereiter, C. (1985). Development of dialectical processes in composition. In D. R. Olson, N. Torrance, & A. Hildyard (Eds.), *Literacy, language, and learning: The nature and consequences of reading and writing* (pp. 307–329). Cambridge, England: Cambridge University Press.

Sinnott, E. W. (1970). The creativeness of life. In P. E. Vernon (Ed.), *Creativity* (pp. 107–115). Middlesex, England: Penguin Books.

Spiro, R. J., & Myers, A. (1984). Individual differences and underlying cognitive processes. In P. D. Pearson (Ed.), *Handbook of reading research* (pp. 471–501). New York: Longman.

Spiro, R. J., Vispoel, W. L., Schmitz, J., Samarapungavan, A., & Boerger, A. (1987). Knowledge acquisition for application: Cognitive flexibility and transfer in complex cognitive domains. In B. C. Britton (Ed.), *Executive control processes.* Hillsdale, NJ: Erlbaum.

Wallas, G. (1970). The art of thought. In P. E. Vernon (Ed.), *Creativity* (pp. 91–97). Middlesex, England: Penguin Books.

CHAPTER 11

The Creative Construction of Rationality

A PARADOX?

David Moshman and Leslie E. Lukin

Is the development of rationality a creative process? Is there something paradoxical about the idea that creativity can result in increasing rationality? We will argue in this chapter that rationality is indeed creatively constructed by the developing individual. If one thinks of creativity as consisting of unconstrained flights of the imagination and of rationality as strict adherence to mechanical rules of reasoning, there is indeed something paradoxical about this conclusion. The paradox dissolves, however, upon reconsideration of the definitions of both rationality and creativity.

This chapter is organized into five major sections. In the first, we present a protocol from a 13-year-old who is ranking seven arguments. We will see (a) that her analysis of the logic becomes increasingly sophisticated over the course of working on the task, and (b) that this improvement is a creative, constructive process. The second section provides a more systematic review of the literature on the development of reasoning, supporting the conclusion that there is systematic progress toward increasing rationality.

The third section considers empiricist (learning) and nativist (innatist) accounts of the development of reasoning. We argue that neither account is adequate and that the problems with each are best addressed by a constructivist view in which creativity is not merely an incidental feature but a fundamental characteristic of development. The fourth section then presents a specific constructivist account of the development of reasoning involving the creative process of *reflective abstraction*.

Finally, we return to the theme of whether creativity can really lead to increasing rationality. We conclude that the developmental picture presented in this chapter, in which development is inherently creative and leads to systematically increasing rationality, has important implications for the nature of both creativity and rationality.

Lori: The Creative Construction of Logic

Lori was a 13-year-old seventh grader who volunteered to participate in a study of conceptions about the nature of logic (Moshman & Franks, 1986, Exp. 1). She was asked to sort and rank argu-

David Moshman and Leslie E. Lukin • Department of Educational Psychology, University of Nebraska, Lincoln, NE 68588.

ments and to explain the bases for her sortings and rankings. The seven arguments, each appearing on a separate index card, were as follows:

1. If elephants are bigger than dogs
   And dogs are bigger than mice
   Then elephants are bigger than mice

2. If adults are older than babies
   And children are older than babies
   Then adults are older than children

3. If dogs are bigger than mice
   And elephants are bigger than mice
   Then dogs are bigger than elephants

4. If dogs are bigger than elephants
   And elephants are bigger than mice
   Then dogs are bigger than mice

5. If babies are older than adults
   And babies are older than children
   Then adults are older than children

6. If mice are bigger than dogs
   And mice are bigger than elephants
   Then dogs are bigger than elephants

7. If elephants are either animals or plants
   And elephants are not animals
   Then elephants are plants

The key concept in the study was validity of inference. An argument is valid if its conclusion follows logically from the given premises, regardless of the empirical truth or falsity of the premises and conclusions. Thus, Arguments 1, 4, and 7 above are valid even though no. 4 has a false premise ("Dogs are bigger than elephants") and no. 7 has not only a false premise ("Elephants are not animals") but a false conclusion as well ("Elephants are plants"). Arguments 2, 3, 5, and 6 are invalid in that their conclusions do not follow necessarily from their premises, even though the conclusions in two cases (nos. 2 and 5) happen to be empirically true.

Most college students showed a clear understanding of validity in sorting and ranking the above arguments, whereas none of the 20 fourth graders in the study did so. Seventh graders spanned the entire range, with some performing like fourth graders and some like college students. Of greatest interest for present purposes are those who initially performed like fourth graders but, by the end of the session, were reasoning like the college students.

Lori was in this latter group. Given multiple opportunities to sort sets of arguments drawn from the above seven, she had consistently failed to distinguish valid from invalid arguments. Instead, she typically sorted arguments by content, distinguishing, for example, arguments about people from arguments about animals. She was then asked to rank the seven arguments from *most logical* to *least logical* and to explain her ranking. In the course of attempting to generate a ranking that satisfied her, she produced a series of six separate rankings.

Lori's initial ranking, from most to least logical, was 1 2 3 4 5 (6 7) (parentheses indicate tie). Her explanation for this ranking was primarily in terms of the number of true statements in each argument. She considered an argument to be most logical if all three statements within it were empirically true, next most logical if it included two true statements, less logical if it included only one true statement, and least logical if it included no true statements. Although she did hint at the concept of validity in explaining why she placed Argument 1 above Argument 2, her articulation of validity was vague and she saw this as a secondary consideration, useful only as a tiebreaker where two arguments had an equal number of true statements within them.

Before the interviewer could move on, however, Lori's focus shifted to the conclusions, and she decided to change her ranking to 1 2 4 5 (3 6 7), explaining that the first four all have true conclusions whereas the latter three are illogical, and equally so, in that their conclusions are empirically false. She still placed no. 1 above no. 2, however, explaining more clearly now that no. 1 "says it in the sentence" whereas in no. 2 you "just know." Thinking this over led her to reconsider her ranking of her first four arguments (those with true conclusions) and resulted in a new ranking: (1 4) (2 5) (3 6 7). Her explanation referred to the fact that in nos. 1 and 4 the conclusion "has to" be, whereas in nos. 2 and 5 it just happens to be "right."

At this point, she began thinking more seriously about no. 7 and decided to move it up to a position just below nos. 1 and 4. Shortly, she put it along with them, arguing that its conclusion "has to be that way" due to the structure of the argument. Finally, she collapsed the distinction between (2 5) and (3 6), noting that in none of these cases is the information sufficient for the conclusion. Thus, she made the transition from an initial ranking based primarily on empirical truth to a final ranking based entirely on validity. This involved a gradual, painstaking differentiation of validity from truth and an increasing sense of the former rather than the latter as the essence of logicality.

It is important to note that at no point in this episode did the interviewer provide any feedback.

His role was exclusively to write down Lori's ranking and explanation. Had Lori been satisfied, this portion of the research would have ended with her explanation of her initial response. Thus, the increasingly explicit recognition and articulation of the concept of validity was an internally generated construction rather than a learned response. Although Lori's previous educational experiences presumably had an impact on her thinking, it appears that her construction of the concept of inferential validity was a genuine act of creativity.

It is also worth noting that the concept of validity did not emerge suddenly from nowhere. Even in her initial ranking, in which Arguments 1 and 2 were seen as the two best because they contained three true statements, Lori placed no. 1 (the valid argument) above no. 2, though she could only articulate vaguely the basis for this decision. As she spontaneously reconstructed her rankings, she became increasingly clear in her account of validity and in differentiating it from empirical truth, leading ultimately to her classifying Argument 7 (with a patently false conclusion) as being just as valid as nos. 1 and 4. Her developmental transition appeared to involve a continuing self-reflection in which an implicit recognition of logical form gradually became the object of explicit awareness and reconstruction, leading to the sophisticated concept of inferential validity. Her creativity appears to reside precisely in this self-reflective process of making the implicit explicit. This conception of development as a creative reconstruction at a higher level of abstraction is a major theme of the chapter to which we will return later.

Lori's construction of validity is thus consistent with our general thesis that rationality is neither learned nor innate but, rather, creatively constructed. In the next section, we will support more systematically the claim that reasoning typically develops in the direction of greater rationality. We will then turn to a more systematic examination of the related claim that creativity, rooted in active self-reflection, is fundamental to this process.

The Development of Reasoning

Reasoning can be divided into at least two major components: *deduction* and *induction*. Deductive reasoning deduces conclusions from given premises; inductive reasoning induces conclusions from empirical observations. Thus, deduction draws conclusions from premises without considering the empirical truth or falsity of those premises; it is concerned exclusively with the internal logic linking sets of propositions. Induction, on the other hand, tests hypotheses against reality; it is concerned not with formal relations but rather with empirical truth. (Note that here we are using the term *induction* in a very broad sense.) We will consider development in each of these two areas.

Development of Deductive Reasoning

Although the development of deductive reasoning is a complex, multifaceted process, it can be usefully construed as consisting of a sequence of four qualitatively distinct stages (Moshman, 1989).

Stage 1: Explicit Content—Implicit Inference. Although Stage 1 children (typically preschoolers) can make correct inferences from a wide variety of premises (Braine & Rumain, 1983; Hawkins, Pea, Glick, & Scribner, 1984), they think about content rather than about the process of making inferences. They do not explicitly grasp the fundamental distinction between premises (the given information) and conclusion (the deduced proposition). That is, they *use* inference but do not think *about* inference.

Consider, for example, the following argument:

8. Sprognoids are either animals or plants
   Sprognoids are not animals
   Therefore, sprognoids are plants

Stage 1 children, given the two premises, will correctly reach the conclusion that sprognoids are plants. They see the conclusion, however, not as a conclusion but as a new fact. They are not thinking about deducing a conclusion from premises; they are thinking about sprognoids, animals, and plants. We as psychologists, of course, can determine that they have in fact engaged in deductive inference. The process of inference is merely implicit in their thinking, however. What they are explicitly aware of is not inference but content (see Table 1).

Stage 2: Explicit Inference—Implicit Logic. Children at this stage, typically in the elementary school years, can think about the process of inference and explicitly grasp the distinction between premises and conclusions. In other words, they recognize their conclusions *as* conclusions, as resulting from inference. This can be seen in the fact that

Table 1.   Development of Deductive Reasoning

	Explicit object of understanding	Knowledge implicit in reasoning (subject)
Stage 1 Explicit content Implicit inference	*Content*	*Inference*: Conclusion deduced and thus distinct from premises
Stage 2 Explicit inference Implicit logic	*Inference:* Conclusion deduced from and thus related to premises	*Logic:* Form of argument distinct from empirical truth of premises and conclusions (necessity)
Stage 3 Explicit logic Implicit metalogic	*Logic*: Relation of argument form and empirical truth of premises and conclusion (validity)	*Metalogic*: Formal logical system distinct from natural language
Stage 4 Explicit metalogic	*Metalogic*: Interrelations of logical systems and natural languages	

they, unlike Stage 1 children, distinguish conclusions that are logically necessary from those that are merely reasonable, plausible, probable, or conventional (Fabricius, Sophian, & Wellman, 1987; Moshman, 1989; Moshman & Timmons, 1982; Pieraut-Le Bonniec, 1980; Somerville, Hadkinson, & Greenberg, 1979) and recognize that inference can be a source of knowledge (Sodian & Wimmer, 1987).

Consider, for example, the following argument:

9. Sprognoids are animals or plants or machines
    Sprognoids are not animals
    Therefore, sprognoids are plants

Stage 2 children will recognize that this argument differs from the previous one in that, although the conclusion has some basis in the premises, it is not logically required by the premises. As psychologists, we might note that the conclusion in Argument 8 is deemed necessary due to the logical form of the argument: X is p or q; X is not p; therefore, X is q. It can be argued that in distinguishing necessary inferences from merely plausible ones Stage 2 children are making use of logical form. However, although Stage 2 children are explicitly aware of making inferences, the form of argument, which is the basis for their judgments of necessity, is merely implicit in their thinking, rather than an object of explicit awareness.

Stage 3: Explicit Logic—Implicit Metalogic. Stage 3 individuals, typically adolescents or adults, are expressly aware of logical form. Because they think about form explicitly, they fully understand

that some forms of argument are valid and others invalid and they sharply distinguish validity from empirical truth (Moshman & Franks, 1986). They understand that to claim an argument is valid means that, due to its form, its conclusion would have to be true *if* its premises were true, but that in fact the premises may be false and, if so, the conclusion may be false as well. Consider, for example, the following argument:

10. Elephants are either animals or plants
     Elephants are not animals
     Therefore, elephants are plants

This argument is identical in form to Argument 8. Whereas Argument 8 presents little difficulty for Stage 1 or Stage 2 children, however, Argument 10 does (Moshman & Franks, 1986). To recognize its validity in the face of the patent falsity of its conclusion requires an explicit awareness of logical form, including a sharp differentiation of logic from empirical truth. Studies of children's natural epistemologies support the view that logical and empirical domains of knowledge are not explicitly differentiated before adolescence (Cummins, 1978; Komatsu & Galotti, 1986; Osherson & Markman, 1975). We have already seen, in the example of Lori, a sample of the transition from Stage 2 to Stage 3.

Stage 4: Explicit Metalogic.   The explicit logic of Stage 3 may be postulated to require implicit metalogical knowledge about the nature of logical systems. Explicit formalization of logical systems involving reflection on the nature of such systems and on their relations with each other and with natural languages may be defined as Stage 4 (Moshman, 1989). Systematic reasoning at this level may be limited to individuals who are engaged in a formal study of logic, though there is evidence of some Stage 4 insights among college undergraduates (Politzer, 1986).

Development of Inductive Reasoning

Although inductive reasoning, especially as we have defined it, is a broad domain, we believe the following account captures some of its fundamental aspects.

Stage 1: Explicit Content—Implicit Subjectivity. The Stage 1 child, typically a preschooler, thinks about content. Although we can infer subjectivity, this is implicit in the child's knowing rather than an object of explicit awareness. Children as old as 3 or 4 seem very limited in their understanding of their own subjectivity. For example, they have great difficulty distinguishing what something "looks like" from what it "really and truly" is, even when researchers have made systematic efforts to use familiar items and circumstances, to ask simple questions, and to teach the relevant concepts (Flavell, 1986; Flavell, Green, & Flavell, 1986; Flavell, Green, Wahl, & Flavell, 1987). Young children view knowledge as something directly absorbed from the world and fail to grasp the role of subjective construction in creating ideas that may differ from person to person and may not directly reflect reality (Broughton, 1978; Clinchy & Mansfield, 1986) (see Table 2).

Stage 2: Explicit Subjectivity—Implicit Theory. Stage 2 children, typically elementary school age, explicitly distinguish knowledge and appearance from reality. They realize the world may be different from what one sees (Flavell, 1986; Flavell *et al.,* 1986) or thinks (Clinchy & Mansfield, 1986). They understand that there is nevertheless a relation between ideas and reality and, if challenged, may defend their ideas by citing evidence consistent with them and/or seeking more such evidence—a *verification strategy.* Although we can view their subjective ideas as theories, they do not think explicitly about theories *as* theories and are thus unsystematic in testing them.

Stage 3: Explicit Theory—Implicit Metatheory. Stage 3 individuals, typically adolescents and adults, have a more explicit grasp of theory and its relation to data. They recognize that theories are not merely more general than data but exist on a different plane, a plane of possibilities as opposed to the realm of realities. The need to test theories is expressly understood. It is recognized that, in an infinite world, theories can never be proven true but can be disproved by a single disconfirming datum. The Stage 3 thinker understands that the key to genuinely testing a theory or hypothesis is not to accumulate supportive data but rather to seek potentially disconfirming data (*falsification strategy*) (Klayman & Ha, 1987; Moshman, 1979a; O'Brien, 1987; O'Brien, Costa, & Overton, 1986; Overton, Ward, Noveck, Black, & O'Brien, 1987; Popper, 1959; Skov & Sherman, 1986). The Stage 3 individual's sophistication in thinking about theories, data, and the relations between them reveals an

Table 2. Development of Inductive Reasoning

	Explicit object of understanding	Knowledge implicit in reasoning (subject)
Stage 1 Explicit content Implicit subjectivity	*Content*	*Subjectivity*: Distinction between appearance and reality
Stage 2 Explicit subjectivity Implicit theory	*Subjectivity*: Relation of appearance and reality (verification strategy)	*Theory*: Distinction between theory and data
Stage 3 Explicit theory Implicit metatheory	*Theory*: Relation of theory and data (falsification strategy)	*Metatheory*: Distinction between metatheory and theory
Stage 4 Explicit metatheory	*Metatheory*: Coordination of theories and metatheories	

implicit metatheoretical competence (Moshman, 1979b), though that competence is implicit in the individual's reasoning about theories rather than itself an object of reflection.

Stage 4: Explicit Metatheory. Some individuals, perhaps in connection with higher education, begin to think explicitly about the metatheoretical assumptions underlying their theories (paradigms) and about their metatheoretical views with respect to the testing of theories (philosophy of science). Recognition that all data are theory-laden and that apparent falsifications of theory can always be explained away through additional assumptions may lead to epistemological relativism, a transitional phase between Stages 3 and 4 in which the possibility of rationally comparing and testing theories is rejected. Further reflection, however, leads to recognition that even if the Stage 3 falsification strategy is inadequate, rational coordination of theory and data leading to genuine progress in understanding reality is nevertheless possible (Broughton, 1978; King, Kitchener, Davison, Parker, & Wood, 1983; Kitchener & King, 1981; Kitchener & Wood, 1987; Welfel & Davison, 1986).

Conclusion: Reasoning and Rationality

The above accounts of stages in the development of deductive and inductive reasoning are both consistent with extensive empirical evidence. They suggest that in each area reasoning genuinely develops in the sense that each new stage is not merely different from the previous one but incorporates and transcends it. With respect to deduction, the increasing differentiation and coordination of premises and conclusions lead to a differentiation of abstract form of argument from empirical truth. With respect to induction, a similar differentiation and coordination of theory and data lead to sophisticated conceptions of truth, falsity, proof, and disproof at increasingly abstract levels of metatheoretical awareness. In both domains, the stages embody a self-reflective trend in which the individual at each level reasons about (reflects on, "knows") the reasoning of the previous level. If we think of rationality as a self-reflective appeal to reasoning (Moshman & Hoover, 1989), the development of reasoning appears to move in the direction of greater rationality.

We can now return to the question of whether this is a creative process. In the next section, we will consider the possibility that it is not. Perhaps so-phisticated reasoning is simply learned from one's environment or, alternatively, is innate in one's genes. We will argue against these views and thus set the stage for a more detailed consideration of the alternative view that the development of reasoning is indeed a creative construction.

Empiricist and Nativist Accounts of the Development of Reasoning

Even if one accepts the empirical evidence that reasoning improves with age, one might argue that this is not the result of a creative process. One alternative is that rationality is learned from one's environment via relatively direct (noncreative) mechanisms of transmission (empiricism). Another possibility is that the observed developmental changes are due to the maturation of abilities programmed in the genes (nativism). We will consider each of these views in turn.

Empiricism

Empiricist accounts of the development of reasoning can be divided into three general categories: physical transmission, social transmission, and linguistic transmission (Moshman, 1979b). First, we will present a rather eclectic empiricist account of the development of reasoning, including mechanisms associated with all three categories. Then we will propose that, although learning undoubtedly plays an important role in the development of reasoning, it is not sufficient for a complete account. In particular, we will argue that it fails to account for (a) conceptions of logical necessity, (b) progression through distinct levels of knowing, (c) increasing rationality, and (d) the origin of genuine novelties. Empiricism thus skirts the central issues of logic, development, rationality, and creativity.

An Empiricist View of the Development of Reasoning. One aspect of an empiricist view is that reasoning develops due to feedback from one's physical environment, that is, via *physical transmission*. For example, when new modes of reasoning are applied to one's problems, they may in some cases be maladaptive. This would lead to nonreinforcing results and would thus tend to extinguish those modes of reasoning. Some new processes, however, would generate adequate solutions leading to results reinforcing to the individual. Such reasoning would be used with increasing frequency. The environment would thereby shape reasoning in the direction of increasing rationality.

Although environmental selection of this sort probably does play a role in the development of reasoning, sophisticated reasoning processes do not lead to consistently reinforcing outcomes. There is little evidence that the sorts of contingencies assumed in this account are sufficiently consistent and have effects of sufficient magnitude to result in substantial increases in rationality in a reasonable period of time. Moreover, the source of new reasoning remains obscure.

The empiricist account of the development of reasoning is greatly enriched when one adds *social transmission*—learning from other people (Bandura, 1977). First, unlike objects in the physical environment, other people actually reason. Although their thinking itself cannot be directly observed, reasoning processes can be and often are externalized and imitated. Such imitation need not be a rote copying of behavior but can involve abstraction of generalizable strategies.

Second, people can provide far more precise and effective feedback on reasoning than can the physical environment. A teacher may consistently and effectively reinforce correct reasoning about math problems by noting the correctness of each right answer and the incorrectness of each wrong answer. Positive or negative evaluation of improper math by the physical environment, by contrast, would be far less direct and consistent.

Finally, people can provide direct instruction. They can explain logical concepts and discuss the rationale for various sorts of reasoning. There is simply no parallel to this in one's dealings with the physical world.

Much social transmission occurs via the vehicle of language: language tremendously facilitates modeling, feedback, and direct instruction. In addition, however, language may itself constitute a major source of reasoning. In fact, language is probably so central to reasoning that it is worth distinguishing a particular aspect of social transmission with a label of its own—*linguistic transmission*. A strong case can be made that, in learning a language, a child learns a set of implicit inference schemata that underlie reasoning throughout the lifespan (Braine, 1978; Braine & Rumain, 1983). A great deal of our reasoning, including most of our automatic deductive inferences, may be in part a result of learning language.

Although there is room for argument about specific mechanisms, it seems clear that learning plays an important role in the development of reasoning (Moshman, 1989). The question is whether learning is *sufficient* to account for the major phenomena that need to be explained. In the next four subsections, we argue that empiricism fails to account for four central (and closely interrelated) phenomena: (1) the logical necessity inherent in advanced reasoning, (2) the progression of reasoning through distinct levels of knowing, (3) the systematic increases in rationality, and (4) the creative production of genuine novelties.

Critique of Empiricism: The Problem of Logic. Progress through the stages of deductive reasoning described above involves increasingly explicit understanding of logical necessity (Moshman, 1989; Moshman & Timmons, 1982). In Stage 2, the child makes accurate judgments regarding whether given premises are sufficient for a conclusion or further information is necessary, thus showing an implicit grasp of necessity. In Stage 3, valid arguments are distinguished from invalid arguments independent of the truth or falsity of premises and conclusions, thus showing a more explicit grasp of necessity as an aspect of logical form. As Lori eventually recognized, the conclusion of a valid argument, even if it is empirically false, "*has to* be that way" (our emphasis). Stage 4 involves further reflection on the role of necessity in diverse logical systems. Available evidence shows Stage 2 understanding as early as age 6 (Somerville *et al.*, 1979) and indicates that Stage 3 understanding is common by early adolescence and spontaneously applied by most college students (Moshman & Franks, 1986). Metalogical comprehension at a Stage 4 level is probably much less common. Even if it were limited to logicians, however, we would have to keep in mind that the logician who devises an explicit theory of necessity is a person whose behavior needs to be explained.

Although the role of logical necessity in the development of inductive reasoning is less obvious, it is equally important (Moshman, 1979b). Theories themselves, of course, are distinguished from logical systems precisely by the fact that they are *not* logically necessary—they can be disconfirmed by empirical evidence. Metatheoretical knowledge concerning the testing of theories, however, does have logical elements. Consider, for example, the Stage 3 insight that, in an infinite world, a hypothesis cannot be conclusively confirmed by any finite number of observations but can be conclusively disconfirmed by a single falsifying datum. This is not simply a theory that happens to work in our universe. On the contrary, it is a logical insight that rests on an understanding of hypotheses as universal statements and of the logical implications of such statements (Popper, 1959). Of course, progress toward Stage 4 complicates matters by putting the testing of simple hypotheses into a broader, explicitly metatheoretical context. Nevertheless, it remains clear that there is a definite logic underlying higher stages of inductive reasoning that provides a basis for using empirical evidence but is itself based not on empirical evidence but on the necessary relations of propositions.

Empiricist efforts to account for logical necessity (of which John Stuart Mill's work is probably the most famous) generally suggest that it is an illusion. Some beliefs, it is argued, are based on more evidence than others. The more evidence we have for a belief, the more strongly we believe it. If the evidence for a belief is sufficiently extensive and consistent, we see it not merely as true but as logically necessary.

This account does not fare well, however, in accounting for the actual phenomena of human belief. The daily rising of the sun, for example, is highly consistent, but there is no temptation to see this as logically necessary. The truths of arithmetic, on the other hand, appear to be disconfirmed every time our checkbooks fail to balance. Nevertheless, we see $2 + 2 = 4$ as logically necessary; instead of rejecting our ''theories'' of arithmetic, we reject the evidence by searching for calculation errors.

Similar empiricist efforts that attempt to account for logical necessity as a social or linguistic convention fare no better (Moshman, 1979b; Moshman & Timmons, 1982). It appears that people do come to distinguish logical from empirical matters and that learning from the physical, social, or linguistic environment cannot explain how this distinction is made.

Critique of Empiricism: The Problem of Development.　　Available evidence suggests a clear directionality to age-related changes in reasoning. The stages earlier described summarize this directionality. As we have seen, each stage includes an explicit differentiation and coordination of what was only implicit in the previous stage. In somewhat broader terms, each stage is a metacognitive reflection on the previous stage. Given this progress toward increasing differentiation and hierarchic integration at higher and higher levels of self-reflec-

tion, it appears that the changes in reasoning are *developmental,* in the strict sense of moving in a systematically progressive direction.

Genuine development is, to say the least, difficult to explain from an empiricist perspective. Instead its existence is typically denied. The empiricist account suggests that children's reasoning changes in whatever direction it is shaped by the environment. The fact that there are certain consistencies in developmental trends is explained as due to similarities in children's environments within any culture or even across cultures.

Thus, for example, an individual who tests hypotheses by seeking verifying information would be expected to use increasingly a falsification strategy to the extent that it is modeled and/or reinforced in the environment. An individual who uses a falsification strategy would be equally likely to reject it in favor of a verification strategy to the extent that the latter is modeled and/or reinforced by the environment. In this account, there is no logic to the falsification strategy that, once understood, makes movement from verification toward falsification more likely than the reverse. Change moves in whatever direction the environment pulls or pushes; there is no genuine development.

The empiricist account is not intuitively very plausible, nor is it consistent with available evidence. Class exercises by the first author over many years show that undergraduates who discuss a difficult hypothesis-testing task (Wason's, 1983, selection task) with no input from the instructor show a strong tendency to move toward falsification, even though the verification approach is initially far more popular. Arguments for falsification presented by fellow students are not initially more frequent or better expressed than arguments for verification, but their inner logic does seem, over a sufficient period of time, to have a greater impact.

Consistent with this informal observation, research in a variety of areas has shown that children are far more likely to be influenced by a model when what is modeled involves a level of reasoning slightly beyond their own than when it involves a level of reasoning below their own (e.g., Walker, 1982). Such evidence is difficult to reconcile with the empiricist view that children are equipotential to move in any direction the environment pulls or pushes. It is more consistent with the view that there is a natural directionality in the development of reasoning.

This is not to say, of course, that people move inexorably through developmental stages regardless of their environments. Learning undoubtedly plays an important role in development. Our argument is that (a) there is a natural, progressive direction of change, (b) reasoning tends to move in this direction in any normal environment, and (c) empiricism cannot account for this.

Critique of Empiricism: The Problem of Rationality. There is no doubt that people can and do learn a variety of modes of reasoning. An empiricist account, however, fails to explicate progress toward rationality. At best, it might suggest that most societies teach good strategies of reasoning, that good reasoning somehow inheres in human languages, and/or that physical environments are sufficiently consistent in reinforcing good reasoning. There are at least three major problems with this account. First, it suggests that a society might just as easily teach irrationality as rationality. Although there is no doubt that environmental factors can hinder the development of reasoning and sharply limit rationality, the empiricist account, as noted above, fails to explain the natural tendency for development to move in the direction of rationality. Second, empiricism has little to say about the self-reflective nature of advanced reasoning. Individuals at or beyond Stage 2 not only reach conclusions but reflect on the fact that they are doing so. Any explanation of rationality must address its self-reflective nature. Third, the empiricist account merely shifts the need for explanation from the individual to language and society. If children learn to be rational via language and social influences, then rationality must be somehow inherent in language and/or in society. It remains unclear how it got there, especially if rationality is not spontaneously produced by the human mind. This leads us directly into the final part of our critique.

Critique of Empiricism: The Problem of Creativity. A major basis for empiricist views is the difficulty of explaining genuine creation of novelty. It is not at all clear how new modes of reasoning or higher levels of rational understanding can be created by the human mind. The empiricist solution is to argue that they are *not* created; rather, they are internalized from the social environment.

This assumes, however, that rationality already exists in language and/or society. But if natural languages include an inherent rationality, how did that come to be there? If society already possesses sophisticated modes of reasoning, where did they come from? It appears the rationality must have

been created by human minds, either individually or in the context of social interaction. But this puts us right back where we started: How does the mind create new and better forms of reasoning? The empiricist account avoids a psychological answer to this question by throwing the problem to linguistics, sociology, or anthropology. But this is (to use the vernacular) a *cop-out:* There is no reason to think that these disciplines are any better equipped to explain creativity than is psychology, or that creativity can ever be explained without reference to psychological considerations.

Again, we are not denying that society and language embody considerable rationality and play an important role in the learning of reasoning by individuals. We do suggest, however, that the human mind is capable of genuine creativity in the construction of rationality. Further, we suggest that this creativity is not limited to brilliant minds that have influenced society or to ancient social interactions that produced language. On the contrary, we suggest that creativity is central to the cognitive development of every individual and is indispensable in explaining the development of reasoning.

The failure of empiricism to account for important aspects of the development of reasoning does not in itself show that a creative process must be involved. In fact, the problems of empiricism have traditionally been taken as arguments for nativism (see Bereiter, 1985; Campbell & Bickhard, 1987). With respect to the specific issues of reasoning, then, we must now turn to the possibility that rationality is innate.

Nativism

A Nativist View of the Development of Reasoning. A nativist account of the development of reasoning stresses its hereditary basis. The simplest version of this, *preformationism,* would propose that mature rationality is directly encoded in the genes. Modern nativists generally reject preformationism in favor of *epigenesis.* The latter is a more developmental conception in that it involves a process of change over some portion of the lifespan. It remains nativist, however, in viewing change as strongly directed by heredity (Kitchener, 1978, 1980).

For example, no modern biologist would suggest that a tiny version of the human heart exists in the DNA of a fertilized human ovum. Rather, the DNA contains genetic instructions that will lead to the development of a heart in any normal (species-appropriate) environment. Although the environment plays a critical role in providing necessary nutriments, it has no effect on the final structure of the heart (except in pathological cases). The structure of the human heart is essentially the same for all humans; its development follows a predetermined path guided by the genes.

A nativist account of the development of reasoning would follow this general framework. Rationality is not directly encoded in the genes; however, human genes do contain precise instructions that, in any normal environment, will result in a sequence of stages of reasoning leading ultimately to mature rationality. Only in pathological cases will there be deviations from this course. Although epigenesis does result in something that was not literally in the genes, the course of development is too directly programmed to be considered creative.

Predetermined epigenesis probably plays an important role in anatomical and physiological development and may have important implications for psychological development. More broadly, we have no quarrel with the view that heredity, like learning, plays an important role in development. The question before us is whether heredity is *sufficient* to account for available evidence concerning the development of reasoning. Again, we think not.

Critique of Nativism. Heredity is often invoked when we cannot account for something in terms of learning. If the observed developmental course of reasoning cannot be explained in terms of the environment, it is tempting to conclude that it was programmed in the genes.

To say something is innate, however, does not explain it. It simply redirects our attention from the ontogenetic (developmental) history of the individual to the phylogenetic (evolutionary) history of the species. It is not obvious that evolutionary mechanisms are any more powerful in accounting for logic, development, or rationality than are developmental mechanisms. Natural selection, for example, is simply an environmental feedback mechanism analogous to operant conditioning. In fact, at the level of phylogenesis, we run into precisely the same difficulty we encountered at the level of ontogenesis: How can empirical experience result in logical necessity? William James noted the problem a century ago: "The experience of the race can no more account for our necessary or *a priori* judgments than the experience of the individual can" (1890/1950, pp. 617–618).

We suggested earlier that, in explaining cognitive novelties as due to learning from society, we are merely foisting on sociology the task of accounting for novelty. Nativism is often an equally unhelpful appeal to biology. It assumes, usually without basis, that evolutionary mechanisms can better explain the creation of novelties than can developmental mechanisms. There is no evidence that sophisticated reasoning of the sort observed in older children and adults has come about through natural selection or any other phylogenetic process or that its development is in any direct sense programmed in human genes. We cannot count on biology, any more than on sociology, to explain the emergence of rationality. We would do better to presume that rationality is creatively constructed by the developing individual and to try to explicate this process.

Interactionism

Before we turn to accounting for the development of reasoning as a creative construction, it is worth saying a word about *interactionism*. In psychological writing, it is common to assert that neither heredity alone nor environment alone can account for development; rather, development involves an interaction of both. In a general sense, this is surely correct. With respect to our current concern, however, the concept of interactionism is not particularly helpful.

One form of interactionism is *statistical interactionism*. This involves the assertion that heredity and environment interact in the statistical sense: The effects of the environment depend on one's genes and the effects of one's genes depend on one's environment. This is no doubt true but of little use for our present purpose in that it says nothing about the *process* of development.

From a developmental point of view, a more useful approach to interactionism is *dynamic interactionism* (Lerner, 1986). This approach includes the concept of statistical interactionism but stresses the actual processes by which the interacting forces of heredity and environment determine the course of development. Such an approach is particularly helpful in explaining the partially unique course of each individual's development in terms of unique and continuing interactions of genes and experience.

With respect to our current concerns, however, even dynamic interactionism is of limited use. Initially, we are concerned primarily with the general course of development in the area of reasoning, not with individual differences. Although the existence of individual differences is beyond dispute, evidence suggests there are also important commonalities in the course of development, summarized in the stages presented earlier, that are worthy of explanation. Dynamic interactionism has little to say about this, focusing instead on individual differences.

Perhaps more important, dynamic interactionism is not itself constructivist, though it is not inconsistent with constructivism. In at least some versions, dynamic interactionism provides an image of the person as a passive space within which heredity and environment interact. The interaction may produce novelties, but there is no *self* actively and purposely producing those novelties. Creation may occur, but no one is responsible for that creativity. It is far from clear that any such process, however interactive it may be, can result in rationality.

Finally, it is important to note that our critique of empiricism was not at all based on its neglect of hereditary factors, nor was our critique of nativism based on its neglect of the individual's environment. Thus, in terms of the question of how reasoning develops, interaction between heredity and environment does not resolve the fundamental inadequacies of each. Once again, we are led to the view that only a conception of reasoning as a creative construction by an active self can explain the progress of rationality.

It is not sufficient, of course, for a constructivist account of reasoning to show the inadequacies of empiricism, nativism, and interactionism. What is needed is a positive explication of how rationality is creatively constructed. It is to this task that we now turn.

A Constructivist Account of Rationality

In general terms, constructivism maintains that development is driven by neither heredity nor environment, nor even by an interaction of the two. In fact, it is not driven at all but, rather, constructed by the active mind. This view is not a specific theory but rather a general metatheoretical approach, or paradigm, within which specific theories can be formulated (Moshman, 1982).

The best-known constructivist theory is that of Jean Piaget. Piaget proposed that development consists of the active construction of a succession of qualitatively distinct stages. The constructivist aspect of his theory revolves around the concept of "equilibration." Most of Piaget's research and theorizing prior to the mid-1960s, however, dealt not with equilibration but with the structure of the various stages of development (e.g., the *groupements* of concrete operations and the complete combinatorial system and INRC group of formal operations). Although Piaget did discuss the process of equilibration and made it clear that the structural stages were the outcome of this process, he was far more clear and detailed in his stage descriptions than in his accounts of the developmental process.

Beginning around the mid-1960s, Piaget's emphasis shifted (see Campbell & Bickhard, 1986). The process of development became a more central focus and its mechanisms (especially equilibration and reflective abstraction) received detailed empirical and theoretical attention. Among the most important of his late works was a 1975 reworking of his theory of equilibration (Piaget, 1985). Piaget proposed that knowing, at any level of development, involves a complex coordination of subject and object. All knowing is subjective in the sense that the reality cannot be directly known; it can only be known by assimilation to the subject's (mental or physical) actions. Nevertheless, increasingly objective knowledge is possible to the extent that one becomes aware of and reconstructs one's subjectivity. Thus, self-understanding and objective knowledge are inextricably linked.

Awareness of one's subjectivity is not an all-or-none matter, however. Campbell and Bickhard (1986) have proposed a general theory of cognitive development that postulates a series of knowing levels, each related to the previous one by a process of reflective abstraction. Knowing Level 1 interacts with the environment. Knowing Level 2 reflects on knowing Level 1. It thus makes explicit what was previously only implicit in the process of knowing the environment. To do this, however, requires construction and application of new knowledge that is only implicit at Level 2. Explicit reflection on knowing Level 2 can only be done from knowing Level 3, which, in turn, involves a newly constructed implicit knowledge knowable only from the perspective of Level 4, and so forth. Ascent through these levels is a very gradual constructive process that takes place in each of various domains of knowing. Rate of progress in the various domains may differ; the sequence of stages within any domain must be consistent, but there need not be consistency across domains.

The knowing levels approach suggests the emergence at each stage of cognitions that are genuinely novel (for the individual) but do not simply appear mysteriously out of nowhere. This approach suggests that the development of reasoning may be a genuinely creative process. Cognitive novelties are actively constructed by the mind but may nevertheless lead to systematically increasing rationality in that each new stage is a systematic reflection on and reconstruction of the stage before. In the next two subsections, we will reconsider the stages of deductive and inductive reasoning proposed earlier from the perspective of a knowing levels approach.

Construction of Deductive Reasoning

Young children think about their environments, including, from a very early age, the content of linguistic propositions. They routinely make a variety of inferences and thus reach conclusions that go beyond the given information. As psychologists, we can reflect on their reasoning and determine that they are using a variety of inference schemata to reach their conclusions. They themselves, however, are not initially aware of their reasoning. They think about content, not about the process of inference.

As their inference schemata become sufficiently efficient and consolidated, however, children begin to reflect on their conclusions, on the distinction between conclusions and premises, on the relation of conclusions and premises, and on the process of inference by which they arrive at conclusions from premises. Their coordination and reconstruction of premises and conclusions, including an explicit awareness of the inference process linking them, does not come from nowhere but rather from reflection on and coordination of what was already implicit in their reasoning. This reflection includes the construction of a new level of understanding in which form of argument is distinguished from content. Only such awareness of form will allow a genuine grasp of the nature of inference, including a sense of the necessity of certain conclusions. Awareness of form, however, is only implicit in Stage 2 thinking. It is part of the framework that allows an explicit grasp of inference but is not itself the object of awareness. It is a newly constructed subject that is used to understand the previous subject, which, accordingly, now becomes the object of understanding.

Although the Stage 2 subject is not an object of reflection, it can become an object of reflection from the next higher level. As the child refines his or her use of argument form to make judgments about conclusions, he or she increasingly grasps the distinction between form and content, until form of argument is sharply distinguished from empirical truth of content. Reflection on the validity of argument forms involves a grasp of formal logic and thus an ability to use a formal logical system (as distinct from a natural language). This requires some degree of (implicit) metalogical knowledge. The construction of such knowledge is central to the construction of Stage 3, and, in turn, may become an object of further reflection, leading to the construction of an explicit grasp of metalogic at Stage 4.

There is no reason in principle for any upper bound on this process, though there may be limits due to inherent information-processing constraints of the human mind. The explicit Stage 4 reflection on metalogic presumably takes place from the perspective of an implicit subjectivity (call it "meta-metalogic" if you like), which, in turn, can become an object of reflection at Stage 5. Not being at Stage 5 ourselves, we have nothing explicit to say about this.

Construction of Inductive Reasoning

A similar account can be provided for the construction of inductive reasoning. Stage 1 children think about content. As psychologists we can see the subjectivity in their thinking and can note the distinction between appearance and reality but children themselves simply know what they know. Knowledge is seen as direct; questions about how it relates to reality, even if put in simple language and contexts, are likely to be viewed with wonderment or simply misconstrued (Broughton, 1978; Flavell, 1986; Flavell et al., 1986).

With rich enough experience, children begin to note that people do not always respond to things the same way as each of them do and that things may even seem different to them at different times. Reflecting on their own subjectivity, children consider the distinction between appearance and reality and the relations between them. They realize that sometimes they need more evidence before they can know that they are correct. Implicit in this Stage 2 orientation toward verification is the idea of testing one's theories.

Further reflection on the subjectivity of knowledge yields an increasingly explicit distinction between theory and data, including the Stage 3 concept that theories are purely hypothetical and must be tested by gathering data that could disconfirm them. This is a metatheoretical view and can itself become the object of further reflection leading (at Stage 4) to explicit conceptions of metatheories and their relation to theories and data. Again, there is no reason in principle why Stage 4 must be the highest stage, but we know of no evidence that anyone proceeds beyond this and, in any event, have nothing substantive to say about "metametatheory."

Conclusions

The specific stages of inductive and deductive reasoning differ. Although a case can be made for a conceptual parallel (e.g., in each sequence, Stage 3 is precisely two reflective abstractions away from the level that interacts directly with reality), typical ages of emergence may not be comparable. What is central for our purposes is that the process is identical in each case. The individual begins with direct (and epistemically naive) interactions with reality, including no awareness of his or her implicit subjectivity in observing, interpreting, or drawing inferences. Through reflection, not on the environment but on his or her own knowing, the individual constructs a new level of understanding that explicitly knows the previous level and thus creates new knowledge via differentiation and coordination of what was only implicit in his or her interactions with the environment. This new level of understanding, however, itself includes knowledge that can become the object of explicit awareness, thus setting the stage (so to speak) for the construction of a still higher level.

This analysis, we believe, accounts for the four phenomena that were so difficult for empiricism and nativism—namely, logic, development, rationality, and creativity. With respect to logic, the problem was to account for how the individual develops a sense that certain things are logically necessary if everything is simply learned from the environment (of the individual or of the species). The constructivist account proposes that not everything is abstracted from the environment. Some knowledge is constructed via reflection on and coordination of the workings of the mind. This allows not merely observation of and generalization from realities but systematic anticipation of all possibilities, thus permitting the construction of a sense of necessity with regard to one's mental operations (Piaget, 1986).

With respect to development, the knowing levels account does explain convincingly the basis for the invariant sequence of stages. Because each level of knowing is a reflection on the previous level, the stages must emerge in the same order for all individuals. Environmental or hereditary factors may determine how rapidly one moves through the stages or how far one gets, but, because each stage is a reflection on the previous one, it would be impossible for the stages to occur in a different order or for a stage to be skipped.

With respect to rationality, the knowing levels approach accounts for the systematic increase suggested by the empirical literature. Each stage constitutes a higher level of rationality than the previous one because it is a reflection that systematically reconstructs the previous stage. Each stage is a reflective awareness of one's reasoning at the previous stage and thus, in an important sense, provides reasons for one's previous reasoning. In highlighting the increasingly self-reflective nature of advanced reasoning, the knowing levels approach justifies the identification of such reasoning as constituting rationality.

Finally, with respect to creativity, the knowing levels approach shows how new ideas can be created that are based on, but nevertheless transcend, earlier knowledge, and that then serve as the basis for further creativity. This conception of creativity allows for genuine novelty but can nevertheless account for systematic progress in rationality.

The Subjective Creation of Objectivity

Creativity and Rationality

Can creativity lead to increasing rationality? The traditional paradigm of rationality is the scientist, who uses the scientific method to gain objective knowledge of the real world. Thus, rationality may be intuitively seen as mechanical conformity to fixed rules of reasoning that guarantee objectivity. A traditional model of creativity, in contrast, is the eccentric and misunderstood artist, whose creative insights spring from the uncharted depths of his or her unconscious mind. Creativity, then, may be construed as consisting of unconstrained flights of fancy deep in the mists of our subjectivity. Given these conceptions, it is indeed difficult to see how rationality could develop via a creative process.

From a constructivist perspective, pure objectivity is impossible not only in fact but in principle. There may indeed be a real world with actual characteristics, but it can be known only through assimilation to one's subjective knowledge and processes of knowing (schemes, schemata, frames, scripts, ideas, theories, strategies, structures, and so forth). Piaget (1985) viewed equilibration, the central process of development, as a continuing renegotiation of the relation between subject (knower) and object (reality as construed by the subject). The object of knowing always remains a function, however, of the knower (subjectivity) as well as a function of reality (objectivity). At no point does it become possible to know reality from a perspective outside one's own knowledge and thus achieve final objectivity (von Glasersfeld, 1979).

It is, however, possible to construct a new framework from which to know one's previous processes or structures of knowing. This process, reflective abstraction, makes it possible to evaluate the contribution of one's earlier subjectivity to one's experience and thus to attain a more objective understanding of the contribution of reality to that experience. The reflection on one's own subjectivity does not, of course, take place from a completely objective perspective. On the contrary, it takes place from a higher level of subjectivity. Nevertheless, the resulting metasubjectivity, in rendering one's previous subjectivity an object of knowing and thus reconstructing and understanding it, constitutes a genuine increase in objectivity. To the extent that the previous knowing involved reasoning, the new stage involves reasoning about that reasoning and thereby constitutes a higher level of rationality. Rationality is thus not a mechanical following of rules but a self-reflective appeal to and coordination of reasoning at levels of understanding that are one or more steps beyond the level that knows the environment.

The construction of each higher level is a genuinely creative act in that the framework for reflecting on one's previous subjectivity is given neither by heredity nor environment, and the resulting explicit reconstruction of what was implicit in that subjectivity involves the creation of genuine novelty. Such creation does take place within the subjective domain in that it involves reflection on one's own subjectivity. It is not a mere flight of fancy, however, but, on the contrary, a systematic abstraction and reconstruction that, by increasing the self-reflective use of reasoning, leads to greater rationality in one's knowing of reality and thus to increasing objectivity.

In this view, creativity is not a trait associated primarily with particular (e.g., gifted or talented) individuals, nor is it a set of skills or abilities that emerge at some point in development. On the contrary, it is a fundamental aspect of development in all normal individuals. The process of development, from this perspective, is inherently creative. This is true even in areas of development, such as reasoning, where progress toward rationality and objectivity is of central concern.

Directions for Research

The suggestion that development is a genuinely creative process suggests avenues of research that might not be considered if one simply assumed that any outcome of development can be entirely explained as a mature version of what was already in the genes (maturation), an internalization of what was already in society (learning), or an interaction of maturation and learning. As a metatheoretical approach, constructivism is less fully reductionist and less committed to an antecedent-consequent sort of mechanical causality than are nativism and empiricism. It even goes beyond most versions of interactionism in these respects. Nevertheless, it can generate specific, testable accounts of development and may even go deeper than alternative approaches in genuinely explaining the underlying process.

In the present case, we have described specific stages of development in two areas of reasoning and explained their emergence via reflective abstraction. One direction for research would be to provide increasingly fine-grained accounts of the stages themselves. This should include microanalysis of substages and of the sequence of transitional states leading from each major stage to the next. The more detailed our understanding of the route(s) development takes and the steps along the way, the better we can guess at plausible mechanisms of transition (Keil, 1984).

There can be no substitute, however, for careful analysis of reasoning during the developmental process itself. Through systematic presentation of challenging problems, it is possible to generate protocols that show how individuals construct and apply new modes of reasoning (Kuhn & Phelps, 1979). Analysis of such protocols (cf. the earlier example of Lori) may not be as straightforward and objective as statistical manipulation of quantitative data in a design with clearly distinguishable independent and dependent variables. Such analysis can, however, be reasonably systematic and can surely yield general and testable conclusions about what goes on in the creative mind.

Creativity and the Limits of Science

Although constructivism thus constitutes a viable research program, it also raises difficult issues. The specific question we have addressed in greatest detail is the question of how rationality can be creatively constructed. A full answer must explain (a) how novel reasoning can be produced by the developing individual, and (b) how this new reasoning can be not merely different from earlier reasoning but in fact more rational, better able to direct the knower toward objective knowledge.

On a psychological level, we have suggested that there is no inherent paradox that renders scientific research along these lines pointless. We have argued that, through repeated reflective abstractions, knowledge implicit in each level of subjectivity can be explicitly differentiated and coordinated at a higher level. The resulting metasubjectivity is more rational due to the self-reflection inherent in its construction and can thus serve as a better basis for objectivity. There is no reason to assume that scientific research cannot further clarify the specifics of these processes.

Nevertheless, constructivism raises challenging questions. Why does reflective abstraction increase rationality? Why is it that metasubjective knowledge is increasingly adapted to objective reality? These are questions that, in some version, have bedeviled every attempt to account for the relation of logical knowledge and empirical reality. As William James (1890/1950, p. 652) put it, one can imagine worlds in which "our logic . . . would form a merely theoretic scheme and be of no use for the conduct of life. But our world is no such world. It is a very peculiar world, and plays right into logic's hands." Constructivism may provide a better approach to these issues than nativism and empiricism in that it does not evade the key questions right from the start, but, at present, it is at best a general approach to looking for the answers.

Although constructivism provides a metatheoretical framework for scientific research, the questions raised here are not merely psychological questions about certain mental processes. They go far deeper in seeking explanations for the fundamentally creative nature of thought and the creative adaptation of thought to reality. Full inquiry into creativity must, at some point, test the limits of empirical science. The fundamental issues of creativity are, ultimately, metaphysical questions about the nature of mind.

ACKNOWLEDGMENTS. We are grateful to Mark Bickhard and Robert Campbell for detailed and thoughtful comments on an earlier draft of this chapter.

References

Bandura, A. (1977). *Social learning theory*. Englewood Cliffs, NJ: Prentice-Hall.

Bereiter, C. (1985). Toward a solution of the learning paradox. *Review of Educational Research, 55*, 201–226.

Braine, M. D. S. (1978). On the relation between the natural logic of reasoning and standard logic. *Psychological Review, 85*, 1–21.

Braine, M. D. S., & Rumain, B. (1983). Logical reasoning. In J. H. Flavell & E. M. Markman (Eds.), *Handbook of child psychology: Vol. 3. Cognitive development* (pp. 263–340). New York: Wiley.

Broughton, J. (1978). Development of concepts of self, mind, reality, and knowledge. In W. Damon (Ed.), *Social cognition* (pp. 75–100). San Francisco: Jossey-Bass.

Campbell, R. L., & Bickhard, M. H. (1986). *Knowing levels and developmental stages*. Basel: Karger.

Campbell, R. L., & Bickhard, M. H. (1987). A deconstruction of Fodor's anticonstructivism. *Human Development, 30*, 48–59.

Clinchy, B. M., & Mansfield, A. F. (1986, April). *The child's discovery of the role of the knower in the known*. Paper presented at the meeting of the Jean Piaget Society, Philadelphia.

Cummins, J. (1978). Language and children's ability to evaluate contradictions and tautologies: A critique of Osherson and Markman's findings. *Child Development, 49*, 895–897.

Fabricius, W. V., Sophian, C., & Wellman, H. M. (1987). Young children's sensitivity to logical necessity in their inferential search behavior. *Child Development, 58*, 409–423.

Flavell, J. H. (1986). The development of children's knowledge about the appearance-reality distinction. *American Psychologist, 41*, 418–425.

Flavell, J. H., Green, F. L., & Flavell, E. R. (1986). Development of knowledge about the appearance-reality distinction. *Monographs of the Society for Research in Child Development, 51*(1, Serial No. 212).

Flavell, J. H., Green, F. L., Wahl, K. E., & Flavell, E. R. (1987). The effects of question clarification and memory aids on young children's performance on appearance-reality tasks. *Cognitive Development, 2*, 127–144.

Hawkins, J., Pea, R. D., Glick, J., & Scribner, S. (1984). "Merds that laugh don't like mushrooms": Evidence for deductive reasoning by preschoolers. *Developmental Psychology, 20*, 584–594.

James, W. (1890/1950). *The principles of psychology* (Vol. 2). New York: Dover.

Keil, F. C. (1984). Mechanisms of cognitive development and the structure of knowledge. In R. J. Sternberg (Ed.),

Mechanisms of cognitive development (pp. 81–99). New York: Freeman.

King, P. M., Kitchener, K. S., Davison, M. L., Parker, C. A., & Wood, P. K. (1983). The justification of beliefs in young adults: A longitudinal study. *Human Development, 26,* 106–116.

Kitchener, K. S., & King, P. M. (1981). Reflective judgment: Concepts of justification and their relationship to age and education. *Journal of Applied Developmental Psychology, 2,* 89–116.

Kitchener, K. S., & Wood, P. K. (1987). Development of concepts of justification in German university students. *International Journal of Behavioral Development, 10,* 171–185.

Kitchener, R. F. (1978). Epigenesis: The role of biological models in developmental psychology. *Human Development, 21,* 141–160.

Kitchener, R. F. (1980). Predetermined versus probabilistic epigenesis: A reply to Lerner. *Human Development, 23,* 73–76.

Klayman, J., & Ha, Y. (1987). Confirmation, disconfirmation, and information in hypothesis testing. *Psychological Review, 94,* 211–228.

Komatsu, L. K., & Galotti, K. M. (1986). Children's reasoning about social, physical, and logical regularities: A look at two worlds. *Child Development, 57,* 413–420.

Kuhn, D., & Phelps, E. (1979). A methodology for observing development of a formal reasoning strategy. In D. Kuhn (Ed.), *Intellectual development beyond childhood* (pp. 45–57). San Francisco: Jossey-Bass.

Lerner, R. M. (1986). *Concepts and theories of human development* (2nd ed.). New York: Random House.

Moshman, D. (1979a). Development of formal hypothesis-testing ability. *Developmental Psychology, 15,* 104–112.

Moshman, D. (1979b). To *really* get ahead, get a metatheory. In D. Kuhn (Ed.), *Intellectual development beyond childhood* (pp. 59–68). San Francisco: Jossey-Bass.

Moshman, D. (1982). Exogenous, endogenous, and dialectical constructivism. *Developmental Review, 2,* 371–384.

Moshman, D. (1989). The development of metalogical understanding. In W. F. Overton (Ed.), *Reasoning, necessity, and logic: Developmental perspectives.* Hillsdale, NJ: Erlbaum.

Moshman, D., & Franks, B. A. (1986). Development of the concept of inferential validity. *Child Development, 57,* 153–165.

Moshman, D., & Hoover, L. M. (1989). Rationality as a goal of psychotherapy. *Journal of Cognitive Psychotherapy, 3,* 31–51.

Moshman, D., & Timmons, M. (1982). The construction of logical necessity. *Human Development, 25,* 309–323.

O'Brien, D. P. (1987). The development of conditional reasoning: An iffy proposition. In H. W. Reese (Ed.), *Advances in Child Development and Behavior* (Vol. 20, pp. 61–90). Orlando, FL: Academic Press.

O'Brien, D. P., Costa, G., & Overton, W. F. (1986). Evaluations of causal and conditional hypotheses. *Quarterly Journal of Experimental Psychology, 38A,* 493–512.

Osherson, D. N., & Markman, E. (1975). Language and the ability to evaluate contradictions and tautologies. *Cognition, 3,* 213–226.

Overton, W. F., Ward, S. L., Noveck, I. A., Black, J., & O'Brien, D. P. (1987). Form and content in the development of deductive reasoning. *Developmental Psychology, 23,* 22–30.

Piaget, J. (1985). *The equilibration of cognitive structures: The central problem of intellectual development.* Chicago: University of Chicago Press.

Piaget, J. (1986). Essay on necessity. *Human Development, 29,* 301–314.

Pieraut-Le Bonniec, G. (1980). *The development of modal reasoning: Genesis of necessity and possibility notions.* New York: Academic Press.

Politzer, G. (1986). Laws of language use and formal logic. *Journal of Psycholinguistic Research, 15,* 47–92.

Popper, K. (1959). *The logic of scientific discovery.* New York: Basic Books.

Skov, R. B., & Sherman, S. J. (1986). Information-gathering processes: Diagnosticity, hypothesis-confirmatory strategies, and perceived hypothesis confirmation. *Journal of Experimental Social Psychology, 22,* 93–121.

Sodian, B., & Wimmer, H. (1987). Children's understanding of inference as a source of knowledge. *Child Development, 58,* 424–433.

Somerville, S. C., Hadkinson, B. A., & Greenberg, C. (1979). Two levels of inferential behavior in young children. *Child Development, 50,* 119–131.

von Glasersfeld, E. (1979). Radical constructivism and Piaget's concept of knowledge. In F. B. Murray (Ed.), *The impact of Piagetian theory: On education, philosophy, psychiatry, and psychology* (pp. 109–122). Baltimore: University Park Press.

Walker, L. J. (1982). The sequentiality of Kohlberg's stages of moral development. *Child Development, 53,* 1330–1336.

Wason, P. C. (1983). Realism and rationality in the selection task. In J. St. B. T. Evans (Ed.), *Thinking and reasoning: Psychological approaches.* London: Routledge & Kegan Paul.

Welfel, E. R., & Davison, M. L. (1986). The development of reflective judgment during the college years: A 4-year longitudinal study. *Journal of College Student Personnel, 27,* 209–216.

CHAPTER 12

Dialectical Thinking and Adult Creativity

Suzanne Benack, Michael Basseches, and Thomas Swan

Perhaps because most work on creativity has originated in personality and social psychology, there has been little attention given to transformations of creativity across the lifespan. Researchers have generally taken one of two approaches. Those interested in deriving nomothetic tests of creative ability or in studying social factors affecting creative performance have focussed on very general features of the creative process equally applicable to people of a wide range of ages and levels of expertise in a domain. Other researchers have been interested in describing the creative process in adults who have made notable creative achievements in public fields, for example, creative artists and scientists. Although both of these approaches have been fruitful to the study of creativity, neither lends itself to the investigation of developmental changes in creative functioning.

Several questions are central to the developmental study of creativity: How does adult creativity differ from creativity in childhood and adolescence? What experiences contribute to the maturing of creativity? How do developments in other realms (cognitive development, affective development,

the acquisition of expertise in specific domains) affect creative functioning? Other chapters in this volume (see Moshman and Lukin, Chapter 11) have addressed this last question by examining the ways in which cognitive development from childhood to adolescence might be related to changes in creativity. In this chapter, we will consider one particular point in the lifespan at which cognitive development and the growth of creativity might be related: namely, the ways in which the development of dialectical thinking in adulthood might facilitate the development of mature forms of creativity.

Adult Cognitive Development: The Move from Formal to Postformal Operations

Piaget's series of stages of cognitive development ends in adolescence with the consolidation of formal operations. Formal operational thinking allows the late adolescent to manipulate the logical relations among abstract propositions, to think about all logically possible states of affairs, and to use the experimental method to test hypotheses. The formal operational thinker solves problems by modeling them as "closed systems" that are made up of a given number of variables that can be related in a finite number of ways. By systematically ma-

Suzanne Benack and Thomas Swan • Department of Psychology, Union College, Schenectady, NY 12308.
Michael Basseches • Massachusetts School of Professional Psychology, and Clinical Developmental Institute, Belmont, MA 02178.

nipulating one variable while controlling the others, all permutations and combinations of the variables' states can be observed and the relations among the variables deduced.

Although this kind of formal analysis is a very powerful cognitive tool, many theorists have argued that it is not an adequate description of mature adult thinking. The important problems of adult thought, it is claimed, are typically ill-defined and open-ended; much of the solution consists of deciding upon a way to model the problem, rather than on applying logical algorithms to the parameters of a given model. In the last decade, a number of authors have described forms of reasoning that develop "beyond formal operations," in late adolescence and adulthood. These "postformal" cognitive structures are hypothesized to retain the analytic power of formal analysis while going beyond its limitations. Although formal operations structure the relations of propositions within a logical system, postformal operations operate on logical systems, relating multiple systems to each other, transforming systems, and evaluating systems.

The claim of this chapter is that by freeing the person from the constraints of formal reasoning, while retaining the power of formal analysis, postformal thinking may facilitate the development of mature forms of creativity. Specifically, we will examine the one particular model of postformal thinking, Basseches's (1984a) depiction of dialectical thinking and its potential relations to creativity.

Dialectical Thinking

Dialectical thinking is a mode of cognition that attempts to comprehend phenomena in the world by seeing them as instances of dialectic. In this sense, to think dialectically is to use a particular model of reality, one that is exemplified in the dialectical philosophical tradition, as manifested in the works of a range of great thinkers, including Hegel (1967), Marx (1967), Darwin (1962), Von Bertalanffy (1968), and Piaget (1952). The claim of the dialectical thinking model is that some adults exhibit patterns of thought that share the underlying assumptions and descriptive categories of the dialectical philosophical outlook. The dialectical worldview is characterized by an emphasis on change, on wholeness, and on constitutive rela-

tions; these three aspects are coordinated in the idea of the dialectical process, that is, the transformation of wholes through interactive and constitutive relations.

Basseches's Dialectical Thinking Framework consists of 24 schemata, or "moves in thought," reflecting different aspects of the dialectical worldview (as summarized in Table 1). There are four major groups of schemata: those reflecting each major aspect of the idea of dialectic—change, wholeness, and relation—and those schemata organizing these three aspects in the notion of the dialectical process. We will briefly describe each aspect of the dialectical worldview and the schema corresponding to them.

Emphasis on Change

A model of reality begins with the question, "What exists?" Many worldviews hypothesize that there are fundamental, unchanging elements making up reality; these elements can enter into various relations with each other, but their fundamental nature remains unchanged. In contrast, dialectical worldviews assume that reality is made up of fundamental processes of change or becoming, in which old forms give way to new emergent forms. Thus, from a dialectical perspective, what currently exists is seen not as fundamental, unchanging reality but as the current moment of an ongoing process of change.

"Motion-Oriented Schemata" reflect the emphasis of dialectical thought on change. They describe moves in thought that function to preserve fluidity in thought, to draw the attention of the thinker to processes of change, or to describe such processes. Schemata 1 and 4 describe a process in thought of moving from reflecting on one idea to reflecting upon its negation—something apart from, contrary to, or excluded from the first idea—and then moving again toward a synthesis, a more inclusive idea that relates the original idea and its negation. Schemata 2, 3, 5, 6, 7, and 8 all function to direct the thinker's attention to processes of change and to counteract the tendency to treat processes as though they were static, fixed "things." For example, Schema 2 affirms that change is fundamental in the nature of things; Schema 6 applies this same notion to thought and asserts that knowledge is fundamentally active and changing. Similarly, Schema 8 understands a present event or situation as part of a larger historical process of change, and Schema 7 involves the rejection of

Table 1. The Dialectical Schemata Framework

A. Motion-oriented schemata

1. Thesis-antithesis-synthesis movement in thought
2. Affirmation of the primacy of motion
3. Recognition and description of thesis-antithesis-synthesis movement
4. Recognition of correlativity of a thing and its other
5. Recognition of ongoing interaction as a source of movement
6. Affirmation of the practical or active character of knowledge
7. Avoidance or exposure of objectification, hypostatization, and reification
8. Understanding events or situations as moments (of development) of a process

B. Form-oriented schemata

9. Location of an element or phenomenon within the whole(s) of which it is a part
10. Description of a whole (system, form) in structural, functional, or equilibrational terms
11. Assumption of contextual relativism

C. Relationship-oriented schemata

12. Assertion of the existence of relations, the limits of separation, or the value of relatedness
13. Criticism of multiplicity, subjectivism, and pluralism
14. Description of a two-way reciprocal relationship
15. Assertion of internal relations

D. Metaformal schemata

16. Location (or description of the process of emergence) of contradictions or sources of disequilibrium within a system (form) or between a system (form) and external forces or elements which are antithetical to the system's (form's) structure
17. Understanding the resolution of disequilibrium or contradiction in terms of a notion of transformation in developmental direction
18. Relating value to (a) movement in developmental direction and/or (b) stability through developmental movement
19. Evaluative comparison of forms (systems)
20. Attention to problems of coordinating systems (forms) in relation
21. Description of open self-transforming systems
22. Description of qualitative change as a result of quantitative change within a form

Table 1. (*Continued*)

23. Criticism of formalism based on the interdependence of form and content
24. Multiplication of perspectives as a concreteness-preserving approach to inclusiveness

---

seeing things as fixed and static when they are actually processes involving change.

Emphasis on Wholeness

Dialectical worldviews reject the separating of reality into fundamentally independent individual elements. Instead, reality is organized into forms, which are coherent wholes. From a dialectical perspective, one cannot think of the parts as separate elements that come together to make up wholes, for the very nature of the parts is determined by the wholes in which they participate. Similarly, the nature of a whole is more than simply the sum of the properties of its parts.

The ''Form-Oriented Schemata'' reflect the dialectical worldview's emphasis on wholeness. These schemata describe moves in thought that (a) direct the thinker's attention to organized or patterned wholes (forms), and that (b) enable the thinker to recognize and describe such forms. Schema 9 directs a thinker's attention from an element or phenomenon being considered to the larger wholes of which it is a part; Schema 10 describes the structural or functional organization of wholes. Schema 11 applies the notion of wholeness to thought and knowledge, by directing the thinker to see particular ideas and values within the context of the larger conceptual frameworks of which those ideas are parts.

Emphasis on Constitutive Relations

If one views reality as made up of independent elements, then one will view the relations those elements enter into as ''external'' to the elements themselves, that is, as not determining what the elements are. In contrast, dialectical outlooks emphasize constitutive relations. The relations among parts within a whole help make the parts what they are, and they also make up the internal structure of the whole.

The ''Relationship-Oriented Schemata'' serve to direct the thinker's attention to relationships and to enable the thinker to conceptualize relationships in ways that emphasize their constitutive nature. Schemata 12 and 13 describe moves in thought that turn the thinker's attention to relationships through the assertion of the existence of relationships, of the limits associated with seeing things as separate, and of the value of bringing things into relation. Schema 14 brings out the interactive aspect of relationships, and Schema 15 describes moves in thought recognizing that relationships help determine the nature of the things being related.

The Notion of Dialectic

The notion of a dialectical process ties together the notions of change, wholeness, and constitutive relations. In a dialectical process, forms or structures exist consisting of elements related in certain ways. Interactive relationships exist both within the form (between the parts of the whole) and between the form and that outside of it (i.e., with the environment). The interactions among the parts and between the whole and its environment eventually lead to change in the whole itself; the whole is transformed, the relations within it are transformed, and thus the nature of the elements is also transformed. Moreover, this transformation is not random change; it goes in a developmental direction, that is, the whole develops toward greater inclusiveness, differentiation, and integration. It becomes, then, a bigger, more complex, more richly organized whole. We can summarize this model of a dialectical process by saying that dialectic is developmental transformation (i.e., developmental movement through forms) occurring via constitutive and interactive relationships.

The "Metaformal Schemata" describe aspects of this notion of dialectical process. Thus, they integrate the categories of relationship, motion, and form. The use of metaformal schemata, then, presupposes an understanding of most of the motion-oriented, form-oriented, and relationship-oriented schemata. Schema 16 describes moves in thought that point out the limits of a system's stability by pointing to contradictions either within the system or between the system and its environment. Schemata 17 18, 21, and 22 are most clearly related to the process of transformation of forms. They direct thought toward instances of systems that are in open interaction with their environments, toward change in developmental directions, and toward the value of developmental chance. Schemata 19, 20, and 24 describe moves in thought that relate systems or

forms to each other, either by coordinating them (Schema 20) or evaluatively comparing them (Schema 19); Schema 24 specifically describes the coordination of systems of thought.

The term *dialectical thinking* is used to refer to a holistic, organized worldview that interprets phenomena in terms of dialectic; this kind of thinking seems not to develop until at least young adulthood, following the consolidation of formal operations (Basseches, 1984a). However, a person can use many of the individual dialectical schemata prior to developing full dialectical thinking. Basseches (1984b) has described four possible phases in the development of dialectical thinking. In the first phase, schemata appear that describe initial understandings of the ideas of form, movement, and relation (Schemata 1, 2, 6, 9, 10, 12, and 16). These schemata often appear in conjunction with or even prior to the development of formal operational thinking in adolescence. Next, "intermediate" level schemata appear in the second phase (Schemata 3, 11, and some forms of 16). In the third phase, "clusters" of more advanced schemata appear. These are oriented around the ideas of form, change, and value. Often people develop two of these clusters while failing to use the schemata that are related to the third. Finally, true dialectical thinking appears; the notions of movement, form, and constitutive relation become organized into a coherent dialectical worldview. At this phase, all three of the clusters of schemata are well represented and Schemata 21 and 22 appear.

Most studies of dialectical thinking have used Basseches's (1984a) original assessment procedure. People are interviewed about complex, open-ended topics, such as the nature of education. The interviews are transcribed, and then use of the 24 schemata is coded. A score of 0–3 is assigned to each schema, indicating whether it is clearly present, probably present, probably absent, or clearly absent. The scores on all 24 schemata are summed to create a Dialectical Index, which can range from 0–72. Some researchers also have used measures of comprehension of and preference for arguments using the dialectical schemata (e.g., Basseches, 1984b; Irwin, in press).

We have described dialectical thinking as an *ontology*, a way of modeling phenomena in the world. Much of what the dialectical thinker does is to see various objects and events in terms of dialectic. For example, one might take a dialectical view of a family, seeing it as a system in which members' identities are determined partly by their relations within the family system, and seeing the family as evolving through the interactions of its members and its interaction with the outside world.

If one applies a dialectical model to the understanding of the nature of thought and knowledge, one derives a dialectical *epistemology*. Dialectical thinkers generally see knowledge as an active process of conceptually organizing and reorganizing phenomena rather than as the accumulation of fixed truths. Knowledge, then, is seen as evolving, as changing in its fundamental structure rather than as simply increasing. Dialectical epistemologies also emphasize the structure and functioning of conceptual systems and collective wholes rather than individual, separate facts and ideas. Several of the dialectical schemata are directly concerned with this application of the idea of dialectic to epistemology (i.e., Schemata 6, 11, 13, and 24).

In the following sections, we consider ways in which dialectical thinking might promote creativity. Specifically, we argue (1) that a dialectical ontology facilitates the creative generation of novelty and the creation of new relations, (2) that a dialectical epistemology supports the kinds of moves in thought necessary for the unconventional, set-breaking, and the synthesizing aspects of creativity, and (3) that the evolution of a metasystematic dialectical perspective facilitates specific forms of mature creativity that are seen in highly functioning creative adults. Before turning to this task, however, it is necessary to have before us a characterization of creativity.

Characteristics of the Creative Process

There seems to be no one commonly accepted definition of creativity. There are, however, core characteristics that recur regularly in descriptions of the creative process or product. The first of these is *novelty;* nearly all definitions of creativity start from the assumption that the creative product is novel, atypical, unusual. This is the dimension most often assessed in tests of creativity, which typically ask the person to generate a large number of unusual responses to standard stimuli (e.g., the Torrance Test of Creative Thinking, 1962, and the Unusual Uses Test of Guilford, 1967). Most definitions of creativity also stipulate that the creative response should meet some criterion of *value*. A creative response must not merely be unusual; it must be effective or useful or an appropriate solution to a problem. The most common definitions of creativity combine these two elements of novelty and value. Rothenberg and Hausman (1976), for example, defined a creative response as one having both "newness" and "value" (p. 6); Amabile (1983) argued that a creative response "is both a novel and appropriate, useful, correct, or valuable response to the task at hand" (p. 33). Bruner (1962) saw creative products as those producing "effective surprise" in the beholder. Barron (1955) proposed that creative responses must have "a certain uncommonness" and be "adaptive to reality" (pp. 478–479).

The criteria of novelty and value focus on the nature of the creative product; other commonly mentioned features of creativity derive from a focus on the creative process. First, creativity is often described as a *response* to an ill-defined problem rather than a well-defined problem—one in which the nature of a solution and the path to a solution are unclear. Amabile (1983) termed these two types of problems "heuristic" and "algorithmic" and claimed that, in a creative response, the problem must be defined by the person as heuristic. Similarly, one of the four characteristics distinguishing creative problem solving for Newell, Shaw, and Simon (1962) was "difficulty in problem formulation." Second, many authors see creative thought as involving the ability to *move away* from past ways of thinking, to "break mental sets." Newell *et al.* (1962), for example, saw creative problem solving as "unconventional"; Henle (1962) referred to this aspect of creativity as "freedom"; Stein (1974) described creativity as a "leap" away from what has previously existed. Third, creativity is often seen as the *forming of relations* among things formerly disconnected. Koestler (1964) saw the essence of creativity as "bisociation," the association of two self-consistent but normally incompatible frames of reference; Henle (1962) called this aspect of creativity "harmony." Finally, some theorists gave particular importance to the role of *contradictions* in the creative process. Creativity is seen as the ability to hold together or bring into relation elements that were previously seen as contradictory. Kuhn (1963), for example, saw divergent thinking in science as a response to anomalies, data contradicting the existing paradigm. Rothenberg (1976) described a process of "Janusian thinking," the holding together of apparently contradictory views as essential to creativity.

The current literature, then, describes creativity as a response to ill-defined problems, involving the breaking away from existing ways of thinking, creating relations among dissociated or even contradictory elements, and resulting in novel and valuable products. Given this characterization of the creative process, how might dialectical thinking contribute to creativity? In the following discussion, we consider the relations among creativity and three aspects of dialectical thinking: (a) the dialectical understanding of reality (dialectical ontology), (b) the dialectical understanding of thought (dialectical epistemology), and (c) the dialectical understanding of the interrelation and evolution of systems (metasystematic perspective).

Dialectical Ontology and Creativity

Many authors posit that, in a creative response, one perceives a given object or event in multiple and novel ways, or brings it into new relations to other objects or events. Using a dialectical perspective to model or understand a phenomenon should support this aspect of creative functioning. In a nondialectical perspective, an object or event is seen as essentially static and separate from other phenomena; a thing unto itself. The same object, viewed from a dialectical perspective, is likely to be seen as a process rather than a thing, changing rather than static, as part of a larger whole, and as fundamentally in relation to other phenomena. Dialectical schemata facilitate creative responses, then, by directing attention from ''the thing itself'' to its history, its future, the systems in which it is embedded, and its relations.

Consider, for example, how a nondialectical thinker and a dialectical thinker might approach designing a birthday cake. The nondialectical thinker starts with an image, perhaps, of a completed birthday cake and considers a number of variables that might be manipulated: the shape, the color, the size, and the type of candles. The dialectical thinker, on the other hand, might think about the birthday cake as a process: its creation, its presentation at the party, its consumption, the memories people will have of it after the party. Moreover, the dialectical thinker might think about the role the cake plays in various contexts and relations: as an act in the life of the person who creates it, as a moment in the process of the party, as an aesthetic object in the scheme of party decorations, as an important object to the birthday child, as food for the other guests at the party, as part of a cultural tradition of birthday cakes, as part of a sequence of birthday cakes across the child's life. Considering

the cake in all these ways and in all these relations helps the dialectical thinker generate a much richer and more novel set of factors to consider in potential cake designs.

To take an example in the realm of adult scientific thought, consider how two psychologists, one a nondialectical and the other a dialectical thinker, might try to explain why adolescents exhibit rebellious behavior. The nondialectical psychologist begins by elaborating a set of truths about the entity ''adolescents'': they have erratic hormone levels associated with pubertal changes, they show high conformity to peer group norms, and they are capable of some forms of abstract reasoning unavailable to children. This psychologist might then consider which set of these factors could cause rebellion. In contrast, the dialectical psychologist will consider the act of rebellion in several contexts and relations: as a part of the overthrowing of childhood ways of functioning, as a strategy in the process of identity formation, as a chapter in the changing parent–child relationship, as a way of negotiating one's relation with the wider society, and as an act within the adolescent peer culture in relation to changes in moral thinking in this period. In all these contexts, rebellion is likely to be seen not as a static phenomenon in itself but as part of the ongoing processes of change.

The use of dialectical schemata to interpret reality, then, provides paths in thought leading from the ''present object'' to a wider set of realities: its past and future history, its contexts and relations. Thus, dialectical ontology ''opens up'' one's perception of reality, lends to it more variety and more connectedness—both central features of the creative process.

Another aspect of dialectical thinking that should support the generation of novel responses is that dialectical thinkers tend to move from a given perception or thought to its antithesis: that which stands outside or in contradiction to it (Schema 1). For example, if it occurs to the dialectical thinker that birthday cakes generally are done in bright, contrasting colors, she or he is likely to consider making a cake in dark, muted colors. If she or he recognizes that, as part of a larger cultural tradition, the candles on birthday cakes should reflect the person's age, she or he might generate an antithesis by saying, ''Perhaps this tradition isn't necessary . . . maybe the candles could symbolize something else.'' Moreover, the dialectical thinker responds to these contradictions by trying to form a synthesis, a new higher order relationship reconciling or relating the opposing ideas or perceptions. The tendency of dialectical thinkers to generate contradictions and then find syntheses reconciling them should support both the novelty-generating and the relationship-creating functions of creativity.

Dialectical Epistemology and Creativity

In adolescence and adulthood, our epistemologies—the models we create of the nature of our own thought—come to play an important role in regulating thought. Our epistemological beliefs tell us how to proceed in solving problems, when to accept solutions as true, and how to feel about events in our mental life, such as discovering contradictions to our beliefs, being uncertain, or finding our beliefs changing. In one sense, then, holding a dialectical view of knowledge is simply one more application of the dialectical worldview to reality; in another sense, however, it has particular importance for directing one's thinking. Basseches (1984a) reflects the special role of a dialectical epistemology in directing thought by including several schemata that specifically reflect the application of dialectical perspectives to the topic of knowledge (Schemata 6, 11, 23, 24). A dialectical model of knowledge is likely to foster creativity, we argue, because it represents the process of thinking as creative. In other words, the features of thought a dialectical model emphasizes and encourages are precisely those described as important to the creative process.

Consider how a nondialectical thinker, using the tools of formal operational analysis, approaches a problem. First, the person already holds some systematic framework from which to approach the problem. This framework will specify a finite number of variables to be considered and will define other aspects of the problem as irrelevant to the solution. The relevant variables are then related in all combinations and permutations of their various values, finding their interrelations through logical deduction and/or experimental manipulation of one variable while holding the others constant. The formal thinker expects this method to produce a single right answer that will hold in all similar circumstances and across time. Contradictions—observations inconsistent with this answer or disagreement from other people—are regarded as a sign that something is wrong with one's solution; the goal is to eliminate them. Internal consistency of one's beliefs and observations is highly valued. The formal operational thinker interprets problems, then, as "algorithmic" in Amabile's terms, as having defined paths leading to clearly and uniquely correct solutions.

This kind of formal analysis is an extremely powerful tool; it is seen by many philosophers of science as the basis of theory testing in science. On the other hand, formal operational analysis does not seem like an adequate description of the creative aspects of scientific thought: that is, of theory creation rather than theory testing. Creativity in fields like science, which are based upon formal analysis, seems to require cognitive operations that, on the one hand, retain the power of systematic thinking while, on the other hand, transcend its limitations. Dialectical thinking may be particularly useful in fostering creativity in these kinds of fields, because the dialectical perspective subsumes formal, closed-system analysis within a broader model describing transformations and interrelations of formal systems. How, then, might holding a dialectical epistemology, a model of the evolution of thought systems, support creativity in these kinds of fields?

First of all, the dialectical thinker sees his or her own thought as in a process of evolution. Where the formal thinker sees the necessity to change his or her thought only if the old view is "in error," the dialectical thinker sees change in his or her thinking as natural, expectable, and valuable. Thus, a dialectical view of knowledge encourages persons to be ready and willing to move away from their past points of view, to do the kind of "set breaking" or "leaping" away from an old tradition that has been seen as characteristic of creative thinkers.

Second, in dialectical epistemology, particular beliefs and values are seen as part of larger thought systems. Differences of opinion exist, then, not because one answer is "right" and the others are "wrong," but because there are many frameworks or perspectives from which to view any problem. This awareness of multiple systematic ways of viewing reality makes one's own view more permeable, more influenceable by other perspectives, perspectives in which the problem is defined in fundamentally different ways. This tendency of dialectical thinkers to be aware of and look to other perspectives than their own should be a source of greater diversity and novelty.

The dialectical thinker sees the evolution of knowledge as resulting from contradictions within a thought system or between a thought system and that which is outside it. For the dialectical thinker, then, contradictions play a key role in intellectual growth. One might expect, therefore, that holding a dialectical epistemology would alter one's response to contradictions that are encountered in problem solving: rather than being signs of trouble, irritants to be ignored when possible and eliminated when necessary, contradictions are opportunities to be sought out and developed.

Finally, a dialectical epistemology directs the person, when encountering contradictions, to look for ways of resolving them in higher order syntheses, by creating new, more complex systems encompassing the old contradictory elements. For those authors who see creativity as involving holding together or relating contradictory ideas or frameworks (e.g., Rothenberg's, 1976, "Janusian thinking" or Koestler's, 1964, "bisociation"), dialectical epistemology serves as a "roadmap" for the creative process.

In sum, then, a dialectical understanding of knowledge gives both cognitive and affective support to the processes many authors see as central to creativity. On the cognitive side, dialectical epistemology might be seen as providing a set of directives to thought: Expect your way of thinking to change. Consider the problem from multiple perspectives: how would people with different frameworks see it? Look out for contradictions and, when you find them, pay close attention to them. Create ways of relating and synthesizing things that seem to be in opposition or inconsistent. All these "habits of thought" foster creativity. On the affective side, a dialectical understanding of the evolution of knowledge helps a person to support the emotional tensions of the creative process: the tension of holding opposing views simultaneously, of sustaining uncertainty, of breaking away from an established way of seeing things, and of tolerating ambiguity. A dialectical view of knowledge helps to support these affective tensions in creative thought, by asserting that these are natural and valuable parts of the evolution of thought, and that they do eventually lead to the creation of new and more adequate knowledge.

Metasystematic Thinking and Creative Work: The Evolving Systems Approach

So far, we have suggested (a) that a dialectical view of objects and events will foster the attention to novelty and relation central to the creative pro-

cess, and (b) that a dialectical view of knowledge will provide ways of retaining the power of formal systematic analysis, while fostering the creative evolution of thought systems. There is one other aspect of dialectical thinking that may be of particular importance to what one might think of as the optimal functioning of creativity, that is, the kind of sustained creative work carried on by adults who are eminent in their fields. Gruber (1981) conducted an intensive study of this kind of sustained creative achievement in the life of Charles Darwin and presented an "evolving systems approach" to creativity (Gruber, 1984). He claimed that significant creative achievement is not so much a matter of a single brilliant insight, but represents the slow development of a "novel point of view." He saw creative production as resulting not from a few dramatic moments of intuition or genius, but from a lifelong organization of work and life leading toward and supporting the evolution of this point of view. He described the creative person as being comprised of three organizational subsystems: the organization of knowledge, the organization of affect, and the organization of purpose. These subsystems overlap and interact, but are to an extent independent. The organization of knowledge consists of a complex hierarchy of beliefs that are constantly being altered in response to new data and new points of view. The organization of affect consists of a "symphony" of affective themes and tones, relating to people's work and to their personal life and needs. The organization of purpose is a complex network of tasks, goals, projects, and enterprises that the person intends to carry out. Each of these subsystems includes several smaller systems that are themselves complexly interrelated, with each subsystem evolving over time. Moreover, Gruber sees the creative person as consciously monitoring and directing the evolution of the three systems and their interrelation.

Far from being an irrational or intutive "leap," then, significant creative achievement, for Gruber, arises from an individual's ability to conceptualize and direct the evolution of a complex organization of thoughts, feelings, and purposes in life, centered around the telos of the creative achievement.

It would seem that formal operations, which act on the relations of propositions and variables within a single system, but cannot manipulate systems as wholes, would be an inadequate cognitive structure for this kind of task. The implication of Gruber's model is that mature, sustained creative effort requires exactly the kinds of cognitive abilities described by the metaformal dialectical schemata: the ability to understand, anticipate, and direct the evolution of a system (Schemata 16, 17, 21, 22) and the ability to relate multiple systems to each other (Schemata 19, 20, 24). The advanced stages in the development of dialectical thinking, then, make it possible for a person to consciously direct his or her own creative process in projects that are extended in both time and scope, such as are characteristic of mature creative achievement in public, organized fields of endeavor.

Summary and Implications for Future Research

We have suggested that the development of dialectical thinking might facilitate the growth of creativity in several ways. First, a dialectical view of objects and events (dialectical ontology) should foster awareness of novelty and of relations among things. Many of the schemata that direct attention to change and relation appear concurrent with or even prior to the acquisition of formal operations. These early dialectical understandings of change and constitutive relation may be related to creativity, then, even in childhood and adolescence. Second, a dialectical view of knowledge seems likely to foster habits of thought that will promote set-breaking, attention to contradiction, and attempts at synthesis, all of which are important features of the creative process. Dialectical epistemologies may be particularly important in promoting creative thought in disciplines that rely heavily on formal analysis. In these contexts, a dialectical epistemology provides the person with a model of creative thought that does not involve relinquishing the power of the formal system, but rather involves integrating the present formal system in a larger view of multiple systems evolving through interrelation with each other and with data. Finally, the development of a coherent, metasystematic dialectical perspective may provide the cognitive operations that are necessary to carry out the kind of conscious management of interrelated evolving systems which Gruber (1984) suggests is characteristic of mature, sustained creative efforts. In sum, then, early dialectical schemata may foster the most basic and general functions of creativity, such as the generation of novelty, whereas the full development of dialectical thinking may make possible mature, specifically adult forms of creativity.

One question future research in this area might address is whether the kinds of processes that Gruber observed in the development of Darwin's thinking are seen in other creative scientists and in creative persons in other fields. Does artistic creativity, for example, also rely on conscious organization of systems of ideas and beliefs and purposeful construction of networks of plans and projects? Case studies of creative achievers in different disciplines could explore whether they use dialectical models to explain and direct the evolution of their thought and work.

A second line of inquiry would be to look across the lifespan at the development of ways in which people become aware of and transcend the limits of various systematizations of experience. Fully developed dialectical thinking, we have seen, enables one to become aware of and transcend the limitations of formal thinking in ways that might foster adult creativity. It may be, however, that children and young adolescents also have ways of coming to understand and go beyond the systems that they use to organize experience and solve problems, and that fostering this kind of critical awareness of their cognitive systems may be important in supporting creativity. For example, one might look at childrens' attention to and understanding of contradictions, their sense of their own thought as static or changing, their tendency to construe problems as closed- or open-ended.

Finally, creativity has generally been studied in arenas where the product is public and discrete—a work of art, a scientific theory, a short story. Often the assessment of creativity rests upon an evaluation of these kinds of products, as though the creativity lay in the thing rather than in the process that produced it. If we take seriously Gruber's perspective, that the creation of a novel point of view is fundamental to the creative process, then it might be relevant to explore people's formation of novel points of view in their conduct of their everyday life, even when this process does not result in public, discrete products. For example, people are "authors" of their moral systems, their sense of personal identity, their views of politics, and their ways of understanding and relating to their children. Surely these are realms in which people are more or less creative, in which some people do and others do not create novel, valuable, and unconventional approaches. Structural-developmental psychologists have developed the techniques of semiclinical interviewing and structural analysis to study people's thinking about these kinds of topics;

we suggest this methodology might prove useful in beginning to look at creativity in people's thought about and conduct of their lives.

In general, the approach to creativity taken in this chapter is to move from a view of creative activity as rooted in a trait of creativity, where some people have more of it than others, to seeing creative activity as reflecting the development and application of specific cognitive and affective capacities. These capacities may be seen as growing out of the interaction of prior cognitive structures (e.g., concrete operations, formal operations) with experiences that confront concrete and formal operational models of phenomena with their limits. Unfortunately, people often tend to avoid and defend against experiences that would challenge the models on which they rely to make sense of themselves and the world, and therefore the development of these dialectical capacities may be rare. However, these capacities can be fostered through adequate educational experience and personal support for the painful disequilibrium and uncertainty of having one's trusted models challenged. Although this poses a major challenge to educationists and other supporters of human development who are concerned with creativity, it opens the door to doing more for creativity than merely marveling at it or measuring it.

References

Amabile, T. M. (1983). *The social psychology of creativity.* New York: Springer-Verlag.

Barron, F. (1955). The disposition toward originality. *Journal of Abnormal and Social Psychology, 51,* 478–485.

Basseches, M. (1984a). *Dialectical thinking and adult development.* Norwood, NJ: Ablex.

Basseches, M. (1984b). Dialectical thinking as a metasystematic form of cognitive organization. In M. L. Commons, F. A. Richards, & C. Armon (Eds.), *Beyond formal operations: Late adolescent and adult cognitive development* (pp. 216–238). New York: Praeger.

Bruner, J. S. (1962). The conditions of creativity. In H. E. Gruber, G. Terrell, & M. Wertheimer (Eds.), *Contemporary approaches to creative thinking* (pp. 1–30). New York: Atherton Press.

Darwin, C. (1962). *Origin of species.* New York: Macmillan.

Gruber, H. (1981). *Darwin on man: A psychological study of scientific creativity.* Chicago: University of Chicago Press.

Gruber, H. E. (1984). The emergence of a sense of purpose: A cognitive case study of young Darwin. In M. L. Commons, F. A. Richards, & C. Armon (Eds.), *Beyond formal operations: Late adolescent and adult cognitive development* (pp. 3–27). New York: Praeger.

Guilford, J. P. (1967). *The nature of human intelligence.* New York: McGraw-Hill.

Hegel, G. W. F. (1967). *The phenomenology of mind.* New York: Harper & Row.

Henle, M. (1962). The birth and death of ideas. In H. E. Gruber, G. Terrell, & M. Wertheimer (Eds.), *Contemporary approaches to creative thinking* (pp. 31–62). New York: Atherton Press.

Irwin, R. (in press). A critique of the proposed stage of dialectical thinking. In M. L. Commons, J. D. Sinnott, F. A. Richards, & C. Armon (Eds.), *Beyond formal operations: Vol. 2. Comparisons and applications of adolescent and adult developmental models.* New York: Praeger.

Koestler, A. (1964). *The act of creation.* New York: Macmillan.

Kuhn, T. S. (1963). The essential tension: Tradition and innovation in scientific research. In F. Barron & C. W. Taylor (Eds.), *Scientific creativity: Its recognition and development* (pp. 341–354). New York: Wiley.

Marx, K. (1967). *Writings of the young Marx on philosophy and society.* L. D. Easton & K. H. Guddat (Eds.). Garden City, NY: Anchor.

Newell, A., Shaw, J., & Simon, H. (1962). The processes of creative thinking. In H. Gruber, G. Terrell, & M. Wertheimer (Eds.), *Contemporary approaches to creative thinking* (pp. 63–119). New York: Atherton Press.

Piaget, J. (1952). *The origins of intelligence in children.* New York: Norton.

Stein, M. I. (1974). *Stimulating creativity* (Vol. 1). New York: Academic Press.

Rothenberg, A. (1976). The process of Janusian thinking in creativity. In A. Rothenberg & C. R. Hausman (Eds.), *The creativity question.* Durham, NC: Duke University Press.

Rothenberg, A., & Hausman, C. R. (Eds.) (1976). *The creativity question.* Durham, NC: Duke University Press.

Torrance, E. P. (1962). *Guiding creative talent.* Englewood Cliffs, NJ: Prentice-Hall.

Von Bertalanffy, L. (1968). *General system theory.* New York: Braziller.

Personalogical Variables and Creativity

Part III is comprised of four chapters, each emphasizing a different element of how personalogical variables influence creativity. Martindale provides a general perspective for thinking about personalogical variables and creativity. Dowd explores a difficult and often controversial topic in his chapter on creativity and the self. Prentky examines the evidence surrounding the notion that creativity may be related to psychopathology. Finally, Heppner, Fitzgerald, and Ball discuss the role of creativity in the therapeutic process.

CHAPTER 13

Personality, Situation, and Creativity

Colin Martindale

Introduction

Because creativity has to do with the production of new ideas, one might think that its study rightly falls within the domain of cognitive psychology. Of course, creativity involves cognition, but it involves a type of cognition that seems only to occur within a matrix of associated motivational, attitudinal, and personalogical traits. Thus, to understand creativity, the person as a whole must be considered. Because of this, theories about the creative process have traditionally been personality theories rather than purely cognitive theories. In 1949, Guilford (1950) pointed out that we did not know enough about creativity. We can never know too much about the creative personality, but we certainly know more than I could hope to cover in this chapter. For more information, the reader may consult the reviews of the literature by Dellas and Gaier (1970), Wallach (1970), Stein (1974), Taylor and Getzels (1975), and Barron and Harrington (1981).

As a point of departure, it is useful to consider—as I have in this chapter—a "composite photograph" or prototype of the creative personality. This gives a general outline but with a good deal of blurring. Thanks to the pioneering work of Helson (e.g., 1973a, 1977), it is known that there are really several rather distinct types of creative personalities. There are also important sex differences to

Colin Martindale • Department of Psychology, University of Maine, Orono, ME 04469-0140.

be taken into account: men and women create in different ways. Again, Helson (e.g., 1973b, 1978) has taken the lead in exploring these differences. Across the last several decades, it has become clear that personality cannot be considered in isolation, but social context must also be taken into account. Although I touch on this issue as it relates to creativity, much more information may be found in Amabile (1983a), Martindale (1975), and Simonton (1984).

Definitions of Creativity

A creative idea is marked by three attributes: It must be original, it must be useful or appropriate for the situation in which it occurs, and it must actually be put to some use. To be counted as creative, it is not enough that an idea be original. Original ideas are common enough, but few of them qualify as creative. The word salad of a hebephrenic is certainly original, but for a variety of reasons it cannot serve as the basis for a poem. By the same token, the delusions of a paranoid are original but hardly serve as a fruitful source of scientific hypotheses. Perfectly normal people also produce original ideas that are useless for a variety of reasons—they are ridiculous, incorrect, and impractical. Even if an original idea is useful, it does not really count as creative unless it is actualized or at least communicated. If I had an original and useful idea about the causes of creativity, we would not count the idea as creative unless I communicated it to others. Or, to take another example, were I to think of the perfect plot for the Great American Novel, this would be of little import unless I actually wrote the novel.

Creative ideas are always new combinations of old ideas. As Poincaré (1913, p. 386) put it, "to create consists of making new combinations of associative elements which are useful." He went on to remark that creative ideas "reveal to us unsuspected kinships between other facts well known but wrongly believed to be strangers to one another. Among chosen combinations the most fertile will often be those formed of elements drawn from domains which are far apart" (p. 386). Consider Einstein's equation, $E = mc^2$. Einstein did not invent the components of the equation *de novo* nor did he invent the concept of energy or the operation of raising a quantity to a power. By the same token, a poet does not generally invent new words but puts old words together in new ways.

Most investigators have defined creativity in the way stated above: There must be a product of some sort and it must be both novel and appropriate or useful in some sense (Barron, 1955; Mednick, 1962; Newell, Shaw, & Simon, 1962; Stein, 1974). As Bruner (1962) put it, a creative product produces "effective surprise" and a "shock of recognition" that the idea is correct. Koestler (1964) made it explicit that creativity often involves not a combination of isolated elements but a connection of two entire "matrices of thought." Amabile (1983b) added the requirement that the idea be produced in a heuristic rather than an algorithmic fashion. An algorithmic task is one in which there is a clear and specifiable method of solution; for example, how differential equations are solved. A heuristic task is one in which there is no known "recipe" for a solution. This is an important point. Many ideas that appear creative to laymen may not be so at all. Experts would recognize that the idea rose from already known algorithms. For example, if one knows nothing about mathematics, it will be impossible to differentiate between creative and uncreative mathematical ideas.

Creativity as a General Trait

Ultimately, all creative products have this quality: old ideas or elements are combined in new ways. This is the case for all domains of creativity. A composer puts together musical tones in new ways, whereas a poet puts together words in new ways. If the ability to recombine elements is a general one, then we do not need different explanations of creativity for different areas of endeavor but only one general explanation. The idea that creativity is a general rather than a domain-specific trait is discussed in detail by Root-Bernstein (1984), Waddington (1969), and Tang (1984).

Combining elements in a new way generally involves perception of an analogy. Consider how Cyrus McCormick invented the grain reaper (Weber, 1969). He noted that grain is like the hair on a person's head. Because mechanical clippers can be used to cut hair, they could also be used to cut shafts of grain. If McCormick had been a poet rather than an inventor, he might have composed a simile rather than creating a machine. I have suggested the following possibility (Martindale, 1981):

Your hair is like the golden grain,
And the dandruff thereupon is but the chaff.

I am quite sure that a better poem could be wrung out of the analogy. The point, however, is that the creative process in poetry and science is really the same thing. In this example, the only difference is what is derived from the newly discovered analogy. Generally, poets and scientists combine different sorts of elements. Energy and mass do not make for good poetry, after all. However, the thought underlying scientific and poetic creativity seems to be quite similar if not identical. A creative physicist, for example, seems to think, talk, and behave more like a creative poet than like an uncreative physicist.

Prerequisites for Creativity

Capacity to Produce Creative Combinations

Before consulting any of the research literature, we can infer some of the necessary conditions for creativity. If creativity involves new combinations of mental elements, then it would certainly seem to be the case that the more mental elements a person had, the more creative he or she should be. Besides having a lot of mental elements, they should also be distributed across a wide spectrum of domains, if Poincaré is correct that remote associations are most likely to give rise to creative ideas. This does seem to be the case. Being an expert in a given specialty does not guarantee that one will be creative in that area (Simon, 1983).

We might guess that intelligence should be a

good predictor of creativity, because the more intelligent one is, the more mental elements one should be able to acquire. However, this may not be the case. Beyond an IQ level of 120 or so, intelligence and creativity are often held not to be closely related (e.g., Barron, 1955). It would seem to be the case that a minimal IQ of 120 or so is necessary for one to be creative in any meaningful sense of the term. However, beyond that level, intelligence does not predict creativity as well as might be expected. One doubts, however, that an IQ of 120 would be sufficient for creative work in all disciplines. Different areas of endeavor most certainly require different minimal levels of intelligence. Once this minimum level is reached, however, creativity and intelligence are not highly correlated (Wallach & Kagan, 1965). By elimination, then, it must be the case that creativity is dependent upon a particular type of cognition, a particular method of combining mental elements. In order to understand creativity, we need to discover what this type of thought is.

Domain-Relevant Skills

A necessary but not sufficient condition for creativity is that one have certain skills or knowledge relevant to the area in which one is working. It is clear enough, for example, that one cannot think of a creative idea about physics if one does not know anything about physics. You cannot very well combine mental elements in a new way if the elements are not known to you in the first place. It is also fairly clear that certain aptitudes or special abilities not directly connected with creativity are necessary (Amabile, 1983b; Feldman, 1980). For example, to be a creative composer, one needs not only ability for creative thinking but also musical talent. Although there are certainly many notable exceptions, creativity is generally confined to a single domain. Michelangelo and Dante Gabriel Rossetti were both poets and visual artists, but they are exceptional. In general, poets are not good painters and painters are not good poets. In fact, many visual artists are rather deficient in their verbal skills. Even though I shall not focus on the issue of domain-specific skills in this chapter, it should be kept in mind that such skills are probably crucial in creative achievement.

Motivational and Personality Factors

Is is possible that creativity could be a purely cognitive matter? That is, is it possible that the only difference between more and less creative people is in the way that they think? We know that this is not the case. As shall be seen, creative cognition tends to occur only within a certain configuration of personality traits. Even if we did not know this, we could be moderately sure that creativity would be connected with certain personality traits. Thomas Alva Edison remarked that genius is 1% inspiration and 99% perspiration. Because inspiration is more interesting than perspiration, it has been studied much more intensively. However, the 1% versus 99% partitioning of the "variance" in creativity is probably close to the mark.

Consider, for example, the production of a scientific article. The idea behind the article—whether creative or not—as likely as not came with little effort. In any event, the effort was slight compared with the time and effort involved in operationalizing the idea, performing the experiment, analyzing the data, and writing the article. A good bit of interest, perseverance, and/or ambition must be present or the article would never be completed. Given that most highly creative scientists produce an average of about 200 articles across the course of their careers (Dennis, 1954), it must be the case that they are driven by very high levels of motivational factors, such as interest, curiosity, or ambition.

Although I am sure it may happen occasionally, it seems unlikely that one would choose a career goal of being a mediocre poet. Rather, if one decides to be a poet, this is almost always a decision to be a great poet. Let the reader consider the competition: one is going up against Shakespeare, Goethe, Milton, and others like them. Once this fact occurs to most people, they are likely to decide upon a rather less challenging line of work. Creative people must have extremely high levels of self-confidence. This does seem to be the case.

Creative people might also be expected to have high levels of self-confidence if we consider the most likely reaction to creative ideas. This reaction is, of course, often extremely negative. Without a good deal of self-confidence, one would hardly be expected to venture toward a goal (production of a creative idea) that if reached would quite likely result in derision, hostility, and so on. Most people simply do not like novelty. It must be the case that creative people do like it, otherwise they would take no pleasure in producing creative ideas and, indeed, would produce none. Except under rather unusual circumstances, people do not, of course, do things that bring them displeasure.

Situational Variables

Studies of creativity have tended to focus upon cognitive and personalogical variables. In light of Mischel's (1979) demonstrations that, at the very least, situation is often as good a predictor of behavior as are personality traits, it would seem that more attention should be paid to situational factors affecting creativity. Common sense tells us that certain situations must be more conducive to creativity than others. It is difficult to imagine creative thought in a situation in which such thought is severely punished or in which, by dint of circumstances, the mental elements one thinks about are not susceptible to creative combinations. If the task at hand were burying one's grandmother, one could think of novel methods, but they would probably not be creative, because they would likely be inappropriate, given that funeral ceremonies are tightly constrained by social and legal restrictions.

Everyone knows that the chance visit of "a person from Porlock" considerably shortened one of the greatest poems ("Kubla Khan") in the English language. Interruption is one of the lethal enemies of creativity (compare Tchaikovsky, 1878/1906). At least some minimal amount of time for solitary contemplation must be a necessary factor in creativity. As we shall see below, other less obvious situational factors also have effects on creativity (Amabile, 1983a; Simonton, 1984).

Conclusions

By necessity, creative people must possess a certain set of traits. On the cognitive level, they must be able to think in some unusual way unavailable to most people, otherwise they would be unable to conceive of creative ideas. In most areas of endeavor, specialized talents, whether learned or innate, must also play a role. On the motivational level, creative people must have high levels of self-confidence and ambition, perseverance, or interest, otherwise, they would be unable to bring their ideas to fruition. Finally, situational factors must foster or hinder creative accomplishment. Note that there is no obvious *a priori* reason to expect the cognitive, special talent, motivational, and situational factors to covary. Yet all these factors must be present if a person is to be creative. Perhaps this is why creativity is so rare. It depends upon the simultaneous presence of a set of traits and factors—none of which is especially rare—that may not, in general, be highly correlated with each another.

The Creative Process

Stages of the Creative Process

Based upon the self-reports of eminently creative people, there is general agreement that the creative process consists of four successive stages. Wallas (1926), drawing heavily upon the observations of Helmholtz (1896), labeled them preparation, incubation, illumination, and verification. Helmholtz (1896) noted that, when confronted with a problem, he as often as not worked intensively on it but came up with no solution. This is the preparation stage: elements presumed to be relevant to the problem are learned and/or manipulated in an intellectual manner. When progress was not made, Helmholtz set the problem aside. This is the incubation stage. After some period of time, often with no clear cause, the solution simply came to his mind. This is the stage of illumination or inspiration. As often as not, it was not the elements that he worked with during the preparation stage that were combined in the flash of illumination, but, rather, some element not before considered relevant that provided the key. After inspiration, the verification stage involved his subjecting the idea to scrutiny and putting it into its final form. For a scientist, this might involve devising and conducting an experiment. For a poet, it might involve putting an image into a form consistent with stylistic rules of the genre within which he works.

Creative Inspiration

The sequence of stages outlined above seems to be very general. Neither scientists nor artists get their creative ideas from purely logical, intellectual work. After reviewing a large number of self-reports of creative people, Ghiselin (1952, p. 5) concluded that "production by a process of purely conscious calculation seems never to occur." This is a very strong statement, but almost everyone who has written about the creative process has drawn a similar conclusion (compare Harding, 1965; Weber, 1969). About the only serious dissenter is Edgar Allan Poe, who held that writing is a purely rational enterprise. Given that much of Poe's output is—to borrow a phrase from Jung—"slime from the unconscious" and that Poe was probably more often inebriated than rational, it is difficult to take his theory very seriously.

Poets and other writers are quite explicit about the effortless and nonintellectual nature of inspiration. Creative inspiration seems to occur in an altered state of consciousness (Martindale, 1981). Nietzsche (1908/1927) described the composition of *Thus Spoke Zarathustra* as follows:

Everything occurs quite without volition, as if in an eruption of freedom, independence, power and divinity. The spontaneity of the images and similies is most remarkable. (p. 897)

William Blake's (1803/1906, p. 115) comment about the composition of his poem on Milton is more extreme: "I have written this poem from immediate dictation, twelve or sometimes twenty or thirty lines at a time without premeditation, and even against my will." Nietzsche and Blake were rather eccentric to put it mildly. Thus, it is reassuring that even the perfectly normal English novelist, William Makepeace Thackeray (1899, p. 97), described a similar possession: "I have been surprised at the observations made by some of my characters. It seems as if an occult power was moving the pen. The personage does or says something, and I ask, how the dickens did he come to think of that?"

It is surprising to many that scientists and mathematicians give very similar descriptions of their experiences, as this example from the French mathematician, Henri Poincaré (1913):

One evening contrary to my custom, I drank black coffee and could not sleep. Ideas rose in crowds; I felt them collide until pairs interlocked, so to speak, making a stable combination. By the next morning I had established the existence of a class of Fuchsian functions, those which come from the hypergeometric series; I had only to write out the results, which took but a few hours. (p. 387)

Scientists who engage in what Kuhn (1962) called revolutionary science uniformly seem to arrive at their ideas in this way. By revolutionary science is meant the sort of theorizing that establishes a new paradigm, for example, Einstein's replacement of the older Newtonian paradigm. Kuhn contrasts this with normal science. Normal scientists engage in "puzzle solving" and do not think in a creative manner. Suppose that an animal runs a maze faster if it has been deprived of food for 24 hours than if it has been deprived for 12 hours. The normal scientist may hypothesize that running speed will be intermediate after 18 hours of food deprivation. Rather clearly, such a hypothesis most likely arose from purely intellectual thought rather than from any blinding flash of inspiration.

The examples of inspiration quoted above do not make explicit exactly what stimulus elicited the creative idea. One may presume that something caused the novel combination of elements, but the creators do not make clear what it was. Let us consider a final example, which concerns how I thought of my theory of aesthetic evolution (Martindale, 1984a). Let us leave aside the question of how creative the theory is; the issue is how it was conceived. The initial problem concerned the history of French poetry—specifically why its content had become more primary process in nature and its metaphors and similes more remote across the course of the last several centuries. The trend in metaphors could be ascribed to a need for novelty, which was rampant among the poets in question. But need for novelty did not explain the regression toward primary process cognition, and need for novelty itself needed to be explained. Although the problem had been laid aside without a satisfactory answer, the solution occurred immediately while I was reading an article by Mednick (1958) on schizophrenia. Mednick argued that schizophrenics have avoidance gradients around anxiety-arousing words and that—for reasons I do not know, since I never finished reading the article—these gradients expand over time. The complete solution to the problem concerning the history of poetry leaped immediately to my mind: of course, poets are faced with continually expanding avoidance gradients around words. Once a simile about a word has been used, it cannot be reused; a more remote associate must be found. How this related to primary process content was apparent as well but need not concern us here. The inspiration was quite effortless and automatic and, in this case, its cause is quite clear. The elements in the Mednick article—avoidance of words, regression (of schizophrenics)—were similar enough to the elements of the poetry problem to draw the latter into consciousness and, at the same time, to solve it. Note a rather embarrassing point: all the elements necessary for the solution were already in my long-term memory. I had simply not simultaneously thought about them before. That is, I knew that poets cannot keep on reusing the same simile, that creativity and regression are related (Kris, 1952), and that creativity and associative gradients are related (Mednick 1962). I expect that all cases of inspiration are similar to this. The difference may be that some third—and forgotten or unnoticed—stimulus served to get the elements combined into a creative idea into consciousness at the same time. In Poincaré's case, for example, let us suppose that combining Elements 1 and 3 led to the insight. Assume that Element 1 was in consciousness. For whatever reason, Element 2 became conscious. It may have been completely unrelated to Element 1 but related enough to Element 3 to bring the latter at least to the fringe of awareness. At that point, the similarity of Elements 1 and 3 immediately became apparent.

Theories of the Creative Process

Primary Process Cognition

Kris (1952) hypothesized that creative individuals are more able to alternate between primary process and secondary process modes of thought than are uncreative people. The primary process–secondary process continuum is the main dimension along which consciousness varies (Fromm, 1978). Primary process cognition occurs in normal states, such as dreaming and reverie, and in abnormal states, such as psychosis and hypnosis. It is autistic, free-associative, and analogical and tends to operate on concrete images rather than abstract concepts. Secondary process thought is the abstract, logical, reality-oriented thought of everyday waking consciousness. According to Kris, creative inspiration involves a "regression" to a primary process state of consciousness. Because primary process cognition is associative, it makes the discovery of new combinations of mental elements more likely. Creative elaboration or verification involves a return to a secondary process state. Because uncreative people are "stuck" at one point on the primary process–secondary process continuum, they are unable to come up with creative ideas. Creation of a very simple creative product may involve on one inspiration–elaboration cycle. More complex productions are likely to require a number of such cycles.

A good deal of evidence is supportive of Kris's (1952) theory that creative people have easier access to primary process modes of thought (see Suler, 1980, for a review). They report more fantasy activity (Lynn & Rhue, 1986; Singer & McCraven, 1961), remember their nighttime dreams better (Hudson, 1975), and are more easily hypnotized than uncreative people (Aston & McDonald, 1985; Bowers & van der Meulen, 1970; Lynn & Rhue, 1986). Wild (1965) showed directly that they are better able to shift between use of primary process and secondary process cognition. Although they used other terms, case studies of eminently creative individuals led nineteenth-century theorists to conclude that what we would call primary process cognition is important for creativity.[1] Lombroso (1901) commented on the "unconsciousness and instinctiveness" of the creative genius: production of creative works seems not to be under conscious control. He also commented on their "somnambulism": composition often occurs in an almost dreamlike state. Nordau (1895) noted a tendency to fall into what he called "inane reverie" and ascribed it to an inability to order, correct, or control the flow of associations or to suppress "irrelevant" associations. He held that the creative genius is subject to the "tyranny of the association of ideas."

It should be noted that a number of cognitive psychologists (e.g., Newell et al. 1962; Perkins, 1981; Weisberg, 1986) argue that creativity involves only secondary process cognition. Their argument is that creative ideas are conceived of in a manner that does not differ from everyday problem solving. This disagreement with Kris seems to be due in part to a misunderstanding of what is meant by primary process cognition. Weisberg (1986), for example, argues that creative ideas almost never occur in dreams, and that creative ideas do not emerge fully formed from "the unconscious." But theorists such as Kris never said that creative products come from dreams or the unconscious. Dreaming is an *extreme* primary process state quite unlikely to produce creative ideas. Secondary process and primary process cognition form the poles of a continuum rather than two discrete types of thought. It is not necessary to dream in order to think in a primary process manner. Furthermore, in its modern usage, primary process thought is not confined to the unconscious; rather, it is a term used to describe the quite conscious thought found, for example, in fantasy and reverie. Thus, it is probably true enough that creative thought does not differ qualitatively from the thought of normal problem solving. However, the latter function probably includes a good bit of what we have called primary process cognition.

Defocused Attention

Mendelsohn (1976) hypothesized that individual differences in how attention is focused are the cause

[1]Throughout this chapter, I have occasion to refer to the writings of Lombroso (1901) and Nordau (1895). Although their explanations of creativity were incorrect, and their phraseology was often intemperate, their observations were particularly acute. They were perfectly well aware of the majority of creative personality traits that we have "discovered" across the course of the last several decades (see Martindale, 1971) as well as of a number of traits that we have not yet rediscovered.

of differences in creativity: ''The greater the attentional capacity, the more likely the combinatorial leap which is generally described as the hallmark of creativity'' (p. 363). To become aware of a creative idea, one must obviously have the elements to be combined in the focus of attention simultaneously. If one could attend to only two things at the same time, only one possible analogy could be discovered at a time. If one could attend to four things at once, six possible analogies could be discovered. Mendelsohn's theory is most relevant to creative inspiration. Creative people may prefer or be prone to states of defocused attention, but they must be capable of focused attention, because the elaboration or verification stage of the creative process calls for this type of attention. In fact, there is a good deal of evidence that uncreative individuals have more narrowly focused attention than do creative ones (Dewing & Battye, 1971; Dykes & McGhie, 1976; Mendelsohn & Griswold, 1966). Based upon case studies of highly creative writers and artists, Nordau (1895) concluded that one of their most common traits was a lack of ability to focus attention. In his typical unsympathetic tone, Nordau remarked about the creative artist that

his want of attention makes him incapable of apprehending the real connecting links between the simplest and most obviously related phenomena, and leads him to deduce them from one or another of the hazy, intangible presentations wavering and wandering in his consciousness. (p. 69)

Flat Associative Hierarchies

Ideas are associated with one another to varying degrees. For example, on a word association task, if the stimulus word is ''table,'' the most likely response is ''chair.'' ''Food'' is a somewhat less probable response, but ''victory'' is far less probable. Because people are fairly consistent in the probabilities of the responses they will make to a stimulus, an associative hierarchy may be plotted for that stimulus. People differ in the steepness of their associative hierarchies. Those with steep hierarchies have only a few responses to make to a stimulus: The mental representation of the stimulus is strongly bonded to only a few other mental representations. On the other hand, people with flat associative hierarchies have more associations to a stimulus. In this case, closer associates are less strongly connected to the stimulus, and more remote associates are more strongly connected to the stimulus than is the case for people with steep associative hierarchies. Mednick (1962) theorized that creative people have relatively flat associative hierarchies,

whereas uncreative people have relatively steep associative hierarchies. This hypothetically accounts for the ability of the creative person to make the remote associations that are the basis of creative ideas. According to Mednick's theory, the ordering of elements on associative hierarchies is proportional to the relative strength of the responses. Research with continuous word association supports this contention (Mednick, 1962). At first, creative and uncreative people tend to give similar responses in a similar order. However, creative people continue to respond at a steady rate, whereas uncreative people run out of responses.

A Cognitive Integration

The theories of Kris (1952), Mednick (1962), and Mendelsohn (1976) are really identical theories expressed in very different vocabularies. Defocused attention is one of the properties of primary process cognition (see Martindale, 1981). Defocused attention and flat associative hierarchies are cognitive and behavioristic ways of describing exactly the same phenomenon (Mendelsohn & Griswold, 1966). The three theories can be restated in cognitive terms (Martindale, 1981).

The consensus is that mind may be represented as a vast set of nodes and relationships among these nodes. The nodes may be activated to varying degrees. The connections between nodes are either excitatory or inhibitory. An activated node influences the activation of nodes with which it is connected via spreading activation or inhibition. Nodes may be identified with neurons or groups of neurons in the neocortex and relationships with the axonal and dendritic connections among these neurons. The nodes may be seen as being partitioned into various ''analyzers''; for example, there seem to be separate analyzers for perception of printed words, faces, spoken words, and so on. The nodes in these analyzers are activated by the presence of the relevant stimulus. Semantic memory hypothetically contains nodes that code concepts and relationships among these concepts. The relationships code attributes of concepts and also connect related concepts to nodes coding superordinate categories. Nodes in all of the analyzers also hypothetically receive nonspecific input from the reticular activating system (Martindale, 1981).

Consciousness corresponds to the set of currently activated nodes. It may be divided into attention (the several most activated nodes) and short-term memory or the fringe of awareness (the remaining, less-activated nodes). Having a flat associative hierarchy or defocused attention corresponds to having a relatively large number of nodes activated—to about the same degree—at the same time. Having a steep associative hierarchy or focused attention corresponds to having fewer nodes activated to differing degrees. In a secondary process state, which corresponds with focused attention and steep associative gradients, a few nodes are highly activated and these nodes inhibit other nodes. In a primary process state, entailing defocused attention and flat associative gradients, more nodes are activated but not activated enough to exert much inhibition. As a rough generality, we may say that inhibition is predominate in secondary process states and disinhibition is predominate in primary process states. The total amount of activation is lower in primary process states of consciousness, but it is spread over a larger number of cognitive nodes. Further, these nodes are not capable of inhibiting each other very much.

Creative inspiration consists of noticing an analogy between at least two things. Another way of putting this is that creative inspiration consists of discovering that these two things share a common superordinate category. The more nodes and relationships that are activated at a given time, the greater the likelihood of this is (Findlay & Lumsden, 1988; Martindale, in press). Of course, this is essentially just a cognitive restatement of the theories described above. Note, however, that the implication is that the capacity of short-term memory *and* attention—rather than just of attention—is held to be greater in creative people than in uncreative people. The cognitive restatement sheds light on the sequence of preparation, incubation, and inspiration. During preparation, attention is probably too focused. One attends to ideas presumed to be relevant to the problem at hand. The difficulty is that the solution lies in ideas thought to be irrelevant. During incubation, the nodes coding the problem remain primed or partially activated on the fringe of awareness. As the creator goes about his business, many other nodes are activated. If one of these nodes happens to be related to the nodes coding the problem, the latter will become activated and leap into attention. This corresponds to inspiration, the discovery of the creative analogy. This would not have occurred if the nodes coding the problem were not already partially activated, because the path connecting the two sets of nodes is presumably long and circuitous. Furthermore, the more nodes that can be simultaneously activated (the more creative the person), the more likely it is

that inspiration will occur, because more paths among nodes can be simultaneously activated.

Campbell (1960) ascribed creativity to a quasi-random combination of mental elements. This makes a good deal of sense if we think of inspiration as an idea in the focus of awareness "pulling" a primed set of ideas into consciousness. Our experiences are not random, but they may be more or less random with respect to whatever problem we are trying to solve. One might think that creative people simply have a lot of original ideas and discard the ones that are not useful. This, however, is definitely not the case. Poincaré (1913) pointed out that "sterile combinations" very seldom occur to the creative genius. This is easy to explain. If the primed elements are not *very* similar to the elements in the focus of attention, they will not become sufficiently activated to enter consciousness. Because of this, sterile combinations are automatically filtered out.

Creativity and Cortical Arousal

In order for a person to be creative, as many nodes as possible must be simultaneously activated. How can this state be reached? The best way it can be reached is by being in a state of low overall cortical arousal. In such a state, more nodes will be activated and to a more equal degree than in a state of higher arousal (Martindale, 1981). The reason for this is that input from the reticular activating system affects activation of nodes in a multiplicative rather than an additive fashion: All nodes receive the same amount of nonspecific input, but this input increases the activation of the more activated nodes much more than the activation of the less activated nodes. The more activated nodes then inhibit the less activated ones. There is also good evidence that primary process thought, defocused attention, and flat associative hierarchies are associated with states of low cortical activation (see Martindale, 1981, for reviews). It must be the case, then, that creativity is related to the level of cortical activation.

Virtually anything that increases arousal causes decrements on tests of creativity. This has been shown to be the case for stress (Dentler & Mackler, 1964), mere presence of other people (Lindgren & Lindgren, 1965), noise (Martindale & Greenough, 1973), extremes of temperature (Lombroso, 1901), and even reward (Amabile, 1983a). It is not the case, however, that creative people are generally in a state of low physiological arousal. They may be more anxious than uncreative people (Maddi & Andrews, 1966) and tend to show slightly higher levels of basal arousal on physiological measures (Martindale, in press). However, as compared with less creative people, those who are more creative do show low levels of cortical arousal while performing creative tasks (Martindale & Hines, 1975). Martindale and Hasenfus (1978) found that the low levels of arousal occur exactly where they should: during creative inspiration rather than during the elaboration stage. It is unlikely that these differences are due to self-control, because creative subjects perform worse than uncreative subjects on biofeedback tasks (Martindale & Armstrong, 1974; Martindale & Hines, 1975). It may be the case that creative people are more variable in their level of arousal than are uncreative people; that is, they may show more extreme fluctuations. This is merely a physiological restatement of Kris's (1952) contention that creative people are more variable on the primary process–secondary process continuum. There are no direct studies of this hypothesis. However, there is evidence that at least some highly creative people tend to fluctuate between states of excessive energy and excessive apathy, abulia, or depression (Lombroso, 1901).

The Creative Personality

Necessary Traits versus Linked Traits

It was argued above that certain cognitive and motivational traits are necessary if one is to be creative. For example, creative people must be able to combine mental elements in a different way than uncreative people. We have just seen that they do have this ability. Can the necessary traits exist in an otherwise ''normal'' personality or are they linked to other traits or personality configurations that are not, in a logical sense, necessary for creativity. Intuition tells us that they must be linked to other traits. After all, the stereotype is that creative geniuses are eccentric and bizarre creatures. It is impossible to picture the mad, sad, and thoroughly bad Lord Byron trying to earn a living as an insurance salesman. But one may immediately recall that Wallace Stevens, whose immense creativity cannot be questioned, did in fact earn his keep as an insurance company executive and, so far as is known, led a thoroughly normal life. Thus, the question comes down to one of probabilities. Are the Stevens or the Byrons more likely?

Cognitive Traits

It is not enough to be able to combine mental elements in a primary process fashion; one must also have the right elements to combine. It takes no research to tell us that most people could not possibly be creative. No possible combination of the ideas with which the ordinary person concerns himself (e.g., what little Johnnie did in school today; where to plant the tulips this fall; the price trajectories of gasoline and lettuce; which team will win the Superbowl) could yield a creative insight. Creative geniuses often exhibit an amazing lack of interest in or concern with the mundane details that constitute virtually the entire fabric of the ordinary person's mental life. Indeed, creative people, in general, tend to be uninterested in details or facts for their own sake (MacKinnon, 1975). To take an example of another sort, no matter how much a person knows about linguistics, he or she will not be able to explain the historical sound changes that seem to occur constantly in all languages unless that person has mental elements drawn from other domains. The reason is that modern linguistics consists almost wholly of statements of rules, and none of these rules pertain to or could cause changes in the phonetic realization of the elements of speech. To solve the problem, our hypothetical linguist would have to know something about psychology, sociology, or physiology, because these neighboring disciplines do have constructs that could explain phonetic change. In short, the more diverse and general a person's store of ideas, the greater is the chance that a creative idea will emerge.

As a rule, creative people do have a very wide range of interests. Among the eminently creative, diversity of interests is rather astounding. Prentky (1980) gives the example of the geneticist Theodosius Dobzhansky, whose interests included music, history, anthropology, philosophy, religion, natural science, and linguistics. Other examples are not difficult to find. Goethe was probably as interested in science as in literature. Edgar Allan Poe believed that his lasting fame would rest not upon his literary works but upon his contributions to cosmological theory. A large number of empirical studies have shown that creative people consistently describe themselves as having a wide range of interests (see Barron & Harrington, 1981). It is very common for creative ideas to arise from combining ideas from different disciplines. Harding (1965) has compiled an extensive list of examples. Based upon her studies, she formulated her "law" of creative thought: an idea will eventually be applied to everything that it is applicable to.

As well as having diverse interests, creative people also seem to categorize ideas in a different way than do less creative people. It would appear that their categorizations are both broader and more idiosyncratic than those of the uncreative. On object-sorting tasks, the categorizations of creative people are as "bizarre" as those of schizophrenics (Dykes & McGhie, 1976). Pettigrew (1958) developed a category-width test. The test consists of items such as the following: "The average religious denomination in the United States has 551 churches." The subject is then asked to guess what the number of churches is for the largest and smallest denomination. A good number of studies have shown that creative people exhibit broader categories on this test (Pettigrew, 1982). It is reasonable to expect that broader categories would allow one to see more items as similar. Perception of similarity where none had been seen before is, of course, the basis of creative insight. It should be noted that broad, diffuse, or hazy categories are an attribute of primary process states of consciousness (compare Werner, 1948).

The concept of category width is somewhat ambiguous. The concept of "animal" is not only broader but also more abstract than the concept of "bird." Research on conceptualization in more and less creative people has not addressed the issue of whether capacity for abstraction or category width *per se* is the crucial variable. At least in the sciences, one is led to suspect that ability for and interest in abstractions must be absolutely crucial for creativity. The reason for thinking this is that the importance—and, hence, the creativity—of a scientific idea is closely related to how general or abstract it is: No matter how ingenious it was, a new theory concerning the causes of creativity in, say, Guatemalans of British descent would not be assessed as very creative unless it could be readily generalized to some wider population. It is surprising that there is no coherent body of research on abstract ability and creativity. Casual observation certainly suggests that uncreative people are often uninterested in and/or incapable of abstraction. Simply put, they cannot see the forest for the trees.

It could well be argued that problem finding is just as creative as problem solving (Mackworth, 1965). After all, there are no explicit problems to be solved in the arts. In science, as often as not, the creator solves not an already existing problem but one that has been discovered. In a study of student artists, Getzels and Csikszentmihalyi (1976) found that creativity was not related to speed or efficiency of problem solving but that it was related to the ability to discover problems. If creative people have very wide categories, they are likely to see exceptions to previously accepted ideas. These exceptions provide new problems; for example, a scientific theory may apply given only certain boundary conditions. For a narrow categorizer, these boundaries may be so constrained that anomalies literally cannot occur: the theory applies only to the things to which it applies. For a wide categorizer, or for someone who thinks on a more abstract level, boundary conditions may be looser. Such a person can discover that a theory does *not* work in a broader context (problem finding) or, perhaps, that it *does* work (simultaneous problem finding and problem solving).

More thought and research are needed on the related issue of problem selection. Creative people seem to have an intuitive knack for selecting important problems. A chemist once described his latest idea to James Bryant Conant with great enthusiasm. The idea had all the marks of a creative breakthrough, save one. Conant's response was that whoever solved the problem would certainly merit a footnote to a footnote in any book on the history of chemistry. Creative people not only need to find problems, they also need to find important ones. Wide categorization, ability for abstraction, and wide interests may help in this respect, but they do not provide a complete explanation. It would be interesting to disentangle motivational and cognitive determinants of problem selection. Are uncreative people really unable to discriminate important from trivial problems, or do they avoid tackling important problems because of low self-confidence or other motivational factors?

Cross-Sexual Interests

Studies have uniformly found that creative people have more cross-sexual or androgynous interests and traits than less creative people; that is, they have interests generally held by members of the opposite sex. They hold these interests in addition to, rather than in place of, interests stereotypically associated with members of their own sex. Thus, a creative woman might be interested in both carpentry and cooking. This pattern of wide-ranging interests has been found for both creative men (Barron, 1957; Kanner, 1976; MacKinnon, 1962) and creative women (Crutchfield, 1962; Helson, 1971). Because of this wider range of interests, creative people may respond in an unusual manner to problems as compared with less creative members of their sex.

Whether this pattern is just an artifact of the wide range of interests in creative people or reflects something deeper is not clear. There is some evidence that creative people tend to have less clear-cut sex-role identities than uncreative people. Besdine (1968) examined the biographies of a number of highly creative men. He found evidence for what he called "Oedipal victory" in a large number of these people. By Oedipal victory he means a situation where the son has replaced the father in the affections of the mother. Freud held that the normal pattern of development involves Oedipal rivalry; for example, around the age of five, the son wants to replace the father in the eyes of his mother. Most children lose this struggle and this leads, as Freud argued, to the establishment of male sex-role identity based upon identification with the father. Identification with the father is also hypothetically the basis for the development of the superego. In the case of Oedipal victory, this would not occur, and we should expect the child to maintain his initial infantile identification with his mother and not to develop a normal superego. The disinhibition or lack of control often found in creative people (see below) would be consistent with weak superego functioning. Another way that a male child can fail to establish a firm masculine sex-role identity is if the father is absent from the home during this crucial period. This would lead to a sort of *de facto* Oedipal victory. In a sample of eminent French and English poets, I found a father-absence rate of 30%—far higher than would be expected for the general population (Martindale, 1972b). Albert (1971) and Goertzel, Goertzel, and Goertzel (1978) have found similar results for other domains of creativity. In spite of popular stereotypes, homosexual subjects are not more creative than heterosexual subjects. In fact, several studies have found trends in the opposite direction (e.g., Domino, 1977). Thus, cross-sexual interests and, perhaps, cross-sexual identification may be related to creativity but homosexuality is not. It seems to be cognitive orientation rather than sexual orientation that is crucial. However, more thorough research is needed before any firm conclusions can be drawn.

Second-Language Learning and Creativity

In a study of creativity in women mathematicians, Helson (1971) found that more of the creative ones were foreign born. Landry (1972) produced evidence that just learning a foreign language enhances creativity. In that study, grammar school children signed up to learn a foreign language. One group began instruction immediately, whereas another group (comparable in terms of intelligence and other possible confounding variables) had to wait. After a period of time, the children taught a second language scored higher on several paper-and-pencil tests of creative ability. Similar results were reported by Lambert, Tucker, and d'Anglejan (1973). Carringer (1974) found that "balanced" bilingual children (i.e., those who had learned two languages about equally well) were more creative than monolingual children. Learning a second language also involves learning associative hierarchies that are "deviant" as compared to those learned for the first language; that is, the connotations of words in different languages are not exactly the same. This factor apparently enhances creativity. But it hardly seems likely that learning a second language would induce very large increases in creativity. However, these results are of interest because they imply that even factors that only slightly increase a person's store of mental elements and associations are positively related to creativity.

Creativity, Age, and Expertise

Creativity exhibits a curvilinear relationship to age (Lehman, 1953; Simonton, 1984). In general, a person's most creative work is done at a fairly early age, and this age of peak productivity varies from field to field. It is fairly early in lyric poetry, mathematics, physics, and chemistry (ages 25–35) and somewhat later in psychology and the social sciences (ages 30–40). Only a few specialties, such as architecture and novel writing show peak performance at later ages (40–45). Not only the best work but the most work is produced at these ages. Output rises rather abruptly to this peak and then declines throughout the rest of a person's career.

Although age *per se* may be a crucial factor in creativity, "age-within-specialty" might also be important: One's most creative work may be done relatively early in one's career within a given specialty, regardless of actual age. A person cannot have any creative ideas until at least some of the elements relevant to a field have been learned. But it would seem that one's best ideas come early—before one becomes an "expert." Once you have become an expert, you may be less likely to be creative. Why? Because being an expert means knowing which elements are important and (the potentially disastrous part) which elements are irrelevant and inappropriate. In other words, the expert may be less likely to make "inappropriate" responses and is consequently less likely to make creative ones. If this line of reasoning is correct, then the way to maintain one's creativity with increasing age is to shift fields. In fact, many consistently creative people do just this. The chemist, Linus Pauling, provides us with a good example of this strategy. Another example would be the psychologist, Leon Festinger. After formulating and testing several important theories in social psychology, Festinger gave up his work in this area completely and began research on visual perception. There is no empirical research on the question of whether age *per se* or age-within-specialty is the main determinant of creativity. Now that mid-life career changes are more common, such a research project is possible. If it turned out that age-within-specialty is the crucial determinant, this would, of course, have profound implications for both individual and social planning.

Even the expertise involved in formal education may, beyond a certain point, be detrimental to creativity. In a study of 301 geniuses in various fields, Simonton (1976) found an inverted-U relationship between creativity and amount of education. Those with a moderate amount of education were most creative. This was the case even in the sciences (Simonton, 1984). Simonton's sample of scientists was small, however. Now that a Ph.D. is more or less required for work in most areas of science, it seems unlikely that an inverted-U relationship would be found. Success in school or college does not seem to be related to creative achievement (MacKinnon, 1960). However, more studies are required before this assertion can be accepted with much confidence. Simonton (1984) gave a number of examples of eminently creative people whose scholastic work was mediocre or poor. He pointed out that time devoted to achieving scholastic excellence may be time made unavailable for acquiring the "irrelevant" knowledge necessary for creativity. He also cited evidence that extremely creative people often dislike formal education and prefer self-education.

Motivational Traits

Creative people appear to have the motivational factors that would seem necessary. It is interesting that these factors are often present in an exacerbated or extreme form. Creative people are indeed self-confident. A large number of studies have shown that, when asked to describe themselves, creative people pick adjectives, such as confident, egotistical, and self-confident (Gough, 1979; Harrington, 1975). Arthur Rimbaud's remark, "I am he who would be God," suggests that self-confidence is often carried a bit far. Recall also Jean Cocteau's remark that "Victor Hugo was a madman who thought he was Victor Hugo," or Paul Valéry's comment that "A man who has never tried to make himself like the gods is less than a man." Lombroso (1901) commented on the "morbid vanity," excessive preoccupation with self, and "megalomania" of the creative genius. Nordau (1895) went even further and used the term "egomania." Perhaps because of their self-confidence, creative people are often not overbearing or obnoxious. Lombroso (1901, p. 46) quotes Alexandre Dumas as observing that Victor Hugo "did not say, 'I am Genius,' but he began to believe firmly that the world would say so."

Creative people also describe themselves with adjectives, such as ambitious, curious, and enthusiastic (Gough, 1979; Harrington, 1975). At high levels of creativity, interest sometimes takes on an almost obsessive quality. Prentky (1980) provides interesting examples of Sir Isaac Newton's absent-mindedness. For example, Newton occasionally left his lodgings having forgotten to get dressed. We may presume that his intense interest in some intellectual problem left no time for such trivial details as putting on his clothes.

Although creative people often describe themselves as energetic (Barron & Harrington, 1981), this contrasts with findings that they tend to be physically inactive (Maddi, 1965) and with a number of well-documented self-reports. Indeed, Lombroso (1901) and Nordau (1895) held, on the basis of such reports, that abulia, apathy, and lack of will are among the most common traits shared by creative artists. Lombroso (1901) argued that the creative genius alternates between erethism and atony—that is, between excitement and inspiration on the one hand and exhaustion and apathy on the other. The journals of Charles Baudelaire and Gustave Flaubert are filled with reports of extreme lack of energy to the point that getting out of bed or beginning to write were seen as almost herculean tasks. Flaubert's behavior is especially enlightening. When he was in bed, he did not have the energy to get up. Once he began writing, he persisted hour after hour—often on the same sentence. Other examples could readily be adduced. We might speculate that creative people have a tendency to persist in whatever state they are in. If they are doing nothing, they find it difficult to begin a task; but if they are performing a task, they find it difficult to stop doing it; they either persevere or perseverate. One wonders whether creative people are *capable* of sustaining attention on a topic for a long period of time or *incapable* of shifting it away from the topic. There is no systematic research on these questions, but it would be well worth undertaking. Interestingly, creative subjects show very slow rates of habituation. Rosen, Moore, and Martindale (1983) measured habituation of skin potential responses to a 60 dB tone. More creative people took twice as long to habituate than did less creative people. This suggests that less creative people may tire quickly of a problem that is not easily solved, whereas the problem may continue to hold the interest or attention of more creative people.

There is also some confusion concerning the relationship between creativity and preference for simplicity versus complexity. If asked to choose between pairs of visual designs, creative people are generally found to prefer the more complex, asymmetric, or ambiguous design (e.g., Barron, 1953; MacKinnon, 1962). On the other hand, creative people have a high need for order (Barron, 1958) and prefer consonant over dissonant tone pairs (Nardi & Martindale, 1981). On the Allport-Vernon-Lindzey Study of Values Scale (1951), creative people, whether artists or scientists, score high on the aesthetic value scale (MacKinnon, 1975). These seemingly contradictory findings make some sense if we consider what it means to have a well-developed aesthetic sense. Almost all aestheticians agree that beauty arises when both unity and variety are maximal (see Martindale, 1984b). That is, a beautiful object is one that unifies a set of diverse elements. It would seem that the goal of the creative person is to produce such an object. For example, a creative scientific theory is beautiful, because it unifies elements that, on the surface, are diverse and unrelated. As the poet Samuel Taylor Coleridge (1817/1907) long ago noted, creativity requires the ability to "exist in ambiguity" or to *tolerate* disorder. However, the ultimate goal is to arrive at an overall synthesis or order.

Wyatt and Campbell (1951) and Bruner and Potter (1964) showed subjects blurred photographic images. The images were gradually focused, and subjects were then asked to guess what they depicted. As compared with people who had not originally seen the very blurred pictures, these subjects' guesses were quite inaccurate. It would seem that their early incorrect guesses led them to fit the "data" to their "hypotheses." Order imposed too early thus led to deformed perceptions. It would be interesting to know if creative people are less prone to such distortion effects on this task, but I am not aware of any research on this topic. Greenwald, Pratkanis, Leippe, and Baumgardner (1986) demonstrated that a quite analogous process can retard progress in science. Amabile (1985) pointed out that keeping options open and suspending judgment would seem to be useful if not necessary skills for creativity. Thus, though a need for order or simplicity must be present in the creative person, it must be counterbalanced by forces that prevent premature imposition of order.

In a series of studies, Amabile (1983a,b, 1985) showed that intrinsic motivation is important for creativity. Intrinsic rewards are those that arise from performing a task; that is, the task is interesting and pleasurable in itself. Extrinsic rewards are those that come from beyond the domain of the task; for example, being paid or praised for working on the task. It would seem that creativity is enhanced by intrinsic rewards and decreased by extrinsic rewards. In one of her studies, Amabile (1985) had poets compose poems under two conditions. In one condition, poets were first led to think about extrinsic rewards that could be important in writing. In the other condition, they were led to ponder the intrinsic rewards of writing. Rated creativity of poems written in the extrinsic-reward condition was significantly lower. Amabile (1979) had other subjects construct collages. One group was told that their products would be evaluated for creativity, whereas the control group was led to believe that the collage was not even the experimenter's primary interest. The control group produced significantly more creative collages. It would seem that extrinsic reward takes the joy (intrinsic reward) out of a task. These findings fit with some of what we know about creativity in the real world. Creative scientists tend to prefer "pure" science and are often reluctant to undertake, or are even disdainful of, practical projects that might yield a good deal of financial remuneration. However, Amabile's findings should not be generalized too far. A poet wants to create a beautiful poem (an intrinsic reward), but this act of creation very often occurs in the context of seeking fame or immortality (extrinsic rewards). A scientist aims to solve important problems not only for their own sake but also in order to obtain some extrinsic reward—for example, a Nobel prize. Indeed, if intrinsic rewards alone were important to creative people, it would be difficult to explain why scientists would bother to publish their findings and why artists would exhibit and sell their paintings.

Openness to Experience and Creativity

I mentioned above that creative people must like novelty. There is some empirical evidence that they do (e.g., Houston & Mednick, 1963). Again, this trait sometimes tends to be carried a bit far in those people of very high creativity. Consider Baudelaire's remark that "the beautiful is always bizarre" or George Moore's (1885/1959) comment, "I am . . . morbid, perverse. But above all perverse, almost everything perverse fascinates me . . . the commonplace, the natural is constitutionally abhorrent" (pp. 59, 61). Salvador Dali complained that the world is not a very interesting place because, among other things, he had never once been served a baked telephone when he ordered lobster in a restaurant. In describing scientific geniuses, Koestler (1959) noted that they have

on the one hand skepticism, often carried to the point of iconoclasm, in their attitude toward traditional ideas, axioms, and dogmas but an open-mindedness that verges on naive credulity towards new concepts. (p. 518)

A number of factor-analytic studies of personality traits have yielded five-factor solutions (e.g., Norman, 1963). The first four factors—neuroticism, extraversion, agreeableness, and conscientiousness—are fairly unambiguous. The fifth factor, which has been labelled variously as culture (Norman, 1963), intelligence (Peabody, 1987), and openness to experience (McCrea & Costa (1985a), seems to be related to creativity. McCrea and Costa (1985b) defined openness to experience as an interest in varied experience for its own sake in a variety of domains, such as fantasy, aesthetics, feelings, actions, ideas, and values. It is argued that such openness is conductive to creativity, and McCrea (1987) has shown that openness to experience, measured by both self-ratings and peer-ratings on both questionnaires and adjective checklists, is correlated with creativity. Hypothetically, those who are not open to experience prefer familiar stimuli and, therefore, are not motivated either to experience or to produce novelty. Thus, to the extent that openness is seen as a cause of creativity, it is a

temperamental or motivational rather than a cognitive cause.

One problem with the construct of openness to experience is that the adjectives that are used to measure it in self- and peer-ratings are not, on the face of it, directly related to openness *per se*. For example, of the adjectives loading on what McCrea and Costa (1987) labeled the openness to experience factor, four refer directly to creativity (original, imaginative, creative, and artistic), six refer to traits often used by creative people to describe themselves (complex, independent, daring, analytical, liberal, and untraditional), and only three are directly or indirectly related to openness (broad interests, curious, and prefer variety). It is not clear to me why the factor is labeled "openness" rather than just "creativity." In other words, openness to experience and creativity would seem to be synonyms that are used to describe the same set of traits. If so, openness cannot be said to explain anything about creativity. Costa and McCrea (1985) have developed a questionnaire measure of openness that is less subject to this criticism. The measure does correlate with paper-and-pencil measures of creativity (McCrea, 1987).

Disinhibition and Creativity

Psychoanalytic theorists (e.g., Kris, 1952; Kubie, 1958) have used the term "regression in the service of the ego" to describe the creative person's access to primary process modes of thought. Such thought is generally pathological, as in schizophrenia, or driven by primitive drives and emotions, as in dreaming. Their idea was that creative people can use primary process thinking to deal with neutral ideas. Is it really the case that creative people have free access to the beneficial aspects of such thought without having to pay the price of suffering from its pathological consequences? It would seem not. Creative people consistently obtain high scores on the Psychoticism scale of the Eysenck Personality Inventory (Eysenck, 1983; Woody & Claridge, 1977) and on related scales on the Minnesota Multiphasic Personality Inventory (MMPI) (Barron, 1969). They either do not or cannot use the defense mechanism of repression (Barron, 1955; Fitzgerald, 1966; Myden, 1959). On object-sorting tasks, highly creative people cannot be differentiated from schizophrenics, although the behavior of both groups is markedly different from that of normal uncreative subjects (Dykes & McGhie, 1976).

In the above discussion, I connected primary process cognition with a relative lack of inhibition. It would seem that the disinhibition of creative people is not confined to cognition but is, rather, a general trait. This is to be expected if creativity is related to low levels of cortical arousal. One of the functions of the cortex is to inhibit lower brain centers. If the cortex is underaroused, it performs this function poorly and lower centers are disinhibited (Eysenck, 1967). The result is a general lack of both cognitive and behavioral inhibition. Creative people are less compliant in laboratory tasks that measure conformity (Barron, 1961), and they are more willing to engage in risk-taking behavior (Anderson & Cropley, 1966; Pankove & Kogan, 1968). When they are asked to describe themselves on adjective checklists, probably the most striking thing is that many of the traits chosen share the common factor of disinhibition. Examples of adjectives picked by highly creative people are gloomy, loud, unstable, bitter, dissatisfied, pessimistic, irritable (Barron, 1952); original, emotional, enthusiastic, impulsive (Van Zelst & Kerr, 1954); and inventive and industrious (MacKinnon, 1962). In contrast, uncreative people describe themselves as gentle, conservative, patient, peaceable (Barron, 1952); contented, conventional (Van Zelst & Kerr, 1954); and virtuous, good, rational, and concerned with others (MacKinnon, 1962). In this case, the common trait is inhibition.

Based upon studies such as the above, Harrington (1975) developed a Composite Creative Personality Scale that includes the adjectives that creative people most consistently use to describe themselves. Note that no matter how narrowly or broadly one defines disinhibition, over half of the adjectives included in this scale have to do with lack of inhibition in one sense or another: active, alert, ambitious, anxious, argumentative, artistic, assertive, capable, clear thinking, clever, complicated, confident, cynical, demanding, egotistical, energetic, enthusiastic, hurried, idealistic, imaginative, impulsive, independent, individualistic, ingenious, insightful, intelligent, interests wide, inventive, original, practical, quick, rebellious, reflective, resourceful, self-confident, sensitive, sharp-witted, spontaneous, unconventional, versatile, *not* conventional, and *not* inhibited. Gough (1979) developed a similar scale based on 12 samples of subjects including 1,700 people. Again, adjectives with connotations of disinhibition are prominent. In-

deed, Anderson and Cropley (1966) have argued that creativity can be explained as due to a general inability or unwillingness to internalize the "stop rules" that people generally learn as they are socialized.

There is an emerging consensus that personal identity or the self is not unitary (e.g., Gergen, 1971; Kihlstrom & Cantor, 1983; Rosenberg & Gara, 1985; Watkins, 1978). The idea is that everyone is to one extent or another a multiple personality. Lombroso (1901) went so far as to list "double personality" as one of the traits of creative genius. I have speculated that the "subselves" of creative people may be more dissociated than those of uncreative people (Martindale, 1980), and that this dissociation arises from the disinhibition found in primary process states of consciousness (Martindale, 1981). The reasons for this contention are several. Creative people are not especially consistent in their traits. Their autobiographical reports often make clear that this inconsistency is not simply disorganization but, rather, a contrast among organized but dissimilar subselves. Also, there is the "dictated" quality of much creative inspiration. William Blake is not alone in saying that his poetry was dictated to him. Robert Louis Stevenson was quite serious when he said that his stories were dictated by "brownies" or "little people." Robert Graves (1966) was firm in his contention that the muse is not at all a metaphor but a real psychic entity and the source of all true poetry. Such statements make sense if we think of the poet as a scribe who copies down the "utterances" of an alien or dissociated subself that has access to "inner speech." If something like this occurs, there is no reason to expect the scribe to understand what he has transcribed and, in fact, he very often does not. Plato noted that poets are "like soothsayers and prophets, who say many fine things but who understand nothing of what they say." To take but one example, T. S. Eliot claimed not to know the meaning of his more obscure images and depended upon literary critics for their explication. These, of course, are extreme cases. It is not clear at present how far, if at all, we should generalize from them. Systematic research on self-identity in more and less creative people needs to be undertaken.

Creativity and Psychopathology

Some theorists have gone so far as to argue that schizophrenia and creativity—both of which involve primary process cognition—are based upon identical cognitive processes that differ only in degree (Forrest, 1976; Hasenfus & Magaro, 1976; Keefe & Magaro, 1980; Prentky, 1980). This argument would seem to be based upon firmer ground than might at first be thought. Several very well-controlled studies (Heston, 1966; Karlsson, 1968, 1978; McNeil, 1971) have shown that the biological relatives of schizophrenics exhibit higher levels of creativity than do matched subjects who are not relatives of schizophrenics. It would seem that the same gene (or genes) may transmit predisposition for a common cognitive and personalogical configuration (compare Eysenck, 1983; Jarvik & Chadwick, 1973). We might speculate that pre-, peri-, and postnatal environments determine whether this configuration is actualized as creativity, schizotypal personality, or schizophrenia.

Several studies have found a higher than normal incidence of bipolar or manic-depressive illness in creative people (Andreason & Cantor, 1974; Jamison, Gerner, & Hammen, 1980). In one study of 30 creative writers, 80% had been treated for mood disorders as compared with 30% of subjects in a matched control group (Holden, 1987). Both people exhibiting bipolar symptoms and their asymptomatic relatives have been found to be more creative than control subjects (Holden, 1987). In this study, creativity was highest in subjects with mild as opposed to severe bipolar mood swings. It is difficult to distinguish periods of intense creative activity from hypomanic episodes (Jamison *et al.,* 1980). Indeed, Isen, Daubman, and Nowicki (1987) have found that induction of positive affect in normal subjects leads to dramatic increases in creative problem-solving abilities.

Predisposition to bipolar mental disorder is genetic, but schizophrenia and bipolar illness are not determined by the same gene or genes. It is not clear at present how findings concerning the relationship between creativity and these two disorders can be tied together aside from the fact that both disorders may be described as involving primary process cognition and disinhibition. Lombroso (1901) produced a large amount of anecdotal evidence that creative people overuse alcohol and other drugs. Recent studies have found high rates of alcoholism in creative writers (Holden, 1987) and positive correlations between creativity and marijuana use (Victor, Grossman, & Eisenman, 1973) and drinking to the point of drunkenness (Martindale, 1972a). Although more extensive studies are

needed, it is of interest that alcohol abuse is often classified as a disinhibition syndrome (e.g., Gorenstein & Newman, 1980).

Conclusions

In order to be creative, one needs access to a primary process state of consciousness involving associative thought, defocused attention, flat associative gradients, and cognitive disinhibition. It would seem that one cannot usually gain access to such a state in an isolated compartment of mind; rather, it is an all-or-none affair. If disinhibition is found in one place, it tends to be found everywhere. If your thoughts are uninhibited, then it is likely that your behavior is also uninhibited. If you will not or cannot conform to the conventional beliefs of science, you are not likely to be any more able to conform to the conventional rules of social behavior. Thus, your disinhibition and unconventionality are likely to be general rather than specific traits. Finally, it is possible that these general traits have brought not only creativity but also all sorts of less desirable traits, ranging from hangovers to bouts of depression. It should be made explicit that the hypothetical linkage between creativity and general disinhibition is not perfect. There are certainly creative people who are not at all uninhibited. Furthermore, if creative people tend to be disinhibited, this in no way implies that people who are disinhibited are necessarily creative.

Situational Variables

Heredity, Environment, and Creativity

Attempts to train people to be more creative have not been very successful (see Stein, 1974, 1975 for reviews). This is rather surprising, as it is clear enough what one needs to do in order to be creative. The problem is not that creativity is difficult to teach but that creativity is impossible to learn. This difficulty in training people to be more creative, as well as the physiological differences that have been found between creative and uncreative people, leads one to doubt that creativity could be determined wholly by environmental factors. The relationship between creativity and genetically transmitted disorders, such as schizophrenia, also leads us to suspect that creativity might be genetically determined. I am aware of four studies that have investigated the heritability of creativity (Barron,

1969; Olive, 1972; Reznikoff, Domino, Bridges, & Honeyman, 1973; and Vandenberg, 1968). The results of these studies are weak and inconsistent. However, all these studies examined paper-and-pencil tests rather than actual creative accomplishments. At present, the extent to which creativity is environmentally determined versus genetically determined is not clear.

Creative Environments

Several theorists (e.g., Crutchfield, 1962; Rogers, 1954) have argued that freedom from external pressure or control and a warm, supportive environment are necessary or at least quite helpful for creativity. Harrington, Block, and Block (1987) have produced empirical evidence that child-rearing practices producing such an environment are correlated with creative potential in both preschool children and adolescents. Amabile's (1983b) contention that extrinsic reward decreases creativity is related to this notion. She also mentions surveillance and externally imposed deadlines as being detrimental to creativity. Naroll, Benjamin, Fohl, Fried, Hildreth, and Schaefer (1971) and Simonton (1975), in historical studies, have found that epochs characterized by political fragmentation produce more creative individuals. It would seem that any sort of control emanating from the environment has negative effects. Given that creative people tend to be disinhibited, one would expect that environmental control of any sort should be especially noxious to them. If a creative person is stuck in such an environment, one would expect lessened creativity. One would also suppose that, if possible, creative people would avoid such environments. As shall be seen below, there are other reasons to expect that creative people may tend to minimize environmental inputs of all sorts—not merely those of a constraining or controlling sort.

Kroeber (1944) argued that the reason that innovations tend to come in waves has to do with emulation: One is more likely to be creative if there are creative role models to emulate or compete with. Simonton (1984) provided strong quantitative evidence for this point of view. There is a very high correlation between the number of eminently creative people in a given generation and the number in the prior generation. Zuckerman (1977) found that over half of the people who win Nobel prizes had previously studied under another Nobel laureate. It seems likely that these findings are due to the provision of role models for already potentially creative people. As mentioned above, attempts to teach people to be creative have not been notably successful.

Oversensitivity and Withdrawal

The stereotype that creative people are oversensitive at both the sensory and the emotional level would seem to be no stereotype at all. The Belgian poet Emile Verhaeren disconnected his doorbell because its ringing caused him physical pain. Marcel Proust withdrew into his cork-lined room because normal levels of light and sound were, he said, painful to him. Lombroso (1901) collected a number of similar self-reports. In fact, creative people do seem to be physiologically overreactive to stimuli. For example, Martindale and Armstrong (1974) found more electroencephalogram (EEG) blocking to onset of a tone in more creative as compared with less creative subjects. Rosen *et al.* (1983) found much larger skin potential responses to noise in more as compared with less creative people. Martindale (1977) asked subjects to rate the intensity of electric shocks: intensity ratings were positively correlated with creativity. Nardi and Martindale (1981) elicited preference judgments for tones varying in intensity. The more creative a subject was, the lower the intensity of his maximally preferred tone. It has also been found that creativity is correlated with augmentation ("amplification" of the intensity of stimulation) on the kinesthetic aftereffect task (Martindale, 1977).

The most common response to oversensitivity would seem to be withdrawal in order to escape overstimulation. The image of the creator in some analogue of Alfred de Vigny's ivory tower is ubiquitous; for example, Flaubert immured at Croisset, Algernon Swinburne at Putney, and Friedrich Hölderlin in the castle tower at Tübingen. Similar withdrawal is found among scientists; the clearest example certainly being Henry Cavendish (see Prentky, 1980). The extreme withdrawal practiced by such creators is a sort of self-imposed sensory deprivation. We know that sensory deprivation causes decreases in cortical arousal and increases in primary process thinking (Schultz, 1965). Thus, it should facilitate creative inspiration. Although creative people do not seem generally to have low levels of arousal, their oversensitivity may drive them to withdraw or to restrict sensory input. This, in turn, would put them in the low-arousal state necessary for creative inspiration.

Research Questions

Throughout this chapter I have tried to point out areas in which research should be undertaken and areas in which further research is needed in order to clarify ambiguities or contradictions in the literature. In this section, three research topics that seem especially promising are outlined. We have seen that the major theories concerning the creative process all involve some variant of the idea that production of creative ideas involves an oscillation between primary process and secondary process cognition. Although there are a number of studies suggesting that creative people do have more access to primary process modes of thought, it is surprising that there are no quantitative studies of verbal reports during problem solving and creative activity. Is there an oscillation between secondary process and primary process content in such reports? Is the oscillation more extreme for more creative subjects? Is it more extreme for creative tasks (e.g., composing a poem) than for standard laboratory puzzles (e.g., the Tower of Hanoi problem)? The existence of validated content analysis measures of primary process versus secondary process content (e.g., Martindale, 1975) would make such research relatively straightforward. As well as being of interest for its own sake, such research might correct the (I believe fallacious) notion of many cognitive psychologists that creative thought does not differ from routine problem solving and that both activities employ purely secondary process cognition.

There are several studies showing attentional differences between more and less creative people. The robustness of these findings needs to be tested using other techniques for measuring attentional capacity. Because differences in capacity of short-term memory are probably even more important than differences in attentional capacity, it is surprizing that there are—to my knowledge—no studies of differences in short-term memory processes between more and less creative people. Invention and creative insight were ascribed above to the ability of creative people to maintain the cognitive units that code a problem in a primed or partially activated state. If activation of cognitive units generally decays less quickly in creative people, they should show exacerbated priming effects. There are a variety of priming techniques that would be of interest to explore. For example, a tachistoscopically presented word is recognized more quickly and more accurately if it is preceded by a related word. Is this effect larger for creative people?

I have argued that inhibition on a number of levels is weaker in creative than in uncreative people. More direct evidence for this now somewhat speculative contention is needed. It is agreed there are a large number of phenomena that are based upon inhibition. Forgetting, for example, is almost universally explained as being due to a process of inhibition. Do creative people forget less rapidly? If so, this would go a long way toward explaining how they come to possess a large number of mental elements and associations. Pavlovian extinction and passive avoidance (suppression of a formerly rewarded response that has come to elicit punishment) are supposedly due to active inhibition. Creative people should extinguish slowly and exhibit deficits on passive avoidance tasks. In short, differences between more and less creative subjects should be found on virtually any task involving inhibition if the generalized disinhibition model of creativity presented above is correct.

Conclusions

Creativity consists of combining previously unrelated mental elements in a new and useful fashion. In order to do this, it is necessary that a person have a large stock of such elements drawn from diverse domains. Intelligence does not interfere with the acquisition of these elements, but, without the presence of certain motivational factors, they will not be learned or remembered in the first place. Purely intellectual or secondary process thought does not seem to produce creative ideas. Rather, a person must have access to an opposite primary process type of cognition that is marked by defocused attention and associative, undirected thinking. At cognitive and neural levels, primary process thought may be explained as involving disinhibition. It would appear that access to primary process thought can only occur within a matrix of personality traits many of which also involve disinhibition. Creativity, then, seems to be a general personalogical trait rather than an isolated cognitive skill.

References

Albert, R. S. (1971). Cognitive development and parental loss among the gifted, the exceptionally gifted and the creative. *Psychological Reports, 29,* 19–26.

Allport, G. W., Vernon, P. E., & Lindzey, G. (1951). *Study of values: Manual of directions.* Boston: Houghton-Mifflin.

Amabile, T. M. (1979). Effects of external evaluation on artistic creativity. *Journal of Personality and Social Psychology, 37,* 221–233.

Amabile, T. M. (1983a). *The social psychology of creativity.* New York: Springer-Verlag.

Amabile, T. M. (1983b). The social psychology of creativity: A componential conceptualization. *Journal of Personality and Social Psychology, 45,* 357–376.

Amabile, T. M. (1985). Motivation and creativity: Effects of motivational orientation on creative writers. *Journal of Personality and Social Psychology, 48,* 393–399.

Anderson, C. C., & Cropley, A. J. (1966). Some correlates of originality. *Australian Journal of Psychology, 18,* 218–227.

Andreason, N. C., & Cantor, A. (1974). The creative writer: Psychiatric symptoms and family history. *Comprehensive Psychiatry, 15,* 123–131.

Aston, M. A., & McDonald, R. D. (1985). Effects of hypnosis on verbal and non-verbal creativity. *International Journal of Clinical and Experimental Hypnosis, 33,* 15–26.

Barron, F. (1952). Personality style and perceptual choice. *Journal of Personality, 20,* 385–401.

Barron, F. (1953). Complexity-simplicity as a personality dimension. *Journal of Abnormal and Social Psychology, 68,* 163–172.

Barron, F. (1955). The disposition toward originality. *Journal of Abnormal and Social Psychology, 51,* 478–485.

Barron, F. (1957). Originality in relation to personality and affect. *Journal of Personality, 25,* 730–742.

Barron, F. (1958). The needs for order and disorder as motives in creative activity. In C. W. Taylor (Ed.), *The 1957 research conference on the identification of creative scientific talent* (pp. 119–128). Salt Lake City: University of Utah Press.

Barron, F. (1961). Creative vision and expression in writing and painting. In *Conference on creative person* (pp. 1–19). Berkeley: Institute of Personality Assessment and Research, University of California.

Barron, F. (1969). *Creative person and creative process.* New York: Holt, Rinehart & Winston.

Barron, F., & Harrington, D. M. (1981). Creativity, intelligence, and personality. *Annual Review of Psychology, 32,* 439–476.

Besdine, M. (1968). The Jocasta complex, mothering, and genius. *Psychoanalytic Review, 55,* 259–277.

Blake, W. (1803/1906). Letter to Thomas Butts. In A. G. B. Russell (Ed.), *The letters of William Blake* (p. 115). London: Methuen.

Bowers, R. S., & van der Meulen, S. (1970). The effect of hypnotic susceptibility on creativity test performance. *Journal of Personality and Social Psychology, 14,* 247–256.

Bruner, J. (1962). The conditions of creativity. In H. Gruber, G. Terrell, and M. Wertheimer (Eds.), *Contemporary approaches to creative thinking* (pp. 1–30). New York: Atherton Press.

Bruner, J., & Potter, M. C. (1964). Interference in visual recognition. *Science, 144,* 424–425.

Campbell, D. T. (1960). Blind variation and selective retention in creative thought as in other knowledge processes. *Psychological Review, 67,* 380–400.

Carringer, D. C. (1974). Creative thinking abilities in Mexican youth. *Journal of Cross-Cultural Psychology, 5,* 492–504.

Coleridge, S. T. (1817/1907). *Biographia literaria.* Oxford: Clarendon Press.

Costa, P. T., Jr., & McCrea, R. R. (1985). *The NEO Personality Inventory manual.* Odessa, FL: Psychological Assessment Resources.

Crutchfield, R. (1962). Conformity and creative thinking. In H. Gruber, G. Terrell, & M. Wertheimer (Eds.), *Contemporary approaches to creative thinking* (pp. 120–140). New York: Atherton Press.

Dellas, M., & Gaier, E. L. (1970). Identification of creativity: The individual, *Psychological Bulletin, 73,* 55–73.

Dennis, W. (1954). Bibliographies of eminent scientists. *Scientific Monthly, 79,* 180–183.

Dentler, R. A., & Mackler, B. (1964). Originality: Some social and personal determinants. *Behavioral Science, 9,* 1–7.

Dewing, K., & Battye, G. (1971). Attention deployment and nonverbal fluency. *Journal of Personality and Social Psychology, 17,* 214–218.

Domino, G. (1977). Homosexuality and creativity. *Journal of Homosexuality, 2,* 261–267.

Dykes, M., & McGhie, A. (1976). A comparative study of attentional strategies of schizophrenic and highly creative normal subjects. *British Journal of Psychiatry, 128,* 50–56.

Eysenck, H. J. (1967). *The biological basis of personality.* Springfield, IL: Charles C Thomas.

Eysenck, H. J. (1983). The roots of creativity: Cognitive ability or personality trait? *Roeper Review, 5(4),* 10–12.

Feldman, D. (1980). *Beyond universals in cognitive development.* Norwood, NJ: Ablex.

Findlay, C. S., & Lumsden, C. J. (1988). The creative mind: Toward an evolutionary theory of discovery and innovation. *Journal of Social and Biological Structures, 11,* 3–55.

Fitzgerald, E. T. (1966). Measurement of openness to experience. *Journal of Personality and Social Psychology, 4,* 655–663.

Forrest, D. V. (1976). Nonsense and sense in schizophrenic language. *Schizophrenia Bulletin, 2,* 286–301.

Fromm, E. (1978). Primary and secondary process in waking and in altered states of consciousness. *Journal of Altered States of Consciousness, 4,* 115–128.

Gergen, K. J. (1971). *The concept of self.* New York: Holt, Rinehart & Winston.

Getzels, J. W., & Csikszentmihalyi, M. (1976). *The creative vision: A longitudinal study of problem finding in art.* New York: Wiley.

Ghiselin, B. (Ed.), (1952). *The creative process.* Berkeley: University of California Press.

Goertzel, M. G., Goertzel, V., & Goertzel, T. G. (1978). *Three hundred eminent personalities.* San Francisco: Jossey-Bass.

Gorenstein, E. E., & Newman, J. P. (1980). Disinhibitory psychopathology: A new perspective and a model for research. *Psychological Review, 87,* 301–315.

Gough, H. G. (1979). A creative personality scale for the Adjective Check List. *Journal of Personality and Social Psychology, 37,* 1398–1405.

Graves, R. (1966). *The white goddess: A historical grammar of poetic myth.* New York: Noonday Press.

Greenwald, A. G., Pratkanis, A. R., Leippe, M. R., & Baumgardner, M. H. (1986). Under what conditions does theory obstruct research progress? *Psychological Review, 93,* 216–229.

Guilford, J. P. (1950). Creativity. *American Psychologist, 14,* 469–479.

Harding, R. (1965). *An anatomy of inspiration.* New York: Barnes & Noble.

Harrington, D. M. (1975). Effects of explicit instructions to ''be creative'' on the psychological meaning of divergent thinking test scores. *Journal of Personality, 43,* 434–454.

Harrington, D. M., Block, J. H., & Block, J. (1987). Testing aspects of Carl Rogers's theory of creative environments:

Child-rearing antecedents of creative potential in young adolescents. *Journal of Personality and Social Psychology, 52,* 851–856.

Hasenfus, N., & Magaro, P. (1976). Creativity and schizophrenia: An equality of empirical constructs. *British Journal of Psychiatry, 129,* 346–349.

Helmholtz, H. von (1896). *Vorträge und Reden.* Brunswick: Friedrich Viewig und Sohn.

Helson, R. (1971). Women mathematicians and the creative personality. *Journal of Consulting and Clinical Psychology, 36,* 210–220.

Helson, R. (1973a). The heroic, the comic, and the tender: Patterns of literary fantasy and their authors. *Journal of Personality, 41,* 163–184.

Helson, R. (1973b). Heroic and tender modes in women authors of fantasy. *Journal of Personality, 41,* 493–512.

Helson, R. (1977). The creative spectrum of authors of fantasy. *Journal of Personality, 45,* 310–326.

Helson, R. (1978). Creativity in women. In J. Sherman & F. Denmark (Eds.), *The psychology of women: Future directions in research* (pp. 553–604). New York: Psychological Dimensions.

Heston, L. L. (1966). Psychiatric disorders in foster home reared children of schizophrenic mothers. *British Journal of Psychiatry, 112,* 819–825.

Holden, C. (1987). Creativity and the troubled mind. *Psychology Today, 21*(4), 9–10.

Houston, J. P., & Mednick, S. A. (1963). Creativity and the need for novelty. *Journal of Abnormal and Social Psychology, 66,* 137–141.

Hudson, L. (1975). *Human beings: The psychology of human experience.* New York: Anchor.

Isen, A. M., Daubman, K. A., & Nowicki, G. P. (1987). Positive affect facilitates creative problem solving. *Journal of Personality and Social Psychology, 52,* 1122–1131.

Jamison, K. R., Gerner, R. H., & Hammen, C. (1980). Clouds and silver linings: Positive experiences associated with primary affective disorders. *American Journal of Psychiatry, 137,* 198–202.

Jarvik, L. F., & Chadwick, S. B. (1973). Schizophrenia and survival. In M. Hammer, K. Salzinger, & S. Sutton (Eds.), *Psychopathology: Contributions from the social and behavioral sciences* (pp. 57–73). New York: Wiley.

Kanner, A. D. (1976). Femininity and masculinity: Their relationships to creativity in male architects and their independence from each other. *Journal of Consulting and Clinical Psychology, 44,* 802–805.

Karlsson, J. L. (1968). Genealogical studies of schizophrenia. In D. Rosenthal & S. S. Kety (Eds.), *The transmission of schizophrenia* (pp. 85–94). Oxford: Pergamon Press.

Karlsson, J. L. (1978). *Inheritance of creative intelligence: A study of genetics in relation to giftedness and its implication for future generations.* Chicago: Nelson-Hall.

Keefe, J. A., & Magaro, P. (1980). Creativity and schizophrenia: An equivalence of cognitive processing. *Journal of Abnormal Psychology, 89,* 390–398.

Kihlstrom, J. F., & Cantor, N. (1983). Mental representations of the self. In L. Berkowitz (Ed.), *Advances in experimental social psychology* (Vol. 17, pp. 1–47). New York: Academic Press.

Koestler, A. (1959). *The Sleepwalkers.* New York: Macmillan.

Kris, E. (1952). *Psychoanalytic explorations in art.* New York: International Universities Press.

Kroeber, A. L. (1944). *Configurations of culture growth.* Berkeley: University of California Press.

Kubie, L. S. (1958). *Neurotic distortion of the creative process.* Lawrence, KS: University of Kansas Press.

Kuhn, T. S. (1962). *The structure of scientific revolutions.* Chicago: University of Chicago Press.

Lambert, W. E., Tucker, G. R., & d'Anglejan, A. (1973). Cognitive and attitudinal consequences of bilingual schooling: The St. Lambert project through grade five. *Journal of Educational Psychology, 65,* 141–159.

Landry, R. G. (1972). The enhancement of figural creativity through second language learning at the elementary school level. *Foreign Language Annals, 4,* 111–115.

Lehman, H. C. (1953). *Age and achievement.* Princeton: Princeton University Press.

Lindgren, H. C., & Lindgren, F. (1965). Brainstorming and orneriness as facilitators of creativity. *Psychological Reports, 16,* 577–583.

Lombroso, C. (1901). *The man of genius* (6th ed.). New York: Charles Scribner's Sons.

Lynn, S. J., & Rhue, J. W. (1986). The fantasy-prone person: Hypnosis, imagination, and creativity. *Journal of Personality and Social Psychology, 51,* 404–408.

MacKinnon, D. W. (1960). The highly effective individual. *Teachers College Record, 61,* 367–378.

MacKinnon, D. W. (1962). The personality correlates of creativity. A study of American architects. In G. S. Nielson (Ed.), *Proceedings of the 14th International Congress of Psychology* (pp. 11–39). Copenhagen: Munksgaard.

MacKinnon, D. W. (1975). IPAR's contribution to the conceptualization and study of creativity. In I. A. Taylor & J. W. Getzels (Eds.), *Perspectives in creativity* (pp. 60–89). New York: Aldine.

Mackworth, N. H. (1965). Originality. *American Psychologist, 20,* 51–66.

Maddi, S. R. (1965). Motivational aspects of creativity. *Journal of Personality, 33,* 330–347.

Maddi, S. R., & Andrews, S. (1966). The need for variety in fantasy and self-description. *Journal of Personality, 34,* 610–625.

Martindale, C. (1971). Degeneration, disinhibition, and genius. *Journal of the History of the Behavioral Sciences, 7,* 177–182.

Martindale, C. (1972a). Anxiety, intelligence, and access to primitive modes of thought in high and low Remote Associates Test scorers. *Perceptual and Motor Skills, 35,* 375–381.

Martindale, C. (1972b). Father absence, psychopathology, and poetic eminence. *Psychological Reports, 31,* 843–847.

Martindale, C. (1975). *Romantic progression: The psychology of literary history.* Washington, DC: Hemisphere.

Martindale, C. (1977). Creativity, consciousness, and cortical arousal. *Journal of Altered States of Consciousness, 3,* 69–87.

Martindale, C. (1980). Subselves: The internal representation of situational and personal dispositions. In L. Wheeler (Ed.), *Review of personality and social psychology* (Vol. 1, pp. 193–218). Beverly Hills: Sage.

Martindale, C. (1981). *Cognition and consciousness.* Homewood, IL: Dorsey.

Martindale, C. (1984a). The evolution of aesthetic taste. In K. Gergen & M. Gergen (Eds.), *Historial social psychology* (pp. 347–370). Hillsdale, NJ: Erlbaum.

Martindale, C. (1984b). The pleasures of thought: A theory of cognitive hedonics. *Journal of Mind and Behavior, 5,* 49–80.

Martindale, C. (in press). Creative imagination and neural activity. In R. Kunzendorf & A. Sheikh (Eds.), *Psychophysiology of mental imagery: Theory, research, and application.* Amityville, NY: Baywood.

Martindale, C. (1988). Innovation, discovery, and evolution. In E. O. Wilson (Ed.), Special issue on the creative mind: Toward an evolutionary theory of discovery and innovation. *Journal of Social and Biological Structures, 11,* 120–122.

Martindale, C., & Armstrong, J. (1974). The relationship of creativity to cortical activation and its operant control. *Journal of Genetic Psychology, 124,* 311–320.

Martindale, C., & Greenough, J. (1973). The differential effect of increased arousal on creative and intellectual performance. *Journal of Genetic Psychology, 123,* 329–335.

Martindale, C., & Hasenfus, N. (1978). EEG differences as a function of creativity, stage of the creative process, and effort to be original. *Biological Psychology, 6,* 157–167.

Martindale, C., & Hines, D. (1975). Creativity and cortical activation during creative, intellectual, and EEG feedback tasks. *Biological Psychology, 3,* 71–80.

McCrea, R. R. (1987). Creativity, divergent thinking, and openness to experience. *Journal of Personality and Social Psychology, 52,* 1258–1265.

McCrea, R. R., & Costa, P. T., Jr. (1985a). Updating Norman's "adequate taxonomy": Intelligence and personality dimensions in natural language and in questionnaires. *Journal of Personality and Social Psychology, 49,* 710–721.

McCrea, R. R., & Costa, P. T., Jr. (1985b). Openness to experience. In R. Hogan & W. H. Jones (Ed.), *Perspectives in personality* (Vol. 1, pp. 145–172). Greenwich, CT: JAI Press.

McCrea, R. R., & Costa, P. T., Jr. (1987). Validation of the five-factor model of personality across instruments and observers. *Journal of Personality and Social Psychology, 52,* 81–90.

McNeil, T. F. (1971). Prebirth and postbirth influences on the relationship between creative ability and recorded mental illness. *Journal of Personality, 39,* 391–406.

Mednick, S. A. (1958). A learning theory approach to schizophrenia. *Psychological Bulletin, 55,* 316–327.

Mednick, S. A. (1962). The associative basis of the creative process. *Psychological Review, 69,* 220–232.

Mendelsohn, G. A. (1976). Associative and attentional processes in creative performance. *Journal of Personality, 44,* 341–369.

Mendelsohn, G. A., & Griswold, B. B. (1966). Assessed creative potential, vocabulary level, and sex as predictors of the use of incidental cues in verbal problem solving. *Journal of Personality and Social Psychology, 4,* 423–431.

Mischel, W. (1979). On the interface of cognition and personality: Beyond the person-situation debate. *American Psychologist, 34,* 740–754.

Moore, G. (1885/1959). *Confessions of a young man.* New York: Capricorn Books.

Myden, W. (1959). Interpretation and evaluation of certain personality characteristics involved in creative production. *Perceptual and Motor Skills, 9,* 139–158.

Nardi, K., & Martindale, C. (1981, April). *Creativity and preference for tones varying in dissonance and intensity.* Paper presented at the Eastern Psychological Association convention, New York.

Naroll, R., Benjamin, E. Fohl, F., Fried, M., Hildreth, R., & Schaefer, J. (1971). Creativity: A cross-historical pilot survey. *Journal of Cross-Cultural Psychology, 2,* 181–188.

Newell, A., Shaw, J., & Simon, H. (1962). The process of creative thinking. In H. Gruber, G. Terrell, & M. Wertheimer (Eds.). *Contemporary approaches to creative thinking* (pp. 63–119). New York: Atherton Press.

Nietzsche, F. (1908/1927). *Ecce Homo.* In *The philosophy of Friedrich Nietzsche.* New York: The Modern Library.

Nordau, M. (1895). *Degeneration* (5th ed.). London: William Heinemann.

Norman, W. T. (1963). Toward an adequate taxonomy of personality attributes: Replicated factor structure in peer nomination personality ratings. *Journal of Abnormal and Social Psychology, 66,* 574–583.

Olive, H. (1972). Sibling resemblances on divergent thinking. *Journal of Genetic Psychology, 120,* 155–162.

Pankove, E., & Kogan, N. (1968). Creative ability and risk-taking in elementary school children. *Journal of Personality, 36,* 420–439.

Peabody, D. (1987). Selecting representative trait adjectives. *Journal of Personality and Social Psychology, 52,* 59–71.

Perkins, D. (1981). *The mind's best work.* Cambridge: Harvard University Press.

Pettigrew, T. (1958). The measurement and correlates of category width as a cognitive variable. *Journal of Personality, 26,* 532–544.

Pettigrew, T. (1982). Cognitive style and social behavior: A review of category width. In L. Wheeler (Ed.), *Review of Personality and Social Psychology* (Vol. 3, pp. 199–224). Beverly Hills: Sage.

Poincaré, H. (1913). *The foundations of science.* Lancaster, PA: Science Press.

Prentky, R. A. (1980). *Creativity and psychopathology: A neurocognitive perspective.* New York: Praeger.

Reznikoff, M., Domino, G., Bridges, C., & Honeyman, M. (1973). Creative abilities in identical and fraternal twins. *Behavior Genetics, 3,* 365–377.

Rogers, C. (1954). Towards a theory of creativity. *ETC: A Review of General Semantics, 11,* 249–263.

Root-Bernstein, R. S. (1984). On paradigms and revolutions in science and art: The challenge of interpretation. *Art Journal, 44,* 109–118.

Rosen, K., Moore, K., & Martindale, C. (1983, September). *Creativity and rate of habituation.* Paper presented at the Eighth International Colloquium on Empirical Aesthetics, Cardiff, Wales, United Kingdom.

Rosenberg, S., & Gara, M. A. (1985). The multiplicity of personal identity. In P. Shaver (Ed.), *Review of personality and social psychology* (Vol. 6, pp. 87–114). Beverly Hills: Sage.

Schultz, D. P. (1965). *Sensory restriction: Effects on behavior.* New York: Academic Press.

Simon, H. A. (1983). Discovery, innovation, and development: Human creative thinking. *Proceedings of the National Academy of Sciences, 80,* 4569–4571.

Simonton, D. K. (1975). Age and literary creativity: A cross-cultural and transhistorical survey. *Journal of Cross-Cultural Psychology, 6,* 259–277.

Simonton, D. K. (1976). Biographical determinants of achieved eminence: A multivariate approach to the Cox data. *Journal of Personality and Social Psychology, 33,* 218–226.

Simonton, D. K. (1984). *Genius, creativity, and leadership: Historiometric inquiries.* Cambridge: Harvard University Press.

Singer, J. L., & McCraven, V. G. (1961). Some characteristics of adult daydreaming. *Journal of Psychology, 51,* 151–164.

Stein, M. (1974). *Stimulating creativity* (Vol. 1). New York: Academic Press.

Stein, M. (1975). *Stimulating creativity* (Vol. 2). New York: Academic Press.

Suler, J. R. (1980). Primary process thinking and creativity. *Psychological Bulletin, 88,* 144–165.

Tang, P. C. C. (1984). On the similarities between scientific discovery and musical creativity: A philosophical analysis. *Leonardo, 17,* 261–268.

Taylor, I. A., & Getzels, J. W. (Eds.). (1975). *Perspectives on creativity*. Chicago: Aldine.

Tchaikovsky, P. (1878/1906). A letter of 1878. In R. Newmarch (Ed.), *Life and letters of Peter Tchaikovsky* (pp. 274–275). London: John Lane.

Thackeray, W. M. (1899). *The works of W. M. Thackeray* (Vol. 12). London: John Murray.

Vandenberg, S. G. (Ed.). (1968). *Progress in human behavior genetics*. Baltimore: Johns Hopkins University Press.

Van Zelst, R. H., & Kerr, W. A. (1954). Personality self-assessment of scientific and technical personnel. *Journal of Applied Psychology, 38,* 145–147.

Victor, H. R., Grossman, J. C., & Eisenman, R. (1973). Openness to experience and marijuana use in high school students. *Journal of Consulting and Clinical Psychology, 41,* 38–45.

Waddington, C. H. (1969). *Beyond appearance: A study of the relationship between painting and the natural sciences in this century*. Edinburgh: Edinburgh University Press.

Wallach, M. A. (1970). Creativity. In P. H. Mussen (Ed.), *Carmichael's manual of child psychology* (Vol. 1), pp. 1211–1272). New York: Wiley.

Wallach, M. A. & Kagan, N. (1965). *Modes of thinking in young children*. New York: Holt, Rinehart & Winston.

Wallas, G. (1926). *The art of thought*. New York: Harcourt, Brace & World.

Watkins, J. G. (1978). *The therapeutic self*. New York: Human Sciences Press.

Weber, J. P. (1969). *The psychology of art*. New York: Delacorte.

Weisberg, R. W. (1986). *Creativity: Genius and other myths*. New York: W. H. Freeman.

Werner, H. (1948). *Comparative psychology of mental development*. New York: International Universities Press.

Wild, C. (1965). Creativity and adaptive regression. *Journal of Personality and Social Psychology, 2,* 161–169.

Woody, E., & Claridge, G. (1977). Psychoticism and thinking. *British Journal of Social and Clinical Psychology, 16,* 241–248.

Wyatt, D. F., & Campbell, D. T. (1951). On the liability of stereotype or hypothesis. *Journal of Abnormal and Social Psychology, 46,* 496–500.

Zuckerman, H. (1977). *The scientific elite*. New York: Free Press.

CHAPTER 14

The Self and Creativity

SEVERAL CONSTRUCTS IN SEARCH OF A THEORY

E. Thomas Dowd

I was invited by the editors of this volume to write a chapter on "creativity and the self." Given the vague and slippery nature of these concepts, this is not an easy task—attempting to be heuristic in my creative thinking about creativity. I shall first define creativity and selfhood, then relate creativity to several person variables and psychological processes. I will then critique the literature and offer some suggestions for a new program of research. Last, I will discuss various ways of fostering creativity in people.

Definition of Creativity

Two constructs seem to emerge from the dictionary definitions of creativity: the act of making or producing and, more specifically, the act of making something new. Unless one produces something, one cannot be creative. Thus, pure mental activity without a resulting product is not creativity. This distinction is important, because people often assume that thought is in itself creative and are willing to pay large sums of money for think tanks from which the product is often minimal. Simply producing is not enough, however; if it were, every assem-

bly line worker could be said to be creative. True creativity is invention, or the process of making something new. This is not as obvious as it seems. What passes for new is often nothing more than a variation on an already existing theme; for example, our assembly line worker may "create" a new method of fastening a fender to an automobile body. Although management might value this change (and even give the worker a bonus), this type of activity is not normally what we mean by creativity. Likewise, what is called *new* is often nothing more than the same technique with a different label or rationale. It is more accurate to refer to these variations as innovative rather than creative. The term *creativity* should be reserved for activities or products that are truly original and break new ground, even though they build to some extent on previous activity. Creative endeavors generally result in strikingly new formulations that are not derived from what preceded them and in that sense represent a discontinuity.

Definition of the Self

The dictionary definition of *self* consists of a number of meanings and is then followed by almost three pages (in small print) of various self-attributes (e.g., self-conscious, self-directed, self-praise,

E. Thomas Dowd • Department of Educational Psychology, Kent State University, Kent OH 44242.

self-satisfied). Two general constructs seem to emerge out of this chaos, however: unity and consistency. Because these two constructs seem especially important, they have been selected for further discussion. The self possesses unity in that the experiencing individual is reflexively aware of only one identity. Although we speak colloquially of a "better self" or a "weaker self," it is tacitly understood that these are only metaphors expressing various aspects of a unified self. Only in the case of true multiple personalities does the unity of selfhood as experienced by the individual break down. There does seem to be a deep human fear, however, that the unit of the self is fragile and can be easily destroyed. The tremendous fascination with Robert Louis Stevenson's Dr. Jekyll and Mr. Hyde, which magnificently expresses this dilemma, may be due in part to this fundamental fear.

The self also possesses consistency in that people seem to themselves and others to be the same person across situations and over time. Although we often speak of "not being ourself today," it is understood that this is only a metaphorical figure of speech and does not reflect reality. Likewise, we assume that people will behave reasonably consistently in a variety of situations and we may regard it as a sign of emotional distress if they do not. Again, as a species, we seem to have a deep fear that this consistency of the self may be fragile, because behavioral and emotional volatility in ourselves or others frightens us. We also become concerned if we change our personality patterns too readily, as we feel that we do not know "who we are" any longer. This attitude is very likely a major source of resistance to psychotherapeutic change. People have a strong need to maintain the consistency of experienced selfhood, even those aspects of the self that are unhelpful or even destructive. Guidano and Liotti (1982), in particular, have referred to the sense of confusion and disorientation of personal identity and resulting fright that often accompanies profound therapeutic change. People strive to maintain consistency of self-experience, even when that consistency may be damaging to them.

Central also to an understanding of the concept of self is its self-reflexive nature. In other words, only by self-reflexively examining our own thinking process, that is, thinking about our own thinking, can we arrive at a sense of self at all. Thus, the self is inextricably intertwined with self-awareness and self-identity. In this capacity for examining the self, humans seem to be unique.

The concept of self has had a tangled history that in part may account for its fuzziness. It belongs to the domain of philosophy as well as to psychology. Adam Smith originally spoke of society as a mirror in which individuals could see themselves as spectators of their own behavior and who therefore could acquire knowledge about themselves. William James and Charles Horton Cooley, in elaborating on this concept, stressed that individuals develop a self-feeling based on how they think they appear to other people. This has been termed the *social self* or the *reflected self* and implicit in this construct is the assumption that people develop their sense of self out of their ongoing interactions with other people.

Carl Rogers is perhaps the psychologist most identified with the concept of self. Rogers (1959) referred to the self as an organized and consistent set of perceptions of the characteristics of "I" or "me" as well as the perceptions of the relationships of this "I" to other people. Thus, although Rogers stresses the internal knowledge and consistency of the sense of self, he also acknowledges that it is at least partially formed through our interactions with others.

Creativity and the Self-Concept

On the surface, it would seem logical that highly creative individuals would also have a positive self-concept and high self-esteem. However, some people also have argued, usually on the basis of selected cases, that there is a strong correlation between creativity and neuroticism. Therefore, this question warrants empirical investigation. Felker and Treffinger (1971) found that high self-concept fourth-grade students scored significantly higher than low self-concept students on self-evaluation of creative abilities and verbal fluency, flexibility, and originality. Jaquish and Ripple (1981) found a relationship between measures of divergent thinking (to be discussed later) and self-esteem across different age groups. Nabi (1979) argued that the creative person possesses self-acceptance to a greater extent than less creative people. On the other hand, Whiteside (1977) found that highly creative females had lower self-esteem than either men or less creative women. Furthermore, she found that highly creative men had self-esteem scores similar to women of minimal creative ability. Williams, Poole, and Lett (1977) found that there were no significant differences between the self-esteem scores of high and low creative individuals. Wright, Fox, and Noppe (1975) found no significant relationship between creativity and self-esteem. They did, however, find a significant relationship between creativity and creative self-concept.

Gifted students may have an especially difficult time forming a positive self-concept. Torrance (1971) argued that gifted children often have difficulty in evolving a self-concept because parents and teachers may suppress their new and often unusual and deviant ideas. By their negative attitudes, these adults may communicate to the gifted child that commonly accepted ideas, values, and concepts are not to be questioned. This problem may affect the vocational development of creative children as well. Holland and Nichols (1964) found significant differences between vocationally decided and undecided boys on overall creativity. The undecided boys not only showed greater creativity but also showed "unusual potential for artistic and persuasive achievement." They concluded that creative boys may need to defer vocational choice because of a slow and complex rate of personal development. This is an important point and one to which I will return later.

What can we conclude from the research on creativity and self-concept? Certainly the evidence is far from clear, in that some studies found a positive relationship whereas others found a negative one. Many of the discrepancies may be due to the use of different measures of creativity and of self-esteem or self-concept. The latter two concepts are not precisely the same, and some of the differences in the results may be due to using the terms interchangeably. In addition, people of different ages were used as subjects in different studies. It may not be appropriate to compare studies using people of different ages because the relationship between creativity and self-esteem/self-concept may vary over the life span. In any event, it is not at all clear that creativity is necessarily related to a good self-concept. But, in a review of the literature, Schubert and Biondi (1977) found no relationship between creativity and maladjustment either. Therefore, it is probably best to say that creativity and the self-concept are moderately positively related at best. Even this conclusion is suspect, however, because of the variety of measures used to assess self-concept.

Creativity and Self-Actualization

Abraham Maslow described self-actualized persons as unusually flexible and tolerant individuals who are able to hold contradictory concepts in their minds simultaneously. They have a rich sense of humor and are able to look at the complexities of life. Although they enjoy the company of others, they tend to be inner-directed. Following Maslow's model, one might expect that creative people would be high on measures of self-actualization; after all, the same attributes could be present in both. Again, the evidence is equivocal. Schubert and Biondi (1977), concluded that there is support for a positive relationship between creativity and self-actualization. Similarly, Damm (1970) found that subjects high in both creativity and intelligence scored significantly higher on self-actualization than subjects who scored high on either creativity or intelligence. There was no significant relationship, however, between creativity and self-actualization only. On the other hand, Murphy, Dauw, Horton, and Fredian (1976) found no relationship between creativity and self-actualization, a finding also reported by Mathes (1978).

Thus, the literature suggests that there is no relation between creativity and self-actualization, at least as measured by such paper-and-pencil tests as the Personal Orientation Inventory. The concept of self-actualization is an especially murky one, however, and this may contribute to the nonsignificant findings. At any rate, the qualities that contribute to self-actualization do not appear to contribute to creativity.

Creativity and Locus of Control

Locus of control, which is a concept developed by Julian Rotter, refers to the degree to which people perceive that they are controlled internally (i.e., by their own efforts or abilities) or externally (i.e., by environmental forces). Individuals possessing an internal locus of control believe that what happens to them is largely governed by such internal attributes as their intelligence, tenacity, or attractiveness. Those possessing an external locus of control believe that what happens to them is largely governed by such external forces as luck, fate, or other people's actions. Although locus of control is, to some degree, situation-specific, there are nevertheless individual differences in the degree to which people attribute outcomes to internal or external forces.

It may seem intuitively obvious that people who possess an internal locus of control would be more creative than those having an external locus of control. After all, creative individuals are commonly assumed to spend hours, perhaps days, in cognitive ruminations and creative activity and appear to be self-contained and self-oriented. One can scarcely imagine an externally oriented creative person. What, after all, would be the point of intense creative activity if outcomes were indeed determined by fate, chance, or luck? Bamber, Jose, and Boice (1975) indeed found that internals had significantly higher scores on the flexibility and fluency measures of the Unusual Uses subtests of the Torrance Tests of Creative Thinking, whereas externals had significantly higher elaboration scores. Glover and Sautter (1976) found very similar results in that internals had higher flexibility and originality scores, whereas externals had higher elaboration scores. They found no differences between internals and externals on fluency. Cohen and Oden (1974) found more mixed results, because creativity was related to internal locus of control only for female kindergarteners. For male students, the reverse was true. DuCette, Wolk, and Friedman (1972) found that internal subjects were more creative than externals regardless of race. On the other hand, Bolen and Torrance (1978) found no differences in creativity as measured by the Unusual Uses subtests of the Torrance Tests of Creative Thinking between internals and externals. Richmond and de la Serna (1980) found that Mexican externals were more creative than internals and suggested that creative college students of the 1970s have a more external orientation than those of a decade ago.

Thus, even though the majority of the studies support the proposition that internals are more creative than externals, there is some doubt as to just how firm these findings are. In particular, it is intriguing to speculate that perhaps there are shifts over time in the relative numbers of internals and externals in the population and, therefore, in the relative numbers of creative people who are internals or externals. The results of Richmond and de la Serna would point to such a conclusion. In any event, it appears that, in general, creativity may be associated with an internal locus of control, although the evidence is somewhat shaky.

Creativity and Divergent Thinking

Divergent thinking is characterized by thought processes that radiate outward and explore new ideas that are generated from the original notion. By its very nature, divergent thinking is tentative, exploratory, and creative and is oriented to the development of possibilities rather than data, to speculation rather than conclusions. Convergent thinking, on the other hand, is characterized by reasoning that brings together the relevant data and arrives at a firm conclusion based on these data. It tends to be deductive rather than inductive. Thus, divergent thinking can be thought of as more intuitive and less data-based (or data-bound) than convergent thinking. Although both types of thinking are necessary under different conditions, it is reasonable to suppose that the ability to engage in divergent thinking should be related to creativity. Therefore, it is frustrating to find that almost no studies have been conducted to examine this relationship. Jaquish and Ripple (1981) found that self-esteem predicted divergent thinking across groups. However, in view of the apparent lack of relationship between self-esteem and creativity (discussed above), it would be premature to make much of these results. Meichenbaum (1975) developed and modeled sets of self-statements that were operationalized from three conceptualizations of creativity and then asked college students to rehearse these statements. The students showed a significant increase in originality and flexibility on tests of divergent thinking as well as an increase in preference for complexity and higher self-concept. Meichenbaum concluded that creativity may be enhanced by getting people to talk to themselves differently.

Despite the lack of research evidence, I would suggest that to engage in divergent thinking comfortably, people need to be able to do several things. First, they must be able to tolerate ambiguity. In general, people feel most comfortable when they can reach cognitive closure on a subject as soon as possible. Their world is therefore more predictable and, hence, safer. Second, they must be able to hold contradictory ideas simultaneously in their minds. Most people search for answers that are "either-or"; creative individuals should be able to think in terms of "both-and." Again, this removes some of the predictability and safety from life and may result in psychological confusion. Third, they must be able to readily incorporate new ideas into their cognitive systems and to modify the constructs by which they organize and make sense of the information which they receive from their environment. People must categorize sensory information into regular and recursive patterns or else they would not be able to generalize and predict behavior across situations and time. Creative people, however, are able to maintain flexible constructs and avoid a premature "hardening of the categories" and "immaculate perception." In this regard, it is noteworthy that Meichenbaum (1975) was able to train individuals to be more original and flexible in their thinking by having them make self-statements that were based on three conceptualizations of creativity. Obviously, this is an area that could benefit from future research.

Creativity and Intrinsic/Extrinsic Motivation

Some evidence indicates that creativity is related to intrinsic motivation. Koestner, Ryan, Bernieri, and Holt (1984) evaluated the impact on intrinsic motivation of informational and controlling limit-setting. They found that controlling limits reduced the quality and creativity of artistic production, but that limits did not undermine intrinsic motivation if these limits were informational in nature. Amabile (1982, 1985) found that creative writings done under an extrinsic motivation orientation were significantly less creative than those written under an intrinsic motivation condition or even in a control condition. These results tend to support the common idea that creative activity is generated and sustained "from within."

Creativity and Openness to Inner Experiences

It is widely supposed that creative people are unusually open to inner experiences in a sort of mystical fashion, and there is research support for such a notion. Schaeffer, Diggins, and Millman (1976) found that male creativity correlated most strongly with openness to theoretical and aesthetic experiences. Female creativity was correlated with openness to inner experiences and sensation seeking. MacKinnon (1964) examined a variety of creative individuals in different fields and concluded, among other things, that creative individuals are especially open to experience of the inner self and

of the outer world. If this is indeed true, then hypnotic ability might be one indicator of creative potential.

Hypnotic ability, or the capacity to enter and experience a hypnotic trance readily, is a relatively stable individual-difference variable that is normally distributed in the population (Bowers, 1976). It is difficult to determine the correlates of hypnotic ability, because most investigations to date have found little or no relationship of hypnotic ability to anything else. It does appear, however, that hypnotic capacity is correlated with the capacity to become imaginatively involved in mental activity and to concentrate on one idea or stimulus while blocking out competing stimuli (Kroger, 1977). People who possess good hypnotic ability report losing all track of time when absorbed in an idea, a capacity attributed to creative people as well. There are also some indications that hypnotic ability may be, in part, genetically based, so that the same might be said of highly creative individuals. In any event, this is another area that is ripe for further exploration.

Creativity and Complex Thinking

There are some hints that creative thought may be more complex than less creative thought. Recall that Holland and Nichols (1964) concluded that creative boys may be characterized by a slow and complex rate of personal development. In a similar vein, Dellas (1978) suggested that the sense of identity of highly creative individuals is tentative, tenuous, and complex. Nabi (1979) argued that the creative person is more complex than the less creative. Meichenbaum (1975) found that subjects who were trained to make creative self-statements showed an increase in preference for complexity. In Piagetian terms, the structural differentiation (differentiation—integration—subsequent integration at a higher level) that characterizes the development of every person may, in the case of creative people, proceed more slowly in a more complex fashion and may involve more layers. This is again a topic that could benefit greatly from further research.

Creativity and Autonomy/Independence

There is a popular stereotype of the creative person as an isolated, socially maladjusted, nonconforming loner. Although this view may provide some comfort for the noncreative individual, it, like all stereotypes, may contain a grain of truth. Nabi (1979) concluded that the creative person demonstrates autonomy and independence. MacKinnon (1964) argued that creative people are independent in thought and action. On the other hand, Williams *et al.* (1977) found that creative individuals did not appear to value highly impulsivity, desire for change, and nonconformity, but valued such qualities as obedience, diligence, attentiveness, and cooperation. The literature discussed earlier under locus of control is also relevant here. It is likely that the creative person, far from being maladjusted, may actually be better adjusted than the less creative.

Critique and Suggestions for Future Research

What can we conclude from the review of the research on creativity and the self? The initial answer is—not much! The reasons for this sad state of affairs can be classified as deficiencies in three areas. First, there is a problem with definitions of key concepts. As noted earlier, creativity itself has been poorly defined, having been confused with innovation or simple extrapolation from existing information or products on one hand and pure mental activity without a definite product on the other. Until we can agree on the definitional parameters of creativity, we will be seriously handicapped in our research efforts on the topic. As a starting point, I would suggest that the definition of creativity focus on the process of divergent thinking. Similarly, the concept of self has been variously defined and is often confused with the concept of identity. Certain of the more humanistic writers have not helped the situation by discussing the self in obscure, almost mystical, terminology. Perhaps a proper definition of this concept might begin with a consideration of the self-reflexive nature of human thinking (e.g., thinking about one's thinking) and the contribution that that process can make to the experience of selfhood. Guidano (1987) has recently described increasing self-knowledge and, therefore, one's experience of selfhood as derived from interactions with other people and a consequent differentiation from those others. This increasing sense of self then becomes a template against which incoming external information is matched and filtered. Thus, selfhood is built out of the recursive and dynamic interaction of two opponent processes; self-perception and perception of the world. It would seem that any definition of the self should take these cognitive processes into account.

Second, there is a problem with the measurement of creativity. Although standardized tests, such as the Torrance Tests of Creative Thinking, have often been used, other assessment devices have ranged from teacher descriptions (Sisk, 1972) to judges' ratings (Amabile, 1982). With such divergent measures, including different types of standardized tests, it is difficult to compare results or to carry out a sustained line of research. We may be faced with a paradox here, however. If creativity involves the production of something new and not merely something different, then it becomes difficult to measure it in advance of an actual creative product. In other words, creativity, by its very nature, may be accessible only after the fact.

Third, the literature on creativity is characterized largely by a collection of one-shot studies that do not seem to be informed by any significant higher-order theoretical constructs or programmatic thrust. The result is that it is difficult to draw firm conclusions regarding the relationship of some common definition of creativity to any other psychological variables. It is absolutely impossible, however, to determine any causal directions between creativity and a host of psychological variables or environmental manipulations. This is a problem shared by other topics of psychological investigation. Thus, it is hoped that it is not too much to expect that journals specializing in studies of creativity (such as the *Journal of Creative Behavior*) will themselves display creativity by fostering the systematic exploration of programmatic research using common definitions, assessment instruments, and theoretical bases.

However, some tentative conclusions can be drawn from the existing research. First, it is apparent that creativity is only weakly related, at best, to such person variables as self-concept and self-actualization. Creativity may be somewhat correlated with internal locus of control, suggesting that creative individuals tend to believe that they are in control of their own destiny and fate. What is not clear, however, is the direction of causality. Are people creative because they are internally controlled or are they internally controlled because they are creative? The answer has implications for fostering creativity. Second, there appears to be a moderate relationship between creativity and such psychological processes as intrinsic motivation, openness to inner experiences, preference for complex thinking, relative autonomy, and the capacity for divergent thinking. Unless creativity is an inborn trait, giving rise to these processes, it is likely that creativity can be fostered by training people, especially children, in such activities as divergent thinking, complex thinking, openness to inner experiences, and the like.

What should an ideal program of research look like in this area? First, a common definition of creativity should be developed so that investigators are dealing with common concepts. I would suggest that the process of divergent thinking should play a central role in this definition. It is intriguing as well as frustrating (despite Guilford's efforts) that almost no research has investigated the relation between creativity and divergent thinking. Likewise, some attention should be paid to a common definition of selfhood. This topic, in particular, has been plagued with much woolly and flatulent excrescences and is badly in need of clear thinking with a solid conceptual base. Newer developments in cognitive psychotherapy (e.g., Guidano, 1987) may provide the integrated theoretical insights needed. Second, common assessment instruments should be developed from these definitions, utilizing multiple measures. For example, behavioral assessments as well as paper-and-pencil instruments should be used. Third, overarching theoretical viewpoints should be used to guide research directions, perhaps involving the comparisons of studies that are derived from differing theoretical orientations. Fourth, leadership should be provided by a significant journal in the field, perhaps by devoting a series of special issues to the presentation of studies reflecting a common theoretical approach. Fifth, more attention should be paid to the investigation of methods of fostering and increasing creativity. Indeed, it could be argued that this is a crucial national need on which our survival as a nation and a society may ultimately depend.

Fostering Creativity

As part of their initial charge, the editors of this volume have given me liberty (or perhaps license) to speculate freely regarding the nature of creativity as it relates to the self. I therefore wish to offer some suggestions for fostering creativity in oneself and in others.

There have been a few attempts to foster creativity. The Meichenbaum (1975) study referred to earlier found that divergent thinking and a preference for complexity can be increased by self-statement training. Sisk (1972) identified a group of gifted children who were also considered by their teachers to be "low creatives" and put them through ten weekly three-hour sessions that included role-playing, creative writing, open discussion, and artistic expression. At the end of the sessions, the teachers reported that the students had become "more aware of their own strengths." They were also getting better grades. Teacher ratings are notoriously unreliable, however, and awareness of strengths seems only tangentially related to creativity. Schempp, Cheffers, and Zaichowsky (1983) tested 208 first through fifth graders who were in physical education classes in which the teacher dominated all classroom decisions or in which the students were encouraged to share in decision making. They found that the shared decision-making group scored significantly higher than the teacher-dominated group on creativity, motor skills, and self-concept. In addition, students allowed to assist in making their own decisions regarding their learning had more positive attitude scores. Amabile (1985) found that students who wrote poems for extrinsic reasons wrote significantly less creative poems than those written for intrinsic reasons. In the same vein, Koestner *et al.* (1984) found that information limits on first and second graders did not undermine intrinsic motivation whereas controlling limits did. These results suggest that creativity can be fostered by reducing authoritarian directions, by involving children and, presumably, adults in decision-making processes, and by deliberately training people in those skills that are thought to be related to creativity.

There are other ways to foster creativity as well. We can encourage people to avoid "premature evaluation" of an issue until they have collected information and taken time to think through the implications of each side. Organized debates are useful for this purpose. Brainstorming seeks to avoid premature evaluation as well. We can encourage complex thinking by encouraging people to become comfortable with ambiguities, unresolved issues, and paradoxes. In fact, explicit training in paradoxical thinking (Dowd & Milne, 1986), in which concepts are true if they are false and false if they are true, might be useful in fostering creativity by giving individuals experience in holding contradictory information in their minds simultaneously.

This is not as easy as it sounds. The psychological press of most people demands that new information be fitted into preexisting categories as rapidly as possible and that a fundamental examination of their conceptual categories be avoided. It is very uncomfortable to suspend judgment or to reevaluate one's habitable patterns of thinking. In addition, most social institutions—family, school, and church—strongly encourage people to follow the rules and avoid questioning of authority and societal norms. The press, both from within and without, is toward the maintenance of existing cognitive concepts and behavior patterns. However, creativity demands that we constantly reevaluate our existing cognitive categories and remain willing to modify or even suspend them on occasion. Thus, there is an ongoing tension between maintaining one's concepts, which is necessary for functioning in the world, and revising these categories, which is necessary for creativity.

Most people engage in convergent thinking, in which they search for the right answer to a problem. Although this may be useful in many circumstances, creative people recognize that there are often many right answers or no right answers. Asking ourselves or others, "What are some other ways of looking at this?" or "What else might I do?" can be useful in fostering divergent thinking and, hence, creativity. Simply asking, "What if . . ? can get one in the habit of thinking divergently. I am reminded here of Robert Kennedy's famous statement, "Some men look at what is and ask why? I look at what is not and ask why not?" Looking for additional possibilities and relationships in everything can foster increased creativity.

From childhood on we are taught to "follow the rules." There are times, however, when we should purposefully discard the rules in order to see through to a new solution. Rules constrain thinking and channel thought processes in certain directions. Without any rules, we would have no way of using past experience to guide and direct our future actions, thus forcing us to treat every situation as a totally new experience. Obviously, this approach would be extremely inefficient as well as psychologically unsettling. However, without the ability to break rules occasionally, we increasingly find ourselves bound by the rigidity of our preexisting rules. Because many of these rules are not consciously known, however, the help of another person is often needed.

Although we are taught to avoid making mistakes whenever possible, creative thinking demands that we not only make mistakes but view them simply as progress-markers toward ultimate success. It is well to remember that the easiest way of avoiding mistakes is to do nothing. Those who aspire to heightened creativity should be told to increase their failure rate in order to increase their success rate.

Humor has been used by many approaches to psychotherapy as a distancing technique—distancing from our problems and from our tendency to take ourselves too seriously. Humor can also foster creativity in that it can help us distance from an overinvolvement in our rules of life, our ways of making sense of the world, and our automatic assumptions. Humor can help us to see the ambiguity in many situations and avoid a premature cognitive closure.

Activities such as meditation may foster creativity as well. During meditation we temporarily suspend the "if-then" linear patterned way of thinking, in which every event has a cause and a result. This linear causal way of thinking is so ingrained in Western culture that it is difficult to realize that other ways of thinking exist. Creativity may be enhanced by adopting a more circular way of thinking in which the focus is on relationships, possibilities, and recursive patterns, rather than on linear causality and single-outcome events. Meditation can help free the mind of old thinking patterns and allow new patterns to develop. In this context, it is interesting to realize how many truly creative activities were the result of serendipity when the individual's mind was on something else. Creative solutions may require that one *not* think about the problem rather than think about it.

Engaging in appropriate leisure activities can also enhance creativity. I have noted (Dowd, 1984) that leisure activities can provide one of the few opportunities for people to engage in exploratory, divergent, and creative activities, rather than problem-solving, goal-directed, and convergent activities. McDowell (1984) argued that leisure activities can provide a heightened sense of self-expression and autonomous control and allow one to explore one's outer ranges of tolerance for novelty, complexity, unfamiliarity, and competence. Iso-Ahola (1984) stated that intrinsic motivation is at the heart of leisure behavior, not unlike creativity, and advocated the deliberate cultivation of intrinsic motivation through the development of perceived competence and self-efficacy by means of leisure experiences. Thus, engaging in leisure experiences that are freely chosen may significantly enhance creativity in all spheres of life.

In one sense, however, creativity cannot be fostered at all. Because creativity is, by definition, unplanned, spontaneous, and divergent, then any planned activity to foster it will render impossible that which is desired. It is similar to the ''Be Spontaneous'' paradox, in which an attempt to comply with the order makes spontaneity impossible. For if the order is obeyed, it cannot be spontaneous, but if it is spontaneous, it must be disobeyed. Only by disobeying the order can it be obeyed. Similarly, we cannot create creativity; we can only set up the conditions for it is hoped its spontaneous occurrence.

I want to offer one caveat, however. Many people do not take kindly to the demonstration of creativity in others and may work to discourage its expression. Creative individuals have been accused of being maladjusted, antisocial, and antireligious. Creative children have earned the animosity of some teachers. Creative people have been villified (Einstein) or even killed (Socrates). Thus, individuals should know that creativity is practiced at some risk to themselves.

I want to close with a final suggestion. People are often urged to be reasonable and logical in their thinking processes, an attitude which is certain death to creativity. Instead, I would like to suggest an attitude that may be more conducive to creativity but that is likely, at the same time, to earn the enmity of others.

The reasonable man adapts himself to his environment.
The unreasonable man persists in adapting his environment to himself.
Therefore, all progress depends on the unreasonable man!

May each of you spend a certain amount of time each day being unreasonable!

References

Amabile, T. M. (1982). Children's artistic creativity: Detrimental effects of competition in a field setting. *Personality and Social Psychology Bulletin, 8,* 573–578.

Amabile, T. M. (1985). Motivation and creativity: Effects of motivational orientation on creative writers. *Journal of Personality and Social Psychology, 48,* 393–397.

Bamber, R. T., Jose, P. E., & Boice, R. (1975). Creativity as affected by differential reinforcements and test instructions. *Bulletin of the Psychonomic Society, 6,* 361–363.

Bolen, L. M., & Torrance, E. P. (1978). The influence on creative thinking of locus of control, cooperation, and sex. *Journal of Clinical Psychology, 34,* 903–907.

Bowers, K. S. (1976). *Hypnosis for the seriously curious.* New York: Norton.

Cohen, S., & Oden, S. (1974). An examination of creativity and locus of control in children. *Journal of Genetic Psychology, 124,* 179–185.

Damm, V. J. (1970). Creativity and intelligence: Research implications for equal emphasis in high school. *Exceptional Children, 36,* 565–569.

Dellas, M. (1978). Creative personality and identity. *Psychological Reports, 43,* 1103–1110.

Dowd, E. T. (1984). Leisure counseling with adults across the life span. In E. T. Dowd (Ed.), *Leisure counseling: Concepts and applications* (pp. 214–233). Springfield, IL: Charles C Thomas.

Dowd, E. T., & Milne, C. R. (1986). Paradoxical interventions in counseling psychology. *The Counseling Psychologist, 14,* 237–282.

DuCette, J., Wolk, S., & Friedman, S. (1972). Locus of control and creativity in black and white children. *Journal of Social Psychology, 88,* 297–298.

Felker, D. W., & Treffinger, D. J. (1971, February). *Self concept, divergent thinking abilities, and attitudes about creativity and problem solving.* Paper presented at the American Educational Research Association convention, New York.

Glover, J. A., & Sautter, F. (1976). An investigation of the relationship of four components of creativity to locus of control. *Social Behavior and Personality, 4,* 257–260.

Guidano, V., & Liotti, G. (1982). *Cognitive therapy and emotional disorders.* New York: Guilford Press.

Guidano, V. F. (1987). *Complexity of the self: A developmental approach to psychopathology and therapy.* New York: Guilford Press.

Holland, J. L., & Nichols, R. C. (1964). The development and validation of an indecision scale: The natural history of a problem in basic research. *Journal of Counseling Psychology, 11,* 27–34.

Iso-Ahola, S. E. (1984). Social psychological foundations of leisure and resultant implications for leisure counseling. In E. T. Dowd (Ed.), *Leisure counseling: Concepts and applications* (pp. 97–125). Springfield, IL: Charles C Thomas.

Jaquish, G. A., & Ripple, R. E. (1981). Cognitive creative abilities and self-esteem across the adult life span. *Human Development, 24,* 110–119.

Koestner, R., Ryan, R. M., Bernieri, F., & Holt, K. (1984). Setting limits on children's behavior: The differential effects of controlling vs. informational styles on intrinsic motivation and creativity. *Journal of Personality, 52,* 233–248.

Kroger, W. S. (1977). *Clinical and experimental hypnosis* (2nd ed.). Philadelphia: J. B. Lippincott.

MacKinnon, D. W. (1964, March). *Identification and development of creative abilities.* Paper presented at the conference on Creativity and the Mentally Gifted, Fresno, CA.

Mathes, E. W. (1978). Self-actualization, metavalues, and creativity. *Psychological Reports, 43,* 215–222.

McDowell, C. F. (1984). Leisure: Consciousness, well-being, and counseling. In E. T. Dowd (Ed.), *Leisure counseling: Concepts and applications* (pp. 5–51). Springfield, IL: Charles C Thomas.

Meichenbaum, D. (1975). Enhancing creativity by modifying what subjects say to themselves. *American Educational Research Journal, 12,* 129–145.

Murphy, J. P., Dauw, D. C., Horton, R. E., & Fredian, A. J. (1976). Self-actualization and creativity. *Journal of Creative Behavior, 10,* 39–44.

Nabi, K. S. (1979). Personality and self: The creativity discussion. *Indian Psychological Review, 18,* 5–8.

Richmond, B. O., & de la Serna, M. (1980). Creativity and locus of control among Mexican college students. *Psychological Reports, 46,* 979–983.

Rogers, C. R. (1959). A theory of therapy, personality, and interpersonal relations, as developed in the client-centered framework. In S. Koch (Ed.), *Psychology: A study of science,* Vol. 3 (pp. 184–256). New York: McGraw-Hill.

Schaeffer, C. E., Diggins, D. R., & Millman, H. L. (1976). Intercorrelations among measures of creativity, openness to experience, and sensation-seeking in a college sample. *College Student Journal, 10,* 332–339.

Schempp, P. G., Cheffers, J. T., & Zaichowsky, L. D. (1983). Influence of decision making on attitudes, creativity, motor skills, and self-concept in elementary children. *Research Quarterly for Exercise and Sport, 54,* 183–189.

Schubert, D. S., & Biondi, A. M. (1977). Creativity and mental health: III. Creativity and adjustment. *Journal of Creative Behavior, 11,* 186–197.

Sisk, D. (1972). Relationship between self-concept and creativity: Theory into practice. *Gifted Child Quarterly, 16,* 229–234.

Torrance, E. P. (1971). Identity: The gifted child's major problem. *Gifted Child Quarterly, 15,* 147–155.

Whiteside, M. (1977). Self-concept differences among high and low creative college students. *Journal of College Student Personnel, 18,* 224–227.

Williams, A. J., Poole, M. E., & Lett, W. R. (1977). The creativity/self-concept relationship reviewed: An Australian longitudinal perspective. *Australian Psychologist, 12,* 313–317.

Wright, R. J., Fox, M., & Noppe, L. (1975). The interrelationship of creativity, self-esteem, and creative self-concept. *Psychology, 12,* 11–15.

CHAPTER 15

Creativity and Psychopathology

GAMBOLING AT THE SEAT OF MADNESS

Robert Prentky

This chapter addresses a topic that has been the subject of intense curiosity throughout civilized history. What are the roots of genius? Are geniuses divinely inspired? Are they mad? What is the nature of their gift? Is it something that can be cultivated? Or perhaps harnessed like a beast of draught? Do geniuses possess a genetic loading for their gift? If the germ of inspiration has a biological component, it would seem that the cornerstone of the creative process remains inaccessible to most of us. If this is the case, it poses an interesting dilemma: Why should a feature of human behavior so critical to the advancement of the species be restricted to so small a segment of the species? After more than 2,500 years of curiosity, we can conclude very little that is definitive. We cannot state with certainty that some genetic contribution enhances creative potential. We cannot state with certainty that creativity can be encouraged, though we undoubtedly can state how it may be discouraged. Despite reams of stories, some farfetched and some true, relating creativity to mental illness, the idea that one must be slightly mad to be creative is so counterintuitive that it is rejected by most sober-minded scientists. And

Robert Prentky • Research Department, The Massachusetts Treatment Center, Bridgewater, MA 02324; and Department of Psychiatry, Boston University School of Medicine, Boston, MA 02118.

rightfully so. It certainly would not be evolutionarily adaptive to wed the curse of mental illness to the gift of creativity. This dilemma was raised by Barron (1958):

> But one cannot readily abandon the idea that to create is in some sense—perhaps in the best sense—to be healthy in mind. Yet how can the maladjustment of many great creative minds be reconciled with the assertion that they are in some respects unusually healthy? (p. 163)

Barron determined, however, that the seeming illogic of associating maladjustment with creativity can be understood from the standpoint of the source of creative inspiration—the unconscious. The creative person is said to be at higher risk for disorder by virtue of gamboling at the seat of disorder.

In the past, theoreticians contributed little in the way of explanation for this farfetched relationship, little, that is, except for the psychodynamic formulation. More recently, investigators have been seriously and productively pursuing other angles (e.g, Cropley & Sikand, 1973; Dykes & McGhie, 1976; Hasenfus & Magaro, 1976; Karlsson, 1978; Keefe & Magaro, 1980; Martindale, 1977–1978, and with his colleagues [with Hasenfus, 1978; with Hines, 1975; and with Hines, Mitchell, & Covello, 1984]; Rothenberg, 1976, 1979, 1983). The crucial question, however, is *not* whether creativity and mental illness are causally linked but whether our knowledge of mental illness offers us any insight into the mechanics of creativity. Does the allegation, be it true or false, that an unusually high percentage of extraordinarily creative people were disturbed help us in any way to comprehend the creative process? I have argued elsewhere that the coincidental association between creativity and real emotional turmoil in a number of highly visible, highly celebrated cases may provide, in a serendipitous fashion, an important key for unlocking one of the secrets of their creativity—specific modes for processing information (Prentky, 1979, 1980). It is *not* my thesis that mental illness is a prerequisite for creativity. It is my thesis that a fruitful theoretical model for understanding the creative process may be in terms of cognitive style (i.e., mode of information processing), and that a genetic predisposition to certain forms of mental illness may be associated with a cognitive style similar to that which promotes creativity. If there is one thing that may characterize all highly creative people, it is the unique manner in which they apprehend their world (i.e., they see things, experience things, or conclude things that the rest of us do not). A disorder of cognition (or information processing) must be present for someone to receive a diagnosis of schizophrenia (Callaway & Naghdi, 1982). Thus, a cardinal feature of *both* creativity and mental illness is information processing. Highly creative people turn into a distinct and productive asset what mentally disturbed people blindly grope for— the ability to absorb and efficiently process information from the environment. The majority of us seem to find sufficient light in the tunnel to navigate without excessive fumbling, though we are rarely blessed with that sudden illumination which, for a split second, makes everything clear. Severely mentally ill people seem to fall at one of two extremes, a constant blinding illumination or a black-out condition. The obvious parsimony of this analogy is intended only to provide a simple heuristic model for looking at two otherwise unrelated phenomena—creativity and mental illness.

In a delightful article on "lunatics, lovers, and poets," Behrens (1975) concluded that "the difference between the schizophrenic act and the act of creation is the difference between Don Quixote (as madman) and author Cervantes (as poet). Madmen take metaphors literally, and the difference is one of awareness" (p. 232). Bronowski (1965) referred to the Pythagorean "Geistesblitz" as "explosions of a hidden likeness" in which the creator fuses two aspects of nature into one. In Behrens's terms, Don Quixote's penchant was to see hidden likeness where likeness clearly did not reside. What we seek to understand is not Quixote's madness nor Sancho Panza's straight vision of reality ("those which appear yonder are not giants, but windmills"), but the genius of those who first thought of harnessing the wind on land using the same sails that harness the wind at sea. Such constructive "likenesses" are discussed in detail elsewhere (Bronowski, 1965; Prentky, 1980).

The aim of this chapter is twofold: (1) to highlight some of the most well-known cases of reputed association between creativity and mental illness, and (2) to review the empirical literature that has examined the personalities and cognitive styles of those defined as creative. Because other chapters in this volume focus on the latter issues (personality and cognitive style), treatment in this chapter will be abbreviated and address the specific question of whether the scientific literature provides any support for an incidence of mental illness among creative people that exceeds chance expectation, and, if so, how that increased incidence may be understood.

An Historical Overview

Alliances or misalliances between "genius" and psychosis have been noted in the literature for at least 2,300 years. One of the earliest references dates back to Aristotle's *Problemata* (ca. 360 B.C.): "Those who have become eminent in philosophy, politics, poetry, and the arts have all had tendencies toward melancholia." Aristotle may have had his eminent predecessor Socrates in mind. The first case study of genius was written about Socrates in 1836 by the psychiatrist Louis-François Lélut (*Du Démon de Socrate*). Becker (1978) stated that "Socrates' inclination 'to take the inspirations of his conscience for the voice of a supernatural agent (his demon),' confirmed, in Lélut's opinion, that Socrates suffered from a 'most undeniable form of madness'" (p. 28). Gibson's (1889) observation was similar. He stated, "Socrates, heathen though he was, was a great philosopher; yet it is credited of him that he acknowledged a tutelary genius or demon, who informed him of coming events and directed—probably in a measure controlled—his behavior" (p. 4).

Despite the often-noted association between "enthousiasmos" (enthusiasm or "mania")—demonic possession or melancholia—and genius during antiquity, Greek "madness" is *not* equatable to modern notions of insanity. According to Aristotle, the "homo melancholicus," depending upon humoral balance, could be divinely distinguished or mad. When black bile was not properly counterbalanced by blood, phlegm, and yellow bile, the result was depression and anxiety. Being of melancholic temperament, however, did not require that one be acutely depressed or anxious. Rosen (1969) cited Phaedrus, a first century A.D. Roman author of fables and reputed translator of some of Aesop's fables, as writing:

The greatest blessing came by way of madness, indeed of madness that is heaven sent. It was when they were made that the prophetess at Delphi and the priestess at Dodona achieved so much for which both states and individuals in Greece are thankful: when sane they did little or nothing. As for the Sibyl and others who by the power of inspired prophesy have so often foretold the future to so many, and guided them aright, I need not dwell on what is obvious to everyone. (p. 84)

This same distinction was made fourteen centuries later, during the Renaissance, where "genio" was described in terms of melancholia and "pazzia" in terms of madness. Pazzia as applied to a sane melancholic genius usually implied such attributes as eccentricity, sensitivity, moodiness, and solitariness (Becker, 1978). None of these qualities was pejorative. The most distinguished artists possessed pazzia. With the arrival of the Enlightenment, the first real change occurred in the conception of genius. Genius was seen as "rational," rooted primarily in the imagination. Rather than humors being balanced, imagination, judgment, and aesthetic "taste" had to be balanced. This change explains why seventeenth-century artists and scholars (e.g., Rubens, Rembrandt, Bernini) generally were not described as melancholic (Wittkower, 1973).

Some 2,100 years after Aristotle, the prevalent conception of genius was that it was allied with degeneracy. This notion was first set forth by Benedict Augustin Morel (ca. 1850), who argued that degeneracy was a state of biological inferiority and that it was inherited. It was conceived that geniuses evolved from the same maladaptive gene pool as the lowliest elements of society—criminals and lunatics. Babcock (1895) enumerated the dire consequences of being born with degenerate genes:

First, and most prominent in the order of frequency is an early death. Second, he may swell the criminal ranks. Third, he may become mentally deranged and ultimately find his way into a

hospital for the insane. Fourth, and least frequently, he startles the world by an invention or discovery in science or by an original composition of great merit in art, music or literature. He is then styled a genius. (p. 752)

Among many others who supported this degeneracy theory was the Italian criminologist Cesare Lombroso.

The first systematic study of the relationship between genius and insanity was published by Lombroso in 1864. Over a quarter of a century later, Lombroso (1891) published his research in book form, concluding that genius was often a "degenerative psychosis of the epileptic group." In a subsequent edition of the same work, Lombroso (1910) stated that

any one who has had the rare fortune to live with men of genius is soon struck by the facility with which they misinterpret the acts of others, believe themselves persecuted, and find everywhere profound and infinite reasons for grief and melancholy.

Nisbet (1912) related genius to no fewer than 40 separate maladies, from apoplexy to vanity, and including such varied afflictions as gout, rheumatism, imbecility, ne'er-do-wellism, opium eating, prodigality, scrofula (tuberculous disorder), sexual passion, and skull shape. Approximately 100 to 125 pages are included in the three separate listings of "insanity," "insane temperament," and "hallucinations." In a somewhat more recent examination, Tsanoff (1949) claimed that "in creative activity, genius is at the ultimate limit of tension, the utmost of reach, of intensity, penetration. . . . But no wonder if it overtakes the physical and mental powers and unbalances the high-strung genius" (p. 29).

The literature is replete with anecdotal and clinical descriptions of the putatively pathological behavior of hundreds of gifted artists, musicians, novelists, poets, and scientists (see Table 1). Grant (1968), in his treatment of "great abnormals," described Kafka as suicidally depressed, probably schizophrenic, van Gogh as a neurotic-hysteric with impulsive and unreasoning rages, Strindberg as a paranoid schizophrenic, and Poe as psychopathic, paranoid, and megalomaniacal. According to Lombroso (1910), Schopenhauer and Tasso might be diagnosed, in contemporary nosology, as bipolar manic-depressives. Chopin, Newton, Gogol, Linnaeus, Pascal, and Swift were all said to suffer from paralytic dementia, whereas Coleridge, Michelangelo, Cromwell, Johnson, Mill, Rossini, Raphael, and Schiller were said to be melancholic

Table 1.   **Presumed Psychiatric Disturbances of Some Eminent Writers, Artists, Composers, and Scientists**[a]

	Schizophrenia	Affective disorders (unipolar and bipolar)		Personality disorders[b]
Writers, poets and philosophers	Baudelaire	Barrie	Lamb	E.B. Browning
	Hölderlin	Balzac	London[c]	R. Browning
	Johnson	Berryman[c]	Lowell	Carlyle
	Kant	Blake	Mill	Comte
	Pound	Boswell	Maupassant	Eddy
	Strindberg	Byron	O'Neill	Eliot
	Swift	Chatterton[c]	Plath[c]	Gogol
		Coleridge	Poe	Heine
		Collins	Roethke	Huxley
		Conrad	Rossetti	Proust
		Cowper	Rousseau	Rimbaud
		Crane[c]	Saroyan	Spencer
		Fergusson	Schiller	Tennyson
		Fitzgerald	Schopenhauer	Zola
		Frost	Sexton[c]	
		Goethe	Shelley	
		Hemingway[c]	Smart	
		Hopkins	Tasso	
		Kafka	Woolf[c]	
Artists	Beil[d]	Crevel[c]		
	Brendel[d]	Michelangelo		
	Cellini	Modigliani[c]		
	Da Vinci	Pollock[c]		
	El Greco	Raphael		
	Goya	Rothko[c]		
	Klotz[d]	Van Gogh[c]		
	Knupfer[d]			
	Moog[d]			
	Neter[d]			
	Orth[d]			
	Pohl[d]			
	Rembrandt			
	Sell[d]			
	Wain			
	Welz[d]			
Composers	Donizetti	Berlioz		Beethoven
	Mendelssohn	Chopin		Schubert
	Rimsky-Korsakov	Elgar		Wagner
		Handel		
		Mahler		
		Rachmaninoff		
		Rossini		
		Schumann		
		Scriabin		
		Tchaikovsky		
		Wolf		
		Wood		

Table 1. (*Continued*)

	Schizophrenia	Affective disorders (unipolar and bipolar)	Personality disorders[b]
Scientists	Cantor Copernicus Descartes Faraday Hamilton Legrange Linnaeus Newton Pascal Swedenborg Weierstrass	Darwin De Forest Mayer Kammerer[c]	Ampere Einstein Freud Heaviside Mendel Nightingale

[a]These "diagnostic classifications" are based almost entirely on presumptive judgments made from archival and anecdotal evidence and should be construed as inferential "best guesses."

[b]This category undoubtedly includes individuals who were highly eccentric but otherwise not psychiatrically disturbed. It also includes others (e.g., Comte, who was described by Nisbet, 1912, as schizophrenic) who rightly belong in a different category.

[c]Suicides.

[d]These ten artists were designated as schizophrenic by Prinzhorn (1972); however, case descriptions strongly suggest that several were affective disorders.

(Tsanoff, 1949). Lombroso (1910) further claimed that many great musicians, including Mozart, Schumann, Beethoven, Handel, Pergolesi, and Donizetti, suffered from "attacks of insanity," including delusions, hallucinations, depression, and mania. Lombroso also included Rousseau, Newton, Comte, and Ampere in this latter category. Lange-Eichbaum (1932), who looked at the temporal relationship of mental illness to creativity, found that many artists become psychotic only after their major contributions were made. He included in this group Baudelaire, Donizetti, Kant, Faraday, Newton, Copernicus, and Linnaeus. Lange-Eichbaum placed the majority of highly creative artists in the "psychopath" category, a term not referring to psychopathy in the Cleckley (1964) sense but to a poorly socialized, schizoid, or schizothymic personality. In this group he included Beethoven, Michelangelo, Schopenhauer, Byron, and Heine.

Beethoven was said to have experienced a variety of subsidiary delusions, ranging from persecution, hero-rescue, fraticide, and sacrifice to birth fantasies (Solomon, 1975). Grillparzer, an Austrian playwright and frequent companion of Beethoven, described Beethoven as "half-crazy" and "a wild beast" when angry (Reichsman, 1981). Larkin's (1970) thorough treatment of Beethoven's medical history suggests that the composer was eccentric,

given to violent tantrums, occasionally very depressed, and often "muddled" or forgetful; however, there is little evidence that he was delusional:

> The picture then is of persistent ill-health, of a prevailing mood of depression, a highly strung, suspicious, "persecuted" man, unstable under stress, hypomanic at times, impulsive to the point of violence, perfectionist, deaf, irritable. Nevertheless, he had enormous charm, and although he might one day drive a visitor away with brutal discourtesy, he would put himself out to be attentive on another occasion. Here is a man who tried to make up for his failings in temperament, breeding, and education, whose tremendous achievements were in spite of cruel handicaps and who did not flounder in self-pity, though not above occasionally being pathetic in letters to women. (p. 460)

Schumann believed that Beethoven and Mendelssohn dictated musical compositions to him from their tombs (Lombroso, 1910). In a recent article about Schumann, Murphy (1979) described the composer's battle with mental illness:

> Robert had been mentally unstable all his life, haunted by fears of insanity since the age of 18.
>
> In 1854, he complained of a "very strong and painful attack" of ear trouble that had bothered him before. This was followed by illusions, such as dictation by angels of a theme on which he wrote some piano variations.
>
> About 16 days later, he asked to be taken to a lunatic asylum, and the next day attempted to drown himself.
>
> In March 1854, he was put in a private asylum in Endenich, where he lived for about 2½ years. Clara was kept from him for fear that her visit would be too disturbing.

She did visit him in July 1856, when it was realized that death was near. He seemed to recognize her, but was unable to speak intelligibly.

He died on July 29, 1856. He was only 46. (p. 5C)

Chopin was described by George Sand as "shutting himself up in his room for whole days, weeping, walking, breaking his pens, repeating and altering a bar a hundred times, spending six weeks on a single page" (Storr, 1976, pp. 65–66). Storr (1971) also cited the case of Wagner:

Wagner had one of the most remarkable creative imaginations of any artist who has ever lived. His originality, the assurance with which he handled his material, and the enormous scale on which the world he created was constructed, are all unparalleled. . . . And yet Wagner, as an individual, was deplorable: Unreliable, selfish, arrogant; a sponger who was constantly in debt, he was quite unscrupulous both sexually and financially. It seems unlikely that this poet of passionate love ever achieved a really satisfactory relationship with a woman; more especially as we know that he retained a strong fetishistic interest in silk and perfume. The personality of Wagner remained infantile; but his creations contained all that he himself lacked. (p. 123)

British playwright Peter Schaffer (1981) dramatized the relationship between Wolfgang Amadeus Mozart and Antonio Salieri in *Amadeus*. Schaffer portrayed Mozart as a childish, conceited, uncouth rival to the more successful Salieri. Salieri, court composer to the Austrian Emperor Joseph II, alone recognized Mozart's genius. Driven by jealousy and aided by Mozart's rude court behavior, Salieri managed to effectively squeeze Mozart out of royal commissions. Mozart died believing that Salieri poisoned him. Mozart's fears were dismissed. Thirty-two years later, Salieri attempted suicide, at which time he confessed to having poisoned Mozart. Salieri's confession was given no more credence than Mozart's accusation. In fact, Mozart's death has been attributed to kidney disease and not to poisoning (Reichsman, 1981). Reichsman quoted from two letters that Mozart wrote to his wife shortly before his death:

If people could see into my heart, I should almost feel ashamed. To me, everything is cold—cold as ice [and] I can't describe what I have been feeling—a kind of emptiness which hurts me dreadfully—a kind of longing which is never satisfied, which never ceases, and which persists, nay, rather increases daily. (p. 293)

Yet another composer, Donizetti, "was during his latter years confined in a lunatic asylum. He died at fifty, leaving a son, like himself, insane" (Nisbet, 1912, p. 170).

Sir James Barrie, the English writer and the creator of the immortal Peter Pan, was beset by obsessions, compulsions, childhood amnesia, and deep depressions (Alston, 1972). William Cowper was said to be manic-depressive, though he composed his verse during periods of quiescence, and Swift "was haunted by the spectre of insanity" throughout his life (Pickering, 1974).

Gibson (1889) commented that:

Swift was a man whose soul could be attuned to the softest, gentlest music, but which could be aroused to the most tempestuous energy. This unhappy condition of Swift's mind was palpably connected in the latter part of his time with diseased brain: giddiness and deafness assaulted him; his memory failed; ungovernable rage followed; and this was succeeded by furious madness. One phase more, and we see him quiet, passionless, idiotic, in which condition death gently overtook him. (p. 45)

Pickering (1974) quoted Nicholson as stating that

Shelley's hallucinations were vivid and detailed. On one occasion, while walking near Pisa, he saw a man coming slowly towards him dressed in a long cloak, with a hood or cowl hiding his face. When the man was only a few yards distant he raised his hood, and Shelley was much startled to see that the man was in fact himself. (p. 292)

Gibson (1889) stated that

with all his faults, Shelley was, perhaps, the grandest metaphysical poet, as he is said to have been one of the best classical scholars, in Europe. Nevertheless, his life was a failure in almost every particular. His nearest relatives rejected him; he suffered torments of mental and bodily pain, and was the subject of extraordinary illusions. No wonder, then, that he had difficulty in bearing up against the mental dejection which fitfully attacked him. (p. 48)

It was suggested by Pickering (1974) that Elizabeth Barrett Browning was "psychoneurotic," though her chronic lung problems (possibly pulmonary tuberculosis), her life-long invalidated condition, and her addiction to morphine certainly complicate any attempt to extract a clear psychiatric diagnosis.

A number of French writers are reputed to have been afflicted by varying degrees of instability. The brilliant Marcel Proust certainly was eccentric and, in later life, a victim of bronchial asthma, a slave to drugs, and a recluse. However, he also has been charged with possessing an implacable superego, evidencing sadistic cruelty and narcissistic self-absorption (Bychowski, 1973). Another apparently disturbed French writer was Guy de Maupassant. Within two years after completion of "Le Horla" in 1887, Maupassant (1900) was "obviously insane," though he did not end up in an asylum until a suicide attempt in 1892 (Dale, 1952). Dale stated that Maupassant's "mental breakdown was attended by migraine, melancholia, obsessions, perversions, hallucinations, and outbreaks of violent, ill-tempered behavior" (p. 237). Louis-François Lélut wrote his second case study on Pascal in 1846 (*L'Amulette de Pascal*). Lélut concluded that Pascal was the victim of mental illness, an opinion later supported by Tsanoff (1949). Yet another French writer, Emile Zola, submitted himself to psychiatric examination. The majority of the panel of 15 psychiatrists concurred that Zola's "genius had its source in the neurotic elements of his temperament" (Trilling, 1950). Zola agreed entirely with their conclusion.

Of the wide variety of psychiatric conditions attributed to the aforementioned individuals, the cluster of conditions subsumed under the category of affective disturbance clearly predominates. This is especially true for writers, poets, philosophers, and composers (see Table 1). Edel (1975) quoted Emerson as saying that "after thirty a man wakes up sad every morning . . . until the day of his death." A nadir of depression has resulted in the suicide of many well-known writers, including the Americans Sylvia Plath, Hart Crane, and Ernest Hemingway and the Britons Virginia Woolf and Thomas Chatterton. Woolf's reflections suggest an association between her depression and her literary inspiration:

If I could stay in bed another fortnight (but there is no chance of that) I believe I should see the whole of "The Waves" . . . I believe these illnesses are in my case—how shall I express it?—partly mystical. Something happens in my mind. It refuses to go on registering impressions. It shuts itself up. It becomes a chrysalis. I lie quite torpid, often with acute physical pain—as last year; only discomfort this. Then suddenly something springs. (Bell, 1972, p. 142)

Although Rousseau did not take his own life, Ellrich (1974) recounted Rousseau's "psychological crisis" (suicidal melancholia). Franz Kafka, Schopenhauer, and Tasso (the greatest Italian poet of the late Renaissance) all had psychological crisis similar to that of Rousseau. Edel's (1975) discussion of depression in the writings of highly creative poets and novelists brings to mind Dr. Benjamin Rush, who viewed the tragedy of artistic madness as "tristimania," a mania of sadness or, technically, agitated depression. Edel found that "nothing is more chronic among writers than their sadness."

As an aside, there is some empirical evidence to support the observation that if creative writers are psychiatrically disturbed, the disturbance is likely to be affective (i.e., unipolar or bipolar depression) (e.g., Andreasen, 1980; Andreasen & Powers, 1975; Andreasen & Canter, 1974; Jamison, 1988; Jamison, Gerner, Hammen & Padesky, 1980). Andreasen and Canter (1974) studied 15 writers from the University of Iowa Writers' Workshop and a matched control group of 15 individuals who were not involved in the arts. Of the 15 writers, four had been hospitalized for a psychiatric problem, compared with none of the controls. Ten of the 15 writers met the diagnostic criteria for affective disorder, compared with two of the controls. Two of the writers were diagnosed as bipolar, compared with none of the controls. For eight of the nine writers who had seen a psychiatrist, the presenting complaint involved affective symptoms. Andreasen and Canter (1974) concluded that

creative writers tend to have a high prevalence of what would normally be called psychiatric illness, that this illness is usually affective disorder, and that their primary relatives also have a high prevalence of affective disorder. (p. 129).

In a subsequent study Andreasen and Powers (1975) compared 15 writers from the Writers' Workshop with 16 manic and 15 schizophrenic inpatients on the Goldstein-Sheerer Object-Sorting Test. The authors reported that the writers resembled the manic patients in conceptual style (i.e., overinclusive thinking) more than they resembled the schizophrenic patients. The schizophrenics examined in this study tended to be underinclusive. Andreasen has expanded her original sample of writers to 30, reporting that the proportion of writers treated for mood disorders in this larger sample is 80%, compared with 30% for the comparison group (Holden, 1987). Forty-three percent of this larger sample evidenced symptoms of manic-depressive illness, compared with 10% of the controls.

Jamison (1988) provided an excellent overview of the clinical and empirical literature on the association of major affective disorder with creativity. She reported on a study conducted in 1983 on 47 of Britain's foremost artists and writers. Jamison found that 38% of her sample had sought treatment for mood disorders, and that approximately three-fourths of those treated had received antidepressants, lithium, or hospitalization. The most severe cases were found among the poets, one-half of whom required medical intervention in the form of hospitalization and/or medication. Jamison pointed out that these rates are even more striking when compared with the base rates in the general population of 1% for bipolar illness and 5% for unipolar illness. According to those base rates, one would have expected, by chance alone, no cases of bipolar illness and 2 cases of unipolar illness in the full sample.

Goertzel, Goertzel, and Goertzel (1978) examined a sample of noted twentieth-century leaders and creators, finding that 5% suicided or attempted suicide. Most of the subsample of suicidal cases were manic-depressive. Goertzel *et al.* noted that psychiatric disturbance was more common among the creators than among the leaders and, within the group of creators, more common among the artists than among the scientists. In a related study, Tomlinson-Keasey, Warren, and Elliott (1986) sought to predict suicide in a sample of 40 women from the Terman Genetic Studies of Genius data base. A total of eight women committed suicide as of 1964. These eight cases were compared with two control groups, 15 women who died of natural causes and were matched on age at death and 17 women who were still living in 1964. More than three-quarters of the entire sample of 40 female "geniuses" experienced transient depression. Among the eight who suicided, the depression was "severe and apparently unremitting."

Phillips (1982) reported on eight cases of manic-depression that he treated with lithium. Contrary to the findings of Jamison, Gerner, and Goodwin (1979), Phillips observed that the lithium seemed to have a beneficial effect on the creativity of his patients. He properly noted, however, that no conclusions could be drawn about creative output and lithium prophylaxis. It is doubtful that a profound disturbance of affect, such as manic-depressive illness, could facilitate the expression of creativity. Indeed, at least one study has provided evidence for a decrement in the functioning of the right cerebral hemisphere that is associated with depressive affect (Tucker, Stenslie, Roth, & Shearer, 1981). However, it may be, as Mitchell (1972) proposed, that creative writers and artists respond to their experiences with greater sensitivity and are thus at higher risk for suffering. Answers to these questions await additional studies with appropriate control groups, a tight operational definition of creativity, and some estimate of base rates. Otherwise it will be impossible to conclude that the observed rate of psychiatric symptoms in experimental groups exceeds the expected rate of those symptoms in the general population.

Scientists do not appear to be exempt from reports of mental illness. At a Donner Laboratory Seminar in Berkeley, California, Karlsson identified a number of highly creative scientists alleged to be mentally ill (Robinson, 1977). Karlsson said of Gregor Mendel, "He wasn't a man of religion. He joined a monastery because he had a nervous breakdown when he was seventeen years old. He continued to have breakdowns and had to get away from the rigors of having to make a living, as he put it" (p. 10). Of Charles Darwin, Karlsson commented that "psychiatrists who have analyzed his life history have concluded that he was manic depressive and not the victim of some exotic disease he may have picked up in South America" (p. 10). Karlsson also related that Sir Isaac Newton "wrote delusional letters which have been preserved, and psychiatrists who read them today say these are the productions of a paranoid schizophrenic" (p. 10). Included in Karlsson's roster of eminent individuals who exhibited signs of mental illness are Michael Faraday, Jack London, and Robert Frost.

Karlsson (1978) elaborated upon this theme in his book on creativity and psychosis:

As part of the present research, a survey was made of famous individuals who were born in the United States west of the Mississippi River before 1890. Since the population of that area was then still relatively small, the total number of men of world fame was found to be rather limited. The ten individuals so identified were Lee DeForest (inventor), T. S. Eliot (poet), Robert Frost (poet), Edwin Hubble (astronomer), Sinclair Lewis (novelist), Jack London (novelist), Edgar Lee Masters (poet), Ezra Pound (poet), Josiah Royce (philosopher), and Mark Twain (humorist). In this group it is reported that T. S. Eliot suffered a nervous breakdown at age thirty-three, Jack London exhibited manic and depressive episodes before committing suicide at age forty, and Ezra Pound was diagnosed as schizophrenic in his mid-fifties. In addition, it is recorded that Lee DeForest and Robert Frost, although apparently never considered psychotic, had episodes of moderately severe depression. Frost's sister and his children suffered from mental illness. Edgar Lee Masters had some kind of nervous exhaustion after writing his famous poems. Mark Twain also became rather melancholic in his later years, and his children exhibited mental disorders. (pp. 135–136)

Not surprisingly, Isaac Newton's mental status has been the subject of much consideration. In discussing several biographies of Newton, Holton (1978) concluded that "these notes and self-imposed exercises [Newton's diaries] are a record of Newton's anxiety, confessions, loneliness, repression of instinctual desires, shame, fantasies of bringing death to his stepfather, mother, and himself—and the dread of punishment for all these" (p. 270). Anthony Storr found that

Newton, particularly, is an apt subject for psychiatric characterization. As you know, Newton was born prematurely, some three months after his father's death. His mother remarried just after his third birthday, leaving him in the care of his grandmother; a betrayal which he never forgave. Newton grew up to be a recluse and a very hypochondriacal, anxious, insecure recluse into the bargain. He was intensely suspicious and quarrelsome, and in 1693 became sufficiently disturbed in mind for rumours of his insanity to gain wide acceptance. . . . The great creators often seem to be more the prey of intrapsychic conflict than most of us; and when we consider those men of genius whose achievements depend especially on a power of abstraction and dissociation from the immediate impact of the physical, like Descartes, Newton and Schopenhauer, it is not difficult to show that their genius and their psychopathology are intimately related. (Krebs & Shelley, 1975, p. 110)

The incident of 1693 has been described elsewhere as "a complete nervous collapse" in which Newton ended relationships, infrequently slept, reported nonexistent conversations, and accused friends of plotting against him (Broad, 1981). Parenthetically, Newton held such undignified titles as the "autocrat of science," "the dictatorial President of the Royal Society," and "the authoritarian Master of the Mint."

Charles Darwin has been the subject of lively debates as to whether he was afflicted by physical or mental illness. The fact that Darwin was healthy and vigorous in his twenties and a recluse in his early thirties was to set a pattern for the remainder of his life. His illness emerged while he was awaiting the departure of the *Beagle* and disappeared during the six years of the voyage. If nothing else can be concluded about Darwin, he was either a hypochondriac or very infirm. Between the years 1890 and 1895, he was said to suffer from prostration, deafness, neuralgia, bronchitis, influenza, lumbago, and liver problems (Winslow, 1971). Darwin also was the victim of chronic insomnia, headaches, "nervousness," and biliousness. All these symptoms, thought to be common to many prominent English, Victorians such as Thomas Huxley, George Eliot (a.k.a. Mary Ann Evans), Robert Browning, Herbert Spencer, and Thomas Carlyle, defined a loosely conceived malaise that Winslow (1971) called *dyspepsia*. Strictly speaking, dyspepsia is an old-fashioned word for indigestion. However, nervous dyspepsia is indigestion brought on by emotional turmoil and usually occurs in high strung, anxious, nervous individuals. Thus, it is not surprising that nervous dyspepsia would be accompanied by any one of a host of psychophysiological disorders.

Although it is strictly a historical aside, there is no more easily demonstrable association of inventive brilliance with the label of madness than that which comes from a group of men who met regularly in Birmingham, England, in the late eighteenth century. Erasmus Darwin (physician), Josiah Wedgwood (pottery manufacturer), James Watt (Scottish engineer), and Matthew Boulton (manufacturer and engineer) were four of the most inventive minds of eighteenth-century England. In fact, it has been said that these four men were the fathers of the Industrial Revolution and, indirectly, of all modern technology. The collective met on the night of a full moon and, hence, earned the name of the Lunar Society. The members of the society, not surprisingly, called themselves *Lunaticks*. Even without evidence that any of these men were in fact "lunatics", there was an irresistible inclination to associate their inventive genius with "lunacy."

Nordau (1900) had his own thoughts on the matter. In referring to the Industrial Revolution, he concluded that "we stand now in the midst of a severe mental epidemic" characterized by "degeneration and hysteria." Nordau believed that Schopenhauer, Nietzsche, Tolstoy, Ibsen, Wagner, and Zola were products of this degenerate, hysterical period.

Another scientist of prolific accomplishment, typically overlooked in discussions of mental disorder, is Sigmund Freud. Despite the libraries written by and about Freud, it is rarely suggested that the man himself was disturbed. One of the best authorities on the subject, Ernest Jones, stated quite unequivocally that "there is ample evidence that for ten years or so—roughly comprising the nineties—[Freud] suffered from a very considerable psychoneurosis" (Pickering, 1974, p. 220). Freud was well aware of his neuroses, as is apparent in a letter written to Fliess on July 7, 1897. In the letter he comments, "What has been going on inside me I still do not know. Something from the deepest depths of my neurosis has been obstructing any progress in the understanding of neuroses" (cited in Pickering, 1974, p. 224). The relationship between Freud's most original contributions and his psychic distress is an interesting one. Freud's writings were, in effect, an insightful reflection of his own turmoil. He stated, "I have long known that I can't be industrious when I am in good health; on the contrary, I need a degree of discomfort which I want to get rid of" (Pickering, 1974, p. 222).

One last case is the remarkable nineteenth-century English reformer and nurse, Florence Nightingale. The case of Nightingale is a most unusual one, rarely cited in psychiatric quarters, typically relegated to romantic tales of a gallant young woman slipping silently from one trench or foxhole to another, holding a flickering paraffin lamp and tending to the agony of the wounded. This image is not entirely incorrect, but it only scratches the surface of a truly remarkable person. During her stay in the Crimea, she undoubtedly endured no less the privations and pain than any of the young men she treated. She was overcome by dysentery, rheumatism, and almost died from Crimean (typhoid) fever. Despite all these distresses, her energy and devotion were boundless. That much of her life is common knowledge.

Her foreign service lasted roughly three years, from the time she took up residence at 1 Harley Street (1853) to her return from the Crimea after the war (1856). During this time, all her afflictions were organic, and she endured them with enormous courage and strength. From 1857 until the end of her life, however, she was invalided with what has been described as neurasthenia (nervous exhaustion or prostration) (Pickering, 1974). Nightingale's attacks of breathlessness and giddiness confined her to a couch or bed but in no way affected the prodigious amount of work she turned out. Indeed, her "illness" insulated her from all unwanted intrusions from the outside world, allowing her to devote every moment to her work.

Apparently, there was no organic basis to the debilitating "nervous" symptoms that incapacitated Nightingale throughout her ninety years. She was a fiery, relentless warrior who constantly gave battle and achieved victory—particularly where her male predecessors had failed. In a thoroughly male-dominated world, she invariably proved to be "a better man than their best" (Pickering, 1974). Although the conflicts that initiated or contributed to her neuroses are speculation, her expenditure of energy seemed to relate to her symptoms. When, in the latter years of her life, the symptoms abated, her extraordinary drive also declined. Her decline was not due exclusively to advanced age because it was visible in 1880 with her mother's death, thirty years before Nightingale died.

The cases and examples discussed thus far are illustrative of the long history of association between exceptional conduct (howsoever it was defined) and abnormal behavior, ranging from eccentricity to psychosis. It is essential to keep in mind that even informal diagnostic classification is inadvisable, and in most instances impossible. Writers have had to rely on archival documents, third-person accounts, and anecdotes. Thus, resulting "diagnoses," sometimes made several thousand years after the person was alive, are unreliable, imprecise, and certainly not compatible with modern nosology. Occasionally, writers even disagree as to the mere presence of pathology. Such a case was Michelangelo, who was given a clean bill of health by Lombroso (1910) but was said to be a melancholic by Tsanoff (1949).

A quick glance through the roster of those alleged to have been mentally disturbed might well leave one with the distinct impression that "everyone who was anyone" was afflicted. As we will see in the second half of this chapter, available research simply does not support such a conclusion. In Havelock Ellis's (1904) well-known study of British "geniuses," for example, he found that out of 1,030 names drawn from the *Dictionary of National Biography,* only 44 individuals (or 4.2%) had a demonstrable mental disorder. Obviously, this percentage would change somewhat if contemporary DSM-III criteria were applied. To play the devil's advocate, one may argue, of course, that the accomplishments of the individuals discussed in the first half of this chapter are of an order of magnitude greater (more creative, more exceptional, more enduring, and more revolutionary) than the accomplishments of most of the 986 sane entries that Ellis examined. This tends to be a moot point as it is difficult enough to define creativity, let alone to rank order degrees of creativity.

Many of Ellis's 986 "normals" may have been more or less deviant in cognitive style, though undeniably sane. Constable held a similar notion in 1905, "I deny the miraculous in genius; it is nothing more than a very exceptional deviation from the average" (quoted in Becker, 1978, p. 61). Too great a deviance in cognitive style will, of course, cast the ominous shadow of mental illness, and there is no reason to suspect that there should not be at least as many genuine cases of psychosis among the highly creative as is found in the general population. Similarly, if we take the incidences of non-psychotic depression, personality disorder, and neurosis found in the general population and include them among the highly creative, we would expect to find that a respectable fraction of creative people had emotional problems.

Research on the Personality Correlates of Creativity

Over the past several decades, a number of investigators have attempted to identify the personality traits most often associated with creativity. Principal research efforts in this regard have been conducted by Cattell and his colleagues using the Sixteen Personality Factor Test (16 PF), MacKinnon, who used the California Psychological Inventory (CPI) and the Minnesota Multiphasic Personality Inventory (MMPI), and Roe, who used the Rorschach and the Thematic Apperception Test (TAT).

The seminal research of Roe (e.g., 1951, 1952, 1953, 1956) sought an answer to the question "What makes a scientist?" through in-depth case histories of scientists who were nominated as eminent by peers. Roe's (1951) first study of 22 physical scientists was later expanded to include biologists, social scientists-psychologists, and anthropologists (1952). Among the multitude of findings drawn from her research, the following points are noteworthy: (1) as children the scientists were highly independent and self-sufficient; they typically enjoyed school and were avid readers; they were slow in social development, shy, introverted; and they admired and respected their fathers; (2) in the child's home there was stability and harmony; the father was usually a professional with advanced education; and there was an intellectual ambience in the home that projected a love of learning and a respect for knowledge; and (3) as adults the scientists were indifferent to religion; they often had the fortune of experiencing one or two outstanding mentors who were highly influential and supportive; and, although they typically performed well on aptitude and intelligence tests, their success was more a function of hard work and dedication than sheer brilliance. Roe (1952) noted that a high proportion (39 out of 64) of the scientists were first-born. In her discussion of birth order, Roe stated, "It seems probable that all this may point to the most important single factor in the making of a scientist—the need and ability to develop personal independence to a high degree" (p. 25). Since first-born children tend to be more dependent than later-born children, Roe suggested that the scientist's pronounced independence may be in reaction to overdependence.

The influential work of Roe and of Terman (1926) was followed, and in good measure supported, by the extensive research efforts of Raymond Cattell and his colleagues using the 16 PF. Drevdahl (1954) compared "creative" and "noncreative" students on the 16 PF (Cattell & Stice, 1957), finding that creative students were significantly more skeptical, aloof, critical, withdrawn, disciplined, insightful, cautious, radical (experimenting, analytic, free-thinking), and resourceful

(cited in Cattell & Drevdahl, 1955). A similar study by Wright (1954) found that men of high scholastic achievement could be distinguished from those of low scholastic achievement by greater skepticism, aloofness, withdrawal, emotional maturity, self-confidence, and tendency to be tense and driven (cited in Cattell & Drevdahl, 1955). Drevdahl (1956) found that creative students were more withdrawn and quiescent than noncreative students, as well as superior in verbal facility, fluency, flexibility, and originality. Drevdahl and Cattell (1958) found large differences when comparing creative artists and writers with the general population. The "creatives" appeared to be stable but living under considerable strain. They were more skeptical, extraverted, radical, self-sufficient, bohemian (unconventional, imaginative, absentminded), and emotionally sensitive than the noncreative controls. Of particular interest was that the artists were even more tense, extraverted, and radical than the writers. Cross, Cattell, and Butcher (1967) also clearly differentiated artists from a matched control group. The artists were low in emotional and superego strength and high in bohemian tendency.

Cattell and Drevdahl (1955) contrasted the general adult population and a university undergraduate population with three groups of scientists: researchers, teachers, and administrators. Researchers, compared with teachers and administrators, were more skeptical, aloof, self-sufficient, emotionally unstable, bohemian, and radical. They were also significantly more assertive, competitive, suspicious or jealous, and withdrawn. The scientists as a whole were significantly more skeptical, aloof, self-sufficient, intellectually adaptable, cautious, withdrawn, and radical than the undergraduate student group and significantly more competitive, assertive, adventurous, sensitive, tolerant, intellectually adaptable, self-confident, emotionally mature, self-indulgent, frivolous, and controlled or compulsive than the general population.

These results generally agree with the Drevdahl (1954) and Wright (1954) studies. The results of these studies are further supported by a subjective assessment of the biographies of 100 distinguished researchers (mostly U.S. and British), in which Cattell (1966) concluded that these researchers would be more skeptical, aloof, intellectually adaptable, self-sufficient, competitive, assertive, suspicious or jealous, and disciplined or conscientious than less-eminent members of the same disciplines. Cattell and Butcher (1968) stated that eminent scientists are skeptical, aloof, emotionally unstable, self-sufficient, and bohemian. The emotional instability of the scientist derives from a high I factor (emotional sensitivity) and not a low C factor (ego weakness). Cattell and Butcher (1968) also cited a study by Tollefson (1961) that provided an equation using "beta weights" that represented correlations between primary factors on the 16 PF and ratings of research contribution. The equation was based on a sample of 53 Ph.D. chemists who were employed in the research department of a large oil company.

$$\text{Research performance} = 0.25B + 0.46C + 0.32E - 0.46I + 0.33N + 0.45Q_1 + 0.29Q_2 - 0.35$$

where, B = general intelligence, C = ego strength, E = dominance, I = emotional sensitivity, N = shrewdness, Q_1 = radicalism, Q_2 = self-sufficiency, and 0.35 = a constant.

Stein (1971) also reported findings on a sample of chemists. He found that the creative chemists were more autonomous, integrative, more "oriented to achievement and acceptance of their own inner impulses," "placed more emphasis on harmony and form and less on mystical values," and "gave more evidence of psychological well-being" than a comparison group of less-creative colleagues.

Thus far we have spoken primarily of research scientists and college students. At least one study clearly demonstrated that 16 PF profiles of 153 writers of fiction ("imaginative literature") bore a striking similarity to profiles of creative scientists (Drevdahl & Cattell, 1958). A similar profile was also found of artists selected from *Who's Who in American Art*. Drevdahl (1956) reported the same finding when looking at liberal arts graduate students who were chosen as highly creative. In a 1966 review chapter, Cattell wrote,

For the present I am inclined to see the general evidence as agreeing with Terman that emotional stability may be low for literary geniuses, but that the average level of ego strength and emotional stability is distinctly higher for effective scientific researchers than for the general population. (p. 122)

This is not surprising if we recall that the origin of the Cattell and Butcher (1968) finding of instability in scientists was emotional sensitivity (high I).

The consistent findings from the 16 PF research are that scientists are more skeptical, detached, critical, intellectually adaptable, and self-sufficient than their comparison groups and that students or artists judged to be creative or high achievers are

more skeptical, detached, and withdrawn than controls judged to be less creative or low achievers. There is a tendency for creative subjects to be more radical and unconventional than noncreative subjects. Findings regarding emotional stability, ego strength, and anxiety are more equivocal.

A similar approach to the 16 PF research deserving mention is the well-known work of the late Donald MacKinnon (1960, 1962a,b, 1965). MacKinnon used the CPI and the MMPI to examine groups of architects rated by professionals in the field as being highly creative. MacKinnon (1960) reported that his creative architects were more interested in symbolic ideas than in concrete ideas and in implications of detail rather than the detail itself. Even though the architects scored high on the psychopathic-deviate (Pd) and schizophrenia (Sc) scales of the MMPI, this was interpreted as indicating greater unusualness of thought process, less inhibition, and freer expression of impulse and imagery (MacKinnon, 1962a). Another prominent feature of the MMPI profiles was a very high peak on the femininity (Mf) scale.

In brief, MacKinnon's research also supports the work of Roe and Terman. He found that creative scientists are introverted, nonconforming, autonomous, yet adaptive, striving and assertive, open-minded or flexible in working style, and intuitive (MacKinnon, 1967, 1972).

The extensive research to come out of Berkeley's Institute of Personality Assessment and Research (IPAR) cannot be done justice here, but it would be inexcusable to omit mention of that massive report prepared by MacKinnon, Crutchfield, Barron, Block, Gough, and Harris in 1958 for the Air Force. The essence of that report was translated into book form by Barron in 1963. Close to 200 personality assessment variables were related to an overall "originality composite" score. The score on the Concept Mastery Test was used to partial out the effect on intelligence. The full sample of 343 officers (all captains) was examined according to an abbreviated originality composite (four of the eight measures) and the Concept Mastery Test score. Two groups were contrasted—one with scores falling one standard deviation above the mean on originality and one sigma (standard deviation) below the mean on intelligence ($N = 15$) and a comparison group with scores falling one sigma below the mean on originality and one sigma above the mean on intelligence. The former ("original") group was characterized by the following adjectives: affected, aggressive, demanding, dependent, dominant, forceful, impatient, initiative, outspoken, sarcastic, strong, and suggestible; the latter (''intelligent'') group was characterized as mild, optimistic, pleasant, quiet, and unselfish.

Another psychometric contribution to the assessment of the creative personality is a 30-item scale devised by Gough (1979). The Adjective Check List (Gough & Heilbrun, 1965) was administered to 12 separate samples comprising 1,701 subjects. Based on an item analysis of the 300-item Adjective Check List, 18 positive and 12 negative items were chosen (positive: capable, clever, confident, egotistical, humorous, individualistic, informal, insightful, intelligent, wide interests, inventive, original, reflective, resourceful, self-confident, sexy, snobbish, and unconventional; negative: affected, cautious, commonplace, conservative, conventional, dissatisfied, honest, narrow interests, mannerly, sincere, submissive, and suspicious). The resulting Creative Personality Scale was then related to six measures of creativity as well as criterion evaluations. This new scale correlated positively and significantly with all six creativity measures but surpassed them with respect to validity.

For a comprehensive discussion of research on personality correlates of creativity as of 1980, the reader is directed to Barron and Harrington's (1981) excellent review article as well as the relevant contributions to this volume for more recent work.

Albert Einstein's remark that scientists are ''rather odd, uncommunicative, solitary fellows'' typifies one common stereotype of the highly creative individual—eccentricity. In the writings of Cattell and his colleagues, ''bohemian tendency'' comes to mind; in the writings of MacKinnon, ''nonconforming'' and ''autonomous.'' It is easy to collect anecdotes and personal statements that seem to support such an idea. Scholander (1978), a noted physiologist, remarked: ''Like a vulgar streaker I shall expose myself in the limelight. I frequently ask myself how has it been possible to live in such an exciting and happy life being such an irregular and irresponsible person?'' (p. 1). In an entirely different context, Ogilvy (1971) commented:

Few of the great creators have bland personalities. They are cantankerous egotists, the kind of men who are unwelcome in the modern corporation. Consider Winston Churchill. He drank like a fish. He was capricious and willful. When opposed, he sulked. He was rude to fools. He was wildly extravagant. He wept on the slightest provocation. His conversation was Rabelaisian. He bullied his subordinates. (p. 208)

It may be of limited value to demonstrate the presence of eccentricity in creative people. First of all, we have no reasonable way of ascertaining the amount of comparable eccentricity found in the general population. Second, eccentricity does not necessarily provide even *prima facie* evidence for the presence of major mental illness. Eccentricity denotes a peculiarity of behavior, and any behavior that deviates sufficiently from the norm or from convention may be viewed as eccentric. In the above examples, Einstein pointed to introversion, Scholander to irresponsibility, and Ogilvy to lability of affect. Perhaps the one least-common denominator, which would be of interest, is the finding that eccentricity could be operationally defined in terms of deviant mood states.

Although it is most challenging to speculate as to what personality traits reliably turn up among highly creative individuals, a note of caution is worth mentioning. As Taylor (1960) pointed out, the relationship between a personality trait and creativity may be dependent upon other traits, perhaps the gestalt of traits, that make up the individual. Furthermore, the trait–creativity relationship may be task- or situation-specific. In other words, we should keep in mind that the interaction of creativity with critical environmental factors is at least as important—maybe more important—than the ''main effect'' of creativity.

From my own perspective, the single most important methodological problem in research on creativity concerns the criterion itself. As Hudson (1970) noted, creativity is now so much a part of our jargon that it has come to refer to everything from performance on a psychological test to one's relationship with one's spouse. The criterion problem was discussed in detail by Shapiro (1970), who spoke of ''ultimate'' and ''concurrent'' criteria of creative activity. An ultimate criterion is based on an individual's total output over a lifetime. This obviously can only be assessed retrospectively or longitudinally in the prospective style of Terman's study. In either case, it does not permit a current assessment of ongoing activity. Thus, concurrent validation became a favored approach. Shapiro discussed three types of concurrent methodology. The first type is exemplified by Guilford's research (e.g., 1950, 1959, 1966, 1968). Guilford assumed that the factor analysis of his tests provided construct validity. A second type uses tests to divide a sample into ''high'' and ''low'' creatives and then contrasts those subgroups on personality tests. If the subgroups separated out as predicted, one could assume that the original tests used for dichotomization (usually of an aptitude nature) were valid. The third type employs a battery of instruments and correlates the resulting scores with some external criterion. All three methods lack one essential ingredient—a truly valid external criterion. Disparate groups fall under the experimental umbrella of creativity, for example, high scorers on a multitude of different instruments, peer nominees, Nobel laureates, and subjects chosen through "consensual validation" (i.e., those "assumed" to be creative) and subjects chosen as a result of some arbitrarily established level of accomplishment (i.e., number of journal articles or books published and contest awards). Studies have examined preschoolers, college students, subjects at the apex of their careers, and subjects at the twilight of their careers. Surely, the creative activity of a preschooler does not fall in the same category as the creative activity of a fifty-year-old seasoned veteran, just as the creative performance of a college sophomore does not fall in the same category as a Nobel laureate.

Creativity is so complex, multifaceted, and heterogeneous that it has all but lost any utility as an empirical construct. It would seem, therefore, that there is an urgent need for empirically derived taxonomic differentiation, wherein we can begin to establish the fundamental attributes of the various products or processes we label as creative. All areas of psychological science have, as Melton (1964) noted, a taxonomic burden; however, the importance of taxonomic differentiation is maximal when the area of inquiry is diverse and amorphous, as is certainly the case with creativity.

Research on Cognitive Aspects of Creativity

Just as the preceding section on personality traits inquires as to the temperamental or motivational aspects of creativity, this section examines the cognitive and intellectual features of creativity. Undoubtedly, the single most important impetus in this area was provided by Guilford (1950, 1956a,b, 1959, 1966, 1968, 1970). Thirty-seven years have elapsed since Guilford (1950) first presented his hypotheses regarding creative thinking. The fecundity of those hypotheses may be measured in more than two decades of fruitful research.

Guilford's mission was to identify primary cognitive traits related to creativity. One primary trait concerned fluency of thinking, which was broken down into "word fluency" (the ability to produce words comprising a certain letter or set of letters), "associational fluency" (the ability to generate words of similar meaning), "expressional fluency" (the ability to generate phrases or sentences), and "ideational fluency" (the ability to generate ideas to fulfill specified requirements in a given time). Another primary trait concerned flexibility of thinking. This was divided into "spontaneous flexibility" (the ability to generate a wide variety of ideas rapidly and without perseveration) and "adaptive flexibility" (the ability to generate unusual solutions for problems). Guilford also proposed, as primary traits, "originality" (the ability to perceive remote associations, generate responses rated as "clever," or produce responses of low frequency in the population), "redefinition" (the ability to reconceptualize a familiar interpretation and apply it in a unique situation), and "elaboration" (the ability to extend a simple design to a more complex or intricate design). The reader may well be correct in surmising that there is little difference between originality and adaptive flexibility. Guilford commented that originality may be a case of adaptive flexibility when verbally meaningful material is involved, whereas nonverbal input is more in keeping with the intention of adaptive flexibility.

Guilford identified three factors that were based upon factor analyses of inventories assessing "thinking interests": tolerance of ambiguity (willingness to accept uncertainty and avoidance of rigidity), convergent thinking (thinking through to one correct answer), and divergent thinking (a search that uncovers several answers). The general line of research that followed pursued the notion that the original person should be one who is tolerant of ambiguity, flexible (as opposed to rigid), and divergent in thinking. In his 1956 review article, Guilford (1956b) concluded that convergent and divergent thinking are complementary aspects of intellectual ability, that the two can be easily distinguished factorially, and that convergent thinking comprised the bulk of most general intelligence tests.

The next step in the development of Guilford's theory of intellect was reported in 1955 (see Guilford, 1966). He grouped 42 factors of intellect into six categories, according to the type of thinking involved. By 1957, the number of intellectual factors had increased to 46 and the number of major categories were reduced to five (cognition [discovery of information], memory, divergent thinking, convergent thinking, and evaluation [testing of information]). These five mental activities or "operations" form one dimension of a three-dimensional cubical model that Guilford called the "structure of intellect." A second dimension consists of six "products" into which information may be converted after processing, and a third dimension consists of four broad types of input that the individual must discriminate between (figural, symbolic, semantic, and behavioral). The cube consists of 120 ($5 \times 6 \times 4$) unique cells, each representing an independent feature of intellectual ability. For present purposes, this complex model will serve only a limited function. A rather small slice of the cube represents creative thinking. According to the three dimensions, that slice would be the divergent-thinking operation cut across most products and including three of the contents (figural, symbolic, and semantic). This means that, at most, 18 of the 120 cells are involved with creative thinking. However, that small slice represents only "classic" creativity (artists, composers, and writers). Guilford (1956a,b, 1966, 1968) has spelled out the range of creative-thinking abilities found in the structure-of-intellect model. The aforementioned classic type provides fluency of verbal expression, spontaneous flexibility, adaptive flexibility, and elaboration. Two other types define scientific or mathematical creativity: convergent thinking, cutting across figural, symbolic, or semantic transformation and yielding "flexibility of closure" or redefinition, and cognition, cutting across figural, symbolic, or semantic implications and yielding "sensitivity to problems."

One interesting note on the relationship between convergent and divergent thinking was provided by Haddon and Lytton (1968). These investigators reported findings that "strongly confirm" the complementary relationship between convergence and divergence, as well as the association between independence and high ability level; that is, convergence and divergence more or less overlap at lower ability levels and become increasingly independent at higher ability levels. Additionally, the authors found strong evidence in support of their hypothesis that informal schools develop qualities of personality that facilitate divergent thinking. The tight rein, firm governance, and rigid schedule of the formal school were more conducive to development of convergent thinking. The sparse literature on the heritability of divergent thinking provides little evidence to support the genetic basis of diver-

gence (Pezzullo, Thorsen, & Madaus, 1972; Vandenberg, 1968), thus lending support to the influence of social learning.

A study that compared Guilford's theory with Mednick's (1962) associative theory of creativity found striking support for the Guilford position (Korb & Frankiewicz, 1979). In brief, Mednick argued that one cognitive process was responsible for creativity, whereas Korb and Frankiewicz found two significant discriminant functions with different variates on each. The investigators looked at 146 college students (juniors or above) who were majoring in art, creative writing, music, or mathematics. The judges (there were 12) determined that 77 of the students were creative, whereas the remainder of the students constituted the noncreative comparison group. The creative writers were "original in a semantic context, fluent and flexible in both the semantic and figural content areas, imaginative, emotionally undisciplined, self-indulgent, interested in reflective thinking and willing to disregard rules" (p. 20). The musicians turned out to be very similar to the writers. The creative artists, however, lacked "fluency and flexibility in both the semantic and figural content areas, while being conscientious, controlled and disinterested in reflective thinking" (p. 20). The mathematicians were similar to the artists, though the authors indicated that the mathematicians did possess an interest in reflective thinking.

In sum, convergent- and divergent-thinking styles blend together at lower levels of ability and separate at higher levels of ability. Creativity may derive from either thinking style, and it may do so with little or no regard to profession (i.e., the divergence of artists and the convergence of scientists). At the outer reaches of sophisticated problem solving and artistic creation, the mode of endeavor is probably an individual characteristic rather than a professional one. As Nicholls (1972) pointed out, the lack of association between tests of divergent thinking and high levels of creativity may well be the failure of the test (i.e., to take convergence into account).

Similarities in cognitive styles between normals and psychotics have been discussed in detail by McConaghy (1960, 1961; McConaghy & Clancy, 1968). McConaghy (1960) distinguished two modes of thinking that reflect predispositions to psychosis. In one case, filtering mechanisms are impaired, thereby permitting the intrusion of irrelevant associations. Thought processes are vague, dominated by intuition. This disorder is said to affect about 10% of the population and carries a warning sign of schizophrenic vulnerability. In the other case, the capacity for making logical attributions is enhanced. Thus, once a conclusion is reached, it is adhered to with greater-than-normal devotion. In this instance logic has been said to triumph over common sense, a condition that may predispose to paranoia.

McConaghy (1961) identified the former mode of thinking as "allusive" (considered to be less pejorative than "loose") and proposed that it may be observed in a wide variety of people, many of whom never become schizophrenic. Allusive thinking is characterized by imprecise (overabstract) and inappropriate speech (similar to overinclusion). McConaghy (1960) found that normal college students with allusive thinking had less difficulty learning the central portion of a word list than students not showing allusive thinking. Because central nervous system (CNS) inhibition impedes serial learning, it was concluded to be weak in allusive cases. Normally, the inhibitory process produces attentional constriction. When inhibition is weak (like blinders removed from a horse), focusing or "tunnel" thinking is impaired. An intrusion of peripheral and irrelevant information produces overabstraction. McConaghy and Clancy (1968) administered a test for allusive thinking to university students and their parents, finding that significantly more students with high scores (presence of allusive thinking) had a parent with a high score than students with low scores. It was concluded that high test scores among family members, as evidenced in samples of both normals (1968) and parents of schizophrenics (1960), supported the hypothesis that the test is measuring allusive thinking in both groups. The latter finding was later replicated by Lidz, Wild, Schafer, Rosman, and Fleck (1963) and Rosman, Wild, Ricci, Fleck, and Lidz (1964).

McConaghy's conceptualizations are based, in good measure, upon the work of Pavlov (1955), who also distinguished two personality types. The artistic type, prone to hysterical or manic-depressive reactions, is intense, vivid, and highly responsive to external stimulation. The thinking type, prone to obsessive-compulsive and schizophrenic reactions, is quiet, ruminative, and hypersensitive to excessive stimulation. It was Pavlov's early writing that led McConaghy (1961), Claridge (1972), and others to attribute allusive thinking to weak levels of CNS inhibition resulting from low cortical excitability.

There is marked resemblance between the cognitive styles characterizing creative thought that Cattell and his colleagues sought to define and the psychotic loosening (or tightening) of ideational boundaries that McConaghy described. In the latter case (McConaghy), the disorder may be called over- or underinclusion, and in the former case (Cattell), the gift is called creativity. The apparent difference between the divergent thinking, loose associations, and irrelevant themes of psychotics and the amazing conceptual leaps, cognitive flexibility, and serendipitous discoveries of creative artists and scientists is one of *control*. Psychotic thinking is unbridled and capricious, whereas creative thinking is rationally directed and purposeful. In sum, it appears that there is reason to suspect a continuity between normal and pathological thinking, a point convincingly argued by Claridge (1972). Thought disorder is not "present or absent" but measured as a single dimension with numerous shades of gray. Thus, typical modes of psychotic thinking are also found in the general (normal) population, only in less severe or debilitating fashion. The existence of such cognitive styles may facilitate creativity as well as reflect a genetic predisposition to psychosis. Claridge (1972) commented that the traits on which creative people distinguish themselves are similar to those traits which possess an increased loading on personality profiles associated with schizophrenia.

There is sparse, though interesting, evidence that associates the Claridge research with the Guilford research. Claridge, Canter, and Hume (1973) looked at personality variation in monozygotic and dizygotic twins, using an extensive battery of psychophysiological tests. The investigators defined a personality dimension of "psychoticism," based on a principal-components analysis of the psychophysiology data. They discovered, among other things, that psychoticism was related to scores on tests of Guilford's divergent thinking. Farmer (1974) also reported that the psychoticism score on Eysenck's Personality Questionnaire (EPQ) was reliably associated with the originality score on one of Guilford's tests (cited in Woody & Claridge, 1977). Woody and Claridge (1977) administered the EPQ and tests of divergent/convergent thinking to university students. The association of divergent thinking with psychoticism (on the EPQ) was strongly confirmed, though the hypothesis of an inverse relationship between psychoticism and convergent thinking was rejected. As Woody and Claridge pointed out, these clear findings may be interpreted two ways. If indeed the psychoticism scale on the

EPQ is valid, the results support the association of disposition to psychosis with divergent thinking. The authors go one step further and suggest that the results relate psychosis to creativity, though it is far from certain that divergent thinking is equatable with creativity. Another way of looking at the same results would be to interpret the data as providing validity for the psychoticism scale. Logically, a heritable predisposition to psychosis should have as a primary feature some distinctive cognitive style. According to the Woody and Claridge study, high-psychoticism students showed marked divergent thinking, though none of the predicted cognitive slowness that is characteristic of many schizophrenics.

Most of the foregoing research is predicated upon two fundamental assumptions. To reiterate: (1) there is a genetic predisposition to psychosis that manifests itself as a nonpsychotic schizoidlike personality in the normal population; and (2) this schizoid profile is, in part, characterized by a thinking style similar to that found in psychosis. Because highly creative individuals may display thinking styles similar to psychotics, it has been theorized that such individuals possess a predisposition to psychosis. This might explain why creative people are frequently perceived as "eccentric," like fish out of place in the normal ocean. This may also explain why so many highly distinguished individuals have been the apparent victims of some form of mental illness.

The second assumption—that similar cognitive, attentional, or information-processing strategies may be found in schizophrenics and creatives—has been examined in several investigations. Dykes and McGhie (1976) predicted that similarities between creativity and psychosis were attributable to common attentional (overinclusive) strategies. Three groups were contrasted: highly creative students, uncreative (equally intelligent) students, and acute nonparanoid schizophrenics. The measure of creativity was Cropley's (1968) paper-and-pencil test. According to two object-sorting tasks and a dichotic-shadowing task, similar strategies were employed by the schizophrenics and the high-creativity students. Both groups took in a wider range of input than the less-creative students. The broad attentional focus of the schizophrenic seemed to be involuntary and unharnessed, resulting in impaired performance, whereas the creative individuals possessed a cognitive flexibility that permitted effective processing of stimulus overload without, as it were, blowing a fuse. The flexibility

of the creative students enabled them to opt for a more convergent strategy when that was deemed more efficient. The authors concluded with an important comment. They noted that narrow attentional focus on key elements of a problem might facilitate problem solving; however, the strategy of encompassing and assimilating a wide range of information is more advantageous when it comes to "original" thinking. Again, it is apparent that the difference, at least on a superficial level, between the creative students and the schizophrenics is one of voluntary control over processing of input. Another interesting point emerged from the Dykes and McGhie study. Presumably the schizophrenics, all inpatients, were medicated, though this fact is not stated. In the event of medication, one would expect "truncated" performance. Free of medication, schizophrenic performance might be considerably more extreme, allowing one to envision a more Gaussian distribution, with schizophrenics not using the "same" strategy as normals but employing an extreme form of that strategy.

Cropley and Sikand (1973) looked at the ways in which the information processing of creatives and schizophrenics differed from normals. Five aspects of information processing (general complexity, flexible complexity, flexibility, differentiation, and general incongruity adaptation level) were examined in 80 adults (40 controls, 20 schizophrenics, and 20 creatives). The creative people were in the arts (as opposed to the sciences) and were so defined according to Eiduson's (1958) criteria—active participation in some field acknowledged as creative and peer recognition. The investigators found that there were useful and reliable ways to differentiate the chronic schizophrenics from the creatives. The creatives were superior to schizophrenics and normals in tolerance for incongruity in information input. On the other hand, schizophrenics differed from creatives and normals in complexity, flexibility, and differentiation. It was speculated that "creative thinkers can tolerate strain (drive for incongruity reduction) and continue to employ broad categorizing strategies in concept formation, whereas non-creatives cannot" (p. 467).

Over the past several decades, there has been a strong attraction to the concept of divergent thinking as an operational construct for defining creativity. It is a clean, simple concept and can be measured easily with a variety of different tests. Additionally, anecdotal reports seem to suggest that something like divergence captures the "essence" of creativity. This enthusiasm survives despite Guilford's own note of caution, as well as the research, indicating that divergent thinking does not correlate highly with creativity (e.g., Nicholls, 1972). There are at least three possible explanations: (1) divergent thinking is only one of several independent cognitive styles that facilitate creativity; (2) divergent thinking interacts with another style, such as convergent thinking; and (3) the criteria used to define or measure creativity failed to capture the intended behavior.

Hasenfus and Magaro (1976) found, in their review of the literature, that "the schizophrenic 'deficit' does in some instances equal creativity" (p. 348). These instances included ideational fluency and overinclusion, as well as word association. In the latter case, it was observed that both schizophrenics and creatives express remote and unusual associations. It was also noted that remote associations are more typical of chronic, nonparanoid schizophrenics, whereas ideational fluency is more characteristic of paranoid schizophrenics. Keefe and Magaro (1980) administered two creativity tests to 10 paranoid and 10 nonparanoid schizophrenics, 10 nonpsychotic psychiatric controls, and 10 normal subjects. The nonparanoid schizophrenics were significantly more creative than the paranoid schizophrenics and the psychiatric controls on the Alternate Uses Test (AUT). In addition, the nonparanoid schizophrenics produced significantly more "highly creative" responses than the normal subjects. No group differences relating to creativity were found on the Revised Art Scale (RAS). Thus, ideational fluency (as measured by the AUT) and not perceptual complexity (as measured by the RAS) provided support for the Hasenfus and Magaro hypothesis that the empirical constructs of schizophrenia and creativity are equivalent. Keefe and Magaro were appropriately prudent in their discussion of the results, pointing out that an equivalence of cognitive processes does not imply an equivalence of mental status. In other words, the Keefe and Magaro findings suggest that certain types of schizophrenics exhibit cognitive processes that are similar to the ones employed by creative people. The study does not provide evidence that creative people are schizophrenic.

A most notable contribution to our understanding of the relationship between creativity and information processing comes from the research of Martindale (1977–1978) and with his colleagues (Martindale & Hasenfus, 1978; Martindale & Hines, 1975; Martindale & Armstrong, 1974; Martindale &

Greenough, 1973; Martindale, Hines, Mitchell, & Covello, 1984). Martindale accumulated evidence that relates creativity (as measured in college students using the Remote Associates Test and the Alternate Uses Test) to low levels of cortical activation, variability in level of activation, and disinhibition. The conclusion drawn by Martindale and Hines (1975) associating disinhibition with creativity appears to be consistent with expectation. Disinhibition, or "dehabituation," is the use of a novel stimulus to revive a habituated orientation reaction. It was a phenomenon ascribed by Pavlov to dissipation of inhibition. An adjunctive, albeit not incidental, feature of this phenomenon may be the recultivating and reconceptualizing of past associations and experiences, giving rise to fresh insights and novel ways of looking at old ideas.

Martindale hypothesized that primary process cognition is associated with either high or low arousal, whereas the secondary process is associated with medium arousal. Efficient task performance is usually optimized at medium levels of arousal, with performance dropping off when arousal is too low or too high. It has been assumed in the past that, as task difficulty increases, the optimal level of arousal decreases. This would suggest that low arousal favors creativity. Such a conclusion assumes that creativity has something to do with task complexity. It makes more sense to suppose that, in cases where "need for solitude" is a prerequisite for creative inspiration, low arousal is facilitatory. As Martindale (1977–1978) pointed out, even the often-noted listlessness of creative individuals can be attributed to either high or low arousal. These findings were integrated by Martindale in the following remarks:

It is hypothesized that highly creative individuals have a high resting level of activation and are thus overreactive to weak stimuli. Highly creative individuals also have a low threshold for protective inhibition so that slightly stronger stimuli elicit a paradoxical reaction; that is, further stimulation elicits decreases in arousal. (1977–1978, p. 80)

In a more recent report, Martindale *et al.* (1984) again hypothesized that creativity involved the use of primary process cognition which would be accompanied by right-hemisphere activation. Three studies supported the hypothesis that highly creative students would exhibit greater right-hemisphere than left-hemisphere EEG activity during creative activity. It is not possible in this chapter to do justice to Martindale's research; however, the findings from his studies draw support from many quarters, including the literatures on evoked responses, lateralization and hemispheric deficit, and input regulation.

A different conception of cognitive process in creativity was provided by Rothenberg (1976, 1979, 1983). Two processes operative in creativity were defined as Janusian and homospatial thinking. The Janusian process "consists of actively conceiving two or more opposite, contradictory, or antithetical concepts, images, or ideas simultaneously" (1976, p. 18). The term derives from the Roman god Janus, who looked in two directions at the same time. The homospatial ("same space") process "consists of actively conceiving two or more discrete entities occupying the same space, a conception leading to the articulation of new identities" (1976, p. 18). Thus, the homospatial process integrates Janusian thoughts. In the former case, logically unrelated entities are conceived of at the same point in time, and, in the latter case, those discrete entities are "superimposed, fused, or otherwise brought together in the mind and totally fill its perceptual space" (p. 18). Thus, the initial and highly distinctive characteristic of creative thought process is the simultaneous conception of two or more antithetical concepts. For this very reason, the process must transcend logic, because the integrated elements are contradictory. The homospatial process is the creation of harmonious coexistence out of opposing and disharmonious ideas.

The putative relationship of these thought processes to psychosis is an interesting one. Homospatial thinking is a process of sophisticated spatial abstraction; it is nonconcrete. At the same time, such thinking does not violate the laws of logic. In fact, Rothenberg calls it "translogical." Psychotic thinking may be characterized by the illogical association of unlike entities. Two points are worth noting. First, creativity often transcends logic, placing emphasis on intuition or speculation. Second, the illogic of psychotic thinking may represent decompensation from a formerly high level of abstraction to a translogical plane devoid of logic. Support for the association between Janusian thinking and creativity and the dissimilarity between the performance of 12 Nobel laureate scientists and 18 mentally ill patients was provided in a more recent study by Rothenberg (1983).

A critical review of the creativity literature by Dellas and Gaier (1970) concluded with the statement that "the roots of creativity do not seem to lie in convergent or divergent thinking, but rather in the personality and motivational aspects of char-

acter" (p. 68). This conclusion illustrates a "transcendentalism" that requires clarification. Personality traits may be confounded with styles of thinking. For instance, personality traits, such as introspective, ruminative, analytical, and cerebral, also suggest a clear style of thinking. The style may be deviant enough to be noteworthy, though obviously not deviant enough to be psychotic. Taken to an extreme, that same style might be labeled underinclusive thought disorder. Logically, where deviance in thinking has not approached the threshold of psychopathology, one would not expect to find a relationship between creativity and mental disorder. Many of the personality and cognitive features that Dellas and Gaier found associated with creativity may be defined alternatively as modes of processing information (such as openness to internal and external stimuli, ideational fluency, discriminative observation, and intuitiveness). In fact, the authors found that the data support the conclusion that the personality traits of creatives "develop fairly early." This would seem to suggest that these traits, whether they relate to personality or cognition, have an endogenous component.

Concluding Thoughts and Speculations

A Metatheoretical Bridge

The intent of this chapter has been to explore the hypothetical relationship between extraordinary creativity and mental illness. At this point, we may fairly conclude that creativity and major mental illness (i.e., psychosis) are *not causally related*. The crucial question, however, is not whether creativity and mental illness are causally linked, but whether our understanding of mental illness offers any insight into the creative process. The question is inspired by the seemingly large number of highly creative individuals who have been sufficiently disturbed to come to the attention of historians. Out of the total pool of, for instance, highly creative writers, if the number who were demonstrably disturbed exceeds the base rate for that disturbance in the general population, then the (possibly) coincidental association between creativity and disturbance in those cases invites plausible explanation.

I have sought to provide (it is hoped) a plausible explanation in the form of a theoretical model based upon a unidimensional, neurocognitive view of thought process (Prentky, 1979; 1980). I proposed that there is an input (information processing) con-

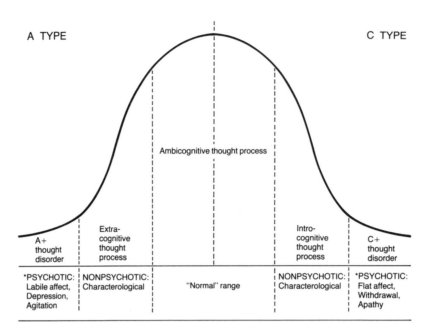

Figure 1. A neurocognitive, unidimensional model for the distribution of thought process in the general population; *illustrative clinical descriptors.

tinuum ranging from extreme constriction to extreme expansion, and that the tendency toward one mode or the other is normally distributed in the population (see Figure 1). The overlap between creativity and mental illness blends somewhere along this continuum. Excess deviation toward either extreme results in thought disorder, whereas some hypothetical "optimum deviation" promotes creativity without risk of major mental illness. When this optimum deviation slides farther out into one of the tails of the distribution, normality slips into abnormality. Because creative people "live" farther from the hypothetical norm and, hence, are closer to the fringes of deviation, there may be a higher incidence of psychopathology among this group. This increased incidence of psychopathology would not be manifested as a major mental illness but rather as a variety of subclinical behavioral "eccentricities." Such eccentricities, depending on their nature, may reflect a genetic predisposition to major mental illness; however, such a contention remains in the realm of speculation. The notion that disordered thinking falls along a continuum with normal thinking and that "thought disorders" are not discrete entities bearing no relation to orderly thinking is certainly not new (Harrow & Quinlan, 1977).

I further proposed that the hypothetical optimum deviation toward constriction or expansion of sensory input defined two distinct profiles, each of which possessed identifiable cognitive, physiological, and clinical characteristics. Each profile was intended to capture a unique constellation of characteristics that, when taken together, promoted creativity. One profile was labeled *A-type* (abstract). A-type is characterized by extensive scanning that often incorporates much peripheral, extraneous information, erratic mental "threshing" of large amounts of information, and a hyperalertness that facilitates the whole process. Such individuals, possessing "strong nervous systems" (e.g., Gray, 1967) that tend to resist (reduce or dampen) stimulation, habituate to stimuli so rapidly that they often pay little or no attention to prior stimuli. In a task situation, one would expect rapid performance with many errors. It was predicted that the A-type would evidence a weak attentional focus, high distractibility, low input registration, easy attentional shift, and relatively poor (diffuse and broad) selection. Clinically, affective symptomatology should predominate, including lability and depression. A-type creativity is characterized by the accumulation of the widest possible array of information. This smorgasbord of data is then harvested, with a keen eye to uncovering previously unobserved relations. If the search is fruitful, and subsequent research (or work) bears out the validity of the observation (or contribution), the discovery (or product) is often relegated to the mystical realm of intuition because no systematic program of research (or work) immediately preceded it. Robinson and Sabat (1977) metaphorically equated the nervous system to radar. In their terms, the A-type functions in a broadband "coasting" mode, responding with reduced resolution to a wide variety of input.

The second profile was labeled *C-type* (concrete). C-type is characterized by the tendency to underinclude or constrict the attentional field. Such individuals, possessing weak nervous systems that tend to augment or magnify stimulation, habituate to stimuli so slowly that they may appear, at the behavioral level, obsessive-compulsive. In a task situation, one would expect slow performance with few errors. It was predicted that C-type would evidence a strong attentional focus, low or normal distractibility, high input registration, and difficult attentional shift. Clinically, schizoidlike symptomatology should predominate, including blunted or flat affect and withdrawal. C-type creativity is characterized by a microscopic, dissectional focus on the separate constituent elements of a problem. The approach to problem solving is to zero in on the absolutely critical relations or the unexpected but meaningful anomalies. Again, the "magic" of intuition arises when no "logical" explanation suffices. I have argued that the fortuitous and accurate association between formerly unrelated elements is no less important to C-type than to A-type. In Robinson and Sabat's terms, the C-type functions under the most band-limited conditions and is thus least variable in response to sequential input.

It was hypothesized that, within the general population, there is an optimum regulation of input that provides for maximally efficient information processing, that insulates against psychiatric disorder, and, tangentially, that reduces the likelihood of extraordinary creativity. As argued, there is also an optimum deviation from this normative regulation of input that increases the likelihood of A-type or C-type cognition while still permitting adequate filtering of stimuli. Too much deviation, in the form of extreme abstraction or concretization, may manifest itself as psychotic thought disorder. It is important to note that I did not propose that creativity and mental illness coexist harmoniously. As mental illness (i.e., psychotic thought disorder)

begins to intrude, creativity typically recedes into the background. In fact, the stress occasionally associated with creativity may help to precipitate breakdown. Kuhn (1970) observed that "some men have undoubtedly been driven to desert science because of their inability to tolerate crisis" (pp. 78–79). Finally, it should be emphasized that a "thought process continuum" remains a hypothetical notion, and that there are no agreed upon anchor points for such a continuum. Thus, it is not possible to quantify "deviation" from the hypothetical mean of such a continuum.

Genetic and Eugenic Considerations

The following dilemma was posed at the beginning of this chapter: Why should a feature of human behavior that is seemingly so critical to the advancement of the species be restricted to so small a segment of the species? The tendency of the human species is to resist change, both genetically and socioculturally. To let up on the biological brakes that regulate extraordinary creativity might threaten the delicate adaptational balance of the species. This would tend to explain the otherwise inexplicable eruption of creativity at isolated moments in history, each moment being separated by at least as long a period of adjustment. This line of reasoning implies, of course, that there is some biological or genetic underpinning to extraordinary creativity. It has been argued, in this regard, that an entire epoch of human inspiration and talent, the golden age of Athens, was attributable to genetics (Darlington, 1969). The forces of heredity alone contrived to initiate (and conclude) that remarkable period of intellectual development. Darlington may actually be correct, but it is all speculation. There is no way of determining the influence of Athenian genes independent of the current zeitgeist. Indeed, it has been argued that the achievements of Periclean Athens were attributed to "the peace of mind allowed by good government . . . [and] intellectual freedom and the consequent encouragement to entertain new ideas, and new art forms" (Pickering, 1974, p. 276). In sum, evidence supporting higher rates of illness in the biological parents or offspring of gifted subjects may imply a diathesis for that illness and suggest *nothing* about the (possibly) coincidental appearance of creativity.

More radical arguments have been made recently, however, suggesting "that the schizophrenia homozygote may some day have the most effective brain" (Karlsson, 1978, p. 188). Jarvik and Chadwick (1973) noted that so maladaptive a condition as schizophrenia, with a high probability of a genetic component, should have declined through natural selection unless it was, in some way, adaptive. Jarvik and Deckard (1977) elaborated upon this theme, arguing that the schizoid-paranoid personality represents a selective advantage. According to Jarvik, these schizoid-paranoid people, who carry the gene or genes predisposing to schizophrenia, have an increased probability of contributing to the gene pool since they, more than their less paranoid cousins, are more likely to survive and ensure the survival of their offspring. The validity of Jarvik's thesis notwithstanding, we have little evidence to suggest that highly creative people are disproportionately schizoid and/or paranoid. McConaghy (1960) did describe a mode of thinking with a predisposition to psychosis that was characterized by paranoia, and Hasenfus and Magaro (1976) reported that paranoid schizophrenics, like creative people, exhibit ideational fluency.

Jarvik's thesis is one possible response to the problem of how an abnormal gene maintains itself given the low fertility of schizophrenics. Other investigators have also sought to identify some compensating selective advantage for schizophrenia. Huxley, Mayr, Osmond, and Hoffer (1964) noted, for example, that schizophrenics are highly resistant to certain physical stressors, such as infectious diseases and severe burns. Carter and Watts (1971) also observed an increased resistance to viral infections early in life among schizophrenics. Such resistance might give individuals with the abnormal gene a selective advantage over normal individuals. There would be no apparent advantage if one was actually schizophrenic; however, normal carriers, those in whom the gene had no penetrance for the disease, would have the selective advantage without the dire outcome of schizophrenia (Alland, 1967). This assumes, of course, that the gene is of low penetrance. It would seem that there are, in fact, at least two plausible theories to explain how a disadvantageous genetic condition is maintained in the population over time despite the reduced fitness of schizophrenics (Slater, Hare, & Price, 1971). One theory is Jarvik's notion that there is a selective advantage for normal (i.e., not psychotic) carriers of the gene. Another theory is that of polygenic inheritance. In this case, a selective advantage for gene carriers would be unnecessary since the "response to natural selection against a polygenic trait associated with lowered marriage and fertility rates would be very slow" (Gottesman & Shields, 1972, p. 329).

If the relevance of the foregoing discussion on genetics has escaped the reader, I will try to recapture a logical progression of thought. The focus of this chapter has been on the presumed similarities between creative cognition and deviant cognition that reflect a predisposition to psychosis. The preceding discussion on genetics presented two lines of argument: in one case, that there is a hypothetical genetic basis to extraordinary creativity; in the other case, that there is a genetic basis to—and possibly a selective advantage for—a predisposition to psychosis. If there is a common biological thread linking creativity with forms of major mental illness, it is argued in this chapter that such a thread may be cognition. Thus, we may make a leap of faith to infer that certain biologically conceived cognitive styles that are peculiar to extraordinary creativity possess common biological ancestry with certain cognitive styles that are associated with a predisposition to major mental illness. Although it is not intuitively (or empirically) obvious that there may be a selective advantage for certain forms of psychosis, the concept itself helps to explain another riddle presented at the beginning of this chapter; namely, how it could be adaptive, from an evolutionary standpoint, to wed the curse of mental illness to the gift of creativity. The outcome of a major mental illness remains a curse and cannot be assumed, in any respect, to be adaptive. There are those who have argued, however, that normal individuals who have the abnormal gene without penetrance for psychosis do in fact have some selective advantage. Thus, even though it makes little sense to wed the outcome of mental illness to creativity, it may make sense to wed a predisposition to mental illness (i.e., "normal" carriers of the aberrant gene) to creativity.

Several very interesting papers offer collateral evidence to support the feasibility of the hypothesis concerning a genetically transmitted cognitive style (or styles) common to highly creative people and those manifesting a predisposition to psychosis with subclinical features. In looking at eye-tracking dysfunctions among 30 sets of dizygotic twins discordant for schizophrenia, 5 of the schizophrenic probands with *good* eye tracking had a healthy co-twin with *bad* eye tracking (Holzman, Kringlen, Levy, Proctor & Haberman, 1977; Holzman, Kringlen, Levy, & Haberman, 1980). In a study involving schizophrenics, manics, and their parents, it was found that a number of schizophrenic probands with *good* eye tracking had nonschizophrenic parents (one or both) with impaired eye tracking (Holzman, Solomon, Levin, & Waternaux,

1984). Although the aforementioned anomalous relation between psychiatric status and eye-tracking performance held for 30% of the schizophrenics, it was present in only 8% of the manic patients. Recently, Matthysse and Holzman proposed a model to explain these seemingly anomalous findings (Matthysse, Holzman, & Lange, 1986; Matthysse & Holzman, 1987). In their genetic latent structure model, the manifest traits of schizophrenia and bad eye tracking are expressions of an inferred latent trait that is genetically transmitted. The latent trait, which is not behaviorally observable, may be expressed as schizophrenia or aberrant eye tracking or both. Matthysse and Holzman (1987) further suggested that the transmission pattern of the latent trait may conform more to Mendelian laws and be of higher penetrance than either of the manifest traits taken separately.

Research on eye movement laterality and creativity lends further support to the aforementioned genetic hypotheses. Harnad (1972) examined ''right movers'' and ''left movers'' (those who look to the right or left) among mathematicians. In the math department, 10 professors and 24 graduate students were questioned about their work. Among those who displayed 80% to 90% unilateral eye movements, 19 were left movers and 13 were right movers. The left movers reported using more imagery and engaging in more artistic activities than the right movers. Because it is assumed that, during introspection, there is a predominance of activity in the hemisphere contralateral to the direction of eye movement, the results suggested that the right hemisphere of the left movers was involved in imagery (though evidence to support greater *creativity* among the left movers was quite weak). Hines and Martindale (1974) also found some support for the association of ''left looking'' with creativity. In two separate studies, left-looking males scored significantly higher on the Remote Associates Test (RAT). These differences did not hold up in a third study with females. Huang and Byrne (1978) used the same lateral eye-movement paradigm to test the hypothesis that ''narrow categorizers,'' being more analytic in the processing of information, would use the left hemisphere and ''broad categorizers,'' being more holistic, would use the right hemisphere. First-year female psychology students were administered Pettigrew's C-W Scale. Those who scored above 90 ($n = 18$) and below 47 ($n = 15$) were selected as broad and narrow categorizers, respectively. The results supported the hypothesis with respect to narrow categorizers. Of the 11 subjects classified as consistent movers (greater than 75% unilateral

movement), 10 moved to the right. Only 5 broad categorizers were consistent enough to be classified. Of those 5, 4 were left movers. The data did not support the hypothesis for this group.

In summary, if we assume that eye tracking reflects, in part, a much more complex process of input regulation, then it is logical to posit that the same latent trait responsible for diminished eye-tracking performance may also be responsible for other deficits in the visual processing of information. In addition, the modes of information processing conferred by that genetically transmitted latent trait may provide an increased advantage for certain types of creativity.

A Taxonomic Consideration

Although all the questions and issues raised here provide fertile ground for future empirical investigation, it is virtually impossible, at present, to draw any reliable conclusions that involve the elastic notion of creativity. Jarvik's hypothesis, like many others, may be supported, or not supported, simply as a function of the way that creativity is defined. Thus, it is imperative that we begin by bringing some definitional order to the constructs we are examining. Given the extraordinary heterogeneity of the domain of behaviors (and products) described as ''creative,'' it is my impression that the first task must be the development of a preliminary taxonomic system that identifies coherent, homogeneous subgroups or types of creative activity. The proliferation of empirical and clinical data on creativity within the last decade has increased the urgency for an organized approach to this extraordinarily complex and diverse behavioral domain. Indeed, the importance of taxonomic differentiation is maximal when the area of inquiry is diverse and amorphous, as is the case with creativity.

On a light note, the interaction of creative cognition with psychiatrically disturbed cognition calls to mind an insightful portent of Captain Ahab: ''My means are sane, my motive and my object mad'' (Melville, 1851). Surely, it was not the harpooner's techniques that were mad but Ahab's fanatical devotion to killing Moby Dick. For present purposes, we may wish to adopt the obverse formula: mad means and sane motives.

ACKNOWLEDGMENTS. The author is grateful to Dan Carter, Raymond Knight, Ruth Rosenberg, and Peg Salamon for critical commentary on earlier versions of this chapter, as well as to Alison Martino for editing and text entry.

References

Alland, A. (1967). *Evolution and human behavior*. Garden City, NY: The Natural History Press.

Alston, E. F. (1972). James Barrie's "M'Connachie"—His "writing half." *American Imago, 29*, 257–277.

Andreasen, N. J. C. (1980). Mania and creativity. In R. H. Belmaker and H. M. Van Praage (Eds.), *Mania: An evolving concept* (pp. 377–386). New York: Spectrum.

Andreasen, N. J. C., & Canter, A. (1974). The creative writer: Psychiatric symptoms and family history. *Comprehensive Psychiatry, 15*, 123–131.

Andreasen, N. J. C., & Powers, P. S. (1975). Creativity and psychosis: An examination of conceptual style. *Archives of General Psychiatry, 32*, 70–73.

Babcock, W. L. (1895). On the morbid heredity and predisposition to insanity of the man of genius. *Journal of Nervous and Mental Disease, 20*, 749–769.

Barron, F. (1958). The psychology of imagination. *Scientific American, 199*, 151–166.

Barron, F. (1963). *Creativity and psychological health*. Princeton, NJ: D. Van Nostrand.

Barron, F., & Harrington, D. M. (1981). Creativity, intelligence, and personality. *Annual Review of Psychology, 32*, 439–476.

Becker, G. (1978). *The mad genius controversy*. Beverly Hills, CA: Sage.

Behrens, R. R. (1975). Lunatics, lovers, and poets: On madness and creativity. *Journal of Creative Behavior, 9*, 228–232.

Bell, Q. (1972). *Virginia Woolf: A biography* (Vol. 2). New York: Harcourt Brace Jovanovich.

Broad, W. J. (1981). Priority war: Discord in pursuit of glory. *Science, 211*, 465–467.

Bronowski, J. (1965). *Science and human values*. New York: Harper & Row.

Bychowski, G. (1973). Marcel Proust and his mother. *American Imago, 30*, 8–25.

Callaway, E., & Naghdi, S. (1982). An information processing model for schizophrenia. *Archives of General Psychiatry, 39*, 339–347.

Carter, M., & Watts, C. A. H. (1971). Possible biological advantages among schizophrenics' relatives. *British Journal of Psychiatry, 118*, 453–460.

Cattell, R. B. (1966). The personality and motivation of the researcher from measurements of contemporaries and from biography. In C. W. Taylor & F. Barron (Eds.), *Scientific creativity: Its recognition and development* (pp. 119–131). New York: Wiley.

Cattell, R. B., & Butcher, H. J. (1968). *The prediction of achievement and creativity*. Indianapolis: Bobbs-Merrill.

Cattell, R. B., & Drevdahl, J. E. (1955). A comparison of the personality profile of eminent researchers with that of eminent teachers and administrators of the general population. *British Journal of Psychology, 46*, 248–261.

Cattell, R. B., & Stice, G. F. (1957). *The 16PF personality factor questionnaire*. Champaign, IL: Institute for Personality and Ability Testing.

Claridge, G. (1972). The schizophrenias as nervous types. *British Journal of Psychiatry, 121*, 1–17.

Claridge, G., Canter, S., & Hume, W. I. (1973). *Personality differences and biological variations: A study of twins*. Oxford, England: Pergamon Press.

Cleckley, H. (1964). *The Mask of Sanity* (4th ed.) St. Louis: C. V. Mosby.

Cropley, A. J. (1968). A note on the Wallach-Kogan test of creativity. *British Journal of Educational Psychology, 38*, 197–201.

Cropley, A. J., & Sikand, J. S. (1973). Creativity and schizophrenia. *Journal of Consulting and Clinical Psychology, 40*, 462–468.

Cross, P., Cattell, R. B., & Butcher, H. J. (1967). The personality pattern of creative artists. *British Journal of Educational Psychology, 37*, 292–299.

Dale, P. M. (1952). *Medical biographies. The ailments of thirty-three famous persons*. Norman: University of Oklahoma Press.

Darlington, C. D. (1969). *The evolution of man and society*. London: George Allen & Unwin.

Dellas, M., & Gaier, E. L. (1970). Identification of creativity: The individual. *Psychological Bulletin, 73*, 55–73.

Drevdahl, J. E. (1954). *An exploratory study of creativity in terms of its relationships to various personality and intellectual factors*. Unpublished doctoral dissertation. University of Nebraska, Lincoln.

Drevdahl, J. E. (1956). Factors of importance for creativity. *Journal of Clinical Psychology, 12*, 21–26.

Drevdahl, J. E., & Cattell, R. B. (1958). Personality and creativity in artists and writers. *Journal of Clinical Psychology, 14*, 107–111.

Dykes, M., & McGhie, A. (1976). A comparative study of attentional strategies of schizophrenics and highly creative normal subjects. *British Journal of Psychiatry, 128*, 50–56.

Edel, L. (1975). The madness of art. *American Journal of Psychiatry, 132*, 1005–1012.

Eiduson, B. T. (1958). Artist and non-artist: A comparative study. *Journal of Personality, 26*, 13–28.

Ellis, H. (1904). *A study of British genius*. London: Hurst & Blackett.

Ellrich, R. J. (1974). Rousseau's account of a psychological crisis. *American Imago, 31*, 80–94.

Farmer, E. W. (1974). *Psychoticism and person-orientation as general personality characteristics of importance for different aspects of creative thinking*. Unpublished Bachelor of Science Thesis, University of Glasgow.

Gibson, C. (1889). *The characteristics of genius. A popular essay*. London: Walter Scott.

Goertzel, M. G., Goertzel, V., & Goertzel, T. G. (1978). *Three hundred eminent personalities*. San Francisco: Jossey-Bass.

Gottesman, I. I., and Shields, J. (1972). *Schizophrenia and genetics: A twin study vantage point*. New York: Academic Press.

Gough, H. G. (1979). A creative personality scale for the adjective check list. *Journal of Personality and Social Psychology, 37*, 1398–1405.

Gough, H. G., & Heilbrun, A. B. (1965). *The adjective check list manual*. Palo Alto, CA: Consulting Psychologists Press.

Grant, V. W. (1968). *Great abnormals*. New York: Hawthorn Books.

Gray, J. A. (1967). Strength of the nervous system, introversion-extraversion, and conditionability and arousal. *Behavior Research and Therapy, 5*, 151–169.

Guilford, J. P. (1950). Creativity. *American Psychologist, 5*, 444–454.

Guilford, J. P. (1956a). The relation of intellectual factors to creative thinking in science. In C. W. Taylor (Ed.), *The identification of creative scientific talent* (pp. 69–95). Salt Lake City: University of Utah Press.

Guilford, J. P. (1956b). The structure of intellect. *Psychological Bulletin, 53*, 267–293.

Guilford, J. P. (1959). Traits of creativity. In H. H. Anderson

(Ed.), *Creativity and its cultivation* (pp. 142–161). New York: Harper.

Guilford, J. P. (1966). Intellectual resources and their values as seen by scientists. In C. W. Taylor & F. Barron (Eds.), *Scientific creativity: Its recognition and development* (pp. 101–114). New York: Wiley.

Guilford, J. P. (1968). *Intelligence, creativity, and their educational implications.* San Diego, CA: Robert R. Knapp.

Guilford, J. P. (1970). Creativity: Retrospect and prospect. *Journal of Creative Behavior, 4,* 149–168.

Haddon, F. A., & Lytton, H. (1968). Teaching approach and divergent thinking abilities. *British Journal of Educational Psychology, 38,* 171–180.

Harnad, S. R. (1972). Creativity, lateral saccades and the nondominant hemisphere. *Perceptual and Motor Skills, 34,* 653–654.

Harrow, M., & Quinlan, D. (1977). Is disordered thinking unique to schizophrenia? *Archives of General Psychiatry, 34,* 15–21.

Hasenfus, N., & Magaro, P. (1976). Creativity and schizophrenia: An equality of empirical constructs. *British Journal of Psychiatry, 129,* 346–349.

Hines, D., & Martindale, C. (1974). Induced lateral eye-movements and creative and intellectual performance. *Perceptual and Motor Skills, 39,* 153–154.

Holden, C. (1987, April). Creativity and the troubled mind. *Psychology Today,* pp. 9–10.

Holton, G. (1978). *The scientific imagination: Case studies.* Cambridge, England: Cambridge University Press.

Holzman, P. S., Kringlen, E., Levy, D. L., Proctor, L. R. & Haberman, S. J. (1977). Abnormal pursuit eye movements in schizophrenia: Evidence for a genetic marker. *Archives of General Psychiatry, 34,* 802–805.

Holzman, P. S., Kringlen, E., Levy, D. L., & Haberman, S. J. (1980). Deviant eye tracking in twins discordant for psychosis: A replication. *Archives of General Psychiatry, 37,* 627–631.

Holzman, P. S., Solomon, C. M., Levin, S., & Waternaux, C. S. (1984). Pursuit eye movement dysfunctions in schizophrenia: Family evidence for specificity. *Archives of General Psychiatry, 41,* 136–139.

Huang, M-s., & Byrne, B. (1978). Cognitive style and lateral eye movements. *British Journal of Psychology, 69,* 85–90.

Hudson, L. (1970). The question of creativity. In P. E. Vernon (Ed.), *Creativity.* Harmondsworth, Middlesex, England: Penguin Books.

Huxley, J., Mayr, E., Osmond, H., & Hoffer, A. (1964). Schizophrenia as a genetic morphism. *Nature, 204,* 220–221.

Jamison, K. R. (in press). Manic-depressive illness and accomplishment: Creativity, leadership, and social class. In F. K. Goodwin & K. R. Jamison, *Manic-depressive illness.* Oxford, England: Oxford University Press.

Jamison, K. R., Gerner, R. H., & Goodwin, F. K. (1979). Patient and physician attitudes toward lithium. *Archives of General Psychiatry, 36,* 866–869.

Jamison, K. R., Gerner, R. H., Hammen, C., & Padesky, C. (1980). Clouds and silver linings: Positive experiences associated with primary affective disorders. *American Journal of Psychiatry, 137,* 198–202.

Jarvik, L. F., & Chadwick, S. B. (1973). Schizophrenia and survival. In M. Hammer, K. Salzinger, & S. Sutton (Eds.), *Psychopathology: Contributions from the social, behavioral sciences* (pp. 57–73). New York: Wiley.

Jarvik, L. F., & Deckard, B. S. (1977). The odyssean person-

ality: A survival advantage for carriers of genes predisposing to schizophrenia? *Neuropsychobiology, 3,* 179–191.

Jones, E. (1958). *The life and work of Sigmund Freud.* New York: Basic Books.

Karlsson, J. L. (1978). *Inheritance of creative intelligence.* Chicago: Nelson-Hall.

Keefe, J. A., & Magaro, P. (1980). Creativity and schizophrenia: An equivalence of cognitive processing. *Journal of Abnormal Psychology, 89,* 390–398.

Korb, R., & Frankiewicz, R. G. (1979, September). *Aptitudes, intellective styles, and personality characteristics as facilitators and differentiators of creativity.* Paper presented at the Annual Meeting of the American Psychological Association, New York.

Krebs, H. A., & Shelley, J. H. (Eds.). (1975). *The creative process in science and medicine.* Proceedings of the C. H. Boehringer Sohn Symposium. Kronberg, Taunus, May 16–17, 1974. New York: American Elsevier.

Kuhn, T. S. (1970). *The structure of scientific revolutions.* Chicago: University of Chicago Press.

Lange-Eichbaum, W. (1932). *The problem of genius* (E. Paul & C. Paul, trans.). New York: Macmillan.

Larkin, E. (1970). Beethoven's medical history. In M. Cooper (Ed.), *Beethoven: The last decade* (pp. 439–466). London: Oxford University Press.

Lélut, L. F. (1836). *Du démon de Socrate, spécimen d'une application de la science psychologique à celle de l'histoire.* Paris: Trinquart.

Lidz, T., Wild, C., Schafer, S., Rosman, B., & Fleck, S. (1963). Thought disorder in the parents of schizophrenic patients: A study utilizing the object sorting test. *Journal of Psychiatric Research, 1,* 193–200.

Lombroso, C. (1891). *The man of genius.* London: Walter Scott.

Lombroso, C. (1910). *The man of genius.* New York: Charles Scribner's Sons.

MacKinnon, D. W. (1960). What do we mean by talent and how do we test for it? In *The search for talent* (pp. 20–29). New York: College Entrance Examination Board.

MacKinnon, D. W. (1962a). The nature and nurture of creative talent. *American Psychologist, 17,* 484–495.

MacKinnon, D. W. (1962b). The personality correlates of creativity: A study of American architects. In G. S. Nielsen (Ed.), *Proceedings of the XIV International Congress of Applied Psychology, Copenhagen, 1961* (Vol. 2, pp. 11–39). Copenhagen: Munksgaard.

MacKinnon, D. W. (1965). Personality and the realization of creative potential. *American Psychologist, 20,* 273–281.

MacKinnon, D. W. (1967). The study of creative persons: A method and some results. In J. Kagan (Ed.), *Creativity and learning* (pp. 20–35). Boston: Beacon Press.

MacKinnon, D. W. (1972). The role of personality traits in the development of scientific abilities. In A. Rosca (Chm.), *Symposium 18: The detection and training of scientific talent* (Vol 1, pp. 515–518). Proceedings, 17th International Congress of Applied Psychology. Liège, Belgium, July 25–30, 1971. Brussels: Editest.

MacKinnon, D. W., Crutchfield, R. S., Barron, F., Block, J., Gough, H. G., & Harris, R. E. (1958, April). *An assessment study of air force officers: Part I. Design of the study and description of variables.* Lackland Air Force Base, TX: Air Force Personnel and Training Research Center. (*Technical Report* WADC-TR-58-91 [I], ASTIA Document No. AD 151040)

Martindale, C. (1977–1978). Creativity, consciousness, and

cortical arousal. *Journal of Altered States of Consciousness, 3,* 69–87.

Martindale, C., & Greenough, J. (1973). The differential effect of increased arousal on creative and intellectual performance. *Journal of Genetic Psychology, 123,* 329–335.

Martindale, C., & Armstrong, J. (1974). The relationship of creativity to cortical activation and its operant control. *Journal of General Psychology, 124,* 311–320.

Martindale, C., & Hasenfus, N. (1978). EEG differences as a function of creativity, stage of the creative process, and effort to be original. *Biological Psychology, 6,* 157–167.

Martindale, C., & Hines, D. (1975). Creativity and cortical activation during creative, intellectual and EEG feedback tasks. *Biological Psychology, 3,* 91–100.

Martindale, C., Hines, D., Mitchell, L., & Covello, E. (1984). EEG alpha asymmetry and creativity. *Personality and Individual Differences, 5,* 77–86.

Matthysse, S., & Holzman, P. S. (1987). Genetic latent structure models: Implication for research on schizophrenia. *Psychological Medicine, 17,* 271–274.

Matthysse, S., Holzman, P. S., & Lange, K. (1986). The genetic transmission of schizophrenia: Application of Mendelian latent structure analysis to eye tracking dysfunctions in schizophrenia and affective disorder. *Journal of Psychiatric Research, 20,* 57–76.

Maupassant, G. de. (1900). *Le horla.* Paris: P. Ollendorff.

McConaghy, N. (1960). Modes of abstract thinking and psychosis. *American Journal of Psychiatry, 117,* 106–110.

McConaghy, N. (1961). The measurement of an inhibitory process in human higher nervous activity: Its relation to allusive thinking and fatigue. *American Journal of Psychiatry, 118,* 125–132.

McConaghy, N., & Clancy, M. (1968). Familial relationships of allusive thinking in university students and their parents. *British Journal of Psychiatry, 114,* 1079–1087.

Mednick, S. A. (1962). The associative basis of the creative process. *Psychological Review, 69,* 220–232.

Melton, A. W. (1964). The taxonomy of human learning: Overview. In A. W. Melton (Ed.), *Categories of human learning* (pp. 325–339). New York: Academic Press.

Melville, H. (1851). *Moby Dick: or, The whale.* New York: Harper & Brothers.

Mitchell, A. R. K. (1972). *Schizophrenia—The meanings of madness.* New York: Taplinger.

Murphy, G. (1979, December 2). Schumann: A short, troubled life. *Rochester Democrat and Chronicle,* p. 5C.

Nicholls, J. G. (1972). Creativity in the person who will never produce anything original and useful: The concept of creativity as a normally distributed trait. *American Psychologist, 27,* 717–727.

Nisbet, J. F. (1912). *The insanity of genius: And the general inequality of human faculty physiologically considered.* London: Stanley Paul.

Nordau, M. (1900). *Degeneration.* New York: D. Appleton.

Ogilvy, D. (1971). The creative chef. In G. A. Steiner (Ed.), *The creative organization* (pp. 119–213). Chicago: University of Chicago Press.

Pavlov, I. P. (1955). [*Selected works*] (S. Belsky, trans.). Moscow: Foreign Languages.

Pezzullo, T. R., Thorsen, E. E., & Madaus, G. F. (1972). The heritability of Jensen's level I and II and divergent thinking. *American Educational Research Journal, 9,* 539–546.

Phillips, R. H. (1982). Mood, creativity, and psychotherapeutic

participation of patients receiving lithium. *Psychosomatics, 23,* 81–87.

Pickering, G. (1974). *Creative malady.* New York: Oxford University Press.

Prentky, R. A. (1979). Creativity and psychopathology: A neurocognitive perspective. In B. A. Maher (Ed.), *Progress in experimental personality research* (Vol. 9, pp. 1–39). New York: Academic Press.

Prentky, R. A. (1980). *Creativity and psychopathology: A neurocognitive perspective.* New York: Praeger.

Prinzhorn, H. (1972). *Artistry of the mentally ill.* New York: Springer-Verlag.

Reichsman, F. (1981). Life experiences and creativity of great composers: A psychosomaticist's view. *Psychosomatic Medicine, 43,* 291–300.

Robinson, D. N., & Sabat, S. R. (1977). Neuroelectric aspects of information processing by the brain. *Neuropsychologia, 15,* 625–641.

Robinson, L. (1977). Visionaries and madmen: Are creativity and schizophrenia linked? *Lawrence Berkeley Laboratory News-Magazine, 2,* 7–10.

Roe, A. (1951). A psychological study of physical scientists. *Genetic Psychology Monographs, 43,* 121–235.

Roe, A. (1952). A psychologist examines 64 eminent scientists. *Scientific American, 187,* 21–25.

Roe, A. (1953). *The making of a scientist.* New York: Dodd, Mead.

Roe, A. (1956). *The psychology of occupations.* New York: Wiley.

Rosen, G. (1969). *Madness in society: Chapters in the historical sociology of mental illness.* New York: Harper & Row.

Rosman, B., Wild, C., Ricci, J., Fleck, S., & Lidz, T. (1964). Thought disorder in the parents of schizophrenic patients: A further study utilizing the object sorting test. *Journal of Psychiatric Research, 2,* 211–221.

Rothenberg, A. (1976). Homospatial thinking in creativity. *Archives of General Psychiatry, 33,* 17–26.

Rothenberg, A. (1979). Creative contradictions. *Psychology Today, 13,* 55–62.

Rothenberg, A. (1983). Psychopathology and creative cognition. *Archives of General Psychiatry, 40,* 937–942.

Schaffer, P. (1981). *Amadeus.* New York: Harper & Row.

Scholander, P. F. (1978). Rhapsody in science. *Annual Review of Physiology, 40,* 1–17.

Shapiro, R. J. (1970). The criterion problem. In P. E. Vernon (Ed.), *Creativity* (pp. 257–269). Harmondsworth, Middlesex, England: Penguin books.

Slater, E., Hare, E. H., & Price, J. S. (1971). Marriage and fertility of psychiatric patients compared with national data. In I. I. Gottesman & L. Erlenmeyer-Kimling (Eds.), *Differential reproduction in individuals with mental and physical disorders. Social Biology, 18,* S60–S73.

Solomon, M. (1975). The dreams of Beethoven. *American Imago, 32,* 113–144.

Stein, M. I. (1971). Several findings of a transactional approach to creativity. In G. A. Steiner (Ed.), *The creative organization.* Chicago: University of Chicago Press.

Storr, A. (1971). Problems of creativity. *Contemporary Psychoanalysis, 7,* 115–133.

Storr, A. (1976). *The dynamics of creation.* Harmondsworth, Middlesex, England: Penguin Books.

Taylor, D. W. (1960). Thinking and creativity. *Annals of the New York Academy of Sciences, 91,* 108–127.

Terman, L. M. (1926). *Genetic studies of genius* (Vols. I, II). Stanford: Stanford University Press.

Tollefson, D. (1961). *Response to humor in relation to other measures of personality*. Unpublished Doctoral Dissertation. University of Illinois.

Tomlinson-Keasey, C., Warren, L. W., & Elliott, J. E. (1986). Suicide among gifted women: A prospective study. *Journal of Abnormal Psychology, 95,* 123–130.

Trilling, L. (1950). *The liberal imagination: Essays on literature and society.* New York: Viking Press.

Tsanoff, R. A. (1949). *The ways of genius.* New York: Harper & Brothers.

Tucker, D. M., Stenslie, C. E., Roth, R. S., & Shearer, S. L. (1981). Right frontal lobe activation and right hemisphere performance. *Archives of General Psychiatry, 38,* 169–174.

Vandenberg, S. (1968). The nature and nurture of intelligence. In D. Glass (Ed.), *Genetics* (pp. 3–58). New York: Rockefeller University Press and the Russell Sage Foundation.

Winslow, J. H. (1971). *Darwin's victorian malady.* Philadelphia: American Philosophical Society.

Wittkower, R. R. (1973). Genius: Individualism in art and artists. In P. P. Wiener (Ed.), *Dictionary of the history of ideas* (pp. 297–312). New York: Scribners.

Woody, E., & Claridge, G. (1977). Psychoticism and thinking. *British Journal of Social and Clinical Psychology, 16,* 241–248.

Wright, S. (1954). *Some psychological and physiological correlates of certain academic underachievers.* Unpublished Doctoral Dissertation, University of Chicago.

CHAPTER 16

Examining Counselors' Creative Processes in Counseling

P. Paul Heppner, Karen Fitzgerald, and Carolyn A. Jones

When working with clients, the process of successful therapy is akin to the process of a continuous weaving, of picking up various colored and textured threads to create a new fabric. (Carolyn Jones, personal communication, January, 1986)

Creative counseling involves feeling connected with the client in a mutual atmosphere of energy, trust and individualized communication. (Helen J. Roehlke, personal communication, January, 1986)

Intense reactions to and awareness of the connections between present difficulties and events in the past will result in the application of new and effective knowledge. (Richard Thoresen, personal communication, January, 1986)

Therapists who have a broad range of knowledge and who are capable of eliciting internal images that capture the essence of a client's situation are constructive and insightful. (Wayne P. Anderson, personal communication, January, 1986)

These are statements from creative, effective therapists who were describing the process which, for them, represents innovative and productive counseling interactions. Their words allude to themes of flexibility, knowledge, confidence, and uniqueness. They describe the process of understanding clients and of intervening in ways that produce constructive change. Although this process is clearly different for each therapist, upon examina-

tion there are underlying elements of spontaneity and intentionality that can be seen in creative counseling behavior.

The purpose of this chapter is to examine the role of counselors' creativity within counseling. The subject of creativity has been examined within a variety of contexts, such as art, scientific inventions, and other public arenas. Little attention, however, has been given to creativity within the therapeutic process. Creativity is often studied in relation to problem solving. Because a counselor's role is to help other people solve problems, the therapeutic process may well be a productive setting within which to examine creativity. Creativity in the counseling process could be examined from several perspectives: (a) from the counselor's point of view, (b) from the client's perspective, or (c) from the interaction between the therapist and the client. In this chapter, we will focus solely on creativity from the counselor's perspective, although the other perspectives merit examination as well. In so doing, we realize that we have artificially divided the counseling process, which has as its foundation the interaction between counselor and client.

We will begin the chapter by briefly defining the term *counseling* and discussing some of the essential characteristics of the counseling process. Next, we will discuss the role of counselor creativity within counseling, suggesting that creativity occurs in at

P. Paul Heppner, Karen Fitzgerald, and Carolyn A. Jones • Department of Psychology, University of Missouri, Columbia, MO 65211.

least two major areas of counseling; namely, understanding a client's problem and facilitating client change. In the third section of the chapter, we will speculate about some of the variables that affect counselor creativity within counseling. Finally, we will conclude by discussing research strategies and how the formal educational training of therapists might provide a unique setting in which to investigate how creativity can be fostered or inhibited in counselor trainees.

The Counseling Process

Counseling has been defined as a psychological specialty in which "practitioners help others improve their well-being, alleviate their distress, resolve their crises, and increase their ability to solve problems and make decisions" (Fretz, 1982, p. 15). Counseling is a process that involves an interaction between client and counselor with the shared goal being client change or growth, often occurring within the context of a highly involving and emotional professional relationship. This goal can be accomplished through various methods derived from the study of human behavior (see Corsini, 1984).

Counseling can also be viewed as an information exchange between the client and the counselor (Heppner & Fitzgerald, 1987). The client attempts to communicate to the counselor the nature of his or her experiences and the difficulties and conflicts that are associated with those experiences. The counselor attempts to understand the client's experiences in the context of this information and to gain an awareness of the client's personality dynamics. In doing this, the counselor utilizes a broad range of knowledge about personality development and dynamics, personal problem solving or coping processes, and communication processes.

Given the counselor's understanding of the client, and the development of a professional working alliance with the client, the focus shifts to client change. The counselor's goal is to help the client change. This is typically done through a variety of interventions that are based on knowledge about counseling techniques and the process of changing human behavior. These interventions can be conceptualized as imparting knowledge and skills as a way of altering maladaptive information-processing patterns that lead to maladaptive behavior. Given their experiences in the world, counselors, too, are subject to change, especially with previous

clients. Although the focus for change is on the client in a counseling situation, experienced counselors acknowledge that they, too, may be affected by the relationship in ways that initially may not be known or not easily controlled.

The counseling process is exceedingly complex, and client change is often difficult to evaluate (Highlen & Hill, 1984). In addition, the possible routes to change are innumerable and many times idiographic. Counseling is also unique in that it involves interaction; this is a special human relationship in which the client and the counselor encounter each other and develop a working alliance. Each counselor–client dyad is unique and establishes idiosyncratic communication patterns within the therapeutic relationship.

Counseling involves scientific and artistic elements. The scientific elements of predictability and rationality are necessary in order to facilitate client change. The artistic side of counseling allows for the uniqueness and vitality of human interaction and includes mystery and evocation. But counselors, unlike artists or scientists, have less control over the medium with which they work. Clients are not frozen in time, waiting for the next intervention, but rather are evolving in an environment of continuous external stimulation. Using the analogy of weaving a new fabric, it is here that new threads are added from the counselor, while threads from within the client are altered. In a sense, creativity within counseling can be the link between the predictable and the mysterious in human interaction, the known and the unknown.

Counselor Creativity within Counseling

Creative thought and behavior are manifested in many ways in the counseling process. Our definition of counselor creativity involves the combination of information, often in unique or novel ways, that is ultimately used to elucidate or solve a client's problem by extending the client's experiential world in some way. A common characteristic of creative events within counseling is "double membership" (Koestler, 1964); that is, creative thought involves seeing events in two frames of reference, which heretofore were seen as unconnected, as part of a theme which then provides new insight into the client's situation for both the client and the counselor. Thus, some kind of transformation of information occurs (Pickard, 1987). This transformation may involve thoughts, feelings, and behaviors that are new or different for the client. Thus, creative events within counseling may require combining events or information in a novel way. This often involves providing a new piece to the client's puzzle and is usually accompanied by a feeling of surprise or a sense of the unexpected.

Another characteristic of creative events pertains to the facilitation of the counseling process. Creative counseling is not simply atypical interventions or novel descriptions of a client. Rather, a critical feature is that the outcome of creative events in counseling is an extension of the client's experiential world and discernible client progress. In other words, the role of creative behavior in counseling is purposeful, not merely interesting or aesthetic. Thus, to evaluate creative processes in a counselor, it is necessary not only to examine how the counselor is processing information but ultimately to estimate the impact on the client as well. (Because the latter point is beyond the scope of this chapter, it will not be discussed much here.) Sometimes client progress may be miniscule; other times the creative integration may result in a major turning point or critical incident in therapy (see Kell & Mueller, 1966). Regardless of the quantity, the presence of change or progress in the client is an essential characteristic in evaluating counselor creativity.

We propose that counselors utilize creative processes in at least two major areas: (a) to understand the essence of the client's problem(s), and (b) to develop interventions to facilitate desired client change. For our immediate purpose, we will delineate the different opportunities for creative expression by counselors in a somewhat temporal and linear fashion. We recognize, however, that this approach does not fully represent the complex nature of creativity within the counseling process where counselor, client, and counselor/client interaction variables are deeply embedded in a contextual matrix. Moreover, the different processes involved in understanding the client's problems and developing interventions are oftentimes intertwined with each other and are highly interdependent in a nonlinear fashion.

A counselor might initially engage in creative processing with a client during the process of case conceptualization. In deriving personality theories, psychologists have used conceptual skills to form broad impressions regarding the healthy development of human beings as well as those attributes that indicate some type of psychological dysfunction or personality disorder. The procedure with individual clients is much the same. This process is similar to the story of the blind men describing an elephant—it is strongly influenced by the perspective of the therapist.

We make use of empathy, intuition, and theoretical and scientific knowledge to create a descriptive image or working model of a client within ourselves. This image, constructed from our experience with the client, is an aid in diagnosis and treatment planning. The challenge lies in creating a balance between an empirically standardized description and an image that does justice to the unique, dynamic aspect of a client.

Understanding the essence of a client's problem involves an accurate representation of the client's difficulties in the context of his or her history and personality dynamics. This often requires perceiving linkages between aspects of client experiences that may seem unrelated. Many times, an experienced and competent counselor can accurately comprehend the essence of a client's problem without a great deal of trouble, and within a relatively few number of counseling sessions. For example, the majority of clients with normal developmental problems pertaining to social relationships, such as dating, studying, career planning, and interpersonal communication, typically present few problems for veteran counselors. Creative thought and behavior may not be required in client assessment in these situations because past experience suggests what the underlying issues are likely to be. Conversely, there are other clients and client problems that present a befuddled array of information, and the counseling process may then reach an impasse. Counselors often acknowledge such situations by noting that they are "feeling stuck," that "something is missing," or that "the pieces don't hang together." The client may appear uncharacteristically "resistant"; the client–counselor interaction may be strained and unproductive; and the counselor may continually discover what seems to be new and unrelated information. In essence, the counselor and the client together are unable to make sense of the relevant information and to integrate that information to pinpoint and understand the nature of the client's difficulties.

An impasse can be a serious obstacle in counseling because progress is blocked. Experienced therapists attempting to circumvent such obstacles often describe periods of intense concentration in which they attend very closely to one or more of their auditory, kinesthetic, or visual senses. In essence, they use whatever modality to obtain more information and then use that information to understand the client's difficulty. Extraneous and nonessential stimuli are blurred in this state of focused attention. Counselors talk about "really hearing the client," and, with this focus, imperceptible nuances or subtleties in the client's "story" may emerge with striking clarity. Counselors may "suddenly have a feeling about the client," perhaps signaling that some key element has yet to be resurrected despite the appearance that everything of importance has been accounted for. They may "feel" affectively to some degree what the client dares not feel as the client tries to avoid painful emotional material and attempts to maintain a sense of control. The counselor's experience of the explicit or implicit feeling state of the client means that he or she "partakes of the quality of the feelings and not the quantity" (Greenson, 1967, p. 368). In working through an impasse, the counselor may also utilize a descriptive image of the client, and as the image "reacts with ideas, feelings, memories or fantasies, etc." (Greenson, 1967, p. 369), the counselor may discover some missing piece in the therapeutic puzzle.

When considering a new piece of information, the experienced therapist will often test his or her hunches or opinions either explicitly with the client (e.g., could it be this?) or implicitly by collecting confirmatory information. Thus, this creative counselor process may occur at once (voila!) or gradually by extended interactions with the client. This additional information allows a more complete integration of the previous information and a more useful picture of the client, so that the counseling process can now proceed in a more productive manner. The composer Brahms described such a process as feeling "vibrations which thrill my whole being . . . [which] assume the form of distinct mental images . . . the ideas flow upon me . . . and not only do I see distinct themes . . . but they are clothed in the right forms" (Abel, 1964, pp. 19–21). In like manner, a novel synthesis of meaningful material can result in an emotional rush for the counselor as a result of the counselor's creative discovery of what was unfamiliar and previously unknown to perhaps both client and counselor.

As the counselor and, in particular, the client better understand the nature of the client's difficulties, and as counseling goals are established, then either implicit or explicit intervention plans are then developed. Depending on the complexity of the client's difficulties and the comprehensiveness of the goal(s), this can be a quick or a very time-consuming process. The task for the counselor is to retrieve a broad array of knowledge about intervention strategies from memory and apply that knowledge to the client's problem at hand. As these plans are "tested out," the counselor can obtain feedback from the client about the effectiveness of the intervention.

Many times an experienced and competent counselor can effectively implement intervention strategies with a client that result in the desired client change. Often these interventions are not especially unique, and there is minimal trial and error involved in the design or the application of the intervention. For example, certain problems, such as phobias, study skills deficits, and lack of assertiveness, can be addressed by relatively standard treatment methods. In these circumstances, there is limited need for more creative thought or behavior on the part of the counselor. However, there are other situations in which the therapist has tried more familiar and logical interventions, all of which have failed. As with problems associated with case conceptualization, counseling may reach another impasse, this time during the intervention phase of the therapeutic process. At such times, counselors often acknowledge feeling frustrated, either with themselves or with the client. This type of impasse during the intervention phase also effectively blocks the therapeutic process and is another opportunity in which creative processes in therapy can be effective.

It is important to note that creative counselor behavior does not only occur during impasses in the counseling process. One therapist mentioned the times when she really felt happy and playful and when the counseling process was "really rolling"; subsequently, she felt inspired to behave very creatively in session. Another spoke of the increased confidence one can feel to take risks when the counseling process is progressing smoothly. However, it seems that some of the most striking creative events occur at points of difficulty when the counselor feels stuck. It may be that these events are simply more meaningful or memorable due to the tension of the impasse and the greater need for a novel, purposeful perspective.

One therapist we spoke to noted her unexpected awareness of feeling sad during a particular counseling sequence. When the therapist reflected that feeling, the client was then able to explore an aspect of herself that effectively opened the door for further change. Other therapists report utilizing spontaneous images that develop in their awareness as a way of synthesizing bits of information obtained from the client. Another therapist described the process of incubation; for example, as he thought about a particular client at times throughout the week, his affective reactions to the client became more pronounced and then served as a basis for an intervention in the next counseling session. Similarly, another therapist described taking a coffee break during a session, primarily to offer himself an opportunity to scan his sensory awareness and integrate new information. In short, it seems that experienced counselors engage in a variety of cognitive and affective processes that allow them to integrate information, sometimes very small pieces of information, which either provides some hints for understanding the client and/or subsequent interventions.

The interactive quality of creativity is essential in understanding its effectiveness. When we choose one way or another to intervene in a client's system, we are taking a step in the "dance" of therapy. Sometimes we may logically or intuitively decide which intervention to use. But sometimes the rationale for an intervention may be difficult to identify, and the client's response may be difficult to predict. Often we express a sense of doing something "on a hunch." In these cases, the reactions of our clients can give us clues as to why we chose a particular intervention or direction and can help us to deepen our understanding of the client.

Sometimes the counselor–client interaction leads to unexpected, unintended, and even unwanted outcomes. Eileen Pickard (personal communication, May 24, 1987) described a "relay of insights" in creative processing, by which she meant that one person's insights may be received quite differently by another and may lead to unintended developments on the part of the initiator. What may begin as uncreative within the intentions of one person may spark creative insights in the receiver, and vice versa. Such "relays" depict the creative processing within counselors and clients.

Variables Affecting Creativity within Counseling

The purpose of this section is to discuss some of the variables that affect a counselor's creativity within counseling. This section is speculative and is based on our own counseling experiences as well as on applied and laboratory problem-solving research. We believe that a number of different variables affect a counselor's creativity within counseling and most likely are interrelated; as a result, our discussion is in no way meant to be exhaustive.

The variables we have identified can be grouped

Table 1. Content and Process Variables Affecting Counselor Creative Processes

Variables	Content	Process
Variables affecting the utilization of knowledge	Breadth and depth of knowledge base	Ability to remain open to new information
	Counselor self-efficacy	Ability to be receptive to one's experiences
Variables affecting the quality of the counseling relationship	Counselor emotional and physical well-being	Counselor effort or involvement

roughly into two categories: (a) variables affecting the utilization of knowledge, and (b) variables affecting the quality of the counseling relationship. We have further divided these categories into content and process variables (see Table 1).

Content refers to variables that are finite and quantifiable, and process refers to more fluid variables and involves the counselor's style of processing information. A critical content variable is the counselor's knowledge base, which seems to us to be the essential foundation of being an effective therapist. A related content variable is a counselor's sense of self-efficacy, which seems to affect how a counselor regulates or uses his or her cognitive, affective, and behavioral responses. Two process variables that are related to knowledge reflect on aspects of the counselor's style of processing information: specifically, (a) remaining open to new information and possibilities, and (b) being receptive to one's experience.

Because counseling is based on interactions between two people, our second group of variables revolves around the interpersonal quality of the therapeutic relationship. A critical content variable within the relationship is the physical and emotional well-being of the therapist. The process variables pertain to the effort or involvement which the therapist invests in the client.

Knowledge Bases

A major variable affecting creativity within counseling is the counselor's knowledge base, including, in particular, knowledge about personality development and dynamics, the change process, and the counseling process. The counselor's knowledge bases directly affect the counselor's abilities in case conceptualization and developing interventions to facilitate desired client change. Research suggests that one's knowledge bases affect the speed and accuracy of processing information (Anderson, 1983); we suspect that this is the case within counseling as well. The more relevant knowledge the counselor has available about counseling activities, the more facile the counselor will be in processing information within the counseling experience. Conversely, the more the counselor labors in the theoretical conceptualization of human behavior and the counseling process, less time, energy, and space will be available to process information about a particular client and his or her unique situation.

In a simplified way, knowledge bases reflect differences along a novice–expert continuum as discussed in the information-processing literature (Anderson, 1983). The counselor's knowledge bases are like a foundation, a base from which to begin. Several of the therapists we interviewed remarked that their experience and reading in the field of psychology (and also great literary works on the human condition) provided an excellent storehouse of information which they could tap into for insight. Large knowledge bases do not guarantee creative behavior within counseling, but high levels of creativity most likely are not achieved without an adequate knowledge base.

Therapist Self-Efficacy

The information in the counselor's knowledge bases is obviously a critical factor within creativity. Another and equally important factor is how the counselor appraises or evaluates his or her counseling knowledge and skills. Such self-evaluation is a metacognitive variable (Butler & Meichenbaum, 1981) and could be conceptualized as self-efficacy (Bandura, 1986). The extent to which a therapist believes in him- or herself (and in the counseling process as well) is a function of previous counseling experience and is most likely correlated with his or her knowledge bases about counseling. We conceptualize self-efficacy as a content variable (rather than a style variable), which is a measurable quantity of belief in oneself as a therapist. A strong belief in oneself as a therapist most likely affects one's performance in a number of ways, such as perseverance, risk-taking, involvement, performance

anxiety, and ability to tolerate confusion and ambiguity (for related problem-solving research, see Heppner, Hibel, Neal, Weinstein, & Rabinowitz, 1982; Heppner, Reeder, & Larson, 1983).

Remaining Open to New Information

There is sometimes a danger in relying exclusively on one's knowledge bases and personality/counseling theories; the therapist may be unable to understand accurately the client's problem or to facilitate client change because the therapist recognizes only information relevant to his or her knowledge bases and theories, thereby restricting or limiting his or her vision. The counselor may be cognitively, perceptually, and emotionally positioned to look for what is already "known" to be a possibility. In short, there sometimes is a risk in knowing, especially when the counselor makes erroneous or biased assumptions about the client (see Havens, 1982). Thus, a critical variable is the manner in which a therapist processes information within counseling so as to remain open to new possibilities. This involves a willingness to set aside one's knowledge, to surrender one's beliefs about a phenomenon, to "not know" in order to learn more deeply about some aspect of a client's life. The ability to tolerate ambiguity and anxiety is important here as one relinquishes predictability. The poet Keats labeled the process "negative capability" and used such phrases to describe this process as removing "barriers to knowledge," "removing the self," "negating or annihilating the self" to permit one to experience reality without the burden of consciousness of "self" (see Bate, 1939; Margulies, 1984). One therapist told of "spontaneous images" that arise when she resists the temptation to assign prematurely categories or labels that she perceives about a client. "Not knowing" means the counselor must resist the lure of status afforded his or her position as an "expert." Paradoxically, the approach of not knowing may allow a counselor to obtain more information to understand more clearly the obstacles a client is experiencing.

Being Receptive to One's Experience

Clients bring problems into counseling that they have been unable to resolve themselves, in part, because they are unaware of their experiences (and, thus, are lacking information), or are unable to find a workable solution. Sometimes counselors can be helpful by "taking on" the client's problem (with high levels of empathy) and using their own reactions to uncover missing information and psychological processes. Or sometimes counselors can obtain information by monitoring how they are personally responding to the client. A therapist talked of the new understanding or the almost "uncanny insights" that emerge when he allows himself to listen "very quietly" to all parts of his experience as he empathizes with the client's situation.

Another process in creativity involves counselors being receptive to their experiences within and between counseling, particularly their respondent, affective, and cognitive processes (for related research, see Klinger, 1971). More experienced counselors talk about reacting to clients with a certain feeling (e.g., sadness, grief, pride) and then using that awareness to facilitate the counseling process in some way. Counselors vary widely in their reception of their own impulses, affects, and ideas. The need to "move beyond words" was expressed by one therapist who makes great use of imagery in his work. Some counselors ignore or are unaware of many of their reactions to clients, or believe them to be inappropriate in that setting, and, thus, are unable to use this information to solve the client's problem. Being receptive to one's inner experiences may be a function of individual difference variables (e.g., introversion-extraversion: Myers & McCaulley, 1985) as well as a learned capacity to use one's inner events. In short, sometimes being creative within counseling involves processing information from several perspectives (counselor, client) as well as several modalities (cognitive, affective) and senses (visual, auditory).

Well-Being

Because counseling is an interpersonal activity, which is often emotionally charged, the emotional and physical well-being of the therapist is an important variable affecting creativity. An emotionally or physically tired therapist often has more difficulty processing information within counseling, and many times is less able to understand the psychological events in the client's life. In short, the well-being of the therapist is a condition that can inhibit or facilitate how the counselor processes information and, consequently, may affect creativity within counseling.

Therapist Effort and Involvement

A critical variable in counseling pertains to the relationship between the counselor and the client

(see Gelso & Carter, 1985). The quality of the relationship will affect the amount of effort expended and the level of involvement by both counselor and client. With a high degree of effort, often there are quantitative and qualitative differences in the amount of information that is processed. Likewise, the counselor's interest and emotional involvement in the client often elicits deep, elaborative cognitive processing within the counselor. In a way, the client becomes a "current concern" (Klinger, 1971) of the counselor. Klinger has noted that creativity often arises from "important" problems; problems that have goals that are meaningful in some way to a person. Thus, a high level of counselor effort and involvement results in a high level of information processing on the part of the counselor, thereby increasing the probability that creative uses of information will occur. This high level of counselor involvement often entails intermittent processing between counseling sessions, or incubating with a problem for a while, until ideas are combined in a unique fashion.

However, sometimes a counselor tries too hard, becomes overinvolved with a client, and his or her focus of attention narrows and results in missed information. Several writers have noted that creative insight occurs during a period of "relaxed tension" (Ghiselin, 1952; Rugg, 1963) so that the solution is not forced (Klinger, 1971). Or sometimes counselors (especially trainees) may be overconcerned about their counseling performance, which not only results in high levels of anxiety or of being overly focused on their emotional responses but also reduces their ability to process information. Sometimes more experienced counselors describe their creative insights as occurring while their senses are involved in a highly charged emotional counseling relationship; yet, concurrently, they are able to remove themselves to cognitively process what is transpiring in the counseling session and the therapeutic process. This phenomenon has been described in other contexts as the capacity to be, at once, both participant and observer (Capra, 1975), and involves the ability to balance internal and external messages.

Conclusion

We have discussed several variables that affect counselors' creativity within counseling. From our experience, there seems to be a curvilinear relationship between most of the variables we have discussed and the creative process; that is, a lack of knowledge, self-efficacy, openness to new information, receptivity to one's experiences, and involvement most likely inhibit creative responses. But high levels of these variables may also inhibit creativity. For example, a large knowledge base about counseling coupled with an exaggerated sense of self-efficacy as a therapist may reduce the therapist's openness to new information and inhibit novel approaches to counseling.

It seems that counselor creativity in counseling is most often a function of some optimal level of information processing by the therapist. Each of the variables we discussed either facilitates or inhibits the therapist in cognitively or affectively processing information relevant to the client's problem. Most likely, counselor creativity within counseling is not simply related to the amount of information processed, but also how the information is processed and combined in novel yet effective ways. It is our hunch that more experienced, highly skilled, and creative therapists have well-differentiated roadmaps of the counseling process for different types of clients, and that they can process information more quickly, accurately, and in nonlinear ways. Their successful experiences may in turn bolster their therapeutic confidence, which in turn allows them greater tolerance for risk taking and ambiguity. Most likely, these counselors can also discriminate between relevant and less relevant information and, subsequently, may have more time to concentrate on finding the missing piece or to combine information in unique and helpful ways.

Final Comments

This chapter discussed the role of counselor creativity within counseling and some of the variables that seem to affect creative counselor behavior. We believe that counseling would provide a productive setting in which to study creativity. In fact, counseling would provide a unique opportunity for studying creativity within the context of an interpersonal relationship. It may prove to be particularly productive to examine creativity in terms of how the counselor processes information and, subsequently, how the client processes information.

There are a number of ways that researchers might proceed. The interpersonal influence research paradigm (see Corrigan, Dell, Lewis, & Schmidt, 1980; Heppner & Dixon, 1981) might also be useful to analyze the effect of a counselor's

information processing (e.g., cognitive, affective, imaging) with problem identification and interventions on the change process (attitudes, cognitions, behaviors) within clients. Investigators could employ methodologies, such as Interpersonal Process Recall (Kagan, 1975), Thought-Listing (Cacioppo & Petty, 1981), Hill's counselor intentions and client reactions (Hill & O'Grady, 1985; Hill, Helms, Spiegel, & Tichenor, 1988), or even Martin's schemata analysis (Martin, 1985). Such methodologies could be used to assess how clients or counselors are processing information, especially during impasses. Comparisons could be made along an expertise dimension (novice trainees, doctoral level interns, experienced and skillful therapists), perhaps initially through intensive single-subject designs and later between groups. Correlational designs could also be utilized to examine the relationships among some of the variables we suggested earlier (e.g., counselor knowledge bases, self-efficacy, remaining open to new information) and creative counselor processes.

Another setting that may be quite fruitful to examine is the formal training of psychotherapists. Much has been written about the impact of formal education on creative behavior in general and on the cognitive processes that are involved in creative production (Burgett, 1982; Simonton, 1983). As yet there has not been a systematic analysis of the manner in which creativity and problem solving are addressed in counselor education programs. Researchers might examine the effects of counselor education on counselor creativity, preferably via a longitudinal analyses, but also through a cross-sectional analysis. A useful research model may be one employed in examining the effect of counselor education on trainees'' research interests (see Royalty, Gelso, Mallinckrodt, & Garrett, 1986). Another approach may be to examine the supervisory process of trainees in relationship to the development of creative processes in counselors. Supervision is widely recognized as one of the most important teaching mechanisms of counselor trainees; within the last five years, there has been a dramatic increase in supervision research, most notably with regard to the developmental processes of trainees (e.g., Heppner & Roehlke, 1984; O'Leary-Wiley & Ray, 1986; Reising & Daniels, 1983). Researchers might examine the relationships between supervisor variables (e.g., supervisor style, supervisor behaviors related to teaching and emotional support, supervisor theoretical orientation and interpersonal values, level of creative processes modeled by the supervisor) with various indices of train-ee creativity (e.g., trainee self-report variables, information processing as indicated above, type and effectiveness of trainee interventions with cli-ents, such as metaphors and novel fantasies) across different trainee developmental levels (see Rabinowitz, Heppner, & Roehlke, 1986, for a model of the latter).

It is our concern that formal education in ad-vanced degree programs may inhibit or discourage the creative capabilities of trainees. For example, trainees are often asked to justify their interven-tions. Although valuable, this challenge process may also discourage divergence and inhibit more creative thinking. In addition, therapists must be ethically responsible for their clients' welfare and safeguard them from harm. Thus, trainees may feel hesitant to consider any approach that is not cus-tomary, or they may be directly cautioned about being creative. Without any assurance of what the reaction to a creative (unique, surprising, nontradi-tional) intervention will be, many counselors (es-pecially novices) hesitate to risk what seems like nonconventional acts. Even though learning the fundamentals of counseling enhances the trainee's ability to be a therapist, the trainee's potential to be intuitive or creative can be inhibited by an over-emphasis on the predictable, traditional methods. Thus, from a research perspective, it may also be useful via some of the research models suggested above to assess if trainees' creative processing in-creases or decreases over time during graduate training.

It is important to note that facilitating creativity in counselor trainees does not need to be done at the expense of the more traditional educational objec-tives. In fact, we believe that counselor educators and supervisors must continue to insist on rigor and demonstrable competence in trainees' academic preparations. A curriculum that fosters the creative capabilities in trainees does not need to be divided along academic/nonacademic lines. Rather, train-ing for creativity and problem solving could be add-ed to the curriculum, with the goal of enhancing the counselor's ability to process information from sev-eral modalities (e.g., thinking, feeling, imaging). In this regard, however, it might be useful to exam-ine the learning objectives most commonly associ-ated with graduate training, with a keen eye toward process versus content objectives, such as ini-tiative, discovery learning, independence, and self-evaluation skills. Anecdotally, it appeared to the first author that some English counselor-training programs were directed more toward such process objectives than were most American programs.

In short, a counselor's role is to help other people solve problems. Because creativity is often studied in problem solving, the training of counseling psy-chologists might be a fertile area to investigate how creativity can be fostered or inhibited in trainees. Likewise, counseling psychologists might provide a population with which to study naturally occur-ring creative events, which could form the basis for descriptive research. It is unfortunate that so little attention has been given to how therapists process information. We know very little how more experi-enced or novice counselors use their cognitive and affective processes, or how they combine informa-tion to develop creative client conceptualizations or therapeutic interventions. Likewise, we know very little about how clients' experiential world is im-pacted by creative counselor responses, and the dy-namic interplay between the two. Perhaps there might be mutual benefits for creative collaborative efforts between cognitive psychologists, who are interested in exploring creative processes, and counseling psychologists, who desire to use cre-ative behavior to create healthy change in their clients.

ACKNOWLEDGMENTS. The authors are grateful to the following therapists for their thoughts regard-ing creativity within counseling: Wayne Anderson, Helen Roehlke, Richard Thoreson. In addition, we would like to thank Helen Roehlke and Eileen Pick-ard for their editorial assistance in preparing this chapter.

References

Abel, A. M. (1964). *Talks with the great composers*. Garmisch-Partenkirchen, Germany: G. E. Schroeder-Verlag.

Anderson, J. R. (1983). *The architecture of cognition*. Cambridge: Harvard University Press.

Bandura, A. (1986). *Social foundations of thought and action: A social cognitive theory*. Englewood Cliffs, NJ: Prentice-Hall.

Bate, W. J. (1939). *Negative capability: The intuitive approach in Keats*. Cambridge: Harvard University Press.

Burgett, P. J. (1982). . . . On creativity. *Journal of Creative Behavior, 16*, 239–249.

Butler, L., & Meichenbaum, D. (1981). The assessment of inter-personal problem-solving skills. In P. Kendall & S. D. Hollon (Eds.), *Assessment strategies for cognitive-behavioral inter-ventions* (pp. 197–225). New York: Academic Press.

Cacioppo, J. T., & Petty, R. E. (1981). Social psychological procedures for cognitive response assessment: The thought-listing technique. In T. V. Merluzzi, C. R. Glass, & M. Genest (Eds.), *Cognitive assessment* (pp. 309–342). New York: Guilford Press.

Capra, F. (1975). *The tao of physics.* Berkeley: Shambala.

Corrigan, J. D., Dell, D. M., Lewis, K. N., & Schmidt, L. D. (1980). Counseling as a social influence process: A review. *Journal of Counseling Psychology, 27,* 395–441.

Corsini, R. (Ed.). (1984). *Current psychotherapies* (3rd ed.). Itasca, IL: F. E. Peacock.

Fretz, B. R. (1982). Perspectives and definitions. *The Counseling Psychologist, 10*(2), 15–19.

Gelso, C. J., & Carter, J. A. (1985). The relationship in counseling and psychotherapy: Components, consequences, and theoretical antecedents. *The Counseling Psychologist, 13*(2), 155–243.

Ghiselin, B. (1952). *The creative process.* New York: New American Library.

Greenson, R. R. (1967). *The technique and practice of psychoanalysis* (Vol. 1). New York: International Universities Press.

Havens, L. (1982). The risks of knowing and not knowing. *Journal of Social Biological Structures, 5,* 213–222.

Heppner, P. P., & Dixon, D. N. (1981). A review of the interpersonal influence process in counseling. *Personnel and Guidance Journal, 59,* 542–550.

Heppner, P. P., & Fitzgerald, K. M. (1987). Human intelligence: Implications for counseling. *Journal of Counseling and Development, 65,* 266–267.

Heppner, P. P., & Roehlke, H. J. (1984). Differences among supervisees at different levels of training: Implications for a developmental model of supervision. *Journal of Counseling Psychology, 31,* 76–90.

Heppner, P. P., Hibel, J. H., Neal, G. W., Weinstein, C. L., & Rabinowitz, F. E. (1982). Personal problem solving: A descriptive study of individual differences. *Journal of Counseling Psychology, 24,* 580–590.

Heppner, P. P., Reeder, B. L., & Larson, L. M. (1983). Cognitive variables associated with personal problem-solving appraisal: Implications for counseling. *Journal of Counseling Psychology, 30,* 537–545.

Highlen, P. S., & Hill, C. E. (1984). Factors affecting client change in individual counseling: Current status and theoretical speculations. In S. D. Brown & R. W. Lent (Eds.), *Handbook of counseling psychology* (pp. 334–396). New York: Wiley-Interscience.

Hill, C. E., & O'Grady, K. E. (1985). A list of therapist intentions illustrated in a case study and with therapists of varying theoretical orientations. *Journal of Counseling Psychology, 32,* 3–22.

Hill, C. E., Helms, J. E., Spiegel, S. B., & Tichenor, V. (1988). Development of a system for categorizing client reactions to therapist interventions. *Journal of Counseling Psychology, 35,* 27–36.

Kagan, N. (1975). Influencing human interaction: Eleven years with IPR. *Canadian Counsellor, 9,* 44–51.

Kell, B. L., & Mueller, W. J. (1966). *Impact and change: A study of counseling relationships.* New York: Appleton-Century-Crofts.

Klinger, E. (1971). *Structure and function of fantasy.* New York: Wiley-Interscience.

Koestler, A. (1964). *The act of creation.* New York: Macmillan.

Margulies, A. (1984). Toward empathy: The uses of wonder. *American Journal of Psychiatry, 141,* 1025–1033.

Martin, J. (1985). Measuring clients' cognitive competence in research on counseling. *Journal of Counseling and Development, 63,* 556–560.

Myers, I. B., & McCaulley, M. H. (1985). *Manual: A guide to the development and use of the Myers-Briggs Type Indicator.* Palo Alto, CA: Consulting Psychologists Press.

O'Leary-Wiley, M., & Ray, P. B. (1986). Counseling supervision by developmental level. *Journal of Counseling Psychology, 33,* 439–445.

Pickard, E. M. (1979). *The development of creative ability.* London: National Foundation for Educational Research.

Rabinowitz, F. E., Heppner, P. P., & Roehlke, H. J. (1986). Descriptive study of process and outcome variables of supervision over time. *Journal of Counseling Psychology, 33,* 292–300.

Reising, G. N., & Daniels, M. H. (1983). A study of Hogan's model of counselor development and supervision. *Journal of Counseling Psychology, 30,* 235–244.

Royalty, G. M., Gelso, C. J., Mallinckrodt, B., & Garrett, K. D. (1986). The environment and the student in Counseling Psychology. *The Counseling Psychologist, 14,* 9–30.

Rugg, H. (1963). *Imagination.* New York: Harper & Row.

Simonton, D. K. (1983). Formal education, eminence, and dogmatism: The curvilinear relationship. *Journal of Creative Behavior, 17,* 149–162.

PART IV

Applications

Part IV of the volume is, by far, the largest of our sections. Three chapters are devoted to various aspects of increasing creativity in writing. Another three chapters focus on creativity in science and social science, and the last two chapters examine procedures whereby creativity may be facilitated at different stages of life.

CHAPTER 17

Foundations for Creativity in the Writing Process

RHETORICAL REPRESENTATIONS OF ILL-DEFINED PROBLEMS

Linda J. Carey and Linda Flower

Introduction: An Approach to Studying Creativity in Writing

A creative act is usually defined as one that has a valuable or interesting product and that is in some way original or surprising (Hayes, 1981). However, whether we characterize a particular act as "creative" clearly depends on the context or circumstances in which it takes place. For example, we evaluate the creativity of a child's drawing using different criteria from those we would apply to a painting by Monet; a creative act may be enriching to one individual or it may have earth-shaking consequences. Although creativity in writing is popularly associated with literary genres, other genres, such as expository writing, also offer opportunities for creative products. For example, a research report, a proposal, or a magazine article could be judged creative if it presents information in a new and valuable way to meet the needs and constraints of its audience and purpose—that is, if the text

Linda J. Carey and Linda Flower • Center for the Study of Writing, Carnegie-Mellon University, Pittsburgh, PA 15238.

presents an innovative solution to a significant rhetorical problem.

In this situational view of creativity, it becomes important to ask not just how did the "genius" class of writers produce traditionally acknowledged (i.e., literary) works, but how do people in that larger class of "effective" writers produce a creative response to a given rhetorical problem? Creative responses to the rhetorical problems raised by school, professions, and public life are necessary on a regular basis for these groups to sustain what others see as quality work. This source of practical creativity, in the face of significant but not infrequent rhetorical problems, is an asset for society that schools, professions, and public groups have to depend upon.

Against this backdrop of practical creativity, which is demonstrated by a wide range of expository writers facing a variety of rhetorical problems, we want to look at the individual writer at work and ask: What are the cognitive processes in expository writing that produce, or at least create an opportunity for, a creative response?

The cognitive research we will discuss does not

try to predict or even account for creativity *per se,* which, we would argue, has multiple sources. Furthermore, the studies we review were not explicitly designed to measure creativity itself but rather to analyze features of expertise. What this research does show us is how certain features of the writing process itself (viz., working with ill-defined problems, task representation, integrating topic and rhetorical knowledge, and strategies for global revision) provide a cognitive mechanism that has the potential to produce a uniquely adaptive response. These features operate as an opportunity or an invitation for creativity—an invitation that writers often decline.

In this chapter, we examine the composing processes of expert writers working in expository genres. We take a problem-solving perspective (see Newell & Simon, 1972; Simon, 1986) which postulates that creativity does not depend on "special" abilities or on unconscious processes and insights, but rather on ordinary cognitive processes that are applied in powerful ways. We draw on research into writers' composing processes and particularly into their planning and revision processes (Flower, Schriver, Carey, Haas, & Hayes, 1987; Hayes, Flower, Schriver, Stratman, & Carey, 1988), which indicates that when expert writers tackle academic or professional expository tasks, they engage in active and complex problem solving in order to define their task and solve their rhetorical problems in unique and interesting ways.

In the first section, we discuss how the ill-defined nature of many writing problems and the cognitive processes experts use to solve these problems interact to provide an opportunity for creative thinking. In the second section, we examine how differences in writers' representation of their task can affect the originality and overall quality of their final products; and in the last two sections, we look at how writers' planning and revision processes can provide opportunities for working creatively in expository genres.

Creativity and Ill-Defined Problems

How do expository writing tasks provide opportunities for creativity? To address this question, we will follow the lead of Newell, Shaw, and Simon (1964) who propose that a creative act is the act of solving an ill-defined problem. These are problems in which solvers have to define the problem for themselves and in which they have to "fill in the

gaps" of the problem with specialist knowledge; each problem-solver's solution will be unique because it reflects the solver's own unique knowledge and values (Hayes, 1981). Thus, the very nature of an ill-defined problem stimulates creativity in the problem solver. Many problems in architecture, in design, and in music would certainly fall under this umbrella of an ill-defined problem (see Reitman, 1964; Simon, 1973) and these are, of course, areas in which we would expect to find expressions of creativity. Similarly, many writing tasks also present a solver with an ill-defined problem and, hence, with a potential for creativity.

Although all writing tasks are ill-defined in comparison with, for example, game problems (such as the Tower of Hanoi problems discussed by Newell & Simon, 1972), some tasks are more ill-defined than others. Such tasks as a routine rejection letter or a lab report for a physics class, for example, may require little active problem solving *if* the writer has already written several of these before and, hence, is very familiar with the discourse conventions. The writer can simply "fill in the blanks" in his or her standard outline (or "script") for the task with appropriate content. Other tasks may only require writers to access their knowledge about a particular topic and to reproduce it on paper. (Reporting the minutes of a meeting would be one obvious example.) Here we will discuss those expository tasks that do require active problem solving. How do good writers develop creative solutions to complex, ill-defined writing tasks and why are student writers' texts often disappointingly routine?

We will address these questions by looking at three processes which our research suggests are crucial to dealing with ill-defined writing tasks: (1) constructing an elaborated and flexible representation of the task; (2) integrating topic knowledge and rhetorical knowledge; and (3) applying and controlling problem-solving strategies.

Constructing a Representation of the Task

By their very nature, ill-defined problems do not present solvers with a ready-made task representation. Rather, in response to vague task specifications, such as "build a house" or "write a research proposal," a problem solver has to take an active role in defining the boundaries of the problem and in specifying a set of goals and criteria for the task. Thus, when faced with an unfamiliar writing task, a writer has to construct his or her own unique representation of the rhetorical problem to be solved

(Flower *et al.*, 1987). Although a topic may be assigned (as in many college writing tasks), or the format may be prespecified (there are standard guidelines for writing a proposal), the conceptual structure the writer creates around a topic, and the function to which those format features are put, reflect the private goals of the writer.

For instance, expert writers spend considerable time and attention elaborating a network of goals, constraints, and criteria as they compose (Flower *et al.*, 1987). They may draw inferences about the audience and set goals for dealing with it, or they may translate format features, such as an obligatory introduction, into goals. These goals, of course, could reflect a conventional plan (e.g., better start out with a topic sentence and some background) or a uniquely adaptive one (e.g., how about showing them, in some subtle way, what they appear to assume?). Setting goals does not guarantee unique goals, but the planning process we have observed goes well beyond a simple selection and transcription of topic knowledge. Even on a ''normal'' academic task, such as that faced by the contributors to this volume, there is likely to be enormous variety in the way the task ''write about creativity in . . .'' is framed and in the top-level goals and constraints writers give themselves. These goals, created in interaction with the writer's topic knowledge, then determine how much of that knowledge is used and how and why it is used.

Because complex writing tasks are quite literally constructed by the writers, people with the same assignments give themselves significantly different rhetorical problems. The very nature of these ill-defined problems—which writers structure and define for themselves—then, is an important basis for creativity in writing. Some writers exploit this potential by giving themselves unique and valued problems to solve. In a study of writers' initial task representations (Carey, Flower, Hayes, Schriver, & Haas, 1986), we found that the nature of the goals that a writer develops in his or her task representation may well affect the quality of the final product and provide an opportunity for creative problem-solving. In a later section, we will discuss how qualitative differences in writers' initial task representations are mirrored by differences in the quality of their final texts.

Building a representation of an ill-defined problem is also a dynamic process (Simon, 1973). Expert writers' representations often change as they progress through the task: new facets of the problem may occur to experts during writing that change

their goals and require them to re-represent the problem or to modify a current representation. For example, in writing a proposal, a writer may realize, on reading the introduction, that the purpose of the research may be clear but not persuasive. The writer may then have to develop a set of unique goals and subgoals for persuading the reader that this particular project is needed and feasible. This process of constructing and reconstructing an image of the task in response to the growing text often leads writers to the discovery of some unique and valuable insights about their task (Flower & Hayes, 1980) and, hence, provides opportunities for creative thinking.

This phenomenon of building a *dynamic* task representation seems to be important to creativity in domains other than writing. For example, a study by Getzels and Csikszentmihalyi (1976) found that artists whose work was rated highly for creativity often discovered new dimensions to a problem as they worked on it; these creative artists were modifying their problem representation in response to their emerging drawings. Or, as Perkins (1981) points out, creative problem solvers remain ready to change their decisions in the light of new knowledge gained from working on the problem and thus remain open to new insights.

The process of constructing and modifying a representation of the task presents inexperienced writers with several difficulties that limit their opportunities for creativity. First, novices may simply ''jump into'' the problem without spending time and effort on re-representing and discovery. The result may be that they are then forced to work with an initial representation which is too abstract or which does not address important features of the task. Certainly, in our work on planning, we found that novice writers tended not to build the complex networks of goals and subgoals that typified the plans of the expert writers (Flower *et al.*, 1987), and, as consequence, their texts failed to address important audience needs.

Second, novices may become committed to one representation of their task and not be open to re-representing the task in light of new discoveries. For example, Beach and Eaton (1984) found that many of their student writers typically relied on the pattern of organization of the ''five-paragraph theme'' and were unable to adapt their texts to the constraints of audience and purpose. Similarly, Britton, Burgess, Martin, McLeod, and Rosen (1975) found that students' representations of rhetorical problems were fixed by their perceptions of the demands of the teacher and school context, rather than by their sense of audience and purpose. As a result, their texts tended to be formulaic and routine and to lack interesting and new angles or perspectives.

Integrating Topic Knowledge and Rhetorical Knowledge

Another opening for creativity in writing is the way in which people manage the constraints of integrating their topic knowledge and rhetorical knowledge. Simply put, writers must often manipulate or transform what they know to meet the constraints of a unique rhetorical situation. If the subject is complex or new, writers will not have available prepackaged or organized pieces of information that can simply be slotted into the text. Rather, they will have to engage in difficult knowledge-transforming operations to adapt what they know to meet the rhetorical goals of, for example, involving and interesting a particular audience (Scardamalia & Bereiter, 1988). This "juggling act" between two different knowledge domains—content knowledge (i.e., about the substance of the text) and rhetorical knowledge (i.e., about the constraints of audience, genre, and purpose) presents an opportunity for expert writers to restructure their knowledge in insightful ways and thus provides a potential for creative expression.

However, this juggling act appears to present difficulties for developing writers. As Scardamalia and Bereiter's study indicates, inexperienced writers often take a "knowledge-telling" approach to expository writing; they simply write all they know about a topic without considering such rhetorical features as audience and purpose. Similarly, Langer (1984) found that having a lot of information on a topic did not necessarily help students to write coherently on that topic; they were unable to structure their knowledge into an appropriate rhetorical pattern to develop, for example, a cause/effect essay. In our studies of planning, we found that writers whose plans mainly consisted of "content plans" produced texts that were less well adapted for audience and purpose than writers who integrated content and rhetorical planning (Carey *et al.*, 1986).

Adults who are capable of adapting what they know to what a reader needs or wants often fail to do so; they report information when the reader needs a recommendation; they define technical concepts

when the learner/textbook reader needs an orientation to the field. In this "writer-based prose," writers take a cognitively less demanding route of talking to themselves (Flower, 1979). For some, this is an efficient first-draft strategy, and they transform their text into "reader-based prose" later. The interaction of rhetorical and content knowledge, then, is both a problem that some writers do not solve and a constraint that generates uniquely adaptive solutions for other writers.

Developing and Applying Problem-Solving Strategies

As we have seen, ill-defined problems require a solver to manage both an evolving set of goals and constraints and a large body of knowledge. To accomplish this management task successfully, a problem solver needs to use strategies for cutting down the search process (Simon, 1973). Our research indicates that expert writers have a wider repertoire of such strategies than do inexperienced writers. For example, we found that our expert planners had several strategies for resolving goal conflicts and for consolidating information; our novices, on the other hand, often simply sidestepped these problems and, as a result, missed opportunities for developing promising aspects of the text (Flower *et al.*, 1987). Similarly, expert revisers seem better equipped to deal with difficult global revision problems because their strategies are more efficient and more flexible; in contrast, novices frequently rely on a time-consuming and risky trial-and-error procedure of rewriting the text until it "sounds better" (Hayes *et al.*, 1988). (We will discuss this work on revision in more detail in the final section.)

Strategies, like some of the other features we have discussed, seem to operate alternatively as a path or a roadblock to creativity. Rose (1984), documented some of the ways in which the possibility for creativity is shut down by the rigid rules and strategies that students bring to writing. Student writers who regularly blocked or failed to do assignments voiced absolutist assumptions about how the writing process should operate (e.g., as a spontaneous and elevated act in which formal preplanning is inappropriate), whereas nonblockers recognized a variety of acceptable approaches determined by the context. The high-blocking students also invoked a variety of rigid "rules" to which a writer must adhere (although they did not agree on the rules). Some of these rules demanded concentration on the surface features of text rather than on the conceptual structure, for instance, and led to premature editing. As one student put it, "I write with the thought . . . that this is going to be it . . . so it had better be good the first time through" (p. 73). Finally, some of the limited strategies students brought to writing, such as depending on the five-paragraph theme, allowed only limited structures of thought, and they led to "incremental" planning in which students planned and composed in small, unconnected segments.

The strategies, assumptions, and rigid rules of the high-blocking students seemed, then, to interfere with their day-to-day functioning as writers in the university. What is interesting for our purpose is that this maladaptive approach to writing seems to operate by shutting down the processes that can foster creativity—the processes of integrating and reintegrating information and of taking a flexible, context-dependent approach to managing strategies. For high-blockers, the constraints that lead creative writers to unique, adaptive plans have ceased to be generative.

Having a repertoire of strategies may not be sufficient to ensure success in solving ill-defined writing problems; a writer must also know *when* to use a particular strategy and be able to monitor and test its effectiveness. This *metacognitive* ability—that is, the ability to regulate one's own strategic action (see Brown, 1980)—allows writers to have more control over their own processes. In our revision research (Hayes *et al.,* 1988), we found that expert revisers made conscious decisions about which strategies to use, based on such criteria as the nature and density of the problems in the text and the pragmatic constraints of the task (e.g., the amount of time available.) The novice writers in our study, however, often failed to deal adequately with text problems because they were inflexible and kept with one strategy, even if it was obviously not working for them. Similarly, research on reading, summarizing, and learning (Brown & Smiley, 1978; Brown, Day, & Jones, 1983), suggests that novices' lack of conscious regulation restricts their ability to use effective comprehension strategies, such as rereading, making inferences, and extracting gists, even if they are aware of these strategies.

To sum up, from the perspective we are taking, many writing tasks are best described as ill-defined problems in which writers construct their own network of goals and plans. The initial representation a writer creates can, of course, be simple and/or conventional, but it can also be an elaborated and unique construction. Hence, the process of writing itself opens the door for creative cognitive acts. Also, the recursive nature of the writing process observed in studies of planning and revision allows, and in fact calls for, re-representation. As writers generate information through the activity of composing itself, they also perceive new goals and constraints, and their image of their task is itself frequently open to transformation. The process opens a door, but whether or not writers do indeed integrate this growing network of goals and topic knowledge into a coherent, much less unique configuration is a question we will look at in the context of specific parts of the process.

In tune with our focus on practical creativity, we are looking at the way the "normal" processes of composing can lead to creative results. We are assuming, as has Simon, that creative acts do not depend on "special" or extraordinary basic processes. In the research we are about to describe, we cannot assert that the written products of the subjects studied would be judged as creative, because public judgment of uniqueness plus value is our standard. The research did not set itself up to study creativity *per se* but expert performance. So the conclusions one can draw are necessarily limited. What we do propose to do is to look more closely at how writers tackle these difficult processes of building a representation of a writing task, of integrating topic and rhetorical knowledge, and of developing and applying problem-solving strategies. We examine these processes in the context of three different kinds of professional and college writing assignments: a task that required interpretation and synthesis of reading materials; one that involved planning and writing a short expository text; and one that was essentially a revision task.

The processes we have chosen have three qualities: they are generative *and* integrative processes and have the potential to affect the top levels of a writer's goal structure. These processes do not, in themselves, produce a creative response to a rhetorical problem, but they do provide, we will argue, the operational foundation for responses that are both novel and highly adaptive to the context for writing. From an educational point of view, these seem to be aspects of the writing process that writers learn to manage with some difficulty, that lead to effective writing, and that have the potential, as high-level generative and integrative processes, to lead to that special effect we label *creative*.

The Effect of Task Representation on Originality

The practical creativity on which we concentrate in this chapter requires an original but highly adaptive response to a rhetorical situation. A creative solution has to function within a considerable set of constraints set by the context. For instance, writing in these situations is often in response to an assignment that is posed by an organization, a manager, or a teacher. The study by Britton *et al.* (1975) of 2,000 samples of school writing in Great Britain, grades 6–12, suggests that school assignments may severely limit opportunities for both originality and imaginative adaptation. By grade 12, 61% of the scripts studied were categorized as papers written by "pupil to examiner," "as a demonstration of material mastered or as evidence of ability to take up a certain kind of style" (p. 122). The terms *assigned* or *school* writing are sometimes used as synonyms for noncreative and purposeless exposition. Sadly enough this may be an apt description for how some teachers use writing (as a test for content knowledge or correctness) and how their students learn to see assigned writing. However, a look at the writing processes of college students suggests that assigned writing is, like any other constraint, subject to interpretation. The task the writer gives him or herself may be a much better predictor of creativity than whether it is assigned and or highly constrained.

As a case in point, we can take a close look at the task representation process itself, as it occurred in a large group of college writers writing a paper on an assigned body of readings.

Alternative Representations of a Standard College Task

In this study, four sections of a freshman class were given a standard, open-ended college assignment that read:

Here are some notes, including research results and observations, on time management. Your task is to read and interpret this data in order to make a brief (1–2 page), comprehensive statement about this subject. Your statement should interpret and synthesize all of the relevant findings in the text.

The text was two pages of notes and conflicting claims taken from various "authorities" on the top-ic of time management, ranging from Alan Lakein on how to "take control of your time and your life," to advice from Cornell's study skills center, to William James's comments on working through fatigue. The assignment was designed to include all the sacred words of college assignments: synthesize, interpret, be comprehensive, and the essay was referred to at the end of the readings as "your statement." The intent was to create a Rorschach assignment that would allow students to examine their own process and interpretation of this college assignment. On the day the assignment was due, students did a self-analysis of how they had viewed the task in terms of the information source they used, the format they thought appropriate, their overall organizing plan, and some of their dominant strategies and goals. This analysis was supported by a checklist based on the results of three prior pilot studies that had shown us a wide range of response to two parallel versions of this assignment. Certain features of these responses are relevant to creativity.

For this assignment, 43% of the freshmen students organized their paper as either a summary of the source texts or as a review and comment—a plan in which the source texts provide a conceptual frame and substance to which the writer can add a commentary at selected spots (Ackerman, in press). Only 25% of the students attempted a synthesis in which their essay was organized around a controlling concept that gave structure and coherence to their discussion. Students who gave themselves the task of synthesis had to invent a concept that could make sense of these data, even though, like normal library research, the information did not fall into a simple or obvious pattern; and they had, at least in theory, to deal with the contradictory claims of these "authorities." An even smaller group, 11%, said that they treated the paper as an interpretation of the source texts, organized around a purpose of their own. To use this plan, writers had to imagine a reader who would find the information useful, or to see an issue or problem to be examined, and use that purpose to organize an interpretation of the relevant material. This plan typically makes heavy use of the writer's own ideas.

When asked to describe their own strategies, 2% of the freshmen said that they used the strategy of "adapting to the reader"; 6% chose to "use the text for my own purpose." However, when they were asked to predict what the experienced, masters level students had done when they did this task, the figures for these adaptive strategies jumped to 24% and 15%. It seems that the students themselves saw that the strategies one used were not a function of the assignment but of the writer. Some students who commented on this difference attributed it to the greater freedom they perceive master's students to have.

Finally, the checklist, though naturally incomplete, also listed a number of goals previous writers had mentioned. The freshmen students identified their goals with choices, such as "presenting learning" (20%), "covering key points" (18%), and "do the minimum" (13%). Zero percent checked the goal of "creativity." Taken together, these analyses show some students giving themselves tasks in which a creative response is unlikely to occur. These data come from the students' own self-analyses; the data based on judges' analyses of the texts showed even lower frequency of syntheses and interpretations. However, these self-reports are interesting because there were clear cases in which students attempted more ambitious tasks, even though the judges were unable to perceive the result of that effort in the written text. The thinking-aloud protocols and the in-class presentations of three of these students can give us a more explicit view of how these interpretations were created (Flower, in press).

Martha was a junior engineering major in one of the pilot studies. Students in the class had done a thinking-aloud protocol of themselves as they read the source texts and wrote their essays. The protocols let them look closely at their own cognition and prepare an in-class presentation on an "interesting feature" of their own writing process. Martha's presentation focused on her own very clear procedure for doing the task. She used what the class came to call the "gist-and-list" strategy: you read through the text with some care, find the key words in each paragraph, and summarize it trying to capture the main idea. You then write a paper organized around this set of gists. The most interesting feature of her plan was its caution rule: Sometimes a new idea will occur to you as you are writing—a new connection, an insight, or new way to organize. If that happens, you must decisively ignore this possibility for it will only confuse you and your paper. Martha's representation of the task placed priority on accurate summarization, efficiency, and coherence. Furthermore, this was a practiced strategy for her, "just like doing a research paper." The task Martha gave herself

seemed very close to the limited "pupil to examiner" recitation of knowledge that Britton's group observed and deplored.

In contrast to Martha, Kate, a beginning graduate student in professional writing, concentrated on the way the audience determined the focus of the paper and defined what information was "relevant." The task she gave herself required adapting her reading to what she imagined her potential readers would be interested in. The following protocol shows us how introducing this additional constraint of audience solved the problem of generating enough to say:

Hmm. Let's see. Ok. I don't see how I'm going to get 1–2 pages out of studies and experts that pretty much back each other up. Damn. I wish I'd never sold my acoustics textbook [reference to an interruption by a roommate.] Well, who are my readers? About 15 people who mostly teach the freshmen course. . . . Yes, so why would anyone care to hear about this? . . . So they want to know how to write better, but maybe more importantly how to teach better. Oh yes, and Linda Flower, but there's no doubt she's interested in that to. Ok. They're my primary audience, so. . . .

As a result of these goals, Kate generates ideas not found in the source and begins her text by telling readers two ways in which her information might be of use to them. This view of writing as an adaptive enterprise is apparently not new to Kate. In her own presentation and in response to Martha's very different plan, Kate remarks that, as a past economics major, she even has a private formula for her procedure: $T = f(A)$. The topic or information she uses is a function of the audience.

Both Kate and Martha appeared to bring well-learned plans for interpreting writing tasks with them. And in one of the pilots, 50% of the students said that they paid no attention to the assignment itself but invoked their standard paper-writing strategies. In light of the clear variety among these representations, one wonders how often the "standard" strategy is the optimal one for all these writers. Our final example shows a student actually negotiating a decision point in her task representation and considering the costs and benefits of alternative interpretations.

"Interpret and synthesize" [student is rereading the assignment].
What the hell does that mean? Synthesize means to pull together, no, to make something up. Why should I want to make something up?
[She then rereads, commenting on the wording of the assignment. . . .]
Synthesis sounds like I'm making a chemical compound. Hmm.

Put together.
[Re-reads] "All of the relevant findings in the text."
How can I do this?

At this point the writer apparently decides that, in fact, she does not want "to make something up" and begins to summarize the readings.

It is not surprising that different representations of a writing task could have the effect of fostering or discouraging original thinking and an adaptive response to the needs of readers. The striking feature of these protocols and presentations is that the students who held these different representations appeared to assume that they were simply doing the task as it was assigned, rather than constructing an interpretation, and were surprised to discover the range of options others considered possible—if not actually mandated by the assignment. Students who were limiting the likelihood of creativity may have done so in the name of least effort, but they appeared to do so in the faith that this was also expected.

Of course, it does not follow that even students who set the goals of being creative will be able to do so. One student in the pilot class said that she habitually set high standards for creativity in her own writing. However, as the protocols made clear, this goal actually functioned as a test that she applied during composing to fledgling ideas and initial bits of prose, which generally failed to pass the test of this rather harsh and premature internal critic. Setting the goal did not seem to promote creativity itself.

To sum up, on a reasonably complex task, such as these college assignments, task representation becomes a critical part of the process. The goals and constraints that students invoke may have sources in unquestioned past experience or in active, inferential efforts at representing features of the task; however, the qualitative differences in these representations point to their constructed nature. Some of these representations shut down the possibility of creativity by giving low priority to the writer's own ideas, by specifying a linear composing process undeflected by those discoveries writing itself engenders, and by eliminating the need for an adaptive transformation of knowledge and treating writing as knowledge-rehearsal rather than as a potentially useful, rhetorical act. Because task representation in writing is (1) a highly interpretive process but (2) often unrecognized and, hence, closed to critical examination, it appears to play an important role in opening the door for creativity in some cases and

closing it in others. In the next section, we will look more closely at the content of the initial task representations of a group of expert and novice writers.

Integrating Topic and Rhetorical Knowledge in Initial Planning

A writer's task representation can, as we have seen, open up possibilities for originality, or confine a writer to producing a routine, standard text. To develop an effective representation of an ill-defined task, writers need to adapt their knowledge about the topic to meet the constraints of audience and purpose. This integration of content and rhetorical knowledge can provide unique opportunities for experienced writers, whereas for others it can be prohibitively difficult. In this section, we will take a closer look at the process of building a task representation of a typical ill-defined professional writing task. What qualitative differences do we see between experts' and novices' task representations that might help account for experts' practical creativity and students' run-of-the-mill responses to many academic or professional writing tasks?

In the study we will discuss here (Flower *et al.,* 1987), five experienced composition teachers and seven student writers with varying degrees of skill were given an expository assignment in which they were asked to write a short article describing their job for *Seventeen* magazine, that is, for an audience of girls aged about thirteen or fourteen. The task was ill-defined in that each writer could draw on and adapt a unique body of personal knowledge about her job and develop a unique set of goals to reach the young readers of the article. Clearly, there was a great variety of ways of approaching this task and, hence, a potential for interesting, adaptive solutions to a complex rhetorical problem. Our writers on this task had to do what many professionals who write for lay audiences have to do:(1) determine their own goals, including representing the audience to themselves and deciding how to meet the audience's needs, and (2) decide what knowledge was relevant, given their goals. For many writers, even the question of defining their job was open to debate. Their answer depended, in part, on their image of the audience and the goals they set for this essay. And that decision, in turn, appeared to depend partly on what information would be easy to access.

We looked at our writers' initial plans, taken from verbal protocols of our subjects' working on our task. (By initial plans, we mean plans articulated before writing a first sentence, see Carey *et al.*, 1986.) We found that even though all our writers developed initial plans for *content* (i.e., for what information they should include), our most successful writers also developed quite complex *rhetorical* plans for their text (e.g., plans related to audience, to overall purpose, or to organizational structure). Although our writers' specific rhetorical goals and plans for the task were diverse (some were personal or even idiosyncratic, e.g., I must change their minds about what an English teacher does), we found that our writers' rhetorical plans included information in these four major categories:

1. *Overall purpose or "theme":* This category encompassed goals and plans for what the essay should accomplish, for an overall focus, or for a unifying idea around which other ideas could be developed. For example, one writing teacher came up with a top-level goal to focus on "how a teacher differs from a professor"; another, on using this essay to "raise (students') horizons and help them to examine their own future."
2. *Audience:* These were plans that developed a representation of the audience for the text. For example, one writer represented her audience as "people like myself, or people like I was, but adjusted for twenty years"; another subject considered their current interests: "they're all in school, they're taking English, for many of them English will be a favorite subject." Many of our experienced writers, in fact, actively struggled with alternative views of their readers.
3. *Structure:* In this category, writers developed goals and plans for organizing or structuring the text. For example, one of our writing teachers came up with a structure that mirrored the important aspects of his job as a writing teacher; "What about a sequence . . . (a writing teacher) reads papers, makes up assignments . . . I want to start with what they think is obvious."
4. *Other rhetorical goals:* In this category, we found diverse plans for addressing this particular audience, for projecting the writer's persona, for the language and tone of the text. For example, given the needs of his readers, one writer decided that "the tone and style in *Seventeen* . . . should be light and lively, filled with slang."

The writers in our study who produced the most successful and innovative texts (in general, but not exclusively, the expert writing teachers) were those who developed plans in all these categories before beginning to write. These writers were able to build what we have termed a *rhetorical representation* of their task that provided an overall framework for generating and selecting information to include in the text. They integrated topic knowledge with rhetorical concerns and interrelated rhetorical goals so that, for example, they saw purpose as closely connected with audience needs. This rhetorical representation provided a unifying and coherent "theory" of the task as they defined it for themselves.

Let us take a look in more detail at how one of our most successful writers built a rhetorical representation of the *Seventeen* magazine task. This writer produced an innovative text that provided an interesting angle on his job as a college writing teacher and that was particularly appropriate to the interests and needs of his readers. The excerpts, taken from a verbal protocol of this writer as he was working on our task, include some of the subject's most important initial planning episodes and our categorization of the goals and plans he is developing.

Clause number	Analysis
Episode 1	
16 Job—English teacher rather than professor.	**Content**
18 In fact that might be a useful thing to to focus on.	**Theme** Defines focus of text
19 . . . how a teacher differs from a professor.	
20 And I see myself as a teacher.	
21 That might help my audience to reconsider their notion of what an English teacher does.	**Theme/Goal** Sets top-level goal

23 (Reads) "young female teenage audience."	
24 They will all have had English.	**Audience**
25 Audience—they're all in school.	Represents relevant background
26 They're taking English.	of readers
27 For many of them English may be a favorite subject.	
29 But for the wrong reason—some of them may have the wrong reasons in that English is good	**Audience** Represents attitudes
30 because it's tidy.	
31 Can be a neat tidy little girl.	
32 Others turned off because it seems too prim.	
33 By God, I can change that notion for them.	**Theme/Goal**

Episode 2

45 All right I'm an English teacher.	
47 I know they are not going to be disposed to hear what I'm saying.	**Audience** Represents attitudes
48 Partly for that reason and partly to put them in the right—the kind of frame of mind,	**Goal**: Prepare audience
49 I want to open with an implied question or a direct one,	**Structure**
50 and put them in the middle of some situation,	Develops skeleton structure
51 then expand from there to talk about my job more generally,	
52 and try to tie it in with their interest.	**Goal: Involve audience**
53 So one question is where to begin.	**Structure**
54 Start in the middle of—probably the first day of class.	Plans introduction
55 They'd be interested.	
56 They'd probably clue into that easily	**Audience**
57 because they would identify with the first days of school,	Represents a shared reference
58 and my first days are raucous affairs.	
59 It would immediately shake 'em up	**Goal**
60 and get them to think in a different context.	Develops audience goals

What features do we see in these excerpts that would lend support to our hypothesis that experts build a rhetorical task representation?

First, this writer's task representation is rich in rhetorical information. In these episodes, he develops plans in all the rhetorical categories discussed above. Not only does he develop plans for specific content to include in his text, but he also develops a theme, a partial structure, a quite detailed representation of his audience, and a set of task-specific goals. For example, he develops a representation of the audience that includes their background (they take English in school and may enjoy it) and their attitudes (they are not going to be disposed to hear what I'm saying.) From this representation he develops a set of goals for his audience—to "shake them up" and make them think in a different context.

Second, the goals that he generates provide an integrated rhetorical framework for his planning. Instead of piecemeal idea generation or brainstorming, we see this writer generating and organizing content to meet his particular persuasive purpose. For example, he starts out with a scenario that will put the audience in the right frame of mind and will help them to think about English teaching in a different context. His text plans are thus adapted to fit with his guiding focus. In addition, many of his goals interact with each other, and two goals may be instantiated by a single text plan. For example, he comes up with the idea to talk about his first day of class because this would further his goal to shake up his audience and because this would be something his readers could identify with. Thus, this one text plan instantiates two of his important goals.

In sum, this writer is generating a set of goals and plans that make this task uniquely his own. Although the task instructions provide him with some loosely defined goals and constraints (the topic, the genre, and the audience), he uses the umbrella of a rhetorical framework to adapt, elaborate, and instantiate these goals. The task that he ends up doing is very much a task that he himself has created. It is a task that results from a coherent theory of the task based on rhetorical principles and concepts.

What alternatives to a rhetorical representation might writers use? We found in our study that several of our inexperienced writers focused their initial planning almost exclusively on generating ideas about what content to include and that they ignored many of the rhetorical features that we found in our experts' initial plans. Thus, they engaged in a type of ''knowledge-driven'' planning without transforming their knowledge to meet the constraints of audience and purpose. Below are some early protocol

Clause number	Analysis
Episode 1	
6 I'm going to assume here I'm an engineer.	**Content**
8 I guess a research—a research engineer.	Defines subject matter of text
10 However, there's a graduate student	**Content** (to end of Episode 1)
11 because I'm a graduate student.	Explores different aspects of job
12 So . . . really my job is I'm going to school.	
13 Let's see—I'm a graduate student,	
14 and I'm an engineer,	
15 and I'm a research engineer.	
16 So everything is there.	
17 So maybe I should explain here instead is that I'm a graduate student pursuing a Ph.D. in engineering.	
20 I do research work.	
22 I teach a course.	
Episode 2	
24 (Reads) "for a thirteen to fourteen teenage audience"	
25 So we have to address the fact that this girl is seventh or eighth grade.	**Audience**
27 Okay so these are all the things going through my head relative to engineering—research engineering.	**Content** Reviews possible
28 These are all the things I'm supposedly doing	details to include
29 and I'm pursuing a Ph.D.	
30 Working on a thesis.	
32 My job here is wrong, the way I'm interpreting my job.	
34 The way I'm interpreting my job means what I'm doing with my life at this moment in time.	**Content** Redefines topic
37 The girl is approximately in seventh or eighth grade.	
38 . . . the assignment has to appeal to a broad range in intellect.	**Goals** Sets very general audience goals
39 It must explain simply what I am doing.	
43 I have to generate an essay.	**Structure**
44 We'll assume it's about two pages.	Specifies genre and length
48 That's not really hard.	
49 I really have my first line	**Process comments**
50 so I'm going to rip off the page here.	
52 I think I can write this out very quickly.	

episodes from one student writer who was working on our *Seventeen* magazine task. This writer's final text was rated eighth out of twelve for quality.

This student's task representation looks different from the expert's in several ways. First, the subject generates few rhetorical goals in contrast to the expert's rich rhetorical planning. Rather, most of the planning is related to features of the topic, for example, the main aspects of his job as a graduate student in engineering and whether being a researcher is in fact his job. He includes no goals for an overall theme or focus to the text; little information about organization beyond a very general sense of the genre and the length; almost no information on his audience's interests or characteristics, beyond that provided in the task instructions; and no goals for the text beyond a rather vague sense that he should ''appeal to a broad range in intellect'' and ''keep the text simple.'' The very general rhetorical goals that he does come up with (e.g., address the fact that this girl is in the 7th or 8th grade) are not further instantiated with subgoals and text plans, and he is unable to build upon them.

Second, we do not see the integrated overall framework to guide his planning process. His planning does not seem to be organized by rhetorical features but rather generated haphazardly by features of the content with which he is struggling. Thus, unable to transform his content to meet the constraints of the assignment and unable to build his own unique set of rhetorical goals for his task, this writer has little option but to ''knowledge-tell.'' His text reflects this limitation as he produces a rather dry description of energy research, which our raters judged to be low in meeting the needs of the audience.

In sum, without any unifying theory of his task, this writer has little choice other than to plunge in and write, letting his topic information drive his planning and generating process. Although he does plan more extensively than many of our other subjects, his plans do not help him to carve out a very appropriate and effective representation of his task.

The two writers we have looked at in detail were typical in many ways of our writers in this study. Several of our subjects built quite complex rhetorical representations of the task, analogous to the one in our first case study, whereas others focused almost exclusively on content plans, as did the writer in the second case. Overall, we found that those writers who engaged in rhetorical planning before writing produced texts that were more successful (particularly in terms of meeting the needs of the audience and in developing an effective rhetorical

purpose) than those who did not. In fact, our writers whose plans were judged to be rich in rhetorical information were judged independently to have the best texts (see Carey *et al.*, 1986). (There was a high positive correlation, $r = .874$, between the quality of initial planning, in terms of the rhetorical features discussed earlier, and text quality.) In addition, we found that:

1. Writers who developed plans in all the rhetorical categories of audience, purpose, theme, and other rhetorical features, as well as content plans, received significantly higher scores for their final text ($p = .0149$, by the Mann-Whitney test) than writers whose planning failed to recognize one or more of these categories; only one of the writers whose text received a score in the lower half of the distribution of scores covered all these categories in his initial plans. In addition, those writers whose plans included goals for an overall focus or ''theme'' for the text received significantly higher scores than those who did not ($p = .0185$). Our weaker writers demonstrated a lack of concern for rhetorical features either because they did not have the appropriate rhetorical knowledge, or because they did not realize the importance of rhetorical planning.

2. Conversely, the writers who produced the more successful texts had a lower percentage of content plans than did writers who produced the poorer texts. (We found a *negative correlation*, $r = -.366$, between the amount of content planning and text quality.) This suggests that writers who focus largely on planning specific content before they begin to write may be missing and/or ignoring important rhetorical goals and constraints, such as adapting a text for the audience.

We want to be cautious about drawing inferences about creativity from differences these studies have shown us between expert and novice writers. However, we have tried to isolate certain features of the writing process that lay a foundation for original and useful solutions to rhetorical problems.

Because creativity is a uniquely adaptive response to such a problem, it seems important that some writers base their effort on first exploring multiple dimensions of the rhetorical problem they face. In response to that situation, they appear to develop a unifying theory of the task that integrates their knowledge with their goals. Insightful adaptive effort is an important part of creativity, but it does not, of course, necessarily involve originality. However, these writers also showed us one of the foundations of such inventiveness. Instead of relying on their prior knowledge and resorting to direct knowledge-telling or relying on standard schemata or conventions, writers who develop a dynamic and rhetorical representation of their task plunged into extended constructive planning. They not only generated fresh inferences, new goals, and adaptive plans but also created a unique configuration of such information adapted to the entire problem as they perceived it. Although the process will not ensure the product, and we must not discount other factors, including domain knowledge, integrative rhetorical planning offers a strong cognitive foundation for rhetorical creativity.

Developing and Applying Problem-Solving Strategies for Revision

Writers who come up with innovative solutions to ill-defined tasks rarely do so without making substantial revisions to their text; in fact, the kind of practical creativity we are discussing in this chapter often requires a writer to spend considerable time and effort on improving, and sometimes rethinking, a text before arriving at a final version. For experienced writers, revising may involve "reseeing" the text on a global level and making major changes to the meaning and to the overall structure (Faigley & Witte, 1981; Sommers, 1980). Our research on the cognitive processes of revision (Hayes *et al.*, 1988) indicates that making these kinds of substantial text changes involves complex problem-solving activities that depend on strategies for pruning down the many options for the text into a productive set of alternatives, and for choosing between these alternatives. In this section, we look in more depth at the kinds of strategies writers develop for revising an expository text.

Text problems that are global in *scope* (i.e., encompassing the whole text or a substantial proportion of it) or that relate to broader and less clear-cut (i.e., global) *issues*, such as audience and purpose, invariably have no easy answers. Both these types of global problems require more than the quick fix procedures that are needed for correcting routine mechanical or grammatical errors; rather, they are difficult for writers to solve because they are themselves ill-defined in that there are many different goals and subgoals that a writer might develop to guide his or her revision and many possible solutions to the problem. The process of solving global revision problems widens a writer's options and thus increases his or her potential for producing an effective and innovative final version of a text.

In our study of revision (Hayes *et al.*, 1988), we found that one important revision process in the repertoire of our expert writers (and a stumbling block for many of our novices) was the ability to diagnose successfully global text problems. We characterize *diagnosis* as building a representation of a text problem that provides a writer with some specific information about the type or category of problem and some possible strategies for improving the text (Flower, Carey, & Hayes, 1985). Sometimes when evaluating a text (either their own or one written by another person) writers will sense that "something does not sound right," that is, they detect a potential trouble spot. If a writer goes on to expand upon such an intuition and explain why the text is poor by coming up with a name or category for the problem, then he or she is making a fully fledged diagnosis. A diagnosis differs from a detection (e.g., "this is terrible") in much the same way that a patient's heartfelt but weakly specified complaint differs from a physician's more multidimensional, high-information diagnosis, involving a problem, symptoms, and solutions. The power of diagnosis resides in identifying the situation as a particular problem type, which, in turn, activates a body of tests and solution procedures. Thus, diagnosis allows for strategic revision.

We will now look at some case studies of writers diagnosing and solving ill-defined text problems. We draw on data from a study of expert and novice writers who were given the task of revising a poorly written rather pedestrian memo from one athletics coach to another about women's sports opportunities on campus. Our subjects were asked to produce a revision of the text that could be given to freshman women students as a one-page handout to introduce them to campus sports (see Hayes *et al.*, 1988). Again, this was a fairly typical professional writing task in that, as well as solving language and organization problems, our writers needed to change the overall focus of the text and adapt it for a new audience who might not be very motivated to read it. We will examine in some depth our writers' diagnoses in relation to a particularly problematic section of the text that was part of larger, whole-text coherence and audience problems, and that also contained several fairly local problems, such as faulty topic focus, negative tone and structure, faulty parallelism, and wordiness. This section of the original text read as follows:

I don't want to infer that the only chance women get for participating in sports is on varsity teams. Intra-mural sports are not the same as varsity sports in which the rules are better, equipment is better, with the techniques of the players being more developed. Irregardless, IM sports may be the choice for many women—they can be just as much fun and take less time.

Our writers represented the problems with this excerpt of text in qualitatively different ways. First, the experts tended to build integrated networks of diagnoses to deal with global text problems. They noticed connections between independent problems at all levels of the text: they saw individual choices of diction, style, and content in terms of a larger multisentence context; they saw concrete evidence of broad global problems in smaller problems. Conversely, the novices tended to see local disconnected problems that were not tied to the larger context; they either did not see the larger problems or did not connect global problems to local ones.

Second, because many of the experts in our study built elaborated representations of text problems, they came up with a variety of solution procedures. The novices, however, tended to build more simple representations that did not allow them to come up with very effective solutions. Because the experts were able to locate these different facets of complex problems in specific text features, they had a wider range of strategies to help them solve both individual local problems and larger global ones.

Case Study 1: Building an Integrated Problem Representation

Although we found interesting individual differences within our subject groups, this case study is especially pertinent to understanding creativity because the two writers typify differences in the amount of integration in our experts' and our novices' problem representations. Figure 1 shows all the diagnostic comments made by one of our teaching experts (BA) about this paragraph, and Figure 2 shows all those made by a novice (ML). For each subject, we distinguished the text level to which the comment applied (i.e., whole text/multiparagraph, paragraph/intersentence, sentence, word level) and the general category of problem mentioned in the comment. We looked specifically at whether the revisers built integrated networks of diagnoses that related text problems and spanned text levels. Where the subjects made explicit connections between diagnoses, either at the same text level or across text levels, the lines on the figures indicate these connections.

Let us take a closer look at our expert's diagnoses in Figure 1. In order to build a representation of the major problems with this excerpt, the expert (BA) relates her concept of the overall purpose of the memo (to recruit for teams in order to lobby for funding—P44–46) with paragraph level diagnoses that focus on: missing information (P43); illogicality in the argument structure (if the memo is recruiting for varsity teams, why talk about intramural teams (P47–48); and unhelpful and unconvincing information about intramural sports that has no purpose (P54–55, 57, 59). She successfully diagnoses some of the individual local problems within this paragraph; however, these diagnoses are closely related to each other and to a larger whole-text problem. By creating this hierarchically structured and integrated representation, BA is able to work at several text levels simultaneously. She can thus analyze the text by working on local examples that contribute to the larger problem.

In contrast, the novice subject (ML) (Figure 2) does not relate this paragraph to the text as a whole in her diagnoses. Rather than seeing one large problem, ML sees several small word-level problems (faulty use of an abbreviation—P50, and faulty word choice—P54, C126) that are not related either to each other or to the sentence-level problems of incoherence (C101) or "negativeness" (C116), which she diagnoses. However, we do see this novice beginning to work more like the expert, though still on a paragraph rather than a whole-text level: she attempts to integrate a rather fuzzy paragraph-level diagnosis that this paragraph contains "negative stuff" (P41) with her diagnosis that a particular sentence seems illogical (What's the good of intramural sorts if they are so bad—C116).

These two writers were fairly typical of the expert and novice writers in our study. In Figure 3, we represent schematically the diagnostic comments made by two other teaching experts and two other novices as they considered the problems in our sample excerpt of the original text. Figure 3 indicates the text levels of the problems that these writers saw, and the extent to which their problem representations were integrated. (The lines on the figure represent explicit connections between the writers' diagnoses and/or detections of text problems.)

The problem representations of the experts and novices (see Figure 3) were very different: first, the experts' diagnoses were integrated, whereas the novices' were more fragmented and independent of each other; second, the experts diagnosed problems at several levels of the text, particularly above the sentence level, whereas the novices focused almost exclusively on sentence and word-level problems; finally, the experts diagnosed global problems (such as audience and purpose), whereas the novices often could *detect* that something global might be wrong with the text (e.g., one subject commented that "this whole paragraph sounds ridiculous") but were unable to come up with a fulfledged diagnosis. Our analysis suggests that experts' ability to integrate diagnoses of local problems with each other and with whole-text diagnoses allows them to see local problems in the context of more global ones. This interaction of the local and the global provides experts with a rich conceptual framework upon which to base their solution procedures. Novices, on the other hand, appear to be driven mainly by the text itself, an approach that does not allow them to import a representation of the unstated purpose of the whole text. Because they often see only the isolated local problems, their solutions are more likely to be *ad hoc* and less goal driven than the experts' solutions.

Case Study 2: Using Diagnosis to Develop Solution Strategies

In this second case study, we look at how one of our experts and one of our novices used their diagnoses of text problems to develop procedures for improving the text. First, we examine some episodes taken from the protocol (P) and cued recall (CR) of an expert writing teacher who effectively diagnosed and solved the problems in our example excerpt. (The statements that are in quotation marks in these episodes indicate where the writer was reading from the original text.) We have selected some key episodes that illustrate how the subject dealt with one of the major problems in the "I don't want to infer" paragraph, a problem he categorized as "negativeness." Notice how he starts by working with the whole paragraph as a single movable unit.

Protocol

P73   What I guess I'd do now is to move this paragraph, or the contents of it

P74   the one about personal benefits, up here.

P75   Continue with the positive things about it rather than the negative.

C163   If you look at these two sentences of which I guess I actually cut everything but about three words.

C164   They are both split in the negative.

C165   "I don't want (to infer)"

C166   "Intramural sports are not"—which I think is not the way a recruiting document should be.

C167   I think you should put in a positive statement.

C168   And secondly, both of them are really lead-ins that don't get you anywhere.

C174   But since we use in addition to varsity sports . . . intramural sports attract these acts and so on

C175   where you tell what it is rather than what it is not.

C176   which is just a delaying tactic.

C188   The paragraph is claiming from the very beginning that she is going to talk about intramural sports,

C189   yet as I said, the first two sentences introduce intramural sports with a negative

C190   and then there's all this information about varsity sports.

C191   So what I tried to do was to substitute information about intramural sports.

C228   . . . either the words or the structure itself, connotation of the words or the structure itself is negative.

C229   It's negative, negative, negative.

C230   I don't have a logical mind.

C231   I can't follow negatives.

C232   I go make them over.

C233   And if I say that I do not want you to think that I don't care about your reluctance, I've lost myself,

C234   because I'm talking about a double negative about a negative mental attitude,

C235   and I can't follow it.

C236   I don't think most people can.

C237   I just changed the structure.

C240   I'm simplifying the sentence structure and making it more direct.

C261   That negative approach thing ("feel that participating in sports is another pressure they don't need.")

C262   They don't need it.

C263   But it's also that I just changed the whole sentence structure.

C264 The sentence structure as the writer had it is that many new students feel that participating in sports is another pressure they don't need.

C266 I set up the structure differently.

C441 Then it seemed to me to emphasize the benefits first as opposed to the reluctance or the problems students feel,

C442 so I brought the—so I changed the order from—

C443 the way this writer had it was the negative to the positive.

C444 I brought the positive to the benefits, to the negative,

C445 which I close with another positive statement to de-emphasize the negatives or the complaints of the problems people feel.

This expert built an elaborated problem representation that provided him with a rich knowledge base for solving the problems in the text. His multifaceted diagnosis sees the "negativeness" problem not only in the words but also in the syntax, in the ordering of information, and in the rhetorical effect of the text. For example, he diagnoses that the connotations of the words and the grammatical structure are both negative (C228); that the "lead-ins," which lead nowhere (C168), highlight inappropriate and negative information; and that the sentences shift the focus to the worst aspects of sports and delay the presentation of the key ideas (C174–176). In addition, he sees these individual problems as symptoms of a larger, more global problem: a negative approach is inappropriate for the overall rhetorical purpose (as he represents it to himself) of the handout, that is, for a recruiting document (C166), and he recognizes recurring patterns of negative structure and tone throughout the whole text (P73–75). In fact, he generalizes about the rhetorical effect of negativeness on readers, that is, that a "double negative about a negative mental attitude" is too difficult for most readers to follow (C234–236).

This writer was able to be very specific in his diagnosis of this complex problem. He effectively locates problems in actual text features at several levels—multiparagraph (P73–78), paragraph (C188–191), and sentence level (C261). This rather difficult "mapping" of general and abstract problems onto the text appears to be an important step in moving from diagnosis to action. This writer's diagnoses enable him to come up with a range of concrete and useful strategies for improving the text that are closely tied to text features. Thus he decides to

1. move the paragraph to continue with the positive statements (P73–75): multiparagraph level
2. put in a positive statement (C167): paragraph level
3. substitute information (in the paragraph) about intramural sports (C191): paragraph level
4. change the order of the statements from negative/positive to positive/negative/positive (C441–445): paragraph level
5. simplify the sentence structure to make it more direct (C240): sentence level

The elaboration and location of problems in the text, which we noted in the expert's diagnoses, provide a contrast to the performance of one of the better and more fluent of the novices. The protocol comments represent this subject's diagnosis of this same problem paragraph.

Protocol

P41 "I don't want" . . . This is all negative stuff. "in which the rules are better, the equipment is better"

P42 It can all be cut.

P45 They (are) a little more casual I guess.

P47 Um this IM down here, I'll go back to that too.

P48 I'll make basic corrections

P49 and then go back and improve.

P50 This IM There's no IM before

P51 so you have to go back

P52 so this should be Intra-mural again.

P54 Irregardless . . . it can't be irregardless.

P55 I guess I've got to change that.

P56 So we'll cut that out

P57 and it should be "IM sports . . .

P58 They can be just as much fun as varsity sports and take less time."

P128	"I don't want to infer" . . . keep varsity,		P181	They tend to be a bit more casual.
P129	intramural sports are . . . tend to be a bit more casual and less demanding.		C114	(Experimenter: You crossed out the whole . . .)
P129a	IM sports may be . . . perhaps a more influential . . .		C115	Well it's just so negative.
P130	Participating is an extra, um let me see . . .		C116	It's like, so what's the good of IM sports
P132	is an addition.		C117	if there so bad.
P133	Oh well, I'll go back to that.		C118	They're just a bit more casual, not as disciplined.
			C125	(Experimenter: And just?")
P179	"I don't want to infer that the only chance women get for participating in sports is on varsity teams." There is also . . . there are also IM sports		C126	I don't like "just" either.
			C127	"Even," "just," and "like," I don't like. (Had commented earlier: "I was always told in any composition class I had that 'like' is just bad to use. So I always put 'such as.')
P180	which are not quite the same as varsity.			

Where the expert's comments show an elaborated representation of the text problems, the novice's comments are sparse and undeveloped. The expert saw an interplay of lexical, syntactic, semantic, genre-related, and rhetorical problems; the novice sees only one—"negative stuff" (P41). Her diagnosis is based on a simulation of a reader's response (C116–C118), a form of diagnosis that normally provides only a very generalized and open-ended definition of the problem. This subject's response is also typical of novice diagnoses in that it depends primarily on the reviser's social or topic knowledge rather than on rhetorical knowledge; she imagines what someone might say about IM sports and rewrites the content of the text to fit her own ideas (P45, C118)

Broad, intentional diagnoses, of the sort both expert and novice were making, pose a built-in problem for the reviser who must map something like a general sense of negativeness or a lack of focus onto specific features in the text. Generally speaking, the more global the diagnosis, the harder it is to locate exactly the problem in the text and the fewer the strategies are available for acting on the diagnosis. Here, while the expert has several procedures operating on different text levels, the novice has few. In fact, she demonstrates a typical novice strategy: first she localizes the problem in a single offending clause (P41); then she solves the problem by deleting (P42) and substituting her own new information (P45). She returns to this section of the text on two later passes and simply rewrites the sentence to fit her own ideas about intramural sports (P128–133; P178–180). In addition, on some occasions in which she is unable to map a general diagnosis to the text (P133), she finally decides to leave the problem alone. We suspect that novice revisers simply may not know how to locate the source of their own responses as readers; they may not see the features of the text that prompted their responses.

These two case studies illustrate the key role of diagnosis in developing effective representations and solutions to ill-defined revision problems. The problem representations our experienced writers built were not just bigger but qualitatively different from the novices' representations. The experts were (1) seeing individual problems as part of a conceptual whole and (2) developing a wider range of effective strategies based on several dimensions of the problem. Overall, we found that our expert writers had several general strategies for dealing with ill-defined revision problems:

1. In the act of building a representation of an ill-defined problem, expert writers are seeing an integrated set of more familiar subproblems. When a global, ill-defined problem is located in features of the text, the diagnosis becomes more operational because it now says something about where and how to proceed. It is the difference between being told to "be more clear" and being told to "define your key terms earlier in the paragraph." Finally, once these abstract problems are given a local context and a name in the form of subgoals and text features, they can lead to text changes, which, though the changes themselves are local, are controlled by a larger, integrated problem and plan.

2. As these writers build their problem representation, they create subgoals that function as tests for success. The novices' criteria tended to be vague, "well it's just so negative," whereas the experts' criteria were much more specific, "the connotations of the words and the structure itself is negative."

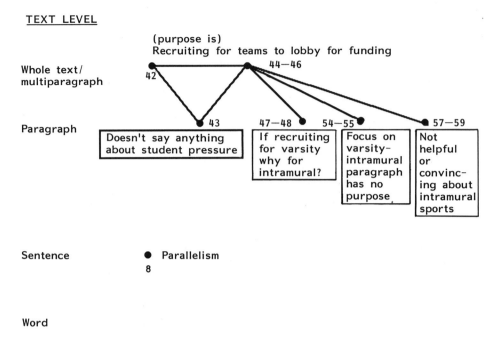

Figure 1. Expert's diagnostic comments.

3. Creating tests and subgoals could have the result that a writer only deals with the isolated local problems and loses sight of the larger context. For example, meeting the goal to introduce some new technical terminology could interact with a more global goal to maintain a chatty, informal tone.

Experts try to maintain this part/whole balance by invoking global tests. For instance, toward the end of the protocol of one of our expert writers, after he has made a number of local revisions, the writer decides to "read (his text) over and see what it sounds like" to test for a potential whole-text prob-

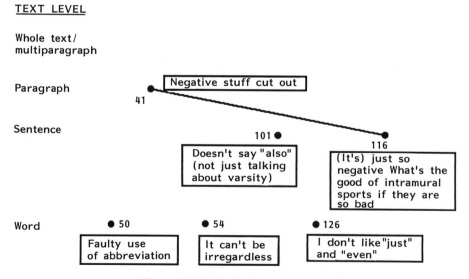

Figure 2. Novice's diagnostic comments.

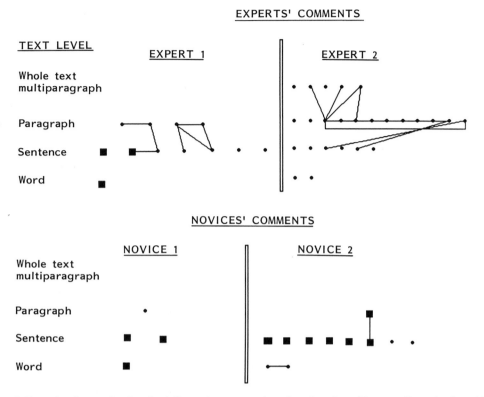

Figure 3. Networks of experts' and novices' diagnostic comments (■ = detection of a problem; • = diagnosis of a problem).

lem: ''I have a feeling there is still a shift in tone. The first paragraph is more formal and it gets less formal as it goes along.'' Thus, the problem solver is able to shift back and forth from representing local problems to seeing their global effects.

4. Finally, a very important expert strategy was a *planning* strategy. Often, when experts are diagnosing and developing solutions to ill-defined problems, they work on a more abstract level with goals and gists rather than with actual text. This allows revisers to integrate various top-level goals before getting into specifics and provides an overall framework for their diagnoses and text changes. Local problems can then be confronted only after a tentative global plan is formulated. Because goals and gists are an effective way to chunk lots of information, revisers can come up with several alternative plans for improving the text. On the other hand, a plan that looked promising in the abstract may not work out at a local level, and the reviser may be pushed back into re-representing the problem. For dealing with complex revision problems where there is not one easy answer, this strategy of plan-

ning with goals and gists gives writers more flexibility than working with prose and allows them to turn vague, amorphous problems into more manageable ones.

In this chapter, we have tried to use recent research in cognition and the composing process to describe some features of this process that help lay a foundation for creativity. Creativity, whether it is practical creativity or genius-type work, clearly rests on many capabilities, including rich knowledge, social expectations, and the context for performance, in addition to cognitive actions. However, our analysis would lead us to contribute two observations to this picture of creativity.

The first observation is that the writing process itself shows us some powerful mechanisms for creativity in the act of building a representation of a problem; in the process of exploring multiple dimensions of that problem and integrating that knowledge into a unifying theory of the task and an integrated plan; and, finally, in the act of using revision as an opportunity to re-envision a text and to deal with individual elements of a text as part of a meaningful, purposeful whole. These powerful but demanding processes in writing are a potential source of both adaptive and original solutions to rich rhetorical problems.

The second observation is that these features—this potential inherent in the cognitive process of experienced writers—is no guarantee of creativity. As educators, on the other hand, it strikes us that many of our students are shutting down this potential in themselves. The strategies that lead them to depend on knowledge-telling, to take limited and tentative looks at their rhetorical problem, to build simplistic images of their task, to invoke rigid rules in the face of a complex situation, and to use revision as a limited tool for repairing local problems all produce a process that does not rise to inventive and generative problem solving when it needs to. Although we cannot guarantee creativity, we can, we believe, help writers develop the strategic, cognitive tools they need to meet situations that demand it.

The focus of this chapter has been on practical creativity—on the variety of creative responses that all sorts of writers bring to many kinds of writing problems, in school and in professional work. It follows that one important line of research growing out of the work we have discussed will pursue the illusive trail of creativity in real-world situations, particularly those situations in which a creative (i.e., a valuable) response to a rhetorical situation is called for, or is likely to make a difference.

Education and writing in school is one place where creativity makes a difference. Our survey suggests some of the following research areas and questions:

1. *Ill-defined tasks.* What is the relation between the expert and novice strategies used in various kinds of writing and the power of those strategies to foster creativity? How do writers with different levels of expertise handle the problem and the potential of ill-defined tasks?
2. *Task representation.* To what extent are students' performances conditioned, on standard school tasks that involve writing, by the ways they represent the task to themselves? Are students sometimes constructing representations that diminish a task or that even obliterate the opportunity for creativity?

What is the role of instruction in fostering a creative approach to ill-defined tasks? For example, how do teachers communicate their expectations of creativity? How can they make the process of thinking creatively operational—an act student writers can work toward? Does instruction sometimes present a romantic view of creative work that fails to recognize the role that energetic and enterprising cognition *can* play?

3. *Planning and revision.* If we turn our attention to teaching, one important question we would like to answer is: Does the more limited problem solving we see in students' writing process and, in particular, in their approach to planning and revision simply reflect what these writers do not do, or what they cannot do? A line of research that we think will be particularly fruitful will be work that focuses directly on the strategies writers use for open-ended tasks and on their own awareness of or metacognition about their options and process.

Currently, we are investigating whether students may have untapped, hidden planning skills which they could draw on, *if* they could be prompted or sensitized to do so. For example, if student writers are explicitly asked to plan on a more expert level (e.g., to focus on rhetorical planning, to elaborate goals, or to deal with conflicts) would we find sharp gains in the sophistication of their planning? Or would we see that applying these strategies, especially in the context of ill-defined tasks, requires better, more direct instruction? The results of this research will, we hope, provide a basis for helping student writers to develop their potential in the classroom. By building on students' hidden strengths as well as focusing on their specific areas of difficulty, we can develop their awareness of powerful cognitive strategies and provide a springboard for a more creative approach to the writing process.

References

Ackerman, J. (in press). Students' self-analyses and judges' perception: Where do they agree? In L. Flower (Ed.), *Reading-to-write: Exploring a cognitive and social process* New York: Oxford University Press.

Beach, R., & Eaton, S. (1984). Factors influencing self-assessing and revising by college freshmen. In R. Beach & L. Bridwell (Eds.), *New directions in composition research* (pp. 149–170). New York: Guilford Press.

Britton, J., Burgess, T., Martin, N., McLeod, A., & Rosen, H. (1975). *The development of writing abilities (11–18).* London: Macmillan.

Brown, A. L. (1980). Metacognitive development and reading. In R. Spiro, B. Bruce, & W. Brewer (Eds.), *Theoretical issues in reading comprehension* (pp. 453–481). Hillsdale, NJ: Erlbaum.

Brown, A. L., & Smiley, S. S. (1978). The development of strategies for studying texts. *Child Development, 49,* 1076–1088.

Brown, A. L., Day, J. D., & Jones, R. S. (1983). The development of plans for summarizing text. *Child Development, 54,* 968–979.

Carey, L. J., Flower, L., Hayes, J. R., Schriver, K., & Haas, C. (1986). *Differences in writers' initial task representations* (ONR Technical Report, No. 2). Pittsburgh, PA: Carnegie-Mellon University.

Faigley, L., & Witte, S. (1981). Analyzing revision. *College Composition and Communication, 32,* 400–414.

Flower, L. (1979). Writer-based prose: A cognitive basis for problems in writing. *College English, 41,* 19–37.

Flower, L. (in press). Task representation. In L. Flower (Ed.), *Reading-to-write: Exploring a cognitive and social process* (Technical Report, Center for the Study of Writing at Berkeley and Carnegie Mellon, New York: Oxford University Press.

Flower, L., & Hayes, J. R. (1980). The cognition of discovery: Defining a rhetorical problem. *College Composition and Communication, 31,* 21–32.

Flower, L., Carey, L. J., & Hayes, J. R. (1985). *Diagnosis in revision: The expert's option* (Communications Design Center Technical Report, No. 27). Pittsburgh PA: Communications Design Center.

Flower, L., Schriver, K., Carey, L. J., Haas, C., & Hayes, J. R. (1987). *Planning in writing: A theory of the cognitive process* (ONR Technical Report, No. 1). Pittsburgh, PA: Carnegie-Mellon, University.

Getzels, J. W., & Csikszentmihalyi, M. (1976). *The creative vision: A longitudinal study of problem finding in art.* New York: Wiley.

Hayes, J. R. (1981). *The complete problem-solver.* Philadelphia, PA: The Franklin Institute Press.

Hayes, J. R., Flower, L., Schriver, K., Stratman, J., & Carey, L. J. (1988). Cognitive processes in revision. In S. Rosenberg (Ed.), *Advances in applied linguistics: Vol. 2. Reading, writing and language process* (pp. 176–240). Cambridge, England: Cambridge University Press.

Langer, J. A. (1984). Where problems start: The effect of available information on responses to school writing tasks. In A. Applebee (Ed.), *Contexts for learning to write* (pp. 135–148). Norwood, NJ: Ablex, 1984.

Newell, A., & Simon, H. A. (1972). *Human problem-solving.* Englewood Cliffs, NJ: Prentice-Hall.

Newell, A., Shaw, J. C., & Simon, H. A. (1962). The process of creative thinking. In H. E. Gruber, G. Terrell, & M. Wertheimer (Eds.), in *Contemporary approaches to creative thinking* (3rd ed., pp. 63–119). New York: Atherton Press.

Perkins, D. N. (1981). *The mind's best work.* Cambridge: Harvard University Press.

Reitman, W. R. (1964). Heuristic decision procedures, open constraints, and the structure of ill-defined problems. In M. W. Shelley & G. L. Bryan (Eds.), *Human judgments and optimality* (pp. 282–315). New York: Wiley.

Rose, M. (1984). *Writer's block: The Cognitive dimension.* Carbondale, IL: Southern Illinois Press.

Scardamalia, M., & Bereiter, C. (1988). Knowledge-telling and knowledge transforming in written composition. In S. Rosenberg (Ed.), *Advances in applied linguistics* (Vol. 2, pp. 142–175). New York: Cambridge University Press.

Simon, H. A. (1973). The structure of ill-structured problems. *Artificial Intelligence, 4,* 181–201.

Simon, H. A. (1986). Some computer models of human learning. In M. Shafto (Ed.), *How we know.* San Francisco, CA: Harper & Row.

Sommers, N. I. (1980). Revision strategies of student and experienced writers. *College Composition and Communication, 31,* 378–387.

CHAPTER 18

Cognition and Writing

THE IDEA GENERATION PROCESS

John A. O'Looney, Shawn M. Glynn, Bruce K. Britton, and Linda F. Mattocks

The interest in ideas and where they come from is an old one, dating back at least to pre-Socratic philosophers and continuing to the present-day theories of creative thinking. The question of where ideas come from has been answered in a variety of ways: ideas can come from the gods, from the imagination, from a mind trained in reasoning, from a haphazard association of memories, from stimulating images, from a subconscious bank of archetypes, from memories transformed by mental schemata, and from attempts to solve problems.

Many of these theories of idea generation are still popular, whereas others have been discarded. The search for a valid theory of idea generation remains important because new curricula for teaching writing, such as Linda Flower's (1981) *Problem-Solving Strategies for Writing,* are being based on particular methods of idea generation. In these new curricula, students are taught how to generate ideas and how to integrate idea generation with other

writing processes, such as organizing, goal setting, translating, and reviewing.

Our purpose is to examine the relationship between cognition and writing, giving particular emphasis to the process of idea generation. We will consider each of the following topics in turn:

1. A human information-processing model
2. Some models of writing that relate idea generation to other subprocesses.
3. Some methods of capturing and manipulating ideas when writing
4. The cognitive constraints imposed on idea generation when writing

We will critically review the literature relevant to idea generation when writing, attempt to pull this literature together theoretically, and identify some remaining research issues that need to be addressed. The writing we speak of here is considered by us to be "creative writing" in that it requires of both novices and experts the production of new and effective ideas, such as those found in good essays, articles, short stories, and novels. We are not speaking of relatively routine writing tasks, such as producing a shopping list.

John A. O'Looney • Department of Language Education, University of Georgia, Athens, GA 30602. Shawn M. Glynn and Linda F. Mattocks • Department of Educational Psychology, University of Georgia, Athens, GA 30602. Bruce K. Britton • Department of Psychology, University of Georgia, Athens, GA 30602.

Human Information-Processing Model

The information-processing model of human behavior holds that a limited capacity "working memory" controls ongoing, conscious mental operations, such as those that enable us to read, write, and solve arithmetic problems (Baddeley, 1978; Britton, Glynn, & Smith, 1985). In *working memory,* new incoming information is maintained temporarily through the process of rehearsal. While maintaining this new information, we can operate on it (e.g., comprehend, infer, or compute), we can integrate it with our existing related knowledge (stored in our long-term memory system), and we can return the product of this integration to our long-term memory system for permanent storage. Working memory is like a cognitive workbench on which we can fashion new intellectual products.

The processing capacity of working memory is limited in terms of (1) the amount of information that can be maintained at one time and (2) the number of cognitive operations that can be performed simultaneously. For present purposes, processing capacity will be defined as "the limited pool of energy, resources, or fuel by which some cognitive operations or processes are mobilized and maintained" (Johnston & Heinz, 1978, p. 422). The processing capacity of a writer's working memory has been found to be related to his or her writing capability (Benton, Kraft, Glover, & Plake, 1984; Tetroe, 1984). With maturation and the acquisition of strategic knowledge on how to manage cognitive resources, the effective capacity of the writer's working memory increases.

Memory Probes

Much of the raw material for our ideas comes from our long-term memory, or our store of referential knowledge. The mode of operation of one's long-term memory has been the subject of numerous experiments by Kintsch and his colleagues (e.g., Kintsch, 1986; van Dijk & Kintsch, 1983). Kintsch (1980), in a discussion of component writing processes, has suggested that the idea generation process begins with a probe of long-term memory. This probe is constrained by information about the topic and the intended audience. Kintsch hypothesized that different topic and audience cues would place different constraints on the search for ideas in one's long-term memory. In particular, a more specific topic or audience would help a writer narrow the search for ideas.

Kintsch's (1980, p. 12) notion of one's long-term memory as a "propositional network that is organized only in the sense that certain relationships exist among the propositional nodes" is essentially a conception of memory as a spatial entity; that is, ideas with strong relationships are stored together and tend to be retrieved together. The stronger the relationship, the more likely one propositional node will be recalled when a node close to it is retrieved.

Polson (personal communication to Kintsch, 1980) found that many writers systematically search their memory along one associative path to a given depth before exploring other branches to the same depth. We have illustrated this strategy in Figure 1. For example, when a mystery writer creates a motive for a murderer, the writer may first consider jealousy in depth before moving on to revenge or greed. This depth-first strategy, Polson speculated, places the least strain on one's working memory. However, though this strategy reduces the demands imposed on the writer, it is possible that following it will lead the writer to neglect other idea paths.

What is particularly important for memory is that the retrieval cues are, to a large extent, under the control of the writer. Manipulation of these cues, Kintsch (1980) suggested, determines a search set that the writer can then explore: "The level of constraint imposed by the retrieval cue and the density of the knowledge space in the area of the search jointly determine how many nodes will be included in the search set" (p. 14). Once the retrieval cues and knowledge base are determined, the search set is automatically constituted. We have illustrated this in Figure 2.

Once an item has been recovered from the search set, the recovered item is added to one's retrieval cues, and the association between the sampled item and the original retrieval cue is heightened. Thus, retrieval cues are continually redirected by the sampled items; however, the direction the search process takes sometimes may not be well suited to the goal of the search.

In an empirical test of Kintsch's model, Caccamise (1981) found a significant difference in idea generation between writers who wrote for an audience of adults (a less constraining task) and those who wrote for children (a more constraining task). Writers who wrote for children had a great deal more difficulty generating and developing ideas. It took them twice as long to write the same number of ideas. Caccamise suggested that in order to maximize idea generation, it may be necessary to first

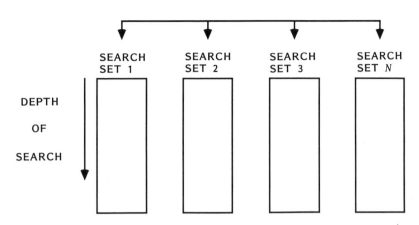

Figure 1. Breadth and depth of memory search.

generate ideas without regard to an audience, and only later reshape ideas to reflect the audience's needs.

Problem Solving

Caccamise (1981) maintained that Kintsch's memory model is best applied to writing when it is combined with a model of a problem-solving system. The resulting general model can be viewed as a serial processor that can only address a small number of inputs and outputs at a time.

Caccamise suggested that generating ideas for writing is a special case of the concept of the "ill-structured problem." Ill-structured problems are not easy to formalize and often demand more from the problem solvers than their limited computational capacities can achieve. An ill-structured problem in writing is one in which a writer must juggle several constraints simultaneously. Consider, for example, when a writer is asked to develop an argument appropriate for an audience whose members vary widely in age, beliefs, and cultural backgrounds. The writer must give extra considera-

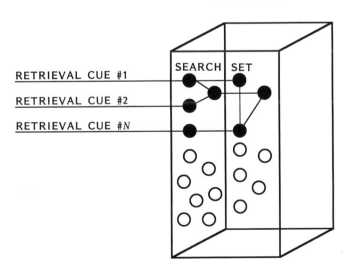

Figure 2. Retrieval cues and knowledge base determine the search set.

tion to these constraints, plus the usual ones, such as idea generation, sentence structure, punctuation, and spelling.

Cooper and Matsuhashi (1983), Flower and Hayes (1980), Young (1981), Newell, Shaw, and Simon (1963) and others also have written of idea generation as a problem-solving process. Young, in particular, has stressed the importance of a task environment that forces a person to formulate the problem, not simply solve already posed problems. Young has suggested that some of the strongest incentives for communication are found in the process of discovering a problem and exploring reasonable solutions to that problem. He also has suggested that discovering real problems and their solutions can be intrinsically rewarding activities for children who are beginning to write.

Beginning writers often encounter the difficult problem of finding sufficient information on a topic in their long-term memory both to begin and sustain a piece of writing. Unlike spoken discourse, in which new ideas can be generated out of a dialectical exchange, writers often have to develop search strategies in order to gain access to information stored in their long-term memories.

Scardamalia, Bereiter, and Goelman (1982) found that fourth-grade writers produced shorter essays than sixth-grade writers. This difference could be explained simply by pointing to a difference in the knowledge base (Voss, Vesonder, & Spilich, 1980) or to differences in the children's ability to manage the demands made on their working memory (Glynn, Britton, Muth, & Dogan, 1982). Scardamalia *et al.*, however, pointed to a third explanation. They suggested that younger children, whose communication experience is predominantly in the spoken mode, rely more on the conversational cues to prompt a memory search for relevant ideas than do older children. To test their hypothesis, Scardamalia *et al.* asked fourth- and sixth-grade children to continue to write after they appeared to have stopped writing. Even though both groups wrote more after being cued, only the younger writers' compositions showed an increase in the coherence of what they wrote. These results suggested that the younger writers had stopped before they had used all the relevant ideas in their memory set. The older children apparently possessed a set of internal cues or prompts that the younger children lacked.

Gagné (1985) has recommended that teachers model self-questioning strategies to help young children acquire internal cues. For example, teachers could write part of a short composition on the board and then step back and ask their class questions about how the composition could be extended; the teachers could then implement the students' suggestions on the board. Gagné has suggested that eventually a child could act as his or her own "surrogate partner" in generating conversational cues for continuing to write.

Purpose

In the human information-processing model, purpose is viewed as driving behavior. Because of the work of Moffett (1968), Britton, Burgess, Martin, McLeod, and Rosen (1975), and Kinneavy (1971), ways of classifying writing into discourse types (e.g., narration and exposition) based on purpose (e.g., description and explanation) are available. Knowledge of discourse types could be considered a heuristic for writers. Understanding the connection between purpose and discourse type could be especially useful to the student writer who is aware of a purpose, but who is in need of a mode in which to pitch his or her voice.

After a writer has determined a purpose and selected the appropriate discourse type for that purpose, specific objectives within the discourse type can be identified. Collins and Gentner (1980) hypothesized four basic objectives that writers have: (1) making the text enticing, (2) making the text comprehensible, (3) making the text memorable, and (4) making the text persuasive. The identification of a clear objective will help a writer narrow the focus of his or her idea generation process.

Models of Writing: Relationship of Idea Generation to Other Writing Subprocesses

Models of writing help us to conceptualize the writing process as a set of component, interrelated subprocesses. We will discuss several models and the role idea generation plays in each. The models are those of Hayes and Flower (1980), Rose (1984), Cooper and Matsuhashi (1983), and Wason (1978).

The Hayes and Flower Model

Hayes and Flower (1980) have described a model (see Figure 3) of writing that has received widespread acceptance among writing theorists. In devising their model, Hayes and Flower posited the

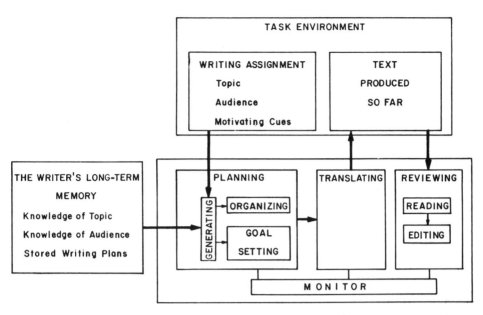

Figure 3. The Hayes and Flower (1980) model of writing. From *Cognitive processes in writing* (p. 11) by L. W. Gregg and E. R. Steinberg, 1980, Hillsdale, NJ: Erlbaum. Copyright 1980 by Lawrence Erlbaum Associates, Inc. Reprinted by permission.

task environment and the writer's long-term memory as the context in which the writing process takes place. The writing process itself consists of planning, translating, and reviewing. Idea generation, organization, and goal-setting are seen as subprocesses of planning. The translating process produces language corresponding to the ideas that are generated and the goals that are set in the planning process; however, the recursive nature of these processes makes it difficult to say where idea generation ends and translating begins.

In the Hayes and Flower model, the function of the generating process is to retrieve from long-term memory items that are relevant to the writing task. Memory probes originate from the task environment, specifically from cues about the topic and the audience. From the first probe, items tend to be retrieved in associative chains. Hayes and Flower contend that most writers will break a retrieval chain when they access one irrelevant item. The most persistent memory searches they observed in verbal report protocols never extended more than three retrievals beyond relevant material.

According to Flower and Hayes (1980), ideas are generated as a response to a rhetorical problem that includes an assignment, an audience, and the writer's personal goals for the reader and text. When generating ideas to solve the rhetorical problem, more successful writers attend to all aspects of the rhetorical situation (i.e., audience, topic, and text). Poor writers tend to limit their solutions (and thus their ideas) to problems in text production, such as format or spelling. In their verbal report protocols, good writers usually make reference to their audience or assignment about twice as often as the poor writers.

Writer's Block and Rose's Model

The study of writer's block by Rose (1984) tends to support the conclusions of Flower and Hayes (1980). Rose found that nonfluent writers, or "high-blockers," tended to plan incrementally; that is, they did not think through the ideas they wanted to express, nor did they write out any organizational approach before beginning a first draft. Rose also found that high-blockers assumed a model of writing as spontaneous, and thus were in a bind when ideas simply did not flow. Furthermore, high-blockers tended to use confusing or conflicting rules, plans, and strategies. Because the conflicts tended to occur at the global level, the poor writers spent much of their composing time on fruitless cogitation rather than on directed idea generation. Rose found that high-blockers paused, on the average, 9.1 more minutes (out of 60) than low-blockers. He concluded that much of the efficiency of low-blockers is rooted in their ability to use flexible rules, appropriate plans, goals to produce first and define later, and in their general absence of conflict. High-blockers, on the other hand, used rigid rules, such as "You must always develop at least three points in your paper." Such a rule, stated as an imperative, can frustrate a novice writer who might only have one argument; and instead of developing the one point he or she does have, the writer is likely to give up entirely (Kean, Glynn, & Britton, 1987).

In his model, Rose (1984) has posited three types of composing subprocesses: rules, interpretive plans, and discourse frames. Rules refer to linguistic, stylistic, rhetorical, and social linguistic processes that are responsive to context and purpose. Good rules flex to match the context; rigid composing rules are enacted without a context. Blocked writers usually have limited, rigid rules.

Interpretive plans influence decisions about how much to write, what to emphasize, what to classify, and what to define. These plans are most fruitfully made in the context of the audience and task. Blocking occurs, Rose has contended, when the writer's interpretive activities are inappropriate to the task or audience.

A third composing subprocess concerns the use of discourse frames. Rose discovered that "incremental planners" planned in that fashion because they knew of no other way to plan. They did not possess control over an array of discourse frames (e.g., description and persuasion). Instead they tended to adapt a few discourse frames to all sorts of content and plans. If a student's knowledge of discourse frames is limited, the complexity and perhaps the fluency of his or her writing will be limited.

The Cooper and Matsuhashi Model

Cooper and Matsuhashi's (1983) model of the composing process is more intricate than that of Rose. These researchers have asserted that there are two main subprocesses of composing: (1) developing global discourse plans, and (2) developing sentence plans. They have argued that a writer's global plans (for a piece of discourse) are influenced by his or her conception of purpose, audience, discourse type, and discourse structure.

Global discourse plans are supported by sentence plans. The basic roles that sentences can play include (a) generalizing roles, such as stating a thesis or restating a proposition; (b) rhetorical roles, such as summarizing and concluding; (c) sequencing roles, such as adding one assertion to the next, replacing a statement with an alternative, and narrating; (d) relationship roles, such as comparison/contrast, inferring, evaluating, cause/result, and qualifying; and (e) development roles, such as exemplifying, defining, and describing. Understanding model patterns of these sentence roles can help a writer to better express his or her ideas.

In order to produce the content of a particular sentence, Cooper and Matsuhashi (1983) have suggested that the writer moves through nine idealized stages of sentence planning:

1. *Formulating a proposition.* In this stage, a writer, guided by a schema for the discourse type, retrieves information from long-term memory and uses the information to form the basis of a message or proposition.

2. *Framing the proposition.* Framing involves choosing an action or state that can be appropriately hung on the objects or people in one's proposition. Chafe (1977) has described such frames as case frames that explicitly determine the role—agentive, affective, recipient, attribute, etc.—each noun will play in the sentence. By placing a noun in various case frames, a writer can change the semantic thrust of the sentence and in doing so generate new ideas.

3. *Placing the proposition.* In this stage, a writer must decide upon what he or she wants to accomplish with respect to his or her audience. Each sentence is generated to accomplish an act (called a "speech act"). Although there are many possible speech acts, a writer's task is facilitated by the knowledge that most nonfiction discourse consists of a relatively small number of representative forms, for example, asserting, commanding, questioning, suggesting, stating, and hinting. Cooper (1984) has argued that the principles writers use to organize content come not from the content, but from writers' intentions expressed as speech acts.

4. *Directing the proposition.* When directing the proposition, the writer must generate an idea as to how his or her theme will be continued in the next sentence. The decision to place certain people or objects in the subject or major theme position in a sentence essentially will decide the direction of the piece of writing. Deciding on a thematic direction also will have consequences for further idea generation: some ideas will be eliminated in the process, whereas others logically will come to the forefront.

5. *Connecting the proposition.* In this stage, the writer takes into account what is given or what has preceded and what is new. In addition to deciding what is given and what is new, at this stage the writer must develop ideas on how to make his or her new ideas cohere with the old. Knowing that cohesion is created through the use of five major types of cohesive ties—reference, substitution, ellipsis, conjunction and lexical reiteration, and collocation—will enable a writer to generate alternative cohesive structures to suit various purposes and modes of discourse (Halliday & Hasan, 1976).

6. *Wording the proposition.* This is the stage whereby the writer codes his or her thoughts into specific lexical sequences. The difficulties writers encounter at this stage have been discussed by Chafe (1977) in terms of the problem of codability. Some objects or events are easy to code because they are part of our common experience (e.g., the colors of a traffic signal). Others are more difficult because they demand specialized knowledge or a unique perspective (e.g., the meaning of an icon of an extinct race). Our choice of words will, as we attempt to write coherently, lay a path for the further generation of ideas. However, this path is circumscribed by (1) our previous choices with regard to discourse type, purpose, functional, and structural sentence roles; (2) our knowledge of the subject; and (3) our vocabulary.

7. *Presenting the proposition.* In this stage, the writer is concerned with issues of usage and grammar; that is, the writer transforms the already composed sentence into proper standard English.

8. *Storing the proposition.* At this stage, the writer's major concern is storing the proposition in his or her memory. A proposition that is longer than a few words must be rehearsed and re-rehearsed to insure it is not lost in the process of transcribing it on paper.

If writers, like speakers, form sentences with clause-size components (Daiute, 1980), one would expect more errors would be found in longer clauses, because producing these clauses would burden a writer's working memory. And, indeed, Daiute (1981) found that the erroneous sentences produced by secondary school students are eight words longer, on the average, than correct sentences. Daiute (1984) suggested that writers who do not make syntax errors have a variety of complex sentence structures stored in long-term memory. These stored schemata for sentence structures help good writers to remember important grammatical information

from prior clauses that fade during recoding.

9. *Transcribing the proposition.* The components of the psychomotor act itself often will dominate the writer's consciousness until they have become somewhat automatic. As Cooper and Matsuhashi (1983) have argued,

a major goal of the development of writing ability is for transcription increasingly to occupy subsidiary awareness, enabling the writer to use focal awareness for other plans and decisions. (p. 33)

Wason's Models

Wason (1978), among others, has noted two rather contradictory models for idea generation when writing. In one model, the writer generates ideas in note or outline form with minimal attention to syntax and style. The writer then translates these notes or outlines into a draft of written discourse. In the other model, the writer composes the first draft using complete sentences and paragraphs, as ideas are generated.

One advantage of the first model, which we will call the *proposition-generating* model, lies in the fact that processing capacity for generating content more likely would be available if that capacity were not being used to generate plans for coordinating patterns of sentence functions, roles, speech acts, and coherence. A second advantage relates to the notion that ideas flow at a rate faster than the writing of prose can capture. Taking notes, then, would have the distinct advantage of keeping pace with the flow of ideas.

One advantage of the second model, which we will call the *sentence-generating* model, is found in its ability to explain how writers often generate ideas by expanding on a point. This process can be seen as the cumulative effect of following a discourse pattern or creating a unique frame, place, direction, connection or wording form a proposition.

A second advantage of the sentence-generating model can be seen among writers who decide not to focus the bulk of their attention on idea production and thereby leave little processing capacity for developing the vehicles that carry ideas to readers (e.g., figurative language). Thus, although proposition generating has the advantage in generating a lot of ideas in rough form, sentence generating has the advantage of generating ideas in the form of good prose.

Cognitive Constraints Imposed on Idea Generation When Writing

Graesser (1984) has identified two sources of writing difficulty: (1) writing makes demands on our limited processing capacity because it requires us to juggle a variety of subprocesses; (2) writing makes demands on our topic knowledge because it calls on us to generate and develop sound ideas. We will discuss these two sources of difficulty in the following sections.

Processing Capacity Limitations

To produce a text, writers must do more than simply generate ideas; they must sequence them, place them into sentences, and comply with the rules of sentence mechanics. According to a cognitive workbench interpretation of text production, each operation imposes a distinct demand on writers' limited processing capacities.

The results of Glynn *et al.* (1982) indicate that, when planning and translating operations are demanded simultaneously from writers, processing capacities are taxed severely. These researchers conducted two experiments on persuasive writing. In their first experiment, production was lowest when preliminary-draft arguments were generated in the form of sentences. Production increased significantly when arguments were generated in the form of ideally sequenced propositions (idea units summarized in several words). Production was highest when arguments were generated in the form of unsequenced propositions. In the latter circumstance, when both the sentence-formation operation and the sequence operation were eliminated, writers were able to allocate more of their capacity to the task of argument production. These findings were later replicated by Hayes and his colleagues (J. R. Hayes, personal communication, April 4, 1985).

In the second experiment by Glynn *et al.*, the availability of additional capacity was found to have no effect on the argument production of writers with low verbal ability. They interpreted their findings as suggesting that additional capacity can provide writers only with the opportunity to draw from their pool of persuasive arguments; the provision of additional capacity cannot by itself remediate deficiencies in the knowledge stores of low-ability writers.

In these experiments, writers' metacognitive knowledge was reflected in a tendency to adopt formats that made possible the effective allocation of processing capacity. The more verbal writers typically used proposition-based formats (e.g., proposition lists, outlines, and diagrams) when constructing a preliminary draft. In each of these formats, a large pool of preliminary draft arguments was displayed in a form that lent itself to rapid identification and comparison of raw ideas. The use of such formats enabled the more verbal writers to reallocate processing capacity and thereby to produce additional arguments. Writers with low verbal ability, on the other hand, used proposition-based formats infrequently.

Freewriting. To cope with their processing capacity limitations, students of writing should be discouraged from attempting to draft finished products on their first try. Advocates of the "freewriting" technique have long discouraged premature editing:

Many people are constantly thinking about spelling and grammar as they try to write. Editing, *in itself,* is not the problem. Editing is usually necessary if we want to end up with something satisfactory. The problem is that editing goes on *at the same time* as producing. The editor is, as it were, constantly fiddling with what he's doing while he's in the middle of trying to do it. (Elbow, 1973, p. 5)

The Glynn *et al.* (1982) experiments provide empirical justification for the use of the freewriting technique. If idea generation is the most important concern of the writer, then perhaps mechanics, sentence formation, and sequence operations should be postponed until later drafts of a document. If these latter operations are postponed, processing capacity can be focused on the production of ideas in simple, proposition-like forms.

It should be kept in mind that good writers are distinguished from poor writers by superior knowledge as well as superior technique. Thus, the freewriting technique alone should not be expected to remediate deficiencies in the idea generation of poor writers. The value of the technique resides solely in its ability to focus processing capacity temporarily on idea generation.

Automaticity. Theorists differ on how much of the writing process can become automatic with practice. Flower and Hayes (1980) have argued that a great deal of writing process, including the production of grammatical sentences, can become automatic and demand very little conscious attention.

Cooper and Matsuhashi (1983) have proposed a contrasting view; they argued that even though planning to produce written discourse can be guided by underlying syntactic and discourse competence . . . it is nearly totally a conscious, non-automatic planning process . . . . [and that] certain phrase and sentence schema may provide local constraints, and a discourse schema may guide the process from a lofty abstraction level; but each clause is still new . . . even the most effortless writing requires close attention to planning every clause and sentence. (p. 34)

It is unlikely that writers can achieve a high level of automaticity in the generation, coordination, and integration of novel, complicated ideas; however, they can achieve it with sentence formation, punctuation, and spelling. The extent to which the latter processes are automated will determine the extent to which additional processing capacity can be dedicated to idea generation while writing. The demands of the writing task, especially in situations in which novice writers have been given tasks requiring more resources than they currently possess, have been known to obstruct the learning of writing skills (Scardamalia, 1981).

We recommend that novice writers be encouraged to cope with their limited processing capacities in two ways: first, by concentrating on idea production and temporarily setting aside the consideration of other subprocesses; and, second, by automatizing sentence formation and mechanics operations to whatever extent is possible. The latter can be achieved by systematic practice and such exercises as "sentence combining."

Topic Knowledge Limitations

Does the amount and organization of a writer's knowledge about a topic influence the quantity and quality of the ideas he or she produces when writing? Relevant to this question are several "biographical" studies in the area of reading comprehension that examined the effect of readers' personal history and life experiences on their construction of meaning (e.g., Anderson, 1977; Goodman & Goodman, 1978; Harste, Burke, & Woodward, 1982). These studies pointed out the ways in which readers' organization of their past experiences affected their responses to new experiences.

Also relevant to the question of topic knowledge are studies that have measured or manipulated students' knowledge of particular domains, and that then asked the students to write about topics in those domains. Voss *et al.* (1980) demonstrated that college students highly knowledgeable about a particular topic, such as baseball, included more elaborative detail and fewer irrelevant shifts of topic in

the essays they wrote. As a result, the essays were more coherent and cohesive.

Perhaps the most sophisticated study of the relationship between topic-specific knowledge and quality of writing was conducted by Langer (1984), who analyzed two sets of papers written for a high school history class. Langer compared the ratings of holistic scores, syntactic complexity, coherence, audience, and function that these papers earned with measures of topic knowledge taken prior to the writing task. Not surprisingly, Langer discovered a strong and consistent relationship between topic-specific background knowledge and the quality of student writing and, moreover, found that the organization of the students' knowledge influenced the quality of their writing:

When the assignment calls for a simple reiteration of facts, or elaboration of a given idea, a large amount of unintegrated (or loosely linked) information will suffice. However, when the student is required to present a thesis, analyze, and defend it, the degree of organization of knowledge, as opposed to simple fluency, will determine success. (p. 41)

The findings of several other studies suggest that poor writers may have difficulty bringing relevant knowledge to bear when writing because they are preoccupied with the more basic skills of spelling, punctuation, and word choice (Atwell, 1981; Birnbaum, 1982; Kellogg, 1987; Pianko, 1979). Good writers, in contrast, are more concerned with their purpose and the representation of their ideas.

Idea Revision. According to Gagné (1985, p. 217–218), revision involves two stages: (1) evaluating what has been written to determine how well it meets one's goals, and then (2) remediating unsuccessful parts of the product. There is a developmental sequence for these two stages. Studies of elementary school children conducted by Bartlett (1982) and by Scardamalia and Bereiter (1983) show that fourth graders are capable of evaluating their writing and recognizing the presence of problems; however, only the children in the higher grades are able to tackle successfully these problems during revision. But even in high school and college, there are some students who fail to evaluate their writing carefully enough to detect problems; and the problems they do detect tend to be related to mechanics rather than ideas (Bridwell, 1980; Faigley & Witte, 1981; Glynn *et al.*, 1982; Stallard, 1974).

Because beginning and remedial writers do not

revise their ideas sufficiently, Cohen and Scardamalia (1983) developed a program of self-diagnostic statements (e.g., "needs an example to explain idea") to prompt revision behavior. The program was successful, with the most frequent revision being the addition of more ideas; it was prompted by the statement "too few ideas."

Besides prompts, there are other things a teacher can do to encourage students to review their written ideas. Gagné (1985) has recommended that the teacher provide students with practice and feedback, and a wide variety of examples and nonexamples of writing problems. In addition, we recommend that students be encouraged to revise other students' writings. Because there is less ego involvement, some students may find it easier to examine critically the work of others. Eventually, they will be able to apply a degree of objectivity to their own work. We further recommend that students be encouraged to give a formal presentation in class based on their written ideas. The questions that listeners raise may signal biases and ambiguities in the speaker's ideas. Later, when the speaker is revising, he or she will be more sensitive to these biases and ambiguities, realizing that it is not possible for readers to ask questions.

Incubation.   Although the effects of an incubation period are well documented in the problem-solving literature, there has been very little direct study of the effects of incubation on idea generation and revision during writing. Quite possibly, an incubation period would allow a writer's biases and idiosyncratic references to become more apparent to him or her.

Bereiter and Scardamalia (1979) have spoken of the supposed benefit of a "cooling-off" period for obtaining a psychological distance between one's initial draft and any subsequent revisions. However, in a study that Bracewell, Bereiter, and Scardamalia (1979) conducted, they did not find that a one-week incubation period for revision led to any significant improvement in papers written by novice writers (over and above what would have been generated if the papers had been revised immediately after being written). More research, employing longer intervals and complicated writing problems, needs to be carried out.

A Framework for Methods of Idea Development

The purpose of this section is to propose a framework to view some of the many methods that are used to capture and develop ideas when writing. It is not possible here to provide in-depth instructions for using each particular method; readers are referred to the original sources cited for that purpose.

Teachers often recommended the following ways of developing ideas:

1. Writing down any ideas related to an assigned topic
2. Keeping a journal of interesting ideas and events
3. Using source materials
4. Thinking in terms of analogies
5. Discussing ideas with a peer or teacher who asks questions (i.e., "conferencing"; Freedman, 1982).

Some beginning writers discover these methods on their own, whereas others rely upon their teachers for an introduction. Bereiter and Scardamalia (1979) have endorsed the teaching of such methods because, they say, beginning writers often are not even aware of which topics they know a little or a great deal about. Relatively simple, informal methods such as these often evolve into complex, formal methods.

We will now discuss some of these formal, complex methods of idea development that are taught to writing students. We propose a framework for viewing these methods: some are derived from a general problem-solving method, based largely on cognitive psychology, whereas others are derived from a general neoclassical invention method, based on traditional schools of rhetoric.

Problem Solving

Problem solving, which is a general method that is rooted in cognitive psychology, has been articulated by Young (1976), Flower and Hayes (1980), Flower (1981), and many others. It revolves around planning processes in writing.

Problem solving has been defined as a movement from a perceived need or sense of difficulty, through the exploration of relevant information and ideas, to the intuition of possible solutions (Young, 1976). After identifying a problem, the writer's next step in his or her problem-solving planning is to define the writing goals (Anderson, 1985). Not all the goals in one's writing relate to content. Bereiter (1980) has identified three basic levels of goal orientation: (1) structure, consisting of text mode, paragraph, and sentence; (2) content, consisting of ideas and their relationships; and (3) purpose, consisting of the goals of the writer and the relationship with the audience.

Idea generation using the problem-solving method involves generating ideas or solutions to problems on syntactic, semantic, and pragmatic levels. Because the problem-solving method is global in scope, Young (1981) has suggested that we regard the more specific ''invention'' techniques as part of this generalized process of inquiry, that is, the problem-solving method. Young argues that, apart from the problem-solving method, invention techniques often function merely as retrieval aids. Within the general problem-solving approach, however, specific invention techniques can contribute to the discovery of new truths and to eventual solutions.

Three specific invention techniques particularly useful within the context of the general problem-solving method are associative listing, brainstorming, and synectics, which will now be discussed.

Associative Listing. Bereiter and Scardamalia (1979) found that simply asking a child to write more could be effective in improving fluency and idea production. Similarly, they found that it was more productive to ask children to list single words associated with a topic than it was to ask them to list ideas. Listing words, it seems, made it possible for the children to access their memories easily while avoiding the syntactic demands that are associated with generating ideas in the form of sentences. A listed word strongly associated with an entire idea can act as a retrieval cue for the idea when it comes time to write. Such listing also allows a freer flow of ideas because writing sentences takes longer than thought and can slow or block idea production.

Similarly, Caccamise (1981) has suggested that writers often believe they are out of ideas when actually they have simply exhausted the contents of one of many possible search sets that hold the activated idea nodes (see Figures 1 and 2). Because working memory limits the number of activated nodes, writers might think that they have come to the end of their ideas, when actually they have only come to the end of one cluster. Perhaps because they have considered the associations incorporated in that cluster in depth, elaborated them, and possibly summarized them, writers will acquire a premature sense of closure. To avoid this sense of closure, Caccamise suggests that writers may want to distribute their idea generation searches over several separate times rather than on one occasion. In this manner, writers will conduct searches that are not limited by previously generated items or by search strategies that have been prematurely closed.

Generating ideas in a simple associative manner may be the most effective planning procedure for children, but Martlew (1983) believes that this type of facilitation overlooks the need to plan and organize text in a cohesive manner. Simple associative memory searches must be integrated with other planning procedures if children are to learn to use appropriate semantic and syntactic structures, economy in organization, and originality of thought (Kroll, 1978; Ochs, 1979). Indeed, unless the teacher is careful, associative listing could reinforce what Bereiter (1980) calls ''associative dumping,'' an immature strategy used by the beginning writer who believes that writing simply involves dumping on paper everything he or she knows about a particular topic.

Brainstorming. A variation of associative listing, the brainstorming technique, involves generating as many ideas as possible, with no immediate judgments about their quality (Osborn, 1953). Johnson, Parrott, and Stratten (1968) demonstrated the effectiveness of brainstorming in a variety of creativity tasks, such as the generation of plot titles. Participants who brainstormed generated a greater number of ideas, including a greater number of high-quality ideas, than participants who were asked to generate only high-quality ideas. Brainstorming does include a judgment component, but it is reserved until later when all possible ideas have been generated. Group and individual brainstorming procedures can be easily implemented in classroom writing situations by teachers who wish to stimulate their students' idea production (Glover, 1979; Glover & Gary, 1976).

Synectics. The technique of synectics capitalizes on analogical reasoning. It requires writers to compare an assigned topic to topics they might not typically consider to be related. For instance, a writer might be asked to describe the similarities between the topic he or she has chosen (e.g., social life in the business office) and a distantly related topic (e.g., the African jungle). In this case, an analogy might be drawn between the office water cooler and the jungle water hole. Even though the analogies often are farfetched and not used in the actual composition, they may help writers to flex or warm up their minds in a way that will help them to perceive a striking and relevant analogy when it does present itself.

The rationale behind synectics is based in part on studies of creative individuals. For cognitive theorists, creativity is not just a result of an individual's unique system of associational bonds but is also an outcome of a person's handling of information and combining of data to develop effective solutions. According to Cropley (1970), creative thinkers tend to take greater risks in their thinking and are more willing to take in large quantities of information. Furthermore, creative individuals also are more likely to code their information (i.e., connect it to prior knowledge so as to make it meaningful) in unusual or novel ways. Cropley believes that the willingness to treat apparently unrelated sets of data as if they were related is a disposition characteristic of creative individuals. This disposition is one aspect of "divergent thinking." The opposite disposition is known as "convergent thinking," which is characteristic of individuals who tend to see a narrower range of connections among data or ideas.

Synectics, then, is a way of stimulating the workings of a creative mind. It is suggested that synectics can help convergent individuals begin to see data equivalences that are not readily apparent to them otherwise.

The importance of invention techniques, such as synectics, has a basis in developmental as well as in cognitive psychology. Growth in the ability to coordinate physical concepts, such as height and weight, has come to be considered a benchmark in cognitive development (Piaget & Inhelder, 1969). As Scardamalia (1981) has pointed out, cognitive development is construed as taking more and more variables into account during single judgmental acts. Training in invention techniques may help beginning writers to learn how to develop their ideas. It is this progressive ability to develop ideas, Scardamalia asserts, that underlies advances in writing, such as the movement from unelaborated to elaborated discourse and the movement from a single-argument thesis defense to a multifaceted defense that anticipates counterarguments.

Techniques in Combination. Specific problem-solving techniques, such as associative listing, brainstorming, and synectics, can be combined into formal, multitechnique methods such as the one proposed by Collins and Gentner (1980), which includes aspects of techniques we have already discussed, plus several others. Altogether, Collins and Gentner recommend seven ways of manipulating a writing topic: (1) identify dependent variables, (2) generate critical cases, (3) compare to similar cases (analogize), (4) compare to dissimilar cases (contrast or differentiate), (5) simulate (by running a model under critical settings of different input variables), (6) taxonomize (by finding a set of constants that provides an underlying explanation for the variation in the critical cases generated), and (7) dimensionalize (by placing a structure on the taxonomy).

Neoclassical Invention

The method of neoclassical invention and the two that follow were identified by Young (1976) in his topographical survey of major invention methods. Neoclassical invention is based on the rhetoric of Aristotle, Cicero, and Quintillian; it involves the art of composing persuasive arguments in support of a proposition. Once a thesis has been determined, the writer makes appeals based on moral character (ethos), based on the audiences' emotions (pathos), and based on logic (logos). Arguments or ideas are discovered by use of topics, or strategic prompts that involve a writer in developing his or her arguments by using definitions, comparison, contrasts, antecedents, consequences, and contraindications (see Table 1). The continuing usefulness of classical invention techniques is attested to by the development of a computer program based on Aristotle's "invention topics" (Burns, 1984).

The Dramatist Method

Whereas the previous method prompted the generation of persuasive arguments, the dramatist method (Burke, 1969) prompts the generation of motives. It relies on a pentad of strategic prompts—

Table 1. Catalogues of Techniques for Idea Generation

Examples of topics
Argument from opposites
A fortiori—argue from less to more (e.g., "care for your family, care for your country")

Dissociation
    appearance/reality
    means/ends
    individual/group
    spirit/letter

Methods of paragraph development
    narrative
    classification

Table 2.   Dramatist Pentad[a]

1. Act: What exactly was done?
2. Scene: Where did it happen?
3. Agent: Who did it?
4. Agency: By what means was it done?
5. Purpose: Why was it done?

[a]Each of the five heuristic probes can be seen as an aspect of the other; for example, war can be an act, a scene, an agency (as a means to an end), a purpose (in schemes proclaiming a cult of war), and as a collective act.

act, scene, agent, agency, and purpose—to evoke statements about the motive implicit in rhetorical acts (see Table 2).

Tagmemics

The method of tagmemics is based on language theory and was specifically developed from axioms of language structure. The method shares a goal common to classical invention, that is, finding arguments that are likely to produce changes in the audience. Moreover, the method assists in the retrieval of information and the analysis of problematic data. Unlike classical invention, however, it is not designed for use with a particular mode of discourse. It involves responding to a series of questions organized under the special organizational concepts called "particle," "wave," and "field" (see Table 3).

Odell (1974) taught a core group of Pike's tagmemic discovery procedures to writing students in order to evaluate the procedures' effectiveness. Specifically, he taught students how to segment

events; contrast a chunk of experience with other units; say how much a thing can change and still be the same; and locate events in a larger class of things, in a temporal sequence, in a physical context, and in a class system. Odell found that the students did learn to examine data more thoroughly and to perform a greater number of intellectual operations on these data. They also learned to present more evidence to support their statements. Odell, however, cautioned that his conclusions are tentative and asked whether other idea development methods might not have had an even greater influence upon students' writing.

Questions to Prompt Future Research

The idea generation process in writing represents an exciting and still largely unexplored area of research. These six questions about the idea generation process can guide the formulation of comprehensive research plans or programs:

1. How does a student become competent at generating ideas during writing?
2. Why do some students become competent in idea generation faster than other students?
3. How do students become, not just competent, but creative in their idea generation?
4. What can a teacher do to help a novice writer become an expert in generating ideas?
5. How should a teacher assess a student's competency and creativity in the skill of idea generation during writing?
6. How should a teacher's assessment pro-

Table 3.   Tagmemic Invention

Knowledge of a thing	(a) Particle	(b) Wave	(c) Field
1. How it differs from everything else	Describe its features (contrast)	What are the features of the novel writing process?	How do the parts of the novel fit together?
2. How much it can change and still be itself	At what point would it become a poem or a report?	How does this process differ from other similar processes?	How does this novel as a system work in contrast to other novels?
3. How it fits into larger systems	How does it relate to a system of literature?	How does the process of the novel fit into the process of literature?	How does the novel as a system relate to the larger system of which it is a part, that is, literature?

cedures change over time as the student becomes increasingly proficient at generating ideas?

Thinking about the preceding fundamental research questions can help in the formulation of plans for future research on the idea generation process. To illustrate, we have formulated a research plan that we present in the next section.

An Illustrational Plan for Future Research

Good writers usually have more ideas to write about than poor writers; however, one should not conclude that good writers are good simply because they may have more ideas. They may be good writers because they can strategically manipulate their ideas and coordinate their manipulations with other writing subprocesses.

To properly test this notion, one could control topic knowledge before examining writers' use of idea manipulation strategies. For example, a class of writers could be taught a body of unfamiliar but related information which they would learn to a given level of mastery. Ideally, this topical information should form a conceptual system (e.g., "photosynthesis" if a science topic was called for).

The writers would then be given a series of writing assignments that would require them to tap primarily this body of information for ideas. During the writing and afterward, writers would be asked to report verbally their thoughts. These verbal reports and associated written products would be analyzed to gain insight into how writers manipulate their ideas. Differences in the quality of the written products would be due largely to variations in the writers' ability to manipulate their ideas and express them in writing.

This plan would also lend itself to an examination of the ways in which the writing process could be used to help students better understand the complicated conceptual systems that they encounter in content areas, such as science, mathematics, and social studies. In other words, this plan could provide additional empirical support for curricula that stress the notions of "writing to learn" and "writing across the content areas."

Summary and Conclusions

This chapter has examined idea generation in the writing process. Our discussion of the human infor-

mation-processing model emphasized the important role of our limited-capacity working memory, the cognitive workbench on which we fashion our ideas while writing. Much of the raw material for our ideas comes from long-term memory, the knowledge base or propositional storehouse that we strategically probe by means of retrieval cues and search sets.

We found that idea generation could be better understood by combining the information-processing model with a model of a problem-solving system. In this combined model, purpose plays an essential role in helping the writer to narrow the focus of his or her idea generation.

The models of writing we discussed helped us to conceptualize the writing process as a set of component, interrelated subprocesses of which idea generation is one. There were some general similarities among the models discussed: for instance, the Hayes and Flower model and the Cooper and Matsuhashi model are hierarchical in nature, with idea generation seen as a subprocess of a higher level subprocess. And all models defined proficient writers as those who could access and coordinate subprocesses in a flexible manner in response to different demands of the writing task, such as those posed by the "assignment," the audience, and the writers' personal goals. All models also stressed the importance of possessing a repertoire of subprocesses that generate not just content ideas, but metacognitive ideas that relate to the overall writing process.

The commonalities of the models are overshadowed, however, by their unique aspects. For example, the Hayes and Flower model assigns special importance to problem solving, viewing the rhetorical situation as a problem that must be solved by juggling rhetorical demands. Rose's model is unique because it stresses the idea-generating behavior of deficient writers, or high-blockers, as much or more than the behavior of proficient writers. The Cooper and Matsuhashi model, with its stress on sentence roles within discourse types, is unique in the weight it gives to the medium as part of the message. And, finally, Wason's two contradictory models, though generic and oversimplified, remind us that more than one model may be necessary to conceptualize the idea generation processes of different writers, or of the same writer in different developmental stages.

In this chapter, we identified two general sources of writing difficulty. One was a writer's processing capacity limitations. We argued that writing is a cognitively demanding process because it can call for a variety of complex subprocesses to be carried out concurrently. Although these subprocesses can severely tax novice writers' limited processing capacities, such procedures as freewriting can help writers to cope with their limitations.

With experience and practice, writers can make some processes highly automatic and, therefore, less demanding on their processing capacities. And even though it may not be possible to achieve automaticity in idea generation, the relative automation of punctuation, spelling, and sentence construction makes it possible to dedicate more processing capacity to idea generation. Thus, we recommend that novice writers cope with their limited processing capacities in two ways: first, by concentrating on idea generation, while temporarily setting aside other subprocesses, and, second, by automatizing mechanics and sentence-formation operations to whatever extent is possible with the aid of appropriate practice exercises.

The second general source of writing difficulty we identified was a writer's topic-knowledge limitations. We suggested that the amount and organization of a writer's topic knowledge influences both the quantity and quality of the ideas produced when writing. We further suggested that poor writers tend to downslide by concentrating on mechanics, whereas good writers tend to upslide by concentrating on ideas.

It was pointed out that revision involves two stages, evaluation and remediation. Beginning and remedial writers may need intensive instruction in one or both stages. The instruction should include self-diagnostic prompts, practice, feedback, examples and nonexamples, revising the writing of others, and speaking in formal settings about the ideas one intends to revise. In addition, allowing ideas to incubate prior to revision may help some writers to better detect biases and ambiguities in their ideas.

We next proposed a framework for viewing the formal methods for capturing and developing ideas when writing. A relatively recent development is the general problem-solving method that incorporates more specific techniques, such as associative listing, brainstorming, and synectics.

Although a complete method of idea generation in the writing process is still to be developed, the methods that are available suggest several ways in which instruction in writing can be improved for individual beginning writers with specific problems. For example, if a student writer has shown thoughtfulness in class discussions but displays a lack of content ideas in a paper, an instructor might recommend one or more of the idea development

methods which we have discussed. On the other hand, if a student seems to have good content ideas that are poorly developed and organized, the instructor might want to show this student writer how to use discourse forms, sentence functions, roles, and plans to develop ideas for organizing and elaborating on existing ideas.

Finally, we posed some fundamental questions for future research. We also presented an illustrational plan: to examine how ideas are manipulated and expressed in writing, students would first master a conceptual system that they would then ''tap'' for a series of writing assignments. This plan could provide additional support for curricula that emphasize ''writing to learn'' and ''writing across the content areas.''

References

Anderson, J. R. (1985). *Cognitive psychology and its implications* (2nd ed.). San Francisco, CA: W. H. Freeman.

Anderson, R. C. (1977). The notion of schemata and the educational enterprise. In R. C. Anderson, R. J. Spiro, & W. E. Montague (Eds.), *Schooling and the acquisition of knowledge*. Hillsdale, NJ: Erlbaum.

Atwell, M. (1981, November). *The evolution of text: The interrelationship of reading and writing in the composing process.* Paper presented at the annual meeting of the National Council of Teachers of English, Boston, MA.

Baddeley, A. D. (1978). The trouble with levels: A reexamination of Craik and Lockart's framework for memory research. *Psychological Review, 85,* 139–152.

Bartlett, E. J. (1982). Learning to revise: Some component processes. In M. Nystrand (Ed.), *What writers know: The language process, and structure of written discourse* (pp. 345–363). New York: Academic Press.

Benton, S. L., Kraft, R. G., Glover, J. A., & Plake, B. S. (1984). Cognitive capacity differences among writers. *Journal of Educational Psychology, 76,* 820–834.

Bereiter, C. (1980). Development in writing. In W. Gregg & E. R. Steinberg (Eds.), *Cognitive processes in writing* (pp. 73–93). Hillsdale, NJ: Erlbaum.

Bereiter, C., & Scardamalia, M. (1982). From conversation to composition: The role of instruction in a developmental process. In R. Glaser (Ed.), *Advances in instructional psychology* (pp. 1–64). Hillsdale, NJ: Erlbaum.

Birnbaum, J. C. (1982). The reading and composing behaviors of selected fourth- and seventh-grade students. *Research in the Teaching of English, 16,* 241–260.

Bracewell, R. J., Bereiter, C., & Scardamalia, M. (1979, April). *A test of two myths about revision.* Paper presented at the annual meeting of the American Educational Research Association, San Francisco.

Bridwell, L. S. (1980). Revising strategies in twelfth-grade students' transactional writing. *Research in the Teaching of English, 14,* 197–222.

Britton, B. K., Glynn, S. M., & Smith, J. W. (1985). Cognitive demands of processing expository text: A cognitive workbench model. In B. K. Britton & J. Black (Eds.), *Understanding expository text* (pp. 227–248). Hillsdale, NJ: Erlbaum.

Britton, J., Burgess, T., Martin, N., McLeod, A., & Rosen, H. (1975). *The development of writing abilities (11–18)*. London: Macmillan.

Burke, K. (1969). *A grammar of motives*. Berkeley, CA: University of California Press.

Burns, M. H. (1984). Recollections of first-generation computer-assisted prewriting. In W. Wresch (Ed.), *The computer in composition instruction* (pp. 15–33). Urbana, IL: National Council of Teachers of English.

Caccamise, D. J. (1981). *Cognitive processes in writing: Idea generation and integration*. Unpublished doctoral dissertation. University of Colorado, Boulder, Colorado.

Chafe, W. (1977). The recall and verbalization of past experience. In R. W. Cole (Ed.), *Current issues in linguistic theory* (pp. 215–246). Bloomington, IN: Indiana University Press.

Cohen, E., & Scardamalia, M. (1983, April). *The effects of instructional intervention in the revision of essays by grade six children*. Paper presented at the annual meeting of the American Educational Research Association, Montreal.

Collins, A., & Gentner, D. (1980). A framework for a cognitive theory of writing. In E. R. Steinberg & L. W. Gregg (Eds.), *Cognitive processes in writing*. Hillsdale, NJ: Erlbaum.

Cooper, C. & Matsuhashi, A. (1983). A theory of the writing process. In M. Martlew (Ed.), *The psychology of written language: Developmental and educational perspectives* (pp. 3–39). New York: Wiley.

Cooper, M. (1984). The pragmatics of form: How do writers discover what to do when? In R. Beach & L. Bridwell (Eds.), *New directions in composition research* (pp. 109–126). London: Guilford.

Cropley, A. J. (1970). S-R psychology and cognitive psychology. In P. E. Vernon (Ed.), *Creativity* (pp. 116–125). Harmondsworth, Middlesex, England: Penguin Books.

Daiute, C. A. (1980). *A psycholinguistic study of writing*. Unpublished doctoral dissertation. Teachers College, Columbia University, New York.

Daiute, C. A. (1981). Psycholinguistic foundations of the writing process. *Research in the Teaching of English, 15*, 5–22.

Daiute, C. (1984). Performance limits on writers. In R. Beach & L. Bridwell (Eds.), *New directions in composition research* (pp. 205–224). London: Guilford.

Elbow, P. (1973). *Writing without teachers*. New York: Oxford University Press.

Faigley, L., & Witte, S. (1981). Analyzing revision. *College Composition and Communication, 32*, 400–414.

Flower, L. S. (1981). *Problem-solving strategies for writing*. New York: Harcourt Brace Jovanovich.

Flower, L. S., & Hayes, J. R. (1980). The cognition of discovery: Defining a rhetorical problem. *College Composition and Communication, 31*, 21–32.

Freedman, S. (1982). The student teacher writer conference: Key techniques. *Journal of English Teaching Techniques, 12*, 38–45.

Gagné, E. D. (1985). *The cognitive psychology of school learning*. Boston: Little, Brown.

Glover, J. A. (1979). The effectiveness of reinforcement and practice for enhancing the creative writing of elementary school children. *Journal of Applied Behavior Analysis, 12*, 487.

Glover, J. A., & Gary, A. L. (1976). Procedures to increase some aspects of creativity. *Journal of Applied Behavior Analysis, 9*, 79–84.

Glynn, S. M., Britton, B. K., Muth, K. D., & Dogan, N. (1982). Writing and revising persuasive documents: Cognitive demands. *Journal of Educational Psychology, 74*, 557–567.

Goodman, D., & Goodman, Y. (1978). *Reading of American children whose language is a stable rural dialect or a language other than English*. (Final Report, Contract No. 100-30087). Washington, DC: National Institute of Education.

Graesser, A. (1984). The impact of different information sources on idea generation: Writing off the top of our heads. *Written Communications, 1*, 341–365.

Gregg, L. W., & Steinberg, E. R. (Eds.). (1980). *Cognitive processes in writing*. Hillsdale, NJ: Erlbaum.

Halliday, M. A. K., & Hasan, R. (1976). *Cohesion in English*. London: Longman.

Harste, J. C., Burke, C. L., & Woodward, V. A. (1982). Children's language and the world: Initial encounters with print. In J. A. Langer & M. Smith-Burke (Eds.), *Reader meets author: Bridging the gap* (pp. 105–131). Newark, DE: International Reading Association.

Hayes, J. R., & Flower, L. S. (1980). Identifying the organization of writing processes. In L. W. Gregg & E. R. Steinberg (Eds.), *Cognitive processes in writing*. Hillsdale, NJ: Erlbaum.

Johnson, D. M., Parrott, G. L., & Stratten, R. P. (1968). Production and judgment of solutions to five problems. *Journal of Educational Psychology, 59* (Monograph Suppl. No. 6).

Johnston, W. A., & Heinz, S. P. (1978). Flexibility and capacity demands of attention. *Journal of Experimental Psychology: General, 107*, 420–435.

Kean, D. K., Glynn, S. M., & Britton, B. K. (1987). Writing persuasive documents: The role of students' verbal aptitude and evaluation anxiety. *Journal of Experimental Education, 55*, 95–102.

Kellogg, R. T. (1987). Effects of topic knowledge on the allocation of processing time and cognitive effort to writing processes. *Memory and Cognition, 15*, 256–266.

Kinneavy, J. L. (1971). *A theory of discourse*. Englewood Cliffs, NJ: Prentice-Hall.

Kintsch, W. (1980, July). *Psychological processes in discourse production*. Paper presented at the workshop on ''Psycholinguistic Models of Production,'' University of Kassel, West Germany.

Kintsch, W. (1986). Learning from text. *Cognition and Instruction, 3*(2), 87–108.

Kroll, B. M. (1978). Cognitive egocentrism and the problem of audience awareness in written discourse. *Research in the Teaching of English, 12*, 269–281.

Langer, J. (1984). The effects of available information on responses to school writing tasks. *Research in the Teaching of English, 18*, 27–44.

Martlew, M. (1983). The development of writing: Communication and cognition. In F. Coulmas & K. Ehlich (Eds.), *Writing in focus* (pp. 257–275). New York: Mouton Publishers.

Moffett, J. (1968). *Teaching the universe of discourse*. Boston: Houghton Mifflin.

Newell, A., Shaw, J. C., & Simon, H. (1963). The processes of creative thinking. In H. E. Gruber, G. Terrell, & M. Wertheimer (Eds.), *Contemporary approaches to creative thinking: A symposium held at the University of Colorado* (pp. 63–119). New York: Atherton Press.

Ochs, E. (1979). Planned and unplanned discourse. In T. Giron (Ed.), *Syntax and semantics, Vol. 12: Discourse and syntax*. New York: Academic Press.

Odell, L. (1974). Measuring the effect of instruction in prewriting. *Research in the Teaching of English, 8,* 228–240.

Osborn, A. F. (1953). *Applied imagination.* New York: Scribners.

Piaget, J., & Inhelder, B. (1969). *The psychology of the child.* New York: Basic Books.

Pianko, S. (1979). A description of the composing processes of college freshmen writers. Research in the Teaching of English, 13, 5–22.

Rose, M. (1984). *Writer's block: The cognitive dimension.* Carbondale, IL: Southern Illinois University Press.

Scardamalia, M. (1981). How children cope with the cognitive demands of writing. In C. H. Frederiksen & J. F. Dominic (Eds.), *Writing: The nature, development and teaching of written communication* (Vol. 2, pp. 81–103). Hillsdale, NJ: Erlbaum.

Scardamalia, M., & Bereiter, C. (1983). The development of evaluative, diagnostic, and remedial capabilities in children's composing. In M. Martlew (Ed.), *The psychology of written language: Developmental and educational perspectives* (pp. 67–95). New York: Wiley.

Scardamalia, M., Bereiter, C., & Goelman, H. (1982). The role of productive factors in writing ability. In M. Nystrand (Ed.), *What writers know: The language process and structure of writers discourse* (pp. 173–210). New York: Academic Press.

Stallard, C. K. (1974). An analysis of the writing behavior of good student writers. *Research in the Teaching of English, 8,* 206–218.

Tetroe, J. (1984, April). *Information processing demand of plot construction in story writing.* Paper presented at the meeting of the American Educational Research Association, New Orleans.

van Dijk, T. A., & Kintsch, W. (1983). *Strategies of discourse comprehension.* New York: Academic Press.

Voss, J. F., Vesonder, G. T. V., & Spilich, G. J. (1980). Text generation and recall by high-knowledge and low-knowledge individuals. *Journal of Verbal Learning and Verbal Behavior, 19,* 651–667.

Wason, P. C. (1978). *Specific thoughts on the writing process.* Paper presented at the Cognitive Processes in Writing—Interdisciplinary Symposium on Cognition, Carnegie-Mellon University.

Young, R. (1976). Invention: A topographical survey. In G. Tate (Ed.), *Teaching composition: 10 bibliographical essays* (pp. 1–43). Fort Worth, TX: Texas Christian University.

Young, R. (1981). Problems and the composing process. In C. H. Frederiksen & J. F. Dominic (Eds.), *Writing: The nature, development, and teaching of written communication* (Vol. 2, pp. 59–66). Hillsdale, NJ: Erlbaum.

CHAPTER 19

Creating the Conditions for Creativity in Reader Response to Literature

Carolyn A. Colvin and Roger Bruning

Introduction

In many classrooms today, the major task of students is to acquire and demonstrate a set of skills that are consistent with instructional objectives. Many educators would agree wholeheartedly with this focus and its implications of goal directedness, objectivity of measurement, and accountability. At the same time, however, an objectives-oriented classroom prescribes a particular role for the student, that of "achiever of objectives." Certainly, the real lives of students are vastly richer in their many dimensions than this narrow role as achiever of objectives can give expression to. To the extent that this role is emphasized and valued over others, students' experiences in schools correspondingly have become circumscribed, even impoverished in their scope. Lying untouched are students' interests, their values, and, indeed, the full array of their capabilities as human beings.

We believe that self-expression is fundamental to all meaningful learning and that the interests and values underlying students' lives must be expressed. It is our contention that, perhaps more than

any other activity that can be offered in an educational setting, the opportunity for students to write can give voice to the self and can channel self-expression to productive, generative, and creative ways. To this end, we focus in this chapter on a particular kind of writing—reader response—in which writing is conceived of as an act of responsive self-expression, of composition, and of creativity. The writing we will describe is not done for evaluation by a teacher, as most school writing currently is, but instead serves as a tool for constructing and negotiating meaning with others. In response writing, students "write to learn" and write to discover what they know. Through the act of writing and by sharing with others their comprehension of what they have read, students begin to understand themselves and to express themselves in creative ways.

In this chapter, we will attempt to show that the writing of reader response not only can create the basic conditions for meaningful learning, but also can play a fundamental role in creativity by helping learners construct new meanings. To reach these goals, however, the process of writing itself must become the focal point—writing not as product but as a creative act of writing to learn, of "making meaning," and of "constructing one's world through writing" (Mayher, Lester, & Prahl, 1983). When the proper conditions are set for stu-

Carolyn A. Colvin • Department of Teacher Education, San Diego State University, San Diego, CA 92182. **Roger Bruning** • Department of Educational Psychology, University of Nebraska, Lincoln, NE 68588-0641.

dents to write in response to what they have read, the elements of creativity become genuine possibilities. These conditions, we will argue, include evoking the subjective reactions of the individual and activating a wide range of cognitive processes. The uniqueness of the individual, his or her experiences, and the materials at hand set the stage for the novel expression of creativity through the writing of reader response.

Reader Response: Responding to Reading by Writing

In the following sections, we will attempt to describe the nature of reader response and outline the features that make it uniquely suited for self-expression and cognitive activation. We will argue that activation of memory for life-events—episodic memory—and generation of affective responses based on one's episodic memory are critical to creative reader response. Further, we will describe the role of the teacher in creating a context in which reader response can be used to foster students' creativity. We will indicate steps by which diversity of reader response through writing can be encouraged; that is, describe ways teachers may be able to create "settings for spontaneity," where students are able to discover, transform, and express the knowledge they have (Rosenblatt, 1976). Finally, we outline an agenda for research in which some of the issues we raise can become areas of inquiry likely to yield information useful to theorists and practitioners.

What Is Reader Response?

At roughly the same time but with seemingly little awareness of the others' work, individuals working in literary theory and in psychology began to reject predominant notions of the objectivity of knowledge and to voice views that emphasized the role of learners' associations, inferences, and interpretations in determining meaning (Cooper, 1985). In psychology, this perspective was advanced against the prevailing behaviorism by individuals such as Bartlett (1932) and Dewey (1938), and later by cognitive theorists, such as Neisser (1967), Bransford (Bransford, Barclay, & Franks, 1972), Rumelhart (1977), and Jenkins (1974).

At issue in literary theory was the emphasis on the dominance of the objective text as a core of study in instruction, a position held most strongly by advocates of the so-called New Criticism, with its focus on objectivity and scientific analysis. Most notable in arguing for the need to shift attention toward what readers do in their responses to literary works was Louise Rosenblatt, whose book *Literature as Exploration* was published in 1938. Although the book received relatively little attention when first published, by the 1960s it had generated a devoted following (Purves, 1976). Currently, in its fourth edition, it is widely regarded as the classic exposition of the role of the reader coming to understand or transact with text.

Within the perspective advocated by Rosenblatt, the term "response to literature" (Cooper, 1985) or simply "reader response" has come to refer to the transactions of readers with literature. Cooper's (1985) and others' use of the term (e.g., Bleich, 1985) suggests the importance of the reader's role, personality, and culture in the reading experience, but without displacing the centrality of the text. Rejected is the idea that a text can be "translated" by the reader; instead, reading is seen as a highly subjective process in which readers understand what they read through the filters of their own experiences and personalities. Emotional reactions are an essential part of reader response.

Our use here of the term *reader response* thus grows out of this general usage (See Tompkins, 1980) and the advocacy of Bleich (1978) and Petrosky (1982) of the position that comprehension is best demonstrated by students' extended written responses to text, followed by discussions and negotiations with others of the subjective meanings of that text. As used in this chapter, then, reader response refers to writing in response to reading within the following general parameters: The immediate stimulus for writing is a written text of some kind; the writing must be extended, usually beyond a paragraph or more; the writing must be personal, involving the subjective perceptions of the individual; and the writing should evolve within the context of a "community of readers and writers" in which it is created, discussed, and revised. Although writing and reading are the key elements, other forms of verbal expression, such as speaking and listening, may be equally important. In our discussion in this chapter, however, we will focus on writing and reading and their relationship to one another and to the creative process.

Why Writing in Response to Reading? When one examines the relationship of writing to reading from a theoretical perspective, it is evident that both reading and writing are based on the construction of meaning (Birnbaum 1986; Birnbaum & Emig, 1983; Harste, Woodward, & Burke, 1984; Petrosky, 1982; Tierney & Pearson, 1983; Salvatori, 1983; Shanahan & Lomax, 1986). Writing and reading are natural companions in the learning process. Readers draw on prior knowledge and experiences, reading strategies, and the extent of their literary sophistication to create meaning from text. They also must be sensitive to the devices and cues used by the author in order to integrate these elements into the meanings they construct from the text.

Texts, in turn, have been formed by authors with a sense of audience, specific and nonspecific intentions, and both directly expressed and tacit messages. In creating text, authors have at their disposal numerous tools of literary expression—choice of vocabulary, sentence structure, cohesive devices, and the like—to give form and meaning to their writing. Ultimately, however, it is in the interaction between reader and the text that comprehension occurs and meaning is created (Langer & Smith-Burke, 1982).

Readers come more or less ably prepared for their interactions with a text (Adams & Bruce, 1982; Harste *et al.*, 1984). For instance, the preparation that readers have had for the reading of a given text (e.g., prior knowledge or experiences) is one determiner of the quality of their transactions with text (Beach & Liebman-Kleine, 1986; Holland, 1975, 1985; Petrosky, 1982). Beyond preparation, the purposes that direct readers in their quest for meaning from the text also will have a powerful influence on their ability to respond actively to text materials. If readers come to a text with expectations that they will be successful in their task, that the reading process will be enjoyable, and that they will create something that will enable them to leave with more than when they began, then the quality of their reading is likely to be far different from that of those who anticipate problems and expect to find the reading tedious. Similarly, readers who are guided by objectives or expect to be quizzed over their reading will read with far more narrow purpose than those who are aiming for personal satisfaction and self-expression as outcomes of the reading task. Most readers fall short of Iser's (1974, 1978) depiction of the ''ideal reader''—ready to participate fully in the reading and to integrate the experiences of reading with the rest of his or her knowledge (Comprone, 1986).

Researchers who have examined the relationship of reading and writing perspectives have suggested that to have readers write in conjunction with their reading may help them become more like Iser's ideal reader (Bleich, 1978; Comprone, 1986; Petrosky, 1982, 1985; Tierney & Leys, 1986). As Petrosky has stated:

> Writing about reading is one of the best ways to get students to unravel their transactions so that we can see how they understand and, in the process, help them elaborate, clarify, and illustrate their responses by reference to the associations and prior knowledge that inform them. (Petrosky, 1982, p. 24)

Petrosky has suggested that when students are asked to write about what they have read, they engage in a creative act of composing. They make meaning from the information available to them, their personal knowledge, and the cultural and contextual frames in which they find themselves (Horton, 1983; Moffett, 1984). Instead of the kind of reading that demands only recall or very little more, Petrosky feels students should be encouraged to provide a structured written response calling on significant prior knowledge and experiences.

Taking up Petrosky's theme, the kind of creative reader response we advocate is one that

> teaches us how to think, lets us read without the pressures of recall and then, when we are finished, it begs us to speak our minds about what we have read and, in the process, it asks us to substantiate our interpretations and opinions—our reading—with evidence from our lives and the texts. (Petrosky, 1982, p. 21)

We believe that virtually all teachers at all educational levels and in all subject areas can use writing in this generative sense. By creating a ''community of readers and writers'' (Tierney & Leys, 1986), they can nurture a new identity in students as individuals whose experiences are valuable in new learning and can create a context, a ''setting for spontaneity'' (Rosenblatt, 1976) in which students can discover, transform, and express the knowledge they have.

Two Examples of Reader Response. To give our readers a fuller flavor of the kind of activities that might be subsumed under the rubric of reader response, we would like you to consider the following two examples. Both are drawn from the general area of literature. In the first case, envision yourself responding to the following instructions in an English class for high school seniors.

Please read the following poem carefully. Then, when you have finished, take 15 or 20 minutes to respond to the following three questions in writing. The questions (Bleich, 1978) are: (1) What do you see in the poem? (2) How do you feel about what you see? and (3) What associations—thoughts and feelings—does the poem create in you?

The River Merchant's Wife: A Letter[1]

While my hair was still cut straight across my forehead
I played about the front gate, pulling flowers.
You came by on bamboo stilts, playing horse,
You walked about my seat, playing with blue plums
And we went on living in the village of Chokan:
Two small people, without dislike or suspicion.

At fourteen, I married My Lord you.
I never laughed, being bashful.
Lowering my head, I looked at the wall.
Called to, a thousand times, I never looked back.

At fifteen I stopped scowling,
I desired my dust to be mingled with yours
For ever and for ever and for ever.
Why should I climb the look out?

At sixteen you departed,
You went into far Ku-to-yet, by the river of swirling eddies
And you have been gone five months.
The monkeys make sorrowful noise overhead.

You dragged your feet when you went out.
By the gate now, the moss is grown, the different mosses
Too deep to clear them away!
The leaves fall early this autumn, in wind.
The paired butterflies are already yellow with August
Over the grass in the West garden;
They hurt me. I grow older.
If you are coming down through the narrows of the river Kiang,
Please let me know beforehand,
And I will come out to meet you
　　　As far as Cho-fu-Sa.

Now further imagine yourself taking your writing, perhaps the next day, to a small group of 2 or 3 of your classmates. There you read what you have written, listen to what others have written, and affirm those things in your own and others' writing that you have found interesting. Finally, imagine again reading the poem and what you have written in response to your reading, then revising your writing, adding any new perceptions and insights gained from your interactions with the group.

This sequence of writing-response activities uses writing to allow students to create an initial meaning for the poem they have just read. Using this composition, the students then have a basis for joining groups of their peers to hear others' responses to

the reading of the Pound poem and for negotiating meanings in their "community" of learners. The initial composing of meaning is critical not only because it is a creative expression of each student's notion of meaning, but also because it forms the basis for further negotiations of meaning. Further elaboration and expression of thought are at the heart of the creative expression described earlier. The initial creative expression enables students to take the next step of making their writing "public" and to carry on further dialogue with their peers. Only after the process of writing, interaction, and rewriting has been played out, we believe, is their writing (which represents the accumulation of their creative expression) ready for evaluation by the teacher.

Our second example also is appropriate to the study of literature, but may be used in a variety of content areas. We have used it, for instance, in demonstrations of reader response for preservice teachers to help them begin to form their philosophies of teaching. It may be used in a similar manner to help students examine their notions of heroes or of influential people in their lives.

We use a children's story as a stimulus, reading it aloud and asking students to access their personal, subjective memories in order to provide an initial written response. Then, once students have composed this response, they are asked to distance themselves from their writing and view it more as an informed reader might. What evolves from this exercise is the kind of writing that acts as a mediator between the subjective, personal response created earlier and the eventual formal statement that expresses the student's philosophy of teaching. The sequence as we have used it is as follows:

The teacher reads aloud from *Ben's Trumpet* by Rachel Isadora (1979). The book is extensively illustrated; the text is relatively brief, describing a boy, Ben, who wants to be a trumpeter, but has only an imaginary instrument.

Ben's Trumpet[2]

In the evening, Ben sits on the fire escape and
listens to the music from the Zig Zag Jazz Club.
He joins in, playing his trumpet.
Sometimes he plays until very late and falls
asleep in the hot night air.
Every day on the way home from school, Ben stops
by the Zig Zag Jazz Club.
He watches the musicians practice.
The pianist, the saxophonist, the trombonist, and the drummer.

---

[1]From *Personae* by Ezra Pound. Copyright 1926 by Ezra Pound. Reprinted by permission of New Directions Publishing Corporation.

[2]From *Ben's Trumpet* by Rachel Isadora. Copyright 1979 by Rachel Isadora Maiorano. Reprinted by permission of Greenwillow Books and the author.

But most of all Ben thinks the trumpeter is the cat's meow.
Ben feels the rhythm of the music all the way home.
He plays for his mama, grandmother and baby brother.
And for his papa and his friends.
One day, Ben is sitting on the stoop and playing his trumpet.
"I like your horn," someone says.
It is the trumpeter from the Zig Zag Club!
Ben smiles and watches him walk to the Club.
The next day, after school, Ben stops and listens
to the musicians practicing a red hot piece.
He starts blasting away with his trumpet.
Some kids in front of the candy store watch him.
"Hey, what ya doing?" they yell.
Ben stops and turns around.
"What you think ya doing?" they ask again.
"I'm playing my trumpet," Ben answers.
"Man, you're crazy! You got no trumpet!"
    They laugh and laugh.
Ben puts his hands in his pockets and walks slowly
home.
He sits on the stoop and watches the blinking
lights of the Zig Zag Club. He sits there a long
time, just watching.
Down the street the band comes out for a break.
The trumpeter comes over to Ben.
"Where's your horn?" he asks.
"I don't have one," Ben says.
The trumpeter puts his hand on Ben's shoulder.
"Come on over to the club," he says,
"and we'll see what we can do."

Once the book has been read, the students are asked to write about the person who has been their "trumpeter." In other words, they are to reflect on the person who has served in a similar capacity as the trumpeter did for Ben and then describe the qualities of that person. The students are asked to think of a particular incident that will exemplify to a reader the importance of this single individual.

Following this composing session and small group discussions, the students are asked to reread their compositions and underline all of the words or phrases that describe this person. To form a bridge between this personal, subjective response and the more abstract philosophy of teaching they are being asked to formulate, students can take these powerful descriptors and use them as a basis for formulating their philosophy statements. Our experience here is that preservice (and inservice) teachers often will write about those "teachers" who have been instrumental in both positive and negative ways in their teaching careers. Those individuals and their qualities also seem to be at the heart of how both novice and mature teachers want to define themselves as teachers in the teaching profession. Once their initial composing is complete, students feel more confident in their reflections, examinations, and reconsiderations of their own thoughts. In giv-

ing life to these thoughts through the act of writing, students are able to better understand what it is they know and feel. Selecting characteristics of their "teacher" for use in their philosophy statements allows them the opportunity to distance themselves from the purely subjective and to consider such things as audience, format, and style. The framework for future writing and revision has been formed by their intensely personal memories that were activated in the initial writing phase.

In both examples, the major elements of reader response are present—a text, reading, writing a response to it, sharing that response with others, and elaborating or modifying that written response. These elements can be replicated in any subject area and with students of almost any age and level of sophistication.

In this basic sequence of events and in its multitude of variations lie the potential for cognitive activation, the construction of new meanings by the learner, and the opportunity for self-discovery and creative self-expression. The written responses composed by the reader come out of reading and rereading both the text and the writing done in response to the text. The response itself may be elaborated or transformed by the reactions of others. In the forward-backward motion of the comprehension process is the creation of meaning. Readers, acting as writers, push forward to create meaning from text.

Creative Dimensions of Reader Response

Writing in response to reading has features few other modes of expression can match for tapping students' potential for creative expression. Some of these lie in its form, others in the cognitive operations that either contribute to writing or can be applied to it. The following section examines some of these features.

Student Self-Expression

A self-evident aspect of any extended writing, self-expression is a fundamental condition for creativity. Although writing, particularly extended writing, currently is a relatively rare component of most classroom interactions (Applebee, 1981, 1984; Birnbaum & Emig, 1983; Bruning, 1984; Good, 1983; Graves, 1983), it has great potential for broadening the role of the student from a passive recipient of information to that of an active learner with an essential role in learning. When directed effectively by teachers, writing requires both production and originality—key building blocks of creative expression.

Activation of Cognitive Processes

Writing activates a wide variety of the cognitive processes of the individual, including perceptual, memorial, and planning and decision-making dimensions (see Carey & Flower, Chapter 17 in this volume; Frase, 1982), and plays an active role in the construction of knowledge and knowledge structures. We will explore each of these in turn.

Dimensions of Cognitive Activation. Flower and Hayes and others (Bracewell, Frederiksen, & Frederiksen, 1982; Flower & Hayes, 1980, 1981, 1984) have described the cognitive processes that are involved in writing as falling into three broad categories: (a) prewriting or *planning,* the stage of generating a conceptual structure that will allow expression of an idea for a specific reader; (b) *translating,* the transformation of the conceptual structure into the actual writing through such activities as vocabulary selection, choosing the language forms through which ideas are expressed, and ordering the expression of ideas into a meaningful sequence; and (c) *revising,* the operations that the writer undertakes to evaluate whether the text is adequate and to make changes to assure its adequacy. Even a cursory evaluation of these three categories of activities makes plain that multiple dimensions of cognitive operations almost certainly are invoked in any extended writing activity.

To write at all, writers minimally must have access not only to the content of what is to be written, but also to the means by which the content might be expressed. Writing must draw on memory, both for semantic knowledge, in the form of specific recall of vocabulary, concepts, and principles, and for knowledge that might more properly be called procedural (Anderson, 1983, 1987), such as morphological, syntactic, and pragmatic aspects of the language expression.

Beyond simple recall, however, is the necessity to recall and to use information in an *organized* fashion, ordered within schemata or frames. The role of such cognitive structures as a critical dimension in guiding comprehension and recall is well established in the literature. Building on the semi-

nal work of Minsky (1975), cognitive theorists and researchers (e.g., Anderson, 1977; Anderson & Pearson, 1984; Rumelhart, 1977, 1980; Rumelhart & Ortony, 1977; Schank & Abelson, 1977; Siefert, McKoon, Abelson, & Ratcliff, 1986) have argued persuasively for the centrality of framelike structural features in human cognitive functioning. In general, their argument is that frames provide a means for information assimilation and direct the cognitive processes of the individual. Readers' frames for key passage concepts and for text structure, for instance, dictate the kind and amount of attention that is devoted to different categories of information in a passage. These structures also underlie the inferences that readers make while reading and assist them in filling in gaps in memory by aiding in the necessary reconstruction of implied information (Anderson & Pearson, 1984). Johnston and Pearson (1982), for instance, have suggested that the influence of such frames is so powerful in reading that prior knowledge about a topic may be a better predictor of reading comprehension than either an intelligence test or a reading test scores.

Just as frames are an integral part of reading and other comprehension activities, so also do they play a powerful role in writing, as writers plan, translate propositions into expression, and edit and revise (Meyer, 1982; Scardamalia & Bereiter, 1982). Among the several kinds of frames that have been suggested as applying to writing (see Bracewell *et al.,* 1982) are story grammars or narrative frames for sequences of events, expository frames for expository text, conversational frames for conversations among characters, and procedural frames for explaining operations and activities. For instance, where one writer may proceed with little attention to reader characteristics and simply concentrate on writing down information recalled, another may take identical information and produce writing crafted toward a specific audience with a specific purpose in mind. The difference between the two writers lies in "framing skills" (Bracewell *et al.,* 1982) that the latter writer brings to bear on the writing task.

From the standpoint of the creative process, then, not only the activation of memory but the nature of that activation is critically important. A large number of studies of creative processes (e.g., see Glover, 1980; Torrance, 1983) have shown the utility for creative activity of stimulating the production of ideas. Indeed, the keystone of most indices of creativity, aside from originality, is simple volume of idea production. What reader response affords is the chance to bring information from memory to consciousness, where it potentially is available for use in the creative act. Then, as the reader/writer struggles with the challenges of writing and with the task of combining information with the structural aspects of what is recalled, the fuller potential of creative responding arises. To write is to activate knowledge about the pragmatic uses of language, understandings of the implied communication between writer and reader, and perceptions of the purposes for writing. To the extent that writing necessitates these cognitive functions, the potential will increase for their creative expression.

Constructive Processes in the Act of Writing. Beyond its ability to mobilize the organized knowledge of the student, reader response stimulates *constructive* aspects of the cognitive processing system—the creation of new meanings. The view of human cognition as actively constructive is not new. The concept of constructive memory is present in the seminal work of Bartlett (1932) and clearly articulated in more recent research (e.g., Bransford *et al.,* 1972; Paris & Lindauer, 1976, 1977). Unless individuals are under explicit instructions to produce it, exact reproduction in recall of events is quite rare. Instead, memory almost always involves transformation of the input by the individual (Loftus & Loftus, 1976).

Constructive models (see Paris & Lindauer, 1977, for a detailed discussion) stress that new information is transformed by affective, social, and cognitive processes of the individual. What is learned is created by each individual; it is as much a product of that persons' existing cognitive structures and affective tones as it is of the material to be learned.

The individual learner in this view is not passive but active. What is learned and subsequently remembered is not reproduced so much as it is created. Information undergoes "blending, condensation, omission, invention, and similar constructive transformations" (Paris & Lindauer, 1977, p. 35). Not only content is transformed, however; equally important are new organizational structures that the individual generates.

The constructivist viewpoint obviously is compatible with that of theorists who see the function of writing, at least in the sense of reader response, as one of creatively constructing new meanings (Tierney & Leys, 1986; Tierney & Pearson, 1983).

When we write, we compose by making meaning from available information, our personal knowledge, and the cultural and contextual frames we happen to find ourselves in. (Petrosky, 1982, p. 26)

In the planning, composing, and revising sequence required by writing, writers somehow must combine the ways in which they have framed their world, the structures of the topic and their knowledge about it, and the demands of the writing task, and must express all these within a framework that can be comprehended by a reader. These are inherently creative acts, and virtually all but the most formulaic of writing tasks require them. Thus, the writing task in reader response can be construed as one of accommodation of knowledge to knowledge and structure to structure. Frameworks of knowledge must be combined with or subsumed within new frames, hierarchically organized knowledge frames must be reconciled with the sequential dimension of writing, and cognitive content and structure must be expressed within the conventions of language.

The act of reader response also has another constructive dimension. Planning, composing, and revision in writing of any length take time and generate a stream of cognitive activity. Although the cognitive processes of writing often have a cyclical quality, in the physical act of writing word must follow word, sentence sentence, and paragraph paragraph. As these activities move ahead, students must relate what they are reading and writing to what is in their memory. Because of the extended time and attention required by writing, discovery of "forgotten" information is likely to be enhanced. With each new activation of information, yet other information is likely to be activated (Anderson, 1983, 1987; Stanovich & West, 1983) and the probability of other recall enhanced, in much the same manner as lively conversation stimulates rich recollections and associations. Further, as writers struggle to reconcile the information encountered in reading with recollections of their experiences in order to express a judgment, partly formed ideas begin to take shape and evolve into new, more complete forms. In order to respond to their reading, writers must make tacit understandings explicit (Petrosky, 1982).

The degree to which such constructive processes occur is no doubt a function of many factors, including the nature of the writing task the readers must complete, the cognitive abilities and the affective resources of readers, and the particular social and cultural contexts in which our readers-as-writers live. What we would argue, however, is that students' resources for responding creatively through writing are vast, far greater than is supposed ordinarily. To tap these resources requires that they be permitted to approach text without artificial restrictions and to respond, especially initially, in their own terms (Rosenblatt, 1976). Only if a teacher has made expression of this kind possible, that is, has created a "setting for spontaneity," can the processes be nurtured in which students can clarify and enlarge their reactions to text.

Creative Interaction with Others through Reader Response

Writing provides a "window into the mind." The self-expressive nature of writing that we are proposing is a part of reader response that provides teachers with an unusual opportunity to enhance students' creative processes. Each event of reader response, beginning with the readers' responding in writing to their reading, followed by their sharing that writing with their peers, and finally concluding with their rewriting what they have written, is an occasion for creative expression and offers teachers the chance to encourage it.

Reader Response as Cognitive Record. Earlier we argued together with Petrosky (1982) that "comprehension arises from an immersion in the particulars of texts, readers' knowledge, and contexts" (p. 22) and that readers' writing reflects that comprehension. In our view, creative reader response must evoke the subjective reactions of the individual in order to activate the widest possible range of cognitive processes. In writing, the processes are moved from inside the head to an outward public reflection of the self.

Writing provides at least a partial record of one's cognition at the time of its creation, a record about which judgments can be made thoughtfully and objectively both by the writer and by others (Bereiter, 1984). To the extent that either students or teachers desire, criteria for judgment of creativity can be invoked in both one's own and others' reactions to the writing.

Reader Response Discussion Groups. In reader response, an important mechanism for providing reactions is that of peer response groups, groups of three or four students who discuss what has been written by each. As typically used in reader response (Murphy, 1987), their function is to provide the readers/writers with an opportunity to share the

meanings they have constructed. Each person in the group ordinarily has a copy of what the group members have written; the leader is the person whose writing is being discussed. In such groups, each individual can obtain assistance in developing ideas, determine if the writing is clear and easy to understand, and, if desired, get advice on such writing mechanics as spelling, grammar, and usage. In Murphy's view, group members should be encouraged to respond to peer writing by complimenting what is effective, asking clarifying questions about the content of the paper, and, as appropriate, making suggestions for additional clarity. The general focus is constructive but is intended to force the students as readers and writers to examine and expand upon thoughts, feelings, and associations that have driven their response. Because the writers' affective reactions and personal knowledge will have been evoked in the writing, such discussion will reveal a variety of perspectives because each group member has seen things differently (Murphy, 1987). Discussion, in turn, creates new perspectives. As Murray (1986) has stated:

> When one says something, lays it out in the open, gathers it up for the speaker and listener, a presence is effected. . . . Whatever the object, once it is said, . . . it now enjoys its own presence in the discussion, has its own meaning, its perspectivalness, its possibilities, and its unfolding history. (p. 81)

Rewriting

Rewriting is a vital part of creative reader response. As fresh perspectives grow out of the interplay among individuals' reading, writing, responding, and rereading and from new possibilities contributed by others, these perspectives can be captured in revisions. In rewriting early drafts students are not asked necessarily to alter their original perceptions, but only to have listened actively to others' perceptions and to have made an honest attempt at describing their own writing and reacting to that of others (Murphy, 1987).

Just as in the original writing of reader response, the goal in revision is to express one's own personal reaction to the text, a reaction with a bias toward one's personal experience and the effect that it has generated. Ideally, the written response will have in it components of a broadened critical perspective that includes the reactions of others both to the text and the student's writing. Others will have shared their personal viewpoints with the reader/writer and thus will have enhanced the potential of what he or she now might write. In practice, of course, helping students to expand and broaden their perspectives may not be a simple matter. As Ritchie (1988) has pointed out, having once struck upon a powerful and personal connection with what they have read, some students are absolutely unwilling and unable to move away from their original writing. Particularly with adolescents and late adolescents, this would not be unexpected for developmental reasons. Nonetheless, they will have been presented with the opportunity to modify their perspective, an opportunity not often available in most current, more traditional approaches to writing.

Enabling Conditions for Creativity in Reader Response

In the foregoing discussion, little has been said about the role of the teacher in reader response classrooms. In one sense, this is appropriate. The emphasis of reader response is on the students' creating their own meaning through their transactions with text. Student experiences and their use of those experiences in responses to text are paramount. Obviously, however, the teacher's actions are critical in creating a "setting for spontaneity."

Creating a Supportive Classroom Culture

The teacher's role in guiding reader response is a complex and exacting one. The first task is contextual—creating a classroom climate in which personal, emotional statements are encouraged and honored. Developing a classroom culture in which personal experiences and self-expression are valued and protected requires a considerable shift in goals from those emphasizing content to those stressing self-expression and individual development. Content need not be abandoned, but the teacher must focus equally on the experiences and identities of the students through which the content is experienced and transformed. As Rosenblatt (1976) has stated, turning attention to the students' backgrounds and temperaments may cause the teacher to fail to do justice to the text, but the students' responses are, as she states with great insight, "part of our teaching materials" (p. 51).

As we indicated at the outset of this chapter, however, making personal expression the centerpiece of classroom process comes into conflict with a strong emphasis in our educational system on uniformity of outcome. Instructional objectives and standard classroom assessment procedures help insure this uniformity. Many teachers also seem to be quite strongly committed to the idea that, even though instructional methods might be individualized, learning objectives should be the same for all. But common objectives for all necessarily fail to be able to account for the interplay of the students' personalities and experiential qualities with the content. To the extent that one embraces a constructive, creative model of learning, the notion of uniform outcome becomes less and less attractive.

Focusing on student expression, particularly a form of student expression that draws upon the fundamental human relationships and emotions known to the student, also is likely to conflict with strongly held student attitudes toward "how education is." Initially, most students are likely to resist, perhaps even strongly, approaches that seem not to offer a clear sense of "what is required" and "what to do" (Murphy, 1987). For many students, too, the opportunity to express one's honest reactions to what has been read will create a great deal of insecurity and uncertainty. As Rosenblatt (1976) has indicated, with the opportunity to express the self comes responsibility. For many students, it is far more comfortable to give this over to a teacher-authority than to take this responsibility on themselves. Teachers also may be well socialized in their roles as information source, critic, and ultimate authority. Consequently they, too, like the students, may unconsciously resist the shift in role necessitated by free student expression in reader response.

Teachers who use the methods of reader response must recognize that students who write with a sense of their own identity, hear the understandings of their work by their peers, and revise—in other words, who participate in a "community of readers and writers"—are less subject to and dependent upon the authority of the teacher. No matter what its potential for student learning and development, change such as this initially may cause great discomfort to many teachers. The rewards are great, however, as both teachers and students begin to value the experiences of their lives and to trust in their own individual expression. Through sharing this expression with others, each can develop greater insights into human life and values and, ultimately, express them in acts of creativity.

Drawing on Students' Episodic Memory

Portraying abstract verbalization and analysis as the "correct" response to literature quickly will destroy responsiveness in virtually all students. Adolescents often are untouched by the appeal of literature because

for them words do not represent keen sensuous, emotional, and intellectual perceptions. This indicates that throughout the entire course of their education, the element of personal insight and experience has been neglected for verbal abstractions. (Rosenblatt, 1976, p. 50)

The strong implication is that, for there to be a potential for creativity, readers who respond must be allowed to take as full advantage as possible of their personal experiences and the emotional responses they generate. These resources lie generally within the realm of episodic memory.

For some time now, memory theorists have proposed that general information, on one hand, and information about specific events, on the other, may be stored in separate memory systems. Tulving (1972, 1983), for instance, has proposed a distinction between *semantic memory* and *episodic memory* that corresponds to these categories. In the semantic representational system is abstract, decontextualized information that has been developed across multiple experiences. Episodic memory, in contrast, is autobiographical and unique, consisting of representations of particular events. Recent formulations of the semantic-episodic distinction (e.g., Whittlesea, 1987) have indicated that it may derive not so much from different stores for the semantic and episodic types of information, but from the encoding and retrieval activities that are used by the individual. In other words, demands of some tasks, contexts, and purposes may lead to the encoding of information with more of the decontextualized features of semantic memory, while other tasks, contexts, and purposes may lead to encoding with strong episodic features (Hintzman, 1986; Whittlesea, 1987).

The Necessary Role of Emotion. Our judgment, for which the rationale is presented below, is that reader response through writing is most likely to create meaning and to enhance creativity when its starting point is in the stimulation of the episodic memory of the reader/writer. Further, it is our strong belief that emotional and not analytical or critical responses on the part of the reader are most likely to stimulate critical expression. In *Literature as Exploration,* Louise Rosenblatt argued persuasively that the reader's response to literature inevitably will be in terms of the student's tempera-

ment, experience, and background. She contended that, at the outset, a literary work will have meaning for a reader *only* in personal terms. These personal responses may be immature, incomplete, or even mistaken, but they nonetheless are the initial meaning of the work to the reader.

Only on the basis of such direct emotional elements, immature though they may sometimes be, can [the reader] be helped to build any sounder understanding of the work. The nature of the student's rudimentary response is, perforce, part of our teaching materials. (Rosenblatt, 1976, p. 51)

The Role of Emotion in Cognition. Current models of cognition lend support to Rosenblatt's assertion. Although by and large the element of emotion had figured only sporadically in earlier theories and models of cognition (see Read, 1984), emotion now has begun to appear as an element in current models of cognitive processes.

One such model is that of Bower and his associates (Bower, 1981; Bower & Cohen, 1982; Gilligan & Bower, 1984). Their perspective, consonant with those of most current models of memory (e.g., Anderson, 1983, 1987; Collins & Loftus, 1975) is that memory can be represented as a rich associative network. This network is composed of concepts, schemata, and events, which form the nodes of the network. These nodes are linked by multiple pathways to one another. Central to the model is the process of spreading activation, in which activation of one or more nodes leads automatically to activation of associated nodes. In such network models, spreading activation is seen as the primary mechanism by which memory is enhanced (e.g., through creating additional associative links through elaboration) and whereby specific information is retrieved from storage and brought into consciousness.

In Bower's model, however, emotions also are central cognitive units, linked like other units to related events and concepts. In the words of Gilligan and Bower (1984), the network contains "emotion nodes" (p. 571) that, once stimulated, activate autonomic response patterns, subjective experiences, and interpretive rules. These units reverberate back to the activated emotion units and cause the activation to persist for some time.

Two features of the emotion nodes are important for our present discussion. First, activation produced by emotion is hypothesized to be unusually persistent in the memory network. Whereas ordinary concepts disappear nearly instantaneously from consciousness when, say, the topic of conversation shifts, activation from emotion continues and only dies out gradually through a natural damping process. That is, the complexity of neurophysiological, motor, and subjective-experiential reactions, once activated, tend to persist much longer than those stemming from "purely cognitive" units.

Second, Bower contends that emotions are stronger sources of activation than conceptual or schematic nodes. As Gilligan and Bower (1984) have stated:

One might think of nodes in the network as small voltage sources (or signal boosters), and that, once aroused, emotion nodes simply send more "voltage" than concept nodes. This would cause an emotion to gain greater control than a thought over the direction and content of subsequent thoughts. (p. 5)

In this conception, then, stimulation of *affective* dimensions of students' episodic memory would be expected to produce activation that is both more durable and more extensive than activation that did not tap this affective component. Thus, when students are asked to link what they have read—a poem, newspaper article, a letter—to their own experience, particularly elements of their experience evocative of emotion, we would argue that engagement and motivation to continue will be high because of the nature of the activation produced. Moreover, not only will it be likely that a relatively larger number of related concepts will be activated, but that their activation will persist longer. To the extent that multiple concepts and schemata continue to be activated and the reader struggles to express the meaning they carry, the fundamental elements are put into place for creative responding.

Although emotion is proposed as an appropriate starting point for student response, reason is not excluded. Reason, to return to Rosenblatt's (1976) view, is equally vital to informed response but should "arise in a matrix of feeling" (p. 227). In her view, rationality is not a force arrayed against emotion, but instead a force applied to emotion in an attempt to understand it. Murray (1986) echoes this same thought:

Provocation, discontinuity, delayed and suspended judgment are ingenious and creative procedures, methods, employed in the process of imaginative thought, but they gain their respect and prove efficacious only within the confines of the structure provided by sound, rational, logical thinking. Neither is successful without the other; both are fruitful when together. (p. 35)

Our argument, then, is that those memories most likely to stimulate the quality of response needed to engender full learner involvement and creativity are likely to be in episodic, not semantic memory. In the former are the directly experienced events of student's lives. These memories, with the full richness of emotion that they can evoke, will provide the best starting point for students' creative transactions with text. In contrast, for the teacher to call for an "understanding" of text based on the abstracted knowledge in semantic memory seems much less likely to evoke from the learner either the vividness of recollection or the motivation to drive a vital interaction between the learner and the text.

To value reading as a highly subjective experience with a strong emotional component, teachers must acknowledge, we believe, the "mine-ness" (Heidegger, 1927/1962) of every students' existence; that each experience, including the hoped-for transaction with text, is comprehended based on self-reference. Often, however, we as teachers behave as if materials we ask students to read have about them a completely objective character—a "truth" to be uncovered by the student or pointed out by us to the student. The origin of meaning in reading, however, arises first from the reader and not from any particular text being read by the reader (Applebee, 1985; Holland, 1968, 1975, 1985; Tierney & Pearson, 1983). Personal experience frames all reading; understanding is created out of who readers are and the responses the text evokes (Beach, 1983; Bleich, 1975a,b).

Another factor, perhaps more speculative, also is likely to make the evocation of episodic memory as a starting point for the reader's transactions with text more productive than attempting to stimulate semantic memory. For younger readers and writers, in particular, we would argue that the contents of episodic memory are much more likely to be large, stably organized, and accessible compared to the contents of semantic memory. Whereas the former reflects the whole body of the student's life experiences, the latter is likely to contain a relatively smaller amount of abstracted qualities of experience organized around selected concepts and topics. The poetry example that was provided earlier illustrates this point; to generate images, to associate feelings, to recall life events when reading this poem is relatively easy to do, no matter what an individual's training. In contrast, however, to "analyze" the poem by applying techniques of literary criticism, or by relating it to other literary works, or somehow to "explain" its meaning is likely to be much more difficult for most readers.

Teaching Methods in Reader Response

An underlying assumption of this chapter is that all reader response is inherently creative from the standpoint of the individual. For a student to respond to reading with extended writing, multiple dimensions of cognition and language must be activated and combined in a creative process. At the same time, however, we would acknowledge that not all student expression in reader response will be judged creative or even divergent from that of others. A "setting for spontaneity" and self-expression through writing are necessary for creative student expression, but not sufficient. When applied to reader response activities, the following dimensions may add to the possibility that the written expression may take new and creative forms.

Arranging Priming Activities

The central act of reader response is readers' transactions with text, transformed through writing. The efficacy of these transactions is based, however, on the assumptions that readers (1) have sufficient knowledge available to have meaningful transactions with the text, (2) have the motivation to engage in meaningful transactions with the text, and (3) have some degree of ease with the act of self-expression. Although some students will have no difficulty on any of these dimensions, many others initially may see no connection between their own experiences and the text and must be helped to see that connection. Still others will have strong predispositions to react "objectively," and not subjectively.

We nonetheless see a number of approaches that teachers can use to prepare their students for their reading. For instance, prior to reading, the teacher may wish to initiate a discussion on the general topic of the reading or writing to establish a preparatory set or, through using analogy or metaphor, link the topic to one familiar to the students. To evoke subjective responses, the teacher may wish to ask students to recollect experiences they have had, images they can visualize, and sensations they have felt. The teacher may ask students to talk to peers, to observe actions of others, to write for information, or to interview individuals. The purpose of all such activities, of course, is to activate the direct sensory experience that will form the basis for the reader response.

Writing for New Audiences

One of the most straightforward ways that writing can be moved into new forms, yet still derive from student experience, is to focus that writing on a new audience. For instance, students in a science class might be asked to use information from a reading in ecology in a letter to a company president, a state senator, or the President (or, for that matter, in letters to pygmys, astronauts, surfers, or real-estate developers). At least implicitly, most writing in the schools is done for the teacher as reader, with little consequent attention to the pragmatic use of language as purposeful and persuasive activity. Simply being forced to express a body of information to a new audience will require transformations of that information and greater personal involvement of the reader/writer. Further variation can be introduced by asking readers to convey their reactions to more than one audience, varying in age, political outlook, or some other significant dimension.

Writing in New Language Forms

When students do write, they ordinarily are taught to value writing as a product. Their writing must be neat, mechanically correct, and well organized. As a consequence, the writing they do is often formulaic. For example, one commonly taught structure for writing essays that is well learned by many students is to present an introductory paragraph containing a thesis sentence, then to give reasons to support that thesis, and then to summarize the argument in a final section. Even though this structure may be useful for some purposes, it is only one of a myriad of possibilities. Instead, the teacher might ask students to create a sequence of their recollections, or imaginary conversations, speeches by historical figures, sets of instructions, product warnings, codes, telegrams, signs, and so on. By letting the students explore new forms of writing, but still requiring them to use their direct experience in responding to the text, new combinations of idea, language, and structure will emerge.

Taking New Perspectives as a Writer

Most writing is from "I" or "we" to "you." Obviously, however, the perspective taken by the writer can be altered. Students can be asked to write as if they were a second person writing to a third, or even as if they were another person, for example, a parent, writing to themselves. They may wish to read and write as visitors from outer space, as a hyperperceptive newborn baby, as the world's oldest person, or as "Star Trek's" Dr. Spock. Nor need their perspective be limited to that of humans—readers can write with their minds' eyes in the roles of a family pet, a radish growing in the garden, a zoo animal being traded to a new zoo, an ancient redwood tree, or an amoeba.

Each change of perspective, of course, will force students to grapple with a new array of cognitive structures and is likely to help stimulate additional points of contact between what they already know and their reading. As they write from a perspective that is new to them, unfamiliar associations and unusual cognitive structures are likely to be generated that will make learning both meaningful and memorable.

Writing with Humor and on Unusual Topics

Creativity, we know, often has a strong component of humor. For most teachers and students, however, learning is seen as serious business and, in school, almost all reading and writing are done with serious purpose on sober-minded topics. Important goals for learning, however, can be reached in many different ways. When process begins to be valued over product, consistent with the constructivist view we have advocated, the specific content and methods of learning are less critical than the processes they engender. For instance, the ability to think freely and well about economic or historical or social issues and about the values inherent in decisions about them may best be developed by whimsy, by humor, through use of metaphor, and by satire. For the typical student, the chance to write a satirical response to an issue may prove to be far more motivating, intellectually stimulating, and ultimately creative than a more "serious" response to that same topic.

Issues for Research in Reader Response

In both literary theory (e.g., Moffett, 1984; Petrosky, 1982; Rosenblatt, 1976, 1978, 1985) and psychological theory (Anderson, 1983; Neisser, 1982; Pearson, 1985), a constructive view of the reader is well accepted. The research consistently has shown that readers' worlds are projected into

what they read. What they comprehend grows not only out of the content and structure of what is read, but out of the readers themselves and their temperaments, intentions, and cultural perspectives (Ronald, 1986).

The general acceptance of a constructive view of learning, however, is not matched by specific knowledge about the impact of writing on reading and on the role each plays in the creation of new knowledge. There seems to be little doubt about the general efficacy for learning and recall of active processing of information (e.g., Glover, Benton, & Bruning, 1983), and the following section is premised on the reasonable assumptions that writing is a way of activating cognitive processes and that such activation is likely to facilitate learning. The present chapter, however, has proposed that a specific pedagogical technique—reader response—is likely to have positive effects on both learning and the probability of creative responding. Whether this is so is, of course, an important issue for research and within that issue are a number of questions of both theoretical and applied interest.

1. Are there distinct differences, both cognitive and affective, in the quality of writing resulting from prereading and prewriting activities presumed to stimulate semantic memory as opposed to those that stimulate episodic memory?

As we have argued throughout this chapter, the "setting for spontaneity" created by the teacher for reader response is likely to be a critical variable. Not only must the teacher create an atmosphere of openness and acceptance, but students must learn how to interact with their peers in constructive and pleasurable ways. Furthermore, the activities that precede reading and writing will determine what students will do. Instructions to recall and write from personal experience in response to a poem, as we have contended, are likely to engender vastly different conditions than instructions that direct readers to their semantic knowledge, for instance, instructions to "read and analyze the poem." Whether, however, the creative consequences of these setting conditions in fact differ is a matter that should be addressed empirically.

2. How does the nature of what is read affect the creative qualities of what is written?

Some materials are inherently more evocative than others. Those written from a "personal" standpoint to which students can readily relate, for instance, may evoke better and more complete writing and discussion than those with more generalized, abstract, textlike structures. Other dimensions of the reading materials that may also greatly affect the potential for creative responding are the extent of imagery used by the author, the strength of point of view taken, the readers interest in the materials, and the familiarity of the topic to the reader.

3. What are the cognitive consequences for creativity of being forced to take different perspectives in writing in response to given text materials?

At present, we know little about the effects on creative expression of having to write from an "unordinary" perspective. Does having to take different perspectives in writing lead to new insights, new cognitive structures, new forms of expression? Does the unusualness of the perspective make a difference? Does the degree with which the reader/writer can identify with the perspective have an impact on the creativity of expression?

4. What are the cognitive consequences for creativity of writing for different audiences?

Development of pragmatic awareness in writers and speakers is an important goal for many teachers. Our interest here, however, is in the creative consequences of writing for varied audiences. Are students, for example, more willing to write creatively for an audience of their peers than for, say, the teacher or for a hypothetical "reader?" Empirical research in which the conditions for writing are systematically varied along this dimension would assist in answering this question.

5. How does what the student initially writes affect subsequent rereadings and rewritings?

Reader response creates an unusually rich interaction among reading, writing, and subsequent rereading and rewriting, and raises interesting questions about how points of view might undergo transformation. Does the substance and structure generated initially and reported in the initial writing persist? That is, are the initial cognitive structures by which the student transacts with the text immutable or can they be transformed by later inputs? What

impact do the reactions of other readers/writers have on what the student does in rewriting and how does this relate to level of cognitive development?

6. What conditions for rewriting will move students in the direction of divergence and what consequences, both cognitive and behavioral, will the divergence have on comprehension of the original text?

For many, perhaps most students, rewriting connotes doing minor editing, and sometimes little more than recopying a messy first draft. What techniques can assist students in making decisions about the need to rewrite and help them transform what they initially have written into something more creative?

7. How does one bridge the gaps between students' experiences, the text, and the task of writing?

In setting conditions for reader response, the teacher frames the task of reading or writing within a particular perspective. What is the impact of that perspective, particularly as metaphors are used to constrain or widen possible reactions to the literary work?

Summary

Writing is a powerful means of expressing the self. Through writing, students can begin to understand their emerging identities and to construct new meanings. When the proper conditions are set for students to respond with writing to what they have read, the elements of creativity become genuine possibilities.

The term *reader response* has come to refer to the transactions of readers with literature, to a point of view in which reading is seen as a highly subjective process whereby readers understand what they read through the filters of their own experiences and personalities, and to a set of related classroom activities in which readers write in response to what they have read, discuss their writing with their peers, and rewrite. The view advanced in this chapter is that reader response provides unique possibilities for creativity. Among these are the opportunity for students to express their own perspective, the extent of cognitive activation that occurs in the kind of writing required in reader response, the interactions with peers about what has been written, and the processes generated by rewriting.

The necessary conditions for creative reader response, we argue, include a supportive classroom culture in which self-expression is valued. It also requires the activation of affective responses from episodic memory, and specific teaching techniques that include appropriate priming activities and planned variations in the assigned writing.

The major research issues raised by this chapter are those relating to the role of emotion in creative reader response and the functional roles of episodic and semantic memory. Other questions include the nature of the interaction among writing, reading comprehension, and rewriting, and the effects of imposing variations in the writing task, such as writing for different audiences and taking different perspectives in writing.

ACKNOWLEDGMENTS. The authors express their sincere gratitude to Robert Brooke and Joy Ritchie of the Department of English at the University of Nebraska-Lincoln for their insightful comments on a preliminary version of this chapter.

References

Adams, M., & Bruce, B. (1982). Background knowledge and reading comprehension. In J. A. Langer & M. T. Smith-Burke (Eds.), *Reader meets author/bridging the Gap. A psycholinguistic and sociolinguistic perspective* (pp. 2–25). Newark, DE: International Reading Association.

Anderson, J. R. (1983). *The architecture of cognition.* Cambridge: Harvard University Press.

Anderson, J. R. (1987). Skill acquisition: Compilation of weak-method problem solutions. *Psychological Review, 94,* 192–210.

Anderson, R. C. (1977). The notion of schemata and the educational enterprise. In R. C. Anderson, R. J. Spiro, & W. E. Montague (Eds.), *Schooling and the acquisition of knowledge* (pp. 415–431). Hillsdale, NJ: Erlbaum.

Anderson, R. C., & Pearson, P. D. (1984). A schema-theoretic view of basic processes in reading comprehension. In P. D. Pearson (Ed.), *Handbook of reading research* (pp. 225–293). New York: Longman.

Applebee, A. N. (1981). *Writing in the secondary school.* Urbana, IL: National Council of Teachers of English.

Applebee, A. N. (1984). *Contexts for learning to write.* Norwood, NJ: Ablex.

Applebee, A. N. (1985). Studies in the spectator role: An approach to response to literature. In C. R. Cooper (Ed.), *Researching response to literature and the teaching of literature: Points of departure* (pp. 87–102). Norwood, NJ: Ablex.

Bartlett, F. C. (1932). *Remembering.* London: Cambridge University Press.

Beach, R. (1983). Attitudes, social conventions and response to literature. *Journal of Research and Development in Education, 16*(1), 47–54.

Beach, R., & Liebman-Kleine, J. (1986). The writing/reading relationship: Becoming one's own best reader. In B. Petersen (Ed.), *Convergences: Transactions in reading and writing* (pp. 64–81). Urbana, IL: National Council of Teachers of English.

Bereiter, C. (1984). Learning about reading from writing. *Written Communication, 1*(2), 163–188.

Birnbaum, J., & Emig, J. (1983). Creating minds, created texts: Writing and reading. In R. P. Parker & F. A. Davis (Eds.), *Developing literacy: Young children's use of language* (pp. 87–104). Newark, DL: International Reading Association.

Birnbaum, J. C. (1986). Reflective thought: The connection between reading and writing. In B. T. Peterson (Ed.), *Convergences: Transactions in reading and writing* (pp. 30–45). Urbana, IL: National Council of Teachers of English.

Bleich, D. (1975a). *Readings and feelings: An introduction to subjective criticism.* Urbana, IL: National Council of Teachers of English.

Bleich, D. (1975b). The subjective character of critical interpretation. *College English, 36*(7), 739–755.

Bleich, D. (1978). *Subjective criticism.* Baltimore: Johns Hopkins University Press.

Bleich, D. (1985). The identity of pedagogy and research in the study of response of literature. In C. Cooper (Ed.), *Researching response to literature and the teaching of literature: Points of departure* (pp. 253–272). Norwood, NJ: Ablex.

Bower, G. H. (1981). Mood and memory. *American Psychologist, 36,* 129–148.

Bower, G. H., & Cohen, P. R. (1982). Emotional influences in memory and thinking: Data and theory. In M. S. Clark & S. T. Fiske (Eds.), *Affect and cognition* (pp. 291–331). Hillsdale, NJ: Erlbaum.

Bracewell, R. J., Frederiksen, C. H., & Frederiksen, J. D. (1982). Cognitive processes in composing and comprehending discourse. *Educational Psychologist, 17*(3), 146–164.

Bransford, J. D., Barclay, J. R., & Franks, J. J. (1972). Sentence memory: A constructive versus interpretive approach. *Cognitive Psychology, 2,* 193–209.

Bruning, R. H. (1984). Key elements of effective teaching in the direct teaching model. In R. L. Egbert & M. Kluender (Eds.), *Using research to improve teacher education: The Nebraska Consortium* (Teacher Education Monograph No. 1, pp. 75–88). Washington, DC: ERIC Clearinghouse on Teacher Education.

Collins, A. M., & Loftus, E. F. (1975). A spreading-activation theory of semantic processing. *Psychological Review, 82,* 407–428.

Comprone, J. J. (1986). Integrating the acts of reading and writing about literature: A sequence of assignments based on James Joyce's "Counterparts." In B. Petersen (Ed.), *Convergences: Transactions in reading and writing* (pp. 215–230). Urbana, IL: National Council of Teachers of English.

Cooper, C. R. (1985). Introduction. In C. R. Cooper (Ed.), *Researching response to literature and the teaching of literature: Points of departure* (pp. ix–xix). Norwood, NJ: Ablex.

Dewey, J. (1938). *Experience and education.* New York: Collier Books.

Flower, L., & Hayes, J. R. (1980). A cognitive process of theory of writing. *College Composition and Communication, 32,* 365–387.

Flower, L., & Hayes, J. R. (1981). Plans that guide the composing process. In C. H. Frederickson & J. F. Dominic (Eds.), *Writing: The nature, development and teaching of written communication* (2nd ed., pp. 39–58). Hillsdale, NJ: Erlbaum.

Flower, L., & Hayes, J. R. (1984). Images, plans and prose: The representation of meaning in writing. *Written Communication, 1*(1), 120–160.

Frase, L. T. (1982). Introduction to special issue on writing. *Educational Psychologist, 17,* 129–130.

Gilligan, S. G., & Bower, G. H. (1984). Cognitive consequences of emotional arousal. In C. E. Izard, J. Kagan, & R. B. Zajonc (Eds.), *Emotions, cognition, and behavior* (pp. 547–588). Cambridge, England: Cambridge University Press.

Glover, J. A. (1980). *Becoming a more creative person.* Englewood Cliffs, NJ: Prentice-Hall.

Glover, J. A., Benton, S., & Bruning, R. H. (1983). Levels of processing: Effects of number of decision on prose recall. *Journal of Educational Psychology, 75,* 382–390.

Good, T. L. (1983). Classroom research: A decade of progress. *Educational Psychologist, 18,* 127–144.

Graves, D. (1983). *Writing: Teachers and children at work.* Exeter, NH: Heinemann.

Harste, J. C., Woodward, V. A., & Burke, C. L. (1984). Examining our assumptions: A transactional view of literacy and learning. *Research in the Teaching of English, 18,* 18.

Heidegger, M. (1962). *Being and time* (J. Macquarrie & E. Robinson, trans.). New York: Harper & Row. (Original work published 1927)

Hintzman, D. L. (1986). "Schema activation" in a multiple-trace memory model. *Psychological Review, 93,* 411–427.

Holland, N. H. (1968). *The dynamics of literary response.* New York: Oxford University Press.

Holland, N. H. (1975). *Five readers reading.* New Haven: Yale University Press.

Holland, N. H. (1985). Reading readers reading. In C. R. Cooper (Ed.), *Researching response to literature and the teaching of literature: Points of departure* (pp. 3–21). Norwood, NJ: Ablex.

Horton, S. R. (1983). *Thinking through writing.* Baltimore, MD: Johns Hopkins University Press.

Isadora, R. (1979). *Ben's trumpet.* New York, NY: Greenwillow Books.

Iser, W. (1974). *The implied reader.* Baltimore, MD: Johns Hopkins University Press.

Iser, W. (1978). *The act of reading. A theory of aesthetic response.* Baltimore, MD: Johns Hopkins University Press.

Jenkins, J. J. (1974). Remember that old theory of memory? Well, forget it! *American Psychologist, 29,* 785–795.

Johnston, P., & Pearson, P. D. (1982). *Prior knowledge, connectivity, and the assessment of reading comprehension* (Tech. Rep. No. 245). Urbana: University of Illinois, Center for the Study of Reading.

Langer, J. A., & Smith-Burke, M. T. (1982). *Reader meets author/bridging the Gap: A psycholinguistic and sociolinguistic Perspective.* Newark, DE: International Reading Association.

Loftus, G. R., & Loftus, E. F. (1976). *Human memory: The processing of information.* New York: Wiley.

Mayher, J. S., Lester, N., & Prahl, G. M. (1983). *Learning to write/writing to learn.* Upper Montclair, NJ: Boynton/Cook.

Meyer, B. F. (1982). Reading research and the composition teacher: The importance of plans. *College Composition and Communication, 33,* 27–49.

Minsky, M. (1975). A framework for representing knowledge. In P. H. Winston (Ed.), *The psychology of computer vision* (pp. 211–277). New York: McGraw-Hill.

Moffett, J. (1984). Reading and writing as meditation. In J. Jensen (Ed.), *Composing and comprehending.* Urbana, IL: ERIC Clearinghouse on Reading and Communication Skills.

Murphy, C. C. (1987). *Enhancing eleventh graders critical comprehension of literary texts.* Unpublished doctoral dissertation, University of Nebraska, Lincoln, NE.

Murray, E. L. (1986). *Imaginative thinking and human existence.* Pittsburgh, PA: Duquesne University Press.

Neisser, V. (1967). *Cognitive psychology.* New York: Appleton-Century-Crofts.

Neisser, V. (1982). *Memory observed: Remembering in natural contexts.* San Francisco: W. H. Freeman and Company.

Paris, S. G., & Lindauer, B. K. (1976). The role of inference in children's comprehension and memory for sentences. *Cognitive Psychology, 8,* 217–227.

Paris, S. G., & Lindauer, B. K. (1977). Constructive aspects of children's comprehension and memory. In R. V. Kail, Jr., & J. W. Hagen (Eds.), *Perspectives on the development of memory and cognition* (pp. 35–58). Hillsdale, NJ: Erlbaum.

Pearson, P. D. (1985). Changing the face of reading comprehension instruction. *Reading Teacher, 38*(8), 724–738.

Petrosky, A. (1982). From story to essay: Reading and writing. *College Composition and Communication, 33,* 19–37.

Petrosky, A. (1985). Response: A way of knowing. In C. R. Cooper (Ed.), *Researching response to literature and the teaching of literature: Points of departure* (pp. 70–83). Norwood, NJ: Ablex.

Pound, E. (1983). The river merchant's wife: A letter. In A. W. Allison, H. Barrows, C. R. Blake, A. J. Carr, A. M. Eastman, & H. M. English (Eds.), *The Norton Anthology of Poetry* (3rd ed., pp. 963–964). New York: W. W. Norton.

Purves, A. C. (1976). Foreword to L. M. Rosenblatt, *Literature as Exploration.* New York: Modern Language Association of America.

Read, P. B. (1984). Forward to C. E. Izard, J. Kagan, & R. B. Zajonc (Eds.), *Emotions, cognition, and behavior.* Cambridge: Cambridge University Press.

Ritchie, J. (1988, March). *Reading, writing, and identity—Connections and misconnections.* Paper presented at the 1988 Conference on College Composition and Communication, St. Louis, MO.

Ronald, K. (1986). The self and the other in the process of composing: Implications for integrating the acts of reading and writing. In B. Peterson (Ed.), *Convergences: Transactions in reading and writing* (pp. 231–245). Urbana, IL: National Council of Teachers of English.

Rosenblatt, L. M. (1976). *Literature as exploration* (3rd ed.). New York: Noble & Noble.

Rosenblatt, L. M. (1978). *The reader, the text, the poem: The transactional theory of the literary work.* Carbondale, IL: Southern Illinois University Press.

Rosenblatt, L. M. (1985). The transactional theory of the literary work: Implications for research. In C. R. Cooper (Ed.), *Researching response to literature and the teaching of literature: Points of departure* (pp. 33–53). Norwood, NJ: Ablex.

Rumelhart, D. E. (1977). Understanding and summarizing brief stories. In E. LaBerge & S. J. Samuels (Eds.), *Basic processes in reading: Perception and comprehension* (pp. 265–303). Hillsdale, NJ: Erlbaum.

Rumelhart, D. E. (1980). Schemata: The building blocks of

cognition. In R. Spiro, B. Bruce, & W. Brewer (Eds.), *Theoretical issues in reading and comprehension* (pp. 33–58). Hillsdale, NJ: Erlbaum.

Rumelhart, D. E., & Ortony, A. (1977). The representation of knowledge and memory. In R. C. Anderson, R. J. Spiro, & W. E. Montague (Eds.), *Schooling and the acquisition of knowledge* (pp. 99–135). Hillsdale, NJ: Erlbaum.

Salvatori, M. (1983). Reading and writing a text: Correlations between reading and writing patterns. *College English, 45*(7), 657–667.

Scardamalia, M., & Bereiter, C. (1982). Assimilative processes in composition planning. *Educational Psychologist, 17*(3), 165–171.

Schank, R. C., & Abelson, R. P. (1977). *Scripts, plans, goals and understanding*. Hillsdale, NJ: Erlbaum.

Shanahan, J., & Lomax, R. G. (1986). An analysis and comparison of theoretical models of the reading-writing relationship. *Journal of Educational Psychology, 78*(2), 116–123.

Siefert, C. M., McKoon, G., Abelson, R. P., & Ratcliff, R. (1986). Memory connections between thematically similar episodes. *Journal of Experimental Psychology: Learning, Memory, and Cognition, 12*, 220–231.

Stanovich, K., & West, R. (1983). On priming by a sentence context. *Journal of Experimental Psychology: General, 112*, 1–36.

Tierney, R., & Leys, M. (1986). What is the value of connecting reading and writing? In B. T. Peterson (Ed.), *Convergences: Transactions in reading and writing* (pp. 15–29). Urbana, IL: National Council of Teachers of English.

Tierney, R., & Pearson, P. D. (1983). Toward a composing model of reading. *Language Arts, 60*(5), 568–579.

Tompkins, J. P. (1980). An introduction to reader-response criticism. In J. Tompkins (Ed.), *Reader-response criticism: From formalism to post-structuralism* (pp. ix–xxvi). Baltimore, MD: Johns Hopkins University Press.

Torrance, E. P. (1983). *Creativity in the classroom*. Washington, DC: National Education Association.

Tulving, E. (1972). Episodic and semantic memory. In E. Tulving & W. Donaldson (Eds.), *Organization of memory* (pp. 382–402). New York: Academic Press.

Tulving, E. (1983). *Elements of episodic memory*. Oxford, England: Oxford University Press.

Whittlesea, B. W. A. (1987). Preservation of specific experiences in the representation of general knowledge. *Journal of Experimental Psychology: Learning, Memory, and Cognition, 13*, 3–17.

CHAPTER 20

Learning via Model Construction and Criticism

PROTOCOL EVIDENCE ON SOURCES OF CREATIVITY IN SCIENCE

John Clement

Introduction

There is growing recognition that mental models play a fundamental role in the comprehension of science concepts. The process of learning via model construction appears to be central to theory formation in science and central for science instruction but is still very poorly understood. This chapter uses evidence from case studies, in which a scientist is asked to think out loud, to argue that nonformal reasoning processes that are neither deductive nor inductive can play an important role in scientific model construction. The construction process is complex and involves repeated passes through a cycle of hypothesis generation, evaluation, and modification.

"Aha" episodes that show that a scientist can generate creative insights via spontaneous analo-

John Clement • Scientific Reasoning Research Institute, University of Massachusetts, Amherst, MA 01003. The research reported in this study was supported by the National Science Foundation under Grants MDR–8470579 and MDR–8751398. Any opinions, findings, and conclusions or recommendations expressed in this chapter are those of the author and do not necessarily reflect the views of the National Science Foundation.

gies and other divergent processes are also examined. It is argued that these insights can involve fairly sudden reorganizations in the structure of a mental model but do not necessarily involve extraordinary or unconscious thought processes. This introduction and a summary of findings at the end constitute an overview of the chapter.

Questions about the Nature of Scientific Theory Formation

Galileo's theory of motion, Faraday's concept of the magnetic field, Darwin's theory of natural selection, and Einstein's theory of relativity are commonly cited examples of creative achievements in science. Each is a major event in the history of scientific ideas, and, in each case, something very new emerged that affected the entire scientific community and subsequently affected civilization as a whole. Analyzing how such achievements take place is a worthwhile goal, but achieving this goal has unfortunately proven to be surprisingly difficult. The universally recognized importance of advances in science has not made the problem of describing the processes by which they were created any easier. In Darwin's case, for example, it is possible to argue that the theory of natural selection was built up gradually through a large number of detailed empirical observations. But, on the other hand, it also is possible to argue that the theory was the result of a mental breakthrough well after the *Beagle*'s voyage in the form of an insight that constituted a sudden reorganization of Darwin's ideas. Thus, even with respect to specific historical examples, disagreement emerges as to the basic sources and pace of theory change in science.

At issue here is an important question concerning the nature of science. Cast in its most global and extreme form, the question is: Does science change in an incremental manner, with a series of many small empirical observations inching it forward, or do occasional large breakthroughs occur in the mind of the scientist in the absence of new data, each causing a great leap forward in the field? One purpose of this chapter is to determine whether the methodology of protocol analysis has the potential to illuminate some aspects of this question by using data from transcripts of scientists solving problems aloud. I will concentrate most on an example of a breakthrough episode in a thinking aloud case study and discuss the senses in which it is or is not an example of a scientific insight or "eureka" event. In particular, the case study is used to address elements of the following more specific questions:

1. What is a scientific insight? Can one identify "insight" events or "eureka" events in thinking aloud protocols? Why do insights occur? Why do periods of slow and fast progress occur in scientific thinking?
2. What processes are involved in the generation of a scientific hypothesis? In particular, are hypotheses always generated as inductions from data? What role do analogies and thought experiments play in creative scientific thinking? What is the role of explanatory models?
3. Are there any parallels between the tensions observed in an individual scientist thinking aloud and the tensions Kuhn describes between an anomaly and a scientific paradigm?
4. What impact do findings relevant to the above questions have on the concepts of "knowledge construction" and "discovery learning" in a theory of instruction?

I will attempt to show that empirical evidence can be collected which speaks to certain aspects of these questions.

Background Questions from Philosophy of Science

The Source and Pace of Theory Change

Eurekaism versus Accretionism. It is useful to separate out two major issues that are involved in the controversy over hypothesis formation, the *pace* of scientific theory change and the *source* of new theories (represented, respectively, in questions 1 and 2, above). With respect to the pace of theory change, one can contrast eurekaist and accretionist positions. A *eurekaist* claims that a theory can be changed at a very fast pace by an insight that reorganizes its structure. In its strongest form, eurekaism is associated with sudden flashes of inspiration, possibly following a period of incubation or nonconscious mental activity. Thus, some ideas may form in and arrive suddenly from the unconscious mind.

An *accretionist* or incremental view of the pace of scientific theory change holds that a scientist gains knowledge in small pieces and puts them together deliberately at a slow and even pace. This process should lead to a smooth progression in the attainment of knowledge—an incremental "march of progress" without large-scale reorganizations.

Rationalism versus Inductivism. A second major issue is the source of new theoretical knowledge. The question of the sources of and justification for new knowledge is a central point of controversy between the rationalist and empiricist traditions in Western thought. The rationalist tradition emphasizes the power of reasoning from prior knowledge and greatly values the consistency and beauty of the resulting theories. Reasoning power, coupled with the prior beliefs of the learner, are emphasized as sources of knowledge. On the other hand, the empiricist tradition emphasizes the importance of careful observation and greatly values the reliability of repeatable experimental procedures. Here the term *induction* will denote a process by which a more general principle is abstracted from a set of empirical observations as the source. I will use the term *inductivism* to refer to the belief that induction is the primary, if not exclusive, source of hypotheses in science. Stated most simply, in this view scientists gradually gather facts, use inductive reasoning to organize them into general statements, and finally build up a pyramid of general empirical laws that summarize all the gathered data. Theory-driven and data-driven approaches in artificial intelligence can, to some extent, be thought of as modern inheritors of the rationalist and inductivist viewpoints.

Although they refer to different issues, the eurekaist versus accretionist and the rationalist versus inductivist controversies are not independent historically but tend to interact. Eurekaism tends to be associated with rationalism, whereas accretionism tends to be associated with inductivism. Thus, it is sometimes useful to refer to an individual position as ''rationalist-eurekaist'' or ''inductivist-accretionist.'' A rationalist–eurekaist view of theory change is associated with the idea that scientists at times must be very creative, whereas the inductivist-accretionist view suggests that scientists can make progress by relying on small changes without large creative breakthroughs. This simplified picture of two opposing camps can be used as a starting point for introducing some important issues concerning the nature of science.

Gould (1980) noted that writers on both sides of this controversy have tried to claim Darwin's theory of evolution as an example. Historically, inductivist-accretionists claimed that it was a prime example of the power of induction, as facts gathered by Darwin during the voyage of the *Beagle* were slowly pieced together into a grand theory. Rationalist-eurekaists claimed that Darwin had a sudden, crucial insight upon reading Malthus's theory of human population constraints.

But both of these positions runs the risk of being oversimplified. As Gould (1980) put it: ''Inductivism reduces genius to dull, rote operations. Eurekaism grants it an inaccessible status more in the domain of intrinsic mystery than in a realm where we might understand and learn from it'' (pp. 60–61). The implied challenge here is to find a less simplistic view that helps to explain creative behavior in a nontrivial way. In this chapter, accounting for the data from the case study leads to a more complex view of scientific discovery than either the extreme eurekaist, accretionist, rationalist, or inductivist positions can provide.

Toward the end of the chapter, I also review some recent historical studies of Darwin's insights that point to the same conclusion.

Philosophical Positions

I give a brief outline here of how these two broad questions concerning the source and pace of scientific theories interact with some of the major twentieth century philosophical positions on the nature

of the scientific enterprise.[1] Prior to this century, empiricists focused on observation as the primary source of knowledge in science, and the twentieth-century logical positivists built on their tradition by attempting to show that scientific knowledge could be grounded firmly in sense experience. In their view, careful observations, and the assumptions of a common scientific observation language and the applicability of the laws of logic and probability, could provide science with knowledge of the utmost reliability, if not certainty. Although the logical positivists concentrated on issues surrounding the justification of theories rather than their origin, their empiricism also affected views of the origins of scientific knowledge. Science was described in an accretionist manner as building and extending theories incrementally, approaching truth in a monotonic way. For example, Rudolph Carnap held the inductivist belief that science advances upward from particular empirical facts to generalizations that summarize or provide an abbreviation for a body of such facts (Suppe, 1974, p. 15n). Certainly positivism has influenced the methodology of other disciplines (e.g., behaviorism in psychology) in this direction.

Important attacks on the positivist position, such as Popper's (1959) success in showing that induction cannot confirm the truth of theories, Hanson's (1958) claim that observations are ''theory laden,'' and Kuhn's (1962) claim that theoretical advances often precede the empirical findings used to support them in science, have raised serious problems by arguing against the empiricist emphasis on sense experience as the pre-eminent basis for knowledge. Popper (1959) held that the proper role for data is in the criticism rather than the confirmation of hypotheses. Hypotheses are conjectures made by scientists rather than certainties abstracted from data. But these conjectures can be reliably criticized and falsified by collecting data. This allows science to make progress via a series of conjectural hypotheses and reliable criticisms. Popper's work provided support for the model shown in Figure 1, the hypothetico-deductive method. There are three

---

[1]Placing different scholars on these two broad spectra ignores many differences between them and requires a number of simplifications. For example, some scholars (e.g., positivists and Popper, 1959) tend to concern themselves with the formal justification of theories, whereas others (e.g., Hanson, 1958, Kuhn, 1962) also focus on their psychological origin; arguments also vary as to whether they refer to science as a whole or to the individual scientist.

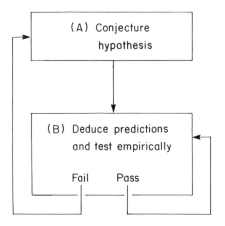

Figure 1. Basic conjecture and empirical evaluation cycle in hypothetico-deductive method.

main stages shown here: (1) a hypothesis is formed by conjecture; (2) predictions deduced from the hypothesis are tested empirically; (3) if the prediction is incorrect, the hypothesis is rejected and the cycle restarted. Popper maintained, contrary to the logical positivists, that a successful empirical test does little to confirm a hypothesis, but that failing such a test is grounds for rejecting a hypothesis. Those hypotheses that survive the gauntlet of repeated testing become accepted laws. Favored laws emerge through the survival-of-the-fittest conjectures, so to speak. However, Popper's emphasis on conjecture also opens up the possibility that a noninductive, nonaccretionist process, or even a eureka event could be involved in hypothesis formation.

Popper's views have in turn been criticized in a number of ways. The most relevant shortcoming for the purposes of the present study is that his classic work does not specify mechanisms for generating hypotheses; he relegates this task to psychology and says only that hypotheses must be conjectural in nature. Also, Hanson's (1958) notion that observations can be "theory-laden" implies that empirical testing in the hypothetico-deductive method may not be fully reliable and sufficient on its own as a means of hypothesis evaluation. (Other means of hypothesis evaluation that are more rationalist in character will be discussed in the next section.)

With regard to the pace of theory change, Kuhn's (1962) ideas of revolution within a scientific discipline and the creative "gestalt switch" that is required for an individual scientist to move outside of his or her own paradigm argue against an accre-

tionist view of theory change. In this view, normal science may be accretionist in character, but revolutionary periods in science involve crisis and reconstruction, implying that science progresses at an uneven pace with periods of slow and fast change. On the other hand, critics of Kuhn, such as Toulmin (1972), have, in turn, questioned the reality of scientific revolutions, arguing for a more continuous view of theory change.[2]

In summary, an inductivist-accretionist view of science sees it as compiling facts and generalizations in a piece-by-piece fashion. Induction is the primary process of hypothesis generation, with a one-directional flow of knowledge from data upward to theories. In a rationalist-eurekaist view, on the other hand, significant theoretical developments can occur when a scientist formulates mental constructions at some distance from existing data and can actually develop new ways of looking at old data. Thus, knowledge can flow downward from a newly invented, general theory to influence the formation of new specific theories, to reorganize one's view of existing data, and to suggest new places to collect important data. Such reorganizations presumably would require a large degree of creativity, perhaps even extraordinary eureka episodes of insight.

These two views have been the subject of continuing controversy. Philosophers have taken various positions between these extremes, and some have attempted to point to examples from the history of science supporting their position. However, in historical studies, it is always difficult to find data saying much in detail about the actual process of hypothesis formation in the individual scientist. In the next section, I consider several descriptions of this process as proposed by philosophers, after which I analyze a thinking-aloud case study to examine these issues from an empirical base at a more detailed level. In this case study, examples of noninductive reasoning in the formation of hypotheses will be examined in order to determine whether these types of data can challenge the inductivist position; and an identified "insight episode" will

[2]Because this chapter focuses on thinking in the individual scientist, I will not discuss here important work that emphasizes social factors in the development of scientific ideas. Although these factors are undoubtedly significant, I believe that studying hypothesis generation processes in the individual scientist is an effective heuristic strategy for investigating a crucial part of the problem.

be examined to determine whether it can provide support for or against a eurekaist position.

Some Possible Views of Hypothesis Formation Processes in the Individual Scientist

How Are Hypotheses Formed?

In this section, it will be useful to concentrate on the more specific question, "What are the mental processes by which hypotheses are formed in an individual?" The answer to this question should involve some sort of model of the mental processes being used. Discussion of this narrower question about individuals may be of some interest to those investigating the broader question about science as a whole, even though the latter issue is more complex. In fact, surprisingly little work has been addressed to this question, especially in comparison to the complementary question, "How are scientific hypotheses tested?" Here I give a brief overview of several possible positions that can be taken on the first question concerning formation.

Popper's (1959) position and the hypothetico-deductive method shown in Figure 1 can be taken as a starting point here in the form of a nonanswer. The method shows one way in which hypotheses might be tested but does not show how they are generated.

Answer 1: Hypothetico-Deductive Method Plus Induction

Popper argued convincingly that induction cannot be used to confirm the truth of scientific theories. However, some modern scholars retain some form of induction in their model of scientific method as a way to suggest hypotheses. This can be represented by the model shown in Figure 2 that combines the hypothetico-deductive method with induction as a source of hypotheses. Here there is no claim for a "logic" of discovery but only for a fallible method for generating hypotheses. Further experiments are performed in order to evaluate the inductions. Such a diagram is commonly implied in everyday characterizations of scientific method as a combination of induction and deduction. Scholars such as Harre (1983), Achinstein (1970), and Gregory (1981) argue that induction can play a role in hypothesis formation. However, they believe that other processes can be involved as well. Recently, Langley (1979) has attempted to develop simula-

tion models of data-driven inductive processes for generating certain scientific laws.

Answer 2: Creative Intuition

Is some form of induction or guessing the only source of scientific hypotheses? A number of recent authors have answered no to this question by pointing to the role of creativity, intuition, and the unconscious in generating hypotheses (Koestler, 1964, Polanyi, 1966; Rothenberg, 1979). Unfortunately, I can only make the briefest mention of these long and detailed works here. Their views can be roughly characterized as replacing the "Hypothesis Formation by Induction" step in Box A of Figure 2 with a process labeled "Hypothesis Formation by Creative Intuition." For example, Polanyi emphasized the role of intuition and tacit knowledge in science. Rothenberg proposed a process of "Janusian thinking," whereby a person is able to juxtapose seemingly contradictory ideas, as a common element in creative thinking. Koestler pointed to "bisociative thought"—the ability to connect normally independent frames of reference—and to the role of the unconscious in accounting for creativity.

An interesting controversy emerged in this area. Perkins (1981) argued that all these descriptions attempt to point to extraordinary thinking processes; they attempt to supplement ordinary reasoning with something more powerful. He countered this idea with the claim that most creative acts can be explained plausibly by a model in which a person uses certain ordinary thinking processes more in-

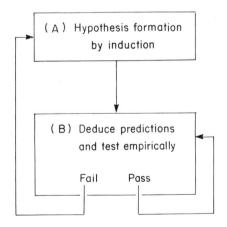

Figure 2. Hypothetico-deductive method with the addition of induction as a source of hypotheses.

tensively, or with special goals in mind. In his view, the difference between a creative and an uncreative person is a difference of degree and purpose, not a difference of kind. Perkins also described authors like Koestler as contributing mainly to the description of the products of creative thinking; a remaining problem is to specify the processes of creative thinking in more detail.

Answer 3: Analogies and Successive Refinement Cycles as Sources of Explanatory Model Hypotheses

The work of another group of scholars in philosophy of science, including Campbell (1920), Harre (1961), Nagel (1961), and Hesse (1966), suggests that analogies may be a source of hypotheses. They argue that scientists often think in terms of theoretical explanatory models, such as molecules, waves, and fields, that are a separate kind of hypothesis from empirical laws. Such models are not simply condensed summaries of empirical observations but rather are inventions that contribute new theoretical terms and images that are part of the scientist's view of the world, and that are not "given" in the data.

As shown in Figure 3, they see a distinction between an empirical law hypothesis summarizing an observed regularity and what I will call an *explanatory model hypothesis*. Campbell's often

cited example is that merely being able to make predictions from the empirical gas law, stating that *PV* is proportional to *RT,* is not equivalent to understanding the explanation for gas behavior in terms of an imagable model of billiard-ball-like molecules in motion. Unlike the empirical law, the model provides a description of a hidden process that explains how the gas works and answers "why" questions about where observable changes in temperature and pressure come from. Causal relationships are often central in such models. The model can not only add significant explanatory power to one's knowledge but can also suggest questions that stimulate the future growth of the theory. In this view, the visualizable model is a major locus of meaning for a scientific theory. (Brief summaries of these views are given in Harre, 1967 and Hesse, 1967.)

The above authors, as well as Black (1979), argue that models involve analogies to familiar situations (e.g., gases are analogous to a collection of colliding balls). In Nagel's (1961) terms, such visualizable analogue models help scientists "make the unfamiliar familiar." This suggests that analogical reasoning may be an important noninductive source for generating such hypothetical models. More recently, theory formation and assessment cycles using analogies have been discussed by Clement (1981), Nersessian (1984), Holland, Holyoak, Nisbett, and Thagard (1986), and Darden and Rada (1988).

Most of the above authors also emphasize a rational (nonempirical) contribution to hypothesis *evaluation,* holding that explanatory models are evaluated also with respect to the criteria of simplicity, aesthetic appeal, and consistency with other accepted models.

The Model Construction Cycle. Figure 4 represents an attempt to bring together several of these features in a single idealized model of the hypothesis development process for constructing scientific models. Typically, such a process would be used to develop an explanation for a newly recognized phenomenon. Essentially, the diagram depicts a cyclical process of hypothesis generation, rational and empirical testing, and modification or rejection. It is difficult to describe so complex a process in a single diagram, but a simplified model will aid in the present analysis. In contrast to Figure 2, in Figure 4, when a hypothesis is evaluated negatively, it can sometimes be improved through modi-

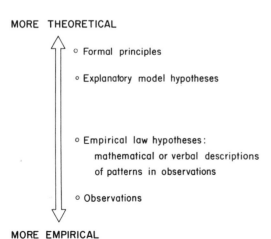

Figure 3. Types of knowledge used in science. Explanatory models are distinguished from empirical laws.

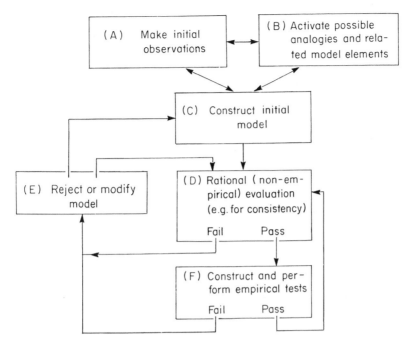

Figure 4. Hypothesis development (model construction) cycle of conjecture, evaluation, and modification or rejection.

fication, instead of being completely rejected. Thus, it may undergo a *series of successive refinements*.

The double-ended arrows, in Figure 4, between "Make Initial Observations," and "Construct Initial Model" represent the idea that not only does model construction respond to observation but that one's focus of attention during observation can be guided by one's initial model. This and other double-ended arrows indicate that the initial model generation process can be highly interactive and complex. It is still poorly understood.

Essentially, the scientist must construct or piece together a conjectured picture of a hidden structure or process that explains why the phenomenon occurred. Peirce (1958) and Hanson (1958) used the term "abduction" (or retroduction) to describe the process of formulating a hypothesis which, if it were true, would account for the phenomenon in question. The hypothesis can be a guess as long as it accounts for (predicts after the fact) the observations collected so far. Empirical law hypotheses that consist only of a recognized regularity or repeated pattern in the variables, such as those discussed by Langley (1979), might be formed via a more data-driven inductive process. This is possi-

ble on those occasions when one has the prior advantage of possessing the right variables, or components of compound variables, to look for. But the explanatory model hypotheses being considered here would be formed by a less data-driven abductive process, possibly for just a single instance of the phenomenon. Such a process might "plagiarize" the knowledge structure from an analogous case in memory to form the starting point or core of a new model. Or it might integrate several related model elements—constructing a new model by combining several existing knowledge structures previously known to the subject.

Hypothesis evaluation can take place in two major ways. Empirical testing can add support to or disconfirm a hypothesis. Rational evaluation can also support or disconfirm a hypothesis, depending, for example, on whether it is found to be consistent or inconsistent with other established theories. Evaluation processes cannot provide full confirmation, but can lead a scientist to have increased or reduced confidence in a theory. Once generated, a hypothesis undergoes repeated cycles of rational and empirical testing and modifications as needed. A limitation of the diagram that is not intended to be part of the model is the order in which rational and empirical evaluations occur; tests can occur in different orders on different cycles.

The endless loops in Figure 4 indicate that, ideally, theories in science are always open to new criticisms. However, as Kuhn (1962) pointed out, scientists will sometimes ignore or discount some criticisms in order to protect a favored theory. In practice, research groups may adopt a "protected core" of theories that they take as givens (Lakatos, 1978).

A missing element in Figure 4 is the influence of the subject's prior theoretical framework. This element is difficult to depict, as it could affect so many of the processes shown. Because the scientist operates from a background of broader theoretical assumptions, these may have an early influence on the model elements and analogies that come to mind, and even (according to Hanson, 1958, and to Kuhn, 1962) on what is observed.[3]

Summary

In summary, little empirical work has been done on the question of hypothesis formation processes in science, but philosophers have proposed several possibilities, including guessing, abduction, induction, and creative leaps. In addition, Campbell (1920) and others have introduced the interesting distinction between empirical law hypotheses that are summaries of perceived patterns in observations and explanatory model hypotheses that introduce visualizable models at a theoretical level and that often contain currently unobservable entities. They suggest that analogies may be an important means of constructing the latter type of hypothesis. A possible synthesis of these ideas was proposed in Figure 4. It allows for the possibility that the hypothetico-deductive method, induction, abduction, analogy, rational evaluation, and hypothesis modification may all play important roles at different times in scientific thought.

The idea that analogies can be involved in hypothesis formation is often used to support a eurekaist view of scientific discovery. If analogy generation is a fast, creative process, and if it is important in

hypothesis formation, then it is a promising candidate for a cognitive process underlying insight or eureka events. This issue will be examined closely in the section following the next one.

Evidence from Thinking Aloud Protocols on Model Construction Cycles Using Analogies

Recently, cognitive psychology has begun to study complex human cognition through the use of protocol analysis. This section uses this method to examine the process of hypothesis generation in thinking-aloud protocols. Several examples of spontaneous analogies will be examined, as well as a breakthrough episode that appears to be an example of insight behavior. Instead of working backward from historical records and outcomes, a more direct analysis of the processes operating in the thinking scientist will be attempted here.

The great difficulty, of course, is to have a video camera trained on the scientist at one of the rare moments when he or she formulates a hypothesis. One way to overcome this difficulty is to pose to the subject conceptually challenging but not overwhelming problems, which allow for the formulation of hypotheses and explanations. The data discussed here were taken from interviews in which advanced doctoral candidates or professors in technical fields were asked to think aloud as they solved such problems. Although the problems do not concern issues on the frontier of science, in many cases they ask subjects to give a scientific explanation of a phenomenon with which they are unfamiliar (i.e., a problem on the frontier of their own personal knowledge). Thus, it is plausible that the thought processes analyzed will share some characteristics with hypothesis formation and model construction processes used on the frontiers of science.

Use of Analogies and Models in Expert Problem Solutions

In this section, evidence will be presented indicating that analogies can be involved in a significant way in generating the solution to a scientific problem, and, more specifically, that they can sometimes lead to a new model of the problem situation.

---

[3]The form of Figure 4 was developed via an extended successive refinement process and was also designed to account for empirical data from protocols (like the ones to be discussed), and not just as a summary of prior literature.

YOU ARE GIVEN THE TASK OF ROLLING A HEAVY WHEEL UP A
HILL. DOES IT TAKE MORE, LESS, OR THE SAME AMOUNT OF
FORCE TO ROLL THE WHEEL WHEN YOU PUSH AT X, RATHER
THAN AT Y?

ASSUME THAT YOU APPLY A FORCE PARALLEL TO THE SLOPE
AT ONE OF THE TWO POINTS SHOWN, AND THAT THERE ARE NO
PROBLEMS WITH POSITIONING OR GRIPPING THE WHEEL.
ASSUME THAT THE WHEEL CAN BE ROLLED WITHOUT SLIPPING
BY PUSHING IT AT EITHER POINT.

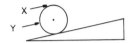

Figure 5. Wheel problem.

Wheel Problem. I will first present a very brief description of a solution to the "wheel problem" illustrated in Figure 5. The question asks whether one can exert a more effective uphill force *parallel to the slope* at the top of a wheel or at the level of the axle (as in pushing on the wheel of a covered wagon, for example).

Subject S2 compared the wheel to the analogous case of pushing on a heavy lever hinged to the hill (Figure 6B). He reasoned that pushing at the point higher up on the lever would require less force. He then made an inference by analogy that the wheel would be easier to push at the top (the correct answer). Here the lever is used as a model in some sense for the wheel.

Use of the Terms Analogy and Model. This initial example motivates the following uses the terms *analogy* and *model.* I will refer to the occurrence of a *spontaneous analogy* when the subject spontaneously shifts his attention to a different situation (called the analogous case) that he believes may have relevant structural similarities to the original problem (also referred to here as the *target*). When this is true, the subject's cognitive structures representing the target and the analogous case will have at least one structural relationship in common. In the discussion that follows, I will refer to the lever situation as the *analogous case* and to the structural similarity relationship between the lever and the wheel as the *analogy relation.*

Some analogies are used casually for "decorative" purposes only. By contrast, the following definition of a scientific model as a predictive analogy is intended to identify analogies that are used for serious scientific purposes. Here, in the broad sense of the term, a *scientific model* will refer to a cognitive structure, where the subject believes that the model situation is analogous to the target situation and believes that one may be able to use the model to predict or account for observations made in the target.

One way in which models are distinguished theoretically from rote facts or procedures is by virtue of having a richer set of relational interconnections within their structure as opposed to being a collection of independent facts. A model M gives the scientist a way of thinking about a target situation T that can predict how T behaves under certain conditions (whether this happens before or after the behavior is observed is not important for the defini-

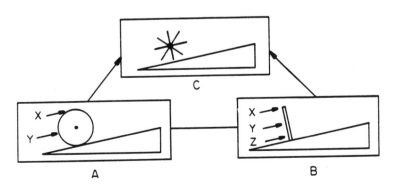

Figure 6. Models used in wheel problem. (A) Original problem, (B) Lever model, (C) Spoked wheel without a rim model.

tion). The lever analogy for the wheel is a scientific model in this sense. Well-developed and successful scientific models are also valued for being precise, unambiguous, general, and predictive (Gentner, 1982). In addition, scientists often prefer models that are visualizable, causal, simple, and that contain familiar entities. (In a later section, the narrower category of an *explanatory* model will be defined as one that posits a material similarity in which elements of *M* are assumed to actually exist as hidden or nonobvious elements in *T*.)

Improving the Model for the Wheel.   The subject was confident that it would be easiest to move the heavy lever in Figure 6B by pushing at point *X*, but he was not so confident that it was a good model for the wheel; he criticized the model by questioning whether there was a valid analogy relationship between it and the case of the wheel. Can one actually view the wheel as a lever, given that the "fulcrum" at the bottom of the wheel is always moving and never fixed? A second improved analogue model described by this subject was the spoked wheel without a rim shown in Figure 6C. The spokes allow one to view the wheel as a collection of many levers, thereby reducing any worries about the moving fulcrum. This is a useful model of the wheel for many purposes, including the present problem.

In summary, after criticizing the "lever" model, the subject was able to produce a second, more elaborate analogous case that provided an improved model. This provides an initial example of a hypothesis generation, evaluation, and modification process leading to the formation and improvement of a mental model via an analogy.

Creative Aspect of Analogies.   As mentioned above, an analogy is a related case that the subject believes is structurally similar to an original case. However, the case also must differ in a significant way from the original problem to be counted as an analogy. By this I mean that one or more features commonly assumed to be fixed in the original problem are different in the related case. In order to generate an analogy like the lever analogy, the subject must break away from the original problem context. This "breaking the set" of the original problem appears to be one of the main reasons that generating an analogy is considered a creative act and is most likely one reason that model construc-

A WEIGHT IS HUNG ON A SPRING. THE ORIGINAL SPRING IS REPLACED WITH A SPRING

- MADE OF THE SAME KIND OF WIRE,
- WITH THE SAME NUMBER OF COILS,
- BUT WITH COILS THAT ARE TWICE AS WIDE IN DIAMETER.

WILL THE SPRING STRETCH FROM ITS NATURAL LENGTH, MORE, LESS, OR THE SAME AMOUNT UNDER THE SAME WEIGHT? (ASSUME THE MASS OF THE SPRING IS NEGLIGIBLE COMPARED TO THE MASS OF THE WEIGHT). WHY DO YOU THINK SO?

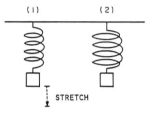

Figure 7. Spring problem.

tion via analogies is not the most common method for solving problems.

Spring Problem.   A second example of a problem illustrating analogy use and model construction is the "spring problem" shown in Figure 7. That the wide spring will stretch farther seems to correspond to most people's initial intuition about this problem. However, carefully answering the question about *why* the wide spring stretches more (and explaining exactly where the restoring force of the spring comes from) is a much more difficult task. Because it asks why, this is largely an explanation question rather than a question with a single, well-defined answer. Thus, it is less like an everyday "puzzle" problem and more like a theoretical "why" question in science in which the answer is an explanation.

In a study of expert qualitative reasoning, I recorded ten professors and advanced graduate students in technical fields while they were solving the spring problem out loud (Clement, 1988). They were told that the purpose of the interview was to study problem-solving methods and were given instructions to solve the problem "in any way you can." After they reached an answer, subjects were asked to give an estimate of their confidence in their answer. They were then asked if there was any way they could increase their confidence, and this often led to further work on the problem. Probing by the

Figure 8. Bending rod model. Longer rod bends more.

interviewer was kept to a minimum, usually consisting of a reminder to keep talking. Occasionally, the interviewer would ask for clarification of an ambiguous statement.

Some of the solutions were quite complex and took up to 50 minutes to complete. All subjects favored the (correct) answer that the wide spring would stretch farther, but the subjects varied considerably in the types of explanations they gave for their prediction. A number of subjects considered the analogous case of a horizontal bending rod (shown in Figure 8) or variations thereof. Most subjects had a strong intuition that a longer rod would bend more than a shorter rod under the same weight; this analogy suggested to them that the wider spring would stretch more. A number of other analogies attempted in this problem are discussed in Clement (1988b), including two foam rubber blocks, one with large and one with small air holes in the foam, springs in series, springs in parallel, series circuits, parallel circuits, and molecules in different crystals. Altogether, 31 significant analogies were observed, and they were generated by seven of the ten subjects. Thus, a large number of spontaneous analogies were generated for this problem.

A Case Study of Hypothesis Generation

In the remainder of this section, I will focus on the case study of subject S2 who appears to develop, criticize, and modify analogous cases for the spring problem until he produces a new hypothesis in the form of an explanatory model for how springs work.

Purpose of Case Study. One of the main reasons for doing an in-depth case study is to develop and refine a basic vocabulary of concepts for describing psychological observations and theories. The initial challenge of such a study is to develop and describe the "units" of behavior to be used in observation and to propose an initial cognitive model in the form of a set of cognitive structures and processes that can account for the behavior and that is both plausi-

ble and consistent. For simpler types of behavior, such modeling can be fairly detailed and, in some cases, can be expressed as a computer simulation. For more complex or poorly understood phenomena, an initial step in modeling can be achieved by formulating a general description of structure and process features—the basic units or cognitive objects to be used, the outline of a model, and a set of "design criteria" that a more detailed model would need to fulfill. The analysis of the case study discussed in the remainder of this chapter will be aimed at the latter level.

S2's Protocol. In the spring problem, subject S2 first generated the model of comparing a long horizontal bending rod with a short one (a weight is attached to the end of each rod), inferring that segments of the wider spring would bend more and therefore stretch more. However, he was concerned about the appropriateness of this model because of the apparent lack of a match between seeing bending in the rod and not seeing bending in the wire in a stretched spring. One can visualize this discrepancy here by thinking of the increasing slope a bug would experience walking down a bending rod and the constant slope the bug would experience walking down the helix of a stretched spring. This discrepancy led him to question whether the bending rod was an appropriate model for the spring. He then constructed the analogous case of the "zigzag spring" shown in Figure 9, apparently in order to attempt to evaluate the analogy relation between the spring and the bending rod and to attempt to construct an improved model. Because the full transcript is quite long, only verbatim excerpts are presented here. (My interpretive comments in the transcript are indicated in brackets.)

Figure 9. Zigzag spring model. Wider spring stretches more.

5   S2:   I have one good idea to start with; it occurs to me that a spring is nothing but a rod wound up uh, and therefore maybe I could answer the question for a rod. But then it occurs to me that there's something clearly wrong with that metaphor because if I actually took spring wire and it was straight instead, it certainly wouldn't hang down like a spring does. . . . It would droop . . . and its slope would steadily increase as you . . . went away from the point of attachment, whereas in a spring, the slope of the spiral is constant.

7   S2:   Why does a spring stretch?. . . I'm still led back to this notion . . . of the spring straightened out [a bending rod] . . . I'm bothered by the fact that the slope doesn't remain constant as you go along it. It seems as though it ought to be a good analogy, but somehow, somehow it doesn't seem to hold up. . . .

23   S2:   I feel I want to reject the straightened spring model—as a bad model of what a spring is like. I feel I need to understand the nature of a spring in order to answer the question. Here's a good idea. It occurs to me that a single coil of a spring wrapped once around is the same as a whole spring. . . . In the one-coil case, I

find myself being tempted back to the straightened spring [rod] model again. . . .

I still don't see why coiling the spring should make any difference. . . . Surely you could coil a spring in squares, let's say, and it . . . would still behave more or less the same. Ah! from squares, visually I suddenly get the idea of a zigzag spring rather than a coiled spring; that strikes me as an interesting idea (draws Figure 9). . . . Might there be something in that idea? . . .

I see a problem with this idea. The problem . . . is that . . . the stretch . . . has to do with . . . the joint. But the springiness of the . . . real spring is a distributed springiness; . . . So . . . I wonder if I can make the [zigzag] spring . . . where the action . . . isn't at the angles . . . it's distributed along the length. . . . And I'm going to do that; I have a visualization. . . . Here's a stretchable bar; (draws modified zigzag spring in Figure 10) a bendable bar, and then we have a rigid connector. . . . And when we do this what bends . . . is the bendable bars . . . and that would behave like a spring. I can imagine that it would.

Here there is evidence that the subject is generating a series of analogue models for the spring—from the rod to the angular zigzag spring to the rectangular zigzag spring with stiff joints. The zigzag spring is eventually dropped, presumably because he was still critical of this model and could not reconcile the bending going on in sections of the

zigzag spring with the lack of change in slope in the original helical spring. However, these attempts do provide evidence for another thought pattern in the form of a repeated dialectic process of model construction, criticism, and modification.

Next, S2 considers the analogy of a double-length spring instead of the double-width spring appearing in the original problem.

Figure 10. Modified zigzag spring model.

37   S2:   This rod here: as the weight moves along, it bends more and more the further out the weight is. . . . Hmmm, what if I imagined moving the weight along the spring . . . would that tell me anything? Would that? I don't know. I don't see why it should. What if the spring were twice as long . . . instead of twice as wide? . . . It seems to me pretty clear that the spring that's twice as long is going to stretch more. . . . Now if this is the same as a

spring that's twice as wide, then that should stretch more. . . . Uhh, but is it the same as a spring that's twice as wide? Again, I just don't see why . . . the coiling [vs. a rod] should make any difference. It just seems geometrically irrelevant to me somehow. . . . But I . . . can't—I have trouble . . . bring that into consonance with the behavior of an actually stretched out spring . . . the slope problem anomaly [increasing slope in the rod, but not in the spring]—if I could resolve that anomaly . . . then I would feel confident of my answer . . . but this anomaly bothers me a lot.

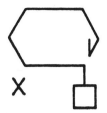

Figure 11. Hexagonal coil model.

Again, he seems critical of the appropriateness of an analogy in the case of the double-length spring.

---

57   S2:   I feel as though I'm reasoning in circles. I think I'll make a deliberate effort to break out of the circle somehow. What else could I use that stretches . . . like rubber bands . . . what else stretches . . . molecules, polyesters, car springs [leaf springs] . . . what about a . . . two-dimensional spiral [watch] spring? That doesn't seem to help.

At this point, the bending rod, double-length spring, and zigzag spring analogies have each pointed him to the correct answer to the problem, yet he remains unsatisfied with his understanding. In line 57, he continues to search unsuccessfully for a more satisfactory analogous case.

Insight Section. Subsequently, subject S2 produces an extremely productive analogy when he generates the idea of the hexagonally shaped coil in Figure 11 and moves from there to the idea of the square-shaped coil in Figure 12. Imagining the stretching of these polygonal coils apparently allowed him to recognize that some of the restoring forces in the spring come from *twisting* in the wire instead of bending—a major breakthrough in the solution that corresponds to the way in which engineering specialists view springs. Much of the remainder of this chapter will focus on this insight.

The impressiveness of the reasoning displayed by different subjects in solving the spring problem

depends on the depth of understanding sought by the subject and on the subject's prior knowledge. The first level of depth in understanding is simply to state an intuition that the wide spring will stretch more; a second level is to give some plausible justification for this. For subjects who have previously learned that there is twisting in the spring wire during stretching, they can, with some effort, achieve a third quantitative level in identifying three causal, linear factors leading to the result that the stretch is proportional to the cube of the coil diameter. Probably the most difficult achievement occurs when the subject does not know about the invisible twisting in the wire, but is somehow able to construct that hypothesis. S2 achieves this in the next section of the protocol to be discussed.

To see why this square coil model is helpful, note that it can, in turn, be understood in terms of two simpler cases, the twisting rod and the bending rod, as shown in Figure 12. That is, pulling the end of the lever "1" down not only bends rod 1, but it also twists rod 2. (One way to comprehend this idea is to view rod 1 as a wrench that is twisting rod 2.) The same is true for all other adjacent rod pairs. Thus, twisting is an important type of deformation in the spring wire in this model.

This part of the protocol is reported in sections as follows:

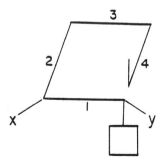

Figure 12. Square coil model.

1. Subject is still in conflict about whether spring wire is bending
2. Subject generates a series of polygonal coil analogies
3. Torsion discovery
4. Subject evaluates and adapts square coil as a preferred model of the spring
5. Subject comments on his increased understanding

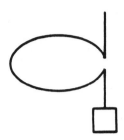

Figure 13. Single spring coil.

Section 1: Subject Is Still in Conflict about Whether Spring Wire Is Bending

57　S2:　I just . . . have the intuition that a . . . straight rod ought to in some sense be a good model for a spring. But there are these anomalies that won't go away. And yet I can't see . . . a better model.

79　S2:　. . . I'm just trying to imagine the coil . . . (traces circle about 7 inches in diameter in air in front of self) a circle with a break in it. . . .

81　S2:　(Has just drawn Figure 13) . . . you could just hold it there . . . and apply a force there, and the spring stretches. . . . I'll be damned if I see why it [the coil] should be any different from that case [the rod]. . . .

87　S2:　. . . if you start with a [stretched] helix and unwind it . . . you should get a bow [bend], but you don't. I mean visually imagining it, you don't. I don't see how you could make the bow go away—just to wind it up—damn it!

111　S2:　Darn it, darn it, darn it . . . why should that [the difference between a rod and a coil] matter? . . . I'm visualizing what will happen when you just take this single coil and pull down on it and it stretches; and it stretches. . . .

(The subject spends a considerable amount of time trying to resolve this issue without making progress.)

Section 2: Subject Generates a Series of Polygonal Coil Analogies

117　S2:　(40 minutes into the protocol) I keep circling back to these same issues without getting anywhere with them. . . . I need to . . . think about it in some radically different way, somehow. Let me just generate ideas about circularity. What could the circularity [in contrast to the rod] do? Why should it matter? How would it change the way the force is transmitted from increment to increment of the spring? Aha! Now let me think about; Aha! Now this is interesting. I imagined; I recalled my idea of the square spring and the square is sort of like a circle and I wonder . . . what if I start with a rod and bend it once (places hands at each end of rod in Figure 8 and motions as if bending a wire) and then I bend it again?

119　S2:　What if I produce a series of successive approximations to . . . the circle by producing a series of polygons? Maybe that would clarify because maybe that, that's constructing a continuous bridge, or sort of a continuous bridge, between the two cases [the rod and the coil]. Clearly there can't be a hell of a lot of difference between the circle, and, say, a hexagon. . . .

121　S2:　. . . or even a triangle . . . square . . . (draws hexagon in Figure 11). . . . Now that, a [hexagon] is essentially a circle. I mean, surely springwise that [hexagon] would behave pretty much like a circle does.

Section 3: Torsion Discovery

121　S2:　Now that's interesting. Just looking at this it occurs to me that when force is applied here, you not only get a bend on this segment, but because there's a pivot here (points to X in Figure 11), you get a *torsion* effect. . . .

122 S2:   Aha! Maybe the behavior of the spring has something to do with twist (moves hands as if twisting an object) forces as well as bend forces (moves hands as if bending an object). That's a real interesting idea. . . . That might be the key difference between this [bending rod] which involves no torsion forces, and this [hexagon]. Let me accentuate the torsion force by making a square where there's a right angle. (Draws Figure 12). I like that. A right angle . . . that unmixes the bend from the torsion.

123 S2:   Now . . . I have two forces introducing a stretch. I have the force that bends this . . . segment [1] and in addition I have a torsion force which twists [segment 2] at vertex, um, X . . . [in Figure 12] (makes motion like turning a doorknob with one hand).

Section 4: Subject Evaluates and Adopts Square Coil as a Preferred Model of the Spring

129 S2:   (b) . . . Does this (points to square-shaped coil) gain in slope—toward the bottom? . . .

130 S2:   (c) . . . Indeed we have a structure here which does not have this increasing slope as you get to the bottom . . . (e) it's only if one looks at the fine structure; the rod between the Y and the X, that one sees the flop effect [downward curvature].

132 S2:   (b) . . . Now I feel I have a good model of sp- of a spring. . . . Now I realize the reason the spring doesn't flop is because a lot of the springiness of the spring comes from torsion effects rather than from bendy [sic] effects. . . .

133 S2:   And now I think I can answer the stretch question firmly by using this . . . square

model of the spring. What does it mean, in terms of the square model, to increase the diameter of the spring? . . . Now making the sides longer certainly would make the [square] spring stretch more.

135 I: How can you tell?

136 S2:   (a) Physical intuition . . . and also recollection . . . the longer the segment (moves hands apart) the more the bendability (moves hands as if bending a rod). . . . (b) Now the same thing would happen to the torsion I think, because if I have a longer rod (moves hands apart), and I put a twist on it (moves hands as if twisting a rod), it seems to me—again physical intuition—that it will twist more. . . .

143 S2:   . . . So . . . doubling the length of the sides . . . it will clearly stretch more. Both for reasons of torsion and for reasons of the segment [bending].

Section 5: Subject Comments on His Increased Understanding

144 S2:   And my confidence is now 99% . . . I now feel pretty good about my understanding about the way a spring works although I realize at the same time I could be quite wrong. Still, there seems to be something to this torsion business; I feel a lot better about it.

178 S2:   Before this torsion insight, my confidence in the answer was 95% but my confidence in my understanding of the situation was way way down, zero. I felt that I did not really understand what was happening; now my confidence in the answer is near 100% and my confidence in my understanding is like 80%.

Analysis of Transcript

Models Used by S2. A hypothesized outline of the cognitive events producing S2's new understanding in this last section is shown in Figure 14. The figure shows hypothesized "snapshots" of a series of S2's final models as they develop over time, with solid lines showing confirmed analogy relations, and dotted lines showing tentative analogy relations. Poorly understood situations are

shown in dotted boxes with well-understood situations shown in solid boxes.

Figure 14A (Line 81): S2 has already reduced the spring situation to the equivalent single circular coil situation as shown by the solid line labeled (1) in the diagram. Also there is a tentative analogy relation shown as a dotted line labeled (2), from the single coil to the well-understood bending rod model.

Figure 14B (Line 117): S2 then recalls his idea of a square spring and generates the model of a hex-

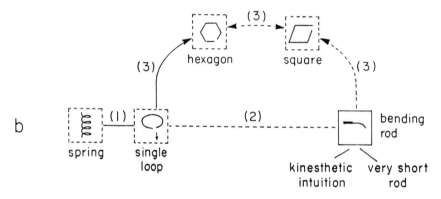

Figure 14. Changes in S2's understanding as he constructs a mental model using analogies.

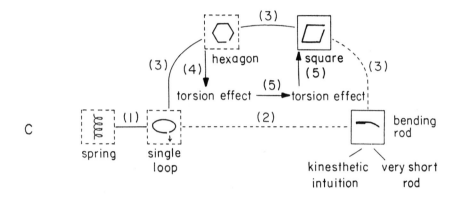

c

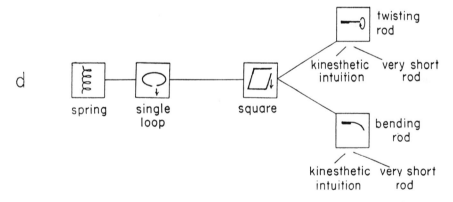

d

Figure 14. (Cont.)

agonal coil. In his words, this is ''constructing a continuous bridge, or sort of a continuous bridge, between the two cases [the rod and the circular coil].''[4]

Figure 14C (Line 121): While analyzing the hexagon in terms of bending effects, it occurs to him (''Aha!'') that there will also be twisting effects. At this point, he shifts to the simpler square model.

Figure 14D (Line 123): By the final stage, S2's understanding of the underlying structure that makes a spring work has changed significantly. He now appears to have a mental model of the spring as working like a square coil that contains elements that bend and twist. His physical intuitions about the difficulty of (1) bending and (2) twisting a long rod versus a short one seem to play a role similar to axioms; they are basic assumptions on which the rest of his conclusions are founded.

In the discussion that follows, I will refer to the square, the hexagonal, and the many sided coil models collectively as *polygonal coil models*. To anticipate, some of the conclusions I wish to draw from this example, in the remainder of this chapter, are the following:

1. The recognition of torsion in the polygonal coil is a significant scientific insight in S2's attempt to understand the spring.
2. S2 uses analogies to invent a model for how the spring works in the form of the polygonal coil.
3. This model can be classified as an explanatory model as opposed to an expedient model because it proposes torsion as a causal factor actually operating in the spring.
4. S2 produces models and insights via a successive refinement process of hypothesis generation, evaluation, and modification or rejection. S2's process is noninductive.
5. The model generation process here is neither a pure eureka phenomenon nor a simple, smooth, methodical buildup of information.
6. Several divergent processes are used in generating hypotheses.
7. The recognition of an anomaly sets up a tension condition that ''drives'' the dialectic process, and that is partially analogous to the

tension between an existing paradigm in the face of anomalies in science.

Insight Behavior.   The short transcript excerpts displayed here do not convey the fact that the subject spent a considerable period of time (about 25 minutes) alternately questioning and trying to justify the initial bending rod model of the spring. Following this frustrating struggle, the invention of the polygonal coil with the subsequent torsion discovery is a candidate for being termed a significant scientific insight for several reasons.[5] First, the idea is productive in the sense that it leads immediately to a considerable amount of cognitive activity. In fact, one is given the impression of a ''flood'' of ideas occurring immediately afterward. Progress is made rapidly, as if the polygonal coil idea were a ''trigger'' that stimulates a series of further ideas. Second, the torsion idea appears fairly quickly, with little warning. Third, the subject changes his hypothesized model of stretching—by considering torsion the subject introduces a new causal factor into the system. Torsion constitutes a very different mechanism from bending for explaining how the spring resists stretching. (S2 is the only subject out of 10 studied who clearly progressed from no awareness of torsion in the spring to an understanding of it as a factor.) Fourth, the subject says that he is now able to resolve the paradox of the apparent lack of bending in a helical spring and states that he feels he has achieved an increase in his understanding of the system. Of course, his ''theory of springs'' could be developed further beyond the polygonal coil idea, but the fact remains that this model is a significant advance over the bending rod models.[6] Fifth, the subject reacts emotionally to his

---

[4]The idea of ''bridging'' between analogous cases with a new intermediate analogous case is an interesting nonempirical strategy in itself for evaluating the validity of the analogy relation between two cases and is discussed in Clement (1986).

[5]There are actually two parts to this insight: the construction of the polygonal coil, and the recognition of torsion in the coil. The first part makes possible the second part, and both are accompanied by ''aha's.'' The first part constitutes the generation of a new representation for the target problem; the second is the new activation of a principle that can be applied to the new representation. In much of the discussion that follows, it will be convenient to treat these together as a single insight.

[6]In fact, twisting is the predominant source of stretching in a helical spring. The idea that the spring wire bends is also partially correct. By imagining the extreme case of a single circular coil of a spring stretched out into an almost straight wire, one can see that stretching produces some unbending as it removes the circular curvature originally put into the wire when it was coiled. However, there is no bending in a vertical plane. Twisting in the square coil can also be used to predict that the stretch varies with the *cube* of the coil diameter.

ideas, calling them "interesting" and exposing a "key difference," as well as producing some emphatic "aha" expressions with a raised tone of voice. Later in this chapter, I will attempt to formulate a more careful definition for the term *insight* that is motivated by these factors.

The Formation of an Explanatory Model via Analogies

Explanatory versus Nonexplanatory Models. As discussed earlier, philosophers of science have developed an important distinction between explanatory models and either empirical law hypotheses or formal quantitative principles, as shown in Figure 3. It will now be useful to specify a more precise definition for the term *explanatory model* in order to say whether S2 has developed one. Recall the proposal to use the term *model* to refer to a cognitive structure M, where the subject believes there is a predictive analogy between some important relational aspects of the model M and some aspects of the target situation T. One kind of model then is merely an expedient and often temporary analogy that predicts some aspects of the target's behavior. M may happen to behave like T, and therefore provide a way of predicting what T will do. Such an expedient model may not provide a satisfying explanation for why T behaves as it does. M may say nothing about the underlying process that explains T's behavior. An explanatory model, on the other hand, should explain how T works, leading to a feeling of "understanding" T.

S2 makes a clear distinction between *confidence in his answer to the problem* and *confidence in his understanding* of the spring:

| 144 | S2: | . . . There seems to be something to this torsion business; I feel a lot better about it. . . . |
| 178 | S2: | Before this torsion insight, my confidence in the answer was 95% but my confidence in my understanding of the situation was way way down, zero. I felt that I did not really understand what was happening; now my confidence in the answer is near 100% and my confidence in my understanding is like 80%. |

This perceived increase in understanding is one indication that the polygonal coil has become an explanatory model for the subject, not just an expedi-

ent analogy for generating the answer to the problem. (Karmiloff-Smith and Inhelder, 1975, have documented a related distinction in children's thinking.)

Hesse (1967) and Harre (1972) identified two types of scientific analogue model: (1) a model that shares only its abstract form with the target (Hesse cites hydraulic models of economic systems as one example); I call this an *expedient model;* and (2) a model that has become in Harre's terms a "candidate for reality," in which a set of material features, instead of only the abstract form, is also hypothesized to be the same in the model and in the target situations. I will refer to the latter type of model M as an *explanatory model* (or *structural hypothesis*), M_e, if some of the basic objects, attributes, and concrete relations in M are hypothesized by the subject to be part of T and to underlie the behavior of interest in T.

This ordinarily means that the subject can attain some degree of ontological commitment to (belief in the reality of) M_e if empirical and rational support are obtained for it. M_e is thought of as a hidden structure within T that provides an explanation for T's behavior. Usually M_e contains some entities that are initially not directly observable or obvious in T at that point in time.

This concept helps to account for the remarkable ability of scientists to formulate and propose hidden structure and processes in nature before they are observed more directly, such as atoms, black holes, and the "bending" of light rays. An explanatory model can allow the scientist to see a phenomenon in a new way via an analogy to a hypothesized visualizable structure that is considered to be hidden in the target situation to be explained. This is something that empirical law hypotheses cannot do.

In the case of the present protocol, the polygonal coil qualifies as explanatory, because the subject believes that twisting and bending effects may actually be operating in the spring wire to produce its behavior. Twisting and bending are concrete features, but they are not ordinarily observed in springs. In this sense, the model expresses for the subject a hypothesis concerning the hidden structure underlying the way stretching produces deformation and restoring forces in the spring wire. Furthermore, the square coil model removes the anomaly of a potentially critical dissimilarity in the original bending rod model—that of the lack of cumulative bending in the spring. All these factors presumably increase S2's feeling of understanding and of having a satisfying explanation for the be-

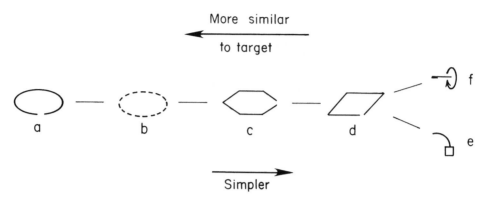

Figure 15. Sequence of models generated by S2.

havior of a spring, as expressed in lines 144 and 178 of the protocol quoted above.

For these reasons, the polygonal coil with torsion model qualifies as an explanatory model that provides a hypothesis about the nature of springs. S2's statements lead one to believe it has become a preferred model of the spring that he will retain in memory. In this sense, S2's protocol is an example of learning via the construction of an explanatory model.[7]

Development of an Explanatory Model from an Initial Nonexplanatory Analogy. A further hypothesis is suggested by S2's problem solution: an expert can develop an explanatory model via the modification and refinement of an initial model that is merely expedient or has low explanatory status. In this view, whether a model is explanatory is a matter of degree. The explanatory status of a model depends on the degree to which one believes that the model contains elements that are like elements hidden in the target to be explained.

It is reasonable that when an analogous case is first proposed, it will often be *unclear* whether it has potential as an explanatory model—whether its elements could be something like the hidden elements in the target or not. Its explanatory status may grow gradually rather than in one decisive jump. Improvements in the model may also raise its explanatory status. Indeed, this seems to be what occurred in S2's case. He used the bending rod early on as a model, which gve him a prediction in which he was highly confident. However, he said his resulting understanding was very low. The recognition of the lack of cumulative bending anomaly appeared to prevent him from accepting it as an explanatory model. Cumulative bending is an important material property that is present in the model but not in the target. A successive refinement process then led to a number of alternative models, culminating with the polygonal coil model. The identification of torsion in the polygonal coil raised S2's feeling of understanding significantly. This is consistent with the interpretation that he had then acquired some confidence that torsion is a real but hidden mechanism operating in the spring. Thus, S2 appears to take an initial, nonexplanatory analogy (the bending rod model) and develop it, via criticisms and modifications, into a model that in fact does have explanatory status for him.

Simplifying Function of Models. In Figure 15, S2 considers a multisided coil but is unable to make further progress in his analysis before quitting. The figure shows the set of polygonal models referred to by S2, placed in order of increasing simplicity or analyzability from left to right. Note that these models attain a higher degree of perceptual resemblance to the spring in the opposite direction from right to left. Of the models shown, the bending and twisting rod models on the right are the simplest to understand, but appear to be least like the spring

---

[7]In one sense, I am appropriating the term *explanatory* here because, as Kuhn (1977) points out, what counts as explanatory is different for Aristotle, Newton, and quantum physics. I am proposing that what counts for S2 in this problem fits the definition given—an analogue model that has material elements that are hypothesized as "candidates for reality." The sharing of material elements between model and target can be termed *material correspondence,* and this assumption seems to be a minimal requirement for something to have potential as an explanation. Whether a satisfying explanation is actually attained, however, will also depend on other factors, such as the support for and comprehensibility of the model.

coil. One might be tempted to call the multigon in (b) the only "really" explanatory model in the sense that it is seen as actually present in the spring, whereas the others are not. But even in the multigon, there are material elements that are not present in the spring, such as fulcrum points and straight-line segments. Apparently, even the multigon model is not a full candidate for the mechanism in the spring.

Hesse (1967) and Harre (1972) described some models in science as *simplifying* models, in which the scientist intentionally uses a model with features that are different from those in *T* in order to make *M* simple enough to analyze. S2's polygonal spring models appear to be simplifying models that are partially explanatory; he sees the spring as probably really twisting, as in the square coil, but not as really square. The square provides a simplifying geometry—but S2 recognizes that ordinary spring coils are not square or polygonal. In summary, this appears to be a case in which modifications of an initial analogy with low explanatory status led to the development of a model with considerably higher explanatory status. However, the polygonal coil model is still a simplifying model, because some of its elements are recognized as not being present in the helical spring.[8]

Three Roles for Analogy. Even the most successful models with no recognizable simplifying assumptions can be questioned as to their ontological status—whether they are "really true" of *T*. It is reasonable to take the point of view that a model can never be fully confirmed as true in a universal sense and should always be open to question. Another way to say this is that even in well-established scientific models, the relation between the idealized model and a real-life example is one of analogy, or partial resemblance, leaving open the possibility that other more refined or useful alternative useful models may be developed in the future.

This means that analogy can play a role in the generation of new hypotheses in at least the following different ways: (1) an analogous case can play a provocative, heuristic role in suggesting new obser-

vations or new explanatory features to attend to; (2) an analogous case can serve as a rough initial model of the target situation that is later developed and refined; (3) a developed explanatory model, whatever its origin, should in the end be linked by an analogy relation to the target situation.

Summary of Evidence for a Model Construction Cycle as a Noninductive Source for Hypotheses

The growth in S2's ideas appears to have occurred via the cyclical process of analogy generation, criticism, and modification (or rejection) that is shown in Figure 16. This is a more general reasoning pattern that can help account for the transitions between the states shown in Figure 14. Table 1 summarizes evidence from the protocol that S2's progress is a result of this kind of cyclical process rather than a result of either a convergent series of deductions or an induction from observations. Figure 16 is therefore a model of the processes that produce the observed behaviors shown in Table 1. Here I assume that the bending rod and zigzag spring models are simplifying models, that the extent to which they are explanatory is unknown to S2 at the time he proposes them, and that they are part of his attempts to develop an explanatory model.

Note that the cycle in Figure 16 corresponds to the nonempirical processes B, C, D, and E in Figure 4, the model construction cycle discussed earlier. Process B is also implicated in the rapid search for analogies, such as "molecules, polyesters, and car springs [leaf springs]" in line 57 of the transcript. Thus, there is evidence in this case study that supports the existence of the nonempirical processes proposed in the model of hypothesis development shown in Figure 4. We therefore appear to be in a position in which real-time protocol evidence can be gathered to evaluate the plausibility of such models of scientific reasoning.

Noninductive Hypothesis Generation. I will now examine more carefully the claim that S2's final model is neither the result of a convergent series of deductions nor an induction from observations. When S2 generates analogue model hypotheses, they appear not to be deduced logically from prior principles; they are essentially reasoned conjectures as to what might be a fruitful representation for analyzing how a spring coil works. The reasoning involved does not carry the certainty associated with deduction.

Nor, apparently are the hypotheses built up inductively as abstract generalizations from observa-

[8]Many sequences of mathematical models, especially in applications of the calculus, have the form shown in Figure 15. In this view, mathematical limit arguments, which examine properties as one passes from an analyzable simpler model and approaches the limit of the target situation, are sophisticated attempts to justify the intuitive validity of the analogy between the model and the target situation. The role of analogies and models in mathematical understanding is discussed by Fischbein (1987).

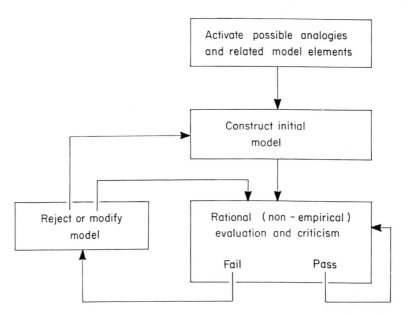

Figure 16. Elements of model construction cycle which are supported by evidence in S2's protocol (see also Table 1).

Table 1. **Location of Evidence for Model Construction Cycle of Hypothesis Generation, Criticism, and Modification or Rejection**

Line	Process[a]	Hypothetical model	Comments
5	G	Horizontal bending rod	Initial analogy
5	C	Horizontal bending rod	Bending in rod, but not in helix
23	G	Square coil	
23	M	Zigzag no. 1	Modifies square to produce zigzag model
23	C	Zigzag no. 1	Joints confounding
23	M	Zigzag no. 2 with stiff joints	Modifies zigzag no. 1 to produce no. 2
	[C][b]		Bending in zigzag, but not in helix
	D	Drops zigzag models	
57	R	Rod model	
87	C	Rod model	Bending in rod, but not in helix
117	R	Square coil	
119	M	Hexagonal coil	
121			Makes torsion discovery in hexagon
122	C	Hexagonal coil	Hexagon geometry too complex
122	R	Square coil	Leads to successful prediction of restoring forces without cumulative bending in spring wire

[a]*Key*: G = Generates hypothesized model; C = Criticizes model; M = Modifies model; R = Reconsiders model; D = Drops or rejects model.
[b]Inferred in absence of direct evidence in protocol.

tions. S2 is unable to collect new data during the interview, and, consequently, his reasoning is independent of new empirical processes. One can also consider whether he might be making new inductions on perceptual memories of *prior* observations, but he does not appear to recall observing bending, twisting, zigzags, or squares in springs; instead these appear to be newly imagined models. The novelty and nonobservability of the polygonal coil with torsion model, and its evolution from criticisms of the earlier horizontal rod model, argue that the hypothesis generation process in this case was an imaginative construction and criticism process rather than one of induction from observations. Quite possibly, S2 would have made some new observations of springs as well, had they been available (although it is doubtful that he would have observed torsion effects). But the present case study demonstrates the possibility that impressive progress in explanatory model construction can be made via noninductive processes.

Of course, it is highly likely that empirical information was involved in the original development of the prior knowledge S2 uses. In attempting to speak to the rationalism versus inductivism issue, it is important to identify the time period of focus. For the purposes of this analysis, the focus is on the new knowledge developed during the hour or so of reasoning in the interview rather than on the origins of the prior knowledge S2 uses. For example, he uses prior knowledge in the form of the concept of twisting. One assumes his earlier learning of the concept of twisting involved empirical experiences with wrenches, cranks, and knobs. His new model of the polygonal spring with torsion uses his old concept of twisting as one of its elements, but the total structure of the model is a larger new construction. The point is that the new knowledge developed by S2— the construction of a new explanatory model hypothesis for how a spring works—was apparently formed by processes during the protocol that were nonempirical.

I do not wish to say here that some form of suggestion from patterns perceived in data cannot be involved in some types of scientific hypothesis formation. Rather, this case study acts more like an "existence proof" in showing the possibility that noninductive construction processes can be very important in the formation of explanatory model hypotheses.

An Explanatory Hypothesis Can Lead to an Empirical Hypothesis.   The final model of the polygonal coil with torsion raises S2's confidence in the empirical law hypothesis that (other factors being equal) wide springs will stretch more than narrow springs. Apparently, this is a case in which the development of a convincing explanatory model hypothesis can establish high confidence in an empirical law hypothesis in the absence of new empirical information. Kuhn (1962) discusses examples of this pattern in the history of science.

Argument for Not Separating the Context of Discovery and the Context of Justification.   Finally, I want to consider a potential criticism of the model construction cycle shown in Figure 4. It is traditional in philosophy to separate the contexts of hypothesis formation and hypothesis testing and evaluation in science. If I claim to be portraying hypothesis *formation* process in Figure 4, then why does it include hypothesis *evaluation* processes as well? The answer concerns the observation that loops in the cycle can at times be traversed extremely rapidly. For example, S2's criticism of the bending rod model in line 5 of Protocol indicates that the time interval between model generation and criticism can be as small as 15 seconds. In addition, his modification of the zigzag spring model in line 23 indicates that an entire generation, criticism, and modification cycle can take place within 90 seconds. Although an evaluation in the form of a carefully designed laboratory experiment can take days or even years, other evaluation processes, such as certain nonempirical checks for consistency, can take place much more rapidly. In this sense, evaluation is an inherent part of the hypothesis formation process. Stated in traditional terms, it may often be impossible to separate the "context of justification" from the "context of discovery." The history of science tends to look at developments over a time scale of years or weeks. From this perspective it may be impossible to separate these two contexts in the early stages of hypothesis formation when the grain size of the time scale that one is using is greater than fractions of an hour.

In addition, generative techniques appear to be used in the service of evaluative goals in this protocol. The initial generation of the zigzag and square spring ideas, for example, appear to be attempts to evaluate the appropriateness of the bending rod model. Subsequently, these become candidates for replacing the rod model.

In sum, the reason that evaluation processes appear in the model of hypothesis formation is that they appear to be an *inherent part* of hypothesis formation down to time periods, on occasion, of less than a single minute. In such cases, one sees a rapid, dialectic interplay between generation and evaluation processes.

Eureka or Accretion? The Presence of Insight in S2's Protocol

I can now move to the second issue outlined in the introduction—the pace of theory change: Does S2's reasoning contain eureka events that involve sudden reorganizations, or does he make progress smoothly in an incremental manner? The answer to this question is not obvious. It seems possible to argue in either direction from this protocol. One can point to what appear to be sudden insights, but, on the other hand, sections precede these insights in which the subject prepares the context and groundwork for having them. Sometimes his methods appear to be systematic, but, at other times, ideas arrive in a rush, as if they are outside of his control. Thus, there seems to be mixed signals in the protocol on this issue.

Defining a Pure Eureka Event

In order to say something useful about the eureka question, one needs to become more precise about the meaning of a eureka event. Here I will propose an initial definition of the extreme case of a *pure eureka event* as an extremely sudden, reorganizing, extraordinary break away from the subject's previous ideas. I use the term *extraordinary* here to refer to processes, such as unconscious or supernormal reasoning, that are different from those used in ordinary thinking. If the appearance of a new hypothesis constitutes a break in the train of thought— if the hypothesis comes "out of the blue" and appears unconnected to the subjects' previous ideas in the protocol—this would constitute one kind of evidence for an extraordinary and probably unconscious thought process. The accretion versus eureka question in extreme form then becomes: Is the subject's accomplishment the result of a smooth, incremental, controlled, buildup from previous ideas? Or is it a sudden, reorganizing, extraordinary break with his previous ideas? I will consider two subissues of this question expressed by the two pairs of key words in it: sudden reorganizing and extraordinary break. In this section, I would like to use the analysis of the protocol as an initial test bed for concepts that are developed to describe the quality and pace of structural change in creative hypothesis generation activities. Some of these concepts may

also prove useful for analyzing structural change in theoretical models in real scientific research.

Is There a Sudden Reorganizing Change in S2's Understanding?

This subquestion itself can be broken down into two parts: Is there a significant structural change? and Is it a sudden change? For the latter part, a pertinent time period must be identified over which the change takes place, and a pertinent concept of "rate of hypothesis formation or modification" must be defined. I will conclude that, although the torsion discovery was not a "blinding insight"— an instantaneous reorganization of his ideas—it certainly was an impressive and relatively sudden breakthrough. The problem is to develop a relatively precise language for saying this.

Is There a Significant Structural Change? One first needs to ask about the size of the change in representation or understanding produced by the torsion insight. Does it simply add on a small new fact or is it a complete reorganization? The type of change in understanding to be discussed here is a structural change (change in relational structure as opposed to surface features) in a currently assumed mental model.

It is clear that the polygonal coil with torsion insight does not constitute a reorganization in S2's understanding of any domain larger than the "theory of springs" (such as the "theory of elastic materials"). However, the insight does appear to add more than a simple fact; it appears to constitute the addition of a significant set of structural relations to the subject's hypothesized model of the spring system, including the new causal chain of weight causing twisting and torsion, which, in turn, causes resistance to stretching; and the new global effect of finding no cumulative effect of bending throughout the square spring.

Can the insight be characterized as a reorganization of the subject's mental model? In some senses it can, although the shift could have been larger. Torsion is a completely different geometric deformation than bending and constitutes a significantly different hypothesis. The case here would be clearer, though, if the subject had switched more completely from the view of spring forces coming from bending to the engineer's view that spring forces come primarily from torsion. S2 did not go this far; instead he switched from using bending alone to using bending and torsion together in his explanations. But he did raise the question of which of these two effects predominates. Although he was unable to reach an answer to this last question, when asked at the end of the interview, about whether the stretch could be due completely to torsion, he felt that it was perfectly plausible. Given more time, the fuller transition might very well have taken place. Clearly, the potential for a complete replacement of the deformation mechanism in the spring was created.

What one can say then is that the subject achieved a major breakthrough in adding a major chain of casual factors to his model of the spring. This can be considered to be a reorganization in the sense that a new system of relationships was created. Thus, the structural change in this subject's model of the spring appears to be of intermediate size. The change process was characterized by imaginative attempts to switch to different problem representations, most of which failed. When a productive representation was found (the polygonal coil), it led to the recognition of a system of new relationships involving force, torsion, and twisting. But it was not a "revolutionary" change in the sense of rejecting and replacing a large, previously assumed body of established knowledge structures. However, it does allow us to imagine the possibility that such a rejection and replacement could occur in science via a similar process.

The Pace of Change in Understanding. I have taken a high rate of change in the currently assumed model as one defining characteristic of a pure eureka event. This rate of change could be defined as the ratio of the size of the change in the model's structure to the time interval over which the change takes place. The latter concept may not be easy to operationalize as an observable variable, depending on the comparisons being made and the complexity of the protocol, but it should at least play a clarifying role at the theoretical level.

It is a challenging task to point to a specific time interval in the protocol representing the "period of insight" because of the difficulty in defining the latter. As an upper limit, the time for the subject's total solution was 52 minutes. Thus, it is certain that the subject changed from the rod model of the spring to the square coil with torsion and bending in a period smaller than this time. Viewed on a large time scale appropriate to the history of science, this would certainly be considered a tiny interval that indicates a relatively sudden structural change.

But much of this time was spent testing the simpler rod model and trying out other analogies, most of which led nowhere. Can one identify a shorter period of insight within the protocol? The bending rod model was proposed within 1 minute after reading the problem. Then a long period without lasting progress in model development of about 40 minutes ensued as the rod model was questioned, the zigzag models were proposed and rejected, and other analogies were tried. Finally, there was a breakthrough in a 4-minute period during which the subject referred to the square hexagonal coils, made the torsion discovery, and incorporated it into his final square coil model of the spring. When the subject finally generated the hexagonal coil toward the end of the protocol, it took less than 80 seconds for him to recognize the torsion effect, and less than another 2 minutes to settle on the square coil as his final model of the spring. This 4-minute period is therefore a candidate for the period of insight.

However, the square coil idea was considered very briefly, only about 6 minutes into the protocol. But it was quickly dropped in order to consider the zigzag spring. Thirty-four minutes later, it was taken up again and led to the torsion insight. Should this 34 minutes between the dropping and re-emergence of an idea be counted as part of the period of insight? I will assume not, because the subject was following separate ideas during this time which turned out to be blind alleys. If one makes this assumption, one can point to this 4-minute segment as a relatively sudden "period of insight." But the difficulties involved in defining the period of insight here are clear. The benefit of this exercise, however, is that it forces one to develop some useful distinctions between concepts, such as structural change in a model, the period of insight, and the rate of structural change in a model.

On the other hand, the insight was not instantaneous, and criticism and modification processes did occur during this 4-minute period as shown in Figure 16 and Table 1. This means that from a microscopic perspective, which looks at the fine grain in the data, the insight appears to be "unpackable" into potentially understandable subprocesses. This leads me to describe it as "fairly sudden," rather than as an extremely sudden "bolt from the blue." This is the first sense in which the insight fails to qualify as a "pure eureka event."

In summary, there appears to be periods in the protocol in which progress is made slowly or not at all and others in which progress is quite rapid. Those periods during which little progress is made are frustrating to the subject but they, in fact, may provide necessary preparation for the later insight.

The pace of structural change is uneven rather than consistent, and progress comes intermittently. When it does come, it is in the form of a relatively sudden breakthrough that involves a significant structural change in the subjects' hypothesized model.

Does the Subject Use Extraordinary Reasoning Processes?

The second major subquestion to the main question of whether there is a pure eureka event in the protocol is whether S2 used extraordinary thought processes during his breakthrough. If the processes are found not to be extraordinary, one can go on to ask the opposite question of whether the subject's thinking is highly controlled in the sense that he always pursues a series of well-defined, conscious plans and procedures. I will conclude that the torsion–polygon insight was neither due to an unexplainable, extraordinary process, nor due solely to a planned, methodological procedure. Rather, it was the result of a dialectic process of conjecture, criticism, and rejection or modification, involving relatively uncontrolled divergent associations and playful transformations on the one hand, as well as relatively controlled strategies for mounting attacks on the problem on the other. But these are all ordinary reasoning processes. S2's association and recognition processes in particular can be viewed as divergent and creative, but these processes are neither conscious plans nor extraordinary.

Extraordinary Thinking. By extraordinary thinking, I mean the use of special processes that are outside of the set of normal reasoning processes used in everyday learning and problem solving. From a psychological point of view, this means I cannot imagine a plausible explanation for a particular thought process that is based on an ordinary sequence of inferences, associations, guesses, estimates and criticisms. Two ways extraordinary thinking could occur during a problem solution are: if the subject performs some supernormal feat of synthesis without preparation; or, more generally, if there is a break in the train of thought, a jump to a new train of thought that has no apparent connection to any previous thought. This last kind of event might be evidence for unconscious processing.

Two Types of Breaks. It is important, however, to distinguish between a break away from the subject's currently assumed model and a break in the train of thought. Clearly, S2 breaks away from his initial model of the problem. The torsion insight represents a real break (in the sense of "breakthrough") with his previous bending rod model for understanding the problem.

On the other hand, S2's work does not contain an obvious break in the train of thought. It does seem possible to construct a believable psychological account of his thought process as a series of connected conscious ideas. The growing series may actually look more like a branching tree or network than a single chain, and there may be jumps of attention from the end of one branch to the end of another, but the essential point is that a new idea does not appear from nowhere; it is always plausible that it was an outgrowth of S2's previous conscious ideas.

Two major parts of S2's insight in the solution are the generation of the square coil analogy and the discovery of torsion. A plausible explanation for the torsion discovery can be given as follows. As S2 was examining adjacent sides in the newly constructed hexagonal coil model, an existing mental schema for dealing with twisting situations was activated. Such a recognition process is a common event in everyday problem solving and should not be considered extraordinary. It does happen to be a key event in the solution to this problem. S2 was not certain about this conjectured recognition at first and needed to examine it critically, which led him to consider a square coil as an easier case.

In the case of the original square coil analogy, it was generated while S2 was thinking about whether there was a difference between a bending rod and a single spring coil:

---

23 S2: Why should the coil have anything to do with—? It's just so arbitrary. Why does it have to be a [circular coil]? Surely you could coil a spring in squares, let's say, and it . . . would still behave more or less the same.

This is a highly creative idea but not one that necessarily involves extraordinary reasoning. Here S2 appears to be imagining ways to bend a piece of wire into a spring. The plausible ordinary process is one of imagining a simple transformation one could perform with one's hands.

The worth of this idea was not recognized immediately. Only after thinking hard about and confirming the lack-of-bending anomaly in the spring does S2 return to the square coil idea in line 117 and use it productively. Here there is a branch in the train of thought, but the return to the square coil idea can be seen as connected to its earlier appearance.

In some cases, the connection to an idea in memory may be a weak one—a loose association or conjectured recognition or playful transformation rather than a deductive inference or a precise subquestion. Associations, transformations, and recognitions in this light are divergent, unpredictable, and sometimes highly creative processes, but not extraordinary ones in the sense of being unconnected to the network of current representations. I consider S2's overall achievement—the marshaling and orchestration of a large number of reasoning processes to produce the invention of a new explanatory model—to be extraordinary in the sense of being unusually productive and creative. However, I can see no evidence that the reasoning processes he uses, taken individually, are extraordinary. The train of thoughts S2 reports weaves a "coherent story" in the sense that each new idea appears connected to previous ideas and is therefore at least weakly constrained by previous ideas.

S2's ideas are also connected by the specific relationships implied in Figure 4, in which new ideas can grow out of modifications of or reactions to past ideas. This is an even more specific sense in which his insight did not emerge from out of the blue, and it will be discussed below in the section on creative processes.

It should be noted that Tweney (1985) cited evidence to discredit the idea that Faraday's discovery of induction was a "bolt from the blue," as some have thought; and Perkins (1981) came to the conclusion, after reviewing the literature on insight in creative thinking, that there is no convincing body of evidence that insights occur via special or extraordinary processes. This does not eliminate the possibility that such special processes might exist, but it does indicate that it is difficult to find convincing evidence for them.

Defining Insight

I have discussed some senses in which S2's protocol does not provide evidence for a pure eureka event. In this section, I will propose some criteria for a less extreme kind of event, which I will term a *scientific insight*. In order to sort out the different senses in which S2's solution is and is not an example of insight behavior, it will be useful to refer to the following list of the features of his polygon with torsion breakthrough that are insight-like.

1. The breakthrough is an important idea.
   (a) It is a key idea—an important component of a solution.
   (b) It overcomes a barrier that blocked progress; it comes after a frustrating series of false leads and blind alleys, after a period in which little progress has taken place; it resolves an anomaly.
2. The breakthrough adds significantly to the subject's knowledge. It produces a large structural change in the subject's model in which he
   (a) Identifies new variables or causal factors in the system
   (b) Identifies a new hypothesized mechanism in the form of an explanatory model; and
   (c) States that it increased his understanding.
3. The subject's ideas are generated fairly quickly during the breakthrough, and he achieves rapid subsequent progress toward a solution.
4. The breakthrough is accompanied by more complex phenomena.
   (a) It is accompanied by indicators of emotional response—surprise, joy, and satisfaction.
   (b) The subject realizes immediately that something important has been discovered in the torsion idea.

The following features are senses in which S2's breakthrough was *not* a pure eureka event.

1. The breakthrough idea was not generated extremely suddenly without preparation.
2. The breakthrough did not involve the total replacement of one hypothesized model with another.
3. The breakthrough is explainable via ordinary reasoning processes; there is little evidence that it was
   (a) An extraordinary thought process,
   (b) An unconscious process, or
   (c) A break with all previous trains of thought.

One can now use the criteria developed in the above list to define three categories of insight behavior. These definitions are, of course, to some extent arbitrary; the goal is to try to define some useful categories that will help to make finer distinctions that can aid in analysis. The categories (designed to refer to hypothesis development activities) are *breakthrough, scientific insight,* and *pure eureka event.* They are defined in increasing order of specificity and unusualness so that the breakthrough category includes scientific insight, and the scientific insight category includes pure eureka events.

A *breakthrough* is a process that produces a key idea—an important component of a solution—and that overcomes a barrier that can block progress toward a solution.

A *scientific insight* is a breakthrough occurring over a reasonably short period of time that leads to a significant structural improvement in one's model of a phenomenon; that is, it constitutes a shift from the subject's previous way of representing the phenomenon and leads to an increase in understanding of the phenomenon, as determined by the evaluation process in Figure 4. This is the descriptor that appears most appropriate for S2's breakthrough.

A *pure eureka event* is a scientific insight in which (1) there is an extremely fast emergence of a new idea with little evidence of preparation; (2) the new idea is a whole structure replacing the subject's previous model or understanding of a situation; (3) the process is not explainable via ordinary reasoning processes; extraordinary thought processes or unconscious thought processes are involved.

This definition recasts the earlier initial definition of a pure eureka event (an extremely sudden, reorganizing, extraordinary break from the subjects' previous ideas) in a way that relates it to other types of insight behavior. For some purposes, reducing everything to these three categories may be less important than having something like the above list of features for describing different ways in which an idea can be insightful. But the three terms may provide a useful shorthand for some purposes.

Summary

This section has attempted to answer the question, Was the polygonal coil with torsion breakthrough more like a sudden eureka event or an example of steady accretion? The case against accretion is the following: When one examines the thinking-aloud case study microscopically over tens of minutes on a small time scale, one sees an arduous dialectic process of conjecture, evaluation, and rejection or modification of hypotheses that precedes the breakthrough, as opposed to an event that takes place instantaneously and effortlessly. Thus, in terms of effort alone, there is certainly a long and steady expenditure of energy on the part of S2. However, the issue of central concern here is not the expenditure of energy but the construction of new knowledge. With respect to the formation of an explanatory model, progress did not take place as a smooth, incremental evolution of new knowledge. Progress appears to be blocked when the subject is "locked into" his current conceptualization of the problem for long and sometimes frustrating periods. Most of the approaches he tries during this period must be thrown away; they are not used later as pieces of the final model. One analogy generated by the subject then led to a fairly sudden insight, which led to the formation of a new hypothesized model. Thus, insight processes were found that are not accretionist in character and that support a view of scientists as being capable of significant reorganizations in a relatively short period of time.

On the other hand, the major case against a pure eureka event is that these processes do not appear to be supernormal or unconscious ones. It was concluded that S2's breakthrough can be considered a relatively sudden and structure-changing event that includes relatively divergent and creative processes, but that there is not evidence for extraordinary processes. The upshot of the present analysis, then, is that rather than being an example of an accretion or eureka process, the pace of progress is uneven, with "more revolutionary" and "less revolutionary" periods of work. S2's breakthrough can be characterized in the above terms as a scientific insight but not as a pure eureka event.

Creative Mental Processes

The various processes in the model construction cycle can be divided into two main categories: the productive processes of generation and modification and the evaluative processes of empirical testing and rational evaluation. In this section, I examine questions about these individual processes and how they interact. Evaluative processes will be discussed first with respect to the role of anomalies, leading to the view that a tension condition indicated in the protocol is partially analogous to the motivating tension between an anomaly and a persistent paradigm in science. In a second section, I discuss the role of transformation and invention in analogue hypothesis generation, processes that create the possibility of provoking the recognition of a new principle in a novel construction. In a final section, I discuss the role of divergence and constraint in productive processes, leading to the view that these processes are less constrained and convergent than established procedures, but more constrained and "intelligent" than a blind selection and variation process.

Anomalies and Persistence in Protocols and Paradigms

In this section, I attempt to provide a deeper level of explanation for the phenomenon of extended periods of little progress between insights in the protocol in terms of the dialectic view of model construction as a cyclical process of generation, evaluation, and modification. Table 1 outlines evidence in the protocol for the presence of such a dialectic process. One of the more subjective observations one can make of S2's overall behavior in the tape is to point to the impressive amount of strenuous activity that he poured into this process. Even for those who admit that analogies can play a role in scientific discovery, a common view is that a subject may be passively reminded of an analogous situation C, and be able to transfer a prediction from C back to the problem. The image is of the insight "coming to the subject" as a passive receiver. In the present case, S2 is much more active and aggressive: inventing tentative analogies, rejecting a number of them, pursuing those that have promise by criticizing them aggressively, and modifying them in a series of thought experiments until he is satisfied he has a valid model. A more apt informal image here than the passive receiver is a constructivist one of the subject "aggressively constructing and testing different models in an effort to capture an understanding of the phenomenon."

What drives all this strenuous activity? In particular, why does S2 persist in criticizing his understanding when he is already 90% sure that the wider spring will stretch more? What drives the hypothesis formulation process and keeps it working in the face of little progress? Why is there a period of very little progress followed by a period of insight in this protocol? For the last question, one could simply say that there are a large number of possible paths to consider and that it is just a matter of luck that determines when one will find a successful path. But there may be a deeper reason connected in at least one way with Kuhn's (1962) idea of intermittent progress in science (periods of normal science and revolution.) In this section, I attempt to speak to these questions in terms of conflict between a persistent model and a perceived anomaly.

Dialectic Tension.   There is a palpable tension obvious in the first section of the videotape that is conveyed only to a limited extent by the transcript: a frustration with not being able to resolve the anomaly of the lack of bending in a helical spring. For example in lines 87 and 111, S2 says:

---

87   S2:   . . . if you start with a [stretched] helix and unwind it . . . you should get a bow [bend], but you don't. I mean visually imagining it, you don't. I don't see how you could make the bow go away—just to wind it up—Damn it!

111 S2:   Darn it, darn it, darn it . . . why should that [the difference between a rod and a coil] matter?

The tension apparently occurs between the rod model and the lack-of-bending anomaly. This tension or disequilibrium condition appears to provide a driving force that keeps S2 actively attacking the problem even though he claims he is already 90% sure of his answer. It bothers him enough to drive him to search for a way to modify the rod model or replace it. This search takes up the better part of the 52-minute interview, and it is peppered with expressions of frustration. Line 178 provides evidence that the reason for his dissatisfaction has to do with an important difference between having a confident prediction and having a feeling of understanding. He speaks of having low confidence in his understanding because the rod model predicts a property that he feels should not occur in real springs, even though he has high confidence in his predicted answer. I take this as an interesting example of a situation in which good performance is not equivalent to deep understanding, and, because of the subsequent events that raise his confidence, I take the important difference to be the lack of a satisfying explanatory model.

Persistence of the Initial Model.   Line 87 of the transcript is indicative of the fact that S2 finds it very difficult to give up the bending rod model. The persistence of this model appears to be an example of an Einstellung effect; a problem space dominates his thinking and prevents him from generating necessary new ideas. In order to make progress, S2 must redescribe the problem using new descriptors; he needs a new problem representation. But the rod model keeps reappearing in the transcript. Even though he proposes rejecting the model several times, he is repeatedly tempted to return to it. It is as if the idea has an autonomous "life of its own."

A Powerful Anomaly. Pitted against this persistent model is a powerful anomaly. Bending in the vertical plane is central to the rod model, but S2 cannot imagine a way for bending to take place in a helical spring. (Here I am using the term *anomaly* in the broad sense of a new finding that conflicts with previous ideas, whereas in some narrower usages, its referent is limited to a new nonconforming observation.) In summary, the symptoms of tension observed in the subject appear to be the result of a conflict between a persistent initial model and a powerful anomaly.

Analogy to the Persistence of a Paradigm. When the polygonal coil with torsion model is found, it appears to finally break the tension. There may be a partial analogy here to Kuhn's (1962) idea of the persistence of a paradigm in science. Even when anomalies are known to exist, it is difficult to reject a paradigm until something better is found to replace it. But this is very difficult to do because it requires breaking out of the current, stable point of view. Here the bending rod model is hard to reject until the better model is found, and this requires a great deal of imaginative effort. Compared to a problem on the frontier of science, the scale here is, of course, very much smaller and easier. For example, there are no social forces to reinforce the stability of the subject's initial model. Nevertheless, this tension between a persistent initial model and a recognized anomaly, which helps to explain the long period of slow progress followed by a period of scientific insight in the protocol, is reminiscent of Kuhn's descriptions.

Tension from an Anomaly as a Source of Motivation. The tension associated with S2's dissatisfaction with his understanding apparently drives him to keep reattacking the problem repeatedly until he makes a breakthrough. In the present situation, the generation of a new or sharply modified model is required in order to break the deadlock; and it is in such cases that analogies should prove to be particularly useful, because they help the subject break away from his current model. When they are successful, they apparently can lead to fairly large and rapid changes in a mental model. S2 considers no less than 12 analogous cases during the protocol, including some that do not appear in the transcript excerpts given here, and this high degree of gener-

ative activity can be seen largely as a response to the tension urging him to find a more satisfying model. Thus, this example suggests that the tension between a previously established model and a prominent anomaly can be a major driving force behind hypothesis generation.

Here it appears to require something as divergent as analogy generation to break out of the Einstellung effect that is formed by a persistent inadequate model. This provides an important connection between the two previous major sections of this chapter on model construction via analogy and the presence of insight in S2's protocol. The process of analogy generation, motivated by the recognition of an anomaly, appears at times to be powerful enough to break away from a persistent but inadequate model or view. This is one way in which a scientific insight can occur. Thus, the phenomenon of intermittent progress that involves periods of little progress punctuated by occasional insights can be seen as a natural outcome of psychological processes.

Transformations, Invention, and Memory Provocation

Transformations as a Source of Creativity. In this section, I move to a discussion of hypothesis generation processes and of analogy generation via transformations in particular. It should be noted that association apparently is not the only source of creative or divergent ideas in this protocol. For example, after considering the bending rod case, S2 says in line 23, "Surely you could coil a spring in squares, let's say, and it . . . would still. . . ." Here he seems to be constructing a new case by transforming the rod into a square coil rather than making an association to an existing idea in memory. Also, in line 37 the double-length spring analogy originates from the transformation of sliding a weight along a wire. A transformation occurs when S2 alters features previously assumed to be fixed in an existing problem representation to create a new representation. In a previous study, it was found that of the analogies generated by 10 subjects in solving the spring problem, more were generated via a transformation than were generated via an association (Clement, 1988). In that study, the term *transformation* was used to refer to a general type of cognitive operation in the form of the alteration of a representation for any situation in working memory, including an original target situation. Thus, the modification process referred to in Figure 4 is a transformation applied to the previously hypothesized scientific model. Although association often is cited as a primary source of creativity, it may be that transformations are just as important, if not more important, in scientific problem solving.

Invention of Analogous Cases.   The novelty of the zigzag and polygonal springs supports the claim that these are invented cases. For example, the square coil was apparently constructed via a transformation, not recalled from memory. Although analogous cases typically are thought of as schemata already in long-term memory that are *activated or retrieved* during problem solving, it can also happen that the analogous case is *invented* along with the analogy relation. Models generated by inventing an analogous case are in this sense even more creative than those generated by being reminded of an analogous case.

The polygonal coil is a new problem representation amenable to a new method of analysis (torsion). In such an instance, the knowledge that one gains from an analogous case C need not be "stored in" C. Thinking about C may activate a useful schema (such as torsion) that has not previously been applied either to the original situation to be explained or to C. This instance provides some support for Black's view that the interaction between the original and analogous cases can produce knowledge in the form of an insight that was not residing beforehand in either the original or the analogous cases: "It would be more illuminating in some of these cases to say that the metaphor creates the similarity than to say that it formulates some similarity antecedently existing" (Black, 1979, p. 37). In the present case study, in contrast to the usual view of analogy generation, the recognition of the key relationship (torsion) in the analogous case occurs *well after* the generation of the analogy. The analogy plays a provocative role in activating a principle whose applicability was previously unrecognized, rather than a "direct source of transferred information" role. This issue is discussed further in Clement (1988b).

Thus, some analogies are invented rather than recalled, and some play a "provocative" role in accessing new information rather than a "direct transfer" role.

Constrained Successive Refinement versus Blind Variation

In this section, I turn to hypothesis generation and modification processes as sources of creativity within the model construction cycle. I want to begin to examine the extent to which these processes are random or constrained. In fact, much of the protocol preceding the torsion insight can be viewed as divergent exploration to find clues for a new direction for analysis. Some relatively unconstrained divergent processes that occur in the protocol are associations, transformations of the problem space, the activation of analogous cases in memory, and the invention of new analogous cases. These processes can lead to multiple suggestions with no guarantee of success or even relevance. They are much less constrained and systematic than an established, convergent procedure for solving a problem. This leads to the following question: Are S2's processes so divergent as to constitute a random trial and error process?

Certainly, S2's divergent thinking seems to be less systematic or formal than either logical deduction or methodical procedures of induction. And yet this less formal method of conjecture, criticism, and modification allows him to make impressive progress in his understanding. In this process, it does not matter so much if one makes a faulty conjecture; it may still be possible to transform it into a successful conjecture by carrying out a series of criticisms and modifications. In this section, I discuss the sense in which this successive refinement process goes beyond a random trial-and-error strategy.

In its weakest form, the cycle in Figure 4 can be described as a *random trial-and-error* process. By this I mean that the old hypothesis is discarded and a totally new random hypothesis is tried on each cycle, without any learning or attempts at modification between cycles. A less divergent strategy would be to modify randomly part of the previous hypothesis and keep the remainder in each cycle. This is analogous to a *random variation* theory of evolution. (See Campbell, 1960, for an exposition of this analogy.) However, there is evidence that the generation and modification processes are not random ones in the case of S2, and that they are more powerful than the above two processes.

The first type of evidence is the general observation of spontaneous analogy generation as a hypothesis generation strategy. Analogous cases are generated by association or transformation processes which means that they are connected in some way to the target. The connection may not be a strong one, but this is better than no connection at all.

The second type of evidence indicates that, at times, a conscious constraint is held in mind when generating a new association or transformation. For example in line 57, S2 appears to focus on the idea of stretching as a constraint as he generates several tentative analogies by association after asking himself, "What else stretches"? In a second example in line 117, he generates polygonal coils while attempting to "generate ideas about circularity. . . . Why should it matter? How would it change the way the force is transmitted" in the spring? The use of conscious constraints during generation is one sense in which the model construction cycle can go beyond a random variation and selection process.

A further type of evidence is the observation of an intelligent modification process in the cycle. Most of the analogies generated by S2 were rejected in the end. But several did clearly serve as stepping stones by preparing the way for suggesting better ideas later on. This gives the cycle the property of successive refinement, in which one can learn from the mistakes of the past. For example, the first zigzag spring in line 23 is criticized as a model because of the contaminating effect of bending at the joints. This is then modified into a second zigzag model with stiff joints, which is aimed at removing the criticism. As a second example, the bending rod model is criticized because of an assumed lack of cumulative bending in the spring. The introduction of the square coil model solved this problem by eliminating the cumulative bending effect. In these instances, the subject seems to generate or search for modifications that remove particular difficulties that the evaluation process has identified in an existing model. Thus, the cycle involves intelligent modification based on information about prior difficulties. This is a particularly powerful way in which generation and modification processes can be constrained. (See Darden, 1983, Rada, 1985, and Darden and Rada, 1988, for further discussion of nonblind hypothesis generation, including the use of interrelations between scientific fields as a heuristic. Also, Holland *et al.,* 1986, discuss goal-weighted summation of activation as a possible mechanism for guiding retrieval of relevant information, and Lenat, 1977, 1983, discusses heuristics for learning by discovery in mathematics. From a broader perspective, in case studies of Faraday's and Darwin's thought, respectively, Tweney (in press) and Gruber (1974) have proposed that breakthroughs which appear to result from a fortunate "chance interaction" of several ideas were in fact significantly favored by a network of prior activities in the scientist's life.)

Finally, it should be noted that comparison and selection between previously generated models can also occur. For example, S2 settles on using the square coil as a model over the hexagonal coil, apparently because the square is simpler to analyze. This is a classic use of rational assessment criterion.

Less Constrained Methods. Not all generation methods are highly systematic or constrained. The generation of the double-length spring analogy in line 37 provides an interesting example. Here the analogy originates from the idea of sliding a weight along a rod. S2 then imagines this transformation happening on the spring itself, as if it were simply an "interesting thing to try." There is some evidence here that he is exploring new and uncertain directions rather than trying to achieve a specific goal using a conscious strategy of generation under constraints. Although the analogy in this case does not lead to a breakthrough, one cannot rule out the possibility that the ability to think playfully in a relatively unconstrained manner would, at times, be a powerful method.

Summary. Thus, I arrive at an intermediate position concerning the nature of the subject's hypothesis generation and modification processes. Compared to a pure eureka event, they form a more ordinary and connected train of thoughts. Compared to a problem-solving process governed by established procedures, they are divergent processes that are relatively unconstrained. They can produce novel inventions like the polygonal coil as well as a presumably infinite variety of other representations. As they occur here within the model construction process however, they often appear as part of an intelligent successive refinement process rather than a blind variation and selection process.

Darwin's Theory of Natural Selection

Having reviewed some philosophical views of hypothesis formation processes in science and having presented some current findings from expert protocols, I will consider briefly a third approach to the study of creativity in science: the analysis of notebooks and other historical documents produced by innovative scientists. I return to the example of Darwin's theory of natural selection mentioned at the beginning of this chapter. Gould (1980) noted that earlier writers had described the origin of this discovery as the net result of a gradual buildup of information—a process of accretion that occurred during Darwin's voyage on the *Beagle,* principally in South America. However, Gruber (1974) debunked this view by pointing to evidence in Darwin's notebooks indicating that after the *Beagle*'s voyage, he, like a number of other naturalists, believed in the existence of evolution (gradual change in species) but still had no model to explain it. He lacked the theory of natural selection. It was only after a year and a half of conceptual struggle after his return to England that Darwin was able to formulate a satisfactory theory. A particularly famous piece of evidence arguing against the accretion view is the important role of an analogy that occurred to Darwin when he read Malthus. In his autobiography (written much later) he wrote:

I happened to read for amusement Malthus on population, and being well prepared to appreciate the struggle for existence which everywhere goes on from long-continued observation of animals and plants, it at once struck me that under these circumstances favorable variations would tend to be preserved, and unfavorable ones to be destroyed. (Darwin 1892/1958, pp. 42–43)

Darwin saw that factors similar to those that limited human population growth (such as a limited food supply) might be the source of a selection factor in a survival of the fittest model for animals. Thus, the accretion by induction view is hard to maintain in Darwin's case.

Does the Malthus episode then provide evidence for a eurekaist view of Darwin's achievement? The recent analyses of Darwin's private notebooks carried out by Gruber (1974) and Schweber (1977) argue against this conclusion as well. They show that Darwin struggled long and hard, considering several hypotheses and gradually modifying and fitting a number of pieces together into the theory of natural selection. The notebooks indicate the analogy from Malthus was only one event in a complicated process of generation, evaluation, and modification.

Darwin read widely in fields outside of biology and apparently drew analogies from these fields in constructing his theory, including the ideas of variation and selection (from breeding in domestic husbandry) and the idea of natural competition (from Malthus) (Darden, 1983). Gould believed Darwin also was influenced by the laissez-faire economics of Adam Smith, which showed that an ordered and efficient economy could emerge from free competition. An analogy can be made to evolution here via the common idea of positive group change coming out of individual struggle. In addition, Gruber (1974) cited Darwin's early geological theories on the growth of the Pacific barrier reefs over tens of thousands of years as fertile preparation for the idea

that small individual forces acting over long periods of time could effect vast changes in nature.

Thus, historical evidence in Darwin's case now supports a more complex view that either inductivism or eurekaism. Both the fertile empirical ground of careful observations and the nonempirical insights formed by key analogies to other fields were apparently crucial in Darwin's case. This analysis suggests that a more realistic hallmark of genius than pure eureka episodes is the ability to generate a variety of tentative analogue models as a starting point and then to carry out the long struggle of repeated conjectures, criticisms, rejections, and modifications necessary to produce a successful new theory. Although the time scale is much longer in Darwin's case, it is interesting that these are the same distinguishing criteria that emerge from the cases of model construction in the protocols discussed earlier. This suggests that perhaps the most viable powerful form of scientific reasoning lies not in the ability to ''hit'' on a perfect model at the outset, but in the ability to engage in such a dialectic, successive refinement cycle.

Features of Creative Thinking and Implications for Future Research

Creative Thinking

To the extent that an extended analysis can remove the initial subjective impressiveness of an event, perhaps I am in danger here of seeming to trivialize the processes of analogy generation, model construction, and insight as hypothesis development activities, and I would therefore like to avoid giving that impression. Clearly, once one has thought through the answer to a problem, the solution process can appear to be less impressive or even obvious from hindsight. While one is actually solving a problem, however, creative reasoning, such as that exhibited by S2, is impressive in a number of ways.

1. First of all, there is the insight in the protocol that seems to lead to a ''flood'' of ideas. The speed of progress during this episode is impressive.

2. S2's central achievement is the generation of a new structural hypothesis—the invention of a new model of hidden mechanisms in the spring that he has never observed. This involves the identification of new causal variables in the system (such as torsion) and new causal chains, as well as the identifi-

cation of a new global effect (lack of cumulative bending).

3. An important factor in producing this achievement is the subject's desire to ask ''why'' questions and to seek a deep level of understanding beyond what is required for the solution of the immediate problem. Presumably, this urge to penetrate surface features and to conceptualize an underlying explanatory model at the core of a phenomenon is a basic motive underlying creative theory formation in science.

4. S2 exhibits a remarkable persistence in this quest in the face of recognized internal inconsistencies and repeated failures. There is something of an existential twist here: although the problem has no practical significance for him, he puts enormous energy into the problem of understanding as a challenge for its own sake.

5. S2's playful and uninhibited inventiveness in producing conjectures and modifications of the problem is impressive. The analogous cases he generated in searching for a better way to represent the problem included the bending rod, polyester molecules, leaf springs, watch springs, two types of zigzag springs, two or more types of polygonal springs, and double-length springs. He displays an ability to think divergently and the flexibility to modify thought forms in novel ways. This kind of flexibility is commonly recognized as a prominent characteristic of creative physicists and inventors.

6. There is a willingness in S2 to criticize vigorously and attack the validity of his own conjectures. He is able to engage in a dialectic conversation with himself, proposing new ideas on the one hand and criticizing them on the other. This seems to require viewing the failure of any single idea as not very important; although, as has been shown, the apparent failure of seven or eight ideas to produce a breakthrough does lead to some degree of frustration for S2.

7. With respect to Figure 4, one can contrast the productive function of the generation and modification processes with the evaluative function of the rational and empirical testing processes. The divergent and creative generation processes (such as the use of analogies) represent a significant departure from the more systematic, rule-governed processes of theory growth that are envisioned by inductionists, who would tend to see them as much too unrestrained to be part of the disciplined scientific enterprise. However, the generation processes are not entirely unconstrained, as has been discussed, and the evaluative processes in Figure 4 provide

some strong restraints that can, in fact, act to control the enterprise of model construction. Thus, alternating between generative and evaluative modes in scientific thinking is seen as a powerful method, even when the generative methods are divergent in character and new empirical tests cannot be performed.

8. Perhaps S2's awareness of his own ability to criticize ideas, and the resulting faith in himself as a self-correcting system, allows him a freer hand— allows him to be more uninhibited in generating conjectures and in considering directions to pursue. It may be that generative ability and critical ability are mutually supporting. Critical ability gives one the freedom to be unusually associative or inventive. Generative inventiveness, or the ability to replace and repair what one removes, gives one the confidence or assurance to be critical of and to tear down, at times, existing ideas. S2 seems willing to consider ''risky'' analogies, such as the double-length spring and the bending rod, that appear to be very different from the original problem. However, it has been shown that, even when a risky initial analogy does not turn out to be explanatory, modifications of it may lead to an explanatory model. Realization of this potential for debugging or redesigning via criticism and modification may allow one to feel freer to explore more imaginative models or a wider range of models. This freedom, in turn, would appear to be an important tool in the difficult job of breaking out of previous conceptions of the target situation. Again, rather than the ability to hit on the best possible idea in one stroke, it may be that it is the ability to engage in a cycle of hypothesis construction and improvement that is the most powerful form of scientific thinking.

These eight qualities are some of the most impressive characteristics of creative thinking visible in the case study.

Implications for Future Research

The conclusions reached here suggest that creative hypothesis formation processes are still poorly understood but are not outside the realm of possible study. Mansfield and Brusse (1981) gave examples of five aspects of the creative process in science: (1) problem selection; (2) extended effort; (3) setting theoretical, empirical, and methodological constraints; (4) changing constraints; and (5) verification and elaboration, including a process of formulating new constraints and testing them. Two areas that the present case study does not address are problem formulation and empirical and methodological constraints.[9] These are important problems for future research.

There are also other areas in which observations were made in the case study that the present analysis has said very little about. The first is the overall complexity in the details of S2's thought processes, including the presence of multiple goals, returns to previously attempted solution paths, the balancing of divergent and convergent processes, and the resolution of competing influences. In addition, each of the subprocesses shown in Figure 4 is in need of much more detailed study. Second, S2 can exhibit an "aha" reaction that something important has been discovered, even before its implications have been developed and articulated. For example, the aha episode upon considering the square coil in line 117 is of this form. Third, subjective observations from the videotape that are hard to capture in print are the exuberance present in his aha episodes and the tone of frustration present during his periods of failure. This adds an emotional dimension to the process that is distinctly human. Fourth, I have only touched on the problem of how "guided" conjecture is guided—why one person's initial conjectures are much more fruitful in the long run than those of others. Fifth, S2's strong drive to ask "why" questions mentioned earlier (a kind of curiosity) certainly has not been explained. Sixth, very little has been said about rational evaluation. Of particular importance is the problem of how one evaluates the validity or appropriateness of a proposed analogy. Matching "important" features is one method, as has been illustrated, but there may be others as well (Clement, 1986). Finally, S2's flexibility in inventing new problem representations is hard to model. His image of the spring appears to be *malleable;* he appears able to modify it into an infinite number of forms and variations. In fact, there are a number of spontaneous imagery reports in the protocol that suggest that certain forms of spatial reasoning on spatial representations may be central to S2's thinking here. Although the discussion of these reports is beyond the scope of this study, it opens up a large and important question for future research on the nature of these processes and the role they play in scientific thinking (Clement, in press a,b).

[9]Getzels and Csikszentmihalyi (1976) have described processes of problem finding in art. Lenat (1983) described an attempt to develop a simulation model for the process of selecting "interesting" problems (theorems for analysis) in mathematics.

The above phenomena are not well understood and indicate that we are far from formulating adequate explanations for many aspects of creative processes. They still inspire awe, pointing to areas in which the science of psychology remains quite weak and in which further research is needed.

Educational Implications

Learning via model construction is an area of utmost importance to mathematics and science education, an area that is very poorly understood. The present study is essentially a study of learning via model construction in scientists. Thus, the study will have interesting educational implications if it can tell us more about processes that need to be fostered when students are learning scientific models.

Essentially, I will propose that the model construction cycle in Figure 4 may be useful as a description of processes that need to take place in students who are learning to comprehend scientific models. Because of space limitations, I can only present a brief sketch of this idea here. The cycle is relevant to three major educational goals: the content goal of comprehending established scientific models; the process goal of learning to solve ill-structured problems; and the even more ambitious process goal of learning scientific method or scientific inquiry skills. By attending to these different content and process goals, educators may be able to design instructional activities more effectively.

Content Goals: Comprehending Scientific Models

With respect to the first goal of comprehending established scientific models, several points can be made. First, as has been discussed, many modern scholars have argued that explanatory models are an essential part of scientific understanding. As shown in Figure 3, explanatory models are a separate type of knowledge from either empirical laws or formal quantitative principles. Easley (1978) and others have noted the unfortunate tendency of educators to associate "real" scientific thinking with only the latter two types of knowledge.

A second point is that students learn complex models via an internal construction process, not via a direct transmission process during lecture. I cannot support this assumption fully here, but current research in science education is providing an increasing amount of evidence in this direction. The complex, tacit, nonobservable, and sometimes counterintuitive nature of scientific models means that misconceptions or ''bugs'' will be the rule rather than the exception during instruction, requiring critical feedback and correction processes. This means that the learning of complex, unfamiliar, or counterintuitive models in science requires a kind of learning by doing and by construction and criticism rather than by listening alone.

In this light, Figure 4 is seen as a potential model for the learning of scientific concepts by construction in the classroom. Educators inspired by Jean Piaget and others have advocated approaches that are based on the processes of disequilibration, accommodation, and the construction of knowledge. Unfortunately, the application of these concepts to instructional design suffers from a lack of precision and consistency. The present approach may lead to a more explicit model of the process of learning scientific models. The findings from this study lend support to an educational strategy in which, rather than ''swallowing packaged ideas as a whole'' in lecture, students are seen as developing partial models, questioning them in face of anomalies, and working from their initial model to construct a more adequate model. The term *knowledge construction* has been much used in discussions of education. Perhaps the concepts of using prior knowledge (e.g., analogies), modifying models, and the successive refinement cycle can provide a more explicit picture of construction processes.

A third point is that explanatory model construction takes place in the scientist via a set of processes that are different from those used either in formal deductive proof, in the manipulation of quantitative expressions, or in inductions from data. The present study speaks perhaps most strongly to this last point. It underscores the importance of processes that aid abduction, such as using analogue models for developing understanding; fostering disequilibrium in order to motivate efforts toward model construction; and fostering criticism and modification (or rejection) processes for overcoming difficulties occurring in students' models that contain misconceptions. Very valuable nonempirical criticism and modification processes can take place when students attempt to give explanations and argue about them in large or small group discussions (Clement *et al.*, 1987). This simple implication is probably greatly underemphasized in instruction. Educators need to distinguish between activities that are aimed at forming explanatory models and those that are aimed at forming empirical law hypotheses or formal quantitative principles, because the cognitive processes involved may be quite different. If this is correct, students are unlikely to learn explanatory models from laboratories that are aimed at inductive reasoning; nor are they likely to learn them from the study of formal quantitative principles.

Problem Solving and Inquiry Skills

Figure 4 can also be thought of as a model of the process of constructing a representation for an ill-structured problem. (Here memories of prior experiences can play a role in empirical testing if no new empirical information is available.) In the case of content goals as discussed above, considerable support might be given by the teacher in guiding students through such a cycle. However, in order to learn problem-solving skills, students eventually need to be able to generate problem representations by going through construction cycles without teacher support. Despite this difference, Figure 4 provides the basis for seeing some significant overlapping in the strategies for achieving content and process (problem solving and inquiry) goals in science education.

Finally, the most ambitious goal in science education is that of teaching scientific investigation or inquiry skills. In fact, it is extremely rare to find a class in which students are asked to propose and test scientific hypotheses for phenomena. Here again, it seems important not to assume that ''discovery learning'' by induction from data is the predominant process in the scientific method. Model criticism and modification processes would seem to be of crucial importance in the design of inquiry activities.

Thus, the most general point to be made is that the cycle outlined in Figure 4 may prove useful as an outline of relevant learning processes for guiding educators in designing and evaluating instructional activities that are concerned with the learning of scientific models. Here I have only been able to sketch some possible implications along these lines; further educational research and development efforts are very much needed.

Summary

This chapter began by posing questions concerning the origins of hypotheses in science and the role of insight or eureka events in creative scientific thinking. I have attempted to show that protocol evidence can be used to argue against an overly inductionist view of the source of hypotheses. It can also be used to argue against either a pure accretionist or a pure eurekaist view of the pace of change in scientific hypothesis formation. Instead, it has led me to take a less simplistic view of hypothesis development as illustrated in Figure 4, emphasizing the possibility of both empirical and nonempirical sources of hypotheses and multiple passes through a cycle of generation, evaluation, and modification (or rejection). In this cycle, hypothesis evaluation can also originate from empirical and nonempirical sources. In such a system, powerful scientific insights can occur when a new model is developed that leads to a "flood" of new ideas. But this can happen without necessarily involving the extraordinary or unconscious reasoning processes that are associated with the term *eureka event*. The present data support the view that the methods that are used by scientists are varied and complex, and that the hypothetico-deductive method, rational evaluation, abduction, analogy, and induction may all play important roles at different times in scientific thought.

Recent work in the philosophy of science was drawn on to make several useful distinctions. The term *scientific model* was used to refer to a predictive analogy. The term *explanatory model* was used to distinguish those scientific models that are intended to represent nonobvious entities that are present in the situation to be explained. The latter term allows one to distinguish between two types of scientific hypothesis: a hypothesis in the form of a predictive, explanatory model that introduces new entities that have not previously been (and may never be) observed directly, and an empirical law hypothesis that summarizes patterns in observations.

These distinctions helped to describe creative processes in the case study of subject S2, who was working on the problem of whether a wide spring stretches more than a narrow spring. S2's central achievement was the generation of an explanatory model—the invention of a new model of hidden mechanisms in the spring that he had not observed. This involved the identification of new causal variables in the system (such as torsion) and new causal chains, as well as the identification and explanation of a global effect (lack of cumulative bending).

The conclusions of the study are organized below into five categories: sources of hypotheses, the role of spontaneous analogies, the eureka versus accre-tion question, creative mental processes, and educational implications.

Sources of Hypotheses

1. A new scientific hypothesis in the form of an explanatory model can be developed via noninductive means in the absence of new empirical information. This lends support to the importance of a noninductive component in the hypothesis generation process.

2. The model construction process proposed was one of successive refinement, involving repeated cycles of generation, evaluation, and modification or rejection. Table 1 summarized evidence from the protocol that S2's progress is a result of this kind of cyclical refinement process rather than a result of either a convergent series of deductions or inductions from observations.

3. Such a cycle can be more powerful than a blind trial and error or a blind variation and evolution process. For example, when difficulties have been identified in an existing model, subsequent generation and modification processes can serve to remove the difficulties.

4. Hypothesis evaluation processes appear to be an *inherent part* of hypothesis formation down to resolution intervals of a single minute on occasion. The history of science tends to look at developments over years or weeks. From this perspective, the case study observation of very small cycle times for the non-empirical criticism and modification loop in Figure 4 (as small as 90 seconds here) makes it very difficult to separate the "context of discovery" from the "context of justification" in the early stages of hypothesis formation. In such cases it is possible to have a rapid, dialectic interplay between generation and evaluation processes.

5. The development of a convincing explanatory model hypothesis can also lead to the formation of an empirical law hypothesis in the absence of new empirical information: in this case, the final model of the polygonal coil with torsion supports the empirical law hypothesis that (other factors being equal) wide springs will stretch more than narrow springs.

Spontaneous Analogies

1. Subjects were observed to generate and use spontaneous analogies as predictive models.

2. Many of the observed analogies apparently

were generated via a transformation of another situation. Although association is often cited as a primary source of creativity, it may be that transformations are just as important, if not more important.

3. In a successful model construction cycle, an initial analogy with low-explanatory status can be developed and modified to become an explanatory model that proposes the presence of a hidden structure operating in the target situation.

4. This means that analogy can play a role in the generation of new hypotheses in at least the following two different ways: (a) an analogous case can serve as a rough initial model of the target situation that is then developed and refined; (b) a developed model, whatever its origin, is linked by an analogy relation to the target situation because it posits that elements and relations in the model are like elements and relations in the target. This appears to contribute to a feeling of understanding when elements in the model are familiar.

5. Rather than always being stored as cases that are activated in memory, some analogies (e.g., revised mental models) are novel, invented cases.

6. In some instances, the knowledge that one gains from an analogy does not come directly from the analogous case. The analogy can play a provocative role by triggering the application of a principle that has never before been applied to either the target or analogous cases. In these instances, the most important relationships in the analogous case is recognized *after* the generation of the analogous case.

The Eureka versus Accretion or Pace of Conceptual Change Question

1. Three possible levels of insight were defined: a breakthrough, which overcomes a barrier that has blocked progress; a scientific insight, which is a relatively sudden breakthrough leading to a significant improvement in a model; and a pure eureka event, which is an insight that is not explainable via ordinary reasoning processes.

2. Aha episodes were observed in association with a scientific insight involving the formation of a new explanatory model. Such an insight can be quite powerful and impressive and can lead to a rapid improvement in conceptual understanding. However, although insights can involve creative thinking, (a) they can involve preparation and confirmation efforts, and (b) they do not necessarily involve unconscious or other extraordinary thought processes that are outside the domain of normal reasoning operations; they do not involve a sudden break in the train of thought that would indicate a pure eureka event. The train of thoughts that S2 reports weaves a ''coherent story'' in the sense that each new idea is connected to previous ideas and is therefore at least weakly constrained by previous ideas. That he appeared to use the processes in Figure 4, in which new ideas can grow out of modifications of or reactions to past ideas, is an even more specific sense in which his insight did not just emerge from out of the blue. This does not prove that important unconscious or nonordinary processes cannot occur—Poincairé's famous insight upon entering a bus may have been one example—but it does indicate that important insights can be generated when there is no evidence for such processing.

3. S2's insight occurred after a long struggle resulting from the conflict between a first-order model and a recognized anomaly. The conflict or disequilibrium condition between a persistent model and an anomaly appears to provide a motivating force for a more intense level of activity for hypothesis development that is not dependent on other external motives. The persistence of the subject's initial model and the tension between it and the perceived anomaly may be partially analogous to the persistence of a paradigm in the face of anomalies in science. An important function of the strategy of searching for analogous cases is that it may help the subject to break away from such a stable persistent model. This helps to explain the presence of intermittent periods of negligible progress and rapid change or insight as a natural outcome of psychological processes.

Creative Mental Processes

1. A subject can use relatively unconstrained, divergent, hypothesis generation processes that can lead to insights, including analogy, association, transformation, and invention processes.

2. Divergent and creative processes represent a significant departure from the more systematic processes of hypotheses generation envisioned by inductionists, who would tend to see the former as much too unrestrained to be part of the scientific enterprise. However, the evaluation processes in Figure 4 can provide some strong restraints. Thus, alternating between generative and evaluative modes in scientific thinking is seen as a powerful method, even when the generative methods are di-

vergent in character and new empirical tests cannot be performed.

3. Divergent processes are relatively unconstrained compared to other processes, but there is evidence that generation and modification processes can be guided by some constraints. This makes the model construction cycle more powerful than a blind selection and variation process.

4. Recent analyses of Darwin's notebooks have suggested that a more indicative hallmark of genius than pure eureka episodes is the ability to generate tentative analogue models as a starting point and then to carry out the long struggle of a cycle of repeated generation, criticism, and modification or rejection that is necessary to construct a successful new theory. In fact, these are the same prominent features that emerged from an analysis of model construction in the thinking-aloud case study. It was conjectured that the most viable powerful form of scientific reasoning may lie in the ability to engage in such a dialectic cycle, rather than in the ability to invent a completed model in one stroke.

5. Thus, the examples discussed here motivate a conception of advanced scientific thinking that includes nondeductive, noninductive, and divergent processes. These processes can play an important role in producing predictive, explanatory models that are novel inventions.

Educational Implications

1. The findings mentioned thus far suggest an educational strategy in which, rather than "swallowing packaged ideas as a whole" in lecture, students are helped to develop partial models, to criticize them, and to work from their initial model to construct a more adequate model.

2. The findings also underscore the importance of: using analogue models for developing understanding; fostering disequilibrium in order to motivate efforts toward model construction; and criticism and modification (or rejection) processes for overcoming difficulties occurring in students' models that contain misconceptions.

3. Explanatory models are an essential part of scientific understanding that is a separate type of knowledge from either empirical laws or formal quantitative principles. Educators need to distinguish between activities that are aimed at forming empirical laws or quantitative principles and those that are aimed at forming explanatory models, because the cognitive processes that are involved may be quite different. For example, students are unlikely to learn explanatory models from laboratories that are aimed at inductive reasoning, or from lectures on formal quantitative principles.

4. The learning process outlined in Figure 4 attempts to give an explicit cognitive meaning for the term *knowledge construction*. As such, it may prove useful as a model of relevant learning processes for guiding curriculum planners and practitioners in designing and evaluating instructional activities in science education.

In conclusion, it appears to be possible to develop models of creative hypothesis formation processes that are tied to empirical information from thinking-aloud protocols. Many aspects of creative reasoning processes remain poorly understood: "guided" conjecture, anticipation in the aha phenomenon, the apparent malleability of the spatial imagination, emotional factors, question asking, and sources of curiosity, to name just a few. They still inspire awe. Nevertheless, creativity is a more accessible object of study than some would claim; it is not always an "instantaneous crystallization transmitted from the unconscious." Current techniques make the process of studying creativity a productive and exciting one: by using protocol analysis and other methods, significant progress can be made in increasing our understanding of it. Exactly how much we will be able to understand and explain in this complex domain—how far our model construction cycles will take us—remains to be seen.

ACKNOWLEDGMENTS. I would like to thank Ryan Tweney, David Perkins, Ernst von Glasersfeld, John Lochhead, and David Brown for their very helpful comments, and, in particular, Lindley Darden for her many insightful criticisms and suggestions.

References

Achinstein, P. (1970). Inference to scientific laws. In R. Stuewer (Ed.), *Minnesota studies in philosophy of science, vol. 5: Historical and philosophical perspectives of science* (pp. 87–104). Minneapolis: University of Minnesota Press.

Ackerman, R. (1965). *Theories of knowledge: A critical introduction.* New York: McGraw Hill.

Black, M. (1979). *More about metaphor.* In A. Ortony (Ed.), *Metaphor and thought* (p. 19–45). Cambridge, England: Cambridge University Press.

Campbell, D. (1960). Blind variation and selective retention in creative thought as in other knowledge processes. *Psychological Review, 67*(6), 380–400.

Campbell, N. (1920). *Physics: The elements.* Cambridge: Cambridge University Press. (Republished in 1957 as *The foundations of science.* New York: Dover.)

Clement, J. (1981). Analogy generation in scientific problem solving. *Proceedings of the Third Annual Meeting of the Cognitive Science Society, 3,* 137–140.

Clement, J. (1982). Analogical reasoning patterns in expert problem solving. *Proceedings of the Fourth Annual Meeting of the Cognitive Science Society, 4,* 79–81.

Clement, J. (1986). Methods for evaluating the validity of hypothesized analogies. *Proceedings of the Eighth Annual Meeting of the Cognitive Science Society, 8,* 223–234.

Clement, J. (1988). Observed methods for generating analogies in scientific problem solving. *Cognitive Science, 12,* 563–586.

Clement, J. (in press a). Nonformal reasoning in experts and in science students: The use of analogies, extreme cases, and physical intuition. In J. Voss, D. Perkins, & J. Siegel, *Informal reasoning and education.* Hillsdale, NJ: Erlbaum.

Clement, J. (in press b). Use of physical intuition in expert problem solving. In D. Tirosch & S. Straus (Eds.), *Implict and explicit knowledge, an educational approach.* Norwood, NJ: Ablex Publishers.

Clement, J. (1987, July), with the assistance of Brown, D., Camp, C., Kudukey, J., Minstrell, J., Palmer, D., Schultz, K., Shimabukuro, J., Steinberg, M., & Veneman, V. Overcoming students' misconceptions in physics: The role of anchoring intuitions and analogical validity. Proceedings of the Second International Seminar on Misconceptions and Educational Strategies in Science and Mathematics (pp. 84–97). Ithaca, NY: Cornell University, Department of Education.

Darden, L. (1982). Artificial intelligence and philosophy of science: Reasoning by analogy in theory construction. *Philosophy of Science Association 2,* 147–165.

Darden, L., & Rada, R. (1988). Hypothesis formation via interrelations. In A. Prieditis (Ed.), *Analogica* (pp. 109–127). Los Altos, CA: Kaufman.

Darwin, C. (1892/1958). In F. Darwin (Ed.), *The autobiography of Charles Darwin and selected letters.* New York: Dover.

Easley, J. (1978). Symbol manipulation reexamined: An approach to bridging a chasm. In B. Presseisen, D. Goldstein, & M. Appel (Eds.), *Topics in cognitive development* (Vol. 2, pp. 99–112). New York: Plenum Press.

Fischbein, E. (1987). Intuition in science and mathematics: An educational approach. Boston, MA: D. Reidel.

Gentner, D. (1982). Are scientific analogies metaphors? In D. Miall (Ed.), *Metaphor: Problems and perspectives* (pp. 106–132). Brighton, Sussex, England: Harvester Press.

Getzels, J., and Csikszentmihalyi, M. (1976). *The creative vision: A longitudinal study of problem finding in art.* New York: John Wiley.

Gould, S. J. (1980). Darwin's middle road. In S. Gould, *The panda's thumb: More reflections in natural history.* New York: Norton.

Gregory, R. (1981). *Mind in science.* Cambridge, England. Cambridge University Press.

Gruber, H. (1974). *Darwin on man.* New York: E. P. Dutton.

Hanson, N. R. (1958). *Patterns of discovery.* Cambridge, England: Cambridge University Press.

Harre, R. (1961). *Theories and things.* London, England: Newman History and Philosophy of Science Series.

Harre, R. (1967). Philosophy of science: History of. In P. Edwards (Ed.), *The encyclopedia of philosophy* (pp. 289–296). New York: Free Press.

Harre, R. (1972). *The philosophies of science.* New York: Oxford University Press.

Harre, R. (1983). *An introduction to the logic of the sciences.* (2nd ed.) New York: St. Martin's Press.

Hesse, M. (1966). *Models and analogies in science.* South Bend, IN: Notre Dame University Press.

Hesse, M. (1967). Models and analogies in science. In P. Edwards (Ed.), *The encyclopedia of philosophy* (pp. 354–359). New York: Free Press.

Holland, J. H., Holyoak, K. J., Nisbett, R. E., & Thagard, P. R. (1986). *Induction: Processes of inference, learning and discovery.* Cambridge, MA: MIT Press.

Karmiloff-Smith, A., & Inhelder, B. (1975). If you want to get ahead, get a theory. *Cognition, 3*(3), 195–212.

Koestler, A. (1964). *The act of creation.* New York: Macmillan.

Kuhn, T. (1962). *The structure of scientific revolutions* (1st ed.). Chicago: University of Chicago Press.

Kuhn, T. (1977). Concepts of cause in the development of physics. In T. Kuhn (Ed.), *The essential tension: Selected studies in scientific tradition and change* (pp. 21–30). Chicago: University of Chicago Press.

Lakatos, I. (1978). The methodology of scientific research programmes. *Philosophical papers* (Vol. 1). Cambridge, England: Cambridge University Press.

Langley, P. W. (1979). Rediscovering physics with BACON 3. *Proceedings of the Sixth International Joint Conference on Artificial Intelligence, 6,* 505–507.

Lenat, D. B. (1977). Automated theory formation in mathematics. *Proceedings of the Fifth International Joint Conference on Artificial Intelligence, 5,* 833–842.

Lenat, D. B., (1983). The role of heuristics in learning by discovery. In T. Mitchell (Ed.), *Machine learning* (pp. 243–306). Palo Alto, CA: Tioga Publishing.

Mansfield, R. S., & Busse, R. V. (1981). *The psychology of creativity and discovery: Scientists and their work.* Chicago: Nelson-Hall.

Nagel, E. (1961). *The structure of science.* New York: Harcourt, Brace, & World.

Nersessian, N. (1984). Faraday to Einstein: *Constructing meaning in scientific theories.* Dordrecht, The Netherlands: Martinas Nijhoff.

Peirce, C. S. (1958). In C. Hartshorne, P. Weiss, & A. Burks (Eds.), *Collected papers* Cambridge: Harvard University Press.

Perkins, D. (1981). *The mind's best work.* Cambridge: Harvard University Press.

Polanyi, M. (1966). *The tacit dimension.* Garden City, NY: Doubleday.

Popper, K. (1959). *The logic of scientific discovery.* London: Hutchinson.

Rada, R. (1985). Gradualness facilitates knowledge refinement. *I.E.E.E. Transactions on Pattern Analysis and Machine Intelligence, 7*(5), 523–530.

Rothenberg, A. (1979). *The emerging goddess.* Chicago: University of Chicago Press.

Schweber, S. (1977). The origin of the Origin revisited. *Journal of the History of Biology, 10,* 229–316.

Suppe, F. (1974). The search for philosophic understanding of scientific theories. In F. Suppe (Ed.), *The structure of scientific theories.* Urbana: University of Illinois Press.

Toulmin, S. (1972). *Human understanding* (Vol. 1). Oxford, England: Oxford University Press.

Tweney, R. (1985). Faraday's discovery of induction: A cognitive approach. In D. Goodling & F. James (Eds.), *Faraday rediscovered: Essays on the life and work of Michael Faraday, 1791–1867* (pp. 189–209). New York: Stockton Press.

Tweney, R. (in press). Fields of enterprise: On Michael Faraday's thought. In D. Wallace and E. Gruber (Eds.), *Creative people at work.* Oxford: Oxford University Press.

CHAPTER 21

Analogical Reasoning and Problem Solving in Science Textbooks

Shawn M. Glynn, Bruce K. Britton, Margaret Semrud-Clikeman, and K. Denise Muth

People's frequent use of analogies to explain everyday phenomena underscores their potential value as instructional tools. Such expressions as "Let me give you an analogy . . . ," "It's just like . . . ," "It's the same as . . . ," "It's no different than . . . ," "Think of it this way . . . ," are commonplace in casual conversation.

The meaningful comprehension of science text is a kind of problem solving: the reader's problem is to understand and elaborate the content of the text. Analogies can help readers to solve this comprehension problem. Authors can provide analogies for readers, and readers can be trained to generate their own analogies. In this chapter, we will focus on the explanatory and creative roles that analogies can play in science textbooks.

Analogical Reasoning and Comprehending Science Text

One of the main purposes of a science text is to explain complex concepts and the relationships among those concepts. Unfortunately, the concepts are often difficult for readers to understand because the concepts are either unfamiliar (e.g., entropy) or are defined somewhat differently than they are in everyday life (e.g., velocity).

Drawing an analogy between concepts in a science text can serve an explanatory function and a creative function. It serves an explanatory function when it puts new concepts and principles into familiar terms. It serves a creative function when it stimulates the solution of existing problems, the identification of new problems, and the generation of hypotheses. Before we explain exactly how an analogy fulfills these functions, we will explain what an analogy actually is, how it works, and what constitutes a good analogy.

What Is an Analogy?

In science and technology, an *analogy* is a correspondence in some respects between concepts, principles, or formulas that are otherwise dissimilar. More precisely, it is a mapping between similar features of those concepts, principles, or formulas. A related term is *analog,* which is a concept, principle, or formula that bears an analogy to something else.

Although the terms *analogy* and *metaphor* are

Shawn M. Glynn and Margaret Semrud-Clikeman • Department of Educational Psychology, University of Georgia, Athens, GA 30602. **K. Denise Muth** • Department of Elementary Education, University of Georgia, Athens, GA 30602. **Bruce K. Britton** • Department of Psychology, University of Georgia, Athens, GA 30602.

frequently substituted for each other, analogy tends to be used more often in scientific and technical contexts. Metaphor is used more often in literary contexts (e.g., she's a breath of fresh air). Because the examples we will present in this chapter are from science textbooks, we will use the term analogy rather than metaphor.

The terms *model* and analogy (or analog) are sometimes used interchangeably. Model is the more inclusive term, referring to a simplified representation of the components, operations, and relations of a more complicated object or process. The representation can take several forms, such as an algebraic equation, a diagram, a flow chart, or a physical replica. An analog is one kind of model; for example, a pump could be used to model the human heart. Models need not be analogs, however. Consider the stick-and-ball models of molecules that are used in chemistry texts. These models are not analogs.

How Do Analogies Work?

Wittrock (1985) conceived of meaningful learning in science as a

student generative process that entails construction of relations, either assimilative or accommodative, among experience, concepts, and higher order principles and frameworks. It is the construction of these relations between and within concepts that produces meaningful learning. (pp. 261–262).

In our view, when an analogy is drawn between science concepts, principles, or formulas, a powerful relation is constructed which leads to the meaningful learning described by Wittrock. An analogical relation is powerful because it comprises, in actuality, an entire *set* of associative relations between features of the concepts, principles, or formulas being compared.

In science texts, analogies are used in a relatively precise fashion to transfer ideas from a familiar conceptual domain to an unfamiliar one. In our explanation of an analogy, we will call the familiar conceptual domain the *analog* and the unfamiliar domain the *target*. The analog, like any concept, has characteristics or *features;* so does the target. If the analog and the target share common or similar features, an analogy can be drawn between them. We have represented an analogy, with its constituent parts, in Figure 1. Note in Figure 1 that the analog and the target are subordinate to a superordinate concept, principle, or formula.

To illustrate our representation of an analogy, we will use the target concept of an *electric circuit,* and the analog concept will be a *hydraulic (water) circuit.* Examine the electric and hydraulic circuit diagrams in Figure 2. An analogy can be drawn between them because they share common or similar features, such as the following:

CIRCUITS

Hydraulic Circuit	*Electric Circuit*
Connecting pipes	Wires
Narrow pipe section	Resistance
Valve	Switch
Pump	Dry cell battery
Flowing water	Electric current
Water molecules	Electrons

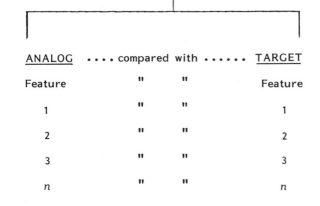

Figure 1. Our representation of an analogy, with its constituent parts. Note that the analog and the target are subordinate to a superordinate concept, principle, or formula.

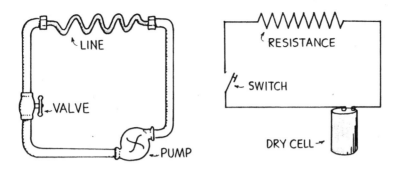

Figure 2. Analogy between a simple hydraulic circuit and an electric circuit. From *Conceptual Physics* (p. 513) by Paul G. Hewitt, 1987, Menlo Park, CA: Addison-Wesley Publishing Company, Inc. Copyright 1987 by Addison-Wesley. Reprinted by permission.

Note that the electric circuit and the hydraulic circuit are both circuits, that is, they are subordinate to the superordinate concept *circuit*. There are other kinds of circuits which, depending upon the number of similar features they share with electric circuits, might also be used to draw an analogy. For example, think of a pinball machine: the pinballs (corresponding to electrons or water molecules) travel a circuit and are pushed by a plunger (corresponding to a battery or a pump). The pinballs even meet "resistance" in the form of bumpers and funnels. We suspect that other analogies, and more creative ones, could be drawn by readers who keep our representation and its constituent parts in mind when thinking about circuits.

Sometimes, there is not a conventional name for the superordinate concept which subsumes an analog and a target. For example, authors of biology texts frequently draw an analogy between the camera and the human eye. Here are some of the similar features:

Camera	Human Eye
Lens	Lens
Inverted image	Inverted image
Film	Retina
Lens cap	Eye lid
Focus	Lens accommodation
Aperture	Pupil dilation

What is the name of the superordinate concept that subsumes the analog "camera" and the target "human eye?" *Optical device* is one candidate, but it certainly is not as familiar a name as *circuit* was in the previous example. Some concepts, particularly infrequently used general ones, do not have labels. Nevertheless, the role of the superordinate concept

(or principle or formula) in the representation of an analogy and its constituent parts is an important one. The identification and naming of the superordinate concept can suggest other analogies; it also can stimulate readers to generalize what they have learned and apply their learning to other contexts. Therefore, even though it might be difficult to identify and name the concept, principle, or formula that subsumes an analog and its target, it is beneficial to do so for purposes of instruction, elaboration, and creativity.

Analogies and Examples

Sometimes readers of a science text confuse an example of a concept with an analogy. An example is an instance of a concept, not a comparison between similar features of two concepts. Consider the relationship between an electric spark and lightning. Lightning is not *like* a big spark, it *is* a big spark! So, lightning is an example of the concept electric spark.

An analogy can be drawn between two examples of the same concept (or the same superordinate concept). Consider the analogy, "A whale is like a dolphin," used in children's science text by an author who wants to point out that both are examples of sea mammals. Now refer to Figure 3 and consider a more elaborate analogy used by the author of a high school physics text who wants to explain the concept of an *electric field:*

Just as the space around the earth and every other mass is filled with an *electric field*—a kind of aura that extends through space. . . . A gravitational force holds a satellite in orbit about a planet, and an electrical force holds an electron in orbit about a proton. In both cases there is no contact between the objects, and the forces are "acting at a distance." Putting this in terms of the

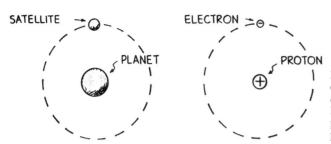

Figure 3. The satellite and the electron both experience forces; they are both in force fields. From *Conceptual Physics* (p. 496) by Paul G. Hewitt, 1987, Menlo Park, CA: Addison-Wesley Publishing Company, Inc. Copyright 1987 by Addison-Wesley. Reprinted by permission.

field concept, we can say that the orbiting satellite and electron interact with the force fields of the planet and the proton and are everywhere in contact with these fields. In other words, the force that one electric charge exerts on another can be described as the interaction between one charge and the electric field set up by the other. (Hewitt, 1987, p. 496)

The superordinate concept in this analogy is *field,* the analog is *gravitational field* (covered by the textbook author in a previous chapter), and the target is *electric field.* The analogy is drawn by comparing similar features of the two kinds of fields: namely, (a) both fields embody forces, (b) the forces influence objects not in contact, and (c) the forces act at a distance. The analogy is also drawn by comparing a planet–satellite relationship, which is an example of a gravitational field, with a proton–electron relationship, which is an example of an electric field. These examples, and their component parts, represent additional similar features on which to base the analogy. In short, an analogy can be drawn between two concepts by comparing examples of those concepts.

What Constitutes a Good Analogy?

How good an analogy is depends upon the purpose for which it is used. In general, analogies can serve two purposes in science text: explanatory and creative. When an analogy is used for an explanatory purpose, the goal is for the reader to fully understand the target by understanding the role each important feature in the target plays. Explanatory analogies are instructional; they can be provided by text authors and generated by the readers themselves.

If an analogy is serving an explanatory purpose, then three criteria can be used to judge its appropriateness: (1) the number of features compared, (2) the similarity of the features compared, and (3) the conceptual significance of the features compared.

The explanatory power of an analogy generally increases as the number of significant, similar features shared by the analog and target increases. However, it is possible to draw a "good" analogy on the basis of a few (or even one!) similar features, if those features are directly relevant to the specific goals of the author. For example, the following analogy is drawn on the basis of only one similar feature, but it is a very important one in terms of the author's goals: the earth rotates on its axis like an ice skater doing a pirouette.

An analogy is considered "bad" if it is difficult to identify and map the important features that are shared by the analog and the target. For example, we have seen cartoons in science textbooks in which an analogy is drawn between the concept of *entropy* and a teenager's messy room. Usually, the author's point is that systems tend to become disordered unless work of some kind is done on them. The author applies this principle to the universe. Unfortunately, the reader is usually confused about the causal agent involved. In the case of the messy room, a teenager is responsible. But who is responsible in the case of the universe? (One wag we know claimed it was still teenagers!) Our point is that a good analogy should not confuse the reader.

If the purpose of the analogy is creative rather than explanatory, then the criteria by which it is judged should be based on the products of the analogy rather than on characteristics of the analogy. In other words, when it comes to judging creativity, the "proof is in the pudding." The criteria that should be applied to an analogy used for creative purposes are: (1) the number of its products, (2) the novelty of its products, and (3) the value of its products.

If an analogy is required to serve an explanatory function and a creative function, then both sets of criteria should be applied. An analogy that serves both functions well would be a very powerful analogy indeed. It is often the case that an analogy can only serve one function well. A particular analogy might be ideal for instructional purposes but might lead to no new ideas because no further correspondences can be found between features of the analog and the target. Or an analogy might suggest new ideas on the basis of one important correspondence, but other correspondences might be lacking, making the analogy a poor choice for authors who want to introduce and explain the target to readers. Thus, some analogies are good for both explanation and creativity, whereas others are good for only one of these purposes.

An Analogy Is a Double-Edged Sword

When used for either an explanatory or a creative purpose, an analogy can be a double-edged sword. It can lead to misunderstanding as well as understanding, and poor predictions as well as good ones. The correspondence of features between two concepts is never identical, otherwise the corresponding concepts would be identical. When authors or readers intentionally or inadvertently compare features that do not correspond to one another, misunderstanding and misdirection can result.

A careful examination of all aspects of an analogy is a prerequisite to using it effectively. All too easily an analogy can lead readers astray. For example, children who believe that electricity in a wire is like water in a hose often conclude, erroneously, that if the wire is cut, the electricity will "leak out."

Of course, one way to guard against misunderstanding and misdirection simply is not to use analogies. There always have been a few scientists and authors who believe that analogies are more trouble than they are worth and that they should not be used at all. Most scientists and authors do use analogies, despite the potential dangers, citing as their reason the significant explanatory and creative potential of analogies.

Occasionally, authors warn readers about the potential dangers of analogies. This is a good practice and we would like to see it adopted by all authors who use analogies. More than 25 years ago, Eric Rogers (1960), in his classic text *Physics for the Inquiring Mind,* introduced his chapter on electric circuits by praising analogies and then cautioning his readers about them:

To this day in teaching elementary electricity we liken electric circuits to hydraulic circuits of water pipes full of water all the way around, with pumps, taps, flowmeters, pressure gauges . . . to correspond to generators, switches, ammeters, voltmeters. . . . Like many uses of analogy in teaching, this does

make things easier for the beginner to understand. . . . Yet saying the electric circuit is "just like" the water circuit does not prove the electric circuit will have such behavior. "Current flow" is a hindsight description, put in after we have found that the electric circuit does have experimental properties which resemble those of a water circuit. As such, it is good teaching, but if misused as an attempted proof, would be bad science. (This seems a long complaint against a teacher's kindly illustration. Yet it was the great mistake of medieval science to argue "what must be" from some authoritarian statement; and present-day popularizers of science make the mistake of building hard-won knowledge into glib analogies from which the science is then apparently produced. Attempts to make physics clearer by analogies may mislead the reader unless he is warned.) (pp. 505–506)

A recent recommendation for the use of analogies, with caution, can be found in *Concepts in Physics,* an introductory physics textbook by Miller, Dillon, and Smith (1980):

Models and analogies can be of great value in physics if they are used with care and discrimination. It is important, for example, to guard against the danger of believing that a model or analogy is an exact representation of some physical system. One should always regard a model critically and remember that an analogy means no more than: under certain special conditions, the physical system being studied behaves as if. . . . (p. 253)

We encourage authors to explain to readers, as Rogers (1960) and Miller *et al.* (1980) did, that analogies are double-edged swords. An analog can be used to explain correctly, even predict, some aspects of the target; however, eventually every analogy breaks down. At that point, miscomprehension and misdirection can begin. Readers must understand this.

Explanatory Function of Analogies

An analogy serves an explanatory function when it puts new ideas into terms with which readers are already familiar. Frequently, authors will use a concept that they covered in an earlier chapter to introduce—by way of analogy—a new concept. Consider the following example in which Paul Hewitt (1987), the author of the text *Conceptual Physics,* uses concepts related to the flow of heat (in his Chapter 21) to introduce concepts related to the flow of electric charge (in his Chapter 34):

Recall in your study of heat and temperature that heat flows through a conductor when a difference in temperature exists across its ends. Heat flows from the end of higher temperature to the end of lower temperature. When both ends reach the same temperature, the flow of heat ceases.

In a similar way, when the ends of an electrical conductor are at different electric potentials, charge flows from the higher potential to the lower potential. Charge flows when there is a *potential difference,* or difference in potential (voltage), across the ends of a conductor. The flow of charge will continue until both ends reach a common potential. When there is no potential difference, no flow of charge will occur. (pp. 509–510)

In the sections that follow, we will present several more analogies and analogy-based problems developed by Paul Hewitt, as we consider his work to be exemplary. Analogies drawn by an author between concepts covered early in a text and concepts covered later are particularly effective because the author can be reasonably confident that the earlier concepts (which function here as analogs) are part of most readers' knowledge base. Also, these analogies are particularly powerful because they prompt readers to connect related concepts and form conceptual systems.

To better understand when and how an analogy should be used to explain a new concept, we examined 43 elementary school, high school, and college science textbooks for examples of *elaborate analogies.* In all the textbooks, we found many examples of simple, one-or-two sentence analogies, such as "Mitochondria are the powerhouses of the cell;" however, elaborate analogies, those that ran on for a paragraph, a page, or several pages, were relatively rare. Elaborate analogies compared and contrasted many features of two major concepts.

High school physics and physical science textbooks appeared to contain the greatest number of elaborate analogies, so we focused our attention on them. Why do high school physics and physical science textbooks have a greater number of elaborate analogies? We have formed some opinions, but keep in mind they are very speculative. We think that elementary school textbook authors use few elaborate analogies because the knowledge base of their readers is so limited and because it is not possible to cover concepts in the depth needed to support analogies. On the other hand, college textbook authors do use elaborate analogies, but not as often as high school textbook authors. College textbook authors may assume that the stronger comprehension capabilities of college students preclude the need for as many analogies. College textbook authors may also be under pressure to cover more material, forcing them to sacrifice some elaborate analogies.

Why do physics textbooks appear to have more elaborate analogies than textbooks in other sciences? Again, we are speculating here. Physics concepts are about very basic phenomena that either do not lend themselves to unaided physical observation (e.g., electrons) or, if they are directly observable, they are often misperceived (e.g., trajectories), or confused with everyday uses of the concept (e.g., speed and velocity). Because of these characteristics, physics concepts need more "conceptual support" when introduced in textbooks. Analogies can provide some of this conceptual support by helping readers to perceive, understand, or reinterpret physics concepts in terms of concepts with which they are already familiar. Although we did find that elaborate analogies were most common in physics textbooks, it is important to keep in mind that textbooks in other sciences, particularly chemistry, included elaborate analogies.

The 19 high school physics and physical science textbooks we examined are listed in Table 1. (Physical science is the study of changes in matter and energy; in addition to physics, it includes areas of study such as chemistry and astronomy.) We identified the elaborate analogies in these texts that involved physics concepts. Some of the texts made relatively extensive use of elaborate analogies, whereas others made little or no use of them. It would be difficult to quantify the amount of analogy use in any meaningful way because the texts varied considerably in their page length, the number of concepts covered, the depth of concept coverage, and the prior knowledge assumed of the reader. In addition, some textbooks were designed for a terminal course, whereas others were intended to be the first course in a science sequence.

It is common for the teacher's edition of high school science textbooks to point out, in the introduction, all the special features that are incorporated into the design of the text. These features are intended to facilitate readers' comprehension of text concepts. Here is a sample of these features: advance organizers; structured overviews; highlighted concept names; margin notes; introductory, adjunct, and review questions; illustrations; cartoons; boxed examples; concept summaries; lists of important terms; conceptual activities; and glossaries. These features, along with supplementary materials, such as laboratory manuals, resource books, videotapes, software, and test item files, are promoted in the teacher's edition as valuable aids to comprehension. Often, the promotion is by an expert in reading comprehension, such as the head of a college or university Department of Reading Education. We believe features such as these can be valuable aids to comprehension, *under certain conditions,* as many research studies have shown (e.g., Britton & Glynn, 1987; Britton, Glynn, Meyer, & Penland, 1982; Glynn, Andre, & Britton, 1986;

Table 1. Physics and Physical Science Textbooks

Beiser, A. (1964) *The science of physics*. Palo Alto, CA: Addison-Wesley.

Dull, C. E., Metcalfe, H. C., & Williams, J. E. (1963). *Modern physics*. New York: Holt, Rinehart & Winston.

Genzer, I., & Younger, P. (1969). *Physics*. Morristown, NJ: Silver Burdett.

Haber-Schaim, U., Dodge, J. H., & Walter, J. A. (1986). *PSSC Physics*. Lexington, MA: D.C. Heath.

Harnwell, G. P., & Legge, G. J. F. (1967). *Physics: Matter, energy, and the universe*. New York: Reinhold.

Hewitt, P. G. (1987). *Conceptual physics*. Menlo Park, CA: Addison-Wesley.

Hirsch, A. J. (1981). *Physics: A practical approach*. Toronto: Wiley.

Hirsch, A. J. (1986). *Physics for a modern world*. Toronto: Wiley.

Johnson, G. P. Barr, B. B., & Leyden, M. B. (1988). *Physical science*. Menlo Park, CA: Addison-Wesley.

Karplus, R. (1969). *Introductory physics*. New York: W. A. Benjamin, Inc.

Krauskopf, K. B., & Beiser, A. (1986). *The physical universe*. New York: McGraw-Hill.

Leyden, M. B., Johnson, G. P., & Barr, B. B. (1988). *Introduction to physical science*. Menlo Park, CA: Addison-Wesley.

Miller, F., Dillon, T. J., & Smith, M. K. (1980). *Concepts in physics*. New York: Harcourt Brace Jovanovich.

Murphy, J. T., & Smoot, R. C. (1972). *Physics principles and problems*. Columbus, OH: Charles E. Merrill.

Pasachoff, J. M., Pasachoff, N., & Cooney, T. M. (1983). *Physical science*. Glenview, IL: Scott, Foresman.

Physical Science Study Committee. (1965). *Physics*. Lexington, MA: D. C. Heath.

Rutherford, F. J., Holton, G., & Watson, F. G. (1975). *Project physics*. New York: Holt, Rinehart & Winston.

Taffel, A. (1986). *Physics: Its methods and meanings*. Newton, MA: Allyn & Bacon.

Wong, H. K., & Dolmatz, M. S. (1984). *Physical science: The key ideas*. Englewood Cliffs, NJ: Prentice-Hall.

Glynn & Britton, 1984; Glynn, Britton, & Tillman, 1985; Glynn & Di Vesta, 1977, 1979). We were surprised to find, however, no mention of analogies in any of the textbook introductions. This was doubly surprising in those textbooks in which authors made excellent use of analogies. Why not promote this valuable aid to comprehension in the introduction to the text?

We think that one reason why analogies are not promoted in introductions to textbooks, even in textbooks that make extensive use of analogies, is that the skill of writing good analogies is, at the present time, what psychologists call "procedural" rather than "declarative." Procedural knowledge is knowledge of "how to do something" rather than "how to explain it in words." Because authors and publishers do not have guidelines or a model for what constitutes a good instructional analogy, the development and evaluation of analogies is fairly subjective. In other words, it is more of an art than a technology. Because the use of analogies is procedural and subjective, authors and publishers may not feel comfortable about promoting them in their textbooks as aids to comprehension, at least not until a model becomes available for designing and evaluating instructional analogies.

The Teaching-with-Analogies (TWA) Model

With the help of members of the faculty in the University of Georgia's Department of Science Education and high school science teachers who were enrolled as graduate students in that department, we reviewed a large number of high school physics, physical science, chemistry, and biology textbooks and subjectively identified the most effective analogies from the standpoint of instructional design. The authors of these analogies performed certain key operations that we have incorporated into a model that can serve as a guide for authors of science textbooks. Our model for using an analogy to explain a science concept contains the following six operations:

1. Introduce target concept
2. Recall analog concept
3. Identify similar features of concepts
4. Map similar features
5. Draw conclusions about concepts
6. Indicate where analogy breaks down

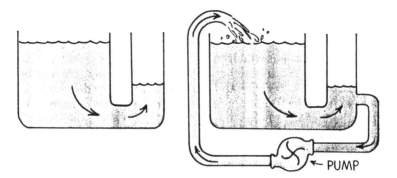

Figure 4. (*Left*) Water flows from the reservoir of higher pressure to the reservoir of lower pressure. The flow will cease when the difference in pressure ceases. (*Right*) Water continues to flow because a difference in pressure is maintained with the pump. From *Conceptual Physics* (p. 510) by Paul G. Hewitt, 1987, Menlo Park, CA: Addison-Wesley Publishing Company, Inc. Copyright 1987 by Addison-Wesley. Reprinted by permission.

The author of a well-designed analogy performs each of these operations for the reader. To illustrate these operations, we present excerpts from Paul Hewitt's (1987) chapters on "Electric Currents" and "Electric Circuits," in which he draws an extended analogy between currents of water (the analog) and currents of electricity (the target):[1]

Electric Current

The last chapter discussed the concept of electric potential, or voltage. This chapter will show that voltage is an "electrical pressure" that can produce a flow of charge, or *current*, within a conductor. The flow is restrained by the *resistance* it encounters. (p. 509)

Flow of Charge

To attain a sustained flow of charge in a conductor, some arrangement must be provided to maintain a difference in potential while charge flows from one end to the other. The situation is analogous to the flow of water from a higher reservoir to a lower one [Figure 4 left]. Water will flow in a pipe that connects the reservoirs only as long as a difference in water level exists. (This is implied in the saying, "Water seeks its own level.") The flow of water in the pipe, like the flow of charge in the wire that connects the Van de Graaff generator to the ground, will cease when the pressures at each end are equal. In order that the flow be sustained, there must be a suitable pump of some sort to maintain a difference in water levels [Figure 4 right]. Then there will be a continual difference in water pressures and a continual flow of water. The same is true of electric current. (pp. 509–510).

Voltage Sources

Charges do not flow unless there is a potential difference. A sustained current requires a suitable "electrical pump" to pro-

---

[1]The excerpts are taken from *Conceptual Physics* by Paul G. Hewitt, 1987, Menlo Park, CA: Addison-Wesley Publishing Company, Inc. Copyright 1987 by Addison-Wesley. Reprinted by permission.

vide a sustained potential difference. Something that provides a potential difference is known as a *voltage source*. (p. 511)

There is often some confusion between charge flowing *through* a circuit and voltage being impressed *across* a circuit. To distinguish between these ideas, consider a long pipe filled with water. Water will flow *through* the pipe if there is a difference in pressure *across* or between its ends. Water flows from the high-pressure end to the low-pressure end. Only the water flows, not the pressure. Similarly, you say that charges flow *through* a circuit because of an applied voltage *across the circuit*. You don't say that voltage flows through a circuit. Voltage doesn't go anywhere, for it is the charges that move. Voltage causes current. (pp. 511–512)

Electrical Resistance

The amount of current that flows in a circuit depends on the voltage provided by the voltage source. It also depends on the resistance that the conductor offers to the flow of charge, or the *electrical resistance*. This is similar to the rate of water flow in a pipe, which depends not only on the pressure behind the water but on the resistance offered by the pipe itself. The resistance of a wire depends on the *conductivity* of the material (that is, how well it conducts) and also on the thickness and length of the wire. (p. 512)

A Battery and a Bulb

It is a bit misleading to say that electrons flow "out of" the battery, or "into" the bulb; a better description is to say they flow *through* these devices. The flow of charge in a circuit is analogous to a pump, the wires to the pipes, and the bulb to any device that operates when the water is flowing. The water flows through both the pump itself and the circuit it connects. It doesn't "squash up" and concentrate in certain regions, but flows continuously. Electric current behaves the same way. (pp. 525–526)

Electric Circuits

Any path along which electrons can flow is a circuit. For a continuous flow of electrons, there must be a complete circuit with no gaps. A gap is usually provided by an electric switch that can be opened or closed to either cut off or allow electron flow.

The water analogy is quite useful for gaining a conceptual

understanding of electric circuits, but it does have some limitations. An important one is that a break in a water pipe results in water spilling from the circuit, whereas a break in an electric circuit results in a complete stop in the flow of electricity. Another difference has to do with turning current off and on. When you *close* an electrical switch that connects the circuit, you allow current to flow in much the same way as you allow water to flow by *opening* a faucet. Opening a switch stops the flow of electricity. An electric circuit must be closed for electricity to flow. Opening a water faucet, on the other hand, starts the flow of water. Except for these and some other differences, thinking of electric current in terms of water current is a useful way to study electric circuits. (pp. 526–527)

In the analogy that Hewitt has drawn between currents of water and currents of electricity, he effectively has performed all the operations specified in our model. In the electric current excerpt, he introduces the target concepts of voltage, current, and resistance. Next, in the flow of charge excerpt, he cues the reader to retrieve from memory information about currents of water. Hewitt realizes that some readers will have only fragmentary knowledge of a water flow system, so he provides a good deal of information about such a system. In the flow of charge excerpt, Hewitt identifies and maps similar features: "The flow of water in the pipe, like the flow of charge in the wire. . . ." Plus, his use of water circuit and electric circuit diagrams (refer back to Figure 2) helps readers to visually identify and map similar features.

In addition to explaining new concepts, analogies can be used to clear up old misconceptions. In the excerpts about "voltage sources" and "a battery and a bulb," Hewitt does exactly this. He uses his analogy to counter some popular misconceptions that readers either already have or are likely to develop. It is important to keep in mind that analogies can be used to straighten out readers' misconceptions, particularly because one of the most popular arguments against using analogies is that they can sometimes cause misconceptions.

Hewitt draws conclusions for readers about the target concepts. For example, in the electrical resistance excerpt, he compares electrical resistance to the resistance water encounters in a pipe and draws the following conclusion for the reader: "The resistance of a wire depends on the *conductivity* of the material . . . and also on the thickness and length of the wire."

Finally, in the electrical circuit excerpt, Hewitt indicates where the analogy breaks down. He explains how a break in an electric circuit differs from that in a water pipe and how an electrical switch differs from a faucet. By doing so, he reduces the

likelihood that his readers will overgeneralize from the analog to the target concept and form some misconceptions.

Hewitt's use of analogies is excellent. He performed all of the six operations specified in our model. If an author were to perform only some of the operations, leaving some to the reader, the technical quality of the analogy would be reduced because it is possible that the reader might fail to perform an operation or might perform it poorly.

In our survey of textbooks of physics and of physical science, we have found many instances where authors suggested an analog to readers, but then left the readers to make sense (or nonsense) out of it for themselves. Under these circumstances, the readers could identify irrelevant features of the target and analog, map them, draw wrong conclusions about the target, and fail to realize where the analogy breaks down. In short, the readers' understanding of the target concept could be both incomplete and incorrect.

The Science Teacher's Use of the Model

Science teachers who keep our model in mind can interpret text analogies for their students. If the author fails to perform some of the operations specified in the model, the teacher can perform these operations for the students. For example, suppose the author of a physical science text draws an analogy between electricity in a wire and water in a hose but fails to point out where this analogy breaks down: namely, that electricity does not spill out if the wire is cut. The teacher can remedy this failure on the author's part by performing this essential operation for the students.

We encourage science teachers to familiarize students with this model so that the students will learn how to interpret, criticize, and extend an author's analogy. When we used our model in science education classes to dissect an author's analogy, the discussions that ensued between the teacher and students, and the students themselves, had some wonderful consequences. The discussion of the analogy enabled the teacher to identify students' misconceptions and knowledge gaps which otherwise would have gone undetected. The discussion also prompted students to tie together concepts that they previously viewed as unrelated.

We also encourage science teachers and students to use the model as a guide when generating their own analogies. They may wish to do this when the text author has not provided an analogy. Or, if the author has provided an analogy, teachers and students may wish to generate another so that they can examine the concept from more than one perspective. For example, the author might use a ''flowing water'' analogy to explain electricity. The teacher and students, however, wishing to view electricity from a different perspective, might generate a ''moving crowd'' analogy, in which electric current is viewed as masses of people, animals, or objects moving through passageways. Consider this version of a moving crowd analogy generated by a student: ''If you increase resistance in the circuit, the current slows down. Now that's like a highway, cars on a highway where . . . as you close down a lane . . . the cars move slower through that narrow point'' (Gentner & Gentner, 1983, p. 111).

The advantage of generating alternative analogies and viewing a concept like electricity from more than one perspective is that each perspective brings particular features of the concept into clearer focus. Thus, the teacher and the students who generate multiple analogies for a concept will have a more comprehensive understanding of that concept and of its relation to other concepts.

Creative Function of Analogies

Analogies serve a creative function when they help readers to solve problems, find problems, and generate hypotheses. Authors prompt readers to use analogies creatively by means of questions, hints, and illustrations. In addition, readers can prompt themselves to use analogies creatively if they are trained to ask certain questions of themselves and perform certain analogical operations.

These prompts are essential because spontaneous analogical problem solving is not common. In a series of experiments, Gick and Holyoak (Gick & Holyoak, 1980, 1983; Holyoak, 1985) demonstrated that 75% of the college students they tested were able to solve a story problem by applying previously learned information *after they received a hint to apply it,* but only about 30% were able to solve the problem without a hint.

The problems used by Gick and Holyoak were embedded in stories about military, medical, firefighting, and other real-life situations. These problems are more difficult than the four-term problems of the form A:B::C:D (e.g., Einstein:Relati-

vity::Darwin:_____) investigated by Sternberg (1977, 1986) and Rumelhart (Rumelhart & Abrahamson, 1973; Rumelhart & Norman, 1981). In the four-term problems, there is a built-in prompt: the student knows that the A-B relationship is relevant and must be mapped to the C-D relationship. With Gick and Holyoak's story problems, in effect the student is given ''C,'' the problem statement, and asked for ''D,'' the problem solution. To solve the problem, the student must notice that some apparently unrelated information (''A-B''), received earlier in the experiment, is relevant to the problem and must apply it without any prompt or hint. Regarding the difficulty of problems such as these that require the spontaneous recognition and application of potentially relevant knowledge from a different domain, Gick and Holyoak (1983) said:

It should be noted that in all of our experiments the critical prior analogs were presented in a context in which their problem-oriented character was incidental. Subjects were never explicitly encouraged to use the stories to learn about a novel kind of problem. In many situations, such as an instructional context, more directive guidance in the application of an analogy is often given. It is quite likely that more intentional learning procedures could improve transfer performance in our paradigm. In particular, explicit guidance might facilitate transfer from a single analog. In the absence of such guidance, failure to derive a general schema from a single instance may only reflect appropriate conservatism; without either further examples or direct instruction, the person may have no principled way to isolate the essential causal aspects of the situation.

Given the difficulty of schema abstraction from a single analog (at least without the guidance of a teacher), one might ask how anyone could spontaneously notice an analogy between one initial analog and a semantically remote transfer problem. (p. 32)

Gick and Holyoak's findings suggest that text authors should play an active role in helping their readers use analogies to solve problems, find problems, and generate hypotheses. We will now examine some of the ways that authors help readers to use analogies creatively.

Analogical Problem Solving

Authors of science textbooks use questions and hints to prompt readers to solve problems by means of analogies. Read the following excerpts from Hewitt's (1985a) *Conceptual Physics* and then tackle the problem posed. The temperature and heat excerpt was extracted from his Chapter 13, and the electrical potential excerpt and the problem posed were extracted from his Chapter 20.

Thermal Energy and Temperature

In this and the following two chapters we are going to investigate more closely the effects of the chaotic and haphazard motion of atoms and molecules that we call *thermal motion*. We begin by considering that which a body has by virtue of this energetic motion: *thermal energy*. . . .

The quantity that tells how warm or cold something is with respect to a standard body is called *temperature*. We say temperature is a measure of the random translational motion of atoms and molecules in a body; more specifically, it is a measure of the *average kinetic energy* of atoms and molecules in a body. We know, for example, that there is twice the thermal energy in 2 liters of boiling water as in 1 liter of boiling water, because 2 liters of boiling water will melt twice as much ice as 1 liter. But the temperatures of both amounts of water are the same because the average kinetic energy of molecules in each is the same. So we see there is a difference between thermal energy, which is measured in joules, and temperature, which we measure in degrees. (pp. 220–221)

Electric Potential Energy and Electric Potential

Rather than dealing with the total potential energy of a charged body, it is convenient when working with electricity to consider the electric *potential energy per charge*. We simply divide the amount of energy in any case by the amount of charge. . . . The concept of potential energy per charge is called *electric potential;* that is,

$$\text{Electric potential} = \frac{\text{Energy}}{\text{Charge}}$$

(p. 333)

Problem

Can we say that a body with twice the electric potential energy of another has twice the electric potential? Why or why not? (*Hint:* Consider the analogy with thermal energy and temperature.) (pp. 337)

Answer and Explanation

We cannot say that a body with twice the electric potential energy of another has twice the electric potential, just as we cannot say that a body with more thermal energy than another has a higher temperature. For example, a barrel full of warm water may have considerably more thermal energy than a cup of hot water. But it doesn't have a higher temperature, or greater KE/molecule. Likewise, the body with twice the electric potential energy (PE) does not necessarily have the greater PE/charge. It is important to distinguish between electric potential energy (PE) and electric potential (PE/charge). The key difference between the two is "*per charge*." (Hewitt, 1985b, p. 156)

As the preceding excerpts illustrate, readers can be prompted to use analogies to connect related bodies of knowledge for purposes of solving a problem. In this illustration, the author simply cued readers to retrieve the appropriate analog from memory. If the author wished to provide the reader with further prompts, he also could have identified the important features of the analog and target and mapped them for the reader.

In the absence of author-provided analogies, can readers generate their own analogies and use them to solve problems in a science text? Certainly! But readers must know what these problem-solving operations are and how to use them. Many, if not most, readers will require training in analogical problem solving. To provide a basis for this training, we will now propose a model of analogical problem solving.

The Analogical Problem Solving (APS) Model

For the kinds of problems readers often encounter in science texts, we propose a model of analogical problem solving involving three major operations, each of which has two suboperations. Here is our APS model:

1. State problem
   A. Represent problem
   B. Identify important features
2. Retrieve analog
   A. Search for analog with similar features
   B. Select analog
3. Solve problem
   A. Map solution
   B. Verify solution

Let us apply this model to the electric potential energy and electric potential problem we just looked at. In the state-the-problem operation, readers state the problem in familiar terms. To do this they must perform two suboperations, the first of which is to form a mental representation of the problem. Problems can be represented as diagrams, or sets of logical statements, or algebraic equations, or geometric figures, or simpler cases, or as examples, or in other ways. In fact, the same problem can often be represented in several ways. In the electric potential energy and electric potential problem, it is important to represent electric potential as electric potential energy *per charge* (PE/charge). It is also important to recognize that the electric potential energy of one body is to be compared with the electric potential of *another body*. If a reader did not attend to this feature of the problem, he or she might think the problem is asking about what the effect of doubling the electric potential energy would be on the electric potential of the *same body*.

In the second suboperation, readers identify the important features of the problem. The key features of this problem are the relationships between the two central concepts, electric potential energy and electric potential. Both have to do with electric energy. More precisely, electric potential energy refers to the *total* potential energy of a charged body, whereas electric potential refers to an *average,* the electric potential energy *per charge*. This average is important because it permits a definite value for electric potential energy per charge (also called "voltage") to be assigned to a location, say, in an electric circuit, regardless of whether or not a charge exists at that location.

Analog retrieval is the readers' next major operation. It consists of two suboperations: searching for an analog with similar features and selecting an analog for evaluation. In the electric potential energy and electric potential problem, the author performed both of these suboperations for the readers by "hinting" that the relationship between thermal energy and heat is analogous to that between electric potential energy and electric potential. Had he not done that, readers would have had to search their memories for analog candidates. They would recognize these candidates on the basis of similar features and select the best candidates for evaluation.

It is hoped that readers would have recognized that some of the relationships between thermal energy and temperature are similar to those between electric potential energy and electric potential. Thermal energy and temperature also have to do with energy. More precisely, thermal energy refers to the *total* random kinetic energy of atoms and molecules in a body, whereas temperature is a measure of the *average* kinetic energy of atoms and molecules in a body.

The final operation, solving the problem, consists of two suboperations, the first of which is mapping a solution. If readers know that a body with more thermal energy than another does not necessarily have a higher temperature, then they can map this information onto the problem as a tentative solution. However, even if the readers do not have this piece of knowledge immediately available, it is still possible for them to induce it and then map this induction to solve the problem.

One way to induce a solution is by generating and mapping an example of the analog to an example of the target. In this case, for thermal energy and temperature, a reader might generate an example such as this: a huge pot of warm soup may have a great deal more thermal energy than a bowl of hot soup, but it does not have a higher temperature. Then, by way of analogy, the reader might generate an exam-

ple for the electric potential energy and electric potential problem: a charged 12-volt automobile battery may have a great deal more electrical potential energy than a balloon rubbed on a hairy head, but it does not have more electric potential. In fact, the balloon might be charged to several thousand volts! However, it has only a tiny amount of electric potential energy, because the charge it carries is less than one millionth of a coulomb.

The final suboperation is to verify the solution generated. For the electric potential energy and electric potential problem, this can be done by testing the solution by means of actual experiments.

For each of the six operations in our analogical problem-solving model, there is associated a potential error that can lead readers to either no solution or to an incorrect solution. First, readers could misrepresent the problem. Second, even if readers correctly represent a problem, it is possible for them to miss an important feature of the problem. Third, the search for an analog could prove fruitless because readers did not search certain domains. For example, with the electric potential energy and electric potential problem, if readers had searched only the domain of mechanics instead of heat, they might not have found a useful analog. Fourth, readers might select and use a relatively poor analog simply because it was the first one they encountered in their search. Fifth, readers might select a good analog, but fail to correctly map important features of the analog to the solution of the problem. Finally, readers might fail to verify that the solution they mapped is, in fact, a valid solution.

If, at any operation in the model, readers detect that they have made an error, it is possible for them to cycle back to an earlier operation and correct their error. For example, a solution that cannot be verified may have been mapped incorrectly, so readers should reexamine their solution mapping. If a solution cannot be mapped, this may be the result of a poor analog, so readers should select a new analog. If readers are unable to find a good analog, it may be the result of searching the wrong domains, so readers should examine other domains. If readers have difficulty finding the right domains, it may be because they have failed to identify important features of the problem or they have focused on unimportant features. And, finally, if readers are not identifying important features, it may be because they have misrepresented the problem, and if so, they should try some alternative ways of looking at it.

The Science Teacher's Use of the Model

We recommend that science teachers train their students to use this model of analogical problem solving. With it, the students can plan, monitor, evaluate, and remediate their problem-solving efforts.

Science teachers should look for opportunities during lectures, demonstrations, and laboratories to "model the model." They should point out to their students when an analogy might be used to gain insight into a problem. The teachers should also demonstrate how to apply the operations in the model to the problem at hand.

Students should be shown how to criticize the analogies they generate, as well as those generated by the teacher and the text author. Those students who learn how to apply the model for themselves will have a powerful intellectual tool they can bring to bear on complex science problems.

Problem Finding and Hypothesis Generation

Analogies can help readers to discover new problems and hypothesize about their solutions. Authors prompt the problem-finding and hypothesis-generating processes of their readers by posing analogical questions in and at the end of chapters. Here are some examples, again from *Conceptual Physics* by Hewitt (1987), in which questions are posed which prompt problem finding and hypothesis generation in readers. The questions are based upon an analogy drawn between gravity and electricity:

* It is said that a gravitational field, unlike an electric field, cannot be shielded. But the gravitational field at the center of the earth cancels to zero. Isn't this evidence that a gravitational field can be shielded?
* How are a gravitational and an electric field similar?
* How is an electric field different from a gravitational field?
* The vectors for the gravitational field of the earth point *toward* the earth; the vectors for the electric field of a proton point *away* from the proton. Explain. (pp. 501, 507–508)

In addition to responding to the author's questions, we believe that readers can and should be trained to generate such questions for themselves; that is, to discover their own problems rather than rely entirely upon the text author to pose them. Having discovered their own problems, the readers can then proceed to hypothesize about possible solutions. This is what it means to read creatively!

Critics of analogies will point out that readers will sometimes generate unreasonable problems and hypotheses, looking for relations between concepts where none exist (as far as we know). Critics will say that the resulting relations will be meaningless, or worse still, confusing to readers.

We agree that the relations made between concepts will be meaningless and confusing at times, but at other times valid relations will be made. We believe the *process* of connecting concepts is important and must be nourished in readers. To reject the process because it sometimes leads to meaningless or incorrect relations is like throwing the baby out with the bath water.

Critics of analogies often believe that a concept, particularly a science concept, should be learned in isolation (from other concepts) so that it is not confused with the other concepts. This is a naive view of how human learning occurs. The process of relating concepts by means of analogy is inherent to human cognition; in effect, analogical reasoning is "hard wired" and it is unreasonable to expect readers not to use it. They will use it. Our concern is that they use it effectively. One way to ensure they use it effectively is to train them in the analogical problem-solving model we presented in the last section, ensuring that readers understand each of the operations, the errors that can result from the operations, and the ways to remediate those errors.

Recently, it has been demonstrated experimentally that analogies function as aids to scientific thought. Gentner and Gentner (1983) showed that college and high school students who used a "flowing fluid" analogy of electricity made different problem-solving inferences than students who used a "moving crowd" analogy. These findings support the view that analogies can serve as important sources of insight.

Many prominent scientists have emphasized the value of analogical reasoning in scientific insight and discovery. For example, Johannes Kepler, the eminent seventeenth-century astronomer, wrote: "And I cherish more than anything else the Analogies, my most trustworthy masters. They know all the secrets of Nature, and they ought to be least neglected in Geometry" (quoted in Polya, 1973, p. 12). Kepler attempted to explain astronomical phenomena, such as the motion of the planets, in terms of precise physical laws. In a letter he wrote in 1605, he drew an analogy between planetary motion and clockwork:

I am much occupied with the investigation of the physical causes. My aim in this is to show that the celestial machine is to be likened not to a divine organism but rather to a clock-work . . . insofar as nearly all the manifold movements are carried out by means of a single, quite simple magnetic force, as in the case of a clockwork, all motions are caused by a simple weight. Moreover, I show how this physical conception is to be presented through calculation and geometry. (Quoted in Rutherford, Holton, & Watson, 1975, Unit 2, p. 68)

Joseph Priestley (1773–1804), a distinguished physical scientist, also found analogies to be useful problem-solving tools. Priestley proposed the "law of electrical force," which was later verified experimentally by the French physicist Charles Coulomb. Here are the events that led to Priestley's proposal:

Priestley verified Franklin's results, and went on to reach a brilliant conclusion from them. He remembered from Newton's *Principia* that gravitational forces behave in a similar way. Inside a hollow planet, the net gravitational force on an object (the sum of all the forces exerted by all parts of the planet) would be exactly zero. This result also follows mathematically from the law that the gravitational force between any two individual pieces of matter is inversely proportional to the square of the distance between them. Priestley therefore proposed that forces exerted by charges vary inversely as the square of the distance, just as do forces exerted by massive bodies. . . . We call the force exerted between bodies owing to the fact that they are charged "electric" force, just as we call the force between uncharged bodies "gravitational" force. . . .
    Priestley's proposal was based on reasoning by analogy, that is, by reasoning from a parallel, well demonstrated case. Such reasoning alone could not *prove* that electrical forces are inversely proportional to the square of the distance between charges. But it strongly encouraged other physicists to test Priestley's hypothesis by experiment. (Rutherford *et al.*, 1975, Unit 4, p. 35)

Perhaps the strongest statement in support of analogies as aids to insight and discovery in science is that of the English physicist N. R. Campbell who, in his 1920 book *Physics, the Elements,* pointed to the billiard ball model of the kinetic theory of gases and argued:

Analogies are not "aids" to the establishment of theories; they are an utterly essential part of theories, without which theories would be completely valueless and unworthy of the name. It is often suggested that the analogy leads to the formulation of the theory, but that once the theory is formulated the analogy has served its purpose and may be removed or forgotten. Such a suggestion is absolutely false and perniciously misleading. (Quoted in Hesse, 1966, p. 4)

Testimonials to the creative potential of analogies are common in the science literature. These testimonials can be found in the personal records of prominent scientists as well as in studies of the history of science (e.g., Darden, 1980; Hesse, 1966). Taken together, these testimonials suggest

that analogies, serving as models, can be valuable aids to scientific explanation and discovery.

Future Research

We have proposed models for using analogies to explain concepts and solve problems in science texts. These models were derived from an analysis of science texts, particularly physics and physical science texts. It is essential, however, that empirical studies be conducted to validate these models. We have initiated a program of studies to do just that. We hope to attract the interest of other researchers who will study and extend these models.

We have encouraged science teachers to familiarize their students with these models. Systematic procedures for training students in the use of these models should be developed, and these procedures should be validated in classroom settings. Ethnographic studies of teacher–student–textbook interactions that involve analogies would be particularly appropriate.

Because the models we proposed were derived from an analysis of science texts, it is not clear to what extent these models generalize across the curriculum to disciplines other than science. We believe the models might generalize to other disciplines; however, textbook surveys and empirical studies must be conducted to verify this.

Finally, a great deal more research is needed on ways to facilitate analogical reasoning and problem solving. More information is needed on how individual differences in cognitive development and content area knowledge influence the generation and use of analogies. More information is also needed concerning the circumstances under which analogies can be counterproductive, resulting in increased confusion instead of comprehension.

Summary and Conclusions

To promote meaningful comprehension, science texts should incorporate features that help readers to relate text content to what they already know. One of the most effective ways for readers to integrate their existing knowledge with text content is to do so by means of analogy. Authors can provide analogies for readers, and readers can be trained to generate their own analogies.

In a science textbook, analogies can serve both

an explanatory and a creative function. They serve an explanatory function when they put new concepts and principles into familiar terms. They serve a creative function when they stimulate the solution of existing problems, the identification of new problems, and the generation of hypotheses.

In science texts, analogies are used to transfer ideas from a familiar conceptual domain (i.e., the analog) to an unfamiliar one (i.e., the target). In our representation of an analogy, the analog and the target are subordinate to a superordinate concept (or principle or formula). The identification and naming of the superordinate concept can suggest other analogies; it can also stimulate readers to generalize what they have learned and apply their learning to other contexts.

When used for either an explanatory or a creative purpose, an analogy can be a double-edged sword. An analog can be used to explain correctly, even predict, some aspects of the target; however, at some point every analogy breaks down. Authors must therefore make readers aware that, at that point, miscomprehension and misdirection may begin.

Analogies drawn by an author between concepts that are covered early in a text and concepts covered later are particularly effective because the author can be sure that the earlier concepts (which function as analogs) are part of every reader's knowledge base. These analogies prompt readers to connect related text concepts and form conceptual systems.

Textbooks of high school physics and of physical science appeared to contain the most elaborate analogies, so we focused our attention on them. We identified the most effective analogies from the standpoint of instructional design. The authors of these analogies performed certain key operations that we incorporated into a model. Our model can serve not only as a guide for authors of science textbooks, but also as a guide for science teachers and students who wish to interpret, criticize, and extend an author's analogy or one of their own.

Analogies serve a creative function when they help readers to solve problems, find problems, and generate hypotheses. Authors prompt readers to use analogies creatively by means of questions, hints, and illustrations. In addition, readers can prompt themselves to use analogies creatively if they are trained to ask certain questions of themselves and perform certain analogical operations. To provide a basis for this training, we proposed a model of analogical problem solving.

The process of relating concepts by means of

analogy is inherent to human cognition; in effect, analogical reasoning is "hard-wired," and it is unreasonable to expect readers not to use it. They will use it. Our concern is that they use it effectively as an aid to understanding and as an insight in science.

We have proposed models for using analogies to explain concepts and solve problems in science texts. Our future research will focus on validating these models and developing procedures for training science students to use them effectively.

ACKNOWLEDGMENTS. We wish to thank Russell Yeany, Chairman of Science Education at the University of Georgia, for surveying textbooks of high school physics and of physical science with us. His comments, along with those of Daryl Adams, Juliet Allan, Alphonse Buccino, Michael Hale, Patrick Kyllonen, Michael Padilla, Joseph Riley, and Paula Schwanenflugel, on the ideas presented in this chapter, were invaluable.

References

Britton, B. K., & Glynn, S. M. (1987). *Executive control processes in reading*. Hillsdale, NJ: Erlbaum.

Britton, B. K., Glynn, S. M., Meyer, B. J. F., & Penland, M. J. (1982). Effects of text structure on use of cognitive capacity during reading. *Journal of Educational Psychology, 74*, 51–61.

Darden, L. (1980). Theory construction in genetics. In T. Nickles (Ed.), *Scientific discovery: Case studies* (pp. 151–170). Dordrecht, The Netherlands: D. Reidel.

Gentner, D., & Gentner, D. R. (1983). Flowing waters or teeming crowds: Mental models of electricity. In D. Gentner & A. L. Stevens (Eds.), *Mental models* (pp. 99–129). Hillsdale, NJ: Erlbaum.

Gick, M. L., & Holyoak, K. J. (1980). Analogical problem solving. *Cognitive Psychology, 12*, 306–355.

Gick, M. L., & Holyoak, K. J. (1983). Schema induction and analogical transfer. *Cognitive Psychology, 15*, 1–38.

Glynn, S. M., & Britton, B. K. (1984). Supporting readers' comprehension through effective text design. *Educational Technology, 24*(10), 40–43.

Glynn, S. M., & Di Vesta, F. J. (1977). Outline and hierarchical organization as aids for study and retrieval. *Journal of Educational Psychology, 69*, 89–95.

Glynn, S. M., & Di Vesta, F. J. (1979). Control of prose processing via instructional cues. *Journal of Educational Psychology, 71*, 595–603.

Glynn, S. M., Britton, B. K., & Tillman, M. H. (1985). Typographical cues in text: Management of the reader's attention. In D. H. Jonassen (Ed.), *The technology of text* (Vol. 2, pp. 192–209). Englewood Cliffs, NJ: Educational Technology Publications.

Glynn, S. M., Andre, T., & Britton, B. K. (1986). The design of instructional text: Introduction to the special issue. *Educational Psychologist, 21*, 245–251.

Hesse, M. B. (1966). *Models and analogies in science*. Notre Dame, IN: University of Notre Dame Press.

Hewitt, P. G. (1985a). *Conceptual physics*. Boston: Little, Brown.

Hewitt, P. G. (1985b). *Instructor's manual to accompany conceptual physics*. Boston: Little, Brown.

Hewitt, P. G. (1987). *Conceptual physics*. Menlo Park, CA: Addison-Wesley.

Holyoak, K. J. (1985). The pragmatics of analogical transfer. In G. H. Bower (Ed.), *The psychology of learning and motivation* (Vol. 19, pp. 59–87). Orlando, FL: Academic Press.

Miller, F., Dillon, T. J., & Smith, M. K. (1980). *Concepts in physics*. New York: Harcourt Brace Jovanovich.

Polya, G. (1973). *Mathematics and plausible reasoning* (Vol. 1.). Princeton, NJ: Princeton University Press.

Rogers, E. M. (1960). *Physics for the inquiring mind*. Princeton, NJ: Princeton University Press.

Rumelhart, D. E., & Abrahamson, A. A. (1973). A model for analogical reasoning. *Cognitive Psychology, 5,* 1–28.

Rumelhart, D. E., & Norman, D. A. (1981). Analogical processes in learning. In J. R. Anderson (Ed.), *Cognitive skills and their acquisition* (pp. 335–339). Hillsdale, NJ: Erlbaum.

Rutherford, F. J., Holton, G., & Watson, F. G. (1975). *Project physics*. New York: Holt, Rinehart & Winston.

Sternberg, R. J. (1977). Component processes in analogical reasoning. *Psychological Review, 84,* 353–378.

Sternberg, R. J. (1986). *Intelligence applied*. New York: Harcourt Brace Jovanovich.

Wittrock, M. C. (1985). Learning science by generating new conceptions from old ideas. In L. H. T. West & A. L. Pines (Eds.), *Cognitive structure and conceptual change* (pp. 259–266). Orlando, FL: Academic Press.

CHAPTER 22

Toward a Model of Creativity Based upon Problem Solving in the Social Sciences

James F. Voss and Mary L. Means

Although creativity manifests itself in all areas of inquiry, most of the cited examples of creative thought involve the thinking of mathematicians, physical and biological scientists, writers, composers, and artists. In typical circumstances, few examples are cited in reference to social scientists. Yet creative acts may be found in virtually any domain, as, for example, in sports, when the forward pass was first used as an offensive weapon in football, or in business, when Henry Ford saw the implications of an assembly line and also realized that mass production would require mass consumption. Similarly, the work of March and Simon (1958) on organizational theory and the theoretical developments of Freud embrace creative work.

Despite the fact that creative acts may be observed in many domains, defining what is meant by creativity and establishing criteria for what constitutes a creative act are certainly nontrivial issues. Indeed, the conceptual complexity of creativity may be demonstrated by asking a few questions. Does a person who is performing a creative act know that he or she is doing just that? If the answer is affirmative, then one must ask how the person is able to know and how knowledge of that act is distinguished from knowledge of other acts. If the answer is negative, then one must ask what criteria establish the act as having been creative. Similarly, to what extent does the product of the mental activity determine whether the mental processes leading to the product constituted a creative act? If the product is quite significant in a theoretical and/or practical sense, does this mean the act was creative? Whereas if the product is relatively insignificant, does this mean the act was not creative? Shakespeare may be regarded as being more creative than Robert Service not because his actual "acts of creativity" were fundamentally different from Service's but because his products demonstrated greater insight into the human condition. Is creativity, therefore, a characteristic of only a limited number of people or are all individuals capable of creative acts? As might be expected, the answer to this question depends upon one's model of the creative process.

Numerous writers have, of course, addressed the issue of creativity (e.g., Bransford & Stein, 1984; Bruner, 1962; Hayes, 1981; Henle, 1962; Koestler, 1964; Perkins, 1981, 1984), and they have shown considerable agreement concerning characteristics ascribed to products that are taken to be the outcome

James F. Voss and Mary L. Means • Department of Psychology, Learning Research and Development Center, University of Pittsburgh, Pittsburgh, PA 15260.

of a creative process. The product characteristics that are most frequently mentioned are novelty, usefulness, and harmony or elegance, with most writers also emphasizing that no single criterion is in itself sufficient in defining a creative product. With respect to the creative process, there is widespread agreement among writers that creativity consists of perceiving an important relation where one had not previously been known or perhaps even suspected. Poincaré (1946), for example, spoke of "an unexpected kinship between facts long known but wrongly believed to be strangers to one another" (p. 386). Other similar statements include "two different lines of thought meet" (Heisenberg, 1958, p. 187); "the connecting of diverse experience" (Bruner, 1962, p. 6); "the emergence of a new and fitting organization" (Crutchfield, 1962, p. 123); "new orderings of facts previously unrelated" (Henle, 1962, p. 38); "seeing unity in variety" (Bronowski, 1956, p. 27); and "making the familiar, unfamiliar and the unfamiliar, familiar" (Murray, 1986, p. 35).

Given the general agreement regarding the products and processes of the creative act, creativity may be taken to refer to a person's relating two previously unrelated concepts and creating a product that is novel as well as elegant and useful. Even though intuitively appealing, this description of a creative act is nevertheless found wanting in at least three ways. First, it fails to take into account the role of context. Creative acts occur in particular contexts; creativity does not come out of "nowhere" (cf. Perkins, 1981). Second, the description, though perhaps missing some components, at the same time may be too all-encompassing. Using the above account, a dog of one of the authors has demonstrated creativity in devising ways to entice the author into playing ball (assuming the process, in its own way, was elegant). Of course, there is nothing to argue against the idea that animals can be creative, except perhaps man's need to feel superior to other species. Third, the idea that creativity involves observing a relationship that was not previously perceived provides little information regarding the processes that underlie the creative act.

In this chapter, we attempt to address some of the complexities of the creative process by presenting a model that views the creative process as a special case of problem solving, and, in particular, as the solving of an ill-structured problem. The model has an information-processing orientation, emphasizing the use of one's prior knowledge and of search processes that act upon the prior knowledge (cf. Newell & Simon, 1972). The model also extends

the information-processing approach by taking into account the function of value and affect.

The assumptions of the model also suggest that a creative act is a function of the various structures and processes that occur in all higher mental activity. Thus, creativity is not taken to be qualitatively different from other types of mental function, and, similarly, creativity is not regarded as a special capacity with which only some people are endowed. This position does not deny individual differences in creativity, with such differences being attributed to the operation of the cognitive and affective mechanisms of mental function.

The idea of viewing creativity in terms of problem solving is, of course, not new (Bransford & Stein, 1984; Hayes, 1981, Henle, 1962; Newell & Simon, 1972; Perkins, 1981). More specifically, Newell, Shaw, and Simon (1962) described creativity as "a special class of problem solving activity characterized by novelty, unconventionality, persistence and difficulty in problem formulation" (p. 66). Hayes (1981) described creativity as "a special kind of problem solving, that is the act of solving an ill-defined problem" (p. 199), whereas Vaughan (1985) indicated that creativity typically "applies to situations which have no single solution" (p. 40). Furthermore, the products sought in the creative process have been regarded as "vaguely and tentatively conceived, groped for, caught at, discovered in the process" (Perkins, 1981, p. 276).

The remainder of this chapter has five sections. We begin in the first section, with an analysis of the solving of ill-structured problems, followed by an "unpacking" of the model that emphasizes the interactive role of prior knowledge and mental search. In the third section, we consider how, within the context of the model, value and affect play a role in the creative process, then in the fourth section, we address the issue of creativity in the social sciences. In the final section, we close with a few remarks regarding how instruction may influence the development of creativity in the social sciences.

On the Solving of Ill-Structured Problems

The Information-Processing Account of Problem Solving

A problem generally is said to exist when an individual wants to reach a particular goal but cannot because of some type of barrier. In information-processing terms, the individual who is confronted by a problem is presumed to be in an initial state, a state consisting of the individual's knowledge of the givens of the problem, of the problem's constraints, and of the goal of the problem, which is viewed as the problem's final state. The problem is presumed to have states intervening between the initial and final states, with the solving of the problem thus consisting of moving from one state to the next until the goal state is achieved. Furthermore, the movement from one state to the next is presumed to take place via use of an operator. If a person is adding a column of digits, for example, each successive addition of a number is a state that is reached by application of the operator "add." Thus, the individual reaches the goal state when all numbers in the column are added.

The information-processing model also uses the terms *task environment* and *problem space*. The task environment refers to the statement of the problem and the environment, external to the individual, in which the problem statement occurs. The problem space refers to a delineated "mental space" that contains all the states that could occur in the solving of a particular problem. In addition, the problem space contains the operators that are available for use in the problem as well as the constraints of the problem. Viewed in this way, the solving of the problem involves a "walk" through the problem space, moving along a "path" from one state to the next until the goal is reached (Newell & Simon, 1972).

In order to solve a problem, the solver needs to determine whether the path being followed is indeed leading to the goal. To do this, the solver uses some type of evaluation strategy. One commonly employed strategy is termed *means–ends analysis,* in which the solver evaluates whether moving into a particular state has moved the solver closer to the goal. This analysis is accomplished by determining whether the discrepancy of the goal and the present state is less than it was when the solver was in the previous state. The final state is thus reached by continuing to reduce the discrepancy. Of course, other strategies exist and some are discussed later in this chapter.

Given the above description, we turn now to how the model has been developed in reference to the solving of complex problems. The solution of complex problems is typically divided into two phases, that of developing the representation of the problem and that of providing the solution to the problem, given the representation. The representation phase consists of the individual's analyzing the problem to determine the givens, the goal, and the constraints of the problem. Such an analysis may take various forms, a common one being to try to classify the problem as belonging to a particular category (a physics mechanics problem) or determining the causes of the problem (a problem of city government to reduce the crime rate). Then, once the representation is developed, the solver provides a solution to the problem. (One can, during the solution phase, "go back" and "re-represent" the problem, although this does not happen frequently.) Having considered the general account of the information-processing view of problem solving, we now consider the distinction of well-structured and ill-structured problems and how solutions are obtained for such problems (cf. Reitman, 1965; Simon, 1973; Voss & Post, 1988).

The Solving of Well-Structured and Ill-Structured Problems

A problem is termed *well structured* when the various components of the problem are well specified and are known to the solver, that is, the goal is well specified, the givens of the problem are either in the problem statement or are well known to the solver, and the constraints also are known to the solver. For example, in proving a geometry theorem, the givens are stated in the problem statement, the "to prove" goal is stated, and the primary constraint is that the solver may use only previously proved theorems in the proof. On the other hand, ill-structured problems are those in which the givens, the goal, and/or the constraints are not well specified or known. Thus, the goal may be poorly specified, the givens may not be in the problem statement and may be unknown to the solver, and the constraints may be unspecified. (The fact that there may be variation in the extent to which the givens and the constraints are specified indicates that the ill-structured, well-structured distinction is a continuum rather than a dichotomy.) Reitman (1965), for example, spoke of a composer's composition of a fugue as an ill-structured problem. In this case, the individual's knowledge of the goal is vague, the givens are the composer's knowledge of the structure of a fugue and knowledge of music theory, with these two factors also constituting constraints. Moreover, as the fugue is composed, additional constraints are set up, such as the key and the fugue passages already written. The idea that constraints are generated during the course of the problem-solving activity is, moreover, a characteristic of the solving of ill-structured problems.

The well-structured, ill-structured distinction is especially important when viewed in relation to whether consensual agreement is established with respect to problem solutions. In particular, well-structured problems typically have solutions that are agreed upon by individuals who have knowledge of the domain in question. Thus, problems found in mathematics and physics texts are well structured, having solutions that are known and agreed upon by mathematicians and physicists. However, ill-structured problems generally do not have known solutions, and experts in the domain of the particular problem frequently not in agreement with respect to whether a particular solution is appropriate. Thus, although in economics there may be some issues upon which economists would agree, there are many problems for which agreement would not be found. Moreover, consensual agreement is found even less frequently in such fields as sociology and political science, as well as in issues of social policy. In fields such as art and music, disagreement generally occurs not in deciding whether, for example, a fugue is a fugue, but in evaluating the quality of the work.

Why are there differences in the structure of problems across various domains? Probably the most important reason is that the data base and the theory of such domains as the physical sciences are relatively well developed, whereas those of social sciences are relatively unrefined with respect to the specificity of concepts, the determination of critical variables, and the development and testing of theory. Furthermore, there is the question of whether social sciences will ever reach such refinement, an issue that is discussed later in this chapter. But this is not to say that domains such as physics are completely well structured. Ill-structured problems may be found at the cutting edge of the research of such domains. A good example of an ill-structured problem in physics is found in the research of Tweney (1985), who has extensively studied the diaries of Michael Faraday. Tweney's analysis shows how Faraday's discovery of electromagnetic induction constituted the solving of an ill-structured problem. Interestingly, Tweney's analysis also points to one of the major differences of the physical sciences and social sciences; namely, that, in the former, hypotheses can be tested by conducting experiments which take a relatively short time to perform whereas, in the latter, experiments, even when they are feasible, may take years to conclude and, more-

over, critical conditions may change during this time.

We now turn to the question of the solving of well-structured and ill-structured problems. Considering the former, Larkin, McDermott, Simon and Simon (1980) have demonstrated that when physics experts are given a problem from a physics textbook, they develop a representation of the problem by analyzing the elements and relations of the problem, sometimes drawing a diagram in the process. Typically, such examination leads to classifying the problem and, once classified, the problem is solved by applying the appropriate equations. Furthermore, in applying the equations, a means–ends analysis is not required because the physicist knows how to solve the problem in question. Thus, this example indicates that the representation phase often consists of a pattern-matching procedure in which the problem statement is considered in terms of its parameters and the relations among the parameters, and these components are matched to a pattern in memory. The physicist, having had previous experience with this type of problem, is able to perform the match and, subsequently, provide the solution. On the other hand, novices in physics often have greater difficulty, for they may not be able to classify the problem and often resort to a process of means–ends analysis in which they try out equations that contain one or more of the parameters found in the problem statement and eventually reach the goal by generating an appropriate sequence of equations (cf. Larkin *et al.*, 1980).

The solving of ill-structured problems is usually more complicated than the solving of well-structured problems. Consider a situation in which a city official is asked to propose a plan for reducing the use of drugs within that particular city. The individual will likely develop a representation of the problem by determining the causes of the drug problem as well as determining the constraints that exist in relation to the problem, constraints that may include budget, staff, and/or time, as well as other factors. The development of the representation may thus involve reading reports of the federal government of the attempts of other cities to deal with the problem, and of the historical development of the problem. In addition, the analysis may involve determining just how extensive drug use is, in reference to age, socioeconomic class, and other factors. The individual may go to drug rehabilitation centers, seeking information and advice. There may be an attempt to determine how the drug trafficking takes place and to determine who seems to profit from the sale of drugs. From the information available, the individual may then conclude that there are three primary causes of the drug problem in that city, or that there is a single cause, for example, economic. Given this representation, the individual may then propose a solution designed to reduce the impact of the perceived causal factor(s). Moreover, the solution, if imaginative and workable, may even be called *creative*.

In solving an ill-structured problem, both the representation and the solution phases involve the process of justification. Evidence for the claims of the representation may be provided, or the individual may develop an argument from which the causes may be inferred. Similarly, the solution is typically justified by indicating why and how the proposed solution would work as well as by indicating why the solution may not work and what can be done to handle possible shortcomings and objections (cf. Voss, Greene, Post, & Penner, 1983). In effect, the justification of the solution points to the important fact that the solution process, taken as a whole, is basically one of rhetoric. Incidentally, an interesting aspect of solving ill-structured problems is that, in the course of developing the representation and of proposing the solution, the solver does not typically provide any verbalizations about the nature of the strategies being pursued. Instead, solvers tend to deal with problems using the specific terminology and context of the problem *per se*.

The sketch of the solving of an ill-structured problem presented in the preceding paragraph suggests the lack of consensual agreement that may occur in relation to solving ill-structured problems. Another official could argue that the causal factors that are derived in the analysis are inaccurate and/or inadequate and could then argue that the problem should, in fact, be represented in a different way. Another person could argue that although the causes seem appropriate, the solution is not because it will not address the causes. Yet another person could argue that though the causes and solution are satisfactory, the solver did not take into account one or more constraints that make the solution unworkable.

Although this account of the "solving" of the city's drug abuse problem provides an example of the solving of an ill-structured problem, other ill-structured problems may have characteristics that vary somewhat from those found in this case. For example, a composer may have the goal of composing a particular type of work, but the point at which the composer feels that the goal has been reached is

somewhat of an arbitrary judgment, in the sense that stopping further revision is not guided by any particular rule except the sense of completion by the composer. The same condition holds for the artist and the writer. A chemist, however, may have a quite precise goal, and when it is achieved, it is well defined.

The idea that creativity may be viewed as a special case of the solving of an ill-structured problem seems reasonable at a descriptive level of analysis. However, to provide a more thorough examination of this view, it is now necessary to consider the nature of solving ill-structured problems in greater detail, providing an analysis of the components of the process.

Prior Knowledge, Search, and Creativity

Prior Knowledge

One of the most critical components of mental functioning in general and problem solving in particular is prior knowledge, and one type of prior knowledge is that of the basic concepts, facts, and principles of a particular subject matter domain. This knowledge is typically declarative in nature (Ryle, 1949) and, though the question of the mental representation of knowledge is an issue currently receiving considerable theoretical attention, we may assume that, for our purposes, such knowledge is stored hierarchically. Furthermore, in addition to declarative knowledge, individuals typically have knowledge of procedures (Ryle, 1949) that are used in a particular domain, as, for example, in the use of subtraction methods in arithmetic or methods of integration in calculus.

A form of procedural knowledge especially important to the present analysis is that of knowledge of strategies. Moreover, the strategies of particular importance are those described by Newell (1980) as weak problem-solving methods. Strong problem-solving methods are characterized as being domain specific, whereas weak methods are not domain specific and include (1) strategies, such as means–ends analysis, analogy, and decomposition, in which a problem is divided into a number of subproblems, (2) conversion, in which one problem is converted into another because the latter is more readily solved, and (3) generate and test, which consists of generating a solution to a problem or subproblem and testing the solution against some criterion. In addition, examining the history of a problem may also be regarded as a weak method. What is particularly important about the weak methods is that, with the possible exception of economics, social sciences have few if any strong methods of problem solving, and the individual must employ weak methods in the solving process. Moreover, what is of critical importance to the present analysis is that the weak methods are fundamental to search, a point that is developed in the next section.

There are two additional points concerning prior knowledge that warrant consideration. First, although having prior knowledge is in itself of critical importance, such knowledge also needs to be accessible; that is, in the course of solving a problem, the knowledge that may be germane to the solution must be accessed, for only if the individual is able to access such knowledge may he or she be able to relate what is being processed and what is in memory. In other words, prior knowledge needs to be a "working" knowledge (cf. Voss, 1987), in the sense that the knowledge needs to be accessible when the individual may need it. How knowledge becomes working knowledge is an important and unresolved issue, but one thing that quite likely makes knowledge more "workable" is its use in a variety of contexts. When used in this way, it raises the likelihood of being accessed in a variety of contexts. The importance of flexibility of access has, of course, been stressed by writers on creativity, such as Perkins (1984) suggesting that expertise in a domain allows for "mobility," and Bruner (1962) suggesting that "flexibility" and "combinatorial playfulness" are important.

Another aspect of prior knowledge that warrants consideration is that though prior knowledge is extremely important to effective problem solving, it also may act to hinder problem solving (Henle, 1962; Perkins, 1981). For example, prior knowledge may set up categorizations that prohibit the individual from viewing problems in new ways. Or prior knowledge may produce a particular highly used problem representation that constrains the individual with respect to looking at the problem in new ways, as in the classical Einstellung effect (e.g., Luchins, 1942).

Search

Although it is important that a person have knowledge and that the knowledge is working, solving ill-structured problems does not take place because all the germane information is available when one first considers the problem. Instead, it is necessary to search, either internally or externally, for information, with the goal of the search being to obtain information germane to the problem at hand. Furthermore, when information is obtained, it also becomes necessary to evaluate the information with respect to its usefulness to the problem at hand. Thus, the process of search is regarded as having two functions, the *operator* function and the *evaluator* function. The operator function, having essentially the same function as that of the previously described operators, refers to the search for information that enables the individual to enter the next problem state. The evaluator function is that of determining the extent to which information that is obtained may be effectively used in the solution process.

Considering the operator function in greater detail, it is assumed that individuals are able to perform this function by using, in part, the previously described weak methods of problem solving. Finding a useful analogy, for example, would constitute a mechanism of search. But other mechanisms are also available when an individual is reasoning about a particular problem. For example, the individual may search for examples to support a given conclusion. Similarly, the individual, in searching externally, may ask questions or go to a library. Also the individual may try out ideas on other people and receive critical feedback. Thus, the individual has a relatively large number of mechanisms that may be used to perform the operator function of the search process.

With respect to the evaluator function, the individual needs criteria that permit acceptance or rejection of the information, and an important aspect of such criteria is that they typically constitute constraints. Thus, in such fields as music, art, and literature, criteria may be aesthetic in nature, with the individual either accepting or rejecting particular information as "looking good," "sounding acceptable," or "feeling right." Such evaluations, moreover, may be accompanied by metastatements, as with a gut-level reaction, but the individual may not be able to verbalize what such statements "mean." In this regard, Perkins (1984) noted that creative individuals have at their disposal personal standards pertaining to creative products that enable them to "strive for products which are elegant, beautiful, and powerful" (p. 4). Interestingly, Getzels and Csikszentmihalyi (1976) found that, in the context of art, individuals who upon finishing a painting tended to view their work as incomplete were subsequently judged in their careers as more successful than individuals who viewed their own products as complete. The authors suggested that creative individuals have a critical capacity that tends to be ahead of their productive capacity, a notion that places strong emphasis upon the importance of the evaluative function.

On the Interaction of Prior Knowledge and Search

In the present section, the interaction of prior knowledge and search is discussed by describing four characteristics of the interaction.

1. *Search is directed, as opposed to random.* The search process is presumed to be directed, and how the direction is established is of importance. However, because goals vary in the extent to which they are defined, the extent to which the search is directed also varies. In addition, search can be constrained by the existence of multiple goals. For example, if an individual is working to develop an arms agreement with the Soviet Union, he or she may have in mind a number of goals that quite likely are ranked in terms of their importance. The goals thus act as a hierarchy of constraints. Moreover, the individual is also constrained by his or her own beliefs and attitudes toward the Soviet Union as well as by the knowledge of the Soviet Union's track record in past agreements, the policies of the current United States administration, the potential political ramifications of any agreement that is reached, and by personal political aspirations. Moreover, in an even more complex way, the constraints may include a type of cultural framework in which historical beliefs held by individuals within their own society may serve as constraints. Thus, all such constraints act to direct the search as well as set criteria for evaluation.

Three points may be made with respect to the role of constraints in the search process. First, whereas in a well-structured domain the constraints may be viewed more or less as rules of the game, the constraints in an ill-structured situation are typically more numerous, not as well defined, and they involve not only situational factors related to the issue but personal factors such as one's own beliefs and goals. Second, during the search, an individual is usually not aware of many of the constraints. Third, the process by which various solutions to goals or subgoals are generated and evaluated involves the

previously described operator and evaluator functions.

One question about the search process that is quite difficult to explain is operator selection, that is, what determines which weak method is to be used. Assume that an individual working in the State Department is confronted by the problem of helping to develop a policy toward South Africa. Of course, this is a complex issue involving such issues as the apartheid policy and United States interests in South Africa. The individual may use a number of strategies, such as looking for historical analogies, either by searching his or her memory or by examining such sources as books that provide accounts germane to the issue. The individual may also focus on the historical roots of the problem as found specifically in South Africa or in Africa as a whole. The individual may also try to adopt the perspective of the government officials of South Africa and try to determine what policies are optimal from that perspective. These various strategies all constitute efforts to expand the search and, more generally, to develop an appropriate problem representation. As previously noted, why one strategy is chosen over another is not clear, but it is likely that operator selection may be based upon past experience such that the use of particular strategies may have been "reinforced." If so, then individuals may have an operator hierarchy that represents the general order in which operators are selected, with the hierarchy being established via prior experience.

2. *Search processes often lead to ambiguous and/or paradoxical propositions.* During the course of the search, it is not uncommon for individuals to find themselves holding to ambiguous propositions in which, for example, two inconsistent solutions seem reasonable. The political scientist analyzing the South African issue may, on the one hand, conclude that the United States should pressure South Africa to drop the apartheid policy immediately but, on the other hand, may also conclude that the policy must be gradually eliminated if the country is to avoid a bloody civil war. The literature on creativity contains many references to the role of ambiguity in the creative process (e.g., Perkins, 1984), and two points are emphasized in this literature. First, creative individuals tend to have a high tolerance for ambiguity (Amabile, 1983; Rothenberg, 1979). Indeed, creative individuals may even seek ambiguities and use the setting up of ambiguities as an important part of the creative process. Such a view, of course, is consistent with the idea that thinking is dialectical in

nature (Bassaches, 1984). Second, creative outcomes often occur as a result of resolving ambiguities (Bruner, 1962).

A critical aspect of ambiguity is that the individual is faced with a difficult processing problem in trying to resolve an ambiguity. There are two sets of constraints that must be dealt with, and the individual must therefore generate a representation or a solution that may likely reject some of the existing constraints while, at the same time, maintaining other constraints. The complexity of such a process, moreover, may be such that not all individuals are capable of conducting such mental gymnastics.

3. *The search process often involves the violation of constraints.* As previously noted, acts that are regarded as creative quite frequently involve violating one or more constraints. Moreover, the constraints often violated in such acts are assumptions; that is, "breakthroughs" occur when an individual rejects a widely held theory by attacking its existing assumptions and formulating an idea based upon different assumptions. Numerous examples of this phenomenon exist, ranging from Stravinsky's "The Rites of Spring" to Paracelsus's insight that disease may be caused by factors external to the body (Boorstin, 1983). Similarly, President Nixon's opening of a dialogue with the People's Republic of China constituted a violation of assumptions regarding the relations between China and the United States. Within the present framework, constraint violation thus reflects a process by which the individual, in obtaining information from the search, is forced to re-represent the problem, and this often happens as a resolution to an ambiguous situation.

4. *Search often involves an alternating immersion and detachment with respect to problem involvement.* Probably the most widely cited phenomenon in the creativity literature is that of the "incubation effect" (Wallas, 1926). This effect refers to the observation that individuals may work on a problem that defies solution and, upon "setting aside" the problem, a solution suddenly occurs to the solver, often upon the occurrence of an apparently extraneous stimulus. The problem is thought to be "incubating" during the period of detachment and somehow the solution is generated during this period. Attempts to explain this effect have been discussed by Perkins (1981).

Within the present framework, the incubation effect is regarded as a continuation of the search process that occurs at a level below the threshold of consciousness (cf. Simon, 1966). At the same time,

however, detachment from a problem also represents a form of perspective-taking, in which an individual may respectively be considering a problem and, at an unconscious level, be considering alternative representations of a problem. The present view does not suggest, however, that there are any special unconscious mechanisms that facilitate problem solution.

A Recapitulation

The interaction of search and prior knowledge, as previously described, is in a sense conceptually quite simple. What makes the process complex, however, is the flexibility of the human mind. The individual has stored in memory an extremely large amount of information, some of which may be germane to the issue being considered. The question then is how to find that information. But, at the same time, finding the information is frequently not enough, for the individual must be able to determine how the information fits in a new context; that is, the information must be related to other concepts to which it has not been previously related. To accomplish this, the individual has at his or her disposal a finite and yet a large number of strategies. Furthermore, the individual needs to evaluate the information and to determine the "fit" of the information to the problem at hand.

Previously in this chapter, we mentioned that the creative process is an act of the human mind that involves the use of processes that occur in virtually everyone in the course of daily existence. Nevertheless, the analysis as thus far presented also indicates that the creative process does not simply involve the use of such mechanisms. To have considerable knowledge, to be able to use what one knows, to define a problem appropriately, to search for information pertaining to the problem, and to evaluate information appropriately are indeed highly complex skills requiring considerable integration. Thus, many people may not be regarded as creative because they lack one or more of these components or because they have not had experience in the use of the mechanisms. One may ask whether we are essentially saying that creativity is the effective use of the operator and evaluator functions in relation to one's prior knowledge. The answer to this question is yes, but————. The "but" refers to the fact that although this statement is true, it is not the whole truth. Thus, we must now consider the roles of value and of affect.

Value, Affect, and the Creative Process

Within the present context, *affect* is regarded as the accuracy of positive or negative feelings that an individual has about a particular idea, object, or event. *Value* is defined as a personalized construct that presumably includes an individual's life-related goals as well as a sense of the means by which goals are to be accomplished. Value is also taken to refer to a sense of quality regarding the goals. When viewed in relation to creativity, one senses that individuals who are creative in virtually any field have a strong interest in that field, accompanied by a goal to excel in that field, although what "to excel" means may vary, of course, from person to person. Furthermore, even though some individuals have such goals in the arts, in science, or in social science and social policy fields, other individuals may have such goals in the office, the factory, or in the professions. However, because creativity can seldom be found in performing what is routine, the observation of creativity is, of necessity, limited primarily to those individuals whose values are such that they strive to excel and who are in fields exposed to the critical eye. Hence, the observation of creativity is quite restricted, and it is not surprising that sometimes creativity has been viewed as a special talent.

We assume that such affect and value relate to creative thinking in the following four ways.

1. *Value and affect influence problem selection.* Some individuals, by their intelligence, curiosity, training, and sense of values, do select problems that are significant, in the sense that the problems have general theoretical significance and/or considerable potential significance to other people (Perkins, 1981). Furthermore, such individuals are presumed to have a relatively strong need to solve the selected problem; this need initially setting up negative affect, negative in the sense that individuals feel a need to obtain a sense of closure concerning the problem. Progress in the solution process then involves positive affect, in the sense that obtaining closure or moving toward it is rewarding. Thus, in a very real sense, the solving of the problem constitutes a strong affective reward (Amabile, 1983). Moreover, although critical recognition of the solution by other individuals may also be important, the more creative individual tends to be motivated more by such internal criteria than by external criteria (Amabile, 1983; Crutchfield, 1962; Perkins, 1981, 1984).

One implication of the role of affect is that individuals who tend to be creative will likely select problems that will generate the previously described negative affect. Moreover, the value structure of such individuals encourages their selection of problems that will be of significance. Thus, the more creative individual seeks out important issues that are challenging and, most importantly, has the ability to discern such issues, a process that once again involves the use of knowledge and search processes. Thus, even though virtually all individuals have affect, that is, negative feelings about some things undone an positive feelings about getting things done, and even perhaps about doing things well, relatively few individuals are attracted to issues that have the previously described general significance.

2. *Value and affect keep the problem at hand in the forefront of consciousness.* Individuals who are working on a problem seem to be continually aware of the problem (cf. Perkins, 1981), and the effect of such awareness is to be searching constantly, internally and externally, for information that is potentially relevant to the problem. The account by Gruber (1981) of Darwin's development of the theory of evolution provides an excellent example of this process, for whenever Darwin observed animals, he apparently did so with some general ideas of animal behavior in mind.

The presumed continual awareness of a problem on the part of the creative individual has some interesting implications. For example, the awareness likely leads to an increased perception of inconsistencies, such inconsistencies being evoked when observations conflict with existing beliefs or hypotheses. Such inconsistencies set up negative affect which may lead to dialectical analysis and resolution. Also, continual awareness leads to an increase in one's knowledge as well as to an increase in the use of search strategies. The latter takes place because the individual needs to interpret new information, and that process requires comparing the information to what already exists in memory. In a sense, the continual awareness of a problem serves as a heuristic that enables the individual to acquire new information and perceive previously unknown relationships.

3. *Value and affect influence persistence.* Another function of value and affect is that they increase persistence in the solution effort. The values of the individual and the related negative feelings that exist when a solution is not forthcoming lead the individual to try new solutions and to search for more information. This point is impor-

tant for it indicates that a close relationship exists between criteria established by one's values and one's persistence. The more creative individual will not tend to be satisfied by achieving something that simply works but will, instead, attain the high standards of performance that are involved. It seems reasonable to assert that most individuals do not have such strong self-expectations.

Value and Affect, Prior Knowledge and Search

When the characteristics of value and affect are considered in relation to prior knowledge and search, it seems clear that the former produce more search, both internal and external, and serve the role of providing feelings regarding the ideas that are developed in the course of the solving process; feelings that can reflect both a sense of accomplishment and a sense of despair. The present model thus depicts the creative individual as an intellectually curious person who is at home when working with uncertainties and paradoxes. This individual has a substantial knowledge base not only of his or her domain of interest but of more general issues and subject matter. This individual is facile in the use of search strategies but quite likely is unable to verbalize when and how they are being used. Finally, although virtually all individuals have such characteristics to some degree and may, to a point, be creative, creative acts that are recognized by the intellectual community are those in which the individual has typically excelled in the integration of these characteristics and has generated a product of theoretical significance and/or practical utility.

Creativity in the Social Sciences

The account of creativity that is developed in this chapter certainly maintains that the nature of the creative process does not vary with the subject matter domain. Differences in content, however, would be expected as a function of domain. The evaluative function performed by the artist, for example, would be different from that performed by the chemist. Given that the general process is consistent across domains while the specific execution varies, the execution of the creative act is taken to be a function of problem context, a matter that is of particular concern when considering creativity in the social sciences.

The question of what contributions in the social sciences have been especially creative were reviewed by Inkeles (1983). He noted that Deutsch, Platt, and Senghass (1971) indicated 62 contributions that were regarded as especially creative and that they used two criteria to make this evaluation. Specifically, a creative act was taken to produce a new perception or new operations, and these had an important influence upon the subsequent development of the field in question. As noted by Inkeles (1983), these criteria largely excluded specific discoveries or demonstrations of important empirical phenomena. Furthermore, Inkeles noted that the procedure of Deutsch *et al.* excluded individuals who did not begin a movement but who made substantive contributions within the field. In contrast, Inkeles pointed out that, in social sciences, creativity has often consisted of work that has provided a conceptual framework for analyzing issues, with such frameworks being neither testable nor falsifiable, for example, socioconscious class. Inkeles also argued that a number of methodological advancements and discoveries have been quite creative. But, perhaps the most interesting point made by Inkeles involves the limitations of social sciences, namely, that three limitations act strongly to influence the nature of creativity. Moreover, because of these three factors, social sciences would be expected to yield fewer creative outcomes than natural sciences. First, social sciences do not attract individuals who are as creative to the extent that such individuals are drawn to the natural sciences. Second, the money provided for social science research is less than that allocated for research in natural sciences. Third, and the one that Inkeles regards as the most fundamental, the subject matter itself contains inherent limitations.

Inkeles ''unpacks'' his third limitation by citing three constraints of social science research. The first constraint is that there is a limit on the size and range of the subject matter. Thus, although natural sciences have expanded their inquiry to the universe as well as to particles, social sciences are limited to the study of the human population. The second constraint is that social science subject matter is conditional, that is, even though conditions of study in the physical sciences remain relatively stable, the conditions of social science phenomena change from one situation to the next. Thus, consistency over social time and social space is rare. The third constraint is that various individuals and public authorities refer to social science work in ideological terms. In this regard, Inkeles notes how, because of a presumed ideology, social science development has been meagre in Socialist countries and also notes politically based constraints that exist in Western countries.

The Inkeles account raises a number of interesting questions regarding creativity in social sciences, and from his comments we are able to gain some idea regarding why examples of creative activity in social sciences are not plentiful. Social sciences seem to evolve not by astounding discoveries but by the growth of concept and method. Social scientists tend to be "concept hunters," in which the delineation and description of a phenomenon are critical endeavors. However, the development of such concepts sometimes appears to be a statement of the obvious and is sometimes regarded as arbitrary and is met with controversy. Thus, relatively few concepts reach a criterion of theoretical significance, in the sense of explanation as opposed to description. In addition, social science developments seldom have met the criterion of having practical significance. Social scientists have not cured a disease, invented television or air conditioning, or developed optic fibers. Indeed, one could question the extent to which social scientists have generally been effective in reducing crime rate, solving international disagreements, and even solving economic problems, although economists would, of course, argue this point. Furthermore, Inkeles's (1983) argument clearly suggests that the issue is not necessarily one of differences in point of development, that is, that the natural sciences are more advanced and that social sciences will eventually "catch up." Instead, the argument is that social sciences, because of their intrinsic nature, may never catch up. Perhaps the best that can be expected is that intelligent individuals will realize that the major problems of the world are in the domain of social sciences, including the social use of technological developments, and that such realizations will lead to a deeper analysis of such issues. At a minimum, social science instruction should help to increase student awareness of the importance of social science questions. The next section presents some suggestions regarding such instruction.

Instruction and Creativity in the Social Sciences

Although generally not recognized as such, social science instruction affords a highly challenging and exceptional opportunity to help develop creative thinking. Furthermore, the nature of such instruction may be derived from the model presented in this chapter. Specifically, the model leads to at least five suggestions. (1) Students need to acquire knowledge of basic facts, concepts, principles, and theory in the domain, and, what is even more important, such learning needs to concentrate upon explanation and rationale. Textbooks currently employed in elementary and secondary school tend to present information in a factual manner with occasional causal information, and greater explanation would be desirable. (2) As acquisition takes place, students need to have experiences in using the knowledge in the solving of problems. This process would help to make knowledge accessible as well as providing experience in the use of the search methods described in this chapter. (3) Students need to develop skills in evaluating arguments, both with respect to their own arguments and with respect to the arguments of others. Such experience should include examining the nature of criteria that are used in evaluation. (4) Controversial issues need to be discussed and the various positions need to be evaluated. There has, of course, been a general tendency to finesse such issues, and such avoidance hardly leads to the development of creative thought. (5) Teachers at the elementary and secondary levels require much more training in social sciences. Although teachers may be well prepared in United States History and sometimes in World History and/or World Cultures, preparation in economics, international relations, and other fields is characteristically poor (Weiss, 1978). Moreover, such training should lead to a deeper consideration and appreciation of the need for creativity in the social sciences.

Summary

In this chapter, we presented a model of creativity that is based upon the solving of social science problems or, more generally, on the solving of ill-structured problems. The model emphasizes the importance of the individual's knowledge base, the effective use of a variety of search mechanisms that provide for obtaining and evaluating information, and the operation of value and affect components that, in a sense, drive the process. We also noted that the cited examples of creativity are usually found in mathematics, natural science, and in the humanities, and are seldom found in social sciences. This fact may be largely attributed to social science research not meeting the criteria that are typically interpreted. Finally, we proposed some suggestions with respect to instruction in social sciences that we hope would lead to an increase of creativity in students.

ACKNOWLEDGMENTS. Preparation of this chapter was supported by the Office of Educational Research and Improvement via Support of the Center for the Study of Learning and of the Learning Research and Development Center of the University of Pittsburgh. The opinions expressed in this chapter do not necessarily reflect those of any of these organizations.

References

Amabile, T. M. (1983). *The social psychology of creativity.* Springer-Verlag.

Bassaches, M. (1984). *Dialectical thinking and adult development.* Norwood, NJ: Ablex.

Boorstin, D. J. (1983). *The discoverers.* New York: Random House.

Bransford, J. D., & Stein, B. S. (1984). *The ideal problem solver.* New York: W. H. Freeman.

Bronowski, J. (1956). *Science and human values.* New York: Julian Messner.

Bruner, J. (1962). The conditions of creativity. In H. E. Gruber (Ed.), *Contemporary approaches to creative thinking* (pp. 1–30). New York: Atherton Press.

Crutchfield, R. S. (1962). Conformity and creative thinking. In H. E. Gruber (Ed.), *Contemporary approaches to creative thinking* (pp. 120–140). New York: Atherton Press.

Deutsch, K. W., Platt, J., & Senghass, D. (1971). Conditions favoring major advances in social sciences. *Science, 171,* 450–458.

Getzels, J. W., & Csikszentmihalyi, M. (1976). *The creative vision: A longitudinal study of problem finding in art.* New York: Wiley.

Gruber, H. E. (1981). *Darwin on man: A psychological study of scientific creativity.* Chicago: University of Chicago Press.

Hayes, J. R. (1981). *The complete problem solver.* Philadelphia: The Franklin Institute Press.

Heisenberg, W. (1958). *Physics and philosophy: The revolution in modern science.* New York: Harper.

Henle, M. (1962). The birth and death of ideas. In H. E. Gruber (Ed.), *Contemporary approaches to creativity.* (pp. 31–62). New York: Atherton Press.

Inkeles, A. (1983). The sociological contribution to advances in the social sciences. *Social Science Journal, 20,* 27–44.

Koestler, A. (1964). *The act of creation.* New York: Dell.

Larkin, J. H., McDermott, J., Simon, D. P., & Simon, H. A. (1980). Models of competence in solving physics problems. *Cognitive Science, 4,* 317–345.

Luchins, A. S. (1942). Mechanization in problem solving. *Psychological Monographs, 54,* (Whole No. 248).

March, J. G., & Simon, H. A. (1958). *Organizations.* New York: Wiley.

Murray, E. L. (1986). *Imaginative thinking and human existence.* Pittsburgh, PA: Duquesne University Press.

Newell, A. (1980). One final word. In D. T. Tuma & F. Reif (Eds.), *Problem solving and education: Issues in teaching and research* (pp. 175–189). Hillsdale, NJ: Erlbaum.

Newell, A., & Simon, H. A. (1972). *Human problem solving.* New Jersey: Prentice-Hall.

Newell, A., Shaw, J. C., & Simon, H. A. (1962). The processes of creative thinking. In H. E. Gruber (Ed.), *Contemporary approaches to creative thinking* (pp. 63–119). New York: Atherton Press.

Perkins, D. N. (1981). *The mind's best work.* Cambridge: Harvard University Press.

Perkins, D. N. (1984). *What else but genius? Six dimensions of the creative mind.* Paper prepared for the symposium on creativity in science, Los Alamos National Laboratory, Los Alamos, New Mexico.

Poincaré, H. (1946). *The foundations of science: Science and hypothesis, the value of science, science and method* (G. G. Halsted, Trans.). Lancaster, PA: Science Press.

Reitman, W. (1965). *Cognition and thought.* New York: Wiley.

Rothenberg, A. (1979). *The emerging goddess.* Chicago: University of Chicago Press.

Ryle, G. (1949). *The concept of mind.* London: Hutchinson.

Simon, H. A. (1966). Scientific discovery and the psychology of problem solving. In R. G. Colodny (Ed.), *Mind and cosmos* (pp. 22–40). Pittsburgh: University of Pittsburgh Press.

Simon, H. A. (1973). The structure of ill-structured problems. *Artificial Intelligence, 4,* 181–201.

Tweney, R. D. (1985). Faraday's discovery of induction: A cognitive approach. In D. Gooding & F. James (Eds.), *Faraday rediscovered* (pp. 189–209). London: Macmillan.

Vaughan, T. D. (1985). The balance of opposites in the creative process. *Gifted Education International, 3,* 38–42.

Voss, J. F. (1987). Learning and transfer in subject matter learning: A problem-solving model. [Special issue]. *International Journal of Education Research, 11,* 607–622.

Voss, J. F., & Post, T. A. (1988). On the solving of ill-structured problems. In M. T. H. Chi, R. Glaser, & M. Farr (Eds.), *The nature of expertise* (pp. 261–285).

Voss, J. F., Greene, T. R., Post, T. A., & Penner, B. C. (1983). Problem solving skill in the social sciences. In G. Bower (Ed.), *The psychology of learning and instruction: Advances in research and theory* (Vol. 17; pp. 165–213). New York: Academic Press.

Wallas, G. (1926). *The art of thought.* New York: Harcourt.

Weiss, I. R. (1978). *Report of the 1977 national survey of science, mathematics, and social studies education.* Report to the National Science Foundation and Contract No. C7619848. Center for Educational Research and Evaluation, Research Triangle Institute.

CHAPTER 23

The Teaching of Creativity to Preschool Children

THE BEHAVIOR ANALYSIS APPROACH

Elizabeth M. Goetz

The presentation of the behavior analysis approach for the teaching of creativity to preschool children requires many subtopics. As a starting point, it will be a fruitful exercise to delineate the obvious differences between the behavior analysis and traditional approaches to training creativity so the reader may be aware of the path to be taken. Before trodding down this path, mention will be made of some other professionals who share with behavior analysts a belief in the early training of creativity, though they have chosen to take different paths.

Crucial to the purpose of this chapter is the definition of creativity, which will be expounded upon in some depth, followed by the determining bases for originality and comments on social and standardized test validation measures for creativity. With the definition of creativity established, given unresolved problems, the major portion of the chapter will be devoted to behavior analysis studies for the training of creativity to preschool children. Basic experimental designs used in these studies will be covered. All the research will be tied to

behavior principles. Finally, a focused environment for the development of creativity in preschool children will be addressed considering the child's home, school, and community.

Characteristics of Behavior Analysis and Traditional Approaches

Is it possible that creativity can be taught to preschool children? Are certain biological prerequisites necessary for such teaching to be effective? The behavior analysis approach addresses these questions in this way. The most important factor in teaching any behavior, even creativity, to any person, even a preschool child, is the congruence of the delivered individualized curriculum with the desired behavioral outcome. Although genetic and biological biochemical variables participate in all behavior, they are considered as givens when teaching creativity. The preschool teacher's role is to assess any child's current degree of creative behavior and train from that point of reference with a positive expectation that is based on the effects of the use of behavior principles.

Traditional ways to training creativity have taken

Elizabeth M. Goetz • The Edna A. Hill Child Development Laboratory Preschools, Department of Human Development, University of Kansas, Lawrence, KS 66045.

a different approach. Here, the focus is on early identification of the creative child followed by placement of that child in an enhancement or acceleration program (Horowitz & O'Brien, 1986). This approach is nowhere more evident than in gifted programs that enroll children based on parent and teacher reports of giftedness (which often includes a component of creativeness) and standardized test scores. This difference in attitude regarding the relationship between established creativity traits and the effectiveness of the succeeding creativity training is but one of the differences that set behavior analysis apart from traditional approaches. Other major distinctions between these two views follow.

First, the assessment of creativity in behavior analysis is criterion-referenced for a class of specifically defined behaviors closely related to a given creative task. Assessment is not based on standardized test scores interpreted in comparison to group norms of creative persons on that test for generic creativity traits. The assignment of the name *creativity* to a group of traits, such as fluency, flexibility, originality, and divergent thinking, and then the reification of that name (creativity) to an entity or process causing those traits is considered a nominal fallacy (cf. Bijou, 1976, p. 85).

Admittedly, both behavior analysts and traditional psychologists recognize that the creative person may excel in the visual and performing arts, dancing and athletics, leadership, creative thinking, or some academic subject with each of these areas requiring somewhat different skills for "the creative act." Yet behavior analysts tend to be more specific in focusing on particular behaviors, either observable or nonobservable (internal verbal behavior), whereas the traditional psychologist tends to be more generic focusing on internal thinking processes or constructs. The rationales behind these different foci are that behavior analysts view both observable and nonobservable behavior as behavior influenced in the same way by environment, whereas traditionalists hold a dualistic view separating them (Day, 1969; Skinner, 1957).

Second, behavior analysts stress the individual analysis of creative behavior that permits the teaching to be particularized for a specific person. Even when there is group training with group data presented in behavior analysis research, the group data represent a compilation of individual data identified as a success or failure of the teaching strategy for each subject. It follows that group statistical analyses, ever present in traditional research, are not prevalent in behavior analysis studies because they identify group norms that tend to mask individual performance.

Third, the behavior analyst's individualized teaching of creativity consists of the precise application of techniques that are based on behavior principles to change operationally defined creative behavior. The traditional approach uses more open-ended teaching to change mental processes, such as hypothesis formation and testing.

Cohorts of Early Training

Before proceeding into the details of the behavior analysis approach, it is proper to acknowledge that behavior analysts are not the only ones to emphasize the teaching of creativity in the early years without undue concern for inherited traits, though their teaching differs from other methods. For example, Torrance's (1962, 1965) major concern, too, has been the training of creativity in early childhood, though the focal point of his training has been the development of a general skill as measured by standardized tests (Winston & Baker, 1985).

On a slightly different tangent, other educators have stressed the early training of basic skills and certain "habits of the mind"—commitment to and pride in hard work and the joy of learning—as the first steps to later creativity. Furthermore, they recommend providing early opportunities to become acquainted with a diversity of pursuits, such as dancing, baseball, and camping.

In his research, Bloom (1985) actually found this recommendation to be wise advice. His data showed that the young and talented had received support (i.e., encouragement and rewards) and instruction in basic skills and habits from parents and teachers before developing their specific creative skills. Therefore, he exhorts this type of early training of the basics and habits along with the freedom to explore a variety of experiences that lead eventually to pairing the child with a highly skilled mentor in the area of promise for that child.

Susuki, founder of the revolutionary system of music instruction and the Yoki Gakuen preschool, also dwells on training basic skills (i.e., reading, writing, and math, as well as music, art, gymnastics, and dance) and the habits of self-discipline and extended on-task behavior (Juan, 1985). He believes that all children are essentially equal in talent and ability at birth, that no child is born gifted, and that the environment forms the child. He espouses repetition at an early age as being the key element in training any behavior. Montessori (1964), also, has long purported this point of view.

Thus, Torrance, Bloom, Susuki, and Montessori do have something in common with the behavior analysis approach—a belief that early environment has a major impact in molding children, possibly even in the area of creativity. What any child can learn, almost all children can learn, given the appropriate conditions of learning. The behavior analysis approach, though, has unique characteristics, which will be set forth.

Definition of Creativity

Original Behavior

By definition, creativity has a connotation of originality, which may be characterized by novelty, difference, ingeniousness, unexpectedness, or inventiveness. In behavior analysis, creative behavior may be original verbal or motor behavior, observed directly or inferred from a product. For instance, a written poem may be the product from which original verbal behavior or thinking is inferred; or a blockbuilding construction may be the product from which original motor behavior is inferred. In either case, behavior or product, a code of objective definitions with related observation rules is used to measure the originality. Reliability between two independent observers, using the same code simultaneously, is needed for the code (and the data obtained from using it) to be acceptable. The determining bases for originality will be detailed in a later section.

Bizarre Behavior

The meaning of the word *creativity* needs some restrictions to disallow the bizarre, random, predictable, imitative, or trained acts from being labeled creative. To eliminate the bizarre act, the creative behavior is required to be relevant to the assigned task. For instance, if the task is blockbuilding, the building of different block forms would be relevant, whereas the throwing of a block at an apple to knock it down from a tree, though ingenious, would not be relevant to the blockbuilding task and would be considered bizarre. In other words, creative behavior needs to be defined in the context of the given task.

Random Behavior

The random or accidental act is not a problem in behavior analysis because intent as a cause is not a part of the behavior analysis perspective. Behavior that occurs is analyzed only in relation to environment, not intent.

Predictable Behavior

Because traditionally creative activity is thought to be intrinsically motivated and personalized from the depth of one's unique self (Ghiselin, 1952), it is an anathema to this notion that predictable, imitative, or trained behavior be considered creative. Therefore, even for behavior analysts, a predictable though novel or original response that is the result of following a routine formula, as, for example, in extracting square roots, is not considered an original response.

Imitative Behavior

Imitative behavior poses a gray area in judging a novel response for a preschool child. First, one may not know whether the response is imitative because at this elementary level a child making a new personal response often makes a response the teacher has seen elsewhere. Is the child reinventing the wheel or just copying it? In the case of a professional creative adult, a response seen elsewhere is considered imitative or derivative, whether it is or is not on the personal level. Second, at this young age, is not a new response on a personal level, though imitative, worthy of commendation as a shaping procedure toward creativity?

Trained Behavior

The training of specific diverse responses, which cumulatively add up to a creativity score, will be subjected to the same criticism as imitative responses. Neither the imitative nor trained response is an original response. But this criticism cannot always be held against the training of various specific responses, because typically, in behavior analysis, the training does not focus as much on the dimensions of the specific responses as it does on the differences among the responses. It is the concept of novelty, doing something different for the first time in a session or across sessions, that is trained. For example, when a preschool blockbuilder initially builds an elaborated balance and is praised for it, that child is not merely praised for the dimensions of this specific form but also for making this form for the first time. This descriptive praise not only emphasizes the novelty of the act but also may serve as a prompt for more novelty, of the child's choosing, thereafter.

Whatever the type of creativity training the behavior analyst pursues, for specific forms or for doing something different, the training itself is viewed as a natural process. To be human is to be shaped by one's environment, planned or unplanned. If this shaping is consistent with the precise application of behavior principles, it will be particularly effective. Because, realistically, life in its entirety cannot be controlled, the interaction of each person's behavioral history with the current environment is bound to be unique, even for those who receive the same training. Therefore, each trained person will bring a personalization to creative behavior that is in keeping with the traditional view.

Determination of Originality

Comparative Base

Not only is originality the hallmark of creativity, but also the actual determination of originality needs a comparative base—the repertoire of an individual, or the norms of a population, society, or culture of which that individual is, or is not, a member. The comparative base could be worldwide and human-history based, and at the professional adult level, where competition reigns, it is. For preschool children, which is the thrust of this chapter, competition is not considered a developmentally appropriate standard (Hendrick, 1975, p. 102). Therefore, the creativity of a preschool child is based typically on that child's own past behavioral history for a given task.

Informal Stimulus Control

In place of the comparative base for judging the originality of creative behavior, some behavior analysts have substituted the stimulus control of a behavior to determine its originality. Creative behavior is considered to be under informal rather than formal stimulus control (Sloane, Endo, & Della

Piana, 1980). Formal stimulus control occurs when a point-by-point correspondence exists between the discriminative stimulus (before the response) and the response—one literal point of reference for each response (i.e., an exact translation). Informal stimulus control occurs when the response is under multiple sources of control (the literal point of reference and one or more tangentially related points of reference for the same response), especially by thematic variables or by sources that are unusual in a given verbal community. It should be noted that the words "a given verbal community" bring one back to the comparative base used for determining originality, which was discussed previously; it may be an impossibility to avoid a comparative base in defining creativity.

Winston and Baker (1985) presented an exemplary illustration of these two types of stimulus control. If the child painted a cityscape in bright colors immediately after viewing a similar picture using similar colors, the painting is under formal control of the other picture. But, if the child decided to use bright colors partly because the city is noisy and exciting, then it is under informal stimulus control. It is doubtful whether one might know the circumstances under which the creative act took place; this hinders one's ability to infer informal or formal stimulus control of a response. Certainly, an audience's statement of the quality of a creative work, which is only known outside of the creator's studio, might be a reaction to the product itself, not the assumed controlling variables.

Because the behavior analyst regards thinking as influenced by environment, as is any other behavior, then the thinking involved in informal stimulus control leading to creative behavior should be able to be trained by manipulating the environment. Indeed, Della-Piana (1978) has done just that in training students to be under informal stimulus control for revision processes in writing poetry.

Della-Piana's students were not preschool children, however, and characteristics of very young children shed a different light on informal stimulus control as a training technique or creativity criterion for them. Because many three- and four-year-old children do not respond differentially to appearance and reality (Flavell, 1986) and think in concrete, not abstract or metaphoric, terms (Lavatelli, 1970), it is unrealistic to try to train them to be under informal stimulus control for creative responding. It follows that informal stimulus control should not be a creativity criterion for them either.

Validation Measures

Social Validation

A possibility for identifying the overall creativity or aesthetic quality of a product or behavior is called *social validation*. Judges thought to be suitable for a specific evaluation are selected. As an example, undergraduate early childhood education majors may be chosen to rate the creativity of drawings by five- and six-year-olds. Social validation has been used by some behaviorists in their studies (Baker & Winston, 1985; Ballard & Glynn, 1975; Maloney & Hopkins, 1973; Maloney, Jacobson & Hopkins, 1973).

In support of social validation, Wolf (1978) exhorts us to be responsible to the fundamental issue of consumer satisfaction. Bushell and Dorsey (1985) feel that social validation sensitizes us to the natural contingencies of reinforcement provided by our appreciative and approving society, and that the effects of training in general will be better maintained when the training incorporates natural contingencies.

Winston (1984) has discussed the weakness of social validation in depth, a major difficulty being that such ratings generally do not constitute an experimental analysis of behavior. For instance, more than one dimension of a child's drawing may be changed by a training procedure, such as contingent reinforcement for form diversity. If judges rate drawings produced after this training as more creative than baseline drawings, this change in ratings may be due to a change in form diversity or a change in some other dimension of the drawings that is correlated with form diversity, such as the resulting overall pattern.

Yet another inadequacy of social validation of creativity is that it is a matter of taste, and taste is fickle, changing from culture to culture and from time to time within a culture. Even within the same culture and the same time period, social validation may be idiosyncratic to the particular group of judges.

Creativity training for preschool children should not be concerned with the social validation of the quality of the resulting product. The process is more important than a polished outcome (Hendrick, 1980, p.136), which might be an unrealistic standard for a preschool child's skill level. Punishing or putting a preschool child on extinction because of poor creative quality based on social validation is obviously undesirable.

Standardized Test Validation

Some researchers using behavior-analytic methodology have included scores on standardized tests, such as the Torrance Tests of Creative Thinking and the Unusual Uses Test, in addition to criterion-referenced creativity measures (Funderbunk, 1976; Glover & Gary, 1976; Glover & Sautter, 1977; Maltzman, Bogartz, & Breger, 1958). In this way, they widen their audience to include those who feel standardized measurement is necessary for validity, and possibly satisfy their own personal conviction.

Standardized tests do not test overall creativity *per se,* however, as shown by their subtests not being highly correlated (Wallach, 1985; Wallach & Kogan, 1965). Furthermore, different creative tasks require different classes of response sets (e.g., blockbuilding response set of arranging hard-edged, three-dimensional shapes and painting response set of drawing fluid one-dimensional lines). If there is a match between a response set(s) on a standardized test and a response set(s) trained, then the use of that test is appropriate. But if not, keep in mind that it is impossible for teachers to be found accountable if they teach one thing and find themselves tested on another.

Unresolved Problems

From the above discussion on the nature of creativity, it is evident that a definitive answer of what it is does not exist. Additionally, at times creativity needs to be viewed in a different light for the preschool child than for the adult. Although both are expected to be original, the comparative base for the child is that same child, whereas the adult is subjected to a broader comparison base of a culture(s). For both the child and adult, bizarre and predictable behavior are not considered creative; but imitative behavior for the child may have some acceptability. The training of creative behavior for both age groups may be seen as fitting as long as the concept of difference or informal stimulus control takes precedence in the training over explicit external control; though training to be under informal stimulus control appears developmentally inappropriate for very young children. Social validation is more appropriate for the adult than the child, but, in either case, it is to be remembered that this measure of taste shifts over time.

Other than the instances of disagreement for the

criteria of creativity, depending on whether the creator is a child or adult, serious problems for either age bracket revolve around the quantity of diversity and the definition of informal stimulus control of the creative behavior or product. The criterion-referenced measures in the behavior analysis of creativity sometimes imply, and other times state outright, that the more diversity in the product, the more creative it is. This is an oversimplification because minimal art, dance, music, and poetry do not rest their creative labels on diversity. A very few forms, movements, musical notes or words can merit rave reviews for creativity from the critics. It is possible that criterion-referenced measures for style rather than amount of diversity are in order.

Winston and Baker (1985) have clearly stated one dispute surrounding the definition of informal stimulus control:

the relationship between the Sloan *et al.* (1980) distinction of formal versus informal control and Skinner's (1957) distinction of formal versus thematic control is not entirely clear. Skinner (1957), for example, treated alliteration in poetry as a formal source of strength, whereas Sloane *et al.* referred to the repetition of sounds as informal control. (pp. 200–201)

Furthermore, another problem in using informal stimulus control as a measure of creativity is that, by adult standards, several persons under the same type of informal stimulus control would be called imitative or derivative, emphasizing the comparative base of a population, society, or culture for creativity. Another contradiction to the informal stimulus control standard for creativity is seen in that adult artists in the realistic movement of the 1970s received worldwide acclaim for almost the exact replication of objects and persons, a point-by-point correspondence between each discriminative stimulus and each response. Informal stimulus control, then, cannot always be the criterion for creativity.

Finally, objectively defining measures for various creative tasks is difficult as implied by the sparse applied research in creativity with preschool children. And, as Winston and Baker (1985) have decried, this applied research has been concerned with short-term specific training rather than the complex chains of behavior that are influenced by one's home, school or work place, and community that would be of tremendous value for our understanding of the long-term development of creativity. In any event, the application of behavior principles does change creative behavior, according to the objective definition of creativity used in short-

term studies, and these changes will be covered further on.

Individual Analysis Experimental Designs

Because behavior analysis research gives prominence to individual data, it is appropriate to present briefly the two common individual analysis experimental designs. These designs are used to demonstrate that the independent variable (the training procedure) of the manipulation of the stimulus before or after the response is actually causing the observed change in the dependent variable (creativity) of the response. All the behavior analytic creativity studies with preschool children to be reviewed used one or a combination of these two basic designs to verify the experimental control of the observed change.

Reversal

A reversal design is used when the behavior might easily reverse or revert to its original pattern if treatment is withdrawn. In a reversal design, the normal or baseline rate of behavior is measured before any attempt is made to change it. For example, if a teacher wished to increase a child's diversity in building block forms, occurrences of each different form in several blockbuilding sessions would be measured before treatment began. Such a baseline measure would be taken until the behavior appeared stable.

During treatment, descriptive verbal praise would be contingent on each different block form per session, and the measurement would continue. If the number of block forms per session increased during treatment, the treatment would be discontinued temporarily to find out whether the treatment might have been the cause of the increase. When the treatment is withdrawn and if the number of block forms decreases or reverses toward the baseline rate, this change would demonstrate that the treatment was the cause of the behavior change. The more reversals, the stronger the experimental control. The reversal procedure may take several forms, such as a return to the baseline condition, differential reinforcement of any other behavior than the creative behavior, or differential reinforcement of incompatible behavior.

In the normal course of using this reversal design, the treatment would be reinstated after the first reversal, and the block forms would once again increase. It has been found that, when behavior is reversed again and again, it usually will not return to the original baseline rate and eventually may not reverse at all. Baer, Rowbury, and Goetz (1976) called this phenomenon the behavior trap; that is, the child finds the changed behavior reinforcing in itself or finds the natural contingencies resulting from that changed behavior reinforcing and continues, therefore, to engage in it in the absence of treatment.

Multiple Baseline

The multiple baseline design is used when teaching a behavior that is not expected to reverse. For instance, if a teacher wished to increase the representational content in a child's drawing by use of self-instructions, the teacher might feel this procedure may not reverse because the child is, to some extent, in control of the treatment, using his or her own self-instructions. Again, as in the reversal design, the normal or baseline rate of the behavior is measured before any attempt is made to change it.

In the case of the multiple baseline design, baselines are taken on the same behavior for more than one child (or, as alternatives, more than one behavior for one child, or in more than one setting for the same behavior for the same child). Then treatment is applied successively to each child. After a definite effect has been observed for the first treatment with the first child, the second treatment with the second child is introduced, and so on. Thus, each successive child will have a longer baseline than the previous child. Each succeeding treatment with a different child serves as a replication of the effects of the previous treatment. The more replications, the stronger the experimental control.

Grouped Individual Data

When group data are presented in a behavior analysis, it is typically a collapsing of individual data in which each individual has had a baseline rate of behavior taken before being treated. The group data may be presented, mentioning how many individuals did or did not follow the group trend. In the reversal design, each subject serves as that subject's own experimental control; in the multiple baseline design, control subjects are the ones with the longer baselines. By contrast, in traditional research with matched subjects, one group might serve as the baseline or control group and another group as the treatment group.

Behavior Principles

Behavior principles are natural laws of behavior that are based on objective data. The application of behavior principles to understand and solve human problems has become an area of research known as applied behavior analysis. Creativity is one of the human endeavors to which behavior principles have been applied.

The concept of operant behavior helps one understand the derivation of behavior principles. The term *operant* refers to a class of related behaviors, a response set. In this instance, operant refers to a class of creative behaviors for each different experimental task (e.g., blockbuilding and easel painting). In general, an operant is a behavior influenced by (1) discriminative stimuli that precede the behavior and signal the probability of reinforcement for the behavior, and/or (2) reinforcing stimuli that follow the behavior. All behavior and the associated preceding or following stimuli are defined objectively for the systematic observation of their occurrence and relationship. Speculation does surround thinking which, though not observable, may be inferred from a related observable behavior or product; it is considered a behavior influenced by the environment in the same way that observable behavior is. But there is no theory regarding hypothetical processes, such as overall creativity, cognition, motivation, or personality; behavior is viewed and analyzed strictly in terms of functional relationships with the environment. The operant learning theory, which is derived from the effects of discriminative stimuli and reinforcing stimuli, is that behavior that is reinforced increases (see Figure 1).

Techniques based on behavior principles are far more numerous than these principles themselves,

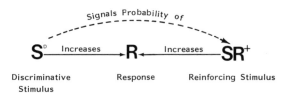

Figure 1. A schematic drawing of the operant learning theory.

which embrace reinforcement, punishment, extinction, schedules of reinforcement, shaping, stimulus control, chaining, generalization, and self-control (see Goetz, 1982a, for a discussion of these principles). For example, some of the techniques based on reinforcement are attention, general praise, descriptive praise, food reinforcers, trinket reinforcers, and token reinforcers.

Characteristics of Effective Teaching of Creativity to Preschool Children

Behavior-analytic studies of creativity for preschool children have focused on the principles of reinforcement, stimulus control, and generalization. Additionally, some of these studies have measured other variables along with behavior principles, such as social validation, material and time limits, maintenance, and a flexible creativity code. In their comprehensive review of behavior-analytic studies of creativity, Winston and Baker (1985) mentioned nineteen such studies with eight of them having preschool (pre-kindergarten) children as subjects. In addition to those eight, five more unpublished studies, many of which were covered by Goetz (1982b), will be touched upon in this chapter.

Reinforcement

Reinforcement, a basic behavior principle, involves the application of an event (a stimulus) after some action (a response) so that the application will cause that action to be repeated or increased (see Figure 2). To be most effective, the stimulus should be applied immediately after the action, although delayed reinforcement in some cases may be effective (Fowler & Baer, 1981; Rogers-Warren & Baer, 1976). A stimulus may be considered reinforcing only in terms of its effect, and not in its extrinsic

physical properties or verbal content. In other words, if a particular contingency increased a behavior, it is a reinforcer (everything else being equal), regardless of what it may otherwise be. What is reinforcing to a given child in a particular situation is determined by that child in that situation, not by the teacher.

Goetz and Baer (1971, 1973): Blockbuilding. The first behavior-analytic creativity study with preschool children was conducted by Goetz and Baer and published in 1971; later, the data were reanalyzed and published in 1973. Descriptive verbal praise was used that was contingent on each different precoded block form built by three children in individual training sessions. Descriptive praise consisted of a detailed account of the form, a statement that the form was different from any form built within that session, and praise (e.g., "That is a very nice arch going up, across, and down, and it is the first time you built it today. Good going!").

Form diversity per blockbuilding session for all the children increased with this intervention. New forms, never before in the child's total prior sequence of blockbuilding sessions, emerged at higher rates during reinforcement of form diversity than during periods of reversals without praise contingent on form diversity. The appearance of new forms was a side effect of reinforcing form diversity per session. This side effect may be viewed as generalization along the gradient underlying block-form inventions.

Goetz and Salmonson (1972): Easel Painting. In 1972, Goetz and Salmonson continued the investigation of the effects of praise on the form-diversity aspect of creativity but used another medium, easel painting, for which forms were precoded. General verbal praise and descriptive verbal praise contingent on form diversity per session were compared. General praise acknowledged a form as being good, but no specific aspect was singled out for comment. Descriptive praise was the same as defined in the foregoing Goetz and Baer study. For three children in individual sessions, descriptive praise resulted in higher form diversity per painting and increased form diversity more quickly than did general praise, though general praise had a slight effect. However, there was no systematic increase of new forms associated with either type of reinforcement.

The stimulus control aspects of the Goetz and Salmonson reinforcement procedures deserve com-

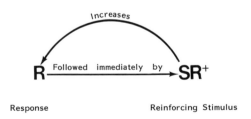

Figure 2. A schematic drawing of the reinforcement paradigm.

ment. Descriptive reinforcement, which included describing the form and denoting its difference from other forms currently present and praise for that form, may have had the stimulus control function of signaling that production of a different form in the future would be reinforced. Perhaps, in addition to the reinforcement procedure, or instead of it, the verbal description of difference and praise for that difference was controlling the probability that future painting responses would be varied. Thus, descriptive reinforcement seemed to have an instructional component for future responding. But general reinforcement did not have descriptive stimuli associated with the experimenter's verbalization and did not increase form diversity as much as descriptive reinforcement.

Romero, Holt, Stella, Baer, and Etzel (1978): Colored Cubes. The comparative effects of general and descriptive praise were again investigated by Romero, Holt, Stella, Baer, and Etzel (1978) with four children. The experimental task was the manipulation of a single layer of colored cubes within a square-shaped container; the surface of various combinations of cubes formed two-dimensional shapes (triangle, line, diamond, and arch). The participating children tended to use one solid-colored side of the cube only, which did not result in making any of the four shapes. Two simple shapes were trained: a triangle and a line. Descriptive praise (e.g., "That's a nice blue triangle") was more effective in increasing the frequency of the triangle and line than general praise (e.g., "That's nice"), which had a small effect compared to baseline performance. These results supported the Goetz and Salmonson (1972) findings that descriptive praise was more effective than general praise and again suggested that descriptive reinforcement has an effective instructional component.

The Romero *et al.* study also had an important side effect. As the children became more skilled in making the two trained shapes during the condition of descriptive reinforcement, their cube designs within the square-shaped container began to display two complex shapes that were never descriptively praised: a diamond and an arch. These two shapes not only increased in number but were also used in different combinations of color and position. The overall appearance of the designs in the set of colored cubes then appeared to be more complex, novel, and symmetrical when compared to initial baseline designs. This side effect—two untrained shapes appearing after two trained shapes—is sim-

ilar to the Goetz and Baer (1973) side effect of new block forms that increased when form diversity within a single product was reinforced.

During the last five sessions of the Romero *et al.* study, a reinforcement fading condition was implemented in an effort to bring the reinforcement contingencies of praise to a level that was thought to be comparable to that of a natural environment. It was found that the complexity of the children's designs was maintained during these last five days and did not differ from the level of complexity under previous reinforcement.

Goetz (1981): Blockbuilding. In two of the preceding studies, creativity training consisted of descriptive reinforcement for each different form (form diversity) in a single block construction or painting. A side effect of reinforcing this form diversity, for one of the studies, was an increase in new forms that appeared for the first time across all sessions of the study. Still, this variation of creativity training was not reinforcing novelty *per se,* because not only new forms were being reinforced across sessions but also some "old" forms that had been reinforced in previous sessions. It was thought that reinforcement for only new forms appearing for the first time in a study would better approximate the reinforcement of "true" novelty. This procedure, however, would result in a thin schedule of reinforcement, and it seemed doubtful that this minimal descriptive praise initially would change a behavior.

Considering the above, Goetz (1981) examined the effects of descriptive praise contingent only on blockbuilding responses that were considered new in relation to all forms in previous experimental sessions—true novelty. Seven of the nine children's new forms increased appreciably during this training. One child's data suggested an increase, and one showed no effects.

Form diversity per construction was analyzed also as a possible side effect of reinforcing only new forms. Four of the nine children showed a corresponding increase in form diversity when new forms were reinforced. One child's data suggested a small increase. Four children's form diversity did not change.

Although the reinforcement schedule was indeed a thin one, often with only one reinforcement per session, this study showed that, overall, minimal descriptive praise produced marked effects. Most children's new forms increased over time, and, in addition, half of the children's form diversity per construction increased. Romero *et al.* (1978) had shown that minimal reinforcement maintained creative behavior during the last days of training. This study demonstrated that minimal reinforcement also could result in initial increases in creative behavior.

Stimulus Control

As previously noted, an operant response may not only be effected by the stimulus that follows and reinforces it but also by the discriminative stimulus that precedes the operant and signals the probability of its reinforcement (see Figure 3). The control of the discriminative stimulus over the following response involves the behavior principle of stimulus control.

The discriminative stimulus may be visual, auditory, or in the form of a teacher's tactile (manual) guidance or modeling. When these prompts, instructions, or models result in a desired response, that response is then reinforced by the teacher. In this way, the prompts, instructions, or models become signals for certain child behaviors that will be reinforced. Instruction, verbal prompts, and modeling are forms of stimulus control that have been used in creativity training.

Reese and LeBlanc (1970): Dance. Reese and LeBlanc (1970) measured motor behavior when they investigated the effects of three types of praise and one type of instruction on the creative spontaneous, not trained, dance movements of a group of four preschoolers. Each child's dance movements were recorded as same, new (several different movements), or none during the first few seconds of a 20-sec time sample for individual children, while they were all dancing in a group to recorded music. Three types of praise were directed to individual children: (1) general praise did not mention the specific movement; (2) descriptive

praise described the movement; and (3) creative praise mentioned that the child was engaged in several different movements, and it could only be given if indeed the child were engaging in different behaviors. The fourth and last condition used creative instruction, which told the children to try to move in different ways. The highest data points for new movement were under the creative instruction condition. Although this pilot study lacked rigid experimental controls (i.e., no reversals or multiple baselines, only sequential conditions) and only presented group data, it is included here because it suggested that children's dance movements may be coded and observed and that instructions may increase diversity in another type of creative behavior, dance.

Figgs, Dunn, and Herbert (1971): Blockbuilding. Four types of verbal prompts were analyzed by Figgs, Dunn, and Herbert (1971) for their effects on form diversity in blockbuilding with a three-year-old subject. The categories of prompts were: (1) suggestions (e.g., "Can you build a farm today?"); (2) difference (e.g., "Let me see you build something different today"); (3) repeat (e.g., "Can you build another one like that?"); and (4) total usage (e.g., "Let's use all the blocks today"). The most effective prompting technique in increasing form diversity per construction was the suggestion to build a specific structure, such as a farm, garage, or fire station, all of which were familiar to the child and had a connotation for a wide variety of possible forms.

In analyzing their results, Figgs *et al.* speculated that perhaps their three-year-old subject did not comprehend the concept of difference, which would explain the ineffectiveness of that category of prompt. To compare these results with the effectiveness of the creative instruction for different dance movements in the Reese and LeBlanc (1970) pilot study, one needs to know that three of their subjects were four-year-olds and one was three-years-old. The suggestion prompt, then, may be the starting point for explaining the concept of difference to a very young child. The suggestion prompt could be tailored to various types of creativity tasks.

Figgs and Herbert (1971): Blockbuilding. Figgs and Herbert (1971) conducted another study with a series of conditions that used separately, or in combination, various types of possible discrimi-

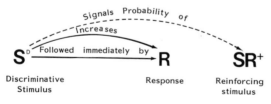

Figure 3. A schematic drawing of the stimulus control paradigm.

native stimuli—modeling, training, and prompts preceding the desired creative behavior—in addition to descriptive praise following the creative behavior. For both their subjects, the combined use of prompts for difference and descriptive praise for difference was the most effective condition for increasing form diversity. These results, however, might have been due to the sequential effects of the preceding modeling and training conditions.

As stated earlier, the Goetz and Salmonson (1972) painting study and the Romero *et al.* (1978) colored-cube study have suggested that descriptive reinforcement has an effective instructional component that is a discriminative stimulus for producing future novel behavior. These findings, like those of Reese and LeBlanc (1970), Figgs *et al.* (1971), and Figgs and Herbert (1971), demonstrated that certain discriminative stimuli preceding a creative behavior may make it more likely to occur. Although prompts for difference, prompts to use all materials, modeling, and training did not seem to be very effective, at least, when used in isolation, suggestions and the instructional component of descriptive reinforcement did seem to be quite effective. The combined use of a prompt for difference and reinforcement for difference seemed to be particularly successful.

Generalization

Generalization is another behavior principle, and it occurs when a behavior is not tightly controlled by the stimuli involved in training that behavior (see Figure 4). Generalization may occur across behaviors (tasks), subjects, settings, trainers, and/or time. When a teacher trains a desirable behavior in a child, the teacher should plan generalization of the behavior to different nontraining conditions for the training to be effective in the child's total life experience.

Does generalization of creative behavior occur? Specifically, when creative behavior change occurs in one type of task, whether through reinforcement or stimulus control training, will there be creative behavior generalization to another task? Several behavior-analytic studies have looked into this question.

Holman, Goetz, and Baer, Experiment 1 (1977): Easel Painting and Blockbuilding. In Experiment 1, Holman, Goetz, and Baer (1977) investigated the generalization of creative behavior from easel painting to blockbuilding. Each day, two chil-

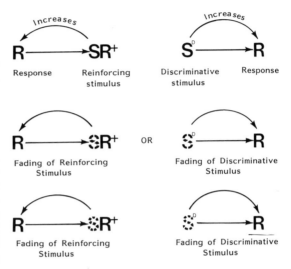

Figure 4. A schematic drawing of the generalization paradigm. Generalization may occur across behaviors, settings, or persons.

dren painted independently at the easel for one experimenter and then built with blocks for another experimenter in another room. The training technique was descriptive verbal reinforcement contingent on each different form painted per picture. There was no training in blocks.

For both children, praise in easel painting increased both form diversity per picture and new forms that appeared for the first time in the study. Blockbuilding form diversity increased during the period in which form diversity in painting was praised—even though there was no praise in blockbuilding—and decreased when the praise for form diversity in painting was discontinued. There was, however, no generalization from the increased number of new forms in easel painting to new forms in blockbuilding. So, there was some generalization (form diversity, but not new forms) from easel painting to blockbuilding, but the generalization was incomplete. Because a different experimenter was present for each task, and the session was conducted in a different room, the experimenter and the setting themselves were not likely to become a discriminative stimulus for making different and/or new forms in the untrained task.

Holman, Goetz, and Baer, Experiment 2 (1977): Felt-Pen Drawing, Easel Painting, Lego Building, and Blockbuilding. In Experiment 2, Holman *et al.* (1977) implemented a more complex experiment on generalization than the above study, which examined creative responding across topograph-ically similar and dissimilar tasks. Each of three children performed four tasks each day, felt-pen drawing and easel painting (similar tasks), and Lego building and blockbuilding (similar tasks). A comparison of dissimilar tasks would be block-building and easel painting or Lego building and felt-pen drawing. Descriptive verbal praise was de-livered contingent on felt-pen drawing only.

Generalization from felt-pen drawing to the topo-graphically similar task of easel painting was shown clearly for two children, and to some extent for the third child, both in form diversity and new forms. Generalization to the topographically dissimilar task of blockbuilding and Lego building was much less evident, though for one child it appeared some-what correlated. One child who later received praise for form diversity in Lego building showed no generalization to its topographically similar task of blockbuilding.

Each child performed all four tasks for the same experimenter in the same setting. Therefore, the experimenter and the setting could have become the discriminative stimuli for the making of different forms in all four tasks. Thus, generalization, depen-dent on a specific skill that had been trained in one task and could be used in the related task, occurred. Postchecks two months later revealed that the two children who had received the greatest number of reinforcement training sessions, within the multi-ple-baseline experimental design, maintained their high levels of form diversity in the directly manipu-lated task and its topographically similar task.

Parsonson and Baer (1978): Tools. The cre-ative operant analyzed in the Parsonson and Baer (1978) study was an improvisation using the three tool classes: hammer, shoelace, and container. Im-provisation was defined as finding a substitute to replace a specifically designed, but currently un-available, tool ordinarily used to solve the problem. The procedure was to present a child with a prob-lem, such as hammering a wooden nail into a board, along with a tray of miscellaneous items for possi-ble improvisation. In the case of hammering a nail, the items might include a small rock, a large rock, a shoe, a block with a drilled hole, a rod that would fit into the drilled hole, and a Styrofoam hammer. Some of these items could be used for hammering the nail into the board, some could not, and others could be combined to do so.

Spontaneous improvisation skills were measured

during baseline, and then each child was trained to improvise by experimenter exemplars within a given class of tools. All five children were trained in hammers, two were trained in two classes of tools, and two were trained in the three classes. All children showed increased improvisation within the trained class, but not across classes. Tools fabri-cated by item combination were rare in baseline but common in training. Follow-up probes immediate-ly after training showed that the effects were main-tained. The same experimenter participated in all sessions and did not have the effect of being a dis-criminative stimulus for improvisation across tool classes.

Lane, Lane, Friedman, Goetz, and Pinkston (1982): Felt-Pen Drawing and Collage Construc-tion. In the Lane, Lane, Friedman, Goetz, and Pinkston (1982) experiment, generalization was ex-amined across tasks and settings. An experimental group of nine children received descriptive praise and tokens contingent on form diversity in felt-pen drawing during individual sessions outside the classroom on Mondays and Wednesdays. On Tues-days, these children joined the control group of nine children for felt-pen drawing, without training just practice, in the classroom. On Thursdays, both ex-perimental and control groups engaged in collage construction, without training, in the classroom.

The experimental children's form diversity in felt-pen drawing increased in the training sessions; but an increase in new forms that appeared for the first time throughout all sessions was not a side effect, which the experimenters speculated might be related to the ability in receptive verbal language of their inner-city black subjects. The experimental group had significantly higher scores for form di-versity during training than the control group. There was some generalization of this increased form diversity to the practice sessions in the class-rooms for felt-pen drawing (generalization across settings) but not for collage construction (gener-alization across tasks). The experimenters were not present in the classroom, and, therefore, they could not be discriminative stimuli for increased form di-versity in the classroom. The two tasks of felt-pen drawing and collage construction were topograph-ically dissimilar, a characteristic which does not seem to facilitate generalization as evidenced by the partial generalization from easel painting to block-building in Experiment 1 of Holman *et al.* (1977); the lack of generalization from felt-pen drawing to blockbuilding or Lego building in Experiment 2 of Holman *et al.* (1977); and the lack of generalization across tool classes in Parsonson and Baer (1978).

In the four preceding studies, generalization was monitored, not specifically planned. From the varying procedures used, it seems that the same experimenter involved in sessions using topographically dissimilar tasks does not become a discriminative stimulus for form diversity across those dissimilar tasks, because specific different skills are used and need to be trained for dissimilar tasks. For example, the specific skill of blockbuilding involves the construction of three-dimensional pieces for different forms. The specific skill of easel painting involves the application of a fluid color on a flat surface for different forms. Generalization across topographically similar tasks, however, was noted in Experiment 2 of Holman *et al.* (1977). Another possibility is that creative behavior may need to be trained in many more different tasks than has been done in these studies before its generalization will occur.

Generalized side effects within the same trained experimental task has occurred, however. Goetz and Baer (1973) and Romero *et al.* (1978) found generalization of new forms as a side effect of increased form diversity per product in blockbuilding and colored cubes. Parsonson and Baer (1978) found that different tools which were fabricated by item combinations increased within the training of a single tool class.

The findings from these studies emphasize the need to plan consciously for generalization using the Stokes and Baer (1977) generalization technology: (1) modify sequentially; (2) introduce to natural maintaining contingencies; (3) train sufficient exemplars; (4) train loosely; (5) use indiscriminate contingencies; (6) program common stimuli; (7) mediate generalization; and (8) train to generalize. Kohler and Greenwood (1986) have provided an extensive discussion for the identification of natural contingencies of reinforcement that seem particularly relevant here for those who are orchestrating generalization in their training as well as for those who champion creativity as a natural process.

Social Validation

Ryan and Winston (1978): Felt-Pen Drawing. Creativity may be evaluated by the community through social evaluation, as was done by Ryan and Winston (1978) with judges who were early childhood education students and parents of preschool children. These experimenters increased color diversity of felt-pen drawing for three children and form diversity for two of the same three with cartoons contingent on each child's reaching an accelerated criterion based on previous session performance. Both the college students and the parents gave higher ratings of creativity for drawings with increased form diversity but not for drawings with increased color diversity.

Ryan and Winston felt that social validation provided information on what behavior to change, specifically in the design of the art curriculum. On the negative side though, they stated that such a narrow conception of creativity is inconsistent with art education as an occasion for a child to engage in relatively unrestricted expression. Nevertheless, social evaluation may advance our understanding of the interaction between children's creative efforts and the social environments, which is an aspect, in itself, of effective teaching. For, if a teacher understands any possible negative reaction of the child's community or of significant others to that child's creative efforts, that teacher may prepare the child to continue the pursuit of individualized creative behavior regardless of the reaction of others.

Material and Time Limits

Several of the previous studies suggest what effect material and time limits might have on training creative behavior. In the Goetz and Baer (1973) blockbuilding study, two of the three children had use of an unlimited number of blocks for building. The third child was limited to using the same 53 blocks for each session. Yet the data for the third child were similar to the data for the other two; form diversity and new forms increased for all the children during reinforcement for different forms per session. In all the other blockbuilding studies, a limited number of blocks, approximately 50, was used, but that limit did not seem to hamper the effectiveness of training.

Three studies used time limits for the experimental creative task. Fallon and Goetz (1975) allowed their children a 3-min limit for felt-pen drawing; Ryan and Winston (1978), a 5-min limit for felt-pen drawing; and Lane *et al.* (1982) a 10-min limit for felt-pen drawing. In all these studies, training produced positive results similar to the Goetz and Salmonson (1972) easel-painting study and the painting and drawing tasks in the Holman *et al.* (1977) studies, none of which used time limits. The crucial factor in the effectiveness of these studies, then, did not appear to be time but rather the contingent reinforcement.

Maintenance

Accountability of teacher performance requires one to assess the maintenance of the behavior trained. Some of these studies shed light on maintenance at various stages. Romero *et al.* (1978) found that creative colored-cube designs were maintained as the contingent reinforcement schedule was thinned during the last five days of training. Parsonson and Baer (1978) reported that there was maintenance of creative improvisation of tools during probes immediately following training. Fallon and Goetz (1975) and Holman *et al.*, Experiment 2 (1977) reported maintenance of increased form diversity several months after training for those children who had received many training trials (8–12) in felt-pen drawing, but not for those who had received fewer trials (5–6). It seems that there is generally short-term maintenance and sometimes long-term maintenance, at least for two months, if the training is of considerable length. Whether maintenance extends beyond several months has not been tested.

At some point, the long-term effects of creativity training in these studies would no longer be appropriate for testing suitable response sets for a child's interests change. For example, a child may build with blocks at ages 3, 4, and 5, but not at age 6, because blockbuilding, at this time, may be considered childish; therefore, a child may no longer be motivated to build with them.

A Flexible Creativity Code

Elliott and Goetz (1971): Blockbuilding. When behaviors are precoded before a study begins, there is always the possibility that a child will engage in experimentally relevant behavior that may not be recorded because it was not defined initially in the observation code. Using descriptive praise contingent on blockbuilding form diversity per construction, Elliott and Goetz (1971) avoided this problem in a single-subject study in which 20 common block forms were used as a starting point, and additional forms were added to the code as the child built them. While the child was building, the experiment-

er made on-the-spot decisions as to what constituted new forms not in the code and praised them if they were appropriate. After each session, the experimenter took a picture of the construction to compare it with all the preceding pictures to determine if that form had ever appeared before. If it had, the form diversity score for a construction would have to be readjusted, but, as it turned out, readjustments did not have to be made. Using this flexible code, the child's form diversity score increased considerably during reinforcement conditions.

A flexible code seems particularly appropriate for creativity research because it can parallel a child's personal spontaneous efforts, the essence of creativity. However, the use of individualized codes for several children does not allow a direct comparison among them. But, for the teacher, who is not a researcher but rather a person who is committed to developing the potential in each child, flexibility in assessment may well be used.

Development of a Focused Environment for Creativity of Preschool Children

Ideally, the child's total environment, including the home, school, and community, should be holistic for a child's creative behavior to occur to the fullest degree. Although this utopia will probably never exist, perhaps one can approximate it and promote creativity within each of these settings and across settings by keeping the following advice in mind.

Prerequisite Behaviors

Children are not miniature adults. Their motor, language, and cognitive skills are elementary. A creative task should be matched to, or on the outer edge of, each child's skill level—a developmentally appropriate task. Therefore, one needs to know the current level of behavior before selecting the next skill in the sequence to be taught. All skills have prerequisite behaviors, though the exact sequence of them may not be invariably fixed.

Any child development text will outline the progressive motor, language, and cognitive skill levels to be considered in selecting a developmentally appropriate task, but that is not the intent here. Generally, one moves from selecting tasks requiring gross motor to fine motor skills, simple to complex expression, and concrete to abstract thinking. That is, a child will be given finger painting before easel painting, a picture book before a storybook, and language-experience story writing before poetry writing.

Selecting creative tasks for children to explore sounds so simple, but it is not quite that easy. Each child is different and surprisingly so. Formulas using ages or stages cannot be used. Furthermore, a child may show a preference for a task that an adult feels is out of reach of that child's skill level, and yet the child's interest in the task may compensate in the effort that is applied for the lack of skill. Always give the child's preference a try. The crucial question is, Is the child primarily participating in this task independently or does the task require inordinate amounts of adult help? The child must participate in the task to learn the creative behavior involved whether at home, in school, or in the community.

Opportunities to Learn

Research has clearly demonstrated that the opportunities to learn are related to the amount of learning (Berliner, 1985). Opportunities to learn may be analyzed as (1) how much time is allocated to a given task; (2) whether the procedure is so structured during that time that the child understands what is to be done; and (3) to what extent the child is engaged with the task during that time. The child needs opportunities to learn to be creative.

Creative activities need to be scheduled with clear instructions of what may be done, and the teacher needs to be aware of the amount of child participation during this time. If the time is allocated and the child is not on task, then perhaps the procedures are unclear or the behavior principles of reinforcement, stimulus control, or generalization are not being implemented properly. Perhaps behavioral techniques that have been used successfully with tasks other than creativity or with slightly older children could be tried, such as delayed reinforcement, praise after and not during the task (Fowler & Baer, 1981; Rogers-Warren & Baer, 1976), or self-instruction, that is, the child instructs himself or herself to be creative (Baker & Winston, 1985).

Finally, the family in the home and teachers in the school or community should capitalize on spontaneous opportunities to learn to be creative. As a case in point, if a child brings a pet gerbil to school one day, a creative maze and obstacle course for the gerbil could be built impromptu.

Disposition

Dispositions are broadly defined as relatively enduring "habits of mind" or characteristic ways of responding to categories of experience across types of situations (Katz, 1985). One's past behavioral history plus current behavioral interactions determine a disposition, given certain biological characteristics. Creativity is an example of a disposition.

Therefore, if one wants a child to have a disposition toward creativity, that is, to respect, admire, and enjoy creative behavior and be desirous of participating in the creative process, one needs to train this disposition. The child may learn this disposition from observation and emulation of models when this emulation is appreciated and acknowledged. The adult who wants children to engage in creative behavior will expose them to creative behavior or its products, model the behavior, and reinforce it. Many opportunities for exposure to creativity exist, such as visits to museums, theaters, buildings of varying architectures, and gardens. Of course, it is a must to have a creative ambience in the school, in the home, and in the community.

Lack of Criticism

Criticism of creative behavior is undoubtedly a punishment that would decrease the behavior. Teachers of young children are not likely to do this, but they should be aware that lack of reinforcement for creative behavior may be construed as criticism, especially in an atmosphere in which children are accustomed to praise for positive behavior.

In his classic brainstorming study, Osborn (1953) found that more original ideas were evoked in group ideation in the absence of criticism or judgment of the value of an idea. An implication of Osborn's results is that lack of criticism in a group of young children seems desirable for an atmosphere in which creativity flourishes without inhibition. Torrance (1980a,b, 1982), in his quality circles, a group of gifted and talented children brainstorming and working together to solve their common problem, similarly downplays criticism to enhance a proliferation of ideas to be evaluated later. Children may be taught not to criticize their peers' efforts toward creative behavior, and teachers and parents should know better.

Climate

In learning creative skills, the child benefits mos from a constant climate that nurtures and sustain that child's creative behavior. Thus, parents in the home and teachers in the school and in the community need to follow the same creativity guidelines of selecting developmentally appropriate tasks, providing opportunities to learn, teaching a disposition, and avoiding criticism.

Furthermore, parents and the school and community teachers need to be aware of what each other is doing. Parents volunteering in school and community activities is fine, but realistically they often cannot and should not be expected to do this. Informal conferences, notes, and telephone calls may suffice to keep them in touch with each other. In this way, the parents can talk with their children about their creative accomplishments in school, and teachers can talk with the children about such accomplishments at home. An open line of communication across the home, school, and community settings will keep the child's climate supportive of that child's creative efforts, which should then generalize from one setting to the other.

Summary and Discussion

Given the foregoing studies in which behavior principles are applied, it seems reasonable to hold that creativity can be taught to preschool children. Even with unresolved problems in defining creativity, it appears that some dimension of creativity, empirically defined, can be taught.

Many techniques that are based on behavior principles, however, have yet to be researched in teaching creativity to preschool children. Delayed reinforcement has not been used and, if successful, would be a practical technique in the typical classroom where a teacher cannot attend to all children immediately. For instance, can a child build with blocks in a corner of the classroom, leave the construction there for a teacher to examine later, and at the end of the school day be praised for any creative efforts exhibited in the blockbuilding with the result of different forms increasing over time?

An intermittent schedule of reinforcement for creativity deserves experimental examination. Again, for the realistic reason that a busy teacher cannot continually monitor a child's creative task, intermittent reinforcement would be a welcomed technique, if it works. As a case in point, can a child work alone at the easel and have a teacher drop in now and then to praise different forms with the result of the number of them increasing?

Self-instruction and self-reinforcement, not yet used in research as training procedures for novelty at this young age, might be other practical techniques for the overworked teacher in that they would require only some initial training and possibly intermittent prompts. These self-control techniques, too, are intriguing because they are germane to the traditional concept of creativity as an expression from the inner self.

Another avenue for scientific study is the function of peers on a preschool child's creativity. For example, can a creative child and a noncreative child be paired at a drawing table with the result that modeling by the creative child and subsequent imitation by the noncreative child take place, leading to the noncreative child's becoming independently creative? Or can the creative child be asked to help the noncreative child with a positive result? Or can the creative child be trained in prompting and reinforcing creativity in the noncreative child with a beneficial effect?

On a different tack, can the types of behavior examined on a one-to-one basis in this chapter be trained in a group setting? As an exemplar, can a teacher have a group of three or four children working on individual collages at the same table, with the teacher circulating around them and praising individual creative acts every so often, and have creativity increase? Additionally, will these children be vicariously reinforced from each other?

Does an overall creative preschool environment, in which creative teachers use creative curriculum activities in a creatively furnished and decorated classroom, foster creativity indirectly as measured by specific tasks? Or is direct teaching that uses precise techniques needed for creativity to increase in those specific tasks?

Finally, long-term maintenance of the types of creative behavior presented here has not been assessed. How long does it maintain? On a kindred issue, does creativity trained on early childhood tasks (e.g., blockbuilding) generalize to creativity on a related middle childhood task (e.g., carpentry)? From the above, it is clear the behavior-analytic research with preschool children has only begun.

If young children are given many developmentally appropriate opportunities to learn to become creative in supportive environments at home, at school, and in the community, and if the principles of behavior are understood and used, the teaching of creativity to all children seems a probability.

References

Baer, D. M., Rowbury, T. G., & Goetz, E. M. (1976). The preschool as a behavioral trap: A proposal for research (pp. 3–

27). *Minnesota Symposium on Learning.* Minneapolis, MN: University of Minnesota Press.

Baker, J. E., & Winston, A. S. (1985). Children's creative drawing: Experimental analysis and social validation of a self-instructional procedure. *Education and Treatment of Children, 8,* 115–132.

Ballard, K. D., & Glynn, T. (1975). Behavioral self-management in story-writing with elementary school children. *Journal of Applied Behavior Analysis, 8,* 387–398.

Berliner, D. C. (1985). Effective classroom teaching: The necessary but not sufficient condition for developing exemplary schools. In G. R. Austin & H. Garber (Eds.), *Research on exemplary schools* (pp. 127–151). Orlando, FL: Academic Press.

Bijou, S. W. (1976). *Child development: The basic stage of early childhood.* Englewood Cliffs, NJ: Prentice-Hall.

Bloom, B. S. (Ed.). (1985). *Developing talent in young people.* New York: Ballantine Books.

Bushell, D., Jr., & Dorsey, D. (1985). Behavioral models of teaching. In T. Husen & T. N. Postlewaite (Eds.), *The international encyclopedia of education* (pp. 437–442). New York: Pergamon.

Day, W. F. (1969). On certain similarities between the philosophical investigations of Ludwig Wittgenstein and the operationism of B. F. Skinner. *Journal of the Experimental Analysis of Behavior, 12,* 489–506.

Della-Piana, G. M. (1978). Research strategies for the study of revision processes in writing poetry. In C. R. Cooper & L. Odell (Eds.), *Research on composing: Points of departure* (pp. 105–134). Urbana, IL: National Council of Teachers of English.

Elliott, C., & Goetz, E. M. (1971). *Creative blockbuilding as a function of social reinforcement using an unrestrictive creativity code.* Unpublished manuscript, University of Kansas.

Fallon, M. P., & Goetz, E. M. (1975). The creative teacher: The effects of descriptive social reinforcement upon the drawing behavior of three preschool children. *School Applications of Learning Theory, 7*(2), 27–45.

Figgs, S., & Herbert, E. (1971). *The effects of training, primes and social reinforcement on creativity in blockbuilding.* Unpublished manuscript, University of Kansas.

Figgs, S., Dunn, J., & Herbert, E. (1971). *The effects of primes on creativity in blockbuilding.* Unpublished manuscript, University of Kansas.

Flavell, J. H. (1986). The development of children's knowledge about the appearance-reality distinction. *American Psychologist, 41,* 418–425.

Fowler, S. A., & Baer, D. M. (1981). Do I have to be good today? The timing of delayed reinforcement as a factor in generalization. *Journal of Applied Behavior Analysis, 14,* 13–24.

Funderbunk, F. R. (1976). Reinforcement control of classroom creativity. In T. Brigham (Ed.), *Behavior analysis in education: Self-control and reading* (pp. 197–204). Dubuque, IA: Kendall/Hunt.

Ghiselin, B. (Ed.). (1952). *The creative process.* New York: Mentor Books.

Glover, J. A., & Sautter, F. (1977). Procedures for increasing four behaviorally defined components of creativity within formal written assignments among high school students. *School Applications of Learning Theory, 9,* 3–22.

Goetz, E. M. (1981). The effects of minimal praise on the creative blockbuilding of three-year-olds. *Child Study Journal, 11,* 55–67.

Goetz, E. M. (1982a). Behavior principles and techniques. In K.

E. Allen & E. M. Goetz (Eds.), *Early childhood education: Special problems, special solutions* (pp. 31–76). Rockville, MD: Aspen Systems.

Goetz, E. M. (1982b). A review of functional analyses of preschool children's creative behaviors. *Education and Treatment of Children, 5,* 157–177.

Goetz, E. M., & Baer, D. M. (1971). Social reinforcement of creative blockbuilding by young children. In G. A. Ramp & B. L. Hopkins (Eds.), *A new direction for education: Behavior analysis* (pp. 72–79). Lawrence, KS, University of Kansas Press.

Goetz, E. M., & Baer, D. M. (1973). Social control of form diversity and the emergence of new forms in children's blockbuilding. *Journal of Applied Behavior Analysis, 6,* 209–217.

Glover, J. A., & Gary, A. L. (1976). Procedures to increase some aspects of creativity. *Journal of Applied Behavior Analysis, 9,* 79–84.

Goetz, E. M., & Salmonson, M. N. (1972). The effect of general and descriptive reinforcement on "creativity" in easel painting. In G. B. Semb (Ed.), *Behavior analysis in education* (pp. 53–61). Lawrence, KS: University of Kansas Press.

Hendrick, J. (1975). *The whole child: New trends in early education.* St. Louis: C. V. Mosby.

Hendrick, J. (1980). *Total learning for the whole child.* St. Louis: C. V. Mosby.

Holman, J., Goetz, E. M., & Baer, D. M. (1977). The training of creativity as an operant and an examination of its generalization characteristics. In B. C. Etzel, J. M. LeBlanc, & D. M. Baer (Eds.), *New directions in behavioral research: Theory, methods and applications. In honor of Sidney W. Bijou* (pp. 441–472). Hillsdale, NJ: Erlbaum.

Horowitz, F. D., & O'Brien, M. (1986). Gifted and talented children: State of knowledge and directions for research. *American Psychologist, 41,* 1147–1152.

Juan, S. (1985). The Yoki Gakuen: The Suzuki philosophy in the preschool. *Childhood Education, 62,* 38–39.

Katz, L. G. (1985). Dispositions in early childhood education. *ERIC/EECE Bulletin, 18*(2), 1, 3.

Kohler, F. W., & Greenwood, C. R. (1986). Toward a technology of generalization: The identification of natural contingencies of reinforcement. *Behavior Analysis, 9,* 19–26.

Lane, T. W., Lane, M. Z., Friedman, B. S., Goetz, E. M., & Pinkston, E. M. (1982). A creativity enhancement program for preschool children in an inner city parent-child center. In A. M. Pinkston, J. L. Levitt, G. R. Green, N. L. Linsk, & T. L. Rzepnicki (Eds.), *Effective social work practice: Advanced techniques for behavioral intervention with individuals, families, and institutional staff* (pp. 435–441). San Francisco, CA: Jossey-Bass.

Lavatelli, C. S. (1970). *Piaget's theory applied to an early childhood curriculum.* Boston: Center for Media Development.

Maloney, K. B., & Hopkins, B. L. (1973). The modification of sentence structure and its relationship to subjective judgements of creativity in writings. *Journal of Applied Behavioral Analysis, 6,* 425–433.

Maloney, K. B., Jacobson, C. R., & Hopkins, B. L. (1973). An analysis of the effects of lectures, requests, teacher praise, and free time on the creative writing behaviors of third grade children. In E. Ramp & G. Semb (Eds.), *Behavior analysis: Areas of research and application* (pp. 244–260). Englewood Cliffs, NJ: Prentice-Hall.

Maltzman, I., Bogartz, W., & Breger, L. (1958). A procedure for increasing word association originality and its transfer effects. *Journal of Experimental Psychology, 56,* 392–398.

Montessori, M. (1964). *The Montessori method.* New York: Schocken Books.

Osborn, A. F. (1953). *Applied imagination.* New York: Scribner's.

Parsonson, B. S., & Baer, D. M. (1978). Training generalized improvisation of tools by preschool children. *Journal of Applied Behavior Analysis, 11,* 363–380.

Reese, N. M., & LeBlanc, J. M. (1970). *Creative dance: Pilot study.* Unpublished research, University of Kansas.

Rogers-Warren, A., & Baer, D. M. (1976). Correspondence between saying and doing: Teaching children to share to praise. *Journal of Applied Behavior Analysis, 9,* 335–354.

Romero, P. M., Holt, W. J., Stella, M. E., Baer, D. M., & Etzel, B. C. (1978, August). *Contingency effects of reinforced and unreinforced forms: Cube design complexity.* Paper presented at the American Psychological Association, Toronto, Canada.

Ryan, B. A., & Winston, A. S. (1978). Dimensions of creativity in children's drawings: A social validation study. *Journal of Educational Psychology, 70,* 651–656.

Skinner, B. F. (1957). *Verbal behavior.* New York: Appleton-Century-Crofts.

Sloane, H. N., Endo, G. T., & Della-Piana, G. (1980). Creative behavior. *Behavior Analyst, 3,* 11–22.

Stokes, T. F., & Baer, D. M. (1977). An implicit technology of generalization. *Journal of Applied Behavior Analysis, 10,* 349–368.

Torrance, E. P. (1962). *Guiding creative talent.* Englewood Cliffs, NJ: Prentice-Hall.

Torrance, E. P. (1965). *Rewarding creative behavior: Experiments in classroom creativity.* Englewood Cliffs, NJ: Prentice-Hall.

Torrance, E. P. (1980a). Lessons about giftedness and creativity from a nation of 115 million overachievers. *Gifted Child Quarterly, 24,* 10–14.

Torrance, E. P. (1980b). Creativity and futurism in education: Retooling. *Education, 100,* 298–311.

Torrance, E. P. (1982). Education for quality circles in Japanese schools. *Journal of Research and Development in Education, 15* (2), 11–15.

Wallach, M. A. (1985). Creativity testing and giftedness. In F. D. Horowitz & M. O'Brien (Eds.), *The gifted and talented: Developmental perspectives* (pp. 99–123). Washington, DC: American Psychological Association.

Wallach, M. A., & Kogan, N. (1965). *Modes of thinking in young children.* New York: Holt, Rinehart & Winston.

Winston, A. S. (1984, August). Beyond reinforcement of novelty. In A. S. Winston & E. M. Goetz (Chairs), *Current issues in the study of creativity as operant behavior.* Symposium conducted at the meeting of the American Psychological Association, Toronto, Canada.

Winston, A. S., & Baker, J. E. (1985). Behavior analytic studies of creativity: A critical review. *Behavior Analyst, 8,* 191–205.

Wolf, M. M. (1978). Social validity: The case for subjective measurement or how applied behavior analysis is finding heart. *Journal of Applied Behavior Analysis, 11,* 203–214.

CHAPTER 24

Mental Management and Creativity

A COGNITIVE MODEL OF TIME MANAGEMENT FOR INTELLECTUAL PRODUCTIVITY

Bruce K. Britton and Shawn M. Glynn

Introduction

Defining Creativity

"Creative" is a term of praise much affected. . . . It is presumably intended to mean original, or something like that, but is preferred because it is more vague and less usual (cf. "seminal"). It has been aptly called a "luscious, round, meaningless word," and said to be "so much in honor that it is the clinching term of approval from the schoolroom to the advertiser's studio." (Fowler, 1965, p. 114)

Creativity is a debased term. *Intellectual productivity* is the best term for what we have in mind in this chapter. Intellectually productive people work to produce useful new ideas. Some examples of intellectually productive people are scientists doing original research, authors writing imaginative literature, political workers devising new solutions to social problems, and mediators proposing ways to resolve conflicts between parties.

Why Intellectually Productive People Need to Manage Their Time

A wise Man should order his Designs, and set all his interests in their proper Places: This Order is often confounded by a foolish Greediness, which, while it puts us upon pursuing so many several Things at once, that in Eagerness for Matters of less consideration, we grasp at Trifles, and let go Things of greater value. (La Rochefoucauld, 1706, p. 43)

Intellectually productive people usually have more things that they would like to do, or need to do, than they have time (Roe, 1952); that is, they do not have enough time to do the things they have to do. One part of the solution to this problem is mental management. To produce large quantities of high-quality mental products, people must effectively manage the limited resource that produces those products: their minds. Managing the mind has several aspects. One aspect, which is considered elsewhere, is memory management (Britton, Smith, & Glynn, 1985). The aspect that this chapter considers is the management of mental time.

The mind can be regarded as a single processor that can do only one thing at a time. The objective of the mental time-management system described in this chapter is to maximize the use of the resource of mental time. The use of mental time is maximized

Bruce K. Britton • Department of Psychology, University of Georgia, Athens, GA 30602. **Shawn M. Glynn** • Department of Educational Psychology, University of Georgia, Athens, GA 30602.

when the largest number of the highest quality intellectual products are produced in the shortest time.

To maximize mental time, it is necessary to make use of a metacognitive system that oversees and supervises the operation of the rest of the cognitive system. Some people have a mental time-management system, and others do not. It is the faith of this chapter that those who have such a system are better off, in the sense that their intellectual productivity is greater. This is called a "faith" because it is based on very little empirical research. The empirical literature on the effects of time management is very small: the only experimental empirical paper we have found is by Hall and Hursch (1982). Literature on the relationship between creativity and time management does not appear to exist (Paul Torrance, personal communication, October 5, 1987). Although there is a large popular literature in this area, it is almost entirely exhortatory in tone, with only anecdotes as evidence. The best example of this literature is Lakein (1973), and though it is very good indeed, the claims it makes are not supported by the kind of evidence usually adduced in behavioral science investigations.

There is, however, a very substantial empirical literature in computer science that demonstrates that the productivity of computers can be substantially increased by applying some of the principles of time management described here. Most present-day computers, like human minds under most circumstances, have a single processor that can do only one thing at a time, and computer scientists have been much concerned with maximizing the use of that resource. This literature was thus the original source of many of the ideas that are presented in this chapter (Greenstein & Rouse, 1982; Pattipati, Kleinman, & Ephrath, 1983; Tulga, 1979; Tulga & Sheridan, 1980).

The alternative to having a mental time-management system is not having one. People who do not have such a system are not supervising their own cognitive system; instead, they are driven by external and internal forces that they do not control.

External forces include deadlines, the goals desired by other people, and the order in which tasks arrive at their desk; internal forces include inertia and momentum. The output of persons who are not in control of their processing resources is likely to be determined fortuitously by the interplay of external and internal forces. In contrast, the output of people who manage their mental time is characterized by the formulation of ordered precedence relations that are relevant to the achievement of specific explicitly formulated goals, and by discrete steps that are taken toward the achievement of those goals.

In the next sections of this chapter, we describe a time-management system that is based on a synthesis of the computer science literature with the popular literature. We then describe the specific time-management problems that intellectually productive people are likely to have. In the concluding sections, we point out that time management is itself an intellectually demanding task for which sufficient time must be set aside. After providing a research agenda, we summarize briefly. An Appendix provides a time-management instrument.

The Time Manager

Top-Level Components

Mental time management is performed by a metacognitive system that has three parts, as shown schematically in Figure 1: the Goal Manager, the Task Planner, and the Scheduler. The Goal Manager takes as input the person's desires and produces as output a list of goals and subgoals with priorities attached.

The Task Planner takes as input the output of the Goal Manager—the prioritized list of goals and subgoals. The planner operates upon those goals and subgoals and produces as output a list of tasks and subtasks with priorities attached. Goals are distinguished from tasks in that goals are objectives, whereas tasks are activities. Objectives are state-

Figure 1. Top-level components of a mental time management system.

ments of a desired end product or a desired state of affairs; objectives are not something that can be "done" with the limbs of the body or the parts of the mind. In contrast, tasks are activities that can be done with the limbs of the body or the parts of the mind. Tasks are instrumental to goals in that they are activities that can bring about a desired state of affairs. For example, a goal could be to achieve the ability to be fluent in French; a task relevant to that goal would be to enroll in a French class.

Subgoals and subtasks are subordinate steps that must be taken to achieve their superordinate goal or task. For example, subgoals of becoming fluent in French are (a) learning French vocabulary and (b) learning French syntax. Subtasks for the task of enrolling in a French class might be (a) looking in the telephone book for educational institutions that might offer French classes, (b) recording their numbers, and (c) dialing the numbers. It is important to note in these examples that these subgoals and subtasks are arranged in precedence relations; that is, certain subgoals must be achieved before others can be achieved. Learning some French vocabulary, for example, is a prerequisite for learning French syntax, and certain subtasks, such as looking up the phone number, must be completed before later ones, such as dialing the number, can be begun.

The third component of the time manager is the Scheduler, which takes as input the output of the Task Planner—the list of tasks and subtasks. The Scheduler produces a "To-Do List," which is used to make the decision about what to do next. This decision is then input to the mind, which then carries out the activity. When each activity is completed, the Scheduler is consulted about what to do next.

Description of Each Time Manager Component

Goal Manager

He who has not directed his life in general to a certain end, for him it is impossible to adjust the separate acts; for him it is impossible to arrange the pieces, who has not a figure of the whole in his head . . . the archer must first know at what he aims, and then adapt his hand, the bow, the string, the arrow, and his motions accordingly. Our judgments go astray if they have no direction and no aim. No wind is fair for the sailor who has no purposed port. (Montaigne, 1925, pp. 48–49)

By far the most important thing about any system is the goals to which it is directed. In the context of time management, this means that the quality of a person's goals is much more important than the efficiency with which they are pursued. Even an optimally efficient time-management system, if it operates to achieve low-quality goals, cannot lead to high-quality results. And even a very poor time-management system can produce important work if it is directed toward important goals. The goals of one's cognitive system are an order of magnitude more important than one's time-management practices. The most efficient possible way of using one's time on a valueless goal is utterly valueless; it is a great deal worse than the least efficient possible way of using one's time on a valuable goal. So the goal-management system is more important than the time-management system; or to put it another way, the time-management system's only purpose is to serve the goals. The importance of high-quality goals is the thing we will be left pointing at after we have said everything we have to say about time management.

People often resist specifying their goals. Frequently stated objections are that they find the task overwhelming or embarrassing, that they feel the task limits their options, or that it takes away some of the creativity, spontaneity, and fun from life (Lakein, 1973). Against these objections must be placed the fact that goals that have not been specified are unlikely to be achieved. The number of paths a life can take is infinite; so the number of end points that can be reached is infinite in number. But the value of those end points differs greatly. So the expected values of the paths differ greatly as well.

The Goal Manager is composed of several parts, as shown schematically in Figure 2.

Goal Generator. When persons want to find out what their goals should be, the first thing they

Figure 2. Components of the Goal Manager.

should do is to produce a long list of possible goals, which can then be narrowed down for the next stage. The input to the Goal Generator is the persons' desires, and everything they know about themselves and the world. The output is a list of candidate goals, which might include, for example, professional goals, such as becoming a prominent psychologist; personal goals, such as learning French; and social, political, intellectual, spiritual, and other types of goals.

Goal Prioritizer. It is obvious that all goals are not of equal importance. Also, because usually the time available is not sufficient to achieve them all, they will have to be placed in order of importance. The Goal Prioritizer orders the goals. The input to the Goal Prioritizer is the list of goals with priorities attached, which can be visualized as a list of goals with the most important ones at the top. The prioritizing is done by heuristics. These heuristics are very important determiners of the quality of the output of all the components described below. A description of these heuristics for the general case is beyond the scope of this chapter, but some heuristics for intellectually productive people are included in later sections.

Subgoal Generator. For each goal, there are usually several prerequisite subordinate goals that have to be achieved in order to achieve the superordinate goal, and often there are several possible routes to the same goal. For example, one might become fluent in French by taking French courses locally or by going to France. The Subgoal Generator takes as input each goal separately, and, using heuristics and knowledge about the world, generates various possible sets of subgoals that could serve as prerequisites to achieve that goal. The output is the various sets of possible subgoals.

Subgoal Prioritizer. Taking the list of possible subgoals, the Subgoal Prioritizer rates them based on feasibility and other constraints. The final output is a prioritized list of subgoals.

Task Planner

The Task Planner has several components, as shown in Figure 3. When beginning work, the planner has a list of prioritized goals and of the subgoals for each goal. For simplicity, we can consider the list as being ordered from top to bottom, with the first goal on the list being the highest priority goal. Underneath each goal is a list of subgoals that must be achieved before the main goal can be achieved. These subgoals are also in priority order. The planner starts with the highest priority goal and looks for its highest priority subgoal. The planner's job is to specify what tasks must be done to achieve that subgoal. It will be useful to recall here that, although goals and subgoals are statements of desired end products, tasks and subtasks are *activities* that can be performed with the limbs of the body or the parts of the mind, often with the help of physical objects or other external resources.

Task Generator. The Task Generator considers the subgoal and thinks of different possible activities that could be performed to accomplish it. In the time available for this phase of planning, the generator then thinks of as many of these activities as is possible and ends up with a list of possible activities that could be done to achieve the goal. In general, these activities are too molar to be performed with specific parts of the body or mind; the Subtask Generator has the responsibility of breaking them down into molecular subcomponents.

Task Prioritizer. On the generated list of possible activities, there will be some that are clearly infeasible or that are very costly in terms of suffering; some that use a scarce resource; and some that are efficient, easy, or pleasant to do. The Task Prioritizer selects which ones are the first choices.

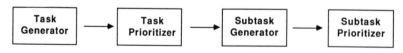

Figure 3. Components of the Task Planner.

Subtask Generator. Starting with the first-choice task, the Subtask Generator breaks it down further into components that can actually be done with parts of the body or the mind. There are many different ways to accomplish the task, and, at this stage, as many possibilities will be generated as time is available.

Subtask Prioritizer. The task possibilities are then narrowed down by the Subtask Prioritizer to produce a list of practical, performable activities.

Task Properties

Up to this point, we have emphasized one property of the goals and tasks: the property we have named *priority*. We need now to consider three other important properties of the tasks. One important property is whether the task has a deadline or not. Whether a particular task has a deadline often depends on whether its superordinate subgoal and goal have a deadline, that is, the deadline property may be "inherited" by any progeny of a goal. For example, one common deadline maintenance goal is to pay one's income taxes by April 15. The deadline property is inherited by its subgoals, like paying both Federal income tax and State income tax, and by their tasks, like gathering one's financial records and procuring the appropriate extra forms from the government, and also by their subtasks, like getting into the car and driving down to the local Internal Revenue Service office to get the forms.

Another important property of tasks is the time required to complete them. Very long tasks need to be treated separately from very short ones. Some tasks should not be begun unless there is sufficient time to complete them on a particular day: waxing the kitchen floor is a maintenance goal of this type. Others can be interrupted and resumed later without penalty. This property is called *interruptibility*.

Another important property is the type of mental resources that a task requires. For some tasks it is necessary to have a very alert, awake, and active mind—high-level intellectually productive work often requires this property. Such tasks can only be done at times of the day when the needed resource is available, for example, in early morning. Other subtasks, such as dealing with one's mail, can often be done with less mental resources, in late afternoon, for example. This property specifies the type

and amount of mental resources that are required to achieve a goal or task.

These additional properties are mentioned here because they are needed as part of the input to the next component of the time-management system, which is the Scheduler. At this point, it will be easy to think back to see how they could have been incorporated into the processing from the very earliest stages. For example, the deadline property could have been attached to certain goals as soon as the Goal Generator produced them, or as soon as some outside force imposed them on the system. The deadline property would then have influenced the work of the Goal Prioritizer and would have been inherited by the goals that are produced by the Subgoal Generator and that are chosen by the Subgoal Prioritizer. In turn, the deadline property would be inherited through the task and subtask planning process. In similar ways, the other properties could have been incorporated into the processing from the earliest stages.

Scheduler

The Scheduler is in charge of choosing a person's next activity. Typically, there are a large number of different things that can be done, but because the person can usually do only one thing at a time, the Scheduler has to decide which it is to be. In making the decision, the Scheduler has access to all the information that is retained from the previous stages, including priorities, deadlines, time required, interruptibility, and mental and other resources. The Scheduler has two components, as shown schematically in Figure 4.

Job Selector. The Job Selector produces a To-Do List for each day. This is a run down of the different things the person has to do that day. Each of the things on the list will be called a *job*. (This new term is used to avoid having to distinguish between subtasks and tasks.) The input to the Job Selector is the list of tasks and subtasks. Each task and subtask has attached to it its entire list of proper-

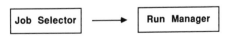

Figure 4. Components of the Scheduler.

ties, including priority, deadlines, time required, interruptibility, and resource requirements. The Job Selector applies to these job properties a heuristic program to select which jobs will be placed on the list for that day.

Run Manager. The To-Do List is then performed by the Run Manager, who decides which job to do first. If that job is not interrupted, it will be completed, and then the Run Manager must decide which job to do next. If there is an interruption, the Run Manager must decide what to do next.

Special Properties of Time Management for the Intellectually Productive

Distinctions between Types of Goals

There are many different types of goals. Intellectual productivity is likely to be associated more with some types of goals than with others.

Intellectual Productivity versus Noncreative Achievement and Maintenance Goals

If people are to achieve the goal of being intellectually productive (creative), then they must set themselves appropriate goals and allow considerable periods of time to work toward achieving them. But most people also have to devote considerable periods of time to tasks that do not lead to intellectual productivity. It is very easy to spend all one's time attending to noncreative or essential maintenance activities, routine tasks, previous commitments, interruptions, and crises (Lakein, 1973). In fact, most people devote all their time to tasks that are not creative. Although these tasks certainly lead to the maintenance of one's body, home, possessions, and relationships, and may also lead to considerable job achievement; they are unlikely to lead to intellectual productivity, except fortuitously.

Personal Goals versus Other Goals and Job Goals

Some goals originate within the self, and other goals are imposed from outside, either by real-world events, such as natural disasters and wars, or by other people who have some influence over us, such as children, spouses, bosses, and political or religious leaders. Conceivably, intellectual productivity can result from any of these goals, but most

intellectual productivity that we know of occurs in response to job goals. This is particularly likely if the job has intellectual productivity as one of its explicit or implicit requirements. However, some jobs have no scope for intellectual productivity or positively discourage it; persons in such jobs are unlikely to be intellectually productive.

Content Goals versus System Goals

Content goals state the content of desired states of affairs, such as knowing French, becoming a prominent psychologist, or owning a sailboat. In contrast, system goals state the operating criteria by which the performance of the cognitive system is to be judged. For example, one common system goal of some people's cognitive system is to maximize the accuracy of the system. Each system goal has associated with it a particular measure of effectiveness; for maximizing the accuracy of the system, the measure of effectiveness would be error rate. Another system goal might be to work as fast as possible, for which one measure of effectiveness would be the number of jobs completed per unit time. Each system goal might be appropriate for a particular profession or job mix. Also, it is possible to combine such goals; for example, one common goal might be to combine speed with accuracy, that is, to be as fast and accurate as one can.

One reason that system goals are mentioned here is to note that the Goal Manager is not concerned with them. The Goal Manager is concerned with content goals. However, system goals can be important to the scheduling system, because the order in which jobs are done can be partly determined by system goals.

The other reason system goals are distinguished from content goals is to point out that intellectually productive people must be concerned primarily with content goals and, moreover, with content goals that lead to intellectually productive results. People who do not intend to be intellectually productive may, however, be concerned primarily with system goals, such as doing a particular job more and more quickly, efficiently, and accurately. But people concerned primarily with system goals will have less time to devote to content goals, and, for that reason, are less likely to be intellectually productive. By the same token, intellectually productive people, because they must concentrate primarily on content goals, will generally have less time to focus on system goals. The result is that their intellectually productive work is sometimes performed slowly and inefficiently, or otherwise does not meet certain desirable system goals.

Intellectual Productivity Effects on Components of the Goal Manager

Goal Generator

People who wish to be intellectually productive need to generate goals that are appropriate to that objective. But because creative ideas are by definition new ones, it is usually impossible to specify in advance what the end point idea to be produced will be, for it has not yet been invented. So intellectually productive people often need to specify problems in place of goals. In such problem–goal statements, the goal idea appears as an unknown entity that is the solution to a particular problem. The generation of such problem–goal statements is often unlikely to occur because the existence of even very imperfect solutions to a problem can cause reasonable people to consider that the problem is already solved. Then the problem becomes part of the background, and it is difficult even to see it as a problem. Intellectually productive people must incorporate heuristics in their goal generators that deal with this.

Goal Prioritizer

If creative products are to result, priority must be given to creative goals. Maintenance goals and noncreative achievement goals must be given lower priority. This particular conflict between goal types is an instance of goal conflict. When people have more things to do than they can possibly do in the time that is available, goal conflict is inevitable. In general, goal conflict can only be resolved by setting priorities.

When creative goals are involved, unique problems arise in setting priorities and in dealing with the other goal and task properties. These can be seen most clearly by considering how priorities are set for maintenance and noncreative achievement goals. The criteria that are used there include threshold considerations of feasibility, practicality, and probability of successful achievement, and also incremental calculations of expected value, resource requirements, and time to achieve. Because maintenance and noncreative achievement goals can be formulated as end-product content statements, it is usually possible to estimate these properties. In contrast, creative goals are unknown solu-

tions, so it is often not possible to calculate any of these properties. Often, the assignment of high priority to creative goals represents a leap of faith.

Subgoal Generator and Prioritizer

The role of the subgoal component is to break down the highest priority goals into subparts to the point where they can be restated as tasks, that is, as activities that can be performed by the limbs or the mind. The breaking down and prioritizing processes are essentially the same whether the goals are creative goals, noncreative achievement goals, or maintenance goals. Of course, some decompositions into subgoals are better than others, in the sense that they will lead to the goal more effectively or more cheaply. The job of figuring out the best decomposition is a problem-solving task that uses essentially the same heuristics whatever the type of goal.

Task Planner

Nothing more will be said about the Task Planner here, except that the planner's operation is the same for creative goals as for any other type of goal.

Scheduling for Intellectual Productivity

Job Selector. On each day in which the To-Do List includes jobs that are priorities for creative work, there is a likelihood that some creative work will be accomplished. On other days, creative products can be achieved only fortuitously. The Job Selector, who is in charge of the To-Do List for each day, must select creative jobs if any progress is to be made toward creative goals.

Run Manager. The Run Manager is in charge of when the selected jobs are to be done during the day. Intellectual productivity typically requires (a) the absorption of large amounts of information, (b) its integration by thinking, and (c) the production of the desired end product. All these activities are performed most effectively by the processor when two conditions are met: the optimum time of day, and large enough blocks of time that are not interrupted by outside forces or by lack of resources needed for the job.

Time of Day. Most people have a certain time of day when they can do intellectually productive work most effectively. For most intellectually productive people with whom we are acquainted, the morning is the best time. Whatever the time, productive work seems usually to be limited in length to no more than a few hours. This time will be called *high time*. During high time, high-quality intellectual work can be performed, whereas at other times it either cannot be performed at all or only with the greatest difficulty and waste of time. People who can schedule their intellectually demanding tasks during high time will achieve more of the tasks than people who cannot.

Large Blocks of Time.   Typically, intellectually productive tasks require the absorption of amounts of information that are very large, the following of chains of thoughts that are very long, and end products whose production is very time consuming. The amounts of time required for these activities are very large. In most cases, the completion of any one unit of an intellectually productive task will require at least all of one day's high time. People who can devote a large amount of their high time to intellectually productive tasks will complete more of them.

Uninterrupted Blocks of Time.   When intellectual activity is interrupted, the task that is in progress must be stored away, along with the results that are reached thus far, and all the information that is required to reactivate the task later on when the interruption has been dealt with. When the task is taken up again, the material needed for its resumption must be reactivated. If the task is not dealt with in this way, it will have to be started from the beginning, or not taken up at all.

Interruptions are particularly disruptive to intellectually productive work because such work often involves lengthy, novel chains of thought that are fragile in the sense that their disruption, even temporarily, can cause a complete loss of critical elements or ordered links between them. Similarly, in intellectually productive work, very large bodies of diverse prior knowledge (driving the production of new ideas) often are configured in novel and therefore very unstable ways, and, when interruptions disrupt these configurations, they may not be recoverable. Thus, interruptions may have a substantial cost if they are permitted to occur during times when intellectually productive activities are in progress.

Two types of interruptions can be distinguished: external interruptions, such as telephone calls or unexpected visits by people, are generally not relevant to the task at hand and are sometimes uncontrollable; whereas job-internal interruptions arise from the progress of the task at hand. Often intellectually productive people will reach a particular point and then find that they need something that is not immediately available: a document, a word, an idea, or some other thing. Usually these needs spawn a new subtask. Sometimes these subtasks are not in themselves intellectually demanding and so can be put off to lower quality time periods. At other times, they are fully as intellectually demanding as the main task in progress and so must be pursued during high time, but they can be put off to later blocks of high time.

Scheduling Creative Subtasks Not Requiring High Time.   Often creative production requires large amounts of tedious work. For example, research psychologists may have to collect, score, and analyze data from subjects. If such work can be delegated to someone who can be trusted to do it right, then time can be saved. But all too often, intellectually productive people have to do tedious tasks themselves because the tasks have never been done before and only they have the understanding to do them right, or because the progress of the tasks is inherently uncertain, and novel decisions must be made in real time. If possible, such tasks should be scheduled at other than high time.

Scheduling Management Time

The most important goal of our cognitive system is to pursue goals that are important to us. The purpose of the entire time-management system described in this chapter is to achieve that goal. Because management of our mental time is itself an intellectually demanding task, high time should be allocated to it. Allocation of a brief period of planning time at the beginning of each high-time period will ensure that the time-management system will have an opportunity to work.

Research Agenda

Research on time management and on intellectual productivity requires measurement and training of time-management practices, skills, and abilities on the one hand, and measurement of intellectual productivity on the other. Britton and Tesser have developed a time-management questionnaire for student populations, which is included in the Appendix. A factor analysis ($N = 90$) yielded three factors, as shown in Table 1. A project is now underway to relate these scores, taken on freshmen, to

Table 1. Items Loading on Three Factors of Time Management Questionnaire

Planning factor

Do you make a list of things you have to do each day? (.80)[a]

Do you plan your day before you start it? (.72)

Do you make a schedule of activities you have to do on work days? (.71)

Do you write a set of goals for yourself each day? (.67)

Do you spend time each day planning? (.66)

Do you have a clear idea of what you want to accomplish during the next week? (.54)

Do you set and honor priorities? (.50)

Grind factor

Do you rarely do things which interfere with your schoolwork? (.63)

Do you feel you are in charge of your own time, by and large? (.60)

On an average day do you spend more time with schoolwork than with personal grooming? (.57)

Do you believe there is little room for improvement in the way you manage your time? (.55)

Do you make constructive use of your time? (.55)

Do you stop unprofitable routines or activities? (.51)

Orderly factor

Do you usually keep your desk clear of everything other than what you are currently working with? (.66)

Do you have a set of goals for the entire quarter? (.49)

The night before a major assignment is due, have you usually completed it? (.47)

When you have several things to do, do you think it is best to do a little bit of work on each one? (.47)

Do you keep your important dates (e.g., exam dates, research paper due dates, etc.) on a single calendar? (.43)

Do you regularly review your class notes, even when a test is not imminent? (.42)

Do you skim reading materials first to see if they are worth reading in depth? (.40)

[a]Factor loadings in parentheses.

cumulative grade point average over the college years as an index of intellectual productivity.

Instruments that are appropriate for business people are contained in Greene (1969) and Bliss (1976). We do not know of any attempts to measure intellectual productivity in connection with these instruments.

The exemplary work on training time-management skills and measuring intellectual productivity can be found in Hall and Hursch (1982). Numerous workshops on training time-management skills are offered at universities (e.g., through the Counseling and Testing Center at the University of Georgia) and by private organizations, but we know of none that has attempted to measure the effectiveness of the programs. Such measurements would be easy to take with the instruments in the Appendix and would provide important information not otherwise available.

A final research tool in this area, which may be useful for both measurement and training, is a computer gamelike program that was devised by Tulga (1979; Tulga & Sheridan, 1980), in which a computer screen display shows several boxes moving right toward a "deadline." Each box represents a task. The length of the box represents the amount of work remaining to do on it; the height of the box represents the number of points gained per unit of work; and the symbols in the box represent various other properties of the task, such as interruptability.

The subject has control of a cursor that can be moved to a box to "work" on it. The subject gets points depending on which task he chooses to work on. For each configuration of boxes (tasks), it is possible to calculate (by enumeration) which task(s) to work on to maximize some criterion. Criteria might be maximizing the number of jobs completed, or the number of points gained, or minimizing the number of jobs that are uncompleted at deadline. The measure of performance is how closely the subject comes to maximizing the chosen criterion.

Such a task is a gamelike simulation of real time management tasks, and could be useful not only for measuring ability but also for training time-management skills.

Summary

A general model for time management is described in detail. Special properties of time management that are particularly relevant to intellectually productive people are pointed out, and some research tools are described. An Appendix provides an instrument for measuring time-management practices.

Appendix

Britton and Tesser Time Management Instrument

This questionnaire includes 35 items that might be descriptive of you. Please read each question and then place a *check mark* in one of the parentheses next to the question, corresponding to the category that best describes how the question applies to you. For example, if the first question *always* applies to you, put a check mark in the parentheses beneath ''always.'' Remember, we are interested in how you think you actually are, not how you would like to be. *Be sure to answer all 35 questions.*

	Always	Frequently	Sometimes	Infrequently	Never
1. Do you believe that there is room for improvement in the way you manage your time?	( )	( )	( )	( )	( )
2. Do you write a set of goals for yourself for each day?	( )	( )	( )	( )	( )
3. On an average class day do you spend more time with personal grooming than doing schoolwork?	( )	( )	( )	( )	( )
4. Do you have a set of goals for the entire quarter?	( )	( )	( )	( )	( )
5. Do you set and honor priorities?	( )	( )	( )	( )	( )
6. Do you usually have a radio, television, or stereo playing while you study?	( )	( )	( )	( )	( )
7. Do you usually keep your desk clear of everything other than what you are currently working with?	( )	( )	( )	( )	( )
8. Are you able to put schoolwork out of your mind when you are socializing?	( )	( )	( )	( )	( )
9. The night before a major assignment is due, are you usually still working on it?	( )	( )	( )	( )	( )
10. Are you able to make minor decisions quickly?	( )	( )	( )	( )	( )
11. Do you clip or xerox articles which, although not presently important to you, may be in the future?	( )	( )	( )	( )	( )
12. Do you smoke an average of at least one pack of cigarettes per day?	( )	( )	( )	( )	( )
13. Do you regularly review your class notes, even when a test is not imminent?	( )	( )	( )	( )	( )
14. Do you keep your important dates (e.g., exam dates, research paper due dates, etc.) on a single calendar?	( )	( )	( )	( )	( )
15. Do you often find yourself doing things which interfere with your schoolwork simply because you hate to say "No" to people?	( )	( )	( )	( )	( )

	Always	Frequently	Sometimes	Infrequently	Never
16. Do you plan your day before you start it?	( )	( )	( )	( )	( )
17. Are you concerned about how well or poorly you use your time?	( )	( )	( )	( )	( )
18. Do you try to schedule your best hours for your most demanding work?	( )	( )	( )	( )	( )
19. Do you make a schedule of the activities you have to do on work days?	( )	( )	( )	( )	( )
20. Do you find yourself waiting a lot without anything to do?	( )	( )	( )	( )	( )
21. Do you skim reading materials first to see if they are worth reading in depth?	( )	( )	( )	( )	( )
22. Do you have a clear idea of what you want to accomplish during the next week?	( )	( )	( )	( )	( )
23. Do you make constructive use of your time?	( )	( )	( )	( )	( )
24. Do you set deadlines for yourself for completing work?	( )	( )	( )	( )	( )
25. Do you spend time each day planning?	( )	( )	( )	( )	( )
26. Do you continue unprofitable routines or activities?	( )	( )	( )	( )	( )
27. Do you keep things with you that you can work on whenever you get spare moments?	( )	( )	( )	( )	( )
28. Do you feel you are in charge of your own time, by and large?	( )	( )	( )	( )	( )
29. Do you have a set of goals for each week ready at the beginning of the week?	( )	( )	( )	( )	( )
30. When you have several things to do, how often do you try to figure out which are most important?	( )	( )	( )	( )	( )
31. When you have several things to do, do you think it is best to do a little bit of work on each one?	( )	( )	( )	( )	( )
32. Each week do you do things as they naturally occur to you, without an effort to make a plan in advance and compulsively follow it?	( )	( )	( )	( )	( )
33. Generally, do you think you can usually accomplish all your goals for a given week?	( )	( )	( )	( )	( )
34. Do you make a list of the things you have to do each day?	( )	( )	( )	( )	( )
35. When you have an idea, do you usually try to remember it mentally until you need it, rather than write it down somewhere?	( )	( )	( )	( )	( )

References

Bliss, E. C. (1976). *Getting things done: The ABCs of Time Management*. New York: Scribner's.

Britton, B. K., Smith, J. W., & Glynn, S. M. (1985). A cognitive workbench model for understanding expository text. In B. K. Britton & J. B. Black (Eds.), *Understanding expository text* (pp. 277–248). Hillsdale, NJ: Erlbaum.

Fowler, H. W. (1965). *A dictionary of modern English usage* (2nd ed.). Oxford: Oxford University Press.

Greene, R. M. (1969). *The management game: How to win with people*. Homewood, IL: Dow Jones-Irwin.

Greenstein, J. S., & Rouse, W. B. (1982). A model of human decision making in multiple process monitor situations. *IEEE Transactions on Systems, Man, and Cybernetics, 12,* 182–193.

Hall, B. L., & Hursch, D. E. (1982). An evaluation of the effects of a time management training program on work efficiency. *Journal of Organizational Behavior Management, 3,* 73–96.

Lakein, A. (1973). *How to get control of your time and your life*. New York: Signet.

La Rochefoucauld, F., Duc de (1706). *Moral maxims and reflections*. London: Sare.

Montaigne, M. (1925). *Essays* (George B. Ives, Trans.). Cambridge: Harvard University Press.

Pattipati, K. R., Kleinman, D. L., & Ephrath, A. R. (1983). A dynamic decision model of human task selection performance. *IEEE Transactions on Systems, Man, and Cybernetics, 13,* 145–166.

Roe, A. (1952). *The making of a scientist*. New York: Dodd, Mead.

Tulga, M. K. (1979). *Dynamic decision making in multi-task supervisory control: Comparison of an optimal algorithm to human behavior*. Unpublished doctoral dissertation, Massachusetts Institute of Technology, Cambridge, MA.

Tulga, M. K., & Sheridan, T. B. (1980). Dynamic decisions and work load in multitask supervisory control. *IEEE Transactions on Systems, Man, and Cybernetics, 10,* 217–232.

Index